Deleted

7

8

9

10

Deleted

11

12

GLOSSARY

MASTER INDEX

Photographer, mechanic and author with 1997 Mustang Cobra

ACKNOWLEDGEMENTS

Wiring diagrams originated by Valley Forge Technical Information Services. Technical writers who contributed to this project include Mike Stubblefield, Jeff Kibler and Jay Storer.

About this manual

ITS PURPOSE

The purpose of this manual is to help you get the best value from your vehicle. It can do so in several ways. It can help you decide what work must be done, even if you choose to have it done by a dealer service department or a repair shop; it provides information and procedures for routine maintenance and servicing; and it offers diagnostic and repair procedures to follow when trouble occurs.

We hope you use the manual to tackle the work yourself. For many simpler jobs, doing it yourself may be quicker than arranging an appointment to get the vehicle into a shop and making the trips to leave it and pick it up. More importantly, a lot of money can be saved by avoiding the expense the shop must pass on to you to cover its labor and overhead costs. An added benefit is the sense of satisfaction and accomplishment that you feel after doing the job yourself.

USING THE MANUAL

The manual is divided into Chapters. Each Chapter is divided into numbered Sections. Each Section consists of consecutively numbered paragraphs.

At the beginning of each numbered Section you will be referred to any illustrations which apply to the procedures in that Section. The reference numbers used in illustration captions pinpoint the pertinent Section and the Step within that Section. That is, illustration 3.2 means the illustration refers to Section 3 and Step (or paragraph) 2 within that Section.

Procedures, once described in the text, are not normally repeated. When it's necessary to refer to another Chapter, the reference will be given as Chapter and Section number. Cross references given without use of the word "Chapter" apply to Sections and/or paragraphs in the same Chapter. For example, "see Section 8" means in the same Chapter.

References to the left or right side of the vehicle assume you are sitting in the driver's seat, facing forward.

Even though we have prepared this manual with extreme care, neither the publisher nor the author can accept responsibility for any errors in, or omissions from, the information given.

➡ **NOTE**

A *Note* provides information necessary to properly complete a procedure or information which will make the procedure easier to understand.

✳ CAUTION

A *Caution* provides a special procedure or special steps which must be taken while completing the procedure where the Caution is found. Not heeding a Caution can result in damage to the assembly being worked on.

✳ WARNING

A *Warning* provides a special procedure or special steps which must be taken while completing the procedure where the Warning is found. Not heeding a Warning can result in personal injury.

Introduction

The Ford Mustang is available in two-door sport coupe or convertible body styles and have a conventional front engine/rear-wheel drive layout.

The available engines on the models covered by this manual are: a 3.8L V6, a Single Over-head Cam two-valves per cylinder (SOHC-2V) 4.6L V8, a Dual Over-head Cam four-valves per cylinder (DOHC-4V) 4.6L V8 or a pushrod 5.0L V8 engine. All models use an electronically controlled multi-port fuel injection system. Later models are equipped with On Board Diagnostic Second generation (OBD II) computerized engine management system. OBD II monitors engine and emissions system operation for malfunctions. The check engine light on the instrument panel will illuminate if any component malfunction occurs.

Power from the engine is transferred through either a five speed manual or four speed automatic transmission and a driveshaft to the differential which is mounted in the solid rear axle assembly. Axles inside the assembly carry power from the differential to the rear wheels.

Suspension is independent in the front, utilizing struts and lower control arms to locate the knuckle assembly at each wheel. Coil springs are mounted between the lower control arm and the frame. The rear suspension features coil springs and shock absorbers.

The steering gear is a power assisted rack and pinion type that is mounted to the front of the engine crossmember with rubber insulators.

The brakes are disc at the front and the rear with vacuum assist as standard equipment. Models equipped with 4.6L DOHC-4V engines utilize hydro boost assisted brakes as standard equipment. Anti-lock Braking Systems (ABS) are optional on all models.

Vehicle Identification Numbers

Modifications are a continuing and unpublicized process in vehicle manufacturing. Since spare parts lists and manuals are compiled on a numerical basis, the individual vehicle numbers are necessary to correctly identify the component required.

VEHICLE IDENTIFICATION NUMBER (VIN)

This very important identification number is stamped on a plate attached to the dashboard inside the windshield on the driver's side of the vehicle (see illustration). The VIN also appears on the Vehicle Certificate of Title and Registration. It contains information such as where and when the vehicle was manufactured, the model year and the body style.

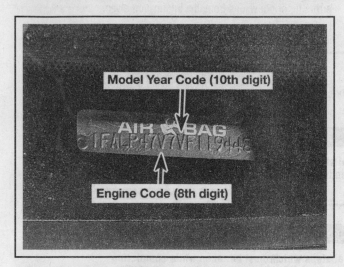

The VIN number is visible through the windshield on the driver's side

VIN ENGINE AND MODEL YEAR CODES

Two particularly important pieces of information found in the VIN are the engine code and the model year code. Counting from the left, the engine code letter designation is the 8th digit and the model year code letter designation is the 10th digit.

On the models covered by this manual the engine codes are:

4	3.8L V6
W, X	4.6L SOHC V8
V	4.6L DOHC V8
T	5.0L H.O. V8
D	5.0L Cobra V8
R	4.6L DOHC V8
Y	4.6L DOHC Supercharged (not covered by this manual)

On the models covered by this manual the model year codes are:

R	1994
S	1995
T	1996
V	1997
W	1998
X	1999
Y	2000
1	2001
2	2002
3	2003
4	2004

The vehicle certification label is affixed the to the driver's side door pillar

The engine identification label is affixed to the valve cover

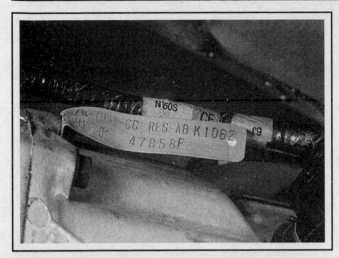

The manual transmission identification tag is retained by a left side engine-to-bellhousing bolt

The rear differential identification tag is bolted to the differential cover

VEHICLE CERTIFICATION LABEL

The Vehicle Certification Label is attached to the driver's side door pillar (see illustration). Information on this label includes the name of the manufacturer, the month and year of production, as well as information on the options with which it is equipped. This label is especially useful for matching the color and type of paint for repair work.

ENGINE IDENTIFICATION NUMBER

Labels containing the engine code, engine number and build date can be found on the valve cover (see illustration). The engine number is also stamped onto a machined pad on the external surface of the engine block.

AUTOMATIC TRANSMISSION IDENTIFICATION NUMBER

The automatic transmission ID number is affixed to a label on the right side of the case.

MANUAL TRANSMISSION IDENTIFICATION NUMBER

The manual transmission ID number is stamped on a tag which is bolted to the driver's side of the bellhousing (see illustration).

REAR DIFFERENTIAL IDENTIFICATION NUMBER

The rear differential ID number is stamped on a tag which is bolted to the differential cover (see illustration).

VEHICLE EMISSIONS CONTROL INFORMATION LABEL

This label is found in the engine compartment. See Chapter 6 for more information on this label.

Buying parts

Replacement parts are available from many sources, which generally fall into one of two categories - authorized dealer parts departments and independent retail auto parts stores. Our advice concerning these parts is as follows:

Retail auto parts stores: Good auto parts stores will stock frequently needed components which wear out relatively fast, such as clutch components, exhaust systems, brake parts, tune-up parts, etc. These stores often supply new or reconditioned parts on an exchange basis, which can save a considerable amount of money. Discount auto parts stores are often very good places to buy materials and parts needed for general vehicle maintenance such as oil, grease, filters, spark plugs, belts, touch-up paint, bulbs, etc. They also usually sell

tools and general accessories, have convenient hours, charge lower prices and can often be found not far from home.

Authorized dealer parts department: This is the best source for parts which are unique to the vehicle and not generally available elsewhere (such as major engine parts, transmission parts, trim pieces, etc.).

Warranty information: If the vehicle is still covered under warranty, be sure that any replacement parts purchased - regardless of the source - do not invalidate the warranty!

To be sure of obtaining the correct parts, have engine and chassis numbers available and, if possible, take the old parts along for positive identification.

Maintenance techniques, tools and working facilities

MAINTENANCE TECHNIQUES

There are a number of techniques involved in maintenance and repair that will be referred to throughout this manual. Application of these techniques will enable the home mechanic to be more efficient, better organized and capable of performing the various tasks properly, which will ensure that the repair job is thorough and complete.

Fasteners

Fasteners are nuts, bolts, studs and screws used to hold two or more parts together. There are a few things to keep in mind when working with fasteners. Almost all of them use a locking device of some type, either a lockwasher, locknut, locking tab or thread adhesive. All threaded fasteners should be clean and straight, with undamaged threads and undamaged corners on the hex head where the wrench fits. Develop the habit of replacing all damaged nuts and bolts with new ones. Special locknuts with nylon or fiber inserts can only be used once. If they are removed, they lose their locking ability and must be replaced with new ones.

Rusted nuts and bolts should be treated with a penetrating fluid to ease removal and prevent breakage. Some mechanics use turpentine in a spout-type oil can, which works quite well. After applying the rust penetrant, let it work for a few minutes before trying to loosen the nut or bolt. Badly rusted fasteners may have to be chiseled or sawed off or removed with a special nut breaker, available at tool stores.

If a bolt or stud breaks off in an assembly, it can be drilled and removed with a special tool commonly available for this purpose. Most automotive machine shops can perform this task, as well as other repair procedures, such as the repair of threaded holes that have been stripped out.

Flat washers and lockwashers, when removed from an assembly, should always be replaced exactly as removed. Replace any damaged washers with new ones. Never use a lockwasher on any soft metal surface (such as aluminum), thin sheet metal or plastic.

Fastener sizes

For a number of reasons, automobile manufacturers are making wider and wider use of metric fasteners. Therefore, it is important to be able to tell the difference between standard (sometimes called U.S.

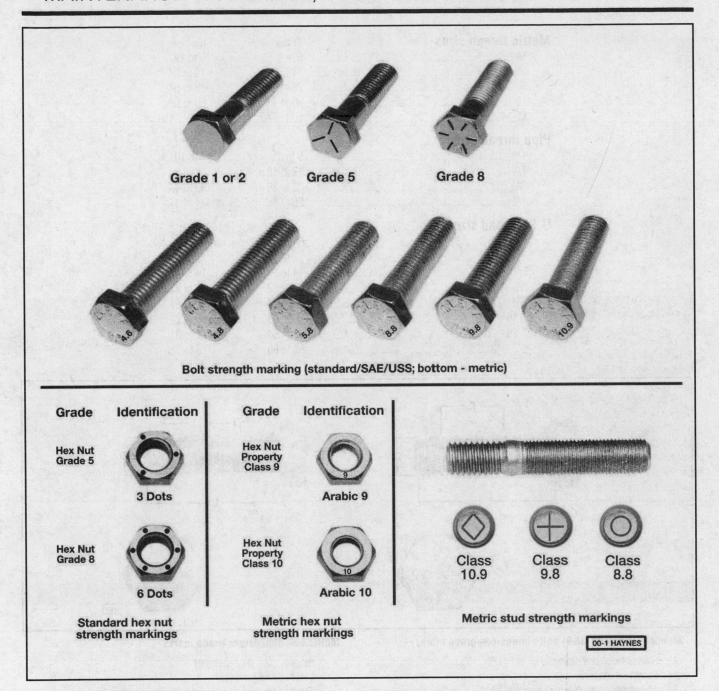

Grade 1 or 2   Grade 5   Grade 8

Bolt strength marking (standard/SAE/USS; bottom - metric)

Grade	Identification	Grade	Identification
Hex Nut Grade 5	3 Dots	Hex Nut Property Class 9	Arabic 9
Hex Nut Grade 8	6 Dots	Hex Nut Property Class 10	Arabic 10

Standard hex nut strength markings

Metric hex nut strength markings

Class 10.9   Class 9.8   Class 8.8

Metric stud strength markings

00-1 HAYNES

or SAE) and metric hardware, since they cannot be interchanged.

All bolts, whether standard or metric, are sized according to diameter, thread pitch and length. For example, a standard 1/2 - 13 x 1 bolt is 1/2 inch in diameter, has 13 threads per inch and is 1 inch long. An M12 - 1.75 x 25 metric bolt is 12 mm in diameter, has a thread pitch of 1.75 mm (the distance between threads) and is 25 mm long. The two bolts are nearly identical, and easily confused, but they are not interchangeable.

In addition to the differences in diameter, thread pitch and length, metric and standard bolts can also be distinguished by examining the bolt heads. To begin with, the distance across the flats on a standard bolt head is measured in inches, while the same dimension on a metric bolt is sized in millimeters (the same is true for nuts). As a result, a standard wrench should not be used on a metric bolt and a metric wrench should not be used on a standard bolt. Also, most standard bolts have slashes

radiating out from the center of the head to denote the grade or strength of the bolt, which is an indication of the amount of torque that can be applied to it. The greater the number of slashes, the greater the strength of the bolt. Grades 0 through 5 are commonly used on automobiles. Metric bolts have a property class (grade) number, rather than a slash, molded into their heads to indicate bolt strength. In this case, the higher the number, the stronger the bolt. Property class numbers 8.8, 9.8 and 10.9 are commonly used on automobiles.

Strength markings can also be used to distinguish standard hex nuts from metric hex nuts. Many standard nuts have dots stamped into one side, while metric nuts are marked with a number. The greater the number of dots, or the higher the number, the greater the strength of the nut.

Metric studs are also marked on their ends according to property class (grade). Larger studs are numbered (the same as metric bolts), while smaller studs carry a geometric code to denote grade.

	Ft-lbs	Nm
Metric thread sizes		
M-6	6 to 9	9 to 12
M-8	14 to 21	19 to 28
M-10	28 to 40	38 to 54
M-12	50 to 71	68 to 96
M-14	80 to 140	109 to 154
Pipe thread sizes		
1/8	5 to 8	7 to 10
1/4	12 to 18	17 to 24
3/8	22 to 33	30 to 44
1/2	25 to 35	34 to 47
U.S. thread sizes		
1/4 - 20	6 to 9	9 to 12
5/16 - 18	12 to 18	17 to 24
5/16 - 24	14 to 20	19 to 27
3/8 - 16	22 to 32	30 to 43
3/8 - 24	27 to 38	37 to 51
7/16 - 14	40 to 55	55 to 74
7/16 - 20	40 to 60	55 to 81
1/2 - 13	55 to 80	75 to 108

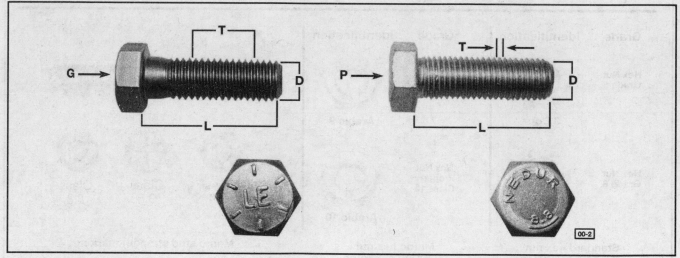

Standard (SAE and USS) bolt dimensions/grade marks

G   Grade marks (bolt strength)
L   Length (in inches)
T   Thread pitch (number of threads per inch)
D   Nominal diameter (in inches)

Metric bolt dimensions/grade marks

P   Property class (bolt strength)
L   Length (in millimeters)
T   Thread pitch (distance between threads in millimeters)
D   Diameter

It should be noted that many fasteners, especially Grades 0 through 2, have no distinguishing marks on them. When such is the case, the only way to determine whether it is standard or metric is to measure the thread pitch or compare it to a known fastener of the same size.

Standard fasteners are often referred to as SAE, as opposed to metric. However, it should be noted that SAE technically refers to a non-metric fine thread fastener only. Coarse thread non-metric fasteners are referred to as USS sizes.

Since fasteners of the same size (both standard and metric) may have different strength ratings, be sure to reinstall any bolts, studs or nuts removed from your vehicle in their original locations. Also, when replacing a fastener with a new one, make sure that the new one has a strength rating equal to or greater than the original.

Tightening sequences and procedures

Most threaded fasteners should be tightened to a specific torque value (torque is the twisting force applied to a threaded component such as a nut or bolt). Overtightening the fastener can weaken it and cause it to break, while undertightening can cause it to eventually come loose. Bolts, screws and studs, depending on the material they are made of and their thread diameters, have specific torque values, many of which are noted in the Specifications at the end of each Chapter. Be sure to follow the torque recommendations closely. For fasteners not assigned a specific torque, a general torque value chart is presented here as a guide. These torque values are for dry (unlubricated) fasteners threaded into steel or cast iron (not aluminum). As was previously mentioned, the size and grade of a fastener determine the amount of torque that can

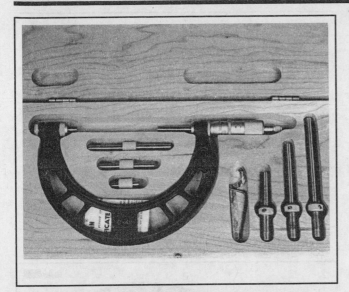

Micrometer set

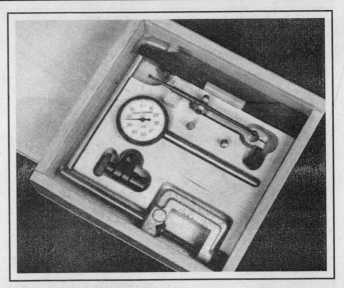

Dial indicator set

safely be applied to it. The figures listed here are approximate for Grade 2 and Grade 3 fasteners. Higher grades can tolerate higher torque values.

Fasteners laid out in a pattern, such as cylinder head bolts, oil pan bolts, differential cover bolts, etc., must be loosened or tightened in sequence to avoid warping the component. This sequence will normally be shown in the appropriate Chapter. If a specific pattern is not given, the following procedures can be used to prevent warping.

Initially, the bolts or nuts should be assembled finger-tight only. Next, they should be tightened one full turn each, in a criss-cross or diagonal pattern. After each one has been tightened one full turn, return to the first one and tighten them all one-half turn, following the same pattern. Finally, tighten each of them one-quarter turn at a time until each fastener has been tightened to the proper torque. To loosen and remove the fasteners, the procedure would be reversed.

Component disassembly

Component disassembly should be done with care and purpose to help ensure that the parts go back together properly. Always keep track of the sequence in which parts are removed. Make note of special characteristics or marks on parts that can be installed more than one way, such as a grooved thrust washer on a shaft. It is a good idea to lay the disassembled parts out on a clean surface in the order that they were removed. It may also be helpful to make sketches or take instant photos of components before removal.

When removing fasteners from a component, keep track of their locations. Sometimes threading a bolt back in a part, or putting the washers and nut back on a stud, can prevent mix-ups later. If nuts and bolts cannot be returned to their original locations, they should be kept in a compartmented box or a series of small boxes. A cupcake or muffin tin is ideal for this purpose, since each cavity can hold the bolts and nuts from a particular area (i.e. oil pan bolts, valve cover bolts, engine mount bolts, etc.). A pan of this type is especially helpful when working on assemblies with very small parts, such as the carburetor, alternator, valve train or interior dash and trim pieces. The cavities can be marked with paint or tape to identify the contents.

Whenever wiring looms, harnesses or connectors are separated, it is a good idea to identify the two halves with numbered pieces of masking tape so they can be easily reconnected.

Gasket sealing surfaces

Throughout any vehicle, gaskets are used to seal the mating surfaces between two parts and keep lubricants, fluids, vacuum or pressure contained in an assembly.

Many times these gaskets are coated with a liquid or paste-type gasket sealing compound before assembly. Age, heat and pressure can sometimes cause the two parts to stick together so tightly that they are very difficult to separate. Often, the assembly can be loosened by striking it with a soft-face hammer near the mating surfaces. A regular hammer can be used if a block of wood is placed between the hammer and the part. Do not hammer on cast parts or parts that could be easily damaged. With any particularly stubborn part, always recheck to make sure that every fastener has been removed.

Avoid using a screwdriver or bar to pry apart an assembly, as they can easily mar the gasket sealing surfaces of the parts, which must remain smooth. If prying is absolutely necessary, use an old broom handle, but keep in mind that extra clean up will be necessary if the wood splinters.

After the parts are separated, the old gasket must be carefully scraped off and the gasket surfaces cleaned. Stubborn gasket material can be soaked with rust penetrant or treated with a special chemical to soften it so it can be easily scraped off.

✹✹ CAUTION:

Never use gasket removal solutions or caustic chemicals on plastic or other composite components.

A scraper can be fashioned from a piece of copper tubing by flattening and sharpening one end. Copper is recommended because it is usually softer than the surfaces to be scraped, which reduces the chance of gouging the part. Some gaskets can be removed with a wire brush, but regardless of the method used, the mating surfaces must be left clean and smooth. If for some reason the gasket surface is gouged, then a gasket sealer thick enough to fill scratches will have to be used during reassembly of the components. For most applications, a non-drying (or semi-drying) gasket sealer should be used.

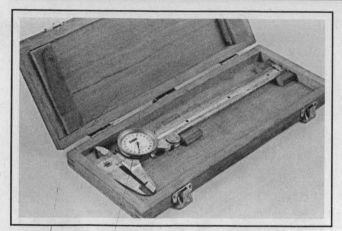

Dial caliper

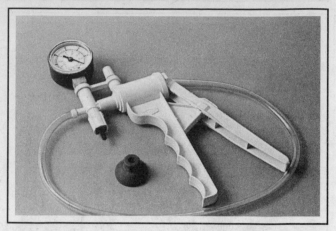

Hand-operated vacuum pump

Timing light

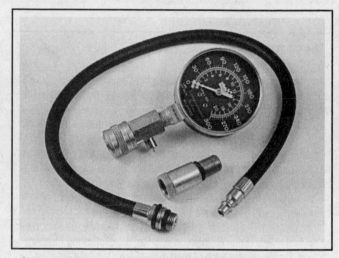

Compression gauge with spark plug hole adapter

Hose removal tips

✳✳ WARNING:

If the vehicle is equipped with air conditioning, do not disconnect any of the A/C hoses without first having the system depressurized by a dealer service department or a service station.

Hose removal precautions closely parallel gasket removal precautions. Avoid scratching or gouging the surface that the hose mates against or the connection may leak. This is especially true for radiator hoses. Because of various chemical reactions, the rubber in hoses can bond itself to the metal spigot that the hose fits over. To remove a hose, first loosen the hose clamps that secure it to the spigot. Then, with slip-joint pliers, grab the hose at the clamp and rotate it around the spigot. Work it back and forth until it is completely free, then pull it off. Silicone or other lubricants will ease removal if they can be applied between the hose and the outside of the spigot. Apply the same lubricant to the inside of the hose and the outside of the spigot to simplify installation.

As a last resort (and if the hose is to be replaced with a new one anyway), the rubber can be slit with a knife and the hose peeled from the spigot. If this must be done, be careful that the metal connection is not damaged.

If a hose clamp is broken or damaged, do not reuse it. Wire-type clamps usually weaken with age, so it is a good idea to replace them with screw-type clamps whenever a hose is removed.

TOOLS

A selection of good tools is a basic requirement for anyone who plans to maintain and repair his or her own vehicle. For the owner who has few tools, the initial investment might seem high, but when compared to the spiraling costs of professional auto maintenance and repair, it is a wise one.

To help the owner decide which tools are needed to perform the tasks detailed in this manual, the following tool lists are offered: *Maintenance and minor repair, Repair/overhaul and Special.*

The newcomer to practical mechanics should start off with the *maintenance and minor repair* tool kit, which is adequate for the simpler jobs performed on a vehicle. Then, as confidence and experience grow, the owner can tackle more difficult tasks, buying additional tools as they are needed. Eventually the basic kit will be expanded into the *repair and overhaul* tool set. Over a period of time, the experienced do-it-yourselfer will assemble a tool set complete enough for most repair and overhaul procedures and will add tools from the special category when it is felt that the expense is justified by the frequency of use.

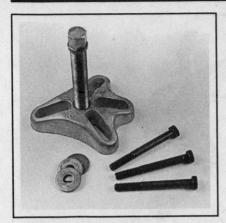

Damper/steering wheel puller

General purpose puller

Hydraulic lifter removal tool

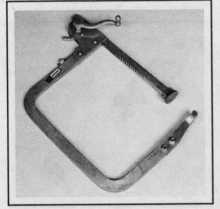

Valve spring compressor

Valve spring compressor

Ridge reamer

Maintenance and minor repair tool kit

The tools in this list should be considered the minimum required for performance of routine maintenance, servicing and minor repair work. We recommend the purchase of combination wrenches (box-end and open-end combined in one wrench). While more expensive than open end wrenches, they offer the advantages of both types of wrench.

Combination wrench set (1/4-inch to 1 inch or 6 mm to 19 mm)
Adjustable wrench, 8 inch
Spark plug wrench with rubber insert
Spark plug gap adjusting tool
Feeler gauge set
Brake bleeder wrench
Standard screwdriver (5/16-inch x 6 inch)
Phillips screwdriver (No. 2 x 6 inch)
Combination pliers - 6 inch
Hacksaw and assortment of blades
Tire pressure gauge
Grease gun
Oil can
Fine emery cloth
Wire brush
Battery post and cable cleaning tool
Oil filter wrench
Funnel (medium size)
Safety goggles
Jackstands (2)
Drain pan

➡Note: If basic tune-ups are going to be part of routine maintenance, it will be necessary to purchase a good quality stroboscopic timing light and combination tachometer/dwell meter. Although they are included in the list of special tools, it is mentioned here because they are absolutely necessary for tuning most vehicles properly.

Repair and overhaul tool set

These tools are essential for anyone who plans to perform major repairs and are in addition to those in the maintenance and minor repair tool kit. Included is a comprehensive set of sockets which, though expensive, are invaluable because of their versatility, especially when various extensions and drives are available. We recommend the 1/2-inch drive over the 3/8-inch drive. Although the larger drive is bulky and more expensive, it has the capacity of accepting a very wide range of large sockets. Ideally, however, the mechanic should have a 3/8-inch drive set and a 1/2-inch drive set.

Socket set(s)
Reversible ratchet
Extension - 10 inch
Universal joint
Torque wrench (same size drive as sockets)
Ball peen hammer - 8 ounce
Soft-face hammer (plastic/rubber)
Standard screwdriver (1/4-inch x 6 inch)
Standard screwdriver (stubby - 5/16-inch)
Phillips screwdriver (No. 3 x 8 inch)
Phillips screwdriver (stubby - No. 2)
Pliers - vise grip

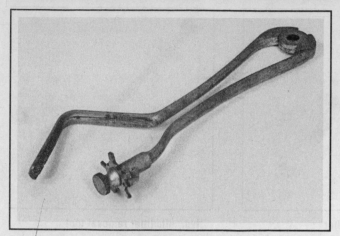

Piston ring groove cleaning tool

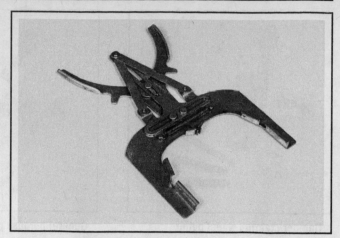

Ring removal/installation tool

Ring compressor

Cylinder hone

Brake hold-down spring tool

Pliers - lineman's
Pliers - needle nose
Pliers - snap-ring (internal and external)
Cold chisel - 1/2-inch
Scribe
Scraper (made from flattened copper tubing)
Centerpunch
Pin punches (1/16, 1/8, 3/16-inch)
Steel rule/straightedge - 12 inch
Allen wrench set (1/8 to 3/8-inch or 4 mm to 10 mm)
A selection of files
Wire brush (large)
Jackstands (second set)
Jack (scissor or hydraulic type)

➡**Note: Another tool which is often useful is an electric drill with a chuck capacity of 3/8-inch and a set of good quality drill bits.**

Special tools

The tools in this list include those which are not used regularly, are expensive to buy, or which need to be used in accordance with their manufacturer's instructions. Unless these tools will be used frequently, it is not very economical to purchase many of them. A consideration would be to split the cost and use between yourself and a friend or friends. In addition, most of these tools can be obtained from a tool rental shop on a temporary basis.

This list primarily contains only those tools and instruments widely available to the public, and not those special tools produced by the vehicle manufacturer for distribution to dealer service depart-

ments. Occasionally, references to the manufacturer's special tools are included in the text of this manual. Generally, an alternative method of doing the job without the special tool is offered. However, sometimes there is no alternative to their use. Where this is the case, and the tool cannot be purchased or borrowed, the work should be turned over to the dealer service department or an automotive repair shop.

Valve spring compressor
Piston ring groove cleaning tool
Piston ring compressor
Piston ring installation tool
Cylinder compression gauge
Cylinder ridge reamer
Cylinder surfacing hone
Cylinder bore gauge
Micrometers and/or dial calipers
Hydraulic lifter removal tool
Balljoint separator
Universal-type puller
Impact screwdriver
Dial indicator set
Stroboscopic timing light (inductive pick-up)
Hand operated vacuum/pressure pump
Tachometer/dwell meter
Universal electrical multimeter
Cable hoist
Brake spring removal and installation tools
Floor jack

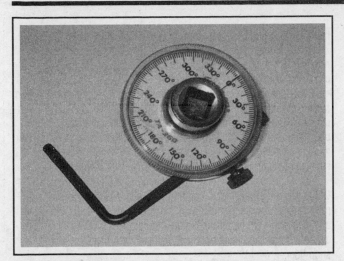

Torque angle gauge

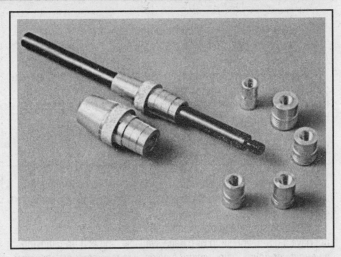

Clutch plate alignment tool

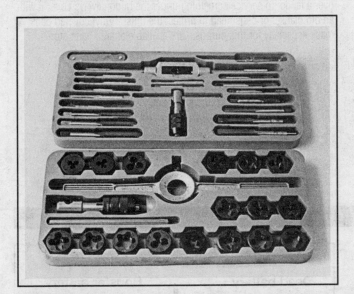

Tap and die set

Buying tools

For the do-it-yourselfer who is just starting to get involved in vehicle maintenance and repair, there are a number of options available when purchasing tools. If maintenance and minor repair is the extent of the work to be done, the purchase of individual tools is satisfactory. If, on the other hand, extensive work is planned, it would be a good idea to purchase a modest tool set from one of the large retail chain stores. A set can usually be bought at a substantial savings over the individual tool prices, and they often come with a tool box. As additional tools are needed, add-on sets, individual tools and a larger tool box can be purchased to expand the tool selection. Building a tool set gradually allows the cost of the tools to be spread over a longer period of time and gives the mechanic the freedom to choose only those tools that will actually be used.

Tool stores will often be the only source of some of the special tools that are needed, but regardless of where tools are bought, try to avoid cheap ones, especially when buying screwdrivers and sockets, because they won't last very long. The expense involved in replacing cheap tools will eventually be greater than the initial cost of quality tools.

Care and maintenance of tools

Good tools are expensive, so it makes sense to treat them with respect. Keep them clean and in usable condition and store them properly when not in use. Always wipe off any dirt, grease or metal chips before putting them away. Never leave tools lying around in the work area. Upon completion of a job, always check closely under the hood for tools that may have been left there so they won't get lost during a test drive.

Some tools, such as screwdrivers, pliers, wrenches and sockets, can be hung on a panel mounted on the garage or workshop wall, while others should be kept in a tool box or tray. Measuring instruments, gauges, meters, etc. must be carefully stored where they cannot be damaged by weather or impact from other tools.

When tools are used with care and stored properly, they will last a very long time. Even with the best of care, though, tools will wear out if used frequently. When a tool is damaged or worn out, replace it. Subsequent jobs will be safer and more enjoyable if you do.

HOW TO REPAIR DAMAGED THREADS

Sometimes, the internal threads of a nut or bolt hole can become stripped, usually from overtightening. Stripping threads is an all-too-common occurrence, especially when working with aluminum parts, because aluminum is so soft that it easily strips out.

Usually, external or internal threads are only partially stripped. After they've been cleaned up with a tap or die, they'll still work. Sometimes, however, threads are badly damaged. When this happens, you've got three choices:

1) *Drill and tap the hole to the next suitable oversize and install a larger diameter bolt, screw or stud.*
2) *Drill and tap the hole to accept a threaded plug, then drill and tap the plug to the original screw size. You can also buy a plug already threaded to the original size. Then you simply drill a hole to the specified size, then run the threaded plug into the hole with a bolt and jam nut. Once the plug is fully seated, remove the jam nut and bolt.*
3) *The third method uses a patented thread repair kit like Heli-Coil or Slimsert. These easy-to-use kits are designed to repair damaged threads in straight-through holes and blind holes. Both are available as kits which can handle a variety of sizes and thread*

patterns. Drill the hole, then tap it with the special included tap. Install the Heli-Coil and the hole is back to its original diameter and thread pitch.

Regardless of which method you use, be sure to proceed calmly and carefully. A little impatience or carelessness during one of these relatively simple procedures can ruin your whole day's work and cost you a bundle if you wreck an expensive part.

WORKING FACILITIES

Not to be overlooked when discussing tools is the workshop. If anything more than routine maintenance is to be carried out, some sort of suitable work area is essential.

It is understood, and appreciated, that many home mechanics do not have a good workshop or garage available, and end up removing an engine or doing major repairs outside. It is recommended, however, that the overhaul or repair be completed under the cover of a roof.

A clean, flat workbench or table of comfortable working height is an absolute necessity. The workbench should be equipped with a vise that has a jaw opening of at least four inches.

As mentioned previously, some clean, dry storage space is also required for tools, as well as the lubricants, fluids, cleaning solvents, etc. which soon become necessary.

Sometimes waste oil and fluids, drained from the engine or cooling system during normal maintenance or repairs, present a disposal problem. To avoid pouring them on the ground or into a sewage system, pour the used fluids into large containers, seal them with caps and take them to an authorized disposal site or recycling center. Plastic jugs, such as old antifreeze containers, are ideal for this purpose.

Always keep a supply of old newspapers and clean rags available. Old towels are excellent for mopping up spills. Many mechanics use rolls of paper towels for most work because they are readily available and disposable. To help keep the area under the vehicle clean, a large cardboard box can be cut open and flattened to protect the garage or shop floor.

Whenever working over a painted surface, such as when leaning over a fender to service something under the hood, always cover it with an old blanket or bedspread to protect the finish. Vinyl covered pads, made especially for this purpose, are available at auto parts stores.

Booster battery (jump) starting

Observe the following precautions when using a booster battery to start a vehicle:

a) *Before connecting the booster battery, make sure the ignition switch is in the Off position.*
b) *Turn off the lights, heater and other electrical loads.*
c) *Your eyes should be shielded. Safety goggles are a good idea.*
d) *Make sure the booster battery is the same voltage as the dead one in the vehicle.*
e) *The two vehicles MUST NOT TOUCH each other!*
f) *Make sure the transmission is in Neutral (manual) or Park (automatic).*
g) *If the booster battery is not a maintenance-free type, remove the vent caps and lay a cloth over the vent holes.*

Connect one jumper lead between the positive (+) terminals of the two batteries (see illustration). Connect the other jumper lead first to the negative (-) terminal of the booster battery, then to a good engine ground on the vehicle to be started. Attach the lead at least 18 inches from the battery, if possible. Make sure the that the jumper leads will not contact the fan, drivebelt or other moving parts of the engine.

Start the engine using the booster battery, then, with the engine running at idle speed, disconnect the jumper cables in the reverse order of connection.

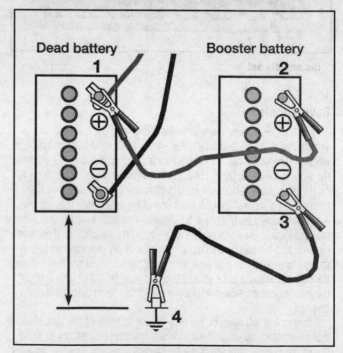

Make the booster battery cable connections in the numerical order shown (note that the negative cable of the booster battery is NOT attached to the negative terminal of the dead battery)

Jacking and towing

JACKING

✳✳ WARNING:

The jack supplied with the vehicle should only be used for changing a tire or placing jackstands under the frame. Never work under the vehicle or start the engine while this jack is being used as the only means of support.

The vehicle should be on level ground. Place the shift lever in Park, if you have an automatic, or Reverse if you have a manual transmission. Block the wheel diagonally opposite the wheel being changed. Set the parking brake.

Remove the spare tire and jack from stowage. Remove the wheel cover and trim ring (if so equipped) with the tapered end of the lug nut wrench by inserting and twisting the handle and then prying against the back of the wheel cover. Loosen the wheel lug nuts about 1/4-to-1/2 turn each.

Place the scissors-type jack under the side of the vehicle and adjust the jack height until it fits in the notch in the vertical rocker panel

Place the jack so it engages the notch in the rocker panel nearest the wheel to be raised

flange nearest the wheel to be changed. There is a front and rear jacking point on each side of the vehicle (see illustration).

Turn the jack handle clockwise until the tire clears the ground. Remove the lug nuts and pull the wheel off. Replace it with the spare.

Install the lug nuts with the beveled edges facing in. Tighten them snugly. Don't attempt to tighten them completely until the vehicle is lowered or it could slip off the jack. Turn the jack handle counterclockwise to lower the vehicle. Remove the jack and tighten the lug nuts in a diagonal pattern.

Install the cover (and trim ring, if used) and be sure it's snapped into place all the way around.

Stow the tire, jack and wrench. Unblock the wheels.

TOWING

As a general rule, the vehicle should be towed with the rear wheels off the ground. If they can't be raised, either place them on a dolly or disconnect the driveshaft from the differential. When a vehicle is towed with the rear wheels raised, the steering wheel must be clamped in the straight ahead position with a special device designed for use during towing The ignition key must be in the OFF position, since the steering lock mechanism isn't strong enough to hold the front wheels straight while towing.

Vehicles equipped with an automatic transmission can be towed from the front only with all four wheels on the ground, provided that speeds don't exceed 35 mph and the distance is not over 50 miles. Before towing, check the transmission fluid level (see Chapter 1). If the level is below the HOT line on the dipstick, add fluid or use a towing dolly. Release the parking brake, put the transmission in Neutral and place the ignition key in the OFF position. There's no distance limitation when towing with either the rear wheels off the ground or the driveshaft disconnected, but don't exceed 50 mph.

Equipment specifically designed for towing should be used. It should be attached to the main structural members of the vehicle, not the bumpers or brackets.

Safety is a major consideration when towing and all applicable state and local laws must be obeyed. A safety chain system must be used at all times. Remember that power steering and power brakes will not work with the engine off.

Automotive chemicals and lubricants

A number of automotive chemicals and lubricants are available for use during vehicle maintenance and repair. They include a wide variety of products ranging from cleaning solvents and degreasers to lubricants and protective sprays for rubber, plastic and vinyl.

CLEANERS

Carburetor cleaner and choke cleaner is a strong solvent for gum, varnish and carbon. Most carburetor cleaners leave a dry-type lubricant film which will not harden or gum up. Because of this film it is not recommended for use on electrical components.

Brake system cleaner is used to remove brake dust, grease and brake fluid from the brake system, where clean surfaces are absolutely necessary. It leaves no residue and often eliminates brake squeal caused by contaminants.

Electrical cleaner removes oxidation, corrosion and carbon deposits from electrical contacts, restoring full current flow. It can also be used to clean spark plugs, carburetor jets, voltage regulators and other parts where an oil-free surface is desired.

Demoisturants remove water and moisture from electrical components such as alternators, voltage regulators, electrical connectors and fuse blocks. They are non-conductive and non-corrosive.

Degreasers are heavy-duty solvents used to remove grease from the outside of the engine and from chassis components. They can be sprayed or brushed on and, depending on the type, are rinsed off either with water or solvent.

LUBRICANTS

Motor oil is the lubricant formulated for use in engines. It normally contains a wide variety of additives to prevent corrosion and reduce foaming and wear. Motor oil comes in various weights (viscosity ratings) from 0 to 50. The recommended weight of the oil depends on the season, temperature and the demands on the engine. Light oil is used in cold climates and under light load conditions. Heavy oil is used in hot climates and where high loads are encountered. Multi-viscosity oils are designed to have characteristics of both light and heavy oils and are available in a number of weights from 5W-20 to 20W-50.

Gear oil is designed to be used in differentials, manual transmissions and other areas where high-temperature lubrication is required.

Chassis and wheel bearing grease is a heavy grease used where increased loads and friction are encountered, such as for wheel bearings, balljoints, tie-rod ends and universal joints.

High-temperature wheel bearing grease is designed to withstand the extreme temperatures encountered by wheel bearings in disc brake equipped vehicles. It usually contains molybdenum disulfide (moly), which is a dry-type lubricant.

White grease is a heavy grease for metal-to-metal applications where water is a problem. White grease stays soft under both low and high temperatures (usually from -100 to +190-degrees F), and will not wash off or dilute in the presence of water.

Assembly lube is a special extreme pressure lubricant, usually containing moly, used to lubricate high-load parts (such as main and rod bearings and cam lobes) for initial start-up of a new engine. The assembly lube lubricates the parts without being squeezed out or washed away until the engine oiling system begins to function.

Silicone lubricants are used to protect rubber, plastic, vinyl and nylon parts.

Graphite lubricants are used where oils cannot be used due to contamination problems, such as in locks. The dry graphite will lubricate metal parts while remaining uncontaminated by dirt, water, oil or acids. It is electrically conductive and will not foul electrical contacts in locks such as the ignition switch.

Moly penetrants loosen and lubricate frozen, rusted and corroded fasteners and prevent future rusting or freezing.

Heat-sink grease is a special electrically non-conductive grease that is used for mounting electronic ignition modules where it is essential that heat is transferred away from the module.

SEALANTS

RTV sealant is one of the most widely used gasket compounds. Made from silicone, RTV is air curing, it seals, bonds, waterproofs, fills surface irregularities, remains flexible, doesn't shrink, is relatively easy to remove, and is used as a supplementary sealer with almost all low and medium temperature gaskets.

Anaerobic sealant is much like RTV in that it can be used either to seal gaskets or to form gaskets by itself. It remains flexible, is solvent resistant and fills surface imperfections. The difference between an anaerobic sealant and an RTV-type sealant is in the curing. RTV cures when exposed to air, while an anaerobic sealant cures only in the absence of air. This means that an anaerobic sealant cures only after the assembly of parts, sealing them together.

Thread and pipe sealant is used for sealing hydraulic and pneumatic fittings and vacuum lines. It is usually made from a Teflon compound, and comes in a spray, a paint-on liquid and as a wrap-around tape.

CHEMICALS

Anti-seize compound prevents seizing, galling, cold welding, rust and corrosion in fasteners. High-temperature anti-seize, usually made with copper and graphite lubricants, is used for exhaust system and exhaust manifold bolts.

Anaerobic locking compounds are used to keep fasteners from vibrating or working loose and cure only after installation, in the absence of air. Medium strength locking compound is used for small nuts, bolts and screws that may be removed later. High-strength locking compound is for large nuts, bolts and studs which aren't removed on a regular basis.

Oil additives range from viscosity index improvers to chemical treatments that claim to reduce internal engine friction. It should be noted that most oil manufacturers caution against using additives with their oils.

Gas additives perform several functions, depending on their chemical makeup. They usually contain solvents that help dissolve gum and varnish that build up on carburetor, fuel injection and intake parts. They also serve to break down carbon deposits that form on the inside surfaces of the combustion chambers. Some additives contain upper cylinder lubricants for valves and piston rings, and others contain chemicals to remove condensation from the gas tank.

MISCELLANEOUS

Brake fluid is specially formulated hydraulic fluid that can withstand the heat and pressure encountered in brake systems. Care must be taken so this fluid does not come in contact with painted surfaces or plastics. An opened container should always be resealed to prevent contamination by water or dirt.

Weatherstrip adhesive is used to bond weatherstripping around doors, windows and trunk lids. It is sometimes used to attach trim pieces.

Undercoating is a petroleum-based, tar-like substance that is designed to protect metal surfaces on the underside of the vehicle from corrosion. It also acts as a sound-deadening agent by insulating the bottom of the vehicle.

Waxes and polishes are used to help protect painted and plated surfaces from the weather. Different types of paint may require the use of different types of wax and polish. Some polishes utilize a chemical or abrasive cleaner to help remove the top layer of oxidized (dull) paint on older vehicles. In recent years many non-wax polishes that contain a wide variety of chemicals such as polymers and silicones have been introduced. These non-wax polishes are usually easier to apply and last longer than conventional waxes and polishes.

CONVERSION FACTORS

LENGTH (distance)

Inches (in)	X	25.4	= Millimeters (mm)	X 0.0394	= Inches (in)
Feet (ft)	X	0.305	= Meters (m)	X 3.281	= Feet (ft)
Miles	X	1.609	= Kilometers (km)	X 0.621	= Miles

VOLUME (capacity)

Cubic inches (cu in; in^3)	X	16.387	= Cubic centimeters (cc; cm^3)	X 0.061	= Cubic inches (cu in; in^3)
Imperial pints (Imp pt)	X	0.568	= Liters (l)	X 1.76	= Imperial pints (Imp pt)
Imperial quarts (Imp qt)	X	1.137	= Liters (l)	X 0.88	= Imperial quarts (Imp qt)
Imperial quarts (Imp qt)	X	1.201	= US quarts (US qt)	X 0.833	= Imperial quarts (Imp qt)
US quarts (US qt)	X	0.946	= Liters (l)	X 1.057	= US quarts (US qt)
Imperial gallons (Imp gal)	X	4.546	= Liters (l)	X 0.22	= Imperial gallons (Imp gal)
Imperial gallons (Imp gal)	X	1.201	= US gallons (US gal)	X 0.833	= Imperial gallons (Imp gal)
US gallons (US gal)	X	3.785	= Liters (l)	X 0.264	= US gallons (US gal)

MASS (weight)

Ounces (oz)	X	28.35	= Grams (g)	X 0.035	= Ounces (oz)
Pounds (lb)	X	0.454	= Kilograms (kg)	X 2.205	= Pounds (lb)

FORCE

Ounces-force (ozf; oz)	X	0.278	= Newtons (N)	X 3.6	= Ounces-force (ozf; oz)
Pounds-force (lbf; lb)	X	4.448	= Newtons (N)	X 0.225	= Pounds-force (lbf; lb)
Newtons (N)	X	0.1	= Kilograms-force (kgf; kg)	X 9.81	= Newtons (N)

PRESSURE

Pounds-force per square inch (psi; lbf/in^2; lb/in^2)	X	0.070	= Kilograms-force per square centimeter (kgf/cm^2; kg/cm^2)	X 14.223	= Pounds-force per square inch (psi; lbf/in^2; lb/in^2)
Pounds-force per square inch (psi; lbf/in^2; lb/in^2)	X	0.068	= Atmospheres (atm)	X 14.696	= Pounds-force per square inch (psi; lbf/in^2; lb/in^2)
Pounds-force per square inch (psi; lbf/in^2; lb/in^2)	X	0.069	= Bars	X 14.5	= Pounds-force per square inch (psi; lbf/in^2; lb/in^2)
Pounds-force per square inch (psi; lbf/in^2; lb/in^2)	X	6.895	= Kilopascals (kPa)	X 0.145	= Pounds-force per square inch (psi; lbf/in^2; lb/in^2)
Kilopascals (kPa)	X	0.01	= Kilograms-force per square centimeter (kgf/cm^2; kg/cm^2)	X 98.1	= Kilopascals (kPa)

TORQUE (moment of force)

Pounds-force inches (lbf in; lb in)	X	1.152	= Kilograms-force centimeter (kgf cm; kg cm)	X 0.868	= Pounds-force inches (lbf in; lb in)
Pounds-force inches (lbf in; lb in)	X	0.113	= Newton meters (Nm)	X 8.85	= Pounds-force inches (lbf in; lb in)
Pounds-force inches (lbf in; lb in)	X	0.083	= Pounds-force feet (lbf ft; lb ft)	X 12	= Pounds-force inches (lbf in; lb in)
Pounds-force feet (lbf ft; lb ft)	X	0.138	= Kilograms-force meters (kgf m; kg m)	X 7.233	= Pounds-force feet (lbf ft; lb ft)
Pounds-force feet (lbf ft; lb ft)	X	1.356	= Newton meters (Nm)	X 0.738	= Pounds-force feet (lbf ft; lb ft)
Newton meters (Nm)	X	0.102	= Kilograms-force meters (kgf m; kg m)	X 9.804	= Newton meters (Nm)

VACUUM

Inches mercury (in. Hg)	X	3.377	= Kilopascals (kPa)	X 0.2961	= Inches mercury
Inches mercury (in. Hg)	X	25.4	= Millimeters mercury (mm Hg)	X 0.0394	= Inches mercury

POWER

Horsepower (hp)	X	745.7	= Watts (W)	X 0.0013	= Horsepower (hp)

VELOCITY (speed)

Miles per hour (miles/hr; mph)	X	1.609	= Kilometers per hour (km/hr; kph)	X 0.621	= Miles per hour (miles/hr; mph)

FUEL CONSUMPTION *

Miles per gallon, Imperial (mpg)	X	0.354	= Kilometers per liter (km/l)	X 2.825	= Miles per gallon, Imperial (mpg)
Miles per gallon, US (mpg)	X	0.425	= Kilometers per liter (km/l)	X 2.352	= Miles per gallon, US (mpg)

TEMPERATURE

Degrees Fahrenheit = (°C x 1.8) + 32

Degrees Celsius (Degrees Centigrade; °C) = (°F - 32) x 0.56

It is common practice to convert from miles per gallon (mpg) to liters/100 kilometers (l/100km), where mpg (Imperial) x l/100 km = 282 and mpg (US) x l/100 km = 235

FRACTION/DECIMAL/MILLIMETER EQUIVALENTS

DECIMALS to MILLIMETERS

Decimal	mm	Decimal	mm
0.001	0.0254	0.500	12.7000
0.002	0.0508	0.510	12.9540
0.003	0.0762	0.520	13.2080
0.004	0.1016	0.530	13.4620
0.005	0.1270	0.540	13.7160
0.006	0.1524	0.550	13.9700
0.007	0.1778	0.560	14.2240
0.008	0.2032	0.570	14.4780
0.009	0.2286	0.580	14.7320
		0.590	14.9860
0.010	0.2540		
0.020	0.5080		
0.030	0.7620		
0.040	1.0160	0.600	15.2400
0.050	1.2700	0.610	15.4940
0.060	1.5240	0.620	15.7480
0.070	1.7780	0.630	16.0020
0.080	2.0320	0.640	16.2560
0.090	2.2860	0.650	16.5100
		0.660	16.7640
0.100	2.5400	0.670	17.0180
0.110	2.7940	0.680	17.2720
0.120	3.0480	0.690	17.5260
0.130	3.3020		
0.140	3.5560		
0.150	3.8100		
0.160	4.0640	0.700	17.7800
0.170	4.3180	0.710	18.0340
0.180	4.5720	0.720	18.2880
0.190	4.8260	0.730	18.5420
		0.740	18.7960
0.200	5.0800	0.750	19.0500
0.210	5.3340	0.760	19.3040
0.220	5.5880	0.770	19.5580
0.230	5.8420	0.780	19.8120
0.240	6.0960	0.790	20.0660
0.250	6.3500		
0.260	6.6040		
0.270	6.8580	0.800	20.3200
0.280	7.1120	0.810	20.5740
0.290	7.3660	0.820	21.8280
		0.830	21.0820
0.300	7.6200	0.840	21.3360
0.310	7.8740	0.850	21.5900
0.320	8.1280	0.860	21.8440
0.330	8.3820	0.870	22.0980
0.340	8.6360	0.880	22.3520
0.350	8.8900	0.890	22.6060
0.360	9.1440		
0.370	9.3980		
0.380	9.6520		
0.390	9.9060		
		0.900	22.8600
0.400	10.1600	0.910	23.1140
0.410	10.4140	0.920	23.3680
0.420	10.6680	0.930	23.6220
0.430	10.9220	0.940	23.8760
0.440	11.1760	0.950	24.1300
0.450	11.4300	0.960	24.3840
0.460	11.6840	0.970	24.6380
0.470	11.9380	0.980	24.8920
0.480	12.1920	0.990	25.1460
0.490	12.4460	1.000	25.4000

FRACTIONS to DECIMALS to MILLIMETERS

Fraction	Decimal	mm	Fraction	Decimal	mm
1/64	0.0156	0.3969	33/64	0.5156	13.0969
1/32	0.0312	0.7938	17/32	0.5312	13.4938
3/64	0.0469	1.1906	35/64	0.5469	13.8906
1/16	0.0625	1.5875	9/16	0.5625	14.2875
5/64	0.0781	1.9844	37/64	0.5781	14.6844
3/32	0.0938	2.3812	19/32	0.5938	15.0812
7/64	0.1094	2.7781	39/64	0.6094	15.4781
1/8	0.1250	3.1750	5/8	0.6250	15.8750
9/64	0.1406	3.5719	41/64	0.6406	16.2719
5/32	0.1562	3.9688	21/32	0.6562	16.6688
11/64	0.1719	4.3656	43/64	0.6719	17.0656
3/16	0.1875	4.7625	11/16	0.6875	17.4625
13/64	0.2031	5.1594	45/64	0.7031	17.8594
7/32	0.2188	5.5562	23/32	0.7188	18.2562
15/64	0.2344	5.9531	47/64	0.7344	18.6531
1/4	0.2500	6.3500	3/4	0.7500	19.0500
17/64	0.2656	6.7469	49/64	0.7656	19.4469
9/32	0.2812	7.1438	25/32	0.7812	19.8438
19/64	0.2969	7.5406	51/64	0.7969	20.2406
5/16	0.3125	7.9375	13/16	0.8125	20.6375
21/64	0.3281	8.3344	53/64	0.8281	21.0344
11/32	0.3438	8.7312	27/32	0.8438	21.4312
23/64	0.3594	9.1281	55/64	0.8594	21.8281
3/8	0.3750	9.5250	7/8	0.8750	22.2250
25/64	0.3906	9.9219	57/64	0.8906	22.6219
13/32	0.4062	10.3188	29/32	0.9062	23.0188
27/64	0.4219	10.7156	59/64	0.9219	23.4156
7/16	0.4375	11.1125	15/16	0.9375	23.8125
29/64	0.4531	11.5094	61/64	0.9531	24.2094
15/32	0.4688	11.9062	31/32	0.9688	24.6062
31/64	0.4844	12.3031	63/64	0.9844	25.0031
1/2	0.5000	12.7000	1	1.0000	25.4000

Regardless of how enthusiastic you may be about getting on with the job at hand, take the time to ensure that your safety is not jeopardized. A moment's lack of attention can result in an accident, as can failure to observe certain simple safety precautions. The possibility of an accident will always exist, and the following points should not be considered a comprehensive list of all dangers. Rather, they are intended to make you aware of the risks and to encourage a safety conscious approach to all work you carry out on your vehicle.

ESSENTIAL DOS AND DON'TS

DON'T rely on a jack when working under the vehicle. Always use approved jackstands to support the weight of the vehicle and place them under the recommended lift or support points.

DON'T attempt to loosen extremely tight fasteners (i.e. wheel lug nuts) while the vehicle is on a jack - it may fall.

DON'T start the engine without first making sure that the transmission is in Neutral (or Park where applicable) and the parking brake is set.

DON'T remove the radiator cap from a hot cooling system - let it cool or cover it with a cloth and release the pressure gradually.

DON'T attempt to drain the engine oil until you are sure it has cooled to the point that it will not burn you.

DON'T touch any part of the engine or exhaust system until it has cooled sufficiently to avoid burns.

DON'T siphon toxic liquids such as gasoline, antifreeze and brake fluid by mouth, or allow them to remain on your skin.

DON'T inhale brake lining dust - it is potentially hazardous (see *Asbestos* below).

DON'T allow spilled oil or grease to remain on the floor - wipe it up before someone slips on it.

DON'T use loose fitting wrenches or other tools which may slip and cause injury.

DON'T push on wrenches when loosening or tightening nuts or bolts. Always try to pull the wrench toward you. If the situation calls for pushing the wrench away, push with an open hand to avoid scraped knuckles if the wrench should slip.

DON'T attempt to lift a heavy component alone - get someone to help you.

DON'T rush or take unsafe shortcuts to finish a job.

DON'T allow children or animals in or around the vehicle while you are working on it.

DO wear eye protection when using power tools such as a drill, sander, bench grinder, etc. and when working under a vehicle.

DO keep loose clothing and long hair well out of the way of moving parts.

DO make sure that any hoist used has a safe working load rating adequate for the job.

DO get someone to check on you periodically when working alone on a vehicle.

DO carry out work in a logical sequence and make sure that everything is correctly assembled and tightened.

DO keep chemicals and fluids tightly capped and out of the reach of children and pets.

DO remember that your vehicle's safety affects that of yourself and others. If in doubt on any point, get professional advice.

ASBESTOS

Certain friction, insulating, sealing, and other products - such as brake linings, brake bands, clutch linings, torque converters, gaskets, etc. - may contain asbestos. Extreme care must be taken to avoid inhalation of dust from such products, since it is hazardous to health. If in doubt, assume that they do contain asbestos.

FIRE

Remember at all times that gasoline is highly flammable. Never smoke or have any kind of open flame around when working on a vehicle. But the risk does not end there. A spark caused by an electrical short circuit, by two metal surfaces contacting each other, or even by static electricity built up in your body under certain conditions, can ignite gasoline vapors, which in a confined space are highly explosive. Do not, under any circumstances, use gasoline for cleaning parts. Use an approved safety solvent.

Always disconnect the battery ground (-) cable at the battery before working on any part of the fuel system or electrical system. Never risk spilling fuel on a hot engine or exhaust component. It is strongly recommended that a fire extinguisher suitable for use on fuel and electrical fires be kept handy in the garage or workshop at all times. Never try to extinguish a fuel or electrical fire with water.

FUMES

Certain fumes are highly toxic and can quickly cause unconsciousness and even death if inhaled to any extent. Gasoline vapor falls into this category, as do the vapors from some cleaning solvents. Any draining or pouring of such volatile fluids should be done in a well ventilated area.

When using cleaning fluids and solvents, read the instructions on the container carefully. Never use materials from unmarked containers.

Never run the engine in an enclosed space, such as a garage. Exhaust fumes contain carbon monoxide, which is extremely poisonous. If you need to run the engine, always do so in the open air, or at least have the rear of the vehicle outside the work area.

If you are fortunate enough to have the use of an inspection pit, never drain or pour gasoline and never run the engine while the vehicle is over the pit. The fumes, being heavier than air, will concentrate in the pit with possibly lethal results.

THE BATTERY

Never create a spark or allow a bare light bulb near a battery. They normally give off a certain amount of hydrogen gas, which is highly explosive.

Always disconnect the battery ground (-) cable at the battery before working on the fuel or electrical systems.

If possible, loosen the filler caps or cover when charging the battery from an external source (this does not apply to sealed or maintenance-free batteries). Do not charge at an excessive rate or the battery may burst.

Take care when adding water to a non maintenance-free battery and when carrying a battery. The electrolyte, even when diluted, is very corrosive and should not be allowed to contact clothing or skin.

Always wear eye protection when cleaning the battery to prevent the caustic deposits from entering your eyes.

HOUSEHOLD CURRENT

When using an electric power tool, inspection light, etc., which operates on household current, always make sure that the tool is correctly connected to its plug and that, where necessary, it is properly grounded. Do not use such items in damp conditions and, again, do not create a spark or apply excessive heat in the vicinity of fuel or fuel vapor.

SECONDARY IGNITION SYSTEM VOLTAGE

A severe electric shock can result from touching certain parts of the ignition system (such as the spark plug wires) when the engine is running or being cranked, particularly if components are damp or the insulation is defective. In the case of an electronic ignition system, the secondary system voltage is much higher and could prove fatal.

Troubleshooting

CONTENTS

ENGINE

1 Engine will not rotate when attempting to start

1 Battery terminal connections loose or corroded. Check the cable terminals at the battery; tighten cable clamp and/or clean off corrosion as necessary (see Chapter 1).

2 Battery discharged or faulty. If the cable ends are clean and tight on the battery posts, turn the key to the On position and switch on the headlights or windshield wipers. If they won't run, the battery is discharged.

3 Automatic transmission not engaged in park (P) or Neutral (N).

4 Broken, loose or disconnected wires in the starting circuit. Inspect all wires and connectors at the battery, starter solenoid and ignition switch (on steering column).

5 Starter motor pinion jammed in driveplate ring gear. Remove starter (Chapter 5) and inspect pinion and driveplate (Chapter 2).

6 Starter solenoid faulty (Chapter 5).

7 Starter motor faulty (Chapter 5).

8 Ignition switch faulty (Chapter 12).

9 Engine seized. Try to turn the crankshaft with a large socket and breaker bar on the pulley bolt.

10 Starter relay (CCRM) faulty (Chapter 4).

11 Transmission Range (TR) sensor out of adjustment or defective (Chapter 6).

2 Engine rotates but will not start

1 Fuel tank empty.

2 Battery discharged (engine rotates slowly).

3 Battery terminal connections loose or corroded.

4 Fuel not reaching fuel injectors. Check for clogged fuel filter or lines and defective fuel pump. Also make sure the tank vent lines aren't clogged (Chapter 4).

5 Faulty distributor components (5.0L engine). Check the cap and rotor (Chapter 1).

6 Low cylinder compression. Check as described in Chapter 2.

7 Water in fuel. Drain tank and fill with new fuel.

8 Defective ignition coil(s) (Chapter 5).

9 Dirty or clogged fuel injector(s) (Chapter 4).

10 Wet or damaged ignition components (Chapters 1 and 5).

11 Worn, faulty or incorrectly gapped spark plugs (Chapter 1).

12 Broken, loose or disconnected wires in the starting circuit (see previous Section).

13 Loose distributor (5.0L engine). Turn the distributor body as necessary to start the engine, then adjust the ignition timing as soon as possible (Chapter 5).

14 Broken, loose or disconnected wires at the ignition coil or faulty coil (Chapter 5).

15 Timing chain failure or wear affecting valve timing (Chapter 2).

16 Fuel injection or engine control systems failure (Chapters 4 and 6).

17 Defective MAF sensor (Chapter 6)

3 Starter motor operates without turning engine

1 Starter pinion sticking. Remove the starter (Chapter 5) and inspect.

2 Starter pinion or driveplate teeth worn or broken. Remove the inspection cover and inspect.

4 Engine hard to start when cold

1 Battery discharged or low. Check as described in Chapter 1.

2 Fuel not reaching the fuel injectors. Check the fuel filter, lines and fuel pump (Chapters 1 and 4).

3 Defective spark plugs (Chapter 1).

4 Defective engine coolant temperature sensor (Chapter 6).

5 Fuel injection or engine control systems malfunction (Chapters 4 and 6).

5 Engine hard to start when hot

1 Air filter dirty (Chapter 1).

2 Fuel not reaching the fuel injection (see Section 4). Check for a vapor lock situation, brought about by clogged fuel tank vent lines.

3 Bad engine ground connection.

4 Defective pick-up coil in distributor (5.0L engine) (Chapter 5).

5 Fuel injection or engine control systems malfunction (Chapters 4 and 6).

6 Starter motor noisy or engages roughly

1 Pinion or driveplate teeth worn or broken. Remove the inspection cover on the left side of the engine and inspect.

2 Starter motor mounting bolts loose or missing.

7 Engine starts but stops immediately

1 Loose or damaged wire harness connections at distributor, coil or alternator.

2 Intake manifold vacuum leaks. Make sure all mounting bolts/nuts are tight and all vacuum hoses connected to the manifold are attached properly and in good condition.

3 Insufficient fuel pressure (see Chapter 4).

4 Fuel injection or engine control systems malfunction (Chapters 4 and 6).

8 Engine 'lopes' while idling or idles erratically

1 Vacuum leaks. Check mounting bolts at the intake manifold for tightness. Make sure that all vacuum hoses are connected and in good condition. Use a stethoscope or a length of fuel hose held against your ear to listen for vacuum leaks while the engine is running. A hissing sound will be heard. A soapy water solution will also detect leaks. Check the intake manifold gasket surfaces.

2 Leaking EGR valve or plugged PCV valve (see Chapters 1 and 6).

3 Air filter clogged (Chapter 1).

4 Fuel pump not delivering sufficient fuel (Chapter 4).

5 Leaking head gasket. Perform a cylinder compression check (Chapter 2).

6 Timing chain(s) worn (Chapter 2).

7 Camshaft lobes worn (Chapter 2).

8 Valves burned or otherwise leaking (Chapter 2).

9 Ignition timing out of adjustment (Chapter 5).

10 Ignition system not operating properly (Chapters 1 and 5).

11 Fuel injection or engine control systems malfunction (Chapters 4 and 6).

9 Engine misses at idle speed

1 Spark plugs faulty or not gapped properly (Chapter 1).
2 Faulty spark plug wires (Chapter 1).
3 Wet or damaged distributor components (5.0L engine) (Chapter 1).
4 Short circuits in ignition, coil or spark plug wires.
5 Sticking or faulty emissions systems (see Chapter 6).
6 Clogged fuel filter and/or foreign matter in fuel. Remove the fuel filter (Chapter 1) and inspect.
7 Vacuum leaks at intake manifold or hose connections. Check as described in Section 8.
8 Incorrect idle speed (Chapter 4).
9 Low or uneven cylinder compression. Check as described in Chapter 2.
10 Fuel injection or engine control systems malfunction (Chapters 4 and 6).

10 Excessively high idle speed

1 Sticking throttle linkage (Chapter 4).
2 Vacuum leaks at intake manifold or hose connections. Check as described in Section 8.
3 Fuel injection or engine control systems malfunction (Chapters 4 and 6).

11 Battery will not hold a charge

1 Alternator drivebelt defective or not adjusted properly (Chapter 1).
2 Battery cables loose or corroded (Chapter 1).
3 Alternator not charging properly (Chapter 5).
4 Loose, broken or faulty wires in the charging circuit (Chapter 5).
5 Short circuit causing a continuous drain on the battery.
6 Battery defective internally.

12 Alternator light stays on

1 Fault in alternator or charging circuit (Chapter 5).
2 Alternator drivebelt defective or not properly adjusted (Chapter 1).

13 Alternator light fails to come on when key is turned on

1 Faulty bulb (Chapter 12).
2 Defective alternator (Chapter 5).
3 Fault in the printed circuit, dash wiring or bulb holder (Chapter 12).

14 Engine misses throughout driving speed range

1 Fuel filter clogged and/or impurities in the fuel system. Check fuel filter (Chapter 1) or clean system (Chapter 4).
2 Faulty or incorrectly gapped spark plugs (Chapter 1).
3 Incorrect ignition timing (Chapter 1).
4 Cracked distributor cap, disconnected distributor wires or damaged distributor components (5.0L engine) (Chapter 1).
5 Defective spark plug wires (Chapter 1).
6 Emissions system components faulty (Chapter 6).
7 Low or uneven cylinder compression pressures. Check as described in Chapter 2.

8 Weak or faulty ignition coil(s) (Chapter 5).
9 Weak or faulty ignition system (Chapter 5).
10 Vacuum leaks at intake manifold or vacuum hoses (see Section 8).
11 Dirty or clogged fuel injector(s) (Chapter 4).
12 Leaky EGR valve (Chapter 6).
13 Fuel injection or engine control systems malfunction (Chapters 4 and 6).

15 Hesitation or stumble during acceleration

1 Ignition system not operating properly (Chapter 5).
2 Dirty or clogged fuel injector(s) (Chapter 4).
3 Low fuel pressure. Check for proper operation of the fuel pump and for restrictions in the fuel filter and lines (Chapter 4).
4 Fuel injection or engine control systems malfunction (Chapters 4 and 6).

16 Engine stalls

1 Idle speed incorrect (Chapter 4).
2 Fuel filter clogged and/or water and impurities in the fuel system (Chapter 1).
3 Damaged or wet distributor cap and wires.
4 Emissions system components faulty (Chapter 6).
5 Faulty or incorrectly gapped spark plugs (Chapter 1). Also check the spark plug wires (Chapter 1).
6 Vacuum leak at the intake manifold or vacuum hoses. Check as described in Section 8.
7 Fuel injection or engine control systems malfunction (Chapters 4 and 6).

17 Engine lacks power

1 Incorrect ignition timing (Chapter 1).
2 Excessive play in distributor shaft (5.0L engine). At the same time check for faulty distributor cap, wires, etc. (Chapter 1).
3 Faulty or incorrectly gapped spark plugs (Chapter 1).
4 Air filter dirty (Chapter 1).
5 Faulty ignition coil(s) (Chapter 5).
6 Brakes binding (Chapters 1 and 10).
7 Automatic transmission fluid level incorrect, causing slippage (Chapter 1).
8 Fuel filter clogged and/or impurities in the fuel system (Chapters 1 and 4).
9 EGR system not functioning properly (Chapter 6).
10 Use of sub-standard fuel. Fill tank with proper octane fuel.
11 Low or uneven cylinder compression pressures. Check as described in Chapter 2.
12 Vacuum leak at intake manifold or vacuum hoses (check as described in Section 8).
13 Dirty or clogged fuel injector(s) (Chapters 1 and 4).
14 Fuel injection or engine control systems malfunction (Chapters 4 and 6).
15 Restricted exhaust system (Chapter 4).

18 Engine backfires

1 EGR system not functioning properly (Chapter 6).
2 Ignition timing incorrect (Chapter 5).

3 Vacuum leak (refer to Section 8).
4 Damaged valve springs or sticking valves (Chapter 2).
5 Vacuum leak at the intake manifold or vacuum hoses (see Section 8).

19 Engine surges while holding accelerator steady

1 Vacuum leak at the intake manifold or vacuum hoses (see Section 8).
2 Restricted air filter (Chapter 1).
3 Fuel pump or pressure regulator defective (Chapter 4).
4 Fuel injection or engine control systems malfunction (Chapters 4 and 6).

20 Pinging or knocking engine sounds when engine is under load

1 Incorrect grade of fuel. Fill tank with fuel of the proper octane rating.
2 Ignition timing incorrect (5.0L engine) (Chapter 1).
3 Carbon build-up in combustion chambers. Remove cylinder head(s) and clean combustion chambers (Chapter 2).
4 Incorrect spark plugs (Chapter 1).
5 Fuel injection or engine control systems malfunction (Chapters 4 and 6).
6 Restricted exhaust system (Chapter 4).

21 Engine diesels (continues to run) after being turned off

1 Idle speed too high (Chapter 4).
2 Ignition timing incorrect (5.0L engine) (Chapter 5).
3 Incorrect spark plug heat range (Chapter 1).
4 Vacuum leak at the intake manifold or vacuum hoses (see Section 8).
5 Carbon build-up in combustion chambers. Remove the cylinder head(s) and clean the combustion chambers (Chapter 2).
6 Valves sticking (Chapter 2).
7 EGR system not operating properly (Chapter 6).
8 Fuel injection or engine control systems malfunction (Chapters 4 and 6).
9 Check for causes of overheating (Section 27).

22 Low oil pressure

1 Improper grade of oil.
2 Oil pump worn or damaged (Chapter 2).
3 Engine overheating (refer to Section 27).
4 Clogged oil filter (Chapter 1).
5 Clogged oil strainer (Chapter 2).
6 Oil pressure gauge not working properly (Chapter 2).

23 Excessive oil consumption

1 Loose oil drain plug.
2 Loose bolts or damaged oil pan gasket (Chapter 2).
3 Loose bolts or damaged front cover gasket (Chapter 2).
4 Front or rear crankshaft oil seal leaking (Chapter 2).
5 Loose bolts or damaged valve cover gasket (Chapter 2).
6 Loose oil filter (Chapter 1).

7 Loose or damaged oil pressure switch (Chapter 2).
8 Pistons and cylinders excessively worn (Chapter 2).
9 Piston rings not installed correctly on pistons (Chapter 2).
10 Worn or damaged piston rings (Chapter 2).
11 Intake and/or exhaust valve oil seals worn or damaged (Chapter 2).
12 Worn valve stems or guides.
13 Worn or damaged valves/guides (Chapter 2).
14 Faulty or incorrect PCV valve allowing too much crankcase airflow.

24 Excessive fuel consumption

1 Dirty or clogged air filter element (Chapter 1).
2 Incorrect ignition timing (5.0L engine) (Chapter 5).
3 Incorrect idle speed (Chapter 4).
4 Low tire pressure or incorrect tire size (Chapter 10).
5 Inspect for binding brakes.
6 Fuel leakage. Check all connections, lines and components in the fuel system (Chapter 4).
7 Dirty or clogged fuel injectors (Chapter 4).
8 Fuel injection or engine control systems malfunction (Chapters 4 and 6).
9 Thermostat stuck open or not installed.
10 Improperly operating transmission.

25 Fuel odor

1 Fuel leakage. Check all connections, lines and components in the fuel system (Chapter 4).
2 Fuel tank overfilled. Fill only to automatic shut-off.
3 Charcoal canister filter in Evaporative Emissions Control system clogged (Chapter 1).
4 Vapor leaks from Evaporative Emissions Control system lines (Chapter 6).

26 Miscellaneous engine noises

1 A strong dull noise that becomes more rapid as the engine accelerates indicates worn or damaged crankshaft bearings or an unevenly worn crankshaft. To pinpoint the trouble spot, remove the spark plug wire from one plug at a time and crank the engine over. If the noise stops, the cylinder with the removed plug wire indicates the problem area. Replace the bearing and/or service or replace the crankshaft (Chapter 2).

2 A similar (yet slightly higher pitched) noise to the crankshaft knocking described in the previous paragraph, that becomes more rapid as the engine accelerates, indicates worn or damaged connecting rod bearings (Chapter 2). The procedure for locating the problem cylinder is the same as described in Paragraph 1.

3 An overlapping metallic noise that increases in intensity as the engine speed increases, yet diminishes as the engine warms up indicates abnormal piston and cylinder wear (Chapter 2). To locate the problem cylinder, use the procedure described in Paragraph 1.

4 A rapid clicking noise that becomes faster as the engine accelerates indicates a worn piston pin or piston pin hole. This sound will happen each time the piston hits the highest and lowest points in the stroke (Chapter 2). The procedure for locating the problem piston is described in Paragraph 1.

5 A metallic clicking noise coming from the water pump indicates worn or damaged water pump bearings or pump. Replace the water

pump with a new one (Chapter 3).

6   A rapid tapping sound or clicking sound that becomes faster as the engine speed increases indicates "valve tapping." This can be identified by holding one end of a section of hose to your ear and placing the other end at different spots along the valve cover. The point where the sound is loudest indicates the problem valve. If the pushrod and rocker arm components are in good shape, you likely have a collapsed valve lifter. Changing the engine oil and adding a high viscosity oil treatment will sometimes cure a stuck lifter problem. If the problem persists, the lifters, pushrods and rocker arms must be removed for inspection (see Chapter 2).

7   A steady metallic rattling or rapping sound coming from the area of the timing chain cover indicates a worn, damaged or out-of-adjustment timing chain. Service or replace the chain and related components (Chapter 2).

COOLING SYSTEM

27   Overheating

1   Insufficient coolant in system (Chapter 1).
2   Drivebelt defective or not adjusted properly (Chapter 1).
3   Radiator core blocked or radiator grille dirty and restricted (Chapter 3).
4   Thermostat faulty (Chapter 3).
5   Cooling fan not functioning properly (Chapter 3).
6   Radiator cap not maintaining proper pressure. Have cap pressure tested by gas station or repair shop.
7   Ignition timing incorrect (5.0L engine) (Chapter 5).
8   Defective water pump (Chapter 3).
9   Improper grade of engine oil.
10 Inaccurate temperature gauge (Chapter 12).

28   Overcooling

1   Thermostat faulty (Chapter 3).
2   Inaccurate temperature gauge (Chapter 12).

29   External coolant leakage

1   Deteriorated or damaged hoses. Loose clamps at hose connections (Chapter 1).
2   Water pump seals defective. If this is the case, water will drip from the weep hole in the water pump body (Chapter 3).
3   Leakage from radiator core or header tank. This will require the radiator to be professionally repaired (see Chapter 3 for removal procedures).
4   Leakage from the coolant reservoir or degas bottle.
5   Engine drain plugs or water jacket freeze plugs leaking (see Chapters 1 and 2).
6   Leak from coolant temperature switch (Chapter 3).
7   Leak from damaged gaskets or small cracks (Chapter 2).
8   Leak from oil cooler or oil cooler adapter housing, 4.6L Cobra models (Chapter 3).

30   Internal coolant leakage

➡Note: Internal coolant leaks can usually be detected by examining the oil. Check the dipstick and inside the rocker arm cover for water deposits and an oil consistency like that of a milkshake.

1   Leaking cylinder head gasket. Have the system pressure tested or remove the cylinder head (Chapter 2) and inspect.
2   Cracked cylinder bore or cylinder head. Dismantle engine and inspect (Chapter 2).
3   Loose cylinder head bolts (tighten as described in Chapter 2).
4   Leakage from internal coolant pipe/hose (4.6L engines) (accessible only with intake manifold removed (Chapter 2B).

31   Abnormal coolant loss

1   Overfilling system (Chapter 1).
2   Coolant boiling away due to overheating (see causes in Section 27).
3   Internal or external leakage (see Sections 29 and 30).
4   Faulty radiator cap. Have the cap pressure tested.
5   Cooling system being pressurized by engine compression. This could be due to a cracked head or block or leaking head gasket(s). Have the system tested for the presence of combustion gas in the coolant at a shop.

32   Poor coolant circulation

1   Inoperative water pump. A quick test is to pinch the top radiator hose closed with your hand while the engine is idling, then release it. You should feel a surge of coolant if the pump is working properly (Chapter 3).
2   Restriction in cooling system. Drain, flush and refill the system (Chapter 1). If necessary, remove the radiator (Chapter 3) and have it reverse flushed or professionally cleaned.
3   Loose water pump drivebelt (Chapter 1).
4   Thermostat sticking (Chapter 3).
5   Insufficient coolant (Chapter 1).

33   Corrosion

1   Excessive impurities in the water. Soft, clean water is recommended. Distilled or rainwater is satisfactory.
2   Insufficient antifreeze solution (refer to Chapter 1 for the proper ratio of water to antifreeze).
3   Infrequent flushing and draining of system. Regular flushing of the cooling system should be carried out at the specified intervals as described in (Chapter 1).

CLUTCH

➡Note: All clutch service information is located in Chapter 8, unless otherwise noted.

34   Fails to release (pedal pressed to the floor - shift lever does not move freely in and out of Reverse)

1   Clutch plate warped, distorted or otherwise damaged.
2   Diaphragm spring fatigued. Remove clutch cover/pressure plate assembly and inspect.
3   Insufficient pedal stroke. Check and adjust as necessary.
4   Lack of grease on pilot bushing.

35 Clutch slips (engine speed increases with no increase in vehicle speed)

1 Worn or oil soaked clutch plate.
2 Clutch plate not broken in. It may take 30 or 40 normal starts for a new clutch to seat.
3 Diaphragm spring weak or damaged. Remove clutch cover/pressure plate assembly and inspect.
4 Flywheel warped (Chapter 2).

36 Grabbing (chattering) as clutch is engaged

1 Oil on clutch plate. Remove and inspect. Repair any leaks.
2 Worn or loose engine or transmission mounts. They may move slightly when clutch is released. Inspect mounts and bolts.
3 Worn splines on transmission input shaft. Remove clutch components and inspect.
4 Warped pressure plate or flywheel. Remove clutch components and inspect.
5 Diaphragm spring fatigued. Remove clutch cover/pressure plate assembly and inspect.
6 Clutch linings hardened or warped.
7 Clutch lining rivets loose.

37 Squeal or rumble with clutch engaged (pedal released)

1 Improper pedal adjustment. Adjust pedal free play.
2 Release bearing binding on transmission shaft. Remove clutch components and check bearing. Remove any burrs or nicks, clean and relubricate before reinstallation.
3 Pilot bushing worn or damaged.
4 Clutch rivets loose.
5 Clutch plate cracked.
6 Fatigued clutch plate torsion springs. Replace clutch plate.

38 Squeal or rumble with clutch disengaged (pedal depressed)

1 Worn or damaged release bearing.
2 Worn or broken pressure plate diaphragm fingers.

39 Clutch pedal stays on floor when disengaged

Sticking cable or release bearing. Inspect cable or remove clutch components as necessary.

MANUAL TRANSMISSION

➡Note: All manual transmission service information is located in Chapter 7A, unless otherwise noted.

40 Noisy in Neutral with engine running

1 Input shaft bearing worn.
2 Damaged main drive gear bearing.
3 Insufficient transmission oil (Chapter 1).

4 Transmission oil in poor condition. Drain and fill with proper grade oil. Check old oil for water and debris (Chapter 1).
5 Noise can be caused by variations in engine torque. Change the idle speed and see if noise disappears.

41 Noisy in all gears

1 Any of the above causes, and/or:
2 Worn or damaged output gear bearings or shaft.

42 Noisy in one particular gear

1 Worn, damaged or chipped gear teeth.
2 Worn or damaged synchronizer.

43 Slips out of gear

1 Transmission loose on clutch housing.
2 Stiff shift lever seal.
3 Shift linkage binding.
4 Broken or loose input gear bearing retainer.
5 Dirt between clutch lever and engine housing.
6 Worn linkage.
7 Damaged or worn check balls, fork rod ball grooves or check springs.
8 Worn mainshaft or countershaft bearings.
9 Loose engine mounts (Chapter 2).
10 Excessive gear end play.
11 Worn synchronizers.

44 Oil leaks

1 Excessive amount of lubricant in transmission (see Chapter 1 for correct checking procedures). Drain lubricant as required.
2 Rear oil seal or speedometer oil seal damaged.
3 To pinpoint a leak, first remove all built-up dirt and grime from the transmission. Degreasing agents and/or steam cleaning will achieve this. With the underside clean, drive the vehicle at low speeds so the air flow will not blow the leak far from its source. Raise the vehicle and determine where the leak is located.

45 Difficulty engaging gears

1 Clutch not releasing completely.
2 Loose or damaged shift linkage. Make a thorough inspection, replacing parts as necessary.
3 Insufficient transmission oil (Chapter 1).
4 Transmission oil in poor condition. Drain and fill with proper grade oil. Check oil for water and debris (Chapter 1).
5 Sticking or jamming gears.

46 Noise occurs while shifting gears

1 Check for proper operation of the clutch (Chapter 8).
2 Faulty synchronizer assemblies. Measure baulk ring-to-gear clearance. Also, check for wear or damage to baulk rings or any parts of the synchromesh assemblies.

AUTOMATIC TRANSMISSION

➡Note: Due to the complexity of the automatic transmission, it's difficult for the home mechanic to properly diagnose and service. For problems other than the following, the vehicle should be taken to a reputable mechanic.

47 Fluid leakage

1 Automatic transmission fluid is a deep red color, and fluid leaks should not be confused with engine oil which can easily be blown by air flow to the transmission.

2 To pinpoint a leak, first remove all built-up dirt and grime from the transmission. Degreasing agents and/or steam cleaning will achieve this. With the underside clean, drive the vehicle at low speeds so the air flow will not blow the leak far from its source. Raise the vehicle and determine where the leak is located. Common areas of leakage are:

a) *Fluid pan: tighten mounting bolts and/or replace pan gasket as necessary (Chapter 1).*
b) *Rear extension: tighten bolts and/or replace oil seal as necessary.*
c) *Filler pipe: replace the rubber oil seal where pipe enters transmission case.*
d) *Transmission oil lines: tighten fittings where lines enter transmission case and/or replace lines.*
e) *Vent pipe: transmission overfilled and/or water in fluid (see checking procedures, Chapter 1).*
f) *Vehicle speed sensor: replace the O-ring where speed sensor enters transmission case.*

48 General shift mechanism problems

Chapter 7 deals with checking and adjusting the shift linkage on automatic transmissions. Common problems which may be caused by out of adjustment linkage are:

a) *Engine starting in gears other than P (park) or N (Neutral).*
b) *Indicator pointing to a gear other than the one actually engaged.*
c) *Vehicle moves with transmission in P (Park) position.*

49 Transmission will not downshift with the accelerator pedal pressed to the floor

Chapter 7 deals with adjusting the throttle valve cable to enable the transmission to downshift properly.

50 Engine will start in gears other than Park or Neutral

Chapter 7 deals with adjusting the Neutral start switch installed on automatic transmissions.

51 Transmission slips, shifts rough, is noisy or has no drive in forward or Reverse gears

1 There are many probable causes for the above problems, but the home mechanic should concern himself only with one possibility; fluid level.

2 Before taking the vehicle to a shop, check the fluid level and condition as described in Chapter 1. Add fluid, if necessary, or change the fluid and filter if needed. If problems persist, have a professional diagnose the transmission.

3 Transmission fluid break down after 30,000 miles.

DRIVESHAFT

➡Note: Refer to Chapter 8, unless otherwise specified, for service information.

52 Leaks at front of driveshaft

Defective transmission or transfer case seal. See Chapter 7 for replacement procedure. As this is done, check the splined yoke for burrs or roughness that could damage the new seal. Remove burrs with a fine file or whetstone.

53 Knock or clunk when transmission is under initial load (just after transmission is put into gear)

1 Loose or disconnected rear suspension components. Check all mounting bolts and bushings (Chapters 7 and 10).

2 Loose driveshaft bolts. Inspect all bolts and nuts and tighten them securely.

3 Worn or damaged universal joint bearings (Chapter 8).

4 Worn sleeve yoke and mainshaft spline.

54 Metallic grating sound consistent with vehicle speed

Pronounced wear in the universal joint bearings. Replace U-joints or driveshaft, as necessary.

55 Vibration

➡Note: Before blaming the driveshaft, make sure the tires are perfectly balanced and perform the following test.

1 Install a tachometer inside the vehicle to monitor engine speed as the vehicle is driven. Drive the vehicle and note the engine speed at which the vibration (roughness) is most pronounced. Now shift the transmission to a different gear and bring the engine speed to the same point.

2 If the vibration occurs at the same engine speed (rpm) regardless of which gear the transmission is in, the driveshaft is NOT at fault since the driveshaft speed varies.

3 If the vibration decreases or is eliminated when the transmission is in a different gear at the same engine speed, refer to the following probable causes:

a *Bent or dented driveshaft. Inspect and replace as necessary.*
b *Undercoating or built-up dirt, etc. on the driveshaft. Clean the shaft thoroughly.*
c *Worn universal joint bearings. Replace the U-joints or driveshaft as necessary.*
d *Driveshaft and/or companion flange out of balance. Check for missing weights on the shaft. Remove driveshaft and reinstall 180-degrees from original position, then recheck. Have the driveshaft balanced if problem persists.*
e *Loose driveshaft mounting bolts/nuts.*
f *Worn transmission rear bushing (Chapter 7).*

56 Scraping noise

Make sure there is nothing, such as an exhaust heat shield, rubbing on the driveshaft.

AXLE(S) AND DIFFERENTIAL

➡Note: For differential servicing information, refer to Chapter 8, unless otherwise specified.

57 Noise - same when in drive as when vehicle is coasting

1 Road noise. No corrective action available.
2 Tire noise. Inspect tires and check tire pressures (Chapter 1).
3 Front wheel bearings loose, worn or damaged (Chapter 1).
4 Insufficient differential oil (Chapter 1).
5 Defective differential.

58 Knocking sound when starting or shifting gears

Defective or incorrectly adjusted differential.

59 Noise when turning

Defective differential.

60 Vibration

See probable causes under Driveshaft. Proceed under the guidelines listed for the driveshaft. If the problem persists, check the rear wheel bearings by raising the rear of the vehicle and spinning the wheels by hand. Listen for evidence of rough (noisy) bearings. Remove and inspect (Chapter 8).

61 Oil leaks

1 Pinion oil seal damaged (Chapter 8).
2 Axleshaft oil seals damaged (Chapter 8).
3 Differential cover leaking. Tighten mounting bolts or replace the gasket as required.
4 Loose filler plug on differential (Chapter 1).
5 Clogged or damaged breather on differential.

BRAKES

➡Note: Before assuming a brake problem exists, make sure the tires are in good condition and inflated properly, the front end alignment is correct and the vehicle is not loaded with weight in an unequal manner. All service procedures for the brakes are included in Chapter 9, unless otherwise noted.

62 Vehicle pulls to one side during braking

1 Defective, damaged or oil contaminated brake pad on one side. Inspect as described in Chapter 1. Refer to Chapter 9 if replacement is required.
2 Excessive wear of brake pad material or disc on one side. Inspect and repair as necessary.
3 Loose or disconnected front suspension components. Inspect and tighten all bolts securely (Chapters 1 and 10).
4 Defective front brake caliper assembly. Remove caliper and inspect for stuck piston or damage.

5 Scored or out of round disc.
6 Loose brake caliper mounting bolts.

63 Noise (high-pitched squeal)

1 Front brake pads worn out. This noise comes from the wear sensor rubbing against the disc. Replace pads with new ones immediately!
2 Glazed or contaminated pads.
3 Dirty or scored disc.
4 Bent support plate.

64 Excessive brake pedal travel

1 Partial brake system failure. Inspect entire system (Chapter 1) and correct as required.
2 Insufficient fluid in master cylinder. Check (Chapter 1) and add fluid - bleed system if necessary.
3 Air in system. Bleed system.
4 Defective master cylinder.

65 Brake pedal feels spongy when depressed

1 Air in brake lines. Bleed the brake system.
2 Deteriorated rubber brake hoses. Inspect all system hoses and lines. Replace parts as necessary.
3 Master cylinder mounting nuts loose. Inspect master cylinder bolts (nuts) and tighten them securely.
4 Master cylinder faulty.
5 Incorrect brake pad clearance.
6 Clogged reservoir cap vent hole.
7 Deformed rubber brake lines.
8 Soft or swollen caliper seals.
9 Poor quality brake fluid. Bleed entire system and fill with new approved fluid.

66 Excessive effort required to stop vehicle

1 Power brake booster not operating properly.
2 Excessively worn brake pads. Check and replace if necessary.
3 One or more caliper pistons seized or sticking. Inspect and rebuild as required.
4 Brake pads contaminated with oil or grease. Inspect and replace as required.
5 Worn or damaged master cylinder or caliper assemblies. Check particularly for frozen pistons.

67 Pedal travels to the floor with little resistance

Little or no fluid in the master cylinder reservoir caused by leaking caliper piston(s) or loose, damaged or disconnected brake lines. Inspect entire system and repair as necessary.

68 Brake pedal pulsates during brake application

1 Wheel bearings damaged, worn or out of adjustment.
2 Caliper not sliding properly due to improper installation or obstructions. Remove and inspect.
3 Disc not within specifications. Check for excessive lateral runout and parallelism. Have the discs resurfaced or replace them with new ones. Also make sure that all discs are the same thickness.

69 Brakes drag (indicated by sluggish engine performance or wheels being very hot after driving)

1 Pushrod adjustment incorrect at the brake pedal or power booster.
2 Obstructed master cylinder compensator. Disassemble master cylinder and clean.
3 Master cylinder piston seized in bore. Overhaul master cylinder.
4 Caliper assembly in need of overhaul.
5 Piston cups in master cylinder or caliper assembly deformed. Overhaul master cylinder.
6 Parking brake assembly will not release.
7 Clogged or internally split brake lines.
8 Wheel bearings defective.
9 Brake pedal height improperly adjusted.

70 Rear brakes lock up under light brake application

1 Tire pressures too high.
2 Tires excessively worn (Chapter 1).
3 Defective proportioning valve.

71 Rear brakes lock up under heavy brake application

1 Tire pressures too high.
2 Tires excessively worn (Chapter 1).
3 Front brake pads contaminated with oil, mud or water. Clean or replace the pads.
4 Front brake pads excessively worn.
5 Defective proportioning valve.

SUSPENSION AND STEERING

➡Note: All service procedures for the suspension and steering systems are included in Chapter 10, unless otherwise noted.

72 Vehicle pulls to one side

1 Tire pressures uneven (Chapter 1).
2 Defective tire (Chapter 1).
3 Excessive wear in suspension or steering components (Chapter 1).
4 Front end alignment incorrect.
5 Front brakes dragging. Inspect as described in Section 71.
6 Wheel bearings improperly adjusted (Chapter 1).
7 Wheel lug nuts loose.

73 Shimmy, shake or vibration

1 Tire or wheel out of balance or out of round.
2 Loose, worn or out of adjustment wheel bearings (Chapter 1).
3 Shock absorbers and/or suspension components worn or damaged (see Chapter 10).

74 Excessive pitching and/or rolling around corners or during braking

1 Defective shock absorbers. Replace as a set.
2 Broken or weak leaf springs and/or suspension components.
3 Worn or damaged stabilizer bar or bushings.

75 Wandering or general instability

1 Improper tire pressures.
2 Incorrect front end alignment.
3 Worn or damaged steering linkage or suspension components.
4 Improperly adjusted steering gear.
5 Out-of-balance wheels.
6 Loose wheel lug nuts.
7 Worn rear shock absorbers.
8 Fatigued or damaged rear leaf springs.

76 Excessively stiff steering

1 Lack of fluid in the power steering fluid reservoir, where appropriate (Chapter 1).
2 Incorrect tire pressures (Chapter 1).
3 Lack of lubrication at balljoints (Chapter 1).
4 Front end out of alignment.
5 Steering gear out of adjustment or lacking lubrication.
6 Improperly adjusted wheel bearings.
7 Worn or damaged steering gear.
8 Interference of steering column with turn signal switch.
9 Low tire pressures.
10 Worn or damaged balljoints.
11 Worn or damaged steering linkage.

77 Excessive play in steering

1 Loose wheel bearings (Chapter 1).
2 Excessive wear in suspension bushings (Chapter 1).
3 Steering gear improperly adjusted.
4 Incorrect front end alignment.
5 Steering gear mounting bolts loose.
6 Worn steering linkage.

78 Lack of power assistance

1 Steering pump drivebelt faulty or not adjusted properly (Chapter 1).
2 Fluid level low (Chapter 1).
3 Hoses or pipes restricting the flow. Inspect and replace parts as necessary.
4 Air in power steering system. Bleed system.
5 Defective power steering pump.

79 Steering wheel fails to return to straight-ahead position

1 Incorrect front end alignment.
2 Tire pressures low.
3 Steering gears improperly engaged.
4 Steering column out of alignment.
5 Worn or damaged balljoint.
6 Worn or damaged steering linkage.
7 Improperly lubricated idler arm.
8 Insufficient oil in steering gear.
9 Lack of fluid in power steering pump.

80   Steering effort not the same in both directions (power system)

1   Leaks in steering gear.
2   Clogged fluid passage in steering gear.

81   Nolsy power steerlng pump

1   Insufficient oil in pump.
2   Clogged hoses or oil filter in pump.
3   Loose pulley.
4   Improperly adjusted drivebelt (Chapter 1).
5   Defective pump.

82   Miscellaneous noises

1   Improper tire pressures.
2   Insufficiently lubricated balljoint or steering linkage.
3   Loose or worn steering gear, steering linkage or suspension components.
4   Defective shock absorber.
5   Defective wheel bearing.
6   Worn or damaged suspension bushings.
7   Damaged leaf spring.
8   Loose wheel lug nuts.
9   Worn or damaged rear axleshaft spline.
10 Worn or damaged rear shock absorber mounting bushing.
11 Incorrect rear axle endplay.
12 See also causes of noises at the rear axle and driveshaft.

83   Excessive tire wear (not specific to one area)

1   Incorrect tire pressures.
2   Tires out of balance.
3   Wheels damaged. Inspect and replace as necessary.
4   Suspension or steering components worn (Chapter 1).
5   Front end alignment incorrect.
6   Lack of proper tire rotation routine. See *Routine Maintenance Schedule*, Chapter 1.

84   Excessive tire wear on outside edge

1   Incorrect tire pressure.
2   Excessive speed in turns.
3   Front end alignment incorrect.

85   Excessive tire wear on inside edge

1   Incorrect tire pressure.
2   Front end alignment incorrect.
3   Loose or damaged steering components (Chapter 1).

86   Tire tread worn in one place

1   Tires out of balance.
2   Damaged or buckled wheel. Inspect and replace if necessary.
3   Defective tire.

Notes

Section

1

TUNE-UP AND ROUTINE MAINTENANCE

1 Ford Mustang Maintenance schedule

The following maintenance intervals are based on the assumption that the vehicle owner will be doing the maintenance or service work, as opposed to having a dealer service department or other repair shop do the work. Although the time/mileage intervals are loosely based on factory recommendations, most have been shortened to ensure, for example, that such items as lubricants and fluids are checked/changed at intervals that promote maximum engine/driveline service life. Also, subject to the preference of the individual owner interested in keeping his or her vehicle in peak condition at all times, and with the vehicle's ultimate resale in mind, many of the maintenance procedures may be performed more often than recommended in the following schedule. We encourage such owner initiative.

When the vehicle is new it should be serviced initially by a factory authorized dealer service department to protect the factory warranty. In many cases the initial maintenance check is done at no cost to the owner (check with your dealer service department for more information).

EVERY 250 MILES OR WEEKLY, WHICHEVER COMES FIRST

Check the engine oil level (Section 4)
Check the engine coolant level (Section 4)
Check the windshield washer fluid level (Section 4)
Check the brake fluid level (Section 4)
Check the tires and tire pressures (Section 5)

EVERY 3000 MILES OR 3 MONTHS, WHICHEVER COMES FIRST

All items listed above, plus:
Check the power steering fluid level (Section 6)
Check the automatic transmission fluid level (Section 7)
Change the engine oil and oil filter (Section 8)
Check the clutch pedal freeplay (Section 9)

EVERY 6000 MILES OR 6 MONTHS, WHICHEVER COMES FIRST

All items listed above, plus:
Check and service the battery (Section 10)
Inspect and replace, if necessary, the windshield wiper blades (Section 11)

Rotate the tires (Section 12)
Check the seat belt operation (Section 13)

EVERY 15,000 MILES OR 12 MONTHS, WHICHEVER COMES FIRST

All items listed above, plus:
Inspect and replace, if necessary, all underhood hoses (Section 14)
Inspect the cooling system (Section 15)
Check the fuel system (Section 16)
Inspect the steering and suspension components (Section 17)
Inspect the brakes (Section 18)
Check the manual transmission lubricant level (Section 19)
Check the rear axle (differential) lubricant level (Section 20)

EVERY 30,000 MILES OR 24 MONTHS, WHICHEVER COMES FIRST

Check the engine drivebelt(s) (Section 21)
Inspect and replace, if necessary, the ignition system components (Section 22)
Replace the air filter (Section 23)*
Check the PCV valve (Section 24)
Replace the fuel filter (Section 25)

INSPECT THE EXHAUST SYSTEM (SECTION 26)

Change the automatic transmission fluid and filter (Section 27)**
Service the cooling system (drain, flush and refill) (Section 28)
Change the brake fluid (Section 29)

EVERY 60,000 MILES OR 48 MONTHS, WHICHEVER COMES FIRST

Replace the spark plugs (Section 30)
Change the manual transmission lubricant (Section 31)
Change the rear axle (differential) lubricant (Section 32)

* Replace more often if is the vehicle is driven in dusty areas
** If the vehicle is operated in continuous stop-and-go driving or in mountainous areas, change at 15,000 miles

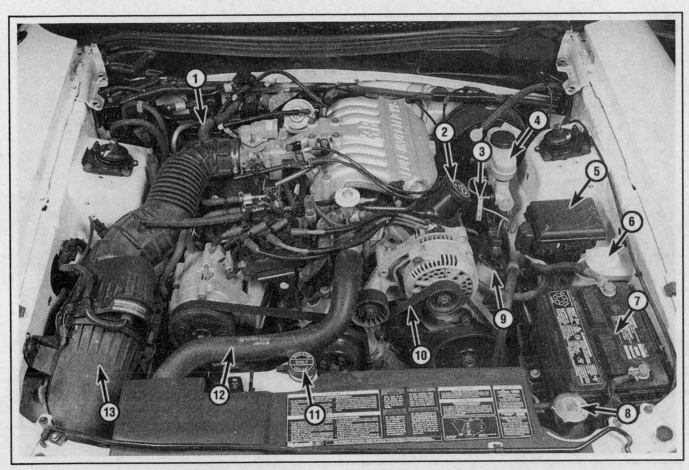

Typical engine compartment components (3.8L V6 engine)

1   Automatic transmission dipstick (not visible)
2   Engine oil filler cap
3   Engine oil dipstick
4   Brake master cylinder reservoir
5   Engine compartment fuse box
6   Windshield washer fluid reservoir
7   Battery

8   Radiator cap
9   Power steering fluid reservoir
10 Drivebelt
11 Engine coolant reservoir
12 Upper radiator hose
13 Air filter housing

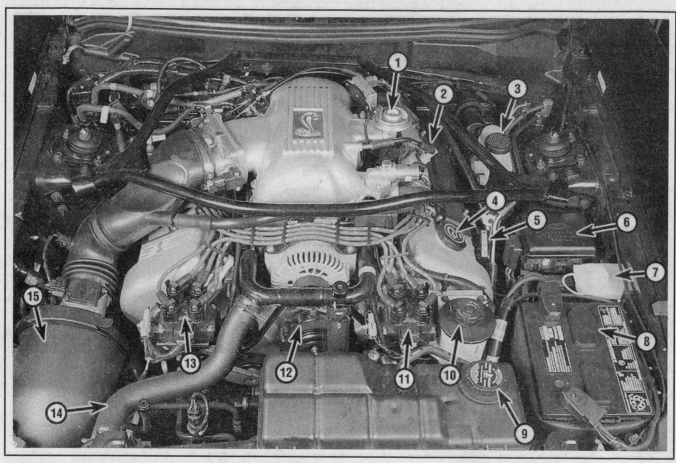

Typical engine compartment components (4.6L engine)

1	EGR valve	6	Fuse block	11	Ignition coil pack B
2	PCV valve	7	Windshield washer fluid reservoir	12	Engine drivebelt
3	Brake fluid reservoir	8	Battery	13	Ignition coil pack A
4	Oil filler cap	9	Coolant expansion tank	14	Upper radiator hose
5	Oil dipstick	10	Power steering fluid reservoir	15	Air filter housing

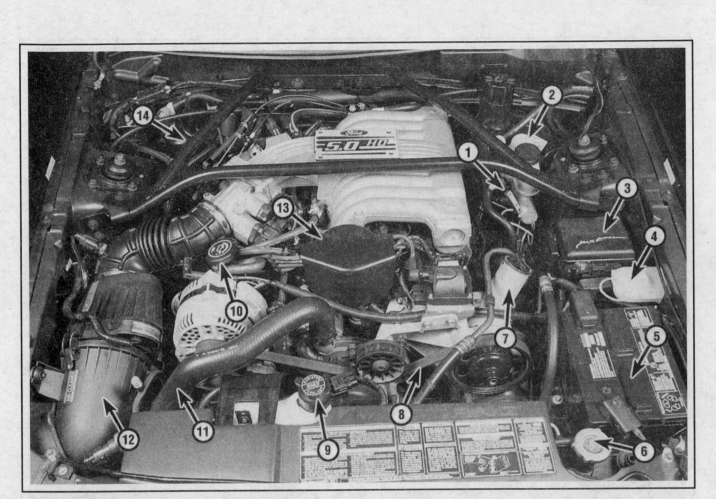

Typical engine compartment components (5.0L V8 engine)

1 Engine oil dipstick
2 Brake master cylinder reservoir
3 Engine compartment fuse box
4 Windshield washer fluid reservoir
5 Battery

6 Radiator cap
7 Power steering fluid reservoir
8 Drivebelt
9 Engine coolant reservoir
10 Engine oil filler cap

11 Upper radiator hose
12 Air filter housing
13 Distributor
14 Automatic transmission dipstick
  (not visible)

Typical engine compartment underside components

1	Lower radiator hose	4	Lower control arm bushing	7	Sway bar end link bushing		
2	Thermostat housing	5	Steering gear mount	8	Sway bar bushing		
3	Oil filter	6	Engine oil drain plug				

Typical rear underside components

1	Gas tank	3	Tail pipe	5	Muffler	7	Rear shock absorber
2	Fuel filter	4	Parking brake cable	6	Control arm bushing		

2 Introduction

This Chapter is designed to help the home mechanic maintain the Ford Mustang with the goals of maximum performance, economy, safety and reliability in mind.

Included is a master maintenance schedule (page 1-2), followed by procedures dealing specifically with each item on the schedule. Visual checks, adjustments, component replacement and other helpful items are included. Refer to the accompanying illustrations of the engine compartment and the underside of the vehicle for the locations of various components.

Servicing the vehicle, in accordance with the mileage/time maintenance schedule and the step-by-step procedures will result in a planned maintenance program that should produce a long and reliable service life. Keep in mind that it is a comprehensive plan, so maintaining some items but not others at the specified intervals will not produce the same results.

As you service the vehicle, you will discover that many of the procedures can - and should - be grouped together because of the nature of the particular procedure you're performing or because of the close proximity of two otherwise unrelated components to one another.

For example, if the vehicle is raised for chassis lubrication, you should inspect the exhaust, suspension, steering and fuel systems while you're under the vehicle. When you're rotating the tires, it makes good sense to check the brakes since the wheels are already removed. Finally, let's suppose you have to borrow or rent a torque wrench. Even if you only need it to tighten the spark plugs, you might as well check the torque of as many critical fasteners as time allows.

The first step in this maintenance program is to prepare yourself before the actual work begins. Read through all the procedures you're planning to do, then gather up all the parts and tools needed. If it looks like you might run into problems during a particular job, seek advice from a mechanic or an experienced do-it-yourselfer.

3 Tune-up general information

The term tune-up is used in this manual to represent a combination of individual operations rather than one specific procedure.

If, from the time the vehicle is new, the routine maintenance schedule is followed closely and frequent checks are made of fluid levels and high wear items, as suggested throughout this manual, the engine will be kept in relatively good running condition and the need for additional work will be minimized.

More likely than not, however, there will be times when the engine is running poorly due to lack of regular maintenance. This is even more likely if a used vehicle, which has not received regular and frequent maintenance checks, is purchased. In such cases, an engine tune-up will be needed outside of the regular routine maintenance intervals.

The first step in any tune-up or diagnostic procedure to help correct a poor running engine is a cylinder compression check. A compression check (see Chapter 2) will help determine the condition of internal engine components and should be used as a guide for tune-up and repair procedures. If, for instance, a compression check indicates serious internal engine wear, a conventional tune-up will not improve the performance of the engine and would be a waste of time and money. Because of its importance, the compression check should be done by someone with the right equipment and the knowledge to use it properly.

The following procedures are those most often needed to bring a generally poor running engine back into a proper state of tune.

MINOR TUNE-UP

Check all engine related fluids (Section 4)
Clean, inspect and test the battery (Section 10)
Check all underhood hoses (Section 14)
Check the cooling system (Section 15)
Check the drivebelt (Section 21)
Inspect the spark plug and coil wires (Section 22)
Check the air filter (Section 23)

MAJOR TUNE-UP

All items listed under Minor tune-up, plus . . .

Check the fuel system (Section 16)
Replace the spark plug and coil wires (Section 22)
Replace the air filter (Section 23)
Replace the PCV valve (Section 24)
Replace the fuel filter (Section 25)
Replace the spark plugs (Section 30)
Check the charging system (Chapter 5)

4 Fluid level checks (every 250 miles or weekly)

1   Fluids are an essential part of the lubrication, cooling, brake and windshield washer systems. Because the fluids gradually become depleted and/or contaminated during normal operation of the vehicle, they must be periodically replenished. See *Recommended lubricants and fluids* at the end of this Chapter before adding fluid to any of the following components.

➡**Note: The vehicle must be on level ground when fluid levels are checked.**

ENGINE OIL

◆ **Refer to illustrations 4.2, 4.4 and 4.6**

2   The oil level is checked with a dipstick, which is located on the left (driver's) side of the engine (see illustration). The dipstick extends through a metal tube down into the oil pan.

3   The oil level should be checked before the vehicle has been

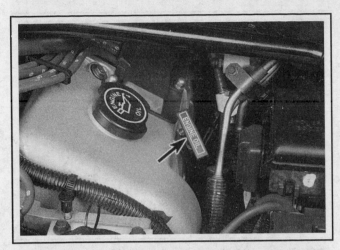

4.2 The oil dipstick is located on the driver side of the engine

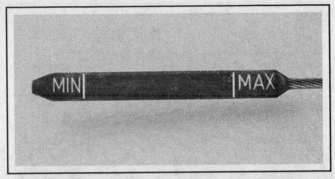

4.4 The oil level should be at or near the MAX area on the dipstick - if it isn't, add enough oil to bring the level to near the MAX mark (it takes one quart of oil to raise the level from the lower to upper mark)

driven, or about 15 minutes after the engine has been shut off. If the oil is checked immediately after driving the vehicle, some of the oil will remain in the upper part of the engine, resulting in an inaccurate reading on the dipstick.

4   Pull the dipstick out of the tube and wipe all the oil from the end with a clean rag or paper towel. Insert the clean dipstick all the way back into the tube and pull it out again. Note the oil at the end of the dipstick. At its highest point, the level should be above the MIN mark, within the hatched marked section of the dipstick (see illustration).

5   It takes one quart of oil to raise the level from the MIN mark to the MAX mark on the dipstick. Do not allow the level to drop below the MIN mark or oil starvation may cause engine damage. Conversely, overfilling the engine (adding oil above the MAX mark) may cause oil fouled spark plugs, oil leaks or oil seal failures.

6   To add oil, remove the filler cap from the valve cover (see illustration). After adding oil, wait a few minutes to allow the level to stabilize, then pull out the dipstick and check the level again. Add more oil if required. Install the filler cap and tighten it by hand only.

7   Checking the oil level is an important preventive maintenance step. A consistently low oil level indicates oil leakage through damaged seals, defective gaskets or past worn rings or valve guides. If the oil looks milky in color or has water droplets in it, the cylinder head gasket(s) may be blown or the head(s) or block may be cracked. The engine should be checked immediately. The condition of the oil should also be checked. Whenever you check the oil level, slide your thumb and index finger up the dipstick before wiping off the oil. If you see small dirt or metal particles clinging to the dipstick, the oil should be changed (see Section 8).

ENGINE COOLANT

▶ Refer to illustration 4.9

✳✳ WARNING:

Do not allow antifreeze to come in contact with your skin or painted surfaces of the vehicle. Flush contaminated areas immediately with plenty of water. Don't store new coolant or leave old coolant lying around where it's accessible to children or pets – they're attracted by its sweet smell. Ingestion of even a small amount of coolant can be fatal! Wipe up garage floor and drip pan spills immediately. Keep antifreeze containers covered and repair cooling system leaks as soon as they're noticed.

4.6 Oil is added to the engine after removing the twist off cap (arrow) located on the valve cover

8   All vehicles covered by this manual are equipped with a pressurized coolant recovery system. A plastic expansion tank located at the front of the engine compartment is connected by a hose to the radiator. As the engine heats up during operation, the expanding coolant fills the tank.

9   The coolant level in the tank should be checked regularly.

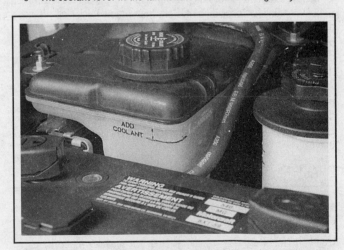

4.9 The coolant expansion tank is located on the front of the engine compartment - keep the level near the arrow at the seam

4.15 The brake fluid level should be near the base of the filler neck of the translucent plastic reservoir

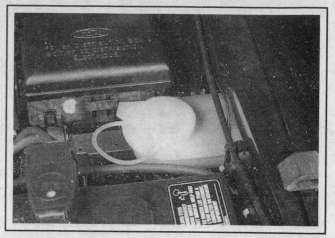

4.22 The windshield washer reservoir is located at the left front corner of the engine compartment next to the battery

✳✳ WARNING:

Do not remove the radiator cap or expansion tank cap to check the coolant level when the engine is warm! The level in the tank varies with the temperature of the engine. When the engine is cold, the coolant level should be at or slightly above the FULL COLD mark on the reservoir. Once the engine has warmed up, the level should be at or near the FULL HOT mark. If it isn't, allow the engine to cool, then remove the cap from the tank and add a 50/50 mixture of ethylene glycol based antifreeze and water (see illustration).

10 Drive the vehicle and recheck the coolant level. Don't use rust inhibitors or additives. If only a small amount of coolant is required to bring the system up to the proper level, water can be used. However, repeated additions of water will dilute the antifreeze and water solution. In order to maintain the proper ratio of antifreeze and water, always top up the coolant level with the correct mixture. An empty plastic milk jug or bleach bottle makes an excellent container for mixing coolant.

11 If the coolant level drops consistently, there may be a leak in the system. Inspect the radiator, hoses, filler cap, drain plugs and water pump (see Section 15). If no leaks are noted, have the radiator cap or expansion tank cap pressure tested by a service station.

12 If you have to remove the radiator cap or expansion tank cap wait until the engine has cooled completely, then wrap a thick cloth around the cap and turn it to the first stop (if you're removing an expansion tank cap, unscrew it slowly, stopping if you hear a hissing noise). If coolant or steam escapes, let the engine cool down longer, then remove the cap.

13 Check the condition of the coolant as well. It should be relatively clear. If it's brown or rust colored, the system should be drained, flushed and refilled. Even if the coolant appears to be normal, the corrosion inhibitors wear out, so it must be replaced at the specified intervals.

BRAKE FLUID

♦ **Refer to illustration 4.15**

14 The brake fluid level is checked by looking through the plastic reservoir mounted on the master cylinder. The master cylinder is mounted on the front of the power booster unit in the left (driver's side) rear corner of the engine compartment.

15 The fluid level should be between the MAX and MIN lines on the side of the reservoir (see illustration).

16 If the fluid level is low, wipe the top of the reservoir and the cap with a clean rag to prevent contamination of the system as the cap is unscrewed.

17 Add only the specified brake fluid to the reservoir (refer to *Recommended lubricants and fluids* at the end of this Chapter or your owner's manual). Mixing different types of brake fluid can damage the system. Fill the reservoir to the MAX line.

✳✳ WARNING:

Brake fluid can harm your eyes and damage painted surfaces, so use extreme caution when handling or pouring it. Do not use brake fluid that has been standing open or is more than one year old. Brake fluid absorbs moisture from the air, which can cause a dangerous loss of braking effectiveness.

18 While the reservoir cap is off, check the master cylinder reservoir for contamination. If rust deposits, dirt particles or water droplets are present, the system should be drained and refilled by a dealer service department or repair shop.

19 After filling the reservoir to the proper level, make sure the cap is seated to prevent fluid leakage and/or contamination.

20 The fluid level in the master cylinder will drop slightly as the brake shoes or pads at each wheel wear down during normal operation. If the brake fluid level drops consistently, check the entire system for leaks immediately. Examine all brake lines, hoses and connections, along with the calipers, wheel cylinders and master cylinder (see Section 18).

21 When checking the fluid level, if you discover one or both reservoirs empty or nearly empty, the brake system should be bled (see Chapter 9).

WINDSHIELD WASHER FLUID

♦ **Refer to illustration 4.22**

22 Fluid for the windshield washer system is stored in a plastic reservoir located at the left (driver's) side of the engine compartment (see illustration).

23 In milder climates, plain water can be used in the reservoir, but it

should be kept no more than 2/3 full to allow for expansion if the water freezes. In colder climates, use windshield washer system antifreeze, available at any auto parts store, to lower the freezing point of the fluid. Mix the antifreeze with water in accordance with the manufacturer's directions on the container.

5   Tire and tire pressure checks (every 250 miles or weekly)

▶ **Refer to illustrations 5.2, 5.3, 5.4a, 5.4b and 5.8**

1   Periodic inspection of the tires may spare you the inconvenience of being stranded with a flat tire. It can also provide you with vital information regarding possible problems in the steering and suspension systems before major damage occurs.

2   The original tires on this vehicle are equipped with 1/2-inch side bands that will appear when tread depth reaches 1/16-inch, but they don't appear until the tires are worn out. Tread wear can be monitored with a simple, inexpensive device known as a tread depth indicator (see illustration).

3   Note any abnormal tread wear (see illustration). Tread pattern irregularities such as cupping, flat spots and more wear on one side than the other are indications of front end alignment and/or balance problems. If any of these conditions are noted, take the vehicle to a tire shop or service station to correct the problem.

4   Look closely for cuts, punctures and embedded nails or tacks. Sometimes a tire will hold air pressure for a short time or leak down very slowly after a nail has embedded itself in the tread. If a slow leak

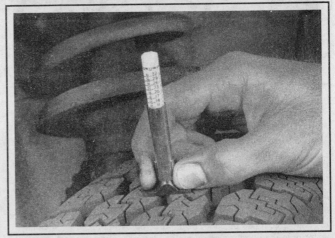

5.2 Use a tire tread depth indicator to monitor tire wear - they are available at auto parts stores and service stations and cost very little

UNDERINFLATION

CUPPING

Cupping may be caused by:

● Underinflation and/or mechanical irregularities such as out-of-balance condition of wheel and/or tire, and bent or damaged wheel.
● Loose or worn steering tie-rod or steering idler arm.
● Loose, damaged or worn front suspension parts.

OVERINFLATION

INCORRECT TOE-IN OR EXTREME CAMBER

FEATHERING DUE TO MISALIGNMENT

5.3 This chart will help you determine the condition of the tires, the probable cause(s) of abnormal wear and the corrective action necessary

5.4a If a tire loses air on a steady basis, check the valve stem core first to make sure it's snug (special inexpensive wrenches are commonly available at auto parts stores)

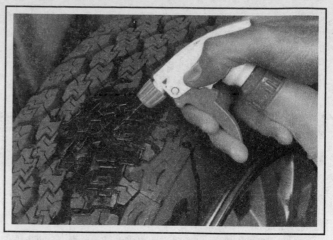

5.4b If the valve stem core is tight, raise the corner of the vehicle with the low tire and spray a soapy water solution onto the tread as the tire is turned slowly - leaks will cause small bubbles to appear

persists, check the valve stem core to make sure it is tight (see illustration). Examine the tread for an object that may have embedded itself in the tire or for a "plug" that may have begun to leak (radial tire punctures are repaired with a plug that is installed in a puncture). If a puncture is suspected, it can be easily verified by spraying a solution of soapy water onto the puncture area (see illustration). The soapy solution will bubble if there is a leak. Unless the puncture is unusually large, a tire shop or service station can usually repair the tire.

5   Carefully inspect the inner sidewall of each tire for evidence of brake fluid leakage. If you see any, inspect the brakes immediately.

6   Correct air pressure adds miles to the life span of the tires, improves mileage and enhances overall ride quality. Tire pressure cannot be accurately estimated by looking at a tire, especially if it's a radial. A tire pressure gauge is essential. Keep an accurate gauge in the glove compartment. The pressure gauges attached to the nozzles of air hoses at gas stations are often inaccurate.

7   Always check tire pressure when the tires are cold. Cold, in this case, means the vehicle has not been driven over a mile in the three hours preceding a tire pressure check. A pressure rise of four to eight pounds is not uncommon once the tires are warm.

8   Unscrew the valve cap protruding from the wheel or hubcap and push the gauge firmly onto the valve stem (see illustration). Note the reading on the gauge and compare the figure to the recommended tire pressure shown on the tire placard on the driver's side door. Be sure to reinstall the valve cap to keep dirt and moisture out of the valve stem

5.8 To extend the life of the tires, check the air pressure at least once a week with an accurate gauge (don't forget the spare!)

mechanism. Check all four tires and, if necessary, add enough air to bring them up to the recommended pressure.

9   Don't forget to keep the spare tire inflated to the specified pressure (refer to your owner's manual or the decal attached to the right door pillar). Note that the pressure recommended for the temporary (mini) spare is higher than for the tires on the vehicle.

6   Power steering fluid level check (every 3000 miles or 3 months)

▶ **Refer to illustrations 6.5a, 6.5b, 6.5c and 6.9**

1   Check the power steering fluid level periodically to avoid steering system problems, such as damage to the pump.

❊❊ CAUTION:

DO NOT hold the steering wheel against either stop (extreme left or right turn) for more than five seconds. If you do, the power steering pump could be damaged.

3.8L V6 AND 5.0L V8 MODELS

2   The power steering pump, located at the front corner of the engine, is equipped with a twist-off cap with an integral fluid level dipstick.

3   Park the vehicle on level ground and apply the parking brake.

4   Run the engine until it has reached normal operating temperature. With the engine at idle, turn the steering wheel back-and-forth several times to get any air out of the steering system. Shut the engine off,

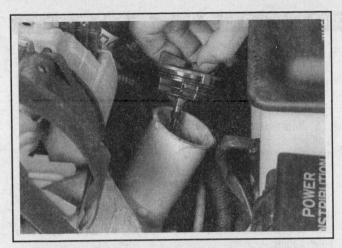

6.5a A dipstick is used to check the power steering fluid level on 3.8L and 5.0L engines

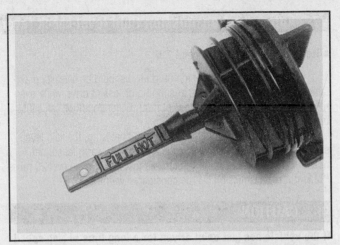

6.5b The dipstick is marked on both sides so the fluid can be checked hot . . .

remove the cap by turning it counterclockwise, wipe the dipstick clean and reinstall the cap. (Make sure it is seated).

5   Remove the cap again and note the fluid level. It must be between the two lines designating the FULL HOT or FULL COLD range (see illustration). Be sure to use the proper temperature range on the dipstick when checking the fluid level - the FULL COLD lines on the reverse side of the dipstick are only usable when the engine is cold (see illustrations).

6   Add small amounts of fluid until the level is correct.

❋❋ CAUTION:

Do not overfill the pump. If too much fluid is added, remove the excess with a clean syringe or suction pump.

7   If additional fluid is required, pour the specified type directly into the reservoir, using a funnel to prevent spills.

4.6L V8 MODELS

8   The fluid reservoir for the power steering pump is mounted the front left corner of the engine block.

9   On these models the reservoir is translucent plastic and the fluid level can be checked visually (see illustration).

10 The fluid level should be kept between the FULL and ADD marks on the reservoir.

11 Add small amounts of fluid until the level is correct.

❋❋ CAUTION:

Do not overfill the reservoir. If too much fluid is added, remove the excess with a clean syringe or suction pump.

ALL MODELS

12 If the reservoir requires frequent fluid additions, all power steering hoses, hose connections, the power steering pump and the steering gear assembly should be carefully checked for leaks.

6.5c . . . or cold

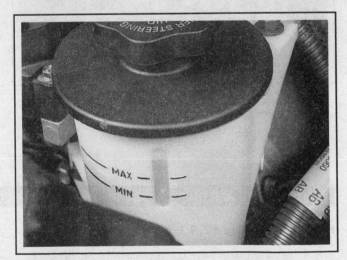

6.9 The power steering fluid reservoir on 4.6L engines is translucent so the fluid level can be checked without removing the cap - unscrew the cap to add fluid

7 Automatic transmission fluid level check (every 3000 miles or 3 months)

▶ **Refer to illustrations 7.4 and 7.6**

1   The automatic transmission fluid level should be carefully maintained. Low fluid level can lead to slipping or loss of drive, while overfilling can cause foaming and loss of fluid. Either condition can cause transmission damage.

2   Since transmission fluid expands as it heats up, the fluid level should only be checked when the transmission is warm (at normal operating temperature). If the vehicle has just been driven over 20 miles (32 km), the transmission can be considered warm.

❊❊ CAUTION:

If the vehicle has just been driven for a long time at high speed or in city traffic in hot weather, or if it has been pulling a trailer, an accurate fluid level reading cannot be obtained.

Allow the transmission to cool down for about 30 minutes. You can also check the transmission fluid level when the transmission is cold. If the vehicle has not been driven for over five hours and the fluid is about room temperature (70 to 95-degrees F), the transmission is cold. However, the fluid level is normally checked with the transmission warm to ensure accurate results.

3   Immediately after driving the vehicle, park it on a level surface, set the parking brake and start the engine. While the engine is idling, depress the brake pedal and move the selector lever through all the gear ranges, beginning and ending in Park.

4   Locate the automatic transmission dipstick tube in the engine compartment (see illustration).

5   With the engine still idling, pull the dipstick from the tube, wipe it off with a clean rag, push it all the way back into the tube and withdraw it again, then note the fluid level.

6   If the transmission is cold, the level should be in the room temperature range on the dipstick (between the two holes); if it's warm, the fluid level should be in the operating temperature range (in the crosshatched area) (see illustration). If the level is low, add the specified automatic transmission fluid through the dipstick tube - use a funnel to prevent spills.

7   Add just enough of the recommended fluid to fill the transmission to the proper level. It takes about one pint to raise the level from the low mark to the high mark when the fluid is hot, so add the fluid a little at a time and keep checking the level until it's correct.

8   The condition of the fluid should also be checked along with the level. If the fluid is black or a dark reddish-brown color, or if it smells burned, it should be changed (see Section 27). If you are in doubt about its condition, purchase some new fluid and compare the two for color and smell.

7.4 The automatic transmission dipstick (arrow) is located at the rear of the engine

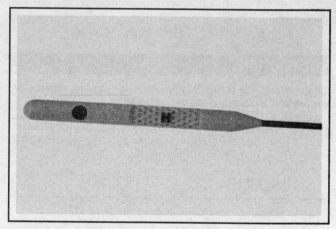

7.6 Check the fluid with the transmission at normal operating temperature - the level should be kept in the HOT range in the cross-hatched area (don't add fluid if the level is anywhere in the cross-hatched area)

8 Engine oil and filter change (every 3000 miles or 3 months)

▶ **Refer to illustrations 8.2, 8.7, 8.12 and 8.16**

1   Frequent oil changes are the most important preventive maintenance procedures that can be done by the home mechanic. As engine oil ages, in becomes diluted and contaminated, which leads to premature engine wear.

2   Make sure that you have all the necessary tools before you begin this procedure (see illustration). You should also have plenty of rags or newspapers handy for mopping up oil spills.

3   Access to the oil drain plug and filter will be improved if the vehicle can be lifted on a hoist, driven onto ramps or supported by jackstands.

❊❊ WARNING:

Do not work under a vehicle supported only by a bumper, hydraulic or scissors-type jack - always use jackstands!

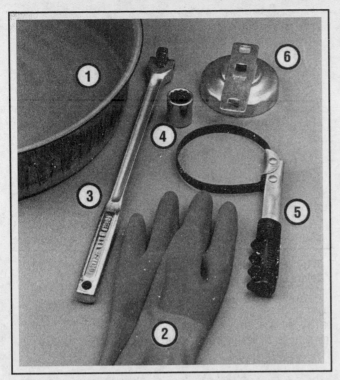

8.2 These tools are required when changing the engine oil and filter

1 *Drain pan* - It should be fairly shallow in depth, but wide to prevent spills
2 *Rubber gloves* - When removing the drain plug and filter, you will get oil on your hands (the gloves will prevent burns)
3 *Breaker bar* - Sometimes the oil drain plug is tight, and a long breaker bar is needed to loosen it
4 *Socket* – To be used with the breaker bar or a ratchet (must be the correct size to fit the drain plug - six-point preferred)
5 *Filter wrench* - This is a metal band-type wrench, which requires clearance around the filter to be effective
6 *Filter wrench* - This type fits on the bottom of the filter and can be turned with a ratchet or breaker bar (different-size wrenches are available for different types of filters)

4   If you haven't changed the oil on this vehicle before, get under it and locate the oil drain plug and the oil filter. The exhaust components will be warm as you work, so note how they are routed to avoid touching them when you are under the vehicle.

5   Start the engine and allow it to reach normal operating temperature - oil and sludge will flow out more easily when warm. If new oil, a filter or tools are needed, use the vehicle to go get them and warm up the engine/oil at the same time. Park on a level surface and shut off the engine when it's warmed up. Remove the oil filler cap from the valve cover.

6   Raise the vehicle and support it on jackstands. Make sure it is safely supported!

7   Being careful not to touch the hot exhaust components, position a drain pan under the plug in the bottom of the engine, then remove the plug (see illustration). It's a good idea to wear a rubber glove while unscrewing the plug the final few turns to avoid being scalded by hot oil.

8   It may be necessary to move the drain pan slightly as oil flow slows to a trickle. Inspect the old oil for the presence of metal particles.

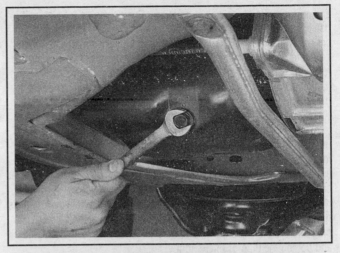

8.7 Use a proper size wrench or socket to remove the oil drain plug and avoid rounding it off

8.12 The oil filter is usually on very tight and will require a special oil filter wrench to remove it - DO NOT use the wrench to tighten the new filter

9   After all the oil has drained, wipe off the drain plug with a clean rag. Any small metal particles clinging to the plug would immediately contaminate the new oil.

10 Clean the area around the drain plug opening, reinstall the plug and tighten it securely, but don't strip the threads.

11 Move the drain pan into position under the oil filter.

12 Loosen the oil filter by turning it counterclockwise with a filter wrench (see illustration). Any standard filter wrench will work.

13 Sometimes the oil filter is screwed on so tightly that it can't be loosened. If it is, punch a metal bar or long screwdriver directly through it, as close to the engine as possible, and use it as a T-bar to turn the filter. Be prepared for oil to spurt out of the canister as it's punctured.

14 Once the filter is loose, use your hands to unscrew it from the block. Just as the filter is detached from the block, immediately tilt the open end up to prevent the oil inside the filter from spilling out.

15 Using a clean rag, wipe off the mounting surface on the block. Also, make sure that none of the old gasket remains stuck to the mounting surface. It can be removed with a scraper if necessary.

16 Compare the old filter with the new one to make sure they are the same type. Smear some engine oil on the rubber gasket of the new filter

and screw it into place (see illustration). Overtightening the filter will damage the gasket, so don't use a filter wrench. Most filter manufacturers recommend tightening the filter by hand only. Normally they should be tightened 3/4-turn after the gasket contacts the block, but be sure to follow the directions on the filter or container.

17 Remove all tools and materials from under the vehicle, being careful not to spill thc oil in the drain pan, then lower the vehicle.

18 Add new oil to the engine through the oil filler cap. Use a funnel to prevent oil from spilling onto the top of the engine. Pour four quarts of fresh oil into the engine. Wait a few minutes to allow the oil to drain into the pan, then check the level on the dipstick (see Section 4 if necessary). If the oil level is in the OK range (hatched area), install the filler cap.

19 Start the engine and run it for about a minute. While the engine is running, look under the vehicle and check for leaks at the oil pan drain plug and around the oil filter. If either one is leaking, stop the engine and tighten the plug or filter slightly.

20 Wait a few minutes, then recheck the level on the dipstick. Add oil as necessary to bring the level into the OK range.

21 During the first few trips after an oil change, make it a point to check frequently for leaks and proper oil level.

22 The old oil drained from the engine cannot be reused in its present state and should be discarded. Oil reclamation centers, auto

8.16 Lubricate the oil filter gasket with clean engine oil before installing the filter on the engine

repair shops and gas stations will normally accept the oil, which can be recycled. After the oil has cooled, it can be drained into a container (plastic jugs, bottles, milk cartons, etc.) for transport to a disposal site.

9 Clutch pedal adjustment (every 3000 miles or 3 months)

1 All vehicles covered by this manual are equipped with a cable operated clutch actuating mechanism which incorporates a self-adjusting device.

2 At the specified intervals, pull up on the clutch pedal to the upmost position. This procedure will separate the adjuster pawl from the adjuster quadrant and allow the clutch mechanisms to self-adjust.

3 It is a good idea to lubricate the clutch linkage at the time of adjustment (see Chapter 8).

10 Battery check, maintenance and charging (every 6000 miles or 6 months)

▶ **Refer to illustrations 10.1, 10.6a, 10.6b, 10.7a and 10.7b**

❊❊ WARNING:

Certain precautions must be followed when checking and servicing the battery. Hydrogen gas, which is highly flammable, is always present in the battery cells, so keep lighted tobacco and all other open flames and sparks away from the battery. The electrolyte inside the battery is actually dilute sulfuric acid, which will cause injury if splashed on your skin or in your eyes. It will also ruin clothes and painted surfaces. When removing the battery cables, always detach the negative cable first and hook it up last!

1 A routine preventive maintenance program for the battery in your vehicle is the only way to ensure quick and reliable starts. But before performing any battery maintenance, make sure that you have the proper equipment necessary to work safely around the battery (see illustration).

2 There are also several precautions that should be taken whenever battery maintenance is performed. Before servicing the battery, always turn the engine and all accessories off and disconnect the cable from the negative terminal of the battery.

3 The battery produces hydrogen gas, which is both flammable and explosive. Never create a spark, smoke or light a match around the battery. Always charge the battery in a ventilated area.

4 Electrolyte contains poisonous and corrosive sulfuric acid. Do not allow it to get in your eyes, on your skin on your clothes. Never ingest it. Wear protective safety glasses when working near the battery. Keep children away from the battery.

5 Note the external condition of the battery. If the positive terminal and cable clamp on your vehicle's battery is equipped with a rubber protector, make sure that it's not torn or damaged. It should completely cover the terminal. Look for any corroded or loose connections, cracks in the case or cover or loose hold-down clamps. Also check the entire length of each cable for cracks and frayed conductors.

6 If corrosion, which looks like white, fluffy deposits (see illustration) is evident, particularly around the terminals, the battery should

10.1 Tools and materials required for battery maintenance

1. **Face shield/safety goggles** - *When removing corrosion with a brush, the acidic particles can easily fly up into your eyes*
2. **Baking soda** - *A solution of baking soda and water can be used to neutralize corrosion*
3. **Petroleum jelly** - *A layer of this on the battery posts will help prevent corrosion*
4. **Battery post/cable cleaner** - *This wire brush cleaning tool will remove all traces of corrosion from the battery posts and cable clamps*
5. **Treated felt washers** - *Placing one of these on each post, directly under the cable clamps, will help prevent corrosion*
6. **Puller** - *Sometimes the cable clamps are very difficult to pull off the posts, even after the nut/bolt has been completely loosened. This tool pulls the clamp straight up and off the post without damage*
7. **Battery post/cable cleaner** - *Here is another cleaning tool which is a slightly different version of Number 4 above, but it does the same thing*
8. **Rubber gloves** - *Another safety item to consider when servicing the battery; remember that's acid inside the battery!*

be removed for cleaning. Loosen the cable clamp bolts with a wrench, being careful to remove the ground cable first, and slide them off the terminals (see illustration). Then disconnect the hold-down clamp bolt and nut, remove the clamp and lift the battery from the engine compartment.

7   Clean the cable clamps thoroughly with a battery brush or a terminal cleaner and a solution of warm water and baking soda (see illustration). Wash the terminals and the top of the battery case with the same solution but make sure that the solution doesn't get into the battery. When cleaning the cables, terminals and battery top, wear safety goggles and rubber gloves to prevent any solution from coming in contact with your eyes or hands. Wear old clothes too - even diluted, sulfuric acid splashed onto clothes will burn holes in them. If the terminals

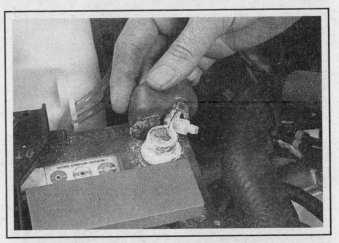

10.6a Battery terminal corrosion usually appears as light, fluffy powder

10.6b Removing the cable from a battery post with a wrench - sometimes special battery pliers are required for this procedure if corrosion has caused deterioration of the nut hex (always remove the ground cable first and hook it up last!)

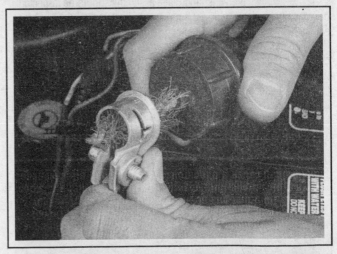

10.7a When cleaning the cable clamps, all corrosion must be removed (the inside of the clamp is tapered to match the taper on the post, so don't remove too much material)

have been extensively corroded, clean them up with a terminal cleaner (see illustration). Thoroughly wash all cleaned areas with plain water.

8   Make sure that the battery tray is in good condition and the hold-down clamp bolts are tight. If the battery is removed from the tray, make sure no parts remain in the bottom of the tray when the battery is reinstalled. When reinstalling the hold-down clamp bolts, do not over-tighten them.

9   Information on removing and installing the battery can be found in Chapter 5. Information on jump starting can be found at the front of this manual.

CLEANING

10   Corrosion on the hold-down components, battery case and surrounding areas can be removed with a solution of water and baking soda. Thoroughly rinse all cleaned areas with plain water.

11   Any metal parts of the vehicle damaged by corrosion should be covered with a zinc-based primer, then painted.

CHARGING

✳✳ WARNING:

When batteries are being charged, hydrogen gas, which is very explosive and flammable, is produced. Do not smoke or allow open flames near a charging or a recently charged battery. Wear eye protection when near the battery during charging. Also, make sure the charger is unplugged before connecting or disconnecting the battery from the charger.

12   Slow-rate charging is the best way to restore a battery that's discharged to the point where it will not start the engine. It's also a good way to maintain the battery charge in a vehicle that's only driven a

10.7b Regardless of the type of tool used on the battery posts, a clean, shiny surface should be the result

few miles between starts. Maintaining the battery charge is particularly important in the winter when the battery must work harder to start the engine and electrical accessories that drain the battery are in greater use.

13   It's best to use a one or two-amp battery charger (sometimes called a "trickle" charger). They are the safest and put the least strain on the battery. They are also the least expensive. For a faster charge, you can use a higher amperage charger, but don't use one rated more than 1/10th the amp/hour rating of the battery. Rapid boost charges that claim to restore the power of the battery in one to two hours are hardest on the battery and can damage batteries not in good condition. This type of charging should only be used in emergency situations.

14   The average time necessary to charge a battery should be listed in the instructions that come with the charger. As a general rule, a trickle charger will charge a battery in 12 to 16 hours.

11 Windshield wiper blade inspection and replacement (every 6000 miles or 6 months)

▶ **Refer to illustrations 11.4 and 11.5**

1   The windshield wiper and blade assembly should be inspected periodically for damage, loose components and cracked or worn blade elements.

2   Road film can build up on the wiper blades and affect their efficiency, so they should be washed regularly with a mild detergent solution.

3   If the wiper blade elements are cracked, worn or warped, or no longer clean adequately, they should be replaced with new ones.

4   Lift the arm assembly away from the glass for clearance, press on the release lever, then slide the wiper blade assembly out of the hook in the end of the arm (see illustration).

5   Use needle-nose pliers to compress the blade element, then slide the element out of the frame and discard it (see illustration).

6   Installation is the reverse of removal.

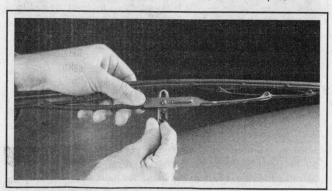

11.4 Press on the release tab and push the blade assembly down out of the hook in the arm

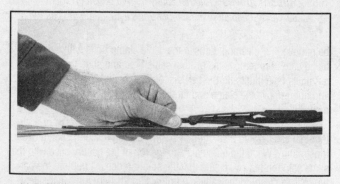

11.5 Use needle-nose pliers to compress the rubber element, then slide the element out - slide the new element in and lock the blade assembly fingers into the notches of the wiper element

12 Tire rotation (every 6000 miles or 6 months)

▶ **Refer to illustration 12.2**

1   The tires should be rotated at the specified intervals and whenever uneven wear is noticed. Since the vehicle will be raised and the tires removed anyway, check the brakes also (see Section 18).

2   Radial tires must be rotated in a specific pattern (see illustration). If your vehicle has a compact spare tire, don't include it in the rotation pattern.

3   Refer to the information in *Jacking and towing* at the front of this manual for the proper procedure to follow when raising the vehicle and changing a tire. If the brakes must be checked, don't apply the parking brake as stated.

4   The vehicle must be raised on a hoist or supported on jackstands to get all four wheels off the ground. Make sure the vehicle is safely supported!

5   After the rotation procedure is finished, check and adjust the tire pressures as necessary and be sure to check the lug nut tightness.

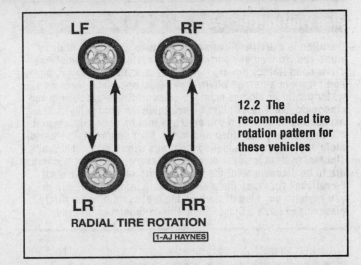

12.2 The recommended tire rotation pattern for these vehicles

13 Seat belt check (every 6000 miles or 6 months)

1   Check seat belts, buckles, latch plates and guide loops for obvious damage and signs of wear.

2   See if the seat belt reminder light comes on when the key is turned to the Run or Start position. A chime should also sound. On passive restraint systems, the shoulder belt should move into position in the A-pillar.

3   The seat belts are designed to lock up during a sudden stop or impact, yet allow free movement during normal driving. Make sure the retractors return the belt against your chest while driving and rewind the belt fully when the buckle is unlatched.

4   If any of the above checks reveal problems with the seat belt system, replace parts as necessary.

14 Underhood hose check and replacement (every 15,000 miles or 12 months)

❄ WARNING:

Replacement of air conditioning hoses must be left to a dealer service department or air conditioning shop that has the equipment to depressurize the system safely. Never remove air conditioning components or hoses until the system has been depressurized.

GENERAL

1   High temperatures under the hood can cause deterioration of the rubber and plastic hoses used for engine, accessory and emission systems operation. Periodic inspection should be made for cracks, loose clamps, material hardening and leaks.

2   Information specific to the cooling system hoses can be found in Section 15.

3   Most (but not all) hoses are secured to the fittings with clamps. Where clamps are used, check to be sure they haven't lost their tension, allowing the hose to leak. If clamps aren't used, make sure the hose has not expanded and/or hardened where it slips over the fitting, allowing it to leak.

PCV SYSTEM HOSE

4   To reduce hydrocarbon emissions, crankcase blow-by gas is vented through the PCV valve in the rocker arm cover to the intake manifold via a rubber hose on most models. The blow-by gases mix with incoming air in the intake manifold before being burned in the combustion chambers.

5   Check the PCV hose for cracks, leaks and other damage. Disconnect it from the valve cover and the intake manifold and check the inside for obstructions. If it's clogged, clean it out with solvent.

VACUUM HOSES

6   It's quite common for vacuum hoses, especially those in the emissions system, to be color coded or identified by colored stripes molded into them. Various systems require hoses with different wall thickness, collapse resistance and temperature resistance. When replacing hoses, be sure the new ones are made of the same material.

7   Often the only effective way to check a hose is to remove it completely from the vehicle. If more than one hose is removed, be sure to label the hoses and fittings to ensure correct installation.

8   When checking vacuum hoses, be sure to include any plastic T-fittings in the check. Inspect the fittings for cracks and the hose where it fits over each fitting for distortion, which could cause leakage.

9   A small piece of vacuum hose (1/4-inch inside diameter) can be used as a stethoscope to detect vacuum leaks. Hold one end of the hose to your ear and probe around vacuum hoses and fittings, listening for the "hissing" sound characteristic of a vacuum leak.

❄ WARNING:

When probing with the vacuum hose stethoscope, be careful not to come into contact with moving engine components such as drivebelts, the cooling fan, etc.

FUEL HOSE

10 The fuel lines are usually under pressure, so if any fuel lines are to be disconnected be prepared to catch spilled fuel.

Refer to Chapter 4 for the fuel system pressure relief procedure.

11 Check all flexible fuel lines for deterioration and chafing. Check especially for cracks in areas where the hose bends and just before fittings, such as where a hose attaches to the fuel pump, fuel filter and fuel injection unit.

12 When replacing a hose, use only hose that is specifically designed for your fuel injection system.

13 Spring-type clamps are sometimes used on fuel return or vapor lines. These clamps often lose their tension over a period of time, and can be "sprung" during removal. Replace all spring-type clamps with screw clamps whenever a hose is replaced. Some fuel lines use spring-lock type couplings, which require a special tool to disconnect. See Chapter 4 for more information on these type of couplings.

METAL LINES

14 Sections of metal line are often used for fuel line between the fuel pump and the fuel injection unit. Check carefully to make sure the line isn't bent, crimped or cracked.

15 If a section of metal fuel line must be replaced, use seamless steel tubing only, since copper and aluminum tubing do not have the strength necessary to withstand vibration caused by the engine.

16 Check the metal brake lines where they enter the master cylinder and brake proportioning unit (if used) for cracks in the lines and loose fittings. Any sign of brake fluid leakage calls for an immediate thorough inspection of the brake system.

15 Cooling system check (every 15,000 miles or 12 months)

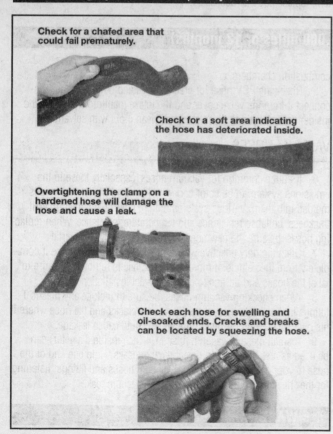

Check for a chafed area that could fail prematurely.

Check for a soft area indicating the hose has deteriorated inside.

Overtightening the clamp on a hardened hose will damage the hose and cause a leak.

Check each hose for swelling and oil-soaked ends. Cracks and breaks can be located by squeezing the hose.

15.4a Hoses, like drivebelts, have a habit of failing at the worst possible time - to prevent the inconvenience of a blown radiator or heater hose, inspect them carefully as shown here

▶ **Refer to illustrations 15.4a and 15.4b**

1 Many major engine failures can be attributed to a faulty cooling system. The cooling system also plays an important role in prolonging transmission life because it cools the fluid.

2 The engine should be cold for the cooling system check, so perform the following procedure before the vehicle is driven for the day or after it has been shut off for at least three hours.

3 If you're working on a vehicle equipped with a 3.8L V6 or a 5.0L V8 engine remove the cap from the radiator. If you're working on a 4.6L V8 engine, remove the cap from the expansion tank. Clean the cap thoroughly, inside and out, with clean water. Also clean the filler neck on the radiator or expansion tank. The presence of rust or corrosion in the filler neck means the coolant should be changed (see Section 28). The coolant inside the radiator should be relatively clean and transparent. If it's rust colored, drain the system and refill it with new coolant.

4 Carefully check the radiator hoses and the smaller diameter heater hoses (see illustration). Inspect each coolant hose along its entire length, replacing any hose which is cracked, swollen or deteriorated. Cracks will show up better if the hose is squeezed. Pay close

attention to hose clamps that secure the hoses to cooling system components. Hose clamps can pinch and puncture hoses, resulting in coolant leaks. Some hoses are hidden from view so sometimes you'll have to trace a coolant leak. For example, on the 4.6L V8 engine the heater hose connects to the water pump under the intake manifold. If it leaks, coolant will run down the rear of the engine (see illustration).

5   Make sure that all hose connections are tight. A leak in the cooling system will usually show up as white or rust colored deposits on the area adjoining the leak. If wire-type clamps are used on the hoses, it may be a good idea to replace them with screw-type clamps.

6   Clean the front of the radiator and air conditioning condenser with compressed air, if available, or a soft brush. Remove all bugs, leaves, etc. embedded in the radiator fins. Be extremely careful not to damage the cooling fins or cut your fingers on them.

7   If the coolant level has been dropping consistently and no leaks are detectable, have the radiator cap and cooling system pressure checked at a service station.

15.4b A leak in the 4.6L V8 engine heater hose means the intake manifold will have to be removed for hose replacement - coolant coming out the back of the engine is the symptom

16 Fuel system check (every 15,000 miles or 12 months)

✳✳ WARNING:

Gasoline is extremely flammable, so take extra precautions when you work on any part of the fuel system. Don't smoke or allow open flames or bare light bulbs near the work area, and don't work in a garage where a gas-type appliance (such as a water heater or clothes dryer) is present. Since gasoline is carcinogenic, wear latex gloves when there's a possibility of being exposed to fuel, and, if you spill any fuel on your skin, rinse it off immediately with soap and water. Mop up any spills immediately and do not store fuel-soaked rags where they could ignite. When you perform any kind of work on the fuel system, wear safety glasses and have a Class B type fire extinguisher on hand. The fuel system is under constant pressure, so, before any lines are disconnected, the fuel system pressure must be relieved. See Chapter 4.

1   If you smell gasoline while driving or after the vehicle has been sitting in the sun, inspect the fuel system immediately.

2   Remove the gas filler cap and inspect if for damage and corrosion. The gasket should have an unbroken sealing imprint. If the gasket is damaged or corroded, install a new cap.

3   Inspect the fuel feed and return lines for cracks. Make sure that the connections between the fuel lines and the fuel injection system and between the fuel lines and the in-line fuel filter are tight.

✳✳ WARNING:

Your vehicle is fuel injected, so you must relieve the fuel system pressure before servicing fuel system components. The fuel system pressure relief procedure is outlined in Chapter 4.

4   Since some components of the fuel system - the fuel tank and part of the fuel feed and return lines, for example - are underneath the vehicle, they can be inspected more easily with the vehicle raised on a hoist. If that's not possible, raise the vehicle and support it on jackstands.

5   With the vehicle raised and safely supported, inspect the gas tank and filler neck for punctures, cracks and other damage. The connection between the filler neck and the tank is particularly critical. Sometimes a rubber filler neck will leak because of loose clamps or deteriorated rubber. Inspect all fuel tank mounting brackets and straps to be sure that the tank is securely attached to the vehicle.

✳✳ WARNING:

Do not, under any circumstances, try to repair a fuel tank (except rubber components). A welding torch or any open flame can easily cause fuel vapors inside the tank to explode.

6   Carefully check all rubber hoses and metal lines leading away from the fuel tank. Check for loose connections, deteriorated hoses, crimped lines and other damage. Repair or replace damaged sections as necessary (see Chapter 4).

17   Steering and suspension check (every 15,000 miles or 12 months)

◆ **Refer to illustrations 17.6, 17.9a, 17.9b, 17.9c and 17.11**

➡**Note: The steering linkage and suspension components should be checked periodically. Worn or damaged suspension and steering linkage components can result in excessive and abnormal tire wear, poor ride quality and vehicle handling and reduced fuel economy. For detailed illustrations of the steering and suspension components, refer to Chapter 10.**

SHOCK ABSORBER CHECK

1   Park the vehicle on level ground, turn the engine off and set the parking brake. Check the tire pressures.

2   Push down at one corner of the vehicle, then release it while noting the movement of the body. It should stop moving and come to rest in a level position within one or two bounces.

3   If the vehicle continues to move up-and-down or if it fails to return to its original position, a worn or weak shock absorber is probably the reason.

4   Repeat the above check at each of the three remaining corners of the vehicle.

5   Raise the vehicle and support it securely on jackstands.

6   Check the shock absorbers and front struts for evidence of fluid leakage (see illustration). A light film of fluid is no cause for concern. Make sure that any fluid noted is from the shocks and not from some other source. If leakage is noted, replace the shocks or struts as a set.

7   Check the shocks and struts to be sure that they are securely mounted and undamaged. Check the upper mounts for damage and wear. If damage or wear is noted, replace the shocks or struts as a set (front or rear).

8   If the shocks or struts must be replaced, refer to Chapter 10 for the procedure.

STEERING AND SUSPENSION CHECK

9   Visually inspect the steering system components for damage and distortion. Look for damaged seals, boots and bushings and leaks of any kind (see illustrations).

10   Clean the lower end of the steering knuckle. Have an assistant

17.6 Check the shocks for leakage at the indicated area (arrow)

17.9a Inspect the tie rod ends and the lower balljoints (not visible) for torn grease seals (arrow)

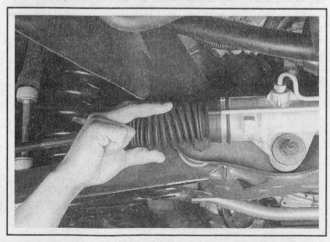

17.9b Check the steering gear boots for cracks and leaking steering fluid

17.9c Check the stabilizer bar bushings (arrows) for deterioration at the front and the rear of the vehicle

grasp the lower edge of the tire and move the wheel in-and-out while you look for movement at the steering knuckle-to-control arm balljoint. If there is any movement the suspension balljoint(s) must be replaced.

11 Grasp each front tire at the front and rear edges, push in at the front, pull out at the rear and feel for play in the steering system components If any freeplay is noted, check the steering gear mounts and the tie-rod ends for looseness (see illustration).

12 Additional steering and suspension system information and illustrations can be found in Chapter 10.

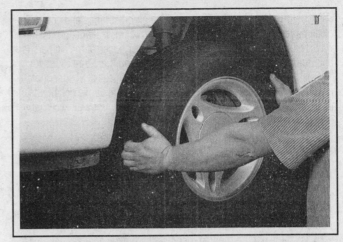

17.11 With the steering wheel in the lock position and the vehicle raised, grasp the front tire as shown and try to move it back-and-forth - if any play is noted, check the steering gear mounts and tie rod ends for looseness

18 Brake check (every 15,000 miles or 12 months)

✳✳ WARNING:

The dust created by the brake system is harmful to your health. Never blow it out with compressed air and don't inhale any of it. An approved filtering mask should be worn when working on the brakes. Do not, under any circumstances, use petroleum-based solvents to clean brake parts. Use brake system cleaner only! Try to use non-asbestos replacement parts whenever possible.

➡**Note: For detailed photographs of the brake system, refer to Chapter 9.**

1 In addition to the specified intervals, the brakes should be inspected every time the wheels are removed or whenever a defect is suspected.

2 Any of the following symptoms could indicate a potential brake system defect: The vehicle pulls to one side when the brake pedal is depressed; the brakes make squealing or dragging noises when applied; brake pedal travel is excessive; the pedal pulsates; brake fluid leaks, usually onto the inside of the tire or wheel.

3 Loosen the wheel lug nuts.

4 Raise the vehicle and place it securely on jackstands.

5 Remove the wheels (see *Jacking and towing* at the front of this book, or your owner's manual, if necessary).

DISC BRAKES

⬧ **Refer to illustrations 18.6 and 18.11**

6 There are two pads (an outer and an inner) in each caliper. The pads are visible through inspection holes in each caliper (see illustration).

7 Check the pad thickness by looking at each end of the caliper and through the inspection hole in the caliper body. If the lining material is less than the thickness listed in this Chapter's Specifications, replace the pads.

➡**Note: Keep in mind that the lining material is riveted or bonded to a metal backing plate and the metal portion is not included in this measurement.**

8 If it is difficult to determine the exact thickness of the remaining pad material by the above method, or if you are at all concerned about the condition of the pads, remove the caliper(s), then remove the pads from the calipers for further inspection (refer to Chapter 9).

9 Once the pads are removed from the calipers, clean them with brake cleaner and re-measure them with a ruler or a vernier caliper.

10 Measure the disc thickness with a micrometer to make sure that it still has service life remaining. If any disc is thinner than the specified minimum thickness, replace it (refer to Chapter 9). Even if the disc has service life remaining, check its condition. Look for scoring, gouging and burned spots. If these conditions exist, remove the disc and have it resurfaced (see Chapter 9).

18.6 You will find an inspection hole (arrow) like this in each caliper - placing a ruler across the hole should enable you to determine the thickness of remaining pad material for both inner and outer pads

11 Before installing the wheels, check all brake lines and hoses for damage, wear, deformation, cracks, corrosion, leakage, bends and twists, particularly in the vicinity of the rubber hoses at the calipers (see illustration). Check the clamps for tightness and the connections for leakage. Make sure that all hoses and lines are clear of sharp edges, moving parts and the exhaust system. If any of the above conditions are noted, repair, reroute or replace the lines and/or fittings as necessary (see Chapter 9).

BRAKE BOOSTER CHECK

12 Sit in the driver's seat and perform the following sequence of tests.

13 With the brake fully depressed, start the engine - the pedal should move down a little when the engine starts.

14 With the engine running, depress the brake pedal several times - the travel distance should not change.

15 Depress the brake, stop the engine and hold the pedal in for about 30 seconds - the pedal should neither sink nor rise.

16 Restart the engine, run it for about a minute and turn it off. Then firmly depress the brake several times - the pedal travel should decrease with each application.

17 If your brakes do not operate as described above when the preceding tests are performed, the brake booster is either in need of repair or has failed. Refer to Chapter 9 for the removal procedure.

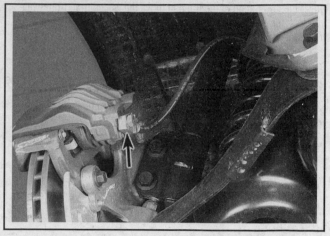

18.11 Check along the brake hoses and at each fitting (arrow) for deterioration and cracks

PARKING BRAKE

18 The parking brake mechanisms on these vehicles are self adjusting and do not require regular scheduled maintenance. For more detailed information on the parking brake assembly see Chapter 9.

19 Manual transmission lubricant level check (every 15,000 miles or 12 months)

19.2 The manual transmission fill plug (A) and drain plug (B) (arrows) are located on the side of the transmission case

▶ **Refer to illustration 19.2**

1 The manual transmission has a filler plug which must be removed to check the lubricant level. If the vehicle is raised to gain access to the plug, be sure to support it safely on jackstands - DO NOT crawl under a vehicle which is supported only by a jack! Be sure the vehicle is level or the check may be inaccurate.

2 Using an open-end wrench, unscrew the plug from the transmission (see illustration) and use a finger to reach inside the housing to determine the lubricant level. The level should be at or near the bottom of the plug hole.

3 If it isn't, add the recommended lubricant through the plug hole with a pump or squeeze bottle.

4 Install and tighten the plug and check for leaks after the first few miles of driving.

20 Differential lubricant level check (every 15,000 miles or 12 months)

▶ **Refer to illustration 20.2**

1 The differential has a check/fill plug which must be removed to check the lubricant level. If the vehicle is raised to gain access to the plug, be sure to support it safely on jackstands - DO NOT crawl under the vehicle when it's supported only by the jack!

2 Remove the check/fill plug from the differential (see illustration).

3   Use your little finger as a dipstick to make sure the lubricant level is even with the bottom of the plug hole. If not, use a syringe to add the recommended lubricant until it just starts to run out of the opening. On some models a tag is located in the area of the plug which gives information regarding lubricant type, particularly on models equipped with a limited slip differential.

4   Install the plug and tighten it securely.

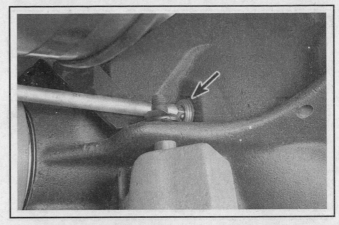

20.2 Use a 3/8-inch drive ratchet or breaker bar and an extension to remove the differential fill plug (arrow)

21 Drivebelt check and replacement (every 30,000 miles or 24 months)

▶ **Refer to illustrations 21.4, 21.5, 21.6 and 21.8**

1   The drivebelts are located at the front of the engine and play an important role in the overall operation of the vehicle and its components. Due to their function and material make-up, the drivebelts are prone to failure after a period of time and should be inspected and adjusted periodically to prevent major engine damage.

2   The vehicles covered by this manual are equipped with a single self-adjusting serpentine drivebelt, which is used to drive all of the accessory components such as the alternator, power steering pump, water pump and air-conditioning compressor.

INSPECTION

3   With the engine off, open the hood and locate the drivebelt at the front of the engine. Using your fingers (and a flashlight, if necessary), move along the belts checking for cracks and separation of the belt plies. Also check for fraying and glazing, which gives the belt a shiny appearance. Both sides of each belt should be inspected, which means you will have to twist the belt to check the underside.

4   Check the ribs on the underside of the belt. They should all be the same depth, with none of the surface uneven (see illustration).

5   The tension of the belt is automatically adjusted by the belt tensioner and does not require any adjustments. Drivebelt wear can be checked visually by inspecting the wear indicator marks located on the side of the tensioner body. Locate the belt tensioner at the front of the engine on the right (passenger) side, adjacent to the lower crankshaft pulley, then find the tensioner operating marks (see illustration). If the indicator mark is outside the operating range, the belt should be replaced.

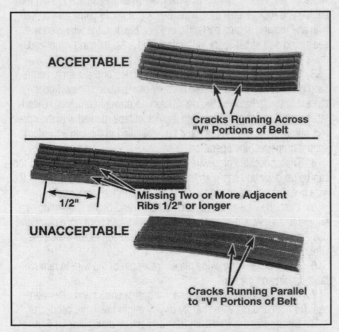

21.4 Small cracks in the underside of a V-ribbed belt are acceptable - lengthwise cracks, or missing pieces that cause the belt to make noise, are cause for replacement

21.5 Belt wear indicator marks are located on the side of the tensioner body - when the belt reaches the maximum wear mark it must be replaced

21.6 Insert a 1/2 inch breaker bar into the tensioner arm, then rotate it clockwise to relieve belt tension

REPLACEMENT

6   To replace the belt, Insert a 1/2 inch breaker bar or ratchet into the square hole located in the tensioner body (see illustration). Rotate the tensioner clockwise to relieve the tension on the belt.

7   Remove the belt from the auxiliary components and carefully release the tensioner.

8   Route the new belt over the various pulleys, again rotating

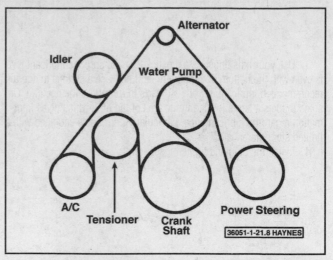

21.8 The routing schematic for the serpentine belt is usually found on the fan shroud (this one's for the 4.6L engine)

the tensioner to allow the belt to be installed, then release the belt tensioner. Make sure the belt fits properly into the pulley grooves - it must be completely engaged.

➡**Note: Most models have a drivebelt routing decal on the upper radiator panel to help during drivebelt installation (see illustration).**

---

22   Ignition system component check and replacement (every 30,000 miles or 24 months)

◆ **Refer to illustrations 22.8, 22.13 and 22.14**

SPARK PLUG WIRES

➡**Note: Every time a spark plug wire is detached from a spark plug, the distributor cap or the coil, silicone dielectric compound (a white grease available at auto parts stores) must be applied to the inside of each boot before reconnection. Use a small standard screwdriver to coat the entire inside surface of each boot with a thin layer of the compound.**

1   The spark plug wires should be checked and, if necessary, replaced at the same time new spark plugs are installed.

22.8 Remove each spark plug wire from the ignition coil packs or distributor on 5.0L engines - check for corrosion and a tight fit

2   The easiest way to identify bad wires is to make a visual check while the engine is running. In a dark, well-ventilated garage, start the engine and look at each plug wire. Be careful not to come into contact with any moving engine parts. If there is a break in the wire, you will see arcing or a small spark at the damaged area. If arcing is noticed, make a note to obtain new wires.

3   The spark plug wires should be inspected one at a time, beginning with the spark plug for the number one cylinder, (the cylinder closest to the radiator on the right bank), to prevent confusion. Clearly label each original plug wire with a piece of tape marked with the correct number. The plug wires must be reinstalled in the correct order to ensure proper engine operation.

4   Disconnect the plug wire from the first spark plug. A removal tool can be used, or you can grab the wire boot, twist it slightly and pull the wire free. Do not pull on the wire itself, only on the rubber boot.

5   Push the wire and boot back onto the end of the spark plug. It should fit snugly. If it doesn't, detach the wire and boot once more and use a pair of pliers to carefully crimp the metal connector inside the wire boot until it does.

6   Using a clean rag, wipe the entire length of the wire to remove built-up dirt and grease.

7   Once the wire is clean, check for burns, cracks and other damage. Do not bend the wire sharply or you might break the conductor.

8   Disconnect the wire from the coil pack or distributor on 5.0L engines. Pull only on the rubber boot. Check for corrosion and a tight fit (see illustration). Reinstall the wire.

9   Inspect each of the remaining spark plug wires, making sure that each one is securely fastened on each end.

10   If new spark plug wires are required, purchase a set for your specific engine model. Pre-cut wire sets with the boots already installed are

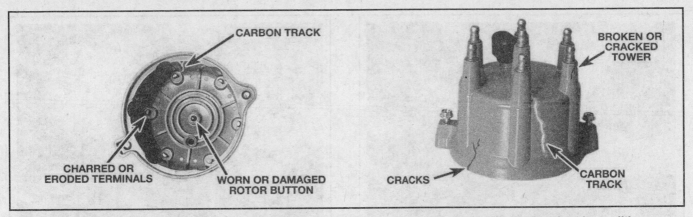

22.13 Shown here are some the common defects to look for when inspecting the distributor cap (if in doubt about its condition, install a new one)

available. Remove and replace the wires one at a time to avoid mix-ups in the firing order. Should a mix up occur, refer to the Specifications at the end this Chapter.

IGNITION COIL PACKS

11 Clean the coil packs with a dampened cloth and dry them thoroughly.

12 Inspect each coil pack for cracks, damage and carbon tracking. If damage exists refer to Chapter 5 for the replacement procedure.

DISTRIBUTOR CAP AND ROTOR (5.0L V8 MODELS)

→Note: It's common practice to install a new distributor cap and rotor each time new spark plug wires are installed. If you're planning to install new wires, install a new cap and rotor also. But if you're planning to reuse the existing wires, be sure to inspect the cap and rotor to make sure that they are in good condition.

13 Remove the mounting screws and detach the cap from the distributor. Check it for cracks, carbon tracks and worn, burned or loose terminals (see illustration).

14 Check the rotor for cracks and carbon tracks. Make sure the center terminal spring tension is adequate and look for corrosion and wear

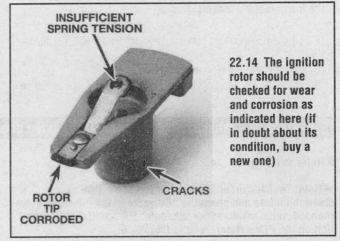

22.14 The ignition rotor should be checked for wear and corrosion as indicated here (if in doubt about its condition, buy a new one)

on the rotor tip (see illustration).

15 Replace the cap and rotor if damage or defects are found. Note that the rotor is indexed so it can only be installed one way. Before installing the cap, apply silicone dielectric compound to the rotor tip (see **Note** at beginning of this Section).

16 When installing a new cap, remove the wires from the old cap one at a time and attach them to the new cap in the exact same location - do not simultaneously remove all the wires from the old cap or firing order mix-ups may occur. Should a mix up occur, refer to the Specifications at the end this Chapter.

23 Air filter replacement (every 30,000 miles or 24 months)

♦ Refer to illustrations 23.2, 23.3 and 23.4

1 Purchase a new filter element for your specific engine type.
2 Remove the air filter housing retaining bolt and retaining clip (see illustration).

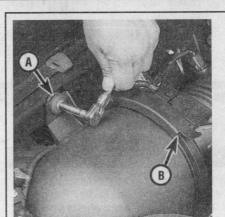

23.2 Remove the air filter housing to body retaining bolt (A) then unfasten the air filter housing to mass air flow sensor retaining clip (B)

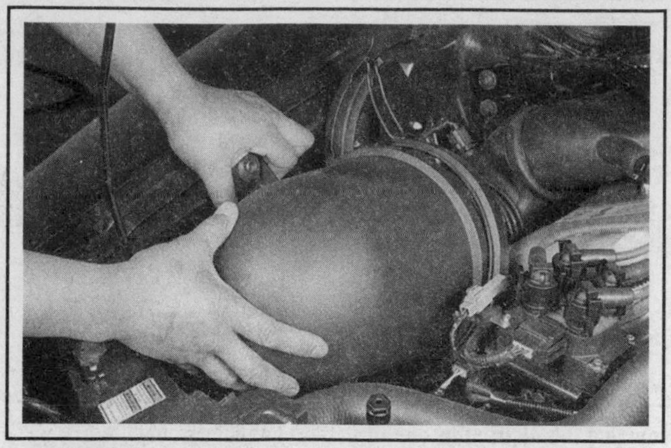

23.3 Use both hands to separate the air filter housing from the lower isolator mounts

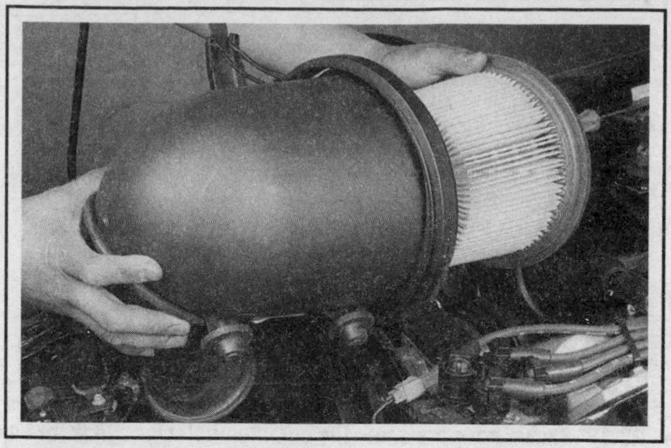

23.4 After detaching the filter housing the filter can be removed and replaced

3 Lift the filter housing out from the inner fenderwell (see illustration).

4 Remove the filter element (see illustration).

5 Place the new air filter element in the housing. Align the tab on the mass air flow sensor with the slot in the air filter housing when reinstalling.

6 The remainder of the installation is the reverse of removal.

24 Positive Crankcase Ventilation (PCV) valve check (every 30,000 miles or 24 months)

Refer to illustration 24.2

Note: To maintain efficient operation of the PCV system, clean the hoses and check the PCV valve at the intervals recommended in the maintenance schedule. For additional information on the PCV system, refer to Chapter 6.

1 On 3.8L and 4.6L SOHC engines the PCV valve is located in the right (passenger's side) valve cover. On 4.6L DOHC engines the PCV valve is located in the left (drivers side) valve cover. On 5.0L engines the PCV valve is located at the rear of the lower intake manifold.

2 Start the engine and allow it to idle, then disconnect the PCV valve from the valve cover or intake manifold and feel for vacuum at the end of the valve (see illustration). If vacuum is felt, the PCV valve/system is working properly (see Chapter 6 for additional PCV system information).

3 If no vacuum is felt, remove the valve and check for vacuum at the hose. If vacuum is present at the hose but not at the valve, replace the valve. If no vacuum is felt at the hose, check for a plugged or cracked hose between the PCV valve and the intake plenum.

4 Check the rubber grommet in the valve cover or intake manifold for cracks and distortion. If it's damaged, replace it.

5 If the valve is clogged, the hose is also probably plugged. Remove the hose between the valve and the intake manifold and clean it with solvent.

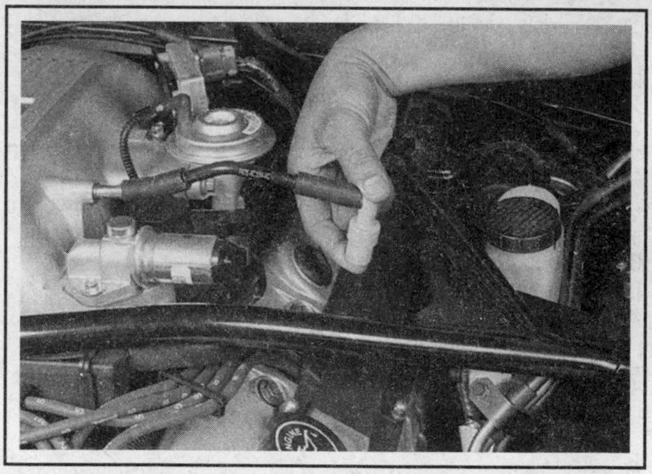

24.2 With the engine running at idle, remove the PCV valve and verify that vacuum can be felt at the end of the valve

6 After cleaning the hose, inspect it for damage, wear and deterioration. Make sure it fits snugly on the fittings.

7 If necessary, install a new PCV valve.

25 Fuel filter replacement (every 30,000 miles or 24 months)

Refer to illustration 25.3

WARNING:

Gasoline is extremely flammable, so take extra precautions when you work on any part of the fuel system. Don't smoke or allow open flames or bare light bulbs near the work area, and don't work in a garage where a gas-type appliance (such as a water heater or clothes dryer) is present. Since gasoline is carcinogenic, wear latex gloves when there's a possibility of being exposed to fuel, and, if you spill any fuel on your skin, rinse it off immediately with soap and water. Mop up any spills immediately and do not store fuel-soaked rags where they could ignite. When you perform any kind of work on the fuel system, wear safety glasses and have a Class B type fire extinguisher on hand.

1   The fuel filter is mounted under the vehicle in front of the gas tank.

2   Inspect the hose fittings at both ends of the filter to see if they're clean. If more than a light coating of dust is present, clean the fittings before proceeding.

3   Relieve the fuel system pressure (see Chapter 4). Removal of the hairpin clip from each fitting is a two-stage procedure. First, spread the two clip legs apart about 1/8-inch to disengage them, then push in on them. Pull on the other end of the clip to detach it from the fitting (see illustration).

❈❈ CAUTION:

If the new filter doesn't include new clips, don't use any tools or you may damage the plastic clips, which will have to be reused. Use your fingers only.

4   Once both hairpin clips are released, grasp the fuel hoses, one at a time, and pull them straight off the filter. Be prepared for fuel spillage.

5   After the hoses have been detached, check the clips for damage and distortion. If they were damaged in any way during removal, new ones must be used when the hoses are reattached to the new filter (if new clips are packaged with the filter, be sure to use them in place of the originals).

6   Use a screwdriver to loosen the clamp, while noting the direction the fuel filter is installed.

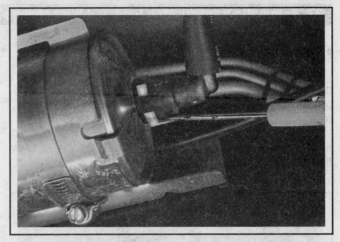

25.3 Use a small screwdriver to pry the fuel line fitting retaining clip off

7   Remove the filter from the bracket and install the new fuel filter in the same direction.

8   Carefully push each hose onto the filter until it's seated against the collar on the fitting, then install the hairpin clips. Make sure the clips are securely attached to the hose fittings - if they come off, the hoses could back off the filter and a fire could result!

9   Start the engine and check for fuel leaks.

26 Exhaust system check (every 30,000 miles or 24 months)

▸ **Refer to illustrations 26.2a and 26.2b**

1   With the engine cold (at least three hours after the vehicle has been driven), check the complete exhaust system from the engine to the end of the tailpipe. Ideally, the inspection should be done with the vehicle on a hoist to permit unrestricted access. If a hoist isn't available, raise the vehicle and support it securely on jackstands.

2   Check the exhaust pipes and connections for evidence of leaks, severe corrosion and damage. Make sure that all brackets and hangers are in good condition and tight (see illustrations).

3   At the same time, inspect the underside of the body for holes, corrosion, open seams, etc. which may allow exhaust gases to enter the passenger compartment. Seal all body openings with silicone or body putty.

4   Rattles and other noises can often be traced to the exhaust system, especially the mounts and hangers. Try to move the pipes, muffler and catalytic converter. If the components can come in contact with the body or suspension parts, secure the exhaust system with new mounts.

5   Check the running condition of the engine by inspecting inside the end of the tailpipe. The exhaust deposits here are an indication of engine state-of-tune. If the pipe is black and sooty or coated with white deposits, the engine may need a tune-up, including a thorough fuel system inspection and adjustment.

26.2a Check the flange connections (arrows) for exhaust leaks - also check that the retaining nuts are securely tightened

26.2b Check the exhaust system hangers (arrow) fo[r] and cracks

27 Automatic transmission fluid and filter change (every 30,000 miles or 24 months)

▶ **Refer to illustrations 27.7, 27.9, 27.10, 27.11 and 27.12**

1 At the specified intervals, the transmission fluid should be drained and replaced. Since the fluid will remain hot long after driving, perform this procedure only after the engine has cooled down completely.

2 Before beginning work, purchase the transmission fluid specified in *Recommended lubricants and fluids* at the end of this Chapter, a new filter and gaskets. Never reuse the old filter or gasket!

3 Other tools necessary for this job include jackstands to support the vehicle in a raised position, a drain pan capable of holding at least eight quarts, newspapers and clean rags.

4 Raise the vehicle and support it securely on jackstands.

5 With the drain pan in place, remove the front and side transmission pan mounting bolts.

6 Loosen the rear pan bolts approximately four turns.

7 Carefully pry the transmission pan loose with a screwdriver, allowing the fluid to drain (see illustration). Don't damage the pan or transmission gasket surfaces or leaks could develop.

8 Remove the remaining bolts, pan and gasket. Carefully clean the gasket surface of the transmission to remove all traces of the old gasket and sealant.

9 Drain the fluid from the transmission pan, clean it with solvent and dry it thoroughly.

➡**Note: Upon initial service most transmissions will have plastic plug lying in the bottom of the pan. This plug was used to keep contamination out of the transmission while on the assembly line. Discard the factory installed dust plug (see illustration).**

10 Remove the old filter from transmission (see illustration).

11 Install a new seal and filter (see illustration).

12 Make sure the gasket surface on the transmission pan is clean, then install a new gasket (see illustration). Put the pan in place against

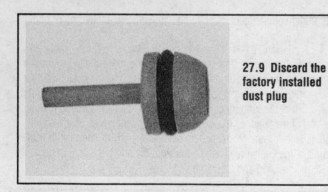

27.7 Pry the pan free of the gasket and allow the fluid to drain

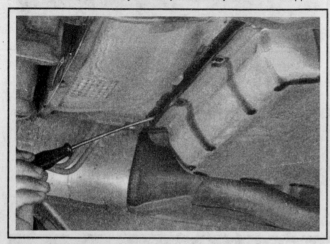

27.9 Discard the factory installed dust plug

27.10 Pull straight down on the filter to remove it

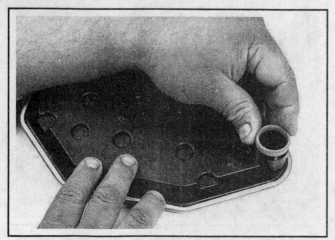

27.11 Install a new seal on the transmission filter

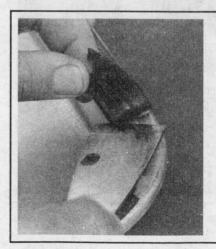

27.12 Be sure to clean all traces of the old gasket from the pan before installing a new one

the transmission and install the bolts. Working around the pan, tighten each bolt a little at a time until the final torque figure listed in this Chapter's Specifications is reached. Don't overtighten the bolts!

13 Lower the vehicle and add four quarts of automatic transmission fluid through the filler tube (see Section 7).

14 With the transmission in Park and the parking brake set, run the engine at a fast idle, but don't race it.

15 Move the gear selector through each range and back to Park. Check the fluid level. Add fluid if needed to reach the correct level.

16 Check under the vehicle for leaks during the first few trips.

28 Cooling system servicing (draining, flushing and refilling) (every 30,000 miles or 24 months)

▶ Refer to illustrations 28.4, 28.5a and 28.5b

✳✳ WARNING:

Do not allow antifreeze to come in contact with your skin or painted surfaces of the vehicle. Rinse off spills immediately with plenty of water. Antifreeze is highly toxic if ingested. Never leave antifreeze lying around in an open container or in puddles on the floor; children and pets are attracted by it's sweet smell and may drink it. Check with local authorities about disposing of used antifreeze. Many communities have collection centers which will see that antifreeze is disposed of safely.

1 Periodically, the cooling system should be drained, flushed and refilled to replenish the antifreeze mixture and prevent formation of rust and corrosion, which can impair the performance of the cooling system and cause engine damage. When the cooling system is serviced, all hoses and the radiator cap should be checked and replaced if necessary.

DRAINING

2 Apply the parking brake and block the wheels. If the vehicle has just been driven, wait several hours to allow the engine to cool down before beginning this procedure.

3 Once the engine is completely cool, remove the radiator cap on vehicles equipped with 3.8L and 5.0L engines or the expansion tank cap on vehicles equipped with 4.6L engines.

4 Move a large container under the radiator drain to catch the coolant. Attach a 3/8-inch diameter hose to the drain fitting to direct the coolant into the container, then open the drain fitting (a pair of pliers may be required to turn it) (see illustration).

28.4 The radiator drain fitting is located at the lower corner of the radiator (arrow)

5 After the coolant stops flowing out of the radiator, move the container under the engine block drain plugs and allow the coolant in the block to drain (see illustrations).

6 While the coolant is draining, check the condition of the radiator hoses, heater hoses and clamps (refer to Section 15 if necessary).

7 Replace any damaged clamps or hoses (refer to Chapter 3 for detailed replacement procedures).

FLUSHING

8 Once the system is completely drained, flush the radiator with fresh water from a garden hose until water runs clear at the drain. The

28.5a The block drain plugs (arrow) are generally located about one to two inches above the oil pan rail - there is one on each side of the engine block

28.5b Remove the air bleed plug (arrow) from the water by-pass tube (4.6L DOHC engines only)

flushing action of the water will remove sediments from the radiator but will not remove rust and scale from the engine and cooling tube surfaces.

9 These deposits can be removed by the chemical action of a cleaner available at auto parts stores. Follow the procedure outlined in the manufacturer's instructions. If the radiator is severely corroded, damaged or leaking, it should be removed (see Chapter 3) and taken to a radiator repair shop.

10 Remove the overflow hose from the coolant recovery reservoir. Drain the reservoir and flush it with clean water, then reconnect the hose.

REFILLING

11 Close and tighten the radiator drain. Install and tighten the block drain plugs.

12 Place the heater temperature control in the maximum heat position.

13 Slowly add new coolant (a 50/50 mixture of water and antifreeze) to the radiator until it is full. Add coolant to the reservoir or expansion tank up to the Full Hot mark.

14 Leave the radiator or expansion tank cap off and run the engine in a well-ventilated area until the thermostat opens (coolant will begin flowing through the radiator and the upper radiator hose will become hot).

15 Turn the engine off and let it cool. Add more coolant mixture to bring the level back up to the lip on the radiator or expansion tank filler neck.

16 Squeeze the upper radiator hose to expel air, then add more coolant mixture if necessary. Replace the radiator or expansion tank cap.

17 Start the engine, allow it to reach normal operating temperature and check for leaks.

29 Brake fluid change (every 30,000 miles or 24 months)

✳✳ WARNING:

Brake fluid can harm your eyes and damage painted surfaces, so use extreme caution when handling or pouring it. Do not use brake fluid that has been standing open or is more than one year old. Brake fluid absorbs moisture from the air. Excess moisture can cause a dangerous loss of braking effectiveness.

1 At the specified intervals, the brake fluid should be drained and replaced. Since the brake fluid may drip or splash when pouring it, place plenty of rags around the master cylinder to protect any surrounding painted surfaces.

2 Before beginning work, purchase the specified brake fluid (see *Recommended lubricants and fluids* at the end of this Chapter).

3 Remove the cap from the master cylinder reservoir.

4 Using a hand suction pump or similar device, withdraw the fluid from the master cylinder reservoir.

5 Add new fluid to the master cylinder until it rises to the base of the filler neck.

6 Bleed the brake system as described in Chapter 9 at all four brakes until new and uncontaminated fluid expels from the bleeder screw. Be sure to maintain the fluid level in the master cylinder as you perform the bleeding process. If you allow the master cylinder to run dry, air will enter the system.

7 Refill the master cylinder with fluid and check the operation of the brakes. The pedal should feel solid when depressed, with no sponginess.

✳✳ WARNING:

Do not operate the vehicle if you are in doubt about the effectiveness of the brake system.

30 Spark plug check and replacement (every 60,000 miles or 48 months)

▶ **Refer to illustrations 30.2, 30.5a, 30.5b, 30.6a, 30.6b, 30.8, 30.9, 30.10a and 30.10b**

➡**Note: If the spark plug heat ranges differ from those listed in this Chapter's Specifications, and if these spark plugs are going to be reused, they must be reinstalled in the exact cylinder from which they were removed. Some spark plugs have only the platinum enhanced ground (side) electrode, while others have only the platinum enhanced center electrode (both electrodes are platinum enhanced on the specified spark plugs). These spark plugs must be installed in the correct cylinder locations for proper ignition operation.**

1 Vehicles equipped with 3.8L and 5.0L engines have the spark plugs located on the sides of the engine. Vehicles equipped with 4.6L engines have the spark plugs located at the top of the engine.

2 In most cases, the tools necessary for spark plug replacement include a spark plug socket which fits onto a ratchet (spark plug sockets are padded inside to prevent damage to the porcelain insulators on the new plugs), various extensions and a gap gauge to check and adjust the gaps on the new plugs (see illustration). A special plug wire removal tool is available for separating the wire boots from the spark plugs, but it isn't absolutely necessary. A torque wrench should be used to tighten the new plugs.

3 The best approach when replacing the spark plugs is to purchase the new ones in advance, adjust them to the proper gap and replace the plugs one at a time. When buying the new spark plugs, be sure to obtain the correct plug type for your particular engine. This information can be found in the Specifications Section a the end of this Chapter, on the Emission Control Information label located under the hood or in the factory owner's manual. If differences exist between the plug specified on the emissions label, Specifications Section or in the owner's manual, assume that the emissions label is correct.

4 Allow the engine to cool completely before attempting to remove any of the plugs. Some engines are equipped with aluminum cylinder heads, which can be damaged if the spark plugs are removed when the engine is hot. While you are waiting for the engine to cool, check the new plugs for defects and adjust the gaps.

5 The gap is checked by inserting the proper thickness gauge between the electrodes at the tip of the plug (see illustration). The gap

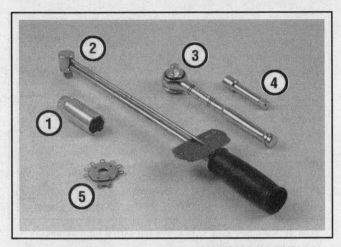

30.2 Tools required for changing spark plugs

1 **Spark plug socket** - *This will have special padding inside to protect the spark plug's porcelain insulator*
2 **Torque wrench** - *Although not mandatory, using this tool is the best way to ensure the plugs are tightened properly*
3 **Ratchet** - *Standard hand tool to fit the spark plug socket*
4 **Extension** - *Depending on model and accessories, you may need special extensions and universal joints to reach one or more of the plugs*
5 **Spark plug gap gauge** - *This gauge for checking the gap comes in a variety of styles. Make sure the gap for your engine is included*

between the electrodes should be the same as the one specified on the Emissions Control Information label. The wire should just slide between the electrodes with a slight amount of drag. If the gap is incorrect, use the adjuster on the gauge body to bend the curved side electrode slightly until the specified gap is obtained (see illustration). If the side electrode is not exactly over the center electrode, bend it with the adjuster until it is. Check for cracks in the porcelain insulator (if any are found, the plug should not be used).

6 With the engine cool, remove the spark plug wire from one spark plug. Pull only on the boot at the end of the wire - do not pull on the wire (see illustrations). A plug wire removal tool should be used if available.

30.5a Spark plug manufacturers recommend using a wire-type gauge when checking the gap - if the wire does not slide between the electrodes with a slight drag, adjustment is required

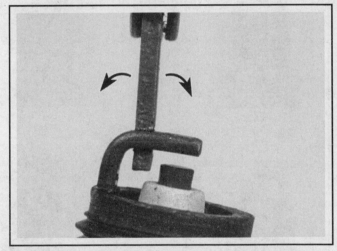

30.5b To change the gap, bend the side electrode only, as indicated by the arrows, and be very careful not to crack or chip the porcelain insulator surrounding the center electrode

30.6a 4.6L DOHC engines require removing a cover to access the spark plugs

30.6b When removing the spark plug wires, pull only on the boot and twist it back-and-forth

7   If compressed air is available, use it to blow any dirt or foreign material away from the spark plug hole. A common bicycle pump will also work. The idea here is to eliminate the possibility of debris falling into the cylinder as the spark plug is removed.

8   Place the spark plug socket over the plug and remove it from the engine by turning it in a counterclockwise direction (see illustration).

9   Compare the spark plug to those shown on this chart to get an indication of the general running condition of the engine (see illustration).

10 Apply a small amount of anti-seize compound to the spark plug threads (see illustration). Install one of the new plugs into the hole until you can no longer turn it with your fingers, then tighten it with a torque wrench (if available) or the ratchet. It is a good idea to slip a short length of rubber hose over the end of the plug to use as a tool to thread it into place (see illustration). The hose will grip the plug well enough to turn it, but will start to slip if the plug begins to cross-thread in the

30.8 Use a spark plug socket wrench with a long extension to unscrew the spark plug

A **normally worn** spark plug should have light tan or gray deposits on the firing tip.

A **carbon fouled** plug, identified by soft, sooty, black deposits, may indicate an improperly tuned vehicle. Check the air cleaner, ignition components and engine control system.

An **oil fouled** spark plug indicates an engine with worn piston rings and/or bad valve seals allowing excessive oil to enter the chamber.

This spark plug has been **left in the engine too long**, as evidenced by the extreme gap- Plugs with such an extreme gap can cause misfiring and stumbling accompanied by a noticeable lack of power.

A **physically damaged** spark plug may be evidence of severe detonation in that cylinder. Watch that cylinder carefully between services, as a continued detonation will not only damage the plug, but could also damage the engine.

A **bridged or almost bridged** spark plug, identified by a build-up between the electrodes caused by excessive carbon or oil build-up on the plug.

30.9 Inspect the spark plug to determine engine running conditions

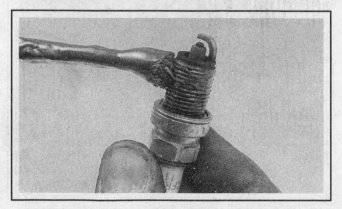

30.10a Apply a thin film of anti-seize compound to the spark plug threads to prevent damage to the cylinder head

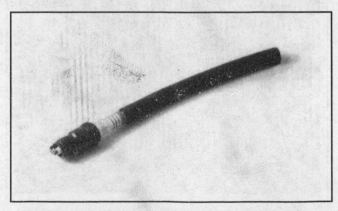

30.10b A length of 3/8-inch ID rubber hose will save time and prevent damaged threads when installing the spark plugs

hole - this will prevent damaged threads and the accompanying repair costs.

11 Before pushing the spark plug wire onto the end of the plug, inspect it following the procedures outlined in Section 22.

12 Attach the plug wire to the new spark plug, again using a twisting motion on the boot until it is seated on the spark plug.

13 Repeat the procedure for the remaining spark plugs, replacing them one at a time to prevent mixing up the spark plug wires.

31 Manual transmission lubricant change (every 60,000 miles or 48 months)

1 Raise the vehicle and support it securely on jackstands.

2 Move a drain pan, rags, newspapers and wrenches under the transmission.

3 Remove the transmission drain plug at the bottom of the case and allow the lubricant to drain into the pan (see illustration 19.2).

4 After the lubricant has drained completely, reinstall the plug and tighten it securely.

5 Remove the fill plug from the side of the transmission case. Using a hand pump, syringe or funnel, fill the transmission with the specified lubricant until it is level with the lower edge of the filler hole. Reinstall the fill plug and tighten it securely.

6 Lower the vehicle.

7 Drive the vehicle for a short distance, then check the drain and fill plugs for leakage.

32 Differential lubricant change (every 60,000 miles or 48 months)

▶ Refer to illustrations 32.4a, 32.4b, 32.4c and 32.6

1 On these models there is no drain plug, so a hand suction pump will be required to remove the differential lubricant through the filler hole. If a suction pump isn't available, or the gasket is leaking, be sure to obtain a new gasket at the same time the gear lubricant is purchased because it will be necessary to remove the cover plate.

2 Raise the vehicle and support it securely on jackstands. Move a drain pan, rags, newspapers and wrenches under the vehicle.

3 Remove the fill plug from the differential (see Section 20). If a suction pump is being used, insert the flexible hose. Work the hose down to the bottom of the differential housing and pump the lubricant out.

4 If the differential is being drained by removing the cover plate, remove the bolts on the lower half of the plate (see illustration). Loosen the bolts on the upper half and use them to keep the cover loosely attached (see illustration). Allow the oil to drain into the pan, then completely remove the cover (see illustration).

32.4a Remove the bolts from the lower edge of the cover . . .

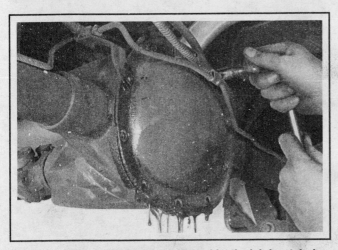

32.4b . . . then loosen the top bolts and let the lubricant drain

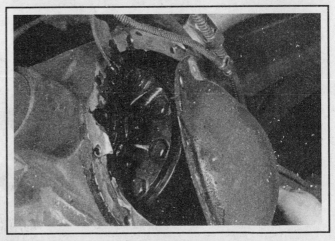

32.4c Once the lubricant has drained, remove the cover

5   Using a lint-free rag, clean the inside of the cover and the accessible areas of the differential housing. As this is done, check for chipped gears and metal particles in the lubricant, indicating that the differential should be more thoroughly inspected and/or repaired.

6   Thoroughly clean the gasket mating surfaces of the differential housing and the cover plate. Use a gasket scraper or putty knife to remove all traces of the old gasket (see illustration).

7   Apply a thin layer of RTV sealant to the cover flange, then press a new gasket into position on the cover. Make sure the bolt holes align properly.

8   Place the cover on the differential housing and install the bolts. Tighten the bolts securely.

9   Use a hand pump, syringe or funnel to fill the differential housing with the specified lubricant until it's level with the bottom of the plug hole.

10   Install the filler plug and make sure it is secure.

32.6 Carefully scrape off the old material to ensure a leak-free seal

Specifications

Recommended lubricants and fluids

➡Note: Listed here are manufacturer recommendations at the time this manual was written. Manufacturers occasionally upgrade their fluid and lubricant specifications, so check with your local auto parts store for current recommendations

Engine oil	
Type	API grade SG or SG/CC multigrade and fuel efficient oil
Viscosity	See accompanying chart

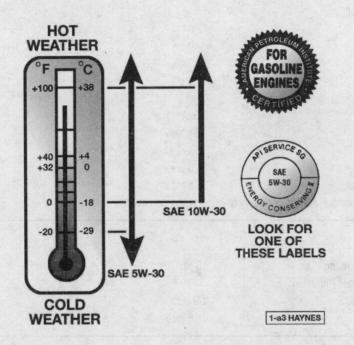

Recommended engine oil viscosity

Fuel	
All except Cobra	unleaded gasoline, 87 octane or higher
Cobra	unleaded gasoline, 91 octane or higher
Engine coolant	50/50 mixture of ethylene glycol based antifreeze and water
Brake fluid	DOT 3 heavy duty brake fluid
Power steering fluid	MERCON automatic transmission fluid
Automatic transmission fluid	
1998 and earlier	MERCON automatic transmission fluid
1999 and later	MERCON V automatic transmission fluid*
Manual transmission fluid	MERCON automatic transmission fluid
Chassis grease	SAE NLGI no. 2 chassis grease
Differential lubricant	SAE 80W-90 GL-5 gear lubricant**

Mercon V is not interchangeable with the regular MERCON fluid.

**Trak-Lok axles add 4 oz. of friction modifier when oil is changed.*

Capacities*

Engine oil (with filter change)

3.8L V6	5.0 qts
5.0L V8	5.0 qts
4.6L V8	
1996 and earlier	5.0 qts
1997 and later	6.0 qts
Fuel tank	15.4 gallons
Cooling system	
V6 models	11.8 qts
V8 models	14.1 qts
Automatic transmission	
AODE	12.5 qts
4R70W	
3.8L V6	13.9 qts
4.6L V8	12.8 qts
Manual transmission	
T5	5.6 pts
T45	6.6 pts
Rear differential	
7.5 inch ring gear	3.25 pts
8.8 inch ring gear	3.75 pts

All capacities approximate. Add as necessary to bring to appropriate level.

General

Radiator cap pressure rating	16 psi
Disc brake pad thickness (minimum)	
1994 through 1997	1/8 inch
1998	1/16 inch

Ignition system

Spark plug type and gap

1994 and 1995	
3.8L V6	Motorcraft AWSF-44PP or equivalent @ 0.052 inch
5.0L V8 (except Cobra)	Motorcraft ASF-42C or equivalent @ 0.052 inch
5.0L V8 (Cobra)	Motorcraft AWSF-32C or equivalent @ 0.052 inch
1996 and later	
3.8L V6	Motorcraft AWSF-44EE or equivalent @ 0.052 inch
4.6L SOHC V8	Motorcraft AWSF-32PP or equivalent @ 0.052 inch
4.6L DOHC V8	Motorcraft AWSF-32EE or equivalent @ 0.052 inch
Firing order	
V6 models	1-4-2-5-3-6
V8 models	1-3-7-2-6-5-4-8

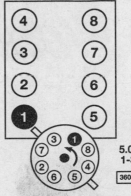

Cylinder location and coil terminal identification diagram - 3.8L engine

Cylinder location and coil terminal identification diagram - 4.6L engine

Cylinder location and distributor rotation diagram - 5.0L engine

Torque specifications	Ft-lbs
Wheel lug nuts	85 to 105
Spark plugs	7 to 14
Oil pan drain plug	
1998 4.6L SOHC	15 to 19
All other models	8 to 12
Automatic transmission pan bolts	10 to 12
Manual transmission drain and fill plug	12 to 22
Rear differential drain and fill plug	12 to 22

Notes

Section

Reference to other Chapters

2A

V6 AND 5.0L V8 ENGINES

1 General information

This Part of Chapter 2 is devoted to in-vehicle repair procedures for the 3.8L V6 and 5.0L V8 engines. All information concerning engine removal and installation and engine block and cylinder head overhaul can be found in Part C of this Chapter.

The following repair procedures are based on the assumption that the engine is installed in the vehicle. If the engine has been removed from the vehicle and mounted on a stand, many of the steps outlined in this Part of Chapter 2 will not apply.

The Specifications included in this Part of Chapter 2 apply only to the procedures contained in this Part. Part C of Chapter 2 contains the Specifications necessary for cylinder head and engine block rebuilding.

2 Repair operations possible with the engine in the vehicle

Many major repair operations can be accomplished without removing the engine from the vehicle.

Clean the engine compartment and the exterior of the engine with some type of pressure washer before any work is done. It will make the job easier and help keep dirt out of the internal areas of the engine.

It may help to remove the hood to improve access to the engine as repairs are performed (refer to Chapter 11 if necessary).

If vacuum, exhaust, oil or coolant leaks develop, indicating a need for gasket or seal replacement, the repairs can generally be made with the engine in the vehicle. The intake and exhaust manifold gaskets, timing cover gasket, oil pan gasket, crankshaft oil seals and cylinder head gaskets are all accessible with the engine in place.

Exterior engine components, such as the intake and exhaust manifolds, the oil pan (and the oil pump), the water pump, the starter motor, the alternator, the distributor and the fuel system components can be removed for repair with the engine in place.

Since the cylinder heads can be removed without pulling the engine, valve component servicing can also be accomplished with the engine in the vehicle. Replacement of the timing chain and sprockets is also possible with the engine in the vehicle.

In extreme cases caused by a lack of necessary equipment, repair or replacement of piston rings, pistons, connecting rods and rod bearings is possible with the engine in the vehicle. However, this practice is not recommended because of the cleaning and preparation work that must be done to the components involved.

3 Top Dead Center (TDC) for number one piston - locating

▶ Refer to illustrations 3.4, 3.6 and 3.7

➡Note: The following procedure applies to the 1994 and 1995 5.0L V8 engine only. The 3.8L V6 does not have a distributor, refer to TDC locating procedure in Chapter 2, Part B for the V6 engine.

1 Top Dead Center (TDC) is the highest point in the cylinder that each piston reaches as it travels up-and-down when the crankshaft turns. Each piston reaches TDC on the compression stroke and again on the exhaust stroke, but TDC generally refers to piston position on the compression stroke. The timing marks on the vibration damper installed on the front of the crankshaft are referenced to the number one piston at TDC on the compression stroke.

2 Positioning the piston(s) at TDC is an essential part of many procedures such as rocker arm removal, valve adjustment, timing chain and sprocket replacement and distributor removal.

3 In order to bring any piston to TDC, the crankshaft must be turned using one of the methods outlined below. When looking at the front of the engine, normal crankshaft rotation is clockwise.

❊❊ WARNING:

Before beginning this procedure, be sure to place the transmission in Neutral and ground the coil wire attached to the center terminal of the distributor cap to disable the ignition system.

a) The preferred method is to turn the crankshaft with a large socket and breaker bar attached to the vibration damper bolt threaded into the front of the crankshaft.

b) A remote starter switch, which may save some time, can also be used. Attach the switch leads to the S (switch) and B (battery) terminals on the starter motor. Once the piston is close to TDC, use a socket and breaker bar as described in the previous paragraph.

c) If an assistant is available to turn the ignition switch to the Start position in short bursts, you can get the piston close to TDC without a remote starter switch. Use a socket and breaker bar as described in Paragraph a) to complete the procedure.

4 Using a felt pen, make a mark on the distributor housing directly below the number one spark plug wire terminal on the distributor cap (see illustration).

3.4 Make a mark on the distributor body directly below the number 1 plug spark plug wire terminal (arrow)

➡Note: The terminal numbers are marked on the spark plug wires near the distributor.

3.6 Turn the crankshaft clockwise until the zero on the vibration damper scale is directly opposite the pointer

3.7 The rotor tip should be pointing at the mark (arrow) on the distributor

5   Remove the distributor cap as described in Chapter 1.

6   Turn the crankshaft (see Paragraph 3 above) until the zero or groove on the vibration damper is aligned with the pointer or TDC mark (see illustration). The pointer or TDC mark and vibration damper are located low on the front of the engine, near the pulley that turns the drivebelt.

7   The rotor should now be pointing directly at the mark on the distributor housing (see illustration). If it isn't, the piston is at TDC on the exhaust stroke.

8   To get the piston to TDC on the compression stroke, turn the crankshaft one complete turn (360-degrees) clockwise. The rotor

should now be pointing at the mark. When the rotor is pointing at the number one spark plug wire terminal in the distributor cap (which is indicated by the mark on the housing) and the ignition timing marks are aligned, the number one piston is at TDC on the compression stroke.

9   After the number one piston has been positioned at TDC on the compression stroke, TDC for any of the remaining cylinders can be located by turning the crankshaft and following the firing order (refer to the Specifications). On the 5.0L V8, turning the crankshaft 90 degrees will bring cylinder number 3 at TDC, and another 90 degrees will reach TDC for number 7.

4   Valve covers - removal and installation

REMOVAL

▸ **Refer to illustrations 4.2, 4.5, 4.7a and 4.7b**

1   Disconnect the cable from the negative battery terminal.

2   Note their locations, then detach the spark plug wire clips from the valve cover studs (see illustration).

3   Detach the spark plug wires from the plugs (see Chapter 1).

Position the wires out of the way.

4   On some vehicles with cruise control, it may be necessary to disconnect the servo linkage at the throttle body and remove the servo bracket.

5   If you're removing the left (driver's side) valve cover, detach the oil fill cap and crankcase vent tube (see illustration) on V6 engines. On 5.0L engines, the upper intake manifold must be removed (refer to Chapter 4) to remove the left valve cover.

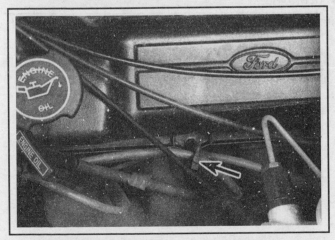

4.2 Remove the spark plug wire clips (arrow) (V6 engine shown, V8 similar)

4.5 Detach the crankcase vent tube (V6 engine shown, V8 similar)

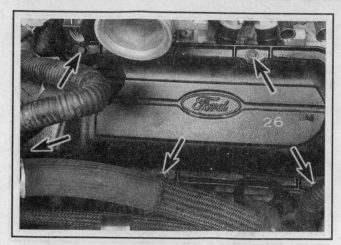

4.7a Remove the bolts and studs (arrows) from each valve cover (V6 engine shown, V8 similar)

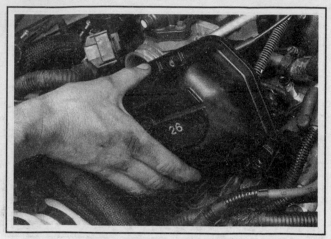

4.7b Move the hoses and slip the cover off (V6 engine shown, V8 similar)

6   If you're removing the right (passenger's side) valve cover, position the air cleaner duct out of the way (see Chapter 4) and remove the PCV valve.

7   Remove the valve cover bolts/nuts (see illustrations), then detach the cover from the cylinder head.

➡**Note: If the cover is stuck to the cylinder head, bump one end with a wood block and a hammer to jar it loose. If that doesn't work, try to slip a flexible putty knife between the cylinder head and cover to break the gasket seal. Don't pry at the cover-to-cylinder head joint or damage to the sealing surfaces may occur (leading to oil leaks in the future). Some valve covers are made of plastic - be extra careful when tapping or pulling on them.**

INSTALLATION

8   The mating surfaces of each cylinder head and valve cover must be perfectly clean when the covers are installed. Use a gasket scraper to remove all traces of sealant and old gasket material, then clean the mat-

ing surfaces with lacquer thinner or acetone. If there's sealant or oil on the mating surfaces when the cover is installed, oil leaks may develop.

9   Clean the mounting bolt threads with a die to remove any corrosion and restore damaged threads. Make sure the threaded holes in the cylinder head are clean - run a tap into them to remove corrosion and restore damaged threads. Apply a small amount of light oil to the bolt threads.

10   The gaskets should be mated to the covers before the covers are installed. Make sure the tabs on the gaskets(s) engage in the slots in the cover(s). On engines that don't have gaskets, apply a 3/16-inch bead of RTV sealant to the cover flange, inside of the bolt holes.

11   Carefully position the cover on the cylinder head and install the bolts/nuts.

12   Tighten the bolts in three or four steps to the torque listed in this Chapter's Specifications. Plastic valve covers are easily damaged, so don't overtighten the bolts!

13   The remaining installation steps are the reverse of removal.

14   Start the engine and check carefully for oil leaks as the engine warms up.

5   Rocker arms and pushrods - removal, inspection and installation

5.2 The rocker arm fulcrum bolts (arrow) may not have to be completely removed - loosen them several turns and see if the rocker arms can be pivoted out of the way to allow pushrod removal

REMOVAL

◆ **Refer to illustrations 5.2 and 5.4**

1   Refer to Section 4 and detach the valve cover(s) from the cylinder head(s).

2   Beginning at the front of one cylinder head, remove the rocker arm fulcrum bolts (see illustration). Store them separately in marked containers to ensure that they will be reinstalled in their original locations.

➡**Note: If the pushrods are the only items being removed, loosen each bolt just enough to allow the rocker arms to be rotated to the side so the pushrods can be lifted out.**

3   Lift off the rocker arms, fulcrums and fulcrum guides (if used). Store them in the marked containers with the bolts (they must be reinstalled in their original locations).

5.4 A perforated cardboard box can be used to store the pushrods to ensure that they are reinstalled in their original locations - note the label indicating the front of the engine

4   Remove the pushrods and store them separately to make sure they don't get mixed up during installation (see illustration).

INSPECTION

▶ **Refer to illustration 5.7**

5   Check each rocker arm for wear, cracks and other damage, especially where the pushrods and valve stems contact the rocker arm faces.

6   Make sure the hole at the pushrod end of each rocker arm is open.

7   Check each rocker arm pivot area and fulcrum for wear, cracks and galling (see illustration). If the rocker arms are worn or damaged, replace them with new ones and use new fulcrums as well.

8   Inspect the pushrods for cracks and excessive wear at the ends. Roll each pushrod across a piece of plate glass to see if it's bent (if it wobbles, it's bent).

INSTALLATION

9   Lubricate the lower end of each pushrod with clean engine oil or moly-base grease and install them in their original locations. Make sure

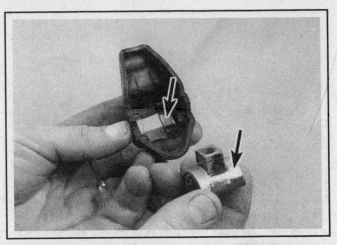

5.7 Check for wear on the rocker arm and fulcrum contact areas (arrows)

each pushrod seats completely in the lifter.

10 Apply moly-base grease to the ends of the valve stems and the upper ends of the pushrods before positioning the rocker arms, fulcrums and guides.

11 Apply moly-base grease to the fulcrums to prevent damage to the mating surfaces before engine oil pressure builds up. Set the rocker arms and guides in place, then install the fulcrums and bolts. Don't tighten the fulcrum bolts at this time.

12 Position the number one cylinder at TDC on the compression stroke (see Section 3). Tighten the number one cylinder rocker arm fulcrum bolts to the torque listed in this Chapter's Specifications. Following the firing order, bring each of the remaining cylinders to TDC on the compression stroke and tighten the respective rocker arm fulcrum bolts.

❋❋ CAUTION:

Tightening a rocker arm fulcrum bolt without the lifter on the base circle of the camshaft lobe may damage the valve train components.

13 Install the valve covers.
14 The remainder of installation is the reverse of removal.

6   Valve springs, retainers and seals - replacement

▶ **Refer to illustrations 6.4, 6.8, 6.9 and 6.16**

➥**Note: Broken valve springs and defective valve stem seals can be replaced without removing the cylinder heads. Two special tools and a compressed air source are normally required to perform this operation, so read through this Section carefully and rent or buy the tools before beginning the job.**

1   Refer to Section 4 and remove the valve cover from the affected

cylinder head. If all of the valve stem seals are being replaced, remove both valve covers.

2   Remove the spark plug from the cylinder which has the defective component. If all of the valve stem seals are being replaced, all of the spark plugs should be removed.

3   Turn the crankshaft until the piston in the affected cylinder is at Top Dead Center on the compression stroke (refer to Section 3 for instructions). If you're replacing all of the valve stem seals, begin with

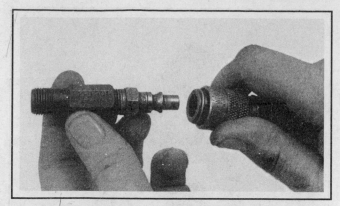

6.4 This is what the air hose adapter that threads into the spark plug hole looks like - they're commonly available from auto parts stores

6.8 Once the spring is depressed, the keepers can be removed with a small magnet or needle-nose pliers (a magnet is preferred to prevent dropping the keepers)

6.9 The seal can be pulled off the guide with a pair of pliers

cylinder number one and work on the valves for one cylinder at a time. Move from cylinder-to-cylinder following the firing order sequence (see this Chapter's Specifications).

4   Thread an adapter into the spark plug hole (see illustration) and connect an air hose from a compressed air source to it. Most auto parts stores can supply the air hose adapter.

➡Note: Many cylinder compression gauges utilize a screw-in fitting that may work with your air hose quick-disconnect fitting.

5   Remove the bolt, fulcrum and rocker arm for the valve with the defective part and pull out the pushrod. If all of the valve stem seals are being replaced, all of the rocker arms and pushrods should be removed (refer to Section 5).

6   Apply compressed air to the cylinder.

✳✳ WARNING:

The piston may be forced down by compressed air, causing the crankshaft to turn suddenly. If the wrench used when positioning the number one piston at TDC is still attached to the bolt in the crankshaft nose, it could cause damage or injury when the crankshaft moves.

7   The valves should be held in place by the air pressure.

8   Stuff shop rags into the cylinder head holes above and below the valves to prevent parts and tools from falling into the engine, then use a valve spring compressor to compress the spring. Remove the keepers with small needle-nose pliers or a magnet (see illustration).

➡Note: A couple of different types of tools are available for compressing the valve springs with the cylinder head in place. One type, shown here, grips the lower spring coils and presses on the retainer as the knob is turned, while the other type utilizes the rocker arm bolt for leverage. Both types work very well, although the lever type is usually less expensive.

9   Remove the spring retainer or rotator, sleeve (used on some intake valves) and valve spring assembly, then remove the valve guide seal (see illustration).

➡Note: If air pressure fails to hold the valve in the closed position during this operation, the valve face or seat is probably damaged. If so, the cylinder head will have to be removed for additional repair operations.

10 Wrap a rubber band or tape around the top of the valve stem so the valve won't fall into the combustion chamber, then release the air pressure.

11 Inspect the valve stem for damage. Rotate the valve in the guide and check the end for eccentric movement, which would indicate that the valve is bent.

12 Move the valve up-and-down in the guide and make sure it doesn't bind. If the valve stem binds, either the valve is bent or the guide is damaged. In either case, the cylinder head will have to be removed for repair.

13 Reapply air pressure to the cylinder to retain the valve in the closed position, then remove the tape or rubber band from the valve stem.

14 Lubricate the valve stem with engine oil and the valve stem tip with polyethylene grease, then install a new guide seal.

15 Install the spring in position over the valve.

16 Install the valve spring retainer or rotator. Some intake valves also have a sleeve that fits inside the retainer. Compress the valve spring and carefully position the keepers in the groove. Apply a small dab of grease to the inside of each keeper to hold it in place (see illustration).

17 Remove the pressure from the spring tool and make sure the keepers are seated.

18 Disconnect the air hose and remove the adapter from the spark plug hole.

19 Refer to Section 5 and install the rocker arm(s) and pushrod(s).

20 Install the spark plug(s) and hook up the wire(s).

21 Refer to Section 4 and install the valve cover(s).

22 Start and run the engine, then check for oil leaks and unusual sounds coming from the valve cover area.

6.16 Apply a small dab of grease to each keeper as shown here before installation - it'll keep them in place on the valve stem as the spring is released

7 Intake manifold - removal and installation

REMOVAL

V6 models

♦ Refer to illustrations 7.5, 7.7 and 7.12

1 Relieve the fuel pressure and remove the air duct assembly (see Chapter 4).

2 Disconnect the negative cable from the battery.

3 Drain the cooling system (see Chapter 1).

4 Remove the upper intake manifold and throttle body (see Chapter 4).

5 Cover the air intake passages with a shop towel (see illustration). Disconnect the upper radiator hose and heater hoses from the intake manifold fittings.

6 Detach any remaining brackets from the intake manifold.

7 Label and disconnect the vacuum and emissions hoses and wire harness connectors attached to the intake manifold (see illustration).

8 Disconnect the heater tube at the intake manifold. Remove the tube support bracket nut.

➡Note: The coolant bypass tube is pressed in and is not serviceable.

9 On models with air conditioning, remove the compressor support bracket.

❋❋ WARNING:

Do not disconnect any refrigerant lines!

10 Remove the fuel injectors and fuel rail assembly (see Chapter 4).

11 Loosen the intake manifold mounting bolts in 1/4-turn increments until they can be removed by hand.

7.5 Cover the air intake with a shop towel to prevent debris from falling into the engine

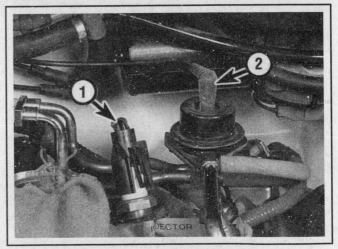

7.7 Label and disconnect the hoses and wiring

1   Sensor connector
2   Vacuum line to fuel pressure regulator

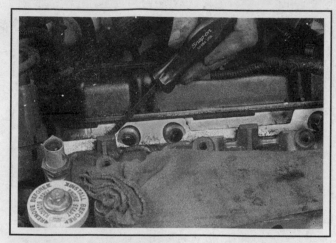

7.12 Pry against a casting protrusion to break the intake manifold loose

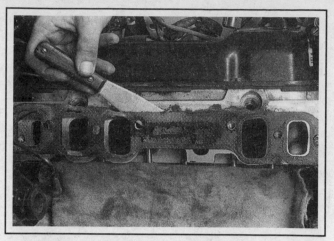

7.25 After covering the lifter valley, use a gasket scraper to remove all traces of sealant and old gasket material from the cylinder head and intake manifold mating surfaces

12 The intake manifold will probably be stuck to the cylinder heads and force may be required to break the gasket seal. A prybar can be positioned under the cast-in lug (see illustration) to pry up the front of the intake manifold, but make sure all bolts have been removed first!

✳✳ CAUTION:

Don't pry between the engine block and intake manifold or the cylinder heads and intake manifold or damage to the gasket sealing surfaces may occur, leading to vacuum and oil leaks.

V8 models

13 Drain the cooling system (see Chapter 1.)

14 Remove the PCV and canister purge hoses.

15 Disconnect the accelerator cable, speed control linkage and automatic transmission cable (if so equipped). Remove the accelerator cable bracket.

16 Label and disconnect the intake manifold vacuum lines.

17 Position the engine to TDC for cylinder number 1 (see Section 3), then mark and remove the distributor (see Chapter 5).

18 Relieve the fuel system pressure (see Chapter 4) and disconnect the fuel supply and return lines.

19 Disconnect the radiator, heater and water pump bypass hoses from the water outlet (see Chapter 3). Disconnect the throttle body cooler hoses.

➡**Note: The heater outlet and coolant bypass tubes are pressed in, and cannot be removed.**

20 Disconnect the electrical connectors from the coolant temperature sending unit, air charge temperature sensor, throttle position sensor, idle speed control solenoid, EGR sensors and fuel injectors (see Chapters 4 and 6).

21 Remove the upper intake manifold (see Chapter 4). Remove the fuel injectors and fuel rail assembly (see Chapter 4).

22 Loosen the lower intake manifold bolts and nuts in 1/4-turn increments until they can be removed by hand.

23 The intake manifold will probably be stuck to the cylinder heads and force may be required to break the gasket seal. A prybar can be used to pry up the intake manifold, but make sure all bolts and nuts have been removed first.

✳✳ CAUTION:

Don't pry between the engine block and manifold or the cylinder heads and intake manifold or damage to the gasket sealing surfaces may occur, leading to vacuum and oil leaks. Pry only at an intake manifold casting protrusion.

INSTALLATION (ALL MODELS)

▶ **Refer to illustrations 7.25, 7.27, 7.30, 7.33a and 7.33b**

✳✳ CAUTION:

The mating surfaces of the cylinder heads, engine block and manifold must be perfectly clean when the manifold is installed. Gasket removal solvents in aerosol cans are available at most auto parts stores and may be helpful when removing old gasket material that's stuck to the cylinder heads and manifold (since the manifold and some V6 engine cylinder heads are made of aluminum, aggressive scraping can cause damage. Be sure to follow directions printed on the container.

➡**Note: The manufacturer recommends the use of guide studs when installing the manifold. To make these, buy four extra intake manifold bolts. Cut the heads off the bolts, then grind a taper and cut a screwdriver slot in the cut ends.**

24 If the manifold was disassembled, reassemble it. Use electrically-conductive sealant on the temperature sending unit threads. Use a new EGR valve gasket.

25 Use a gasket scraper to remove all traces of sealant and old gasket material (see illustration), then clean the mating surfaces with lacquer thinner or acetone. If there's old sealant or oil on the mating surfaces when the manifold is installed, oil or vacuum leaks may develop. When working on the cylinder heads and block, cover the lifter valley with shop rags to keep debris out of the engine. Use a vacuum cleaner to remove any gasket material that falls into the intake ports in the cylinder heads.

26 Use a tap of the correct size to chase the threads in the bolt holes, then use compressed air (if available) to remove the debris from the holes.

7.27 Cut the heads off four old intake manifold bolts to use as guide studs - cut a slot in the end to allow use of a screwdriver to remove them and install the studs at each corner

✳✳ WARNING:

Wear safety glasses or a face shield to protect your eyes when using compressed air!

Remove excessive carbon deposits and corrosion from the exhaust and coolant passages in the cylinder heads and manifold.

27 Install the four manifold alignment studs you have made, one at each of the four corner mounting holes (see illustration).

28 Apply a 1/8-inch wide bead of RTV sealant to the four corners where the manifold, block and cylinder heads converge.

➡ **Note: This sealant sets up in 15 minutes. Do not take longer to install and tighten the manifold once the sealant is applied, or leaks may occur.**

29 Apply a small dab of contact adhesive to the manifold gasket mating surface on each cylinder head. Position the gaskets on the cylinder heads, over the alignment studs. The upper side of each gasket will have a TOP or THIS SIDE UP label stamped into it to ensure correct installation.

30 Position the end seals on the engine block, then apply a 1/8-inch wide bead of RTV sealant to the four points where the end seals meet

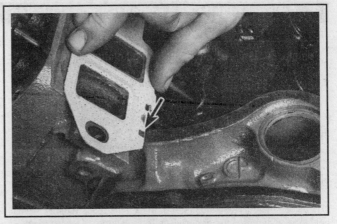

7.30 Apply a bead of RTV sealant to the corners where the engine block, cylinder heads and intake manifold converge, then position the gaskets and end seals in place and apply an additional bead of RTV sealant where the end seals and intake manifold gasket meet (arrow)

the intake manifold gasket (see illustration).

31 Make sure all intake port openings, coolant passage holes and bolt holes are aligned correctly.

32 Carefully set the manifold in place while the sealant is still wet.

✳✳ CAUTION:

Don't disturb the gaskets. The alignment studs will keep the manifold from moving fore-and-aft after it contacts the seals on the engine block. Make sure the end seals haven't been disturbed.

33 Lightly oil the manifold bolts, install them and tighten to the torque listed in this Chapter's Specifications, following the recommended sequence (see illustrations). Work up to the final torque in three steps. When all but the corner bolts have been installed hand-tight, remove the alignment studs and replace them with bolts before tightening any bolts to the final torque.

34 The remaining installation steps are the reverse of removal. Start the engine and check carefully for oil and coolant leaks at the intake manifold joints.

35 Recheck the mounting bolt torque.

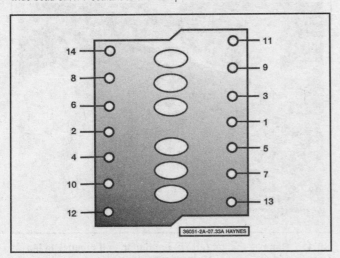

7.33a Intake manifold bolt tightening sequence - V6 engine

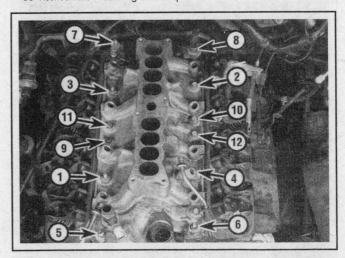

7.33b Intake manifold tightening sequence - 5.0L V8 engine

8 Exhaust manifolds - removal and installation

REMOVAL

♦ **Refer to illustrations 8.5, 8.11a and 8.11b**

1 Disconnect the negative battery cable from the battery.

2 Disconnect the oxygen sensor electrical connector and remove the spark plugs (see Chapter 1).

3 Raise the vehicle and support it securely on jackstands.

4 Working under the vehicle, apply penetrating oil to the exhaust pipe-to-manifold studs and nuts (they're usually rusty).

5 Remove the nuts holding the exhaust crossover pipe to the exhaust manifold(s) (see illustration). In extreme cases you may have to heat them with a propane or acetylene torch in order to loosen them.

Right (passenger's side) manifold

6 Remove the air cleaner duct assembly (see Chapter 4).

7 Disconnect the ignition secondary wire from the coil and distributor.

8 Disconnect the EGR tube.

9 On vehicles with an automatic transmission, the automatic trans-

mission dipstick and tube must be removed. Plug the hole to prevent dirt from entering the engine.

Left (driver's side) manifold

10 If it's in the way, remove the oil dipstick and tube.

Both manifolds

11 Bend back the locking tabs (if equipped). Remove the mounting bolts and separate the exhaust manifold(s) from the cylinder head (see illustrations). Note the locations of the bolts and studs, and remove the old gaskets.

INSTALLATION

12 Check the exhaust manifold for cracks and make sure the bolt threads are clean and undamaged. The exhaust manifold and cylinder head mating surfaces must be clean before the manifolds are reinstalled - use a gasket scraper to remove all carbon deposits and old gasket material.

➡**Note: If the exhaust manifold is being replaced with a new one, remove the oxygen sensor. Clean the threads of the oxygen sensor with a wire brush and coat the threads with high-temperature anti-seize compound before transferring the sensor to the new exhaust manifold.**

13 Position the exhaust manifold and gasket on the cylinder head and install the mounting bolts.

➡**Note: Exhaust manifold warpage is common on the V6 engine. Although some were built without gaskets, we recommend installing them.**

If you're working on a V6 engine, install the pilot bolts first. Sometimes it's necessary to elongate (with a round file) some holes in the exhaust manifolds to start the bolts - but never file out the pilot bolt holes!

14 When tightening the mounting bolts, work from the center to the ends and be sure to use a torque wrench. Tighten the bolts in three equal steps until the torque listed in this Chapter's Specifications is reached.

15 The remaining installation steps are the reverse of removal.

16 Start the engine and check for exhaust leaks.

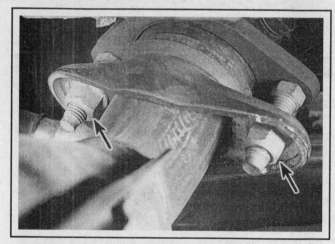

8.5 From below, remove the two exhaust pipe-to-manifold nuts (arrows)

8.11a Remove the exhaust manifold bolts and studs (V6 engine, right manifold); also remove the bolt holding the dipstick holder (A)

8.11b Remove the nut (arrow) holding the oil dipstick to the left exhaust header on the 5.0L V8

9 Cylinder heads - removal and installation

❄ CAUTION:

The engine must be completely cool when the cylinder heads are removed. Failure to allow the engine to cool off could result in cylinder head warpage.

REMOVAL

1 Disconnect the cable from the negative battery terminal.
2 Remove the valve covers (see Section 4).
3 Remove the pushrods and rocker arms (see Section 5).
4 Remove the upper intake manifold (see Chapter 4) and the lower intake manifold (see Section 7).

Left (driver's side) cylinder head

⯈ Refer to illustration 9.7

5 Unbolt the power steering pump and tie it aside in an upright position. Leave the hoses connected (see Chapter 10).
6 Remove the exhaust manifold (see Section 8).
7 Disconnect the alternator wiring (see Chapter 5). Unbolt the alternator and power steering bracket (see illustration).
8 If only the left cylinder head is being removed, proceed to Step 13.
9 On 5.0L V8 engines, remove the air conditioning compressor and position it out of the way (see Chapter 3). DO NOT disconnect the hoses!

Right cylinder head

10 On V6 engines, remove the air conditioning compressor and position it out of the way (see Chapter 3). DO NOT disconnect the hoses! On V8 engines, unbolt the alternator bracket.
11 Remove the exhaust manifold (see Section 8).

Both cylinder heads

⯈ Refer to illustration 9.13

12 Loosen the cylinder head bolts in 1/4-turn increments until they can be removed by hand. Work from bolt-to-bolt in a pattern that's the reverse of the tightening sequence.

➡Note: Head bolts should not be reused. Remove the bolts and discard them - new bolts must be used when installing the cylinder head(s).

13 Lift the cylinder head(s) off the engine. If resistance is felt, DO NOT pry between the cylinder head and engine block as damage to the mating surfaces will result. To dislodge the cylinder head, place a wood block against the end of it and strike the wood block with a hammer or place a prybar against a casting protrusion (see illustration). Store the cylinder heads on blocks of wood to prevent damage to the gasket sealing surfaces. Do not slide them across the floor or workbench.
14 Cylinder head disassembly and inspection procedures are covered in detail in Chapter 2, Part C.

INSTALLATION

⯈ Refer to illustrations 9.18, 9.21a and 9.21b

15 The mating surfaces of the cylinder heads and engine block must be perfectly clean when the cylinder heads are installed. Use a gasket scraper to remove all traces of carbon and old gasket material, then clean the mating surfaces with lacquer thinner or acetone. If there's oil on the mating surfaces when the cylinder heads are installed, the gaskets may not seal correctly and leaks may develop. When working on the engine block, cover the lifter valley with shop rags to keep debris out of the engine. Use a vacuum cleaner to remove any debris that falls into the cylinders.
16 Check the engine block and cylinder head mating surfaces for nicks, deep scratches and other damage. If damage is slight, it can be removed with a file - if it's excessive, machining may be the only alternative.
17 Use a tap of the correct size to chase the threads in the cylinder head bolt holes. Dirt, corrosion, sealant and damaged threads will affect torque readings.
18 Position the new gasket(s) over the dowel pins in the engine

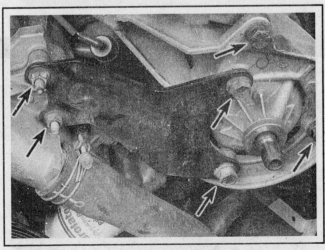

9.7 Power steering/alternator mount bolts (arrows) on the left (driver's) side of a typical V6 engine

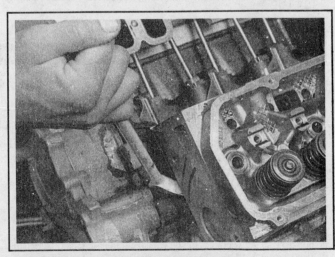

9.13 Using a prybar, carefully lever it against a casting protrusion to lift the cylinder head and break the gasket seal

9.18 Locating dowels (arrows) are used to position the gaskets on the engine block - make sure the mark (circled) is correctly oriented

block (see illustration). Make sure it's facing the right way.

19 Carefully position the cylinder head(s) on the engine block without disturbing the gasket(s).

20 Before installing the new V6 engine cylinder head bolts, coat the

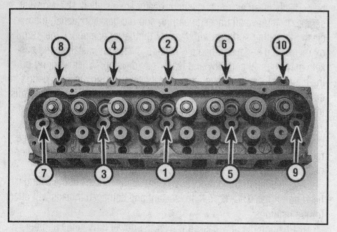

9.21b Cylinder head bolt tightening sequence - 5.0L V8 engine

9.21a Cylinder head bolt tightening sequence - V6 engine

threads of the four short bolts with pipe sealant (Ford part no. D8AZ-1955 8-A or equivalent). Lightly oil the threads of the remaining V6 engine cylinder head bolts. If you're working on a V8 engine, new bolts must also be used, with light oil applied to the threads of all of the bolts.

21 Install the bolts in their original locations and tighten them finger tight. Follow the recommended sequence and tighten the bolts, in the recommended steps, to the torque listed in this Chapter's Specifications (see illustrations).

> ### ✳✳ CAUTION:
>
> **When following the torque sequence for the V6 engine, at Step 4, do not loosen all the bolts at the same time or the gasket will not seal properly. Loosen the first bolt in the sequence, tighten it to the final torque (Steps 5 and 6) then go on to the next bolt in sequence, loosening and tightening the bolts until the sequence is completed.**

22 The remaining installation steps are the reverse of removal.

23 Change the engine oil and filter (see Chapter 1), then start the engine and check carefully for oil and coolant leaks.

10 Timing chain cover - removal and installation

REMOVAL

1 On V6 models, refer to Chapter 3 and remove the fan, fan shroud and water pump. On V8 models, perform all water pump removal steps except actual removal of the pump. The pump may be removed or left attached to the timing chain cover with four nuts. On all engines, disconnect the radiator and heater hoses.

2 Drain the engine oil and remove the oil filter (see Chapter 1).

3 Remove the crankshaft vibration damper (see Section 16).

4 Unbolt and remove all accessory brackets attached to the timing chain cover. When unbolting the power steering pump (see Chapter 10), tie it aside with the hoses still connected. On air-conditioned models, remove the compressor front support bracket, leaving the compressor in place (see Chapter 3).

V6 models

5 Position the number one piston at TDC on the compression stroke (see Section 3), then disconnect the electrical connector at the camshaft position sensor and remove the camshaft position sensor (see Chapter 6).

6 Remove the oil pan and oil pump pickup (see Section 14).

7 Unbolt the ignition timing indicator or pointer.

V8 models

8 Remove the oil pan-to-timing chain cover bolts.

9 Use a razor knife or single-edged razor blade to cut the oil pan gasket flush with the engine block face, by inserting the blade behind the bottom corners of the front cover-to-block mating surfaces. The idea is to make a clean cut of the oil pan gasket so that cover removal doesn't tear the original gasket.

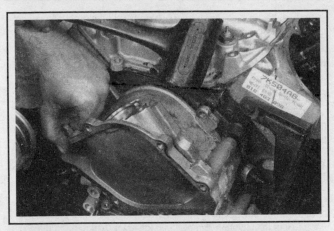

10.10a Gently tap the timing chain cover loose with a soft-face hammer (V6 engine shown)

All models

♦ Refer to illustrations 10.10a, 10.10b, 10.10c and 10.10d

10 Remove the bolts and separate the timing chain cover from the engine block. If it's stuck, tap it gently with a soft-face hammer (see illustrations).

✳✳ CAUTION:

DO NOT use excessive force or you may crack the cover. If the cover is difficult to remove, double check to make sure all of the bolts have been removed.

On V6 models, the bolt under the oil filter housing is easy to miss, and on V8 models, don't overlook the two cover bolts at the top (see illustrations).

INSTALLATION

11 On V8 models, remove the circular rubber seal from the front of the oil pan and stuff a shop rag into the oil pan opening to keep debris out of the engine.

12 Use a gasket scraper to remove all traces of old gasket material and sealant from the cover, oil pan and engine block, then clean them with lacquer thinner or acetone.

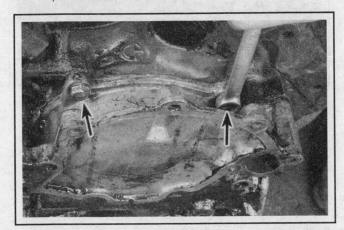

10.10d . . . there are two cover bolts (arrows) that are at the top, behind the water pump area

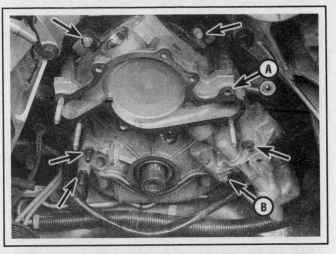

10.10b Timing chain cover bolts and studs (arrows) on V6 engines, shown before oil pan is removed - Bolt A should be coated with sealant before installation, and don't overlook bolt B behind the oil pump

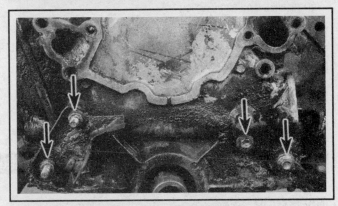

10.10c On V8 models, with the water pump bolts and oil pan-to-cover bolts removed, these four bolts (arrows) hold the cover to the engine block, but . . .

V6 models

♦ Refer to illustration 10.14

13 The oil pump is mounted in the timing chain cover and driven by the intermediate shaft, which is driven by the camshaft position sensor. See Section 15 for oil pump information.

14 To install the intermediate shaft in the timing chain cover, make

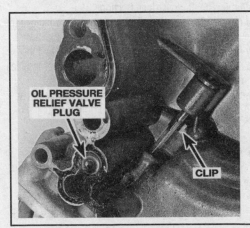

10.14 Install the clip with the top just below the mark (V6 engine only)

a mark one inch from the end. Insert the shaft until it seats in the oil pump and snap the clip onto the shaft with the top of the clip just below the mark on the shaft (see illustration).

15 While the cover is off the engine, it's a good idea to install a new crankshaft front seal (see Section 16).

16 Lubricate the timing chain and front crankshaft oil seal lips with engine oil.

17 Apply a thin coat of RTV sealant to the engine block side of the new gasket, then position it on the engine. The dowel pins will hold it in place as the cover is installed.

18 Apply a thin coat of RTV sealant to the gasket surface of the cover and attach it to the engine. The dowel pins will position it correctly. Don't damage the seal and make sure the gasket remains in place.

19 Install the bolts finger tight. Tighten them to the torque listed in this Chapter's Specifications only after the water pump has been installed (some of the water pump bolts also hold the timing chain cover in place).

➡Note: When installing the water pump, be sure to coat the threads of the water pump bolt with sealant (see illustration 10.10b).

20 Install the oil pan (Section 14).

V8 models

21 Cut two front sections from new oil pan side gaskets to install between the oil pan side rails and timing chain cover.

22 Attach the gasket sections to the oil pan with contact adhesive (Ford part no. D7AZ-19B508-A or equivalent).

23 Apply a 1/8-inch bead of RTV sealant to the oil pan-to-block joints.

24 Install a new circular rubber oil pan seal in the groove in the bottom of the front cover.

➡Note: Clean the groove thoroughly with lacquer thinner first, then use contact adhesive to hold the seal in place.

25 Lubricate the timing chain and front crankshaft oil seal lips with engine oil.

26 Apply a thin coat of RTV sealant to the engine block side of the new cover gasket, then position it on the engine. The dowel pins will hold it in place as the cover is installed.

27 Apply a thin coat of RTV sealant to the gasket surface of the cover and attach it to the engine. Don't dislodge the circular rubber seal or the gaskets.

28 It may be necessary to compress the rubber seal by forcing the cover down before installing the cover bolts to the engine block. Temporarily slip the vibration damper onto the crankshaft to align the cover.

29 Apply Teflon pipe sealant to the threads, then install the bolts. Tighten the oil pan-to-cover bolts to the torque listed in this Chapter's Specifications while aligning the cover with the damper. Make sure the gaskets and seal stay in place.

30 Tighten the cover-to-block bolts and tighten the bolts to the torque listed in this Chapter's Specifications, then remove the vibration damper.

All models

31 Install the remaining parts in the reverse order of removal.

➡Note: When reinstalling the damper on V8 models, apply a dab of RTV sealant to the keyway in the damper first.

32 Add engine oil and coolant (Chapter 1).
33 Run the engine and check for leaks.

---

11 Timing chain and sprockets - inspection, removal and installation

INSPECTION

1 Disconnect the negative battery cable from the battery.

V6 models

▶ Refer to illustration 11.4

2 Refer to Section 3 and position the number one piston several degrees before TDC on the compression stroke.

3 Remove the right valve cover (Section 4).

4 Attach a dial indicator to the cylinder head with the plunger in-line with and resting on the rocker arm (see illustration).

5 Remove the timing chain cover (see Section 10).

6 Temporarily remove the timing chain and sprockets to remove the chain tensioner (see below).

7 Temporarily install the timing chain and sprockets without the tensioner and slip the timing chain cover and vibration damper in place to provide timing marks.

8 Turn the crankshaft clockwise until the number one piston is at TDC (Section 3). This will take up the slack on the right side of the chain.

9 Zero the dial indicator.

10 Slowly turn the crankshaft counterclockwise until the slightest movement is seen on the dial indicator. Stop and note how far the number one piston has moved away from TDC by looking at the ignition timing marks.

11 If the mark has moved more than 6 degrees, install a new timing chain and sprockets.

11.4 Install a dial indicator to measure timing chain deflection (V6 engine) - use a short length of vacuum hose to hold the plunger on the pushrod, or set the indicator on the pushrod end of the rocker arm

V8 models

▶ Refer to illustration 11.14

12 Rotate the crankshaft in a counterclockwise direction to take up the slack in the left side of the chain.

13 Remove the timing chain cover (Section 10).

14 Establish a reference point on the engine block and measure from

11.14 On V8 models, to check the timing chain deflection establish a reference point on the engine block and measure from that point to the chain

11.20 Align the timing marks on the crankshaft and camshaft sprockets (arrows) before removing the sprockets from the shafts

11.22 Remove the camshaft sprocket and chain from the camshaft

11.23 On V6 models, if you're planning to remove the camshaft, slide the spacer off the camshaft

that point to the chain (see illustration).

15 Reinstall the vibration damper bolt. Using this bolt, turn the crankshaft clockwise with a wrench until the slack is taken up on the right side of the chain.

16 Force the left side of the chain out with your fingers and measure the distance between the reference point and the chain. The difference between the two measurements is the deflection.

17 If the deflection exceeds 1/2-inch, install a new timing chain and sprockets.

REMOVAL AND INSTALLATION

▶ **Refer to illustrations 11.20, 11.22, 11.23, 11.24 and 11.25**

Removal

18 Position the number one piston at TDC on the compression stroke (Section 3).

19 Remove the timing chain cover (Section 10). Try to avoid turning the crankshaft during vibration damper removal.

20 Make sure the crankshaft and camshaft sprocket timing marks are aligned (see illustration). If they aren't, install the vibration damper bolt and use it to turn the crankshaft clockwise until the two marks are aligned.

21 Remove the camshaft sprocket mounting bolt (all models) and camshaft position sensor drive gear (V6 model only).

22 Pull the sprocket/chain off the camshaft and detach the chain from the crankshaft sprocket (see illustration). Don't lose the pin in the end of the camshaft (V8 models only).

23 If you intend to remove the camshaft on a V6 engine, slip the spacer off the camshaft (see illustration).

24 On V6 models, pry back the tensioner and insert a pin punch to cage the spring (see illustration).

11.24 On V6 models, push the spring in the chain tensioner back and insert a pin punch to hold it in place

11.25 If the camshaft and/or the crankshaft sprockets are stuck, pry with two opposing screwdrivers to remove them

11.29 Slip the chain over the crankshaft sprocket and attach the camshaft sprocket to the camshaft

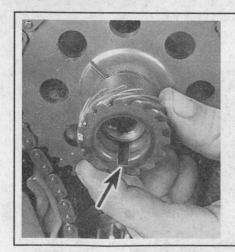

11.31 On V6 models, align the keyway (arrow) on the camshaft position sensor drive gear with the Woodruff key on the camshaft

11.27 Position the crankshaft with the key facing up (12 o'clock)

➡Note: If the tensioner assembly was removed earlier for checking chain deflection, replace it now and pin it back.

25 The crankshaft sprocket can be levered off with two large screwdrivers or a pry bar (see illustration).

Installation

▶ Refer to illustrations 11.27, 11.29 and 11.31

26 Align the keyway in the crankshaft sprocket with the Woodruff key in the end of the crankshaft. Press the sprocket onto the crankshaft with the vibration damper bolt, a large socket and some washers or tap it gently into place until it's completely seated.

❋❋ CAUTION:

If resistance is encountered, DO NOT hammer the sprocket onto the shaft. It may eventually move into place, but it may be cracked in the process and fail later, causing extensive engine damage.

27 Turn the crankshaft until the key is facing up (12 o'clock position) (see illustration).

28 Reinstall the spacer on the camshaft, if removed.

29 Drape the chain over the camshaft sprocket and turn the sprocket until the timing mark faces down (6 o'clock position). Mesh the chain with the crankshaft sprocket and position the camshaft sprocket on the end of the camshaft (see illustration). If necessary, turn the camshaft so the dowel pin fits into the sprocket hole (V8 engine) or the bolt holes in the sprocket are aligned with the offset threaded holes in the camshaft flange (V6 engine).

30 When correctly installed, a straight line should pass through the center of the camshaft, the camshaft timing mark (in the 6 o'clock position), the crankshaft timing mark (in the 12 o'clock position) and the center of the crankshaft (see illustration 11.20). DO NOT proceed until the valve timing is correct!

31 On V6 models, install the camshaft position sensor drive gear (see illustration).

32 Apply a non-hardening thread locking compound to the threads and install the camshaft sprocket bolt. Tighten the bolt to the torque listed in this Chapter's Specifications.

33 Reinstall the remaining parts in the reverse order of removal.

12 Valve lifters - removal, inspection and installation

REMOVAL

▶ **Refer to illustrations 12.3a, 12.3b, 12.3c, 12.4a and 12.4b**

1   Remove the intake manifold (see Section 7).

2   Remove the rocker arms and pushrods (see Section 5).

3   Before removing the lifters, arrange to store them in a clearly labeled box to ensure that they're reinstalled in their original locations. Remove the lifter guide retainer and guide plates (see illustrations).

4   There are several ways to extract the lifters from the bores. Special tools designed to grip and remove lifters are manufactured by many tool companies and are widely available (see illustration), but may not be needed in every case. On newer engines without a lot of varnish buildup, the lifters can often be removed with a small magnet (see illustration) or even with your fingers. A machinist's scribe with a bent end can be used to pull the lifters out by positioning the point under the retainer ring in the top of each lifter.

❊❊ CAUTION:

Don't use pliers to remove the lifters unless you intend to replace them with new ones (along with the camshaft). The pliers may damage the precision machined and hardened lifers, rendering them useless.

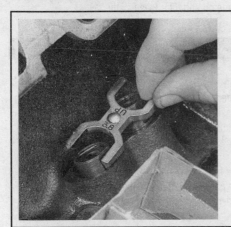

12.4a If the lifters are difficult to remove, you may have to remove them with a special puller . . .

12.3a Remove the lifter guide retainer bolts . . .

On engines with a lot of sludge and varnish, work the lifters up and down, using carburetor cleaner spray to loosen the deposits.

INSPECTION

▶ **Refer to illustrations 12.6 and 12.7**

5   Clean the lifters with solvent and dry them thoroughly without

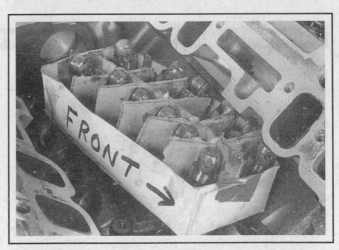

12.3b . . . and the guide plates

12.3c Be sure to store the lifters in an organized manner to make sure they're reinstalled in their original locations

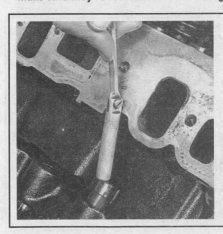

12.4b . . . or you may be able to remove the lifters with a magnet

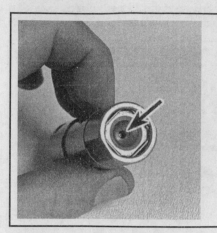

12.6 Inspect the pushrod seat (arrow) in the top of each lifter for wear

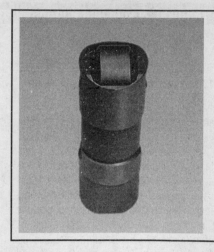

12.7 The roller must turn freely - check for wear and excessive play as well

mixing them up.

6   Check each lifter wall and pushrod seat for scuffing, score marks and uneven wear. If the lifter walls are damaged or worn (which isn't very likely), inspect the lifter bores in the engine block as well. If the pushrod seats (see illustration) are worn, check the pushrod ends.

7   Check the roller carefully for wear and damage and make sure they turn freely without excessive play (see illustration).

8   If any lifters are found to be defective, they can be replaced with new ones without having to replace the camshaft (unlike conventional, non-roller lifters), but if the camshaft is being replaced due to high mileage, all the lifters should be replaced as well.

INSTALLATION

9   The original lifters, if they're being reinstalled, must be returned to their original locations. Coat them with moly-base grease or engine assembly lube.

10 Install the lifters in the bores.

11 Install the guide plates and guide retainer.

12 Install the pushrods and rocker arms.

13 Install the intake manifold and valve covers.

14 Change the engine oil and filter (see Chapter 1).

13   Camshaft and bearings - removal, inspection and installation

CAMSHAFT LOBE LIFT CHECK

1   In order to determine the extent of cam lobe wear, the lobe lift should be checked prior to camshaft removal. Refer to Section 4 and remove the valve covers. The rocker arms must also be removed (Section 5), but leave the pushrods in place.

2   Position the number one piston at TDC on the compression stroke (see Section 3).

3   Beginning with the number one cylinder, mount a dial indicator on the engine and position the plunger in-line with and resting on the first rocker arm (see illustration 11.4).

4   Zero the dial indicator, then very slowly turn the crankshaft in the normal direction of rotation until the indicator needle stops and begins to move in the opposite direction. The point at which it stops indicates

maximum cam lobe lift.

5   Record this figure for future reference, then reposition the piston at TDC on the compression stroke.

6   Move the dial indicator to the remaining number one cylinder pushrod and repeat the check. Be sure to record the results for each valve.

7   Repeat the check for the remaining valves. Since each piston must be at TDC on the compression stroke for this procedure, work from cylinder-to-cylinder following the firing order sequence (see Section 3).

8   After the check is complete, compare the results to the Specifications. If camshaft lobe lift is less than specified, cam lobe wear has occurred and a new camshaft should be installed.

REMOVAL

▶ **Refer to illustrations 13.11 and 13.12**

9   Refer to the appropriate Sections and remove the pushrods, the valve lifters and the timing chain and camshaft sprocket. The radiator should be removed as well (Chapter 3). You also may have to remove the air conditioning condenser and the grille as well, but wait and see if the camshaft can be pulled out of the engine.

10 Check the camshaft end play with a dial indicator aligned with the front of the camshaft. Insert a camshaft sprocket bolt and use it to pull the camshaft fore and aft. If the play is greater than specified, replace the thrust plate with a new one when the camshaft is reinstalled.

11 Remove the camshaft thrust plate bolts. A T-30 Torx bit is required for the bolts on the V6 engine (see illustration).

13.11 V6 models use T-30 Torx screws to retain the camshaft thrust plate (arrows)

13.12 Carefully guide the camshaft out of the engine block to avoid nicking the bearings with the lobes

12 Carefully pull the camshaft out. Support the cam so the lobes don't nick or gouge the bearings as it's withdrawn (see illustration).

INSPECTION

▶ **Refer to illustration 13.14**

13 After the camshaft has been removed, clean it with solvent and dry it, then inspect the bearing journals for uneven wear, pitting and evidence of seizure. If the journals are damaged, the bearing inserts in the engine block are probably damaged as well. Both the camshaft and bearings will have to be replaced. Replacement of the camshaft bearings requires special tools and techniques which place it beyond the

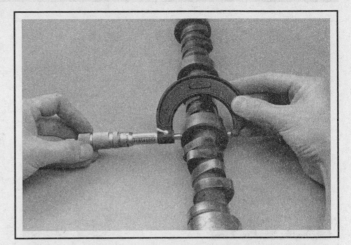

13.14 The camshaft bearing journal diameters are checked to pinpoint excessive wear and out-of-round conditions

scope of the home mechanic. The engine block will have to be removed from the vehicle and taken to an automotive machine shop for this procedure.

14 Measure the bearing journals with a micrometer (see illustration) to determine whether they are excessively worn or out-of-round.

15 Inspect the camshaft lobes for heat discoloration, score marks, chipped areas, pitting and uneven wear. If the lobes are in good condition and if the lobe lift measurements are as specified, you can reuse the camshaft.

INSTALLATION

▶ **Refer to illustration 13.16**

16 Lubricate the camshaft bearing journals and cam lobes with camshaft installation lube (see illustration).

➡**Note: If the camshaft on a V6 is being replaced, remove the Woodruff key from the old camshaft and slide off the spacer ring. Clean, lubricate and install the ring on the new camshaft and install the Woodruff key.**

17 Slide the camshaft into the engine. Support the cam near the engine block and be careful not to scrape or nick the bearings.

18 Apply moly-base grease or engine assembly lube to both sides of the thrust plate, then position it on the engine block with the oil grooves in (against the engine block). Install the bolts and tighten them to the torque listed in this Chapter's Specifications.

19 Refer to the appropriate Sections and install the lifters, pushrods, rocker arms, timing chain/sprocket, timing chain cover and valve covers.

20 The remaining installation steps are the reverse of removal.

21 Before starting and running the engine, change the oil and install a new oil filter (see Chapter 1).

13.16 Apply camshaft installation lube to the camshaft lobes and journals prior to installation

14 Oil pan - removal and installation

➡**Note: The following procedure applies only to the 1994 and 1995 5.0L V8 models. The procedure for the V6 engine oil pan removal is virtually identical as the 4.6L V8, which is covered in Part B of this Chapter.**

REMOVAL

▶ **Refer to illustration 14.18**

1 Removal of the oil pan is a difficult procedure, involving dis-

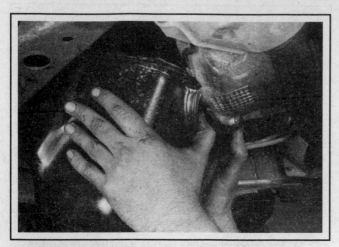

14.18 Slip the oil pan out, turning it slightly to clear the flywheel/driveplate

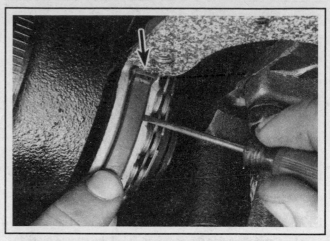

14.22 Press the front and rear end seals firmly into their grooves, then apply a dab of RTV sealant to the joints (arrow) where the side gaskets and end seals meet

connection of several front suspension components for clearance. An engine support "cradle" and a transmission jack will be necessary to complete this procedure and can often be rented at an equipment rental yard.

2 Disconnect the cable from the negative battery terminal.

3 Remove the oil dipstick.

4 Remove the air cleaner assembly (see Chapter 4).

5 Remove the two bolts retaining the fan shroud to the radiator and pull the shroud loose from the lower retaining clips.

6 Attach an engine support fixture (Ford tool no. D88L-6000-A or equivalent) to the engine lifting eyes on the engine.

7 Raise the vehicle and place it securely on jackstands.

8 Position a drain pan under the engine, drain the oil and remove the engine oil filter (refer to Chapter 1).

9 Refer to Chapter 5 and remove the starter. Refer to Section 8 and disconnect the exhaust pipes from the headers. Lower the exhaust pipes.

10 Remove the engine mount through-bolts.

11 Refer to Chapter 7 and remove the rear transmission mount.

12 Raise the engine about two inches with the support fixture.

13 Remove the power steering cooler line retaining clips.

14 Remove the bolt securing the transmission lines to the right side of the engine block.

15 Disconnect the electrical connector from the low oil level sensor located in the oil pan if so equipped.

16 Disconnect the steering flex coupling and remove the two long bolts that retain the rack-and-pinion steering unit to the crossmember. Pull the unit forward and down, without disconnecting the lines (see Chapter 10).

17 Remove the engine oil pan retaining bolts.

18 Unbolt the oil pump/pick-up tube assembly, place it in the oil pan and remove the oil pan with the pickup (see illustration). The hex oil pump driveshaft will also come out with the oil pump.

19 Empty any residual oil from the oil pan.

INSTALLATION

▸ **Refer to illustration 14.22**

20 Use a gasket scraper or putty knife to remove all traces of old gasket material and sealant from the pan and engine block.

21 Clean the mating surfaces with lacquer thinner or acetone. Make sure the bolt holes in the engine block are clean.

22 Use a dab of gasket adhesive to hold the front and rear rubber seals in the front cover and rear main cap, using a small screwdriver to force the new seal tightly into the groove (see illustration). Stick the side gaskets in place on the engine block with a few dabs of adhesive and tuck the front and rear tabs into the slots in the ends of the front and rear rubber seals. Apply a dab of RTV sealant to the four corners where the side gaskets meet the end seals.

23 Position the oil pump/pickup inside the oil pan, maneuver the pan in position and bolt the oil pump to the engine block. It may help to have an assistant holding the pan in place while you bolt up the pump.

➡**Note: Insert the hex driveshaft into the pump before bolting the pump to the engine.**

24 Carefully position the pan against the engine block and install the bolts finger tight. Make sure the gaskets haven't shifted, then tighten the bolts to the torque listed in this Chapter's Specifications. Start at the center of the pan and work out toward the ends in a spiral pattern.

25 The remaining steps are the reverse of removal.

✳ CAUTION:

Don't forget to refill the engine with oil before starting it (see Chapter 1).

26 Start the engine and check carefully for oil leaks at the oil pan. Drive the vehicle and check again.

15 Oil pump - removal and installation

➡️**Note: If there is insufficient oil pressure, see Chapter 2, Part C for oil pressure testing.**

V6 MODELS

▶ **Refer to illustrations 15.3, and 15.11**

1 The oil pump is mounted externally on the timing chain cover.

2 Detach the oil filter (Chapter 1).

3 Detach the cover and gasket, then remove the gears from the cavity in the timing chain cover (see illustration). Discard the gasket.

4 Clean and inspect the oil pump cavity. If the oil pump gear pocket in the timing chain cover is damaged or worn, replace the timing chain cover.

5 Remove all traces of gasket material from the oil pump cover, then check it for warpage with a straightedge and feeler gauges. If it's warped more than 0.0016-inch, replace it with a new one.

6 To remove the pressure relief valve, first detach the timing chain cover from the engine (Section 10). Drill a hole in the plug (see illustration 10.14), then pry it out or remove it with a slide hammer and screw adapter. Remove the spring and valve from the bore.

7 Remove all metal chips from the bore and the valve, then check them carefully for wear, score marks and galling. If the bore is worn or damaged, a new timing chain cover will be required. The valve should fit in the bore with no noticeable side play or binding.

8 If the spring appears to be fatigued or collapsed, replace it with a new one. The tension can be measured and compared to this Chapter's Specifications to determine its condition.

9 Apply clean engine oil to the valve and install it in the bore, small end first. Insert the spring, then install a new plug. Carefully tap it in until it's 0.010-inch below the machined surface of the cover.

10 Intermediate shaft removal and installation is covered in Section 10.

11 The oil pump pickup is inside the oil pan. For access, remove the oil pan (see Section 14). Remove the pick-up tube nut and the two mounting bolts (see illustration).

12 Installation is the reverse of removal.

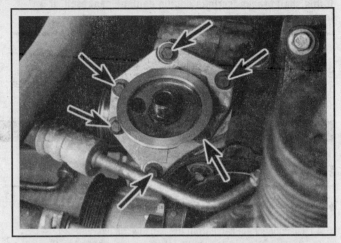

15.3 After the filter is removed, the V6 engine oil pump cover bolts are accessible (arrows)

✳️ CAUTION:

Be sure to pack the oil pump with petroleum jelly before installing the cover (DO NOT use any lubricant other than petroleum jelly). It must fill all voids between the gears, cavity and cover. If this isn't done, the pump may fail to prime when the engine is started.

Install a new cover gasket and tighten the bolts to the torque listed in this Chapter's Specifications in a criss-cross pattern. Use a new pick-up tube gasket and tighten the mounting bolts securely.

V8 MODELS

▶ **Refer to illustration 15.17**

13 Unbolt and lower the oil pan as described in Section 14.

14 Remove the oil pick-up tube-to-main bearing cap nut.

15 Remove the oil pump mounting bolts.

16 Lower the oil pump assembly into the oil pan and remove the oil pan from the vehicle with the oil pump inside. If the pump is faulty, or you suspect that it's faulty, install a new one - do not attempt to repair the original.

17 The oil pump hex driveshaft will come out with the pump. Examine the distributor end of the hex for signs of wear (see illustration).

15.11 To detach the V6 engine pickup tube, remove the nut and bolt (arrows)

15.17 There is serious wear on the distributor end (arrow) of this hex drive - it should be replaced

18 Prime the oil pump prior to installation. Pour clean oil into the pickup and turn the pump shaft by hand.

19 If you separate the pump from the pick-up tube, use a new gasket and tighten the bolts securely when reattaching them.

20 Fit the oil pump driveshaft into the pump. It must seat all the way. DO NOT try to force it. If it doesn't align, turn the pump slightly and try again.

21 Install the oil pump/pickup and drive with the oil pan as described in Section 14. Tighten the mounting nuts/bolts to the torque listed in this Chapter's Specifications.

22 The remainder of installation is the reverse of removal.

16 Crankshaft oil seals - replacement

FRONT SEAL - TIMING CHAIN COVER IN PLACE

▸ **Refer to illustrations 16.4, 16.5, 16.6, 16.8 and 16.10**

1 Disconnect the cable from the negative battery terminal.
2 Remove the electric cooling fan/shroud assembly (see Chapter 3).

3 Remove the drivebelts (see Chapter 1).
4 Mark the crankshaft pulley and vibration damper so they can be reassembled in the same relative position. This is important, since the damper and pulley are initially balanced as a unit. Unbolt and remove the pulley (see illustration).
5 Remove the bolt from the front of the crankshaft, then use a puller to detach the vibration damper (see illustration).

Clean the crankshaft nose and the seal contact surface on the vibration damper with lacquer thinner or acetone. Leave the Woodruff key in place in the crankshaft keyway.

➡**Note: The damper to crankshaft bolt is very tight. Have an assistant hold the flywheel from turning while removing the bolt, or hold the damper with a special strap-wrench designed for this purpose.**

6 Carefully remove the seal from the cover with a screwdriver or seal removal tool (see illustration). Be careful not to damage the cover or scratch the wall of the seal bore. If the engine has accumulated a lot of miles, apply penetrating oil to the seal-to-cover joint and allow it to soak in before attempting to remove the seal.
7 Check the seal bore and crankshaft, as well as the seal contact

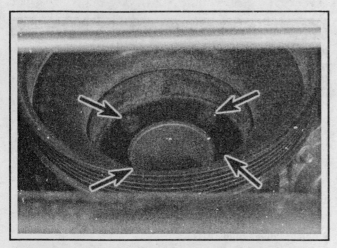

16.4 Mark the pulley and vibration damper before removing the four bolts (arrows) - the large vibration damper bolt in the center (not seen here) is usually very tight, so use a six-point socket and a breaker bar to loosen it

16.5 Use the recommended puller to remove the vibration damper - if a puller that applies force to the outer edge is used, the damper will be damaged!

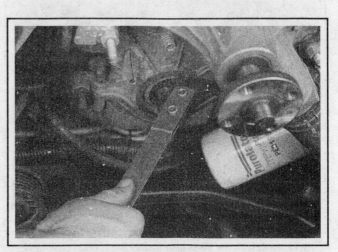

16.6 Use a screwdriver or seal removal tool (shown) to work the seal out of the timing chain cover - be very careful not to damage the cover or nick the crankshaft!

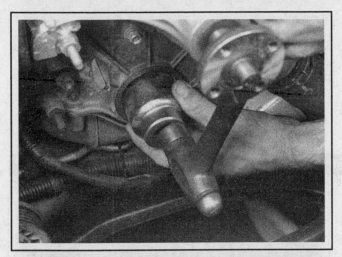

16.10 A soft-face hammer can be used to tap the vibration damper onto the crankshaft - don't use a steel hammer!

16.8 Clean the bore, then apply a small amount of oil to the outer edge of the new seal and drive it squarely into the opening with a large socket and a hammer - don't damage the seal in the process and make sure it's completely seated

surface on the vibration damper for nicks and burrs. Position the new seal in the bore with the open end of the seal facing IN. A small amount of oil applied to the outer edge of the new seal will make installation easier - don't overdo it!

8   Drive the seal into the bore with a large socket and hammer until it's completely seated (see illustration). Select a socket that's the same outside diameter as the seal (a section of pipe can be used if a socket isn't available).

9   Apply moly-base grease or clean engine oil to the seal contact surface of the vibration damper and coat the keyway (groove) with a thin layer of RTV sealant.

➡**Note: If a new vibration damper is being installed, balance pins must be located in the new damper in the same relative positions as the original. Also, the pulley must be attached to the damper with the same orientation to the pins as on the original.**

10   Install the damper on the end of the crankshaft. The keyway in the damper bore must be aligned with the Woodruff key in the crankshaft nose. If the damper can't be seated by hand, tap it into place with a soft-face hammer (see illustration) or slip a large washer over the bolt, install the bolt and tighten it to press the damper into place. Remove the large washer, then install the bolt and tighten it to the torque listed in this Chapter's Specifications.

11   Install the remaining parts removed for access to the seal.

12   Start the engine and check for leaks at the seal-to-cover joint.

FRONT SEAL - TIMING CHAIN COVER REMOVED

13   Use a punch or screwdriver and hammer to drive the seal out of the cover from the back side. Support the cover as close to the seal bore as possible. Be careful not to distort the cover or scratch the wall of the seal bore. If the engine has accumulated a lot of miles, apply penetrating oil to the seal-to-cover joint on each side and allow it to soak in before attempting to drive the seal out.

14   Clean the bore to remove any old seal material and corrosion. Support the cover on blocks of wood and position the new seal in the bore with the open end of the seal facing IN. A small amount of oil applied to the outer edge of the new seal will make installation easier - don't overdo it!

16.17 If you're very careful not to damage the crankshaft or the seal bore, the rear seal can be pried out with a screwdriver - normally a special puller is used for this procedure

15   Drive the seal into the bore with a large socket and hammer until it's completely seated. Select a socket that's the same outside diameter as the seal (a section of pipe can be used if a socket isn't available).

REAR MAIN SEAL

⬧ **Refer to illustration 16.17**

16   Refer to Chapter 7 and remove the transmission, then detach the flywheel or driveplate and the rear cover plate from the engine (Section 17).

17   The old seal can be removed by prying it out with a screwdriver (see illustration) or by making one or two small holes in the seal flange with a sharp pick, then using a screw-in type slide-hammer puller. Be sure to note how far the seal is recessed into the bore before removing it; the new seal will have to be recessed an equal amount.

※※ **CAUTION:**

Be very careful not to scratch or otherwise damage the crankshaft or the bore in the housing or oil leaks could develop!

18   Clean the crankshaft and seal bore with lacquer thinner or

acetone. Check the seal contact surface very carefully for scratches and nicks that could damage the new seal lip and cause oil leaks. If the crankshaft is damaged, the only alternative is a new or different crankshaft.

19 Make sure the bore is clean, then apply a thin coat of engine oil to the outer edge of the new seal. Apply moly-based grease to the seal lips. The seal must be pressed squarely into the bore, a special seal installation tool (Ford tool no. T82L-6701-A) is highly recommended.

Hammering it into place is not recommended. If you don't have access to the special tool, you may be able to tap the seal in with a large section of pipe and a hammer. If you must use this method, be very careful not to damage the seal or crankshaft! And work the seal lip carefully over the end of the crankshaft with a blunt tool such as the rounded end of a socket extension.

20 Reinstall the engine rear cover plate, the flywheel or driveplate and the transmission.

17 Flywheel/driveplate - removal and installation

▶ **Refer to illustration 17.4**

1 Raise the vehicle and support it securely on jackstands, then refer to Chapter 7 and remove the transmission. If it's leaking, now would be a very good time to replace the front pump seal/O-ring (automatic transmission only).

2 Remove the pressure plate and clutch disc (see Chapter 8) (manual transmission equipped vehicles). Now is a good time to check/replace the clutch components and pilot bearing.

3 Look for factory paint marks that indicate flywheel-to-crankshaft alignment. If they aren't there, use a center-punch or paint to make alignment marks on the flywheel/driveplate and crankshaft to ensure correct alignment during reinstallation.

4 Remove the bolts that secure the flywheel/driveplate to the crankshaft (see illustration). If the crankshaft turns, use a flywheel-holding tool or wedge a screwdriver through the starter opening to jam the flywheel.

5 Remove the flywheel/driveplate from the crankshaft. Since the flywheel is fairly heavy, be sure to support it while removing the last bolt.

✳✳ WARNING:

The flywheel is heavy and the ring gear teeth may be sharp, wear gloves to protect your hands.

6 Clean the flywheel to remove grease and oil. Inspect the surface for cracks, rivet grooves, burned areas and score marks. Light scoring can be removed with emery cloth. Check for cracked and broken ring gear teeth. Lay the flywheel on a flat surface and use a straightedge to check for warpage.

7 Clean and inspect the mating surfaces of the flywheel/driveplate and the crankshaft. If the crankshaft rear seal is leaking, replace it

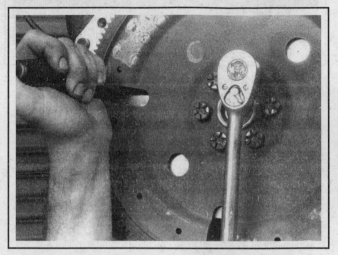

17.4 On automatic transmission driveplates, insert a prybar through a hole to keep the crankshaft from turning when loosening/tightening the bolts

before reinstalling the flywheel/driveplate.

8 Position the flywheel/driveplate against the crankshaft. Be sure to align the marks made during removal. Note that some engines have an alignment dowel or staggered bolt holes to ensure correct installation. Before installing the bolts, apply Teflon thread sealant to the threads.

9 Use a flywheel-holding tool or wedge a screwdriver through the starter motor opening to keep the flywheel/driveplate from turning as you tighten the bolts to the torque listed in this Chapter's Specifications.

10 The remainder of installation is the reverse of the removal procedure.

18 Engine mounts - check and replacement

1 Engine mounts seldom require attention, but broken or deteriorated mounts should be replaced immediately or the added strain placed on the driveline components may cause damage or wear.

CHECK

2 During the check, the engine must be raised slightly to remove the weight from the mounts.

3 Raise the vehicle and support it securely on jackstands, then position a jack under the engine oil pan. Place a large wood block

between the jack head and the oil pan, then carefully raise the engine just enough to take the weight off the mounts.

✳✳ WARNING:

DO NOT place any part of your body under the engine when it's supported only by a jack!

4 Check the mounts to see if the rubber is cracked, hardened or separated from the metal plates. Sometimes the rubber will split right

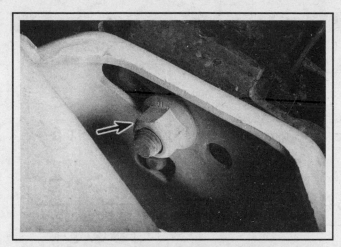

18.9 Remove the nut from the mount-to-crossmember stud, shown here from below the crossmember

18.13a On V6 models, remove the three bolts, two shown here, (arrows) holding the mount to the engine block - it isn't necessary to remove the other bolts, which hold the motor mount bracket to the engine

down the center. Rubber preservative should be applied to the mounts to slow deterioration.

5   Check for relative movement between the mount plates and the engine or frame (use a large screwdriver or pry bar to attempt to move the mounts). If movement is noted, lower the engine and tighten the mount fasteners.

REPLACEMENT

▶ **Refer to illustrations 18.9, 18.13a and 18.13b**

6   Disconnect the cable from the negative battery terminal.

7   Detach the air cleaner duct.

8   Support the bottom of the engine with a floor jack and wood block under the oil pan. Take a slight amount of weight off the engine by raising the jack.

9   Remove the engine mount stud nuts on the bottom side of the front suspension crossmember (see illustration).

10 Disconnect the shift linkage where it connects the transmission to the body (see Chapter 7).

11 Remove the accessories and oil cooler line retaining clips from the engine mount brackets.

12 Raise the engine high enough to clear the brackets. Do not force the engine up too high. If it touches anything before the mounts are free, remove the part for clearance. Temporarily place a wood block between the oil pan and sub-frame as a safety precaution.

13 Unbolt the mount from the engine block and remove it from the vehicle (see illustrations).

➡**Note: On vehicles equipped with self-locking nuts and bolts, replace them with new ones whenever they are disassembled. Prior to assembly, remove hardened residual adhesive from the engine block holes with an appropriate-size bottoming tap.**

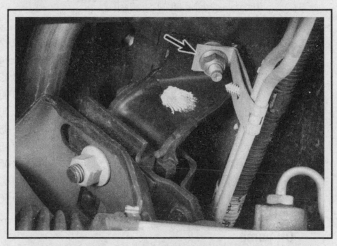

18.13b On V8 models, remove the two fasteners, one show here, (arrow) holding the mount to the engine block

14 If a new mount is being installed on a V6 model equipped with a bracket between the mount and the engine block, remove only the mount-to-bracket bolts. Leave the bracket bolted to the engine block.

15 Attach the new mount to the engine block and install the bolts and stud/nuts in the appropriate locations. Tighten the fasteners securely.

16 Lower the engine into place. Install the large mount-to-crossmember nuts and tighten them securely.

17 Complete the installation by reinstalling all parts removed to gain access to the mounts.

Specifications

V6 ENGINE

General

Displacement	3.8 liters (232 cubic inches) or 3.9 liters (238 cubic inches)
Cylinder numbers (front-to-rear)	
Left (driver's) side	4-5-6
Right side	1-2-3
Firing order	1-4-2-5-3-6

3.8L V6 Engines
1-4-2-5-3-6

36051-2A-specs HAYNES

Cylinder and coil terminal locations - V6 engine

Camshaft and lifters

Lobe lift	
Intake	0.245 inch
Exhaust	0.259 inch
Theoretical valve lift @ zero lash	
Through 2003	
Intake	0.424 inch
Exhaust	0.447 inch
2004 (intake and exhaust)	0.45 inch
Allowable lobe lift loss	0.005 inch (maximum)
Endplay	0.001 to 0.006 inch
Journal diameter (all)	2.0515 to 2.0505 inches
Cam bearing inside diameter	2.0535 to 2.0525 inches
Journal-to-bearing (oil) clearance	0.001 to 0.003 inch
Journal runout limit	0.002 inch
Journal out-of-round limit	0.001 inch

Oil pump

Relief valve spring tension	17.1 to 15.2 lbs at 1.20 inches
Relief valve-to-bore clearance	0.0017 to 0.0029 inch
Gear backlash	0.008 to 0.0012 inch
Gear radial clearance	0.002 to 0.0055 inch
Gear height (beyond housing)	0.0005 to 0.0055 inch

Torque specifications* Ft-lbs (unless otherwise indicated)

Camshaft sprocket bolt	30 to 36
Camshaft thrust plate bolts	72 to 120 in-lbs
Timing chain cover-to-block bolts	15 to 22
Water pump-to-timing chain cover bolts	15 to 22
Oil pan mounting bolts	84 to 108 in-lbs

Torque specifications* (continued)   Ft-lbs (unless otherwise indicated)

Oil pump and filter body to front cover
    8-mm bolt   17 to 23
    6-mm bolt   72 to 96 in-lbs
Cylinder head bolts
    1994 and 1995
        Step 1   15
        Step 2   29
        Step 3   37
        Step 4   Loosen 2 to 3 turns (DO NOT loosen all the bolts at the same time, from this point on work on one bolt at a time) (see text)

        Step 5
            Long bolts   11 to 19
            Short bolts   7 to 15
        Step 6   Tighten an additional 90-degrees
    1996 and later
        Step 1   15
        Step 2   29
        Step 3   36
        Step 4   Loosen 2 to 3 turns (DO NOT loosen all the bolts at the same time, from this point on work on one bolt at a time) (see text)

        Step 5
            Long bolts   29 to 37
            Short bolts   11 to 18
        Step 6   Tighten an additional 180-degrees
Rocker arm fulcrum bolts
    1994 and 1995
        Step 1   44 in-lbs
        Step 2   19 to 25
    1996 and later
        Step 1   44 in-lbs
        Step 2   22 to 29
Intake manifold-to-cylinder head bolts
    1994 and 1995
        Step 1   96 in-lbs
        Step 2   15
    1996 through 2003
        Step 1   72 in-lbs
        Step 2   108 in-lbs
    2004
        Step 1   44 in-lbs
        Step 2   89 in-lbs
Exhaust manifold bolts   23 to 26
Crankshaft pulley-to-vibration damper bolts   20 to 28
Valve cover bolts   72 to 108 in-lbs
Vibration damper bolt   103 to 132
Flywheel/driveplate mounting bolts   54 to 64

*Note: Refer to Part C for additional specifications.

5.0L V8 ENGINE

General

Displacement	5.0 liters (302 cubic inches)
Cylinder numbers (front to rear)	
Left (driver's) side	5-6-7-8
Right side	1-2-3-4
Firing order	1-3-7-2-6-5-4-8

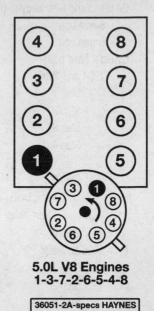

**5.0L V8 Engines
1-3-7-2-6-5-4-8**

36051-2A-specs HAYNES

**Cylinder location and distributor rotation
- 5.0L V8 engine**

Camshaft

Lobe lift (intake and exhaust)	
H.O.	0.2780 inch
Cobra	0.2822 inch
Theoretical valve lift @ zero lash	
H.O.	
Intake	0.442 inch
Exhaust	0.442 inch
Cobra	
Intake	0.4797 inch
Exhaust	0.4797 inch
Allowable lobe lift loss	0.005 inch (maximum)
Endplay	
Standard	0.0005 to 0.0055 inch
Service limit	0.009 inch
Journal diameter	
No. 1	2.0805 to 2.0815 inches
No. 2	2.0655 to 2.0665 inches
No. 3	2.0505 to 2.0515 inches
No. 4	2.0355 to 2.0365 inches
No. 5	2.0205 to 2.0215 inches
Bearing inside diameter	
No. 1	2.0825 to 2.0835 inches
No. 2	2.0675 to 2.0685 inches
No. 3	2.0525 to 2.0535 inches
No. 4	2.0375 to 2.0385 inches
No. 5	2.0225 to 2.0235 inches
Journal-to-bearing (oil) clearance	
Standard	0.001 to 0.003 inch
Service limit	0.006 inch
Runout limit	0.005 inch
Out-of-round limit	0.0005 inch
Camshaft gear backlash	0.006 to 0.011 inch
Front bearing location	0.005 to 0.020 inch below front face of block

Torque specifications*   Ft-lbs (unless otherwise indicated)

Camshaft sprocket bolt	40 to 45
Camshaft thrust plate-to-engine block bolts	108 to 144 in-lbs
Timing chain cover bolts	12 to 18
Cylinder head bolts	
Step 1	25 to 35
Step 2	45 to 55
Step 3	Tighten an additional 90 degrees
Vibration damper-to-crankshaft bolt	110 to 130
Exhaust manifold bolts	26 to 32
Intake manifold-to-cylinder head bolts	
Step 1	96 in-lbs
Step 2	16
Step 3	23 to 25
Oil filter insert-to-engine block adapter bolt	20 to 30
Oil pan mounting bolts	110 to 144 in-lbs
Oil pump mounting bolts	22 to 32
Oil pick-up tube-to-oil pump bolts	12 to 18
Oil pick-up tube-to-main bearing cap nut	22 to 32
Drivebelt pulley-to-vibration damper bolts	35 to 50
Rocker arm fulcrum bolts	18 to 25
Flywheel/driveplate mounting bolts	75 to 85
Front engine mount nuts	72 to 98

*Note: Refer to Part C for additional specifications.

Notes

Section

Reference to other Chapters

2B

4.6L V8 ENGINES

1 General information

This Part of Chapter 2 is devoted to in-vehicle repair procedures for the 4.6L Single Overhead Cam (SOHC) engine and the 4.6L Double Overhead Cam (DOHC) version of the engine, installed only in the Cobra models. The two engines are very similar, except for the cylinder heads and timing chain designs. The SOHC version has one camshaft per cylinder head and two valve per cylinder, while the DOHC Cobra engine has two camshaft per cylinder head and four valves per cylinder. All information concerning engine removal and installation and engine block and cylinder head overhaul can be found in Part C of this Chapter.

The following repair procedures are based on the assumption that the engine is installed in the vehicle. If the engine has been removed from the vehicle and mounted on a stand, many of the steps outlined in this Part of Chapter 2 will not apply.

The Specifications included in this Part of Chapter 2 apply only to the procedures contained in this Part. Part C of Chapter 2 contains the Specifications necessary for cylinder head and engine block rebuilding.

2 Repair operations possible with the engine in the vehicle

Many major repair operations can be accomplished without removing the engine from the vehicle.

If possible, clean the engine compartment and the exterior of the engine with some type of pressure washer before any work is started. It will make the job easier and help keep dirt out of the internal areas of the engine.

It may help to remove the hood to improve access to the engine as repairs are performed (refer to Chapter 11 if necessary).

If vacuum, exhaust, oil or coolant leaks develop, indicating a need for gasket or seal replacement, the repairs can generally be made with the engine in the vehicle. The intake and exhaust manifold gaskets, timing cover gasket, oil pan gasket, crankshaft oil seals and cylinder head gaskets are all accessible with the engine in place.

Exterior engine components, such as the intake and exhaust manifolds, the oil pan, the water pump, the starter motor, the alternator and the fuel system components can be removed for repair with the engine in place.

Since the cylinder heads can be removed without pulling the engine, valve component servicing can also be accomplished with the engine in the vehicle. Replacement of the timing chain and sprockets and oil pump is also possible with the engine in the vehicle.

In extreme cases caused by a lack of necessary equipment, repair or replacement of piston rings, pistons, connecting rods and rod bearings is also possible with the engine in the vehicle. However, this practice is not recommended because of the cleaning and preparation work that must be done to the components involved.

3 Top Dead Center (TDC) for number one piston - locating

◆ **Refer to illustration 3.1**

Refer to Chapter 2, Part A for the TDC locating procedure, but use the illustration provided with this Section for the appropriate reference marks and the following exceptions:

a) *Disable the ignition system by disconnecting the primary electrical connectors at the ignition coil pack/modules (see Chapter 5).*

b) *Remove the spark plugs and install a compression gauge in the number one cylinder. Turn the crankshaft clockwise with a socket and breaker bar as described in Chapter 2.*

c) *When the piston approaches TDC, compression will be noted on the compression gauge. Continue turning the crankshaft until the notch in the crankshaft damper is aligned with the TDC mark on the front cover (see illustration). At this point number one cylinder is at TDC on the compression stroke.*

3.1 When placing the engine at Top Dead Center (TDC), align the notch in the crankshaft damper (arrow) with the TDC indicator on the timing chain cover

4 Valve covers - removal and installation

REMOVAL

Right valve cover

▶ Refer to illustrations 4.2a, 4.2b, 4.6 and 4.7

1   Disconnect the cable from the negative battery terminal.
2   On Cobra models, remove the engine compartment brace (see illustrations).
3   Refer to Chapter 4 and remove the air cleaner outlet tube.
4   On 4.6L-SOHC models, disconnect the electrical connectors from the MAF (Mass Air Flow) and IAT (Intake Air Temperature) sensors (see Chapter 6). Raise the air conditioning hose and pull the wire harness out of the way.
5   Disconnect the spark plug wires, and remove any clips or bolts retaining the wire separators to the valve covers. On 4.6L-DOHC models, remove the spark plug wire covers from the valve cover to access the spark plug wires (see Chapter 1).
6   Remove the PCV valve and hose from the valve cover (see illustration).
7   Remove the valve cover bolts (see illustration).
8   Remove the right valve cover from the cylinder head.

➡ **Note: If the valve cover is stuck to the cylinder head, bump one end with a wood block and a hammer to jar it loose. If that doesn't work, try to slip a flexible putty knife between the cylinder head and valve cover to break the gasket seal. Don't pry at the valve cover-to-cylinder head joint or damage to the sealing surfaces may occur (leading to oil leaks in the future). Some valve covers are made of plastic - be extra careful when tapping or pulling on them.**

Left valve cover

▶ Refer to illustrations 4.12 and 4.14

9   Remove the air cleaner outlet tube.
10 Disconnect the PCV hose.
11 On 4.6L-SOHC models, Disconnect the cruise control cable at the throttle body, and disconnect the electrical connectors from the oil pressure sensor and variable orifice sensor.

4.2a On Cobra models, the engine compartment brace must be removed - remove the three bolts (arrows) at each shock tower and . . .

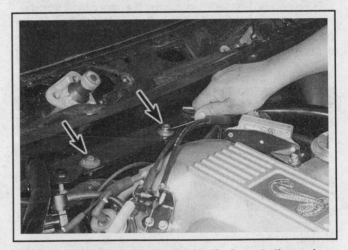

4.2b . . . two bolts (arrows) retaining the brace to the cowl

4.6 Remove the PCV valve and hose, then remove the valve cover bolts (arrows) - 4.6L-SOHC

4.7 Remove the valve cover bolts (arrows) - 4.6L-DOHC

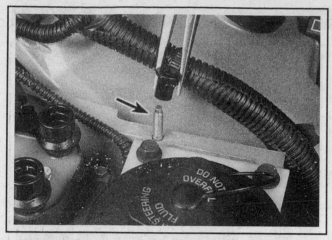

4.12 Disconnect the wiring harness from the studs (arrow indicates one at the front of the valve cover) and position the wiring harness aside

12 On 4.6L-DOHC models, Remove the wiring harness clips from the studs and position the harness out of the way (see illustration).

13 On both models, the left valve cover is a more difficult removal procedure than for the right valve cover. On the 4.6L-SOHC models, the fuel lines are routed over the valve cover, but there is enough clearance to maneuver the valve cover out carefully without disconnecting the fuel lines.

✳✳ WARNING:

Do not disconnect the fuel lines without relieving the fuel system pressure first (see Chapter 4).

14 Remove the valve cover bolts, making note of which ones are studs, and remove the valve cover (see illustration). On 4.6L-DOHC models, take your time to avoid scratching the valve cover in the tight quarters.

INSTALLATION

▶ **Refer to illustrations 4.16 and 4.17**

15 The mating surfaces of each cylinder head and valve cover must be perfectly clean when the valve covers are installed. Remove all

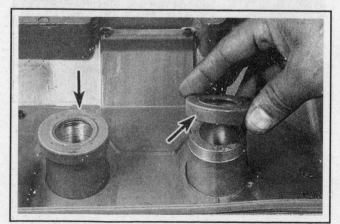

4.16 On 4.6L-DOHC models, install new spark plug seals (arrows) before reinstalling the valve cover

4.14 When removing the left valve cover fasteners on a 4.6L-DOHC engine, remove the nut (arrow) retaining the oil dipstick tube and position the tube aside

traces of sealant, and clean the mating surfaces with lacquer thinner or acetone. If there's sealant or oil on the mating surfaces when the valve cover is installed, oil leaks may develop.

16 The valve cover gaskets should be mated to the valve covers with gasket adhesive before the valve covers are installed. Make sure the gasket is pushed all the way into the groove in the valve cover. Install new spark plug sealing gaskets on 4.6L-DOHC models (see illustration). No sealer or adhesive is required to install the spark plug seals.

17 At the mating joint (two spots per cylinder head) between the timing chain cover and cylinder head, apply a dab of RTV sealant before installing the valve cover (see illustration).

18 Carefully position the valve cover on the cylinder head and install the nuts and bolts.

➡**Note: Install the covers within five minutes of applying the RTV sealant.**

19 Tighten the fasteners in two steps to the torque listed in this Chapter's Specifications. Wait two minutes between the first and the second round of tightening. Tighten the bolts/nuts in a sequence starting in the center and working alternately toward each end of the valve cover.

✳✳ CAUTION:

Be careful with the plastic valve covers, don't over tighten the bolts!

20 The remaining installation steps are the reverse of removal.
21 Start the engine and check for oil leaks as the engine warms up.

4.17 Apply a dab of RTV sealant to the mating joints (arrows) between the timing cover and the cylinder head just before installing the valve cover

5 Crankshaft pulley/vibration damper - removal and installation

REMOVAL

◆ **Refer to illustrations 5.2 and 5.3**

1 Remove the accessory drivebelt (see Chapter 1).

2 Remove the flywheel inspection cover (see Chapter 7) and with the help of an assistant, wedge a large screwdriver into the starter ring gear teeth to prevent the crankshaft from turning. Remove the large center bolt from the crankshaft pulley with a breaker bar and socket (see illustration).

3 Using a suitable puller, detach the vibration damper (see illustration). Leave the Woodruff key in place in the crankshaft keyway.

✳✳ CAUTION:

Don't use a puller with jaws that grip the outer edge of the vibration damper. The puller must be the type shown in the illustration that utilizes bolts to apply force to the vibration damper hub only.

INSTALLATION

◆ **Refer to illustration 5.4**

4 Lubricate the oil seal contact surface of the vibration damper hub (see illustration) with moly-base grease or clean engine oil. Apply a dab of RTV sealant to the front end of the keyway in the vibration damper before installation.

5.2 With the crankshaft being held by an assistant, use a breaker bar and socket to remove the crankshaft pulley bolt (arrow)

5 Install the vibration damper on the end of the crankshaft. The keyway in the vibration damper must be aligned with the Woodruff key in the crankshaft. If the vibration damper cannot be seated by hand, slip the large washer over the bolt, install the bolt and tighten it to pull the vibration damper into place. Tighten the bolt to the torque listed in this Chapter's Specifications.

6 The remaining installation steps are the reverse of removal.

7 Check the oil level. Run the engine and check for oil leaks.

5.3 Remove the vibration damper with a puller that bolts to the vibration damper hub to prevent damage to the vibration damper

5.4 Inspect the vibration damper for signs of damage or excessive wear

1 Oil seal surface   2 Woodruff keyway

6   Timing chain cover - removal and installation

REMOVAL

▶ **Refer to illustrations 6.10, 6.11a, 6.11b, 6.11c, 6.12a, 6.12b and 6.13**

1   Disconnect the cable from the negative battery terminal.
2   Drain the engine oil and remove the oil filter (see Chapter 1).
3   Remove the drive belt and the water pump pulley. Remove the crankshaft pulley/vibration damper (see Section 5). On 4.6L-DOHC engines, remove the lower water pump mounting bolt for clearance (see Chapter 3).
4   Refer to Section 4 and remove both valve covers.

➡**Note: On 4.6L-DOHC engines, the engine compartment brace must be removed.**

5   On 4.6L-DOHC models, drain the cooling system (see Chapter 1) and remove the upper radiator hose and bypass pipes (see Chapter 3).
6   Remove the engine cooling fan/shroud assembly (see Chapter 3).
7   On 4.6L-SOHC models, remove the oil pan (see Section 14).
8   Disconnect the electrical connectors to the camshaft sensor and the crankshaft sensor (see Chapter 6). Disconnect and remove both ignition coil packs (one is attached to each side of the timing chain cover, see Chapter 5).
9   Remove the bolts securing the power steering pump to the engine (see Chapter 10).

➡**Note: The front lower bolt on the power steering pump will not come all the way out.**

Position the pump aside and secure it out of the way.
10   Unbolt and set aside the power steering fluid reservoir (see illustration).
11   Remove the ignition coil brackets. (see illustrations).
12   Remove the timing chain cover-to-engine block bolts (see illustration).

➡**Note: On 4.6L-DOHC models, be sure to remove the four oil pan-to-timing chain cover bolts from underneath (see illustration).**

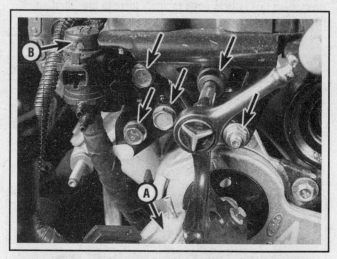

6.11a Remove the bolts and nut (arrows) retaining the right coil bracket to the front cover - when the bolts are removed, set aside the diverter valve (A) and bracket and the bypass valve (B)

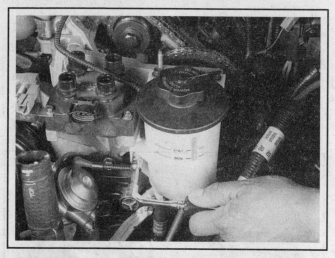

6.10 Unbolt and set aside the power steering fluid reservoir

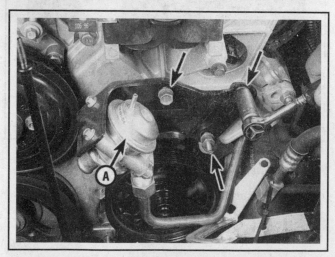

6.11b On 4.6L-DOHC models, remove the two bolts and one nut (arrows) and set aside the diverter valve (A) and bracket . . .

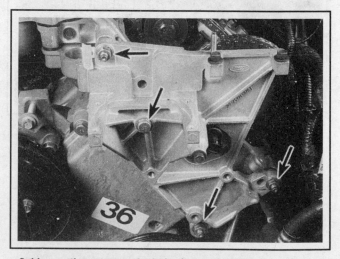

6.11c . . . then remove the bolts (arrows) and the combination mounting bracket

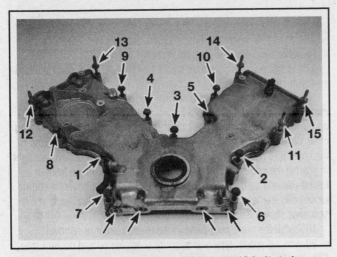

6.12a Including the oil pan bolts, there are 19 bolts to be removed (note the locations of studs/nuts in your application) before the timing chain cover can be removed

13 Separate the timing chain cover from the engine block (see illustration). If it's stuck, tap it gently with a soft-face hammer to break the gasket bond.

✳✳ CAUTION:

DO NOT use excessive force or you may crack the cover. If the cover is difficult to remove, double check to make sure all of the bolts have been removed.

INSTALLATION

▶ **Refer to illustrations 6.15, 6.16a and 6.16b**

14 Clean the mating surfaces of the timing chain cover, engine block and cylinder heads to remove all traces of old gasket material, oil and dirt. Final cleaning should be with lacquer thinner or acetone. On 4.6L-DOHC models, do not use a scraper near the bottom of the engine block, or you could damage the front portion of the existing oil pan gasket.

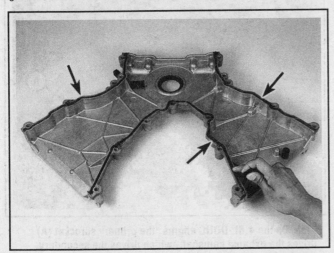

6.15 Install three new gaskets (arrows) into the grooves in the back of the timing chain cover

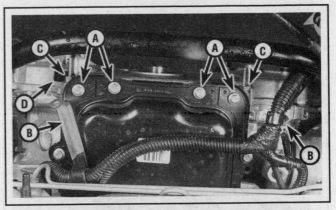

6.12b Remove the crankshaft position sensor (D) - on 4.6L-DOHC engines, remove the four oil pan bolts (A), and disconnect the two wiring harness clips (B) from the studs (C) on the lower front cover

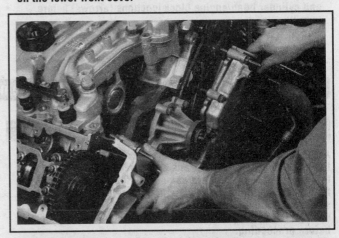

6.13 Separate the timing chain cover from the engine, using a soft-faced hammer if necessary to break the gasket seal

✳✳ WARNING:

Be careful when cleaning any of the aluminum components. Use of a metal scraper could cause scratches or gouges that could lead to an oil leak later.

15 Adhere the three new gaskets to the backside of the timing chain cover (see illustration).

16 Apply a 1/8-inch bead of RTV sealant to the junctions of the oil

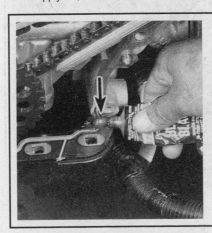

6.16a Apply a small bead of RTV sealant to the mating edges of the engine block, timing chain cover and oil pan - shown are the lower corners on 4.6L-DOHC, with oil pan in place

6.16b Apply a dab of RTV at the cylinder head/valve cover and cylinder head/engine block junctions (arrows) before installing the timing chain cover

pan, timing chain cover and engine block (see illustration). Apply a small dab of RTV where the timing chain cover and engine block meet at the valve cover surface (see illustration).

17 Lubricate the timing chains and the lip of the front crankshaft oil seal with clean engine oil.

18 Install the timing chain cover on the engine. On 4.6L-SOHC models, push the cover straight in onto the engine's dowel pins, but on the 4.6L-DOHC model, position the bottom/front edge of the timing chain cover flush with the front edge of the oil pan and "tilt" the top of the cover into place against the engine. Do not shove the cover straight in against the engine or the sealant may be scraped off the front of the oil pan and cause a leak. Tighten the timing chain cover-to-engine block bolts to the torque listed in this Chapter's Specifications, in the sequence shown (see illustration 6.12a).

19 Install the remaining parts in the reverse order of removal.

20 Add the proper type and quantity of engine oil and coolant (see Chapter 1). Run the engine and check for leaks.

7   Timing chains, tensioners and sprockets - removal, inspection and installation

❊❊ CAUTION:

At no time, once the timing chain(s) have been removed, can the crankshaft or the camshafts be rotated. If moved, damage to the valves and/or pistons can occur. Special tools, available from your local Ford dealer, are necessary to prevent the camshafts from moving when the timing chain is removed. Read through the entire procedure and obtain the necessary tools before proceeding.

➡ Note: Because this is an "interference" engine design, if the chain has broken, there will be damage to the valves and/or pistons and will require removal of the cylinder heads.

REMOVAL

▶ Refer to illustrations 7.3a, 7.3b, 7.4, 7.5a, 7.5b, 7.5c, 7.5d, 7.6a, 7.6b, 7.8, 7.11, 7.12a, 7.12b and 7.13

1   Disconnect the cable from the negative battery terminal.

2   Position the number one cylinder on TDC (see Section 3).

3   Remove the timing chain cover (see Section 6) and the valve covers (see Section 4). Two long timing chains connecting the crankshaft to the camshafts (see illustration). On the 4.6L-DOHC engine, there are two smaller additional timing chains (secondary chains, one on each cylinder head) that connect the intake camshafts to the exhaust camshafts (see illustration).

7.3a Both engine types have two long primary timing chains with two main tensioners (arrows) - 4.6L-SOHC shown

7.3b On the 4.6L-DOHC engine, the primary sprocket (A) drives the exhaust camshaft, which drives the secondary timing chain (B) and the intake camshaft (C)

7.4 The crankshaft sensor tooth wheel has a specific direction to be installed, look for the word "rear" stamped in (arrow)

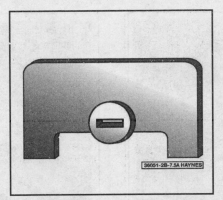

7.5a Camshaft positioning tool used on the 4.6L-SOHC engine

7.5b The camshaft positioning tool is installed at the rear of the camshaft and inserts into a flat-sided hole (arrow)

4 Remove the crankshaft position sensor toothed-wheel (see illustration) by sliding it off the end of the crankshaft nose. Note the stamped word "rear" on the wheel to be sure it's reinstalled in the correct direction.

5 Install the appropriate camshaft retaining tools (see illustrations). The tool locks the camshaft(s) in position when the timing chains are removed.

✳✴ CAUTION:

The camshaft(s) MUST be retained exactly at TDC. If the valve timing is off when the timing chain(s) are reinstalled, severe engine damage could result.

The retaining and positioning tools, available at most auto parts stores, are installed into the rear of the camshaft and hold the cam in place by locking into the specially shaped hole in the rear of the camshaft. This will prevent any movement of the camshafts in either direction, due to valve spring pressure, when the timing chains are removed.

6 Remove the right side timing chain tensioner (see illustrations).

7.5c On 4.6L-DOHC models, the positioning tool (arrow) (one tool is required for each cylinder head) fits into the D-slots on the rear of the camshafts to position the camshafts at TDC

7.5d After positioning the camshafts at TDC, install the retaining tool (arrow) to lock the camshafts

7.6a To remove the timing chain tensioner from the engine block, remove the two bolts from the tensioner (arrows) . . .

7.6b . . . and detach the guide assembly from the dowel at the opposite end

7.8 The stationary chain guide is removed by removing the bolts (arrows) at the mount plate

7.11 Remove the bolt on 4.6L-DOHC engines, then take off the larger primary camshaft sprocket

7.12a Compress the 4.6L-DOHC secondary tensioner with a C-clamp . . .

7 Remove the right timing chain from the crankshaft and camshaft sprockets.

8 Remove the stationary guide (see illustration).

9 Remove the left side timing chain tensioner. Remove the chain

from the crankshaft and camshaft sprockets.

10 Remove the left side stationary guide.

11 On 4.6L-DOHC engines, remove the bolt and the large primary camshaft sprocket (see illustration).

12 The secondary (smaller) timing chain on the 4.6L-DOHC engine has a tensioner between the two sprockets. Compress the tensioner with a C-clamp, then insert two pins to lock the tensioner in position (see illustrations). Remove the tensioner, and repeat for the opposite cylinder head.

>※※< **CAUTION:**

The plunger is spring-loaded, do not remove the tensioner from the engine without pinning it, or it could drop out and be damaged.

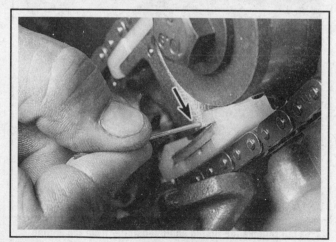

7.12b . . . then insert a drill bit or pin (arrow) to hold the tensioner in the compressed position

13 Remove the camshaft sprocket bolt and large washer from the intake camshaft (4.6L-DOHC) and slip both camshaft sprockets (and their spacers) off with the secondary chain (see illustration).

14 If necessary, remove the crankshaft sprockets, camshaft sprockets and camshaft sprocket spacers, noting the position of each sprocket so it may be reinstalled in its original location. The camshaft sprockets on

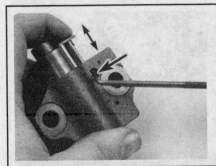

7.16a To fully retract the primary tensioner, release the plunger lock (arrow) and push the plunger into the tensioner body

7.13 With both camshaft sprocket bolts removed on 4.6L-DOHC engines, slide the sprockets off with the secondary chain

7.16b Check the tensioner oil feed hole (arrow) to be sure it's not plugged by debris

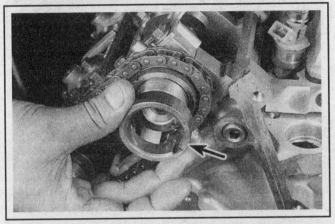

7.18 With the secondary chain and sprockets in place on 4.6L-DOHC engines, be sure to reinstall the spacer (arrow), washer and bolt in the intake camshaft

the 4.6L-SOHC should only be removed from the camshafts if replacement of one of the components is necessary.

INSPECTION

▶ **Refer to illustrations 7.16a and 7.16b**

15 Inspect the individual sprocket teeth and keyways for wear and damage. Check the chain for cracked plates, pitted or worn rollers. Check the wear surface of the chain guides for wear and damage. Replace any excessively worn or defective parts with new ones.

❋❋ CAUTION:

If excessive plastic material is missing from the chain guides, the oil pan should be removed and cleaned of all debris (see Section 14). Check the oil pick-up tube and screen. Replace the assembly if it is clogged.

16 Check the primary tensioners for proper operation:
a) *Release the plunger lock (see illustration) and make sure the piston moves freely.*
b) *Submerge the tensioner in a can of oil or solvent, remove from the fluid and depress the plunger to make sure the oil feed oil is not plugged (see illustration).*

➡Note: Also inspect the oil feed hole in the engine block to be certain it's not plugged.

INSTALLATION

▶ **Refer to illustrations 7.18, 7.19, 7.20a, 7.20b and 7.23**

17 Install the stationary chain guides, for both sides, and tighten the bolts to the torque listed in this Chapter's Specifications.

18 On 4.6L-DOHC models, install the secondary timing chain with its camshaft sprockets and spacers onto the two camshafts (on each cylinder head), then install the tensioner (see illustration). Do not remove the pins from the secondary tensioners until both secondary camshaft sprockets are in place.

19 If removed, install the left crankshaft sprocket on the crankshaft with the beveled hub of the sprocket facing forward. When the two sprockets are placed correctly the hubs will be facing each other and

7.19 When both are installed, the two crankshaft sprockets should align like this; here the left sprocket is installed bevel forward, and the right sprocket (in hand) is ready to install with its bevel (arrow) toward the other sprocket

7.20a When installing the timing chain, align one of the bright links in the timing chain with the dimple on the primary camshaft sprocket (arrows) - sprocket should also align with the keyway in the camshaft

7.20b Align the bright link at the lower end of the chain with the timing mark on the crankshaft sprocket (it should be at 6 o'clock) then bolt the primary camshaft sprocket to the camshaft - both primary chains are aligned here

there will be the maximum space possible between the two sprockets. The timing marks on each sprocket will also align (see illustration). For now, only install the inner (left chain) crankshaft sprocket, with its bevel forward.

20 Install the left timing chain on the camshaft sprocket, aligning the bright link with the dimple (see illustration). Loop the timing chain under the crankshaft sprocket and align the bright link with the alignment mark on the crankshaft sprocket. The timing marks on the crankshaft sprocket should be in the 6 o'clock position (see illustration).

➡**Note: If the plated links on your chain aren't noticeable, lay the chain down on the bench where the chain is exactly halved. Paint a bright mark on the two links at each end, then use those marks for alignment.**

21 Install the cam sprocket and chain on the camshaft. Install the camshaft sprocket bolt and tighten the bolt to the torque listed in this

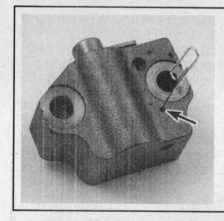

7.23 Lock the primary timing chain tensioner in the fully retracted position by placing a paper clip into the hole in the tensioner body (arrow)

Chapter's Specifications. Install the right chain and sprocket in the same manner. Verify that all timing marks are in alignment, at each primary camshaft sprocket and both crankshaft sprockets.

22 Install the primary timing chain stationary guides, if removed earlier.

➡**Note: The longer bolts are the ones that hold the guide to the cylinder head, the shorter ones go to the engine block.**

23 The steps for installing the timing chain tensioner/guide are the same for both sides, either side can be done first. Before assembling the tensioner with the chain guide, compress the tensioner and lock it in this position with a straightened paper clip, Allen wrench or drill bit (see illustration).

24 Remove the slack from the chain with a C-clamp or by hand, and install the tensioner and guide assembly to the engine block in the retracted position. Tighten the bolts to the torque listed in this Chapter's Specifications.

25 Remove the paper clip and apply pressure against the tensioner chain guide so the tensioner fully extends against the chain guide and all slack is removed from the chain. Also remove the pins from the secondary tensioners (4.6L-DOHC only).

26 Recheck all the timing marks to make sure they are still in alignment (see illustrations 7.20a and 7.20b).

27 Remove the camshaft positioning tools (and retaining tool on 4.6L-DOHC).

28 Slowly rotate the crankshaft in the normal direction of rotation (clockwise) at least two revolutions and again bring the engine to TDC. If you feel any resistance, stop and find out why. Check all alignment marks to verify that everything is properly assembled.

29 The remainder of installation is the reverse of removal.

8   Rocker arms and valve lash adjusters - removal, inspection and installation

There are two methods of removing the rocker arms and lash adjusters on these engines. The method recommended by the manufacturer accomplishes the removal of the camshaft roller followers without the removal of the camshaft(s) by using two special tools specified by the manufacturer; a valve spring spacer and a valve spring compressor which are made specifically for the overhead cam engine (check with your local auto parts store or specialty tool dealer for availability). The

valve spring compressor uses the camshaft as a pivot point and, with a ratchet or bar attached, pushes down on the spring to release tension on the cam follower. The spring spacer keeps the spring from collapsing too far and hitting the valve stem seal. The alternative method requires the removal of the camshaft (see Section 9) in order to remove the cam followers. Either method will achieve the same results, but it is much easier using the manufacturers tools, if they can be located.

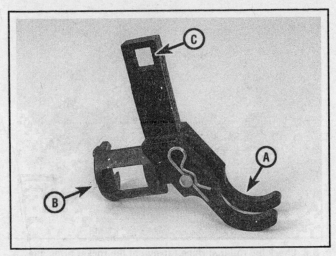

8.4a This type of valve spring compressor hooks under the camshaft at (A), pushes on the valve spring retainer at (B), and is operated by a 1/2-inch drive breaker bar placed at (C)

REMOVAL

♦ **Refer to illustrations 8.4a, 8.4b and 8.5**

1 Remove the valve cover(s) (see Section 4).

2 Because of the interference design of these 4.6L engines, the pistons must be positioned off TDC before compressing the valve springs to remove the rockers arms or lash adjusters. On the 4.6L-SOHC engine, set the crankshaft at TDC for number 1 piston, then turn the crankshaft counterclockwise 45 degrees. In this position, looking at the front of the crankshaft, the keyway in the crankshaft will point at the 9 o'clock position, and all pistons will be positioned below the block deck.

3 On the 4.6L-DOHC engine, each cylinder being worked on will have to be set to the bottom of its stroke. This is easiest to do by setting the engine to TDC for cylinder number 1 (see Section 3), then turning the engine 90 degrees further. This is BDC (Bottom Dead Center) for cylinder number 1. The same position for the rest of the firing can be achieved by turning 90 degrees each time and following the firing order in this Chapter's Specifications. The cam followers for the cylinder being worked on should be on the base of each camshaft lobe.

4 Install a valve spring compressor and compress the spring enough to remove the rocker arm (see illustrations). Camshaft rocker arms and hydraulic lash adjusters, MUST be reinstalled with the same camshaft lobe that they were removed from. Label and store all components to avoid confusion during reassembly.

> ❈❈ **CAUTION:**
>
> On 4.6L-SOHC engines, a valve spring spacer, available at most auto parts stores, should be inserted into the coils of the spring before compressing it. If the spacer isn't in place between one of the valve coils, the spring can be compressed too far and the valve seal may be damaged.

5 Remove the hydraulic lash adjuster (see illustration). If there are many miles on the vehicle, the adjusters may have become varnished and difficult to remove. Apply a little penetrating oil around the lash adjuster to help loosen the varnish.

➡ **Note: Keep the rocker arm and lash adjuster for each valve together in a marked plastic sandwich bag.**

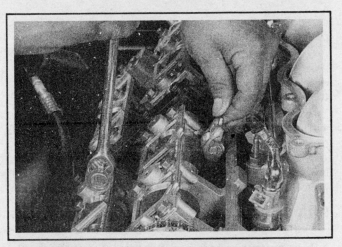

8.4b Compress the valve spring with the tool until you can slip the rocker arm out - keep the rocker arms and lash adjusters matched to their original location

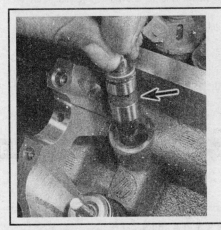

8.5 Pull the lash adjuster straight up and out of the cylinder head

INSPECTION

♦ **Refer to illustrations 8.6 and 8.8**

6 Inspect each adjuster carefully for signs of wear or damage. The areas of possible wear are the ball tip that contacts the cam follower and the sides of the adjuster that contacts the bore in the cylinder head (see illustration). Since the lash adjusters frequently become clogged as mileage increases, we recommend replacing them if you're con-

8.6 Inspect the lash adjuster for signs of excessive wear or damage, such as pitting, scoring or signs of overheating (bluing or discoloration), where the tip contacts the camshaft follower (1) and the side surfaces that contact the lifter bore in the cylinder head (2)

cerned about their condition or if the engine is exhibiting valve "tapping" noises.

7   A thin wire or paper clip can be placed in the oil hole to move the plunger and make sure it's not stuck.

➡**Note: The lash adjuster must have no more than 1/16-inch of total plunger travel.**

It's recommended that if replacement of any of the adjusters is necessary, that the entire set be replaced. This will avoid the need to repeat the repair procedure as the others require replacement in the future.

8   Inspect the rocker arms for signs of wear or damage. The areas of wear are the ball socket that contacts the lash adjuster and the roller where the follower contacts the camshaft (see illustration).

INSTALLATION

9   Before installing the lash adjusters, bleed as much air as possible out of them. Stand the adjusters upright in a container of oil. Use a thin wire or paper clip to work the plunger up and down. This "primes" the adjuster and removes most of the air. Leave the adjusters in the oil until ready to install.

10 Lubricate the valve stem tip, rocker arm, and lash adjuster bore with clean engine oil.

11 Install the lash adjusters and, with the valve spring depressed as in Step 3, install each rocker arm.

12 The remainder of installation is the reverse of the removal procedure.

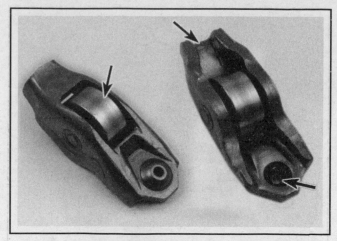

8.8 Check the roller surface (arrow) of the rocker arms and the areas where the valve stem and lash adjuster contact the rocker (arrows at right)

13 When re-starting the engine after replacing the adjusters, the adjusters will normally make some "tapping" noises, until all the air is bled from the lash adjusters. After the engine is warmed-up, raise the speed from idle to 3,000 rpm for one minute. Stop the engine and let it cool down. All of the noise should be gone when it is restarted.

9   Camshaft(s) - removal, inspection and installation

REMOVAL

▶ **Refer to illustrations 9.3, 9.4 and 9.7**

1   Remove the valve covers (see Section 4), and the timing chain cover (see Section 6).

2   Remove the timing chains, camshaft sprockets and spacers (see Section 7).

9.3 Camshaft end play can be checked by setting up a dial indicator off the front of the camshaft and prying the cam gently forward and back

❉❉ CAUTION:

Don't mix up the sprockets, they are marked, as RB (right bank) and LB (left bank), and must go back on the appropriate camshaft.

3   Measure the thrust clearance (endplay) of the camshaft(s) with a dial indicator (see illustration). If the clearance is greater than the value listed in this Chapter's Specifications, replace the camshaft and/or the cylinder head.

4   There are two "camshaft cap clusters", for each camshaft. The configuration of the two cap clusters are different and must be placed in their original locations. Mark the camshaft cap clusters with a front and rear indication, for both the left and right cylinder heads.

9.4 Each camshaft has two "camshaft cap clusters," rather than individual bearing caps, that hold the camshaft in place on the cylinder head. Note the position of the bolts (arrows)

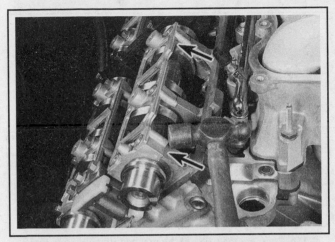

9.7 If the camshaft cap clusters seem to be stuck, tap lightly under these spots to loosen them, then lift straight up

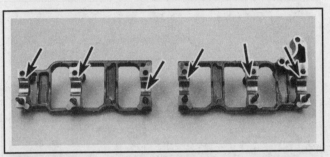

9.9b Inspect the bearing surfaces of the "camshaft cap clusters" (arrows) for signs of excessive wear, damage or overheating

➥**Note: Two bolts used on one of the camshaft cap clusters are different than the others (see illustration), be sure they go back in the same locations on reassembly.**

5   Before removing the camshaft caps and camshafts, rotate the crankshaft 45-degrees counterclockwise (as you are facing the engine) from TDC. This will place the crankshaft keyway in the 9 o'clock position. Once at this position it ensures that all pistons are below the level of the engine block deck, and low enough in the cylinders to avoid valve contact.

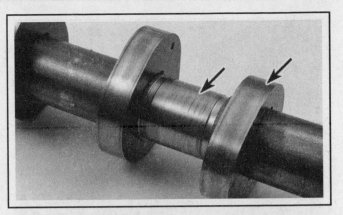

9.9a Areas to look for excessive wear or damage on the camshafts are; the bearing surfaces and the camshaft lobes (arrows)

➥**Note: The camshaft positioning and retaining tools used in Section 7 must be removed to turn the crankshaft to the "non-interference" position.**

6   It's IMPORTANT to loosen the bearing cap cluster bolts only 1/4-turn at a time, following the reverse of the tightening sequence (see illustrations 9.16a and 9.16b), until they can be removed by hand.

7   Remove the two cap clusters and lift the camshaft off the cylinder head. You may have to tap lightly under the camshaft caps to jar them loose (see illustration). Don't mix up the camshafts or any of the components. They must all go back on the same positions, and on the same cylinder head they were removed from.

8   Repeat this procedure for removal of the remaining camshaft(s).

INSPECTION

▸ **Refer to illustrations 9.9a, 9.9b, 9.10a, 9.10b, 9.10c, 9.11a, 9.11b and 9.13**

9   Visually examine the cam lobes and bearing journals for score marks, pitting, galling and evidence of overheating (blue, discolored areas). Look for flaking of the hardened surface of each lobe (see illustrations).

10   Using a micrometer, measure the diameter of each camshaft journal and the lift of each camshaft lobe (see illustrations). Compare your

9.10a Measuring the camshaft bearing journal diameter

9.10b Measure the camshaft lobe at its greatest dimension . . .

9.10c . . . and subtract the camshaft lobe diameter at its smallest dimension to obtain the lobe lift specification

9.11a Lay a strip of Plastigage on each of the camshaft journals

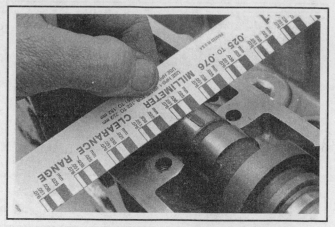

9.11b Compare the width of the crushed Plastigage to the scale on the envelope to determine the oil clearance

9.13 Oil is delivered to the timing chain tensioner by a feed tube and reservoir in the cylinder head

1   Tensioner oil feed tube
2   Reservoir

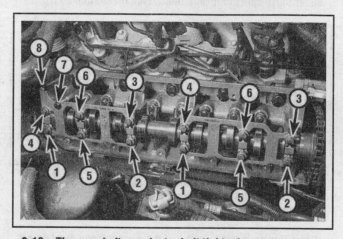

9.16a The camshaft cap cluster bolt tightening sequence, 4.6L-SOHC models - notice that each cap is tightened separately and has its own sequence

measurements with the Specifications listed at the end of this Chapter, and if the diameter of any one of these is less than specified, replace the camshaft.

11 Check the oil clearance for each camshaft journal as follows:

a) Clean the bearing surfaces and the camshaft journals with lacquer thinner or acetone.
b) Carefully lay the camshaft(s) in place in the cylinder head. Don't install the rocker arms or lash adjusters and don't use any lubrication.
c) Lay a strip of Plastigage on each journal (see illustration).
d) Install the camshaft cap clusters.
e) Tighten the cluster cap bolts, a little at a time, to the torque listed in this Chapter's Specifications.

➡**Note: Don't turn the camshaft while the Plastigage is in place.**

f) Remove the bolts and detach the caps.
g) Compare the width of the crushed Plastigage (at its widest point) to the scale on the Plastigage envelope (see illustration).
h) If the clearance is greater than specified, and the diameter of any journal is less than specified, replace the camshaft. If the journal diameters are within specifications but the oil clearance is too great, the cylinder head is worn and must be replaced.

12 Scrape off the Plastigage with your fingernail or the edge of a credit card - don't scratch or nick the journals or bearing surfaces.

13 Finally, be sure to check the timing chain tensioner oil feed tube and reservoir before installing the cam cap cluster (see illustration). it must be absolutely clean and free of all obstructions or it will affect the operation of the timing chain tensioner.

INSTALLATION

▸ **Refer to illustrations 9.16a and 9.16b**

14 If the lash adjusters and/or camshaft followers have been removed, install them in their original locations (see Section 8).

15 Apply moly-base grease or camshaft installation lube to the camshaft lobes and bearing journals, then install the camshaft(s).

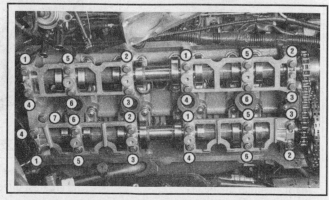

9.16b Camshaft cap tightening sequence - 4.6L-DOHC models

16 Install the camshaft cap clusters in the correct locations, and following the correct bolt tightening sequence (see illustrations), tighten the bolts in 1/4 turn increments to the torque listed in this Chapter's Specifications.

17 Rotate the crankshaft 45-degrees clockwise, to bring it back to top dead center (TDC). Reinstall the camshaft positioning and retaining tools (see Section 7) to set the camshafts at TDC before reinstalling the timing chain(s).

18 Install the camshaft sprockets, timing chain(s), tensioners and timing chain cover (see Section 7).

19 The remainder of installation is the reverse of the removal procedure.

10 Valve springs, retainers and seals - replacement

Broken valve springs and/or defective valve stem seals can be replaced without removing the cylinder heads. There are two methods described in this Section. The method recommended by the manufacturer accomplishes the removal of the valve springs and seals without the removal of the camshafts; however, this method does require the use of two special tools, a valve spring spacer and a valve spring compressor which are made specifically for the overhead cam engine. They are available at most auto parts stores. The valve spring compressor uses the camshaft as a pivot point and, with a ratchet attached, pushes down on the spring to release tension on the cam follower. The spring spacer keeps the spring on 4.6L-SOHC engines from collapsing too far and hitting the valve stem seal. The alternative method uses a more commonly-available tool, but will require the removal of the camshaft (see Section 9) in order to remove the valve spring. Either method will achieve the same results, but it is much easier using the manufacturer's recommended procedure, if the correct tools can be located.

In either repair procedure, a compressed air source is normally required to perform this operation, so read through this Section carefully and rent or buy the tools before beginning the job.

REMOVAL

▶ **Refer to illustration 10.4**

1 Remove the valve cover (see Section 4).

2 Remove the spark plug from the cylinder with the defective component. If all of the valve stem seals are being replaced, remove all the spark plugs.

3 Turn the crankshaft until the piston in the affected cylinder is at Top Dead Center (TDC) on the compression stroke (see Section 3). If you're replacing all of the valve stem seals, begin with cylinder number one and work on the valves for one cylinder at a time. Move from cylinder-to-cylinder following the firing order sequence (see this Chapter's Specifications).

4 Thread an air hose adapter into the spark plug hole (see illustration) and connect an air hose from a compressed air source to it. Most auto parts stores can supply the air hose adapter.

➡ **Note: Many cylinder compression gauges utilize a screw-in fitting that may work with your air hose quick-disconnect fitting.**

5 Apply compressed air to the cylinder.

✴✴ WARNING:

The piston may be forced down by compressed air, causing the crankshaft to turn suddenly. If the wrench used when positioning the number one piston at TDC is still attached to the bolt in the crankshaft nose, it could cause damage or injury when the crankshaft moves.

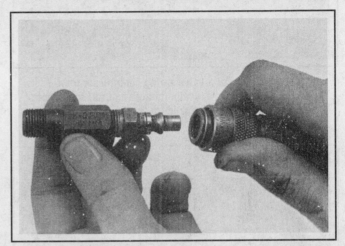

10.4 This is the air hose adapter that threads into the spark plug hole - they're commonly available from auto parts stores

6 The valves should be held in place by the air pressure.

7 Stuff shop rags into the cylinder head holes above and below the valves to prevent parts and tools from falling into the engine.

8 Install a valve spring compressor and, on 4.6L-SOHC models, a valve spring spacer, available at most auto parts stores.

✴✴ CAUTION:

If the spacer isn't in place between one of the valve coils on the 4.6L-SOHC engine, the spring can be compressed too far and damage the valve seal.

9 Compress the spring and remove the rocker arm (see Section 8). Rocker arms and hydraulic lash adjusters MUST be reinstalled with the same camshaft lobe that they were removed from. Label and store all components to avoid confusion during reassembly.

10 Keeping the spring compressed, remove the keepers with small needle-nose pliers or a magnet (see illustration 10.13). Remove the spring retainer and valve spring. Remove the valve stem seal (see illustration 10.15). If air pressure fails to hold the valve in the closed position during this operation, the valve face and/or seat is probably damaged. If so, the cylinder head will have to be removed for additional repair operations.

Alternative procedure

▶ **Refer to illustrations 10.12, 10.13 and 10.15**

11 Remove the camshaft(s) (see Section 9).

10.12 Installation of a valve spring compressor more commonly available at local automotive parts stores (note the camshaft must be removed for the use of this type of valve spring compressor)

10.13 Once the spring is compressed remove the keepers with a needle-nose pliers or a magnet, as shown here

10.15 Use pliers, of any type, to firmly grasp the old seal and pull it off the valve guide

10.20a The valve stem seals combine a seal with the valve spring seat

12 Install the commonly-available clamp-type valve spring compressor (see illustration).

13 Compress the spring and remove the keepers with small needle-nose pliers or a magnet (see illustration).

14 Remove the spring retainer and valve spring.

15 Remove the stem seal (see illustration). If air pressure is being used, and it fails to hold the valve in the closed position during this operation, the valve face and/or seat is probably damaged. If so, the cylinder head will have to be removed for additional repair operations.

INSTALLATION

♦ **Refer to illustrations 10.20a, 10.20b and 10.22**

16 Wrap a rubber band or tape around the top of the valve stem so the valve won't fall into the combustion chamber, then release the air pressure.

17 Inspect the valve stem for damage. Rotate the valve in the guide and check the end for eccentric movement, which would indicate that the valve is bent.

18 Move the valve up-and-down in the guide and make sure it

doesn't bind. If the valve stem binds, either the valve is bent or the guide is damaged. In either case, the cylinder head will have to be removed for repair.

19 Reapply air pressure to the cylinder to retain the valve in the closed position, then remove the tape or rubber band from the valve stem.

20 Lubricate the valve stem with engine oil and install a new seal (see illustration). There is a special tool for the installation of the valve

10.20b This is a special valve seal installation tool, available at most auto parts stores, but a deep socket that fits over the seal can be used to gently tap the seal into place

seal, available at most auto parts stores. If the tool isn't available, a socket that will fit over the seal and is deep enough to make contact with the seat (see illustration), can be used to carefully tap the new seal into place.

❉❉ CAUTION:

The valve seal used on the 4.6L engines is a combination seal and spring seat. Never place a valve spring directly against the aluminum cylinder head (without a seal/spring seat), the hardened spring would damage the cylinder head.

21 Install the spring in position over the valve.

22 Install the valve spring retainer. Compress the valve spring and carefully position the keepers in the groove. Apply a small dab of grease to the inside of each keeper to hold it in place if necessary (see illustration).

23 Remove the pressure from the spring tool and make sure the keepers are seated.

24 Disconnect the air hose and remove the adapter from the spark plug hole.

10.22 Apply a small dab of grease to each keeper as shown here before installation - it'll hold them in place on the valve stem as the spring is released

25 If the camshaft(s) were removed, reinstall them at this time (see Section 9).

26 Install the spark plug(s) and connect the wire(s).

27 The remaining installation steps are the reverse of removal.

28 Start and run the engine, then check for oil leaks and unusual sounds coming from the valve cover area.

11 Intake manifold - removal and installation

REMOVAL

4.6L-SOHC models

▶ **Refer to illustration 11.22**

1   Relieve the fuel system pressure (see Chapter 4). Disconnect the cable from the negative battery terminal.

2   Drain the cooling system and remove the drivebelt (see Chapter 1).

3   Disconnect the radiator, heater and water pump bypass hoses from the water outlet (see Chapter 3).

4   Remove the thermostat housing (see Chapter 3). The thermostat housing bolts also retain the intake manifold.

5   Remove the air inlet tube.

6   Label and disconnect the intake manifold vacuum lines.

7   Remove the PCV and canister purge hoses from the valve covers (see Section 4).

8   Disconnect the accelerator cable, automatic transmission cable and speed control linkage (if so equipped).

9   Disconnect the ignition wire brackets, boots and wires and set them out of the way.

➡**Note: Pull the spark plug wire separators from their mounts on the valve cover studs and lay the wires out of the way.**

10 Disconnect the alternator electrical connectors and remove the alternator (see Chapter 5).

11 Remove the bolts retaining the alternator bracket to the intake manifold (see Chapter 5).

12 Disconnect both ignition coils (see Chapter 5).

13 Disconnect the electrical connectors from the camshaft sensor, coolant temperature sending unit, air charge temperature sensor, throttle positioner, idle speed control solenoid, EGR sensors and fuel injectors (see Chapter 5).

14 Disconnect the throttle and cruise control cables, and remove the throttle body (see Chapter 4).

15 Separate the wire loom bracket at the rear of the manifold.

16 Raise the vehicle with a jack and place it securely on jack stands.

17 Disconnect the EGR tube from the right exhaust manifold (see Chapter 4).

18 Disconnect the electrical connector at the oil pressure sending unit (see Chapter 2, Part C).

19 Lower the vehicle and position the harness out of the way.

20 Disconnect the fuel supply and return lines and cap the open fittings (see Chapter 4).

21 Loosen the intake manifold bolts and nuts in 1/4-turn increments, following the reverse order of the tightening sequence (see illustration 11.37a), until they can be removed by hand. The injectors and fuel rails can be left on the intake manifold during removal.

22 Lift the intake manifold from the cylinder heads (see illustration). The manifold may be stuck to the cylinder heads and force may be required to break the gasket seal. A prybar can be used to pry up the manifold, but make sure all bolts and nuts have been removed first!

11.22 Make sure there is nothing attached to the intake manifold and remove the manifold from the engine

11.27 The coolant bypass tube assembly is retained at the front of the intake manifold by two nuts (arrows)

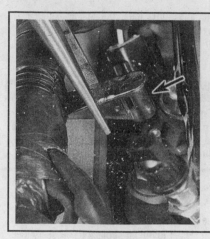

11.28 Remove the clips (arrows) retaining the wiring harnesses along the sides of the intake manifold and position the wire harness aside

> ❉❉ **CAUTION:**
>
> The intake manifold is plastic. Don't pry between the engine block and manifold or the cylinder heads, or damage to the gasket sealing surface may occur, leading to vacuum and oil leaks. Pry only at the manifold protrusion.

23 Remove the intake manifold gaskets and clean all traces of gasket or sealant material from the sealing surfaces of the cylinder heads and intake manifold.

4.6L-DOHC models

♦ Refer to illustrations 11.27 and 11.28

24 Refer to Section 4 and remove the engine compartment brace and spark plug wire covers from the valve covers. Disconnect the spark plug wires from the spark plugs and position the wires aside.

25 Relieve the fuel system pressure and disconnect the fuel lines (see Chapter 5). Disconnect all wiring harnesses, cables and vacuum hoses attached to the intake manifold plenum.

26 Remove the alternator (see Chapter 5).

27 Drain the cooling system (see Chapter 1). Disconnect the electrical connectors from the two coolant temperature sensors. Remove the upper radiator hose and coolant bypass tube assembly (see illustration).

28 Disconnect the wiring harness retainers from the intake manifold

11.34 Check the condition of the water pump hose (arrow) and replace it if necessary

studs and position the harness aside (see illustration).

29 Remove the bolts from the intake manifold in the reverse of the tightening sequence (see illustration 11.37b).

➡**Note: Make marks or otherwise keep track of the location of the fasteners and studs.**

30 Refer to Chapter 6 and disconnect the cables to the Intake Manifold Runner Control (IMRC), and remove the lower intake manifolds.

31 Remove the left and right intake manifold runner control sections and remove the gaskets from the cylinder heads.

➡**Note: For more information on the Intake Manifold Runner Control (IMRC) system, see Chapter 6).**

INSTALLATION

All models

♦ Refer to illustrations 11.34, 11.35a, 11.35b, 11.37a and 11.37b

> ❉❉ **CAUTION:**
>
> The mating surfaces of the cylinder heads, engine block and intake manifold must be perfectly clean. Gasket removal solvents in aerosol cans are available at most auto parts stores and may be helpful when removing old gasket material that's stuck to the cylinder heads and intake manifold. Since the cylinder heads are aluminum and the intake manifold is aluminum or plastic, aggressive scraping can cause damage! Be sure to follow directions printed on the container, and use only a plastic-tipped scraper, not a metal one.

32 If the intake manifold was disassembled, reassemble it or if you are replacing it, transfer all components to the new intake manifold. On 4.6L-DOHC models, transfer the IMRC components to the new intake manifold. Use electrically-conductive sealant on the temperature sending unit threads. Use a new EGR valve gasket.

33 Remove the old gaskets, then clean the mating surfaces with lacquer thinner or acetone. If there's old sealant or oil on the mating surfaces when the intake manifold is installed, oil or vacuum leaks may develop. When working on the cylinder heads and engine block, cover the open engine areas with shop rags to keep debris out of the engine. Use a vacuum cleaner to remove any gasket material that falls into the intake ports in the cylinder heads.

34 Use a tap of the correct size to chase the threads in the bolt holes, then use compressed air (if available) to remove the debris from the holes.

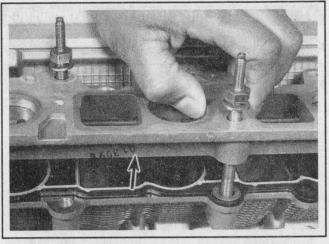

11.35a Install the new intake manifold gaskets to the cylinder head, aligning the plastic pins (arrow) to their holes in the cylinder head

11.35b On 4.6L-DOHC models, use punches or studs to align the intake manifold runner control sections (arrow) to the gasket and cylinder head

Remove excessive carbon deposits and corrosion from the exhaust and coolant passages in the cylinder heads and intake manifold.

➡**Note: If the vehicle has many miles on it, replace the water pump hose (normally hidden by the intake manifold) before replacing the manifold (see illustration).**

35 Install the gaskets on the cylinder heads (see illustration). Make sure all alignment tabs, intake port openings, coolant passage holes and bolt holes are aligned correctly. The gasket that goes on the cylinder head will have projecting plastic pins to align it with holes in the cylinder head. On 4.6L-DOHC models, place the intake manifold runner control sections on each cylinder head and align them with the cylinder head and lower gaskets by using a tapered punch or one of the mounting studs for alignment (see illustration).

36 Carefully set the intake manifold in place. Don't disturb the gaskets and don't move the manifold fore-and-aft after it contacts the gaskets on the engine block.

37 Install the intake manifold bolts and, following the recommended tightening sequence (see illustrations), tighten them to the torque listed in this Chapter's Specifications. Replace the O-ring seal on the thermostat housing. Install the thermostat housing and tighten the bolts to the torque listed in Chapter 3 Specifications.

38 On 4.6L-DOHC models, refer to Chapter 4 for installation of the upper intake plenum.

➡**Note: Use a new gasket and make sure the plastic, load-limiting spacers are In place before installing the upper plenum.**

39 The remaining installation steps are the reverse of removal. Start the engine and check carefully for oil and coolant leaks.

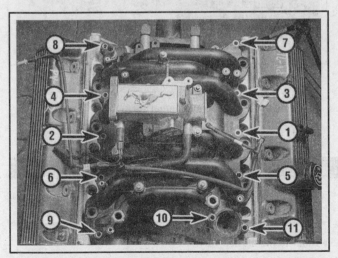

11.37a Intake manifold bolt tightening sequence - 4.6L-SOHC

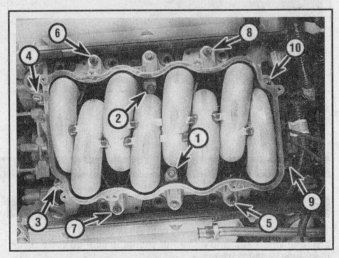

11.37b Intake manifold bolt tightening sequence - 4.6L-DOHC

12 Exhaust manifolds - removal and installation

REMOVAL

▶ **Refer to illustrations 12.8a and 12.8b**

1   Disconnect the cable from the negative battery terminal.

2   Refer to Section 4 for removal of the engine compartment brace, if equipped.

3   Raise the vehicle and support it securely on jackstands.

4   Working under the vehicle, apply penetrating oil to the exhaust pipe-to-manifold studs and nuts (they're usually corroded or rusty). Also apply some to the EGR pipe fitting on the left exhaust manifold.

5   Remove the nuts retaining the exhaust pipes to the manifolds and drop the Y-pipe assembly (see Chapter 4).

6   Remove the starter motor (see Chapter 5) for removal of the right exhaust manifold.

7   Disconnect the steering shaft from the steering gear and position the shaft away from the left exhaust manifold (see Chapter 10).

❋❋ **CAUTION:**

Do not allow the steering column shaft to rotate with the steering gear disconnected or damage to the airbag sliding contact assembly could occur. Lock the steering column and remove the key.

12.8a Disconnect the EGR tube (arrow) from the left exhaust manifold

8   Remove the EGR pipe fitting from the left exhaust manifold. Remove the eight mounting nuts from each manifold (see illustrations).

➡**Note: The exhaust manifold nuts are difficult to access. You'll need a flex-socket and various-length 3/8-inch drive or 1/4-inch drive extensions to reach all the bolts.**

If necessary, remove the motor mount through bolts and using a floor jack or engine hoist, raise the engine slightly to allow sufficient clearance for manifold removal.

INSTALLATION

9   Check the exhaust manifolds for cracks. Make sure the bolt threads are clean and undamaged. The exhaust manifold and cylinder head mating surfaces must be clean before the exhaust manifolds are reinstalled - use a gasket scraper to remove all carbon deposits.

10   Position a new gasket in place and slip the exhaust manifold over the studs on the cylinder head. Install the mounting nuts.

11   When tightening the mounting nuts, work from the center to the ends on 4.6L-SOHC models, and from the rear to the front on 4.6L-DOHC models. Tighten the bolts in three equal steps to the torque listed in this Chapter's Specifications.

12   The remaining installation steps are the reverse of removal.

13   Start the engine and check for exhaust leaks.

12.8b With the steering shaft secured aside remove the mounting nuts (arrows indicate two) and maneuver the manifold out of the engine compartment

13 Cylinder heads - removal and installation

❋❋ **CAUTION:**

The engine must be completely cool when the cylinder heads are removed. Failure to allow the engine to cool off could result in cylinder head warpage.

➡**Note: Cylinder head removal is a difficult and time-consuming job requiring several special tools, rear through the procedure and obtain the necessary tools before beginning.**

REMOVAL

▶ **Refer to illustration 13.7**

1   Disconnect the negative battery cable and drain the cooling system (see Chapter 1).

2   Remove the intake manifold (see Section 11).

3   Remove the exhaust manifolds (see Section 12).

4   Remove the timing chain cover (see Section 6).

13.7 Several cylinder head bolts can't be completely removed from the cylinder head while it's in the vehicle, pull them out just until the threads clear the engine block and tape them at this height (arrow) - remove the bolts along with the cylinder head

5   The cylinder heads can be removed with the camshafts, rocker arms and lash adjusters in place. Remove the primary timing chains, tensioners and guides (see Section 7).

✳✳ CAUTION:

Use the required camshaft retaining fixtures to lock the camshafts and leave the tools in place.

6   If the cylinder head is to be completely overhauled, refer to Section 8 and remove the rocker arms, and Section 9 for removal of the camshafts.

7   Following the reverse of the tightening sequence (see illustration 13.18a), use a breaker bar to remove the cylinder head bolts. Loosen the bolts in sequence 1/4-turn at a time.

➡**Note: Several cylinder head bolts cannot be fully removed while the engine is in the vehicle. These include the lower rear bolts on the left side, and two of the lower bolts on the right side interfere with the shock tower. Pull the bolts up until their threads clear the engine block, then apply tape to the bolts to hold them up (see illustration). Remove the bolts with the cylinder head.**

8   Use a pry bar at the corners of the cylinder head-to-engine block mating surface to break the cylinder head gasket seal. Do not pry between the cylinder head and engine block in the gasket sealing area.

9   Lift the cylinder head(s) off the engine. If resistance is felt, place a wood block against the end and strike the wood block with a hammer. Store the cylinder heads on wood blocks to prevent damage to the gasket sealing surfaces.

10 Remove the cylinder head gasket(s). Before removing, note which gasket goes on which side, they are different and cannot be interchanged.

11 Cylinder head disassembly and inspection procedures are covered in detail in Chapter 2, Part C.

INSTALLATION

✳✳ CAUTION:

New cylinder head bolts must be used for reassembly. Failure to use new bolts may result in cylinder head gasket leakage and engine damage.

◆ **Refer to illustrations 13.15, 13.16, 13.18a and 13.18b**

12 The mating surfaces of the cylinder heads and engine block must be perfectly clean when the cylinder heads are installed. Use a gasket scraper to remove all traces of carbon and old gasket material, then clean the mating surfaces with lacquer thinner or acetone. If there's oil on the mating surfaces when the cylinder heads are installed, the gaskets may not seal correctly and leaks may develop. When working on the engine block, cover the open areas of the engine with shop rags to keep debris out during repair and reassembly. Use a vacuum cleaner to remove any debris that falls into the cylinders.

13 Check the engine block and cylinder head mating surfaces for nicks, deep scratches and other damage.

14 Use a tap of the correct size to chase the threads in the cylinder head bolt holes. Dirt, corrosion, sealant and damaged threads will affect torque readings.

15 Make sure the new gaskets are installed on the correct cylinder banks (see illustration). They are not interchangeable.

16 Position the new gasket(s) over the alignment dowels (see illustration) in the engine block.

17 Before placing the cylinder heads on the engine block, rotate the

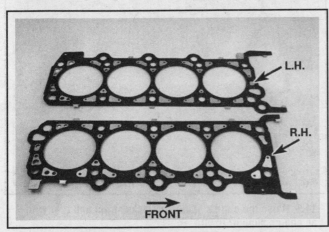

13.15 Identify the left and right cylinder head gaskets, the shapes are different and cannot be interchanged

13.16 Position the gaskets on the correct cylinder banks, push them down over the alignment dowels

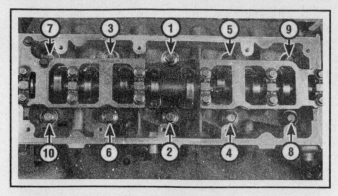

13.18a Cylinder head bolt tightening sequence - SOHC and DOHC models

crankshaft counterclockwise, as you are facing the engine, so the crankshaft keyway is in the 9 o'clock position.

✳✳ CAUTION:

If the crankshaft isn't placed in the position described, damage will occur to either pistons and/or valve train parts.

18 Carefully position the cylinder heads on the engine block without disturbing the gaskets. Make sure that the hard-to-remove cylinder head bolts are installed in the cylinder head, with tape around them (see Step 7). Install NEW cylinder head bolts (the cylinder head bolts are torque-to-yield design and cannot be reused). Following the recommended sequence (see illustration), tighten the cylinder head bolts, in the steps, to the torque listed in this Chapter's Specifications.

13.18b Mark each cylinder head bolt with a paint stripe (arrows) and using a breaker bar and socket, tighten the bolts in sequence the additional 1/4-turn (90-degrees)

➡**Note: The method used for the cylinder head bolt tightening procedure is referred to as "torque-angle" or "torque-to-yield" method. Follow the procedure exactly.**

Tighten the bolts in the first step using a torque wrench, then use a breaker bar and a special torque-angle adapter (available at most auto parts stores) to tighten the bolts the required angle. If the adapter is not available, mark each bolt with a paint stripe to aid in the torque angle process (see illustration).

19 The remaining installation steps are the reverse of removal.

20 Change the engine oil and filter (see Chapter 1), then start the engine and check carefully for oil and coolant leaks.

14 Oil pan - removal and installation

➡**Note: The following procedure applies to both the 4.6L V8 engines as well as the 3.8L V6 engine. The manufacturer's procedure calls for supporting the engine from above while disconnecting and lowering the front suspension crossmember to gain the necessary clearance, a difficult job for the home mechanic. The procedure outlined below, does not require lowering the suspension.**

REMOVAL

◆ **Refer to illustrations 14.6, 14.8 and 14.15**

1 Disconnect the negative battery cable from the battery.
2 Remove the air cleaner duct assembly (see Chapter 4).
3 Remove the wiper arms and module (see Chapter 12).
4 Remove the weatherstrip and plastic covering from the cowl.
5 Remove the crankshaft position sensor shield, if equipped.
6 Attach an engine support fixture (available at most equipment rental yards) to the engine lifting eyes adjacent to the exhaust manifolds.

➡**Note: Many equipment rental yards rent the engine support fixture (see illustration).**

14.6 Raise the engine about two inches front and rear with an engine support fixture

14.8 Disconnect the electrical connector at the oil pan for the oil level sensor

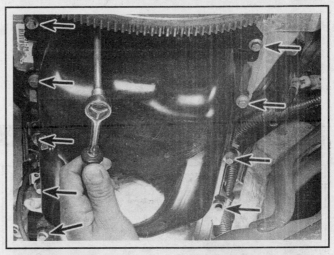

14.15 Remove the bolts from around the perimeter of the oil pan (arrows) and lower the pan to the frame crossmember

7   Raise the vehicle and support it securely on jackstands.

8   Remove the oil level dipstick and disconnect the oil level sensor on the side of the oil pan (see illustration).

9   Drain the engine oil and remove the oil filter (see Chapter 1).

10 If you're working on a vehicle with an automatic transmission, disconnect the transmission cooler lines at the radiator (see Chapter 3).

11 Remove the starter motor (see Chapter 5), wire harness and ground strap.

12 Remove the large engine mount-to-crossmember nuts from the front engine mounts (see Section 18).

13 Remove the transmission (see Chapter 7). Remove the flywheel/driveplate (see Section 16).

14 Raise the engine a little at a time with the support fixture, keeping the engine relatively level (raising the back as much as the front) and watching for interference with any engine compartment components. When the engine is raised about two inches, place short lengths of 2x4 lumber between the motor mounts and the crossmember for extra safety.

15 Remove the oil pan mounting bolts (see illustration), including the oil pan-to-bellhousing bolts (V6 only).

16 Carefully separate the pan from the engine block. Don't pry between the engine block and pan or damage to the sealing surfaces

may result and oil leaks could develop. Instead, dislodge the pan with a large rubber mallet or a wood block and a hammer.

INSTALLATION

▶ **Refer to illustrations 14.19 and 14.20**

17 Use a gasket scraper or putty knife to remove all traces of old gasket material and sealant from the pan and engine block.

❊❊ CAUTION:

Be careful not to damage the delicate aluminum surfaces.

18 Clean the mating surfaces with lacquer thinner or acetone. Make sure the bolt holes in the engine block are clean.

19 Use RTV sealant to hold the new rear rubber seal in place on the V6 engine. On 4.6L V8 models, apply a bead of RTV sealant to the four corner seams where the rear seal retainer meets the engine block, and the front cover meets the engine block (see illustration).

20 Carefully position the pan against the engine block and install the

14.19 On 4.6L V8 engines, apply a dab of RTV sealant at the corners of the front cover, and at the rear-seal retainer-to-engine block joints (arrows) before installing the oil pan

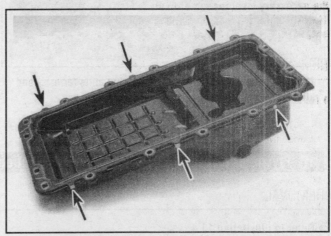

14.20 Place the gasket on the oil pan, the locating tabs (arrows) on each side of the gasket will keep the gasket aligned during installation

bolts finger tight. Make sure the gaskets haven't shifted, then tighten the bolts to the torque listed in this Chapter's Specifications (see illustration). Start at the center of the pan and work out toward the ends in a spiral pattern.

21 The remaining steps are the reverse of removal.

22 Start the engine and check carefully for oil leaks at the oil pan. Drive the vehicle and check again.

15 Oil pump - removal and installation

15.2 Remove the two bolts (arrows) retaining the pickup tube to the oil pump

▶ **Refer to illustrations 15.2, 15.4 and 15.6**

➡**Note: The oil pump is available as a complete replacement unit only. No service parts or repair specifications are available from the manufacturer.**

1 Unbolt and lower the oil pan as described in Section 14. It's not necessary to completely remove the oil pan.

➡**Note: It is possible on 4.6L-DOHC engines to remove the oil pump without removing or lowering the oil pan (a difficult procedure), but you must be careful not to drop the two pickup tube bolts.**

2 Remove the two bolts that attach the oil pump pick-up tube to the oil pump (see illustration).

3 Remove the timing chain cover, timing chains, chain guides and crankshaft sprockets (see Sections 6 and 7).

4 Remove the four oil pump mounting bolts (see illustration) and separate the pump from the engine block.

5 Prime the oil pump prior to installation. Pour clean oil into the pick-up port and turn the pump by hand.

6 Inspect the O-ring gasket on the pick-up tube (see illustration). If damaged replace it.

7 Install the oil pump to the engine and tighten the bolts to the torque listed in this Chapter's Specifications.

8 The remainder of installation is the reverse of removal procedure.

9 Fill the engine with the correct type and quantity of oil. Start the engine and check for leaks.

15.4 Remove the four oil pump mounting bolts (arrows) and oil pump from the engine block

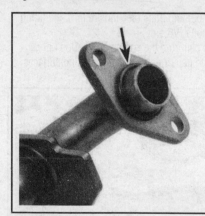

15.6 Before bolting the pickup tube back into the oil pump, inspect the O-ring (arrow) and replace it if necessary

16 Flywheel/driveplate - removal and installation

REMOVAL

▶ **Refer to illustration 16.4**

1 Disconnect the cable from the negative battery terminal.
2 Raise the vehicle and support it securely on jackstands.
3 Refer to Chapter 7 and remove the transmission. Inspect the

transmission. If it's leaking, now would be a very good time to have the transmission front pump seal/O-ring replaced.

➡**Note: On models with automatic transmissions, the driveplate-to-torque converter bolts can be accessed for removal through the large rubber plug on the right rear of the engine block.**

16.4 Make an alignment mark (arrow), if not already on the driveplate, to reassure proper reassembly

4   Look for factory paint marks that indicate driveplate-to-crankshaft alignment. If they aren't there, scribe or paint marks on the driveplate and crankshaft to ensure correct alignment during reassembly (see illustration).

5   Remove the bolts that secure the flywheel/driveplate to the crankshaft (see illustration 16.3). Use a flywheel-retaining tool to keep the crankshaft from turning while loosening the flywheel/driveplate bolts.

➡**Note: There are six flywheel retaining bolts on 4.6L-SOHC models, and eight on 4.6L-DOHC models.**

6   Remove the flywheel/driveplate from the crankshaft. Be sure to support it while removing the last bolt.

✲✲ WARNING:

The teeth on the flywheel may be sharp, and the manual transmission flywheel is heavy. Be sure to hold it with gloves or rags.

➡**Note: After the driveplate is removed, there is a reinforcement/mounting plate that is located between the engine block and the driveplate. It doesn't need to be removed, unless necessary.**

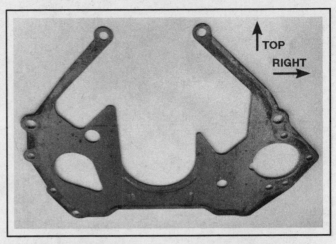

16.7 If the reinforcement plate is removed, for any reason, it should be reinstalled in the direction shown here

INSTALLATION

▶ **Refer to illustration 16.7**

7   If removed, be sure the reinforcement plate is installed as shown (see illustration), so it is correctly positioned for the starter installation.

8   Clean and inspect the mating surfaces of the driveplate and the crankshaft. If the crankshaft rear seal is leaking, replace it before reinstalling the driveplate (see Section 17).

9   Check for cracked, broken or missing ring gear teeth. If any of these conditions are found, replace the flywheel/driveplate.

10 Install the flywheel/driveplate to the engine, aligning the marks made during removal. Note that some engines have an alignment dowel or staggered bolt holes to ensure correct installation. Before installing the bolts, apply Teflon thread sealant to the threads.

11 Use a flywheel-retaining tool to keep the driveplate from turning as you tighten the bolts to the torque listed in this Chapter's Specifications.

12 The remainder of installation is the reverse of the removal procedure.

17 Crankshaft oil seals - replacement

FRONT SEAL

▶ **Refer to illustrations 17.4 and 17.6**

1   Disconnect the negative battery cable.

2   Remove the drivebelt (see Chapter 1).

3   Remove the crankshaft pulley/vibration damper (see Section 5).

4   Carefully remove the seal from the cover with a seal removal tool (see illustration). If a seal removal tool is not available, carefully use a screwdriver. If the timing cover is removed, use a chisel or small punch and hammer to drive the seal out of the cover from the back side. Support the cover as close to the seal bore as possible with two wood blocks. Be careful not to damage the cover or scratch the wall of the seal bore.

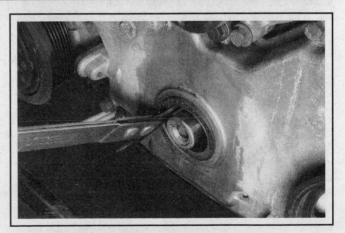

17.4 Using a special seal removal tool or screwdriver, remove the front crankshaft oil seal, be very careful not to scratch the crankshaft during seal removal

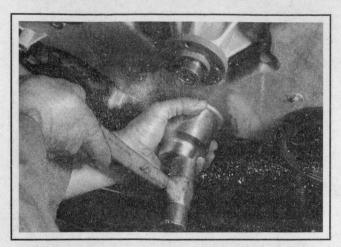

17.6 There is special tool for installing the front oil seal into the timing chain cover, but if the tool is unavailable a large socket (the same diameter as the seal) can be used to drive the seal into place

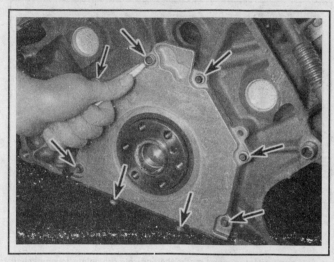

17.15 Remove the eight bolts (arrows) and separate the seal retainer from the engine block

17.16 Support the seal retainer on two wood blocks and drive out the old seal with a blunt punch and hammer

17.17 Support the seal retainer and drive the new seal into the housing with a wood block or a section of pipe, be sure not to cock the seal in the bore while installing

5   Check the seal bore and crankshaft, as well as the seal contact surface on the vibration damper for nicks and burrs. Position the new seal in the bore with the open end of the seal facing IN. A small amount of oil or grease applied to the outer edge of the new seal will make installation easier - but don't overdo it!

6   Drive the seal into the bore with a large socket and hammer until it's completely seated (see illustration). If the cover is removed, support the cover on wood blocks. Select a socket that's the same outside diameter as the seal (a section of pipe can be used if a socket isn't available).

7   Lubricate the lip of the seal with clean engine oil and install the damper on the end of the crankshaft. The keyway in the damper bore must be aligned with the Woodruff key in the crankshaft nose.

➥**Note: Before reinstalling the damper, apply as small dab of RTV sealant to the front end of the crankshaft key groove.**

8   If the damper can't be seated by hand, tap it into place with a soft-face hammer, or install the bolt and washer and tighten it to press the damper into place.

9   Tighten the damper bolt to the torque listed in this Chapter's Specifications.

10 Install the drivebelt.
11 Install the remaining parts removed for access to the seal.
12 Start the engine and check for leaks.

REAR SEAL

▶ **Refer to illustrations 17.15, 17.16, 17.17 and 17.18**

13 Disconnect the cable from the negative battery terminal. Refer to Chapter 7 and remove the transmission.

14 Remove the flywheel/driveplate and the rear cover plate from the engine (Section 16).

15 Remove the bolts, detach the seal retainer (see illustration) and clean off all the old gasket and/or sealant material from both the engine block and the seal retainer.

16 Support the seal and retainer assembly on wood blocks and drive the old seal out from the back side with a drift punch and hammer (see illustration).

17 Drive the new seal into the retainer with a wood block (see illustration).

18 Clean the crankshaft and seal bore with lacquer thinner or acetone. Check the seal contact surface on the crankshaft very carefully for scratches or nicks that could damage the new seal lip and cause oil leaks (see illustration). If the crankshaft is damaged, the only alternative is a new or different crankshaft.

19 Lubricate the crankshaft seal journal and the lip of the new seal with engine oil.

20 Place a 1/16-inch wide bead of anaerobic sealant on either the engine block or the seal retainer.

21 Install the oil seal retainer by slowly and carefully pushing the seal onto the crankshaft. The seal lip is stiff, so work it onto the crankshaft with a smooth object such as the end of a socket extension as you push the retainer against the engine block.

22 Install and tighten the retainer bolts to the torque listed in this Chapter's Specifications.

23 Reinstall the engine rear cover plate, driveplate and the transmission.

24 The remaining steps are the reverse of removal.

25 Check the oil level and add if necessary, run the engine and check for oil leaks.

17.18 Inspect the seal contact surface on the crankshaft (arrow) for signs of excessive wear or grooves

18 Engine mounts - check and replacement

CHECK

▶ **Refer to illustration 18.4**

1 Engine mounts seldom require attention, but broken or deteriorated mounts should be replaced immediately or the added strain placed on the driveline components may cause damage or wear.

2 During the check, the engine must be raised slightly to remove the weight from the mounts.

3 Raise the vehicle and support it securely on jackstands, then position a jack under the engine oil pan. Place a large wood block between the jack head and the oil pan, then carefully raise the engine just enough to take the weight off the mounts.

4 Check the mounts to see if the rubber is cracked, hardened or separated from the metal plates (see illustration). Sometimes the rubber will split right down the center.

5 Check for relative movement between the mount plates and the engine or frame (use a large screwdriver or pry bar to attempt to move the mounts). If movement is noted, lower the engine and tighten the mount fasteners.

6 Rubber preservative should be applied to the mounts to slow deterioration.

REPLACEMENT

▶ **Refer to illustrations 18.9a, 18.9b, 18.10 and 18.13**

7 Disconnect the negative battery cable.

8 Refer to Section 4 for removal of the engine compartment brace, if equipped.

9 On the right side, remove the starter motor (refer to Chapter 5) and on the left side disconnect the two nuts retaining the oxygen sensor

18.4 Inspect the engine mount components for cracked rubber insulators (arrow), missing bolts or cracked metal brackets

18.9a On the left engine mount, remove the nut (arrow) and move the ground cable and oxygen sensor cable bracket aside

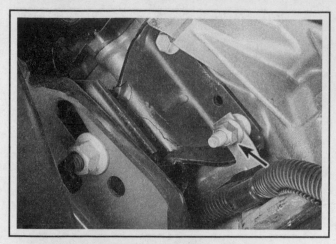

18.9b Remove the nut (right-side mount) retaining the wiring harness

18.10 With the engine raised, remove the crossmember nuts (arrow) and remove the engine mount

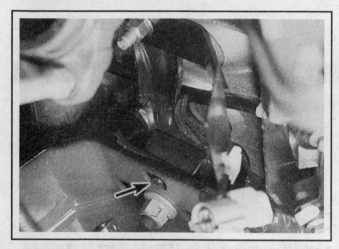

18.13 Make sure the projecting nub on the engine mount is located in the hole (arrow) in the crossmember before tightening the mounting bolts

electrical cable and ground cable to motor mount studs (see illustrations).

10 Remove the large nuts securing the engine mount studs to the front crossmember (see illustration).

11 Once the nuts have been removed from the mounts on both sides of the engine, raise the engine up with a jack and wood block under the crankshaft damper until the studs clear the crossmember.

12 Remove the mount-to-engine block bolts and detach the mount.

13 Installation is the reverse of removal. Replace the heat shields, if equipped, in the same relationship to the mount as originally installed. Tighten the bolts to the torque listed in this Chapter's Specifications.

➞**Note: The engine mounts have a rounded locating projection that fits into a hole in the front crossmember when the engine is lowered. Look from below the crossmember to see that the projection is seated in the hole (see illustration).**

Specifications

General

Displacement	4.6 liters (281 cubic inches)
Bore and stroke	3.5539 X 3.5460 inches
Cylinder numbers (front to rear)	
Right side	1-2-3-4
Left (driver's) side	5-6-7-8
Firing order	1-3-7-2-6-5-4-8

4.6L V8 Engines
1-3-7-2-6-5-4-8

36051-2A-specs HAYNES

Cylinder and coil
terminal location

Camshaft

Lobe lift	
4.6L-SOHC	
Intake	0.2594 inch
Exhaust	0.2594 inch
4.6L-DOHC	
Intake, primary	0.21839 inch
Intake, secondary	0.21877 inch
Exhaust	0.21856 inch
Endplay	
Standard	0.00098 to 0.00649 inch
Service limit	0.00748 inch maximum
Journal diameter (all)	1.0615 to 1.06047 inches
Bearing inside diameter (all)	1.06346 to 1.06248 inches
Journal-to-bearing (oil) clearance	
Standard	0.00098 to 0.002992 inch
Service limit	
4.6L-SOHC	0.00476 inch maximum
4.6L-DOHC	0.00394 inch maximum
Camshaft sprocket bolts	82 to 95

Torque specifications

	Ft-lbs (unless otherwise indicated)
Camshaft caps to cylinder head	71 to 106 in-lbs
Timing chain cover bolts	15 to 22
Drive belt idler and tensioner bolts	15 to 22
Cylinder head bolts	
4.6L-SOHC and 1998 and later 4.6L-DOHC	
Step 1	28 to 31
Step 2	Tighten an additional 90-degrees
Step 3	Loosen one turn
Step 4	28 to 31
Step 5	Tighten an additional 90-degrees
Step 6	Tighten an additional 90-degrees
1997 and earlier 4.6L-DOHC	
Step 1	28 to 31
Step 2	Tighten an additional 90-degrees
Step 3	Tighten an additional 90-degrees

Torque specifications — Ft-lbs (unless otherwise indicated)

Vibration damper-to-crankshaft bolt	
1996	114 to 121
1997 and later	
Step 1	66
Step 2	Loosen one full turn
Step 3	36
Step 4	Tighten an additional 90-degrees
Valve cover bolts	71 to 106 in-lbs
Oil pan-to-engine block bolts	
1996	15 to 22
1997 and later	
Step 1	15
Step 2	Tighten an additional 60-degrees
Exhaust manifold-to-cylinder head nuts	14 to 16
Intake manifold-to-cylinder head bolts	
4.6L-SOHC	15 to 22*
4.6L-DOHC	
Upper plenum to intake	71 to 106 in-lbs
Intake to lower side plates (2 small bolts)	71 to 106 in-lbs
Intake/side plates assembly to cylinder head	
Step 1	15 to 22
Step 2	Tighten an additional 90-degrees
Oil filter adapter bolts	15 to 22
Oil cooler-to-filter adapter insert	
1996	59 to 74
1997 and later	41 to 53
Oil pump-to-engine block mounting bolts	71 to 106 in-lbs
Oil pick-up tube-to-main bearing cap nut	15 to 22
Oil pick-up tube-to-oil pump bolts	71 to 106 in-lbs
Flywheel/driveplate mounting bolts	59 to 64
Ignition coil brackets to front cover	15 to 22
Timing chain tensioners/guides	15 to 22
Engine mount-to-engine block bolts/studs	25 to 33
Engine mount stud to crossmember nuts	95 to 126
Engine compartment brace bolts	15 to 22
Rear seal retainer plate	89 in-lbs

*After assembly, retorque with the engine hot

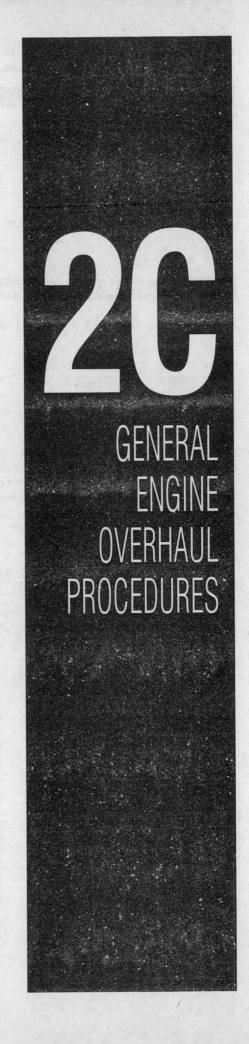

2C

GENERAL
ENGINE
OVERHAUL
PROCEDURES

1 General information

Included in this portion of Chapter 2 are the general overhaul procedures for the cylinder head(s) and internal engine components.

The information ranges from advice concerning preparation for an overhaul and the purchase of replacement parts to detailed, step-by-step procedures covering removal and installation of internal engine components and the inspection of parts.

The following Sections have been written based on the assumption that the engine has been removed from the vehicle. For information concerning in-vehicle engine repair, as well as removal and installation of the external components necessary for the overhaul, see Parts A and B of this Chapter and Section 7 of this Part.

The Specifications included in this Part are only those necessary for the inspection and overhaul procedures which follow. Refer to Parts A and B for additional Specifications.

2 Engine overhaul - general information

▶ **Refer to illustrations 2.4a, 2.4b, 2.4c and 2.4d**

It is not always easy to determine when, or if, an engine should be completely overhauled, as a number of factors must be considered.

High mileage is not necessarily an indication that an overhaul is needed, while low mileage does not preclude the need for an overhaul. Frequency of servicing is probably the most important consideration. An engine that has had regular and frequent oil and filter changes, as well as other required maintenance, will most likely give many thousands of miles of reliable service. Conversely, a neglected engine may require an overhaul very early in its life.

Excessive oil consumption is an indication that piston rings and/or valve guides are in need of attention. Make sure that oil leaks are not responsible before deciding that the rings and/or guides are bad. Test the cylinder compression (see Section 3) or have a leak down test performed by an experienced tune-up mechanic to determine the extent of the work required.

If the engine is making obvious knocking or rumbling noises, the connecting rod and/or main bearings are probably at fault. To accurately test oil pressure, temporarily connect a mechanical oil pressure gauge in place of the oil pressure sending unit (see illustrations). Compare the reading to the pressure listed in this Chapter's Specifications. If the pressure is extremely low, the bearings and/or oil pump are probably worn out.

Loss of power, rough running, excessive valve train noise and high

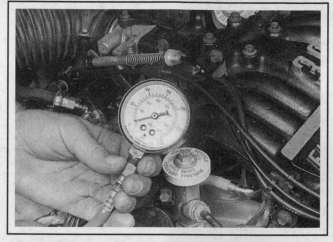

2.4a Remove the oil pressure sending unit and attach an oil pressure gauge - be sure the fittings you use have the same thread as the sender

fuel consumption rates may also point to the need for an overhaul, especially if they are all present at the same time. If a complete tune-up does not remedy the situation, major mechanical work is the only solution.

2.4b The oil pressure sending unit is located at the lower left (driver's side) corner of the engine, near the oil filter (4.6L SOHC engine shown, 5.0L engine similar)

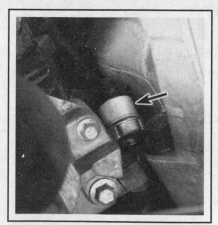

2.4c Oil pressure sender location, 3.8L V6 - left side of the block, under the power steering pump

2.4d On 4.6L DOHC engines, the oil pressure sending unit (arrow) is located on the oil filter adapter, just behind the oil cooler

An engine overhaul involves restoring the internal parts to the specifications of a new engine. During an overhaul, the piston rings are replaced and the cylinder walls are reconditioned (rebored and/or honed). If a re-bore is done, new pistons are required. The main bearings, connecting rod bearings and camshaft bearings are generally replaced with new ones and, if necessary, the crankshaft may be reground to restore the journals. Generally, the valves are serviced as well, since they are usually in less-than-perfect condition at this point. While the engine is being overhauled, other components, such as the distributor, starter and alternator, can be rebuilt as well. The end result should be a like-new engine that will give many trouble free miles.

→Note: Critical cooling system components such as the hoses, the drivebelts, the thermostat and the water pump MUST be replaced with new parts when an engine is overhauled. The radiator should be checked carefully to ensure that it isn't clogged or leaking. Some engine rebuilding shops will not honor their engine warranty unless you have had the radiator replaced or professionally cleaned. If in doubt, replace it with a new one. Also, we do not recommend overhauling the oil pump - always install a new one when an engine is rebuilt.

Before beginning the engine overhaul, read through the entire procedure to familiarize yourself with the scope and requirements of the job. Overhauling an engine is not difficult, but it is time consuming.

Plan on the vehicle being tied up for a minimum of two weeks, especially if parts must be taken to an automotive machine shop for repair or reconditioning. Check on availability of parts and make sure that any necessary special tools and equipment are obtained in advance. Most work can be done with typical hand tools, although a number of precision measuring tools are required for inspecting parts to determine if they must be replaced. Often an automotive machine shop will handle the inspection of parts and offer advice concerning reconditioning and replacement.

→Note: Always wait until the engine has been completely disassembled and all components, especially the engine block, have been inspected before deciding what service and repair operations must be performed by an automotive machine shop. Since the block's condition will be the major factor to consider when determining whether to overhaul the original engine or buy a rebuilt one, never purchase parts or have machine work done on other components until the block has been thoroughly inspected. As a general rule, time is the primary cost of an overhaul, so it does not pay to install worn or substandard parts.

As a final note, to ensure maximum life and minimum trouble from a rebuilt engine, everything must be assembled with care in a spotlessly clean environment.

3   Cylinder compression check

▶ **Refer to illustration 3.6**

1   A compression check will tell you what mechanical condition the upper end (pistons, rings, valves, head gaskets) of your engine is in. Specifically, it can tell you if the compression is down due to leakage caused by worn piston rings, defective valves and seats or a blown head gasket.

→Note: The engine must be at normal operating temperature for this check and the battery must be fully charged.

2   Begin by cleaning the area around the spark plugs before you remove them (compressed air works best for this). This will prevent dirt from getting into the cylinders as the compression check is being done.

3   Remove all of the spark plugs from the engine (see Chapter 1).

4   Block the throttle wide open.

5   Disable the ignition system by disconnecting the primary (low voltage) wires from the coil(s).

6   With the compression gauge in the number one spark plug hole, crank the engine over at least four compression strokes and watch the gauge (see illustration). The compression should build up quickly in a healthy engine. Low compression on the first stroke, followed by gradually increasing pressure on successive strokes, indicates worn piston rings. A low compression reading on the first stroke, which does not build up during successive strokes, indicates leaking valves or a blown head gasket (a cracked head could also be the cause). Record the highest gauge reading obtained.

7   Repeat the procedure for the remaining cylinders and compare the results to the Specifications.

8   Add some engine oil (about three squirts from a plunger-type oil can) to each cylinder, through the spark plug hole, and repeat the test.

9   If the compression increases after the oil is added, the piston rings are definitely worn. If the compression does not increase significantly, the leakage is occurring at the valves or head gasket. Leakage past the valves may be caused by burned valve seats and/or faces or

3.6 A compression gauge with a threaded fitting for the spark plug hole is preferred over the type that requires hand pressure to maintain the seal - be sure to open the throttle valve as far as possible during the compression check

warped, cracked or bent valves.

10   If two adjacent cylinders have equally low compression, there is a strong possibility that the head gasket between them is blown. The appearance of coolant in the combustion chambers or the crankcase would verify this condition.

11   If the compression is unusually high, the combustion chambers are probably coated with carbon deposits. If that is the case, the cylinder heads should be removed and decarbonized.

12   If compression is way down or varies greatly between cylinders, it would be a good idea to have a leak-down test performed by an automotive repair shop. This test will pinpoint exactly where the leakage is occurring and how severe it is.

4   Vacuum gauge diagnostic checks

A vacuum gauge provides valuable information about what is going on in the engine at a low-cost. You can check for worn rings or cylinder walls, leaking head or intake manifold gaskets, incorrect carburetor adjustments, restricted exhaust, stuck or burned valves, weak valve springs, improper ignition or valve timing and ignition problems.

Unfortunately, vacuum gauge readings are easy to misinterpret, so they should be used in conjunction with other tests to confirm the diagnosis.

Both the absolute readings and the rate of needle movement are important for accurate interpretation. Most gauges measure vacuum in inches of mercury (in-Hg). The following references to vacuum assume the diagnosis is being performed at sea level. As elevation increases (or atmospheric pressure decreases), the reading will decrease. For every 1,000 foot increase in elevation above approximately 2000 feet, the gauge readings will decrease about one inch of mercury.

Connect the vacuum gauge directly to intake manifold vacuum, not to ported (throttle body) vacuum. Be sure no hoses are left disconnected during the test or false readings will result.

Before you begin the test, allow the engine to warm up completely. Block the wheels and set the parking brake. With the transmission in Park, start the engine and allow it to run at normal idle speed.

❊❊ WARNING:

Carefully inspect the fan blades for cracks or damage before starting the engine. Keep your hands and the vacuum gauge clear of the fan and do not stand in front of the vehicle or in line with the fan when the engine is running.

Read the vacuum gauge; an average, healthy engine should normally produce about 17 to 22 inches of vacuum with a fairly steady needle. Refer to the following vacuum gauge readings and what they indicate about the engine's condition:

1   A low steady reading usually indicates a leaking gasket between the intake manifold and cylinder head(s) or throttle body, a leaky vacuum hose, late ignition timing or incorrect camshaft timing. Check ignition timing with a timing light and eliminate all other possible causes, utilizing the tests provided in this Chapter before you remove the timing chain cover to check the timing marks.

2   If the reading is three to eight inches below normal and it fluctuates at that low reading, suspect an intake manifold gasket leak at an intake port or a faulty fuel injector.

3   If the needle has regular drops of about two-to-four inches at a steady rate, the valves are probably leaking. Perform a compression check or leak-down test to confirm this.

4   An irregular drop or down-flick of the needle can be caused by a sticking valve or an ignition misfire. Perform a compression check or leak-down test and read the spark plugs.

5   A rapid vibration of about four in.-Hg vibration at idle combined with exhaust smoke indicates worn valve guides. Perform a leak-down test to confirm this. If the rapid vibration occurs with an increase in engine speed, check for a leaking intake manifold gasket or head gasket, weak valve springs, burned valves or ignition misfire.

6   A slight fluctuation, say one inch up and down, may mean ignition problems. Check all the usual tune-up items and, if necessary, run the engine on an ignition analyzer.

7   If there is a large fluctuation, perform a compression or leak-down test to look for a weak or dead cylinder or a blown head gasket.

8   If the needle moves slowly through a wide range, check for a clogged PCV system, incorrect idle fuel mixture, carburetor/throttle body or intake manifold gasket leaks.

9   Check for a slow return after revving the engine by quickly snapping the throttle open until the engine reaches about 2,500 rpm and let it shut. Normally the reading should drop to near zero, rise above normal idle reading (about 5 in.-Hg over) and then return to the previous idle reading. If the vacuum returns slowly and doesn't peak when the throttle is snapped shut, the rings may be worn. If there is a long delay, look for a restricted exhaust system (often the muffler or catalytic converter). An easy way to check this is to temporarily disconnect the exhaust ahead of the suspected part and redo the test.

5   Engine removal - methods and precautions

If you have decided that an engine must be removed for overhaul or major repair work, several preliminary steps should be taken.

Locating a suitable work area is extremely important. A shop is, of course, the most desirable place to work. Adequate work space, along with storage space for the vehicle, will be needed. If a shop or garage is not available, at the very least a flat, level, clean work surface made of concrete or asphalt is required.

Cleaning the engine compartment and engine before beginning the removal procedure will help keep tools clean and organized.

An engine hoist or A-frame will be needed. Make sure that the equipment is rated in excess of the combined weight of the engine and its accessories. Safety is of primary importance, considering the potential hazards involved in lifting the engine out of the vehicle.

If the engine is being removed by a novice, a helper should be available. Advice and aid from someone more experienced would also be helpful. There are many instances when one person cannot simultaneously perform all of the operations required when lifting the engine out of the vehicle.

Plan the operation ahead of time. Arrange for or obtain all of the tools and equipment you will need prior to beginning the job. Some of the equipment necessary to perform engine removal and installation safely and with relative ease are (in addition to an engine hoist) a heavy duty floor jack, complete sets of wrenches and sockets as described in the front of this manual, wooden blocks and plenty of rags and cleaning solvent for mopping up spilled oil, coolant and gasoline. If the hoist is to be rented, make sure that you arrange for it in advance and perform beforehand all of the operations possible without it. This will save you money and time.

Plan for the vehicle to be out of use for a considerable amount of time. A machine shop will be required to perform some of the work which the do-it-yourselfer cannot accomplish due to a lack of special equipment. These shops often have a busy schedule, so it would be wise to consult them before removing the engine in order to accurately estimate the amount of time required to rebuild or repair components that may need work.

Always use extreme caution when removing and installing the engine. Serious injury can result from careless actions. Plan ahead, take your time and a job of this nature, although major, can be accomplished successfully.

6 Engine - removal and installation

✳✳ WARNING 1:

The air conditioning system is under high pressure. DO NOT loosen any fittings or remove any components until after the system has been discharged. Air conditioning refrigerant should be properly discharged into an EPA-approved container at a dealer service department or an automotive air conditioning repair facility. Always wear eye protection when disconnecting air conditioning system fittings.

✳✳ WARNING 2:

Gasoline is extremely flammable, so take extra precautions when you work on any part of the fuel system. Don't smoke or allow open flames or bare light bulbs near the work area, and don't work in a garage where a gas-type appliance (such as a water heater or a clothes dryer) is present. Since gasoline is carcinogenic, wear latex gloves when there's a possibility of being exposed to fuel, and, if you spill any fuel on your skin, rinse it off immediately with soap and water. Mop up any spills immediately and do not store fuel-soaked rags where they could ignite. The fuel system is under constant pressure, so, if any fuel lines are to be disconnected, the fuel pressure in the system must be relieved first (see Chapter 4 for more information). When you perform any kind of work on the fuel system, wear safety glasses and have a Class B type fire extinguisher on hand.

REMOVAL

▶ **Refer to illustrations 6.6, 6.26, 6.28 and 6.29**

1 Relieve the fuel system pressure (see Chapter 4).

2 Disconnect the negative cable from the battery.

3 Cover the fenders and cowl and remove the hood (see Chapter 11). Special pads are available to protect the fenders, but an old bedspread or blanket will also work.

4 Remove the air cleaner assembly.

5 Drain the cooling system (see Chapter 1).

6 Label the vacuum lines, emissions system hoses, electrical connectors, ground straps and fuel lines that would interfere with engine removal, to ensure correct reinstallation, then detach them. Pieces of masking tape with numbers or letters written on them work well (see illustration). If there's any possibility of confusion, make a sketch of the engine compartment and clearly label the lines, hoses and wires.

7 Label and detach all coolant hoses from the engine.

8 Remove the cooling fan/shroud and radiator (see Chapter 3).

9 Remove the drivebelt(s) (see Chapter 1).

10 Disconnect the accelerator cable, and Throttle Valve (TV) linkage/speed control cable from the engine (see Chapter 4).

6.6 Label each wire before unplugging the connector

11 Unbolt the power steering pump (see Chapter 10). Leave the lines/hoses attached and make sure the pump is kept in an upright position in the engine compartment (use wire or rope to restrain it out of the way).

12 On air conditioned models, unbolt the compressor (see Chapter 3) and set it aside. Do not disconnect the hoses.

13 Remove the air inlet tube.

14 On 4.6L engine models, remove the 42-pin connector from the retaining bracket on the vacuum booster and separate the 42-pin connector from the transmission harness and position it out of the way.

15 Drain the engine oil (see Chapter 1) and remove the filter.

16 Remove the starter motor (see Chapter 5).

17 Remove the alternator (see Chapter 5).

18 Unbolt the exhaust system from the engine (see Chapter 2, Part A or B, whichever applies to the engine being worked on).

19 If you're working on a model with an automatic transmission, remove the torque converter access cover and remove the torque converter-to-driveplate fasteners (see Chapter 7B).

20 Support the transmission with a jack. Position a block of wood between them to prevent damage to the transmission. Special transmission jacks with safety chains are available - use one if possible.

21 Attach an engine sling or a length of sturdy chain to the engine and then to the engine hoist.

➡**Note: Some engines have lifting brackets already installed on them, usually on the exhaust manifold studs. Other engines do not have them, but they are available separately from Ford dealer parts departments.**

22 Roll the hoist into position and connect the sling or chain to it. Take up the slack in the sling or chain, but don't lift the engine.

6.26 Use a prybar or a large screwdriver and pry the engine from the transmission bellhousing

❄❄ WARNING:

DO NOT place any part of your body under the engine when it's supported only by a hoist or other lifting device.

23 Remove the transmission-to-engine block bolts (see Chapter 7).

24 Remove the engine mount through-bolts or mounting stud nuts from both sides (see Chapter 2, Part A or B, depending which engine is being worked on).

25 Recheck to be sure nothing is still connecting the engine to the transmission or vehicle. Disconnect anything still remaining.

26 Raise the engine slightly. Carefully work it forward to separate it from the transmission (see illustration). If you're working on a vehicle with an automatic transmission, be sure the torque converter stays in the transmission (clamp a pair of vise-grips to the transmission housing to keep the converter from sliding out). Slowly raise the engine out of the engine compartment. Check carefully to make sure nothing is hanging up.

27 Remove the driveplate (see Part A or B of this Chapter).

28 Mount the engine on an engine stand (see illustration).

29 Once the engine is removed, support the transmission with a piece of pipe that crosses from side to side to hold the transmission as the floor jack is removed (see illustration).

INSTALLATION

30 Check the engine and transmission mounts. If they're worn or damaged, replace them.

31 Carefully lower the engine into the engine compartment - make sure the engine mounts line up.

32 Guide the torque converter into the crankshaft following the procedure outlined in Chapter 7B. Don't pull the converter away from the transmission; let the engine move back against the transmission.

33 Install the transmission-to-engine bolts and tighten them securely.

6.28 Use long, high-strength bolts (arrows) to hold the engine block on the engine stand - make sure they are tight before lowering the hoist and placing the entire weight of the engine on the stand

6.29 Use a piece of pipe to support the transmission once the engine has been removed, then remove the floor jack that supported the transmission during engine removal

❄❄ CAUTION:

DO NOT use the bolts to force the transmission and engine together!

34 Reinstall the remaining components in the reverse order of removal.

35 Add coolant and oil as needed. Run the engine and check for leaks and proper operation of all accessories, then install the hood and test drive the vehicle.

7 Engine rebuilding alternatives

The do-it-yourselfer is faced with a number of options when performing an engine overhaul. The decision to replace the engine block, piston/connecting rod assemblies and crankshaft depends on a number of factors, with the number one consideration being the condition of the block. Other considerations are cost, access to machine shop facilities, parts availability, time required to complete the project and the extent of prior mechanical experience on the part of the do-it-yourselfer.

Some of the rebuilding alternatives include:

Individual parts - If the inspection procedures reveal that the engine block and most engine components are in reusable condition, purchasing individual parts may be the most economical alternative. The block, crankshaft and piston/connecting rod assemblies should all be inspected carefully. Even if the block shows little wear, the cylinder bores should be surface honed.

Crankshaft kit - This rebuild package consists of a reground crankshaft and a matched set of pistons and connecting rods. The pistons will already be installed on the connecting rods. Piston rings and the necessary bearings will be included in the kit. These kits are commonly available for standard cylinder bores, as well as for engine blocks which have been bored to a regular oversize.

Short block - A short block consists of an engine block with a crankshaft and piston/connecting rod assemblies already installed. All new bearings are incorporated and all clearances will be correct. The existing cylinder head(s), camshaft, valve train components and external parts can be bolted to the short block with little or no machine shop work necessary.

Long block - A long block consists of a short block plus an oil pump, oil pan, cylinder head(s), valve cover(s), camshaft and valve train components, timing sprockets, belt or chain and timing cover. All components are installed with new bearings, seals and gaskets incorporated throughout. The installation of manifolds and external parts is all that is necessary.

Give careful thought to which alternative is best for you and discuss the situation with local automotive machine shops, auto parts dealers or parts store countermen before ordering or purchasing replacement parts.

8 Engine overhaul - disassembly sequence

❊❊ CAUTION:

The cylinder head bolts on the 5.0L and 4.6L engines are "torque-to-yield" bolts and are NOT reusable. A predetermined stretch of the bolt gives the even clamping load needed to seal the cylinders properly. Once removed they must be replaced. New head bolts are also recommended on V6 engines for maximum sealing potential.

1 It's much easier to disassemble and work on the engine if it's mounted on a portable engine stand. A stand can often be rented quite cheaply from an equipment rental yard. Before the engine is mounted on a stand, the flywheel/driveplate should be removed from the engine.

2 If a stand isn't available, it's possible to disassemble the engine with it blocked up on the floor. Be extra careful not to tip or drop the engine when working without a stand.

3 If you're going to obtain a rebuilt engine, all external components must come off first, to be transferred to the replacement engine, just as they will if you're doing a complete engine overhaul yourself. These include:

Alternator and brackets
Emissions control components
Distributor or camshaft position sensor (if equipped)
Spark plug wires and spark plugs
Thermostat and housing cover
Water pump
EFI components
Intake/exhaust manifolds
Oil filter (replace)
Engine mounts
Driveplate

Engine rear plate
Crankshaft damper

➡ **Note: When removing the external components from the engine, pay close attention to details that may be helpful or important during installation. Note the installed position of gaskets, seals, spacers, pins, brackets, washers, bolts and other small items.**

4 If you're obtaining a short block, which consists of the engine block, crankshaft, pistons and connecting rods all assembled, then the cylinder head(s), oil pan and oil pump will have to be removed as well. See *Engine rebuilding alternatives* for additional information regarding the different possibilities to be considered.

5 If you're planning a complete overhaul, the engine must be disassembled and the components removed in the following order:

Driveplate
Valve covers
Intake manifold
Exhaust manifolds
Rocker arms and pushrods (3.8L and 5.0L engines)
Camshafts and followers (4.6L engines)
Valve lifters (3.8L and 5.0L engines)
Vibration damper
Timing chain cover
Timing chain(s), sprockets, guides and tensioners
Camshaft (5.0L engines)
Valve lifters (4.6L engines)
Cylinder heads
Oil pan
Oil pump (replace)
Piston/connecting rod assemblies
Crankshaft and main bearings (replace)

6   Before beginning the disassembly and overhaul procedures, make sure the following items are available. Also, refer to *Engine overhaul - reassembly* sequence for a list of tools and materials needed for engine reassembly.

Common hand tools
Small cardboard boxes and plastic bags for storing parts
Gasket scraper
Ridge reamer
Vibration damper puller
Micrometers
Telescoping gauges
Dial indicator set
Valve spring compressor
Cylinder surfacing hone
Piston ring groove cleaning tool
Electric drill motor
Tap and die set
Wire brushes
Oil gallery brushes
Cleaning solvent

9   Cylinder head - disassembly

♦ **Refer to illustrations 9.1, 9.2 and 9.3**

➡**Note: New and rebuilt cylinder heads are commonly available for most engines at dealerships and auto parts stores. Due to the fact that some specialized tools are necessary for the disassembly and inspection procedures, and replacement parts may not be readily available, it may be more practical and economical for the home mechanic to purchase replacement head(s) rather than taking the time to disassemble, inspect and recondition the original(s). However, most machine shops will not have a core set of 4.6L DOHC cylinder heads, so chances are you will have to wait until the rebuilding work is done to your heads.**

1   Cylinder head disassembly involves removal of the intake and exhaust valves and related components. If they're still in place, remove the rocker arm nuts, pivot balls and rocker arms from the cylinder head studs. Label the parts or store them separately (see illustration) so they can be reinstalled in their original locations and in the same valve guides they are removed from.

2   Compress the springs on the first valve with a spring compressor and remove the keepers (see illustration). Carefully release the valve spring compressor and remove the retainer, sleeve (if used), the spring and the spring seat (if used).

3   Pull the valve out of the head, then remove the oil seal from the guide. If the valve binds in the guide (won't pull through), push it back into the head and deburr the area around the keeper groove with a fine file or whetstone (see illustration).

4   Repeat the procedure for the remaining valves. Remember to

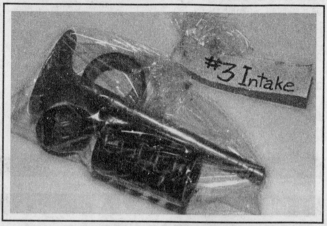

9.1 A small plastic bag, with an appropriate label, can be used to store the valve train components so they can be kept together and reinstalled in the original position

keep all the parts for each valve together so they can be reinstalled in the same locations.

5   Once the valves and related components have been removed and stored in an organized manner, the head should be thoroughly cleaned and inspected. If a complete engine overhaul is being done, finish the engine disassembly procedures before beginning the cylinder head cleaning and inspection process.

9.2 Use a valve spring compressor to compress the spring, then remove the keepers from the valve stem with needle-nose pliers or a magnet, as shown here on a 4.6L SOHC engine

9.3 If the valve won't pull through the guide, deburr the edge of the stem end and the area around the top of the keeper groove with a file or whetstone

10 Cylinder head - cleaning and inspection

1 Thorough cleaning of the cylinder head(s) and related valve train components, followed by a detailed inspection, will enable you to decide how much valve service work must be done during the engine overhaul.

➡ **Note: If the engine was severely overheated, the cylinder head is probably warped (see Step 12).**

CLEANING

2 Scrape all traces of old gasket material and sealing compound off the head gasket, intake manifold and exhaust manifold sealing surfaces. Be very careful not to gouge the cylinder head. Special gasket removal solvents that soften gaskets and make removal much easier are available at auto parts stores.

3 Remove all built up scale from the coolant passages.

4 Run a stiff wire brush through the various holes to remove deposits that may have formed in them.

5 Run an appropriate-size tap into each of the threaded holes to remove corrosion and thread sealant that may be present. If compressed air is available, use it to clear the holes of debris produced by this operation.

❊❊ WARNING:

Wear eye protection when using compressed air!

6 Clean the exhaust manifold stud threads, if equipped.

7 Clean the cylinder head with solvent and dry it thoroughly. Compressed air will speed the drying process and ensure that all holes and recessed areas are clean.

➡ **Note: Decarbonizing chemicals are available and may prove very useful when cleaning cylinder heads and valve train components. They are very caustic and should be used with caution. Be sure to follow the instructions on the container.**

8 Clean the valvetrain components with solvent and dry them thoroughly (don't mix them up during the cleaning process).

➡ **Note: Compressed air will speed the drying process and can be used to clean out the oil passages.**

9 Clean all the valve springs, spring seats, keepers and retainers with solvent and dry them thoroughly. Work the components from one valve at a time to avoid mixing up the parts.

10 Scrape off any heavy deposits that may have formed on the valves, then use a motorized wire brush to remove deposits from the valve heads and stems. Again, make sure the valves don't get mixed up.

INSPECTION

➡ **Note: Be sure to perform all of the following inspection procedures before concluding that machine shop work is required. Make a list of the items that need attention.**

Cylinder head

▸ **Refer to illustrations 10.12 and 10.14**

11 Inspect the head very carefully for cracks, evidence of coolant leakage and other damage. If cracks are found, check with an automotive machine shop concerning repair. If repair isn't possible, a new cylinder head should be obtained.

12 Using a straightedge and feeler gauge, check the head gasket mating surface for warpage (see illustration). Check the head both straight across and corner-to-corner. If the warpage exceeds the limit listed in this Chapter's Specifications, it can be resurfaced at an automotive machine shop.

➡ **Note: If the 5.0L cylinder heads are resurfaced, the intake manifold flanges will also require machining.**

13 Examine the valve seats in each of the combustion chambers. If they're pitted, cracked or burned, the head will require valve service that's beyond the scope of the home mechanic.

14 Check the valve stem-to-guide clearance by measuring the lateral movement of the valve stem with a dial indicator attached securely to the head (see illustration). The valve must be in the guide and approximately 1/16-inch off the seat. The total valve stem movement indicated by the gauge needle must be divided by two to obtain the actual

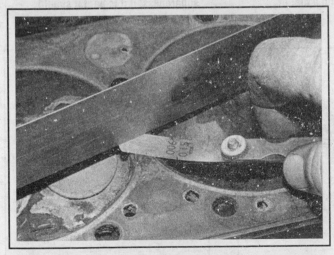

10.12 Check the cylinder head gasket surface for warpage by trying to slip a feeler gauge under the straightedge (see this Chapter's Specifications for the maximum warpage allowed and use a feeler gauge of that thickness)

10.14 Lay the head on its edge, pull each valve out about 1/8 inch, set up a dial indicator with the probe touching the valve stem, wiggle the valve and measure its movement

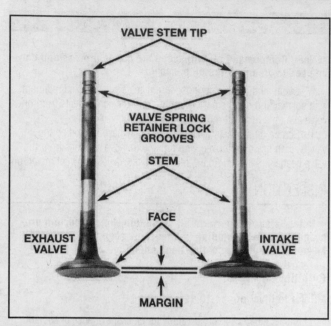

10.15 Check for valve wear at the points shown here

clearance. After this is done, if there's still some doubt regarding the condition of the valve guides they should be checked by an automotive machine shop (the cost should be minimal).

Valves

▶ **Refer to illustrations 10.15 and 10.16**

15 Carefully inspect each valve face for uneven wear, deformation, cracks, pits and burned areas (see illustration). Check the valve stem for scuffing and galling and the neck for cracks. Rotate the valve and check for any obvious indication that it's bent. Look for pits and excessive wear on the end of the stem. The presence of any of these conditions indicates the need for valve service by an automotive machine shop.

16 Measure the margin width on each valve (see illustration overleaf). Any valve with a margin narrower than 1/32-inch will have to be replaced with a new one.

Valve components

▶ **Refer to illustrations 10.17 and 10.18**

17 Check each valve spring for wear (on the ends) and pits. Measure the free length and compare it to the Specifications (see illustration). Any springs that are shorter than specified have sagged and should not

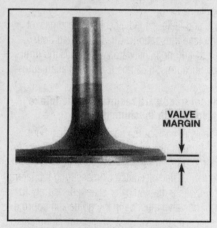

10.16 The margin width on each valve must be as specified (if no margin exists, the valve cannot be reused)

10.17 Measure the free length of each valve spring with a dial or vernier caliper

10.18 Check each valve spring for squareness; if it is bent it should be replaced

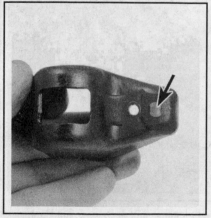

10.22a On 5.0L and 3.8L engines, check the rocker arms where the pushrod rides (arrow) . . .

10.22b . . . the fulcrum seats (arrows) in the top of the rocker arm . . .

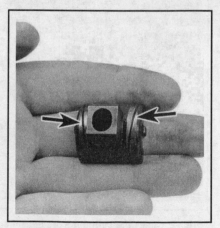

10.22c . . . and the fulcrums themselves for wear and galling (arrows)

be reused. The tension of all springs should be checked with a special fixture before deciding that they're suitable for use in a rebuilt engine (take the springs to an automotive machine shop for this check).

18 Stand each spring on a flat surface and check it for squareness (see illustration). If any of the springs are distorted or sagged, replace all of them with new parts.

19 Check the spring retainers and keepers for obvious wear and cracks. Any questionable parts should be replaced with new ones, as extensive damage will occur if they fail during engine operation.

Rocker arm components

♦ **Refer to illustrations 10.22a, 10.22b, 10.22c and 10.22d**

20 Clean all the parts thoroughly. Make sure all oil passages are open.

21 Check the rocker arm faces (the areas that contact the pushrod ends and valve stems) for pits, wear, galling, score marks and rough spots.

22 Check the rocker arm pivot contact areas and fulcrums. Look for cracks in each rocker arm and bolt (see illustrations).

23 Inspect the pushrod ends for scuffing and excessive wear. Roll each pushrod on a flat surface, like a piece of plate glass, to determine if it's bent.

24 Check the rocker arm studs in the cylinder heads (3.8L and 5.0L) for damaged threads and secure installation.

25 Any damaged or excessively worn parts must be replaced with new ones.

26 If the inspection process indicates that the valve components are in generally poor condition and worn beyond the limits specified, which is usually the case in an engine that's being overhauled, reassemble the valves in the cylinder head and refer to Section 11 for

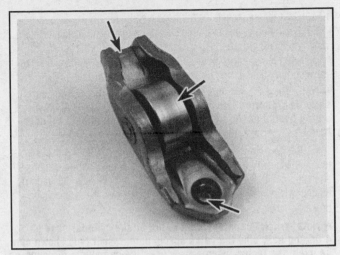

10.22d On 4.6L engines, check the rocker arms for wear (arrows) at the valve stem end, roller and the pocket that contacts the lash adjuster

valve servicing recommendations.

27 Clean all the parts thoroughly. Make sure all oil passages are open.

28 Any damaged or excessively worn parts must be replaced with new ones.

29 If the inspection process indicates that the valve components are in generally poor condition and worn beyond the limits specified, which is usually the case in an engine that's being overhauled, reassemble the valves in the cylinder head and refer to Section 11 for valve servicing recommendations.

11 Valves - servicing

1 Because of the complex nature of the job and the special tools and equipment needed, servicing of the valves, the valve seats and the valve guides, commonly known as a valve job, should be done by a professional.

2 The home mechanic can remove and disassemble the head, do the initial cleaning and inspection, then reassemble and deliver it to a dealer service department or an automotive machine shop for the actual service work. Doing the inspection will enable you to see what condition the head and valve train components are in and will ensure that you know what work and new parts are required when dealing with an automotive machine shop.

3 The dealer service department or automotive machine shop will

remove the valves and springs, recondition or replace the valves and valve seats, recondition the valve guides, check and replace the valve springs, spring retainers or rotators and keepers (as necessary), replace the valve seals with new ones, reassemble the valve components and make sure the installed spring height is correct. The cylinder head gasket surface will also be resurfaced if it's warped.

4 After the valve job has been performed by a professional, the head will be in like-new condition. When the head is returned, be sure to clean it again before installation on the engine to remove any metal particles and abrasive grit that may still be present from the valve service or head resurfacing operations. Use compressed air, if available, to blow out all the oil holes and passages.

12 Cylinder head - reassembly

♦ **Refer to illustrations 12.3a, 12.3b, 12.6, 12.7a, 12.7b and 12.9**

1 Regardless of whether or not the head was sent to an automotive repair shop for valve servicing, make sure it's clean before beginning reassembly.

2 If the head was sent out for valve servicing, the valves and related

components will already be in place. Begin the reassembly procedure with Step 9.

3 On all engines, lubricate and install the valves, then install new seals on each of the valve guides. Using a hammer and deep socket, gently tap each seal into place until it's seated on the guide (see illustrations). Don't twist or cock the seals during installation or they will not seat properly on the valve stems.

4   On 4.6L engines, reinstall the valve lifters.

5   Beginning at one end of the head, lubricate and install the first valve. Apply moly-base grease or clean engine oil to the valve stem.

6   Drop the spring seat or shim(s) over the valve guide and set the valve spring, retainer and sleeve (if used) in place.

➡**Note: On 4.6L engines, the valve seal has the spring seat/ shim incorporated into one piece (see illustration). A valve spring should never sit directly against an aluminum cylinder head.**

7   Apply a small dab of grease to each keeper to hold it in place (see illustration). Compress the springs with a valve spring compressor and carefully install the keepers in the upper groove (see illustration), then slowly release the compressor and make sure the keepers seat properly.

➡**Note: When the camshafts are not on the cylinder head on 4.6L engines, only the valve spring compressor type shown can be used; the factory compressor uses the camshafts for leverage and is used during disassembly only (see Part B of this Chapter).**

8   Repeat the procedure for the remaining valves. Be sure to return the components to their original locations - don't mix them up!

12.3a On pushrod models with the type of seal shown, use a hammer and a seal installer (or a deep socket, as shown here) to drive the seal onto the valve guide/head casting boss (umbrella-type seals don't need to be driven into place)

12.3b Installing a valve stem seal on a 4.6L engine - the socket must contact the flange (spring seat) of the seal

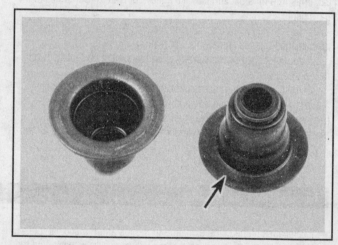

12.6 4.6L engines use valve stem seals that are a valve spring seat and seal combined into one part - make sure replacement parts are the same as the ones removed earlier

12.7a Apply a small dab of grease to each keeper as shown here before installation - it'll hold them in place on the valve stem as the spring is released

12.7b Compress the springs with a valve spring compressor and position the keepers in the upper groove, then slowly release the compressor and make sure the keepers seat properly

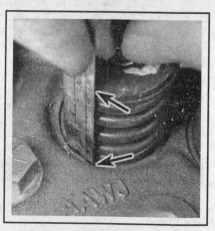

12.9 Valve spring installed height is the distance from the spring seat on the head to the bottom of the spring retainer

9   Check the installed valve spring height with a ruler graduated in 1/32-inch increments or a dial caliper. If the head was sent out for service work, the installed height should be correct (but don't automatically assume that it is). The measurement is taken from the top of each spring seat or shim(s) to the bottom of the retainer (see illustration). If the height is greater than the figure listed in this Chapter's Specifications, shims can be added under the springs to correct it.

10 Apply moly-base grease to the rocker arm faces and the fulcrums, then install the rocker arms and fulcrums on the cylinder head studs.

13 Pistons/connecting rods - removal

▶ **Refer to illustrations 13.1, 13.3, 13.4, 13.6a, 13.6b, 13.7 and 13.8**

➥**Note: Prior to removing the piston/connecting rod assemblies, remove the cylinder head(s), the oil pan and the oil pump (on 5.0L engines) by referring to the appropriate Sections in Chapter 2, Part A or Part B, depending which engine is being overhauled.**

13.1 A ridge reamer is required to remove the ridge from the top of each cylinder - do this before removing the pistons!

1   Use your fingernail to feel if a ridge has formed at the upper limit of ring travel (about 1/4-inch down from the top of each cylinder). If carbon deposits or cylinder wear have produced ridges, they must be completely removed with a special tool (see illustration). Follow the manufacturer's instructions provided with the tool. Failure to remove the ridges before attempting to remove the piston/connecting rod assemblies may result in piston breakage.

➥**Note: Do not let the tool cut into the ring travel area more than 1/32-inch.**

2   After the cylinder ridges have been removed, turn the engine upside-down so the crankshaft is facing up.

3   Before the connecting rods are removed, check the endplay with a dial indicator or with feeler gauges (see illustration). Slide them between the first connecting rod and the crankshaft throw until the play is removed. The endplay is equal to the thickness of the feeler gauge(s). If the endplay exceeds the service limit, new connecting rods will be required. If new rods (or a new crankshaft) are installed, the endplay may fall under the specified minimum (if it does, the rods will have to be machined to restore it - consult an automotive machine shop for advice if necessary). Repeat the procedure for the remaining connecting rods.

4   Check the connecting rods and caps for identification marks. If they aren't plainly marked, use a small center-punch, number stamping die (see illustration), or scribe, to make the appropriate number of indentations, or marks, on each rod and cap (1, 2, 3, etc., depending on the engine type and cylinder they're associated with).

13.3 Check the connecting rod side clearance (endplay) with a dial indicator or a feeler gauge

13.4 Mark the rod bearing caps in order from the front of the engine to the rear (numbers can be used or use one mark for the front cap, two for the second one and so on)

5   Loosen each of the connecting rod cap nuts 1/2-turn at a time until they can be removed by hand.

6   Remove the connecting rod cap and bearing insert (see illustrations). Don't drop the bearing insert out of the cap.

➡Note: The 4.6L engine uses a different method, referred to as "fractured cap method", to more accurately match the rod cap to the connecting rod. The mating line of the rod and cap (see illustration) is made by breaking ("fracturing") the cap from the rod. This is supposed to ensure a perfect match once reassembled with its corresponding rod.

7   If the connecting rod has studs with attaching nuts (rather than cap bolts as shown in illustration 13.6a) slip a short length of plastic or rubber hose over each connecting rod cap bolt to protect the crankshaft journal and cylinder wall as the piston is removed (see illustration).

8   Remove the bearing insert and push the connecting rod/piston assembly out through the top of the engine. Use a wooden or plastic hammer handle to push on the upper bearing surface in the connecting rod (see illustration). If resistance is felt, double-check to make sure that all of the ridge was removed from the cylinder.

9   Repeat the procedure for the remaining cylinders.

10   After removal, reassemble the connecting rod caps and bearing inserts in their respective connecting rods and install the cap nuts finger tight. Leaving the old bearing inserts in place until reassembly will

13.6a Remove the rod and bearing insert together

help prevent the connecting rod bearing surfaces from being accidentally nicked or gouged.

11   Don't separate the pistons from the connecting rods (see Section 18 for additional information).

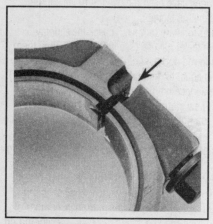

13.6b On 4.6L engine connecting rods the method used to manufacture and machine the rod cap is unique; they "fracture" (break) the cap from the rod to give a perfect match upon reassembly

13.7 To prevent damage to the crankshaft journals and cylinder walls, slip sections of hose over the rod bolts (if assembled with this type of rod nut and bolt) before removing the piston/rod assemblies

13.8 Use a hammer handle to drive the piston and connecting assembly down and out of the cylinder block, being very careful not to nick the crankshaft on the way out

14   Crankshaft - removal

▶ Refer to illustrations 14.1, 14.3 and 14.4

➡Note: The crankshaft can be removed only after the engine has been removed from the vehicle. It's assumed that the flywheel or driveplate, vibration damper, timing chain(s) or gears, oil pan, oil pump and piston/connecting rod assemblies have already been removed.

1   Before the crankshaft removal procedure is started, check the endplay. Mount a dial indicator with the stem in line with the crankshaft and just touching the end of the crankshaft (see illustration).

2   Push the crankshaft all the way to the rear and zero the dial indicator. Next, pry the crankshaft to the front as far as possible and check the reading on the dial indicator. The distance that it moves is the endplay. If it's greater than limit listed in this Chapter's Specifications, check the crankshaft thrust surfaces for wear. If no wear is evident, new main bearings should correct the endplay.

3   If a dial indicator isn't available, feeler gauges can be used. Gently pry or push the crankshaft all the way to the front of the engine. Slip feeler gauges between the crankshaft and the front face of the thrust main bearing to determine the clearance (see illustration).

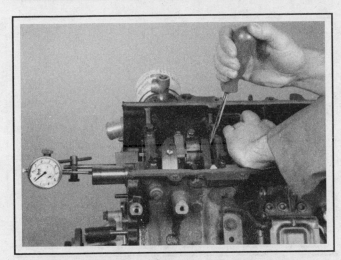

14.1 Checking crankshaft endplay with a dial indicator

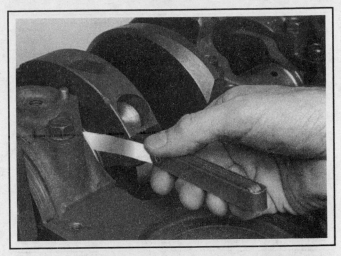

14.3 Checking crankshaft endplay with a feeler gauge

4   Check the main bearing caps to see if they're marked to indicate their locations (see illustration). They should be numbered consecutively from the front of the engine to the rear. If they aren't, mark them with number stamping dies or a center-punch. Main bearing caps generally have a cast-in arrow, which points to the front of the engine.

3.8L AND 5.0L ENGINES

➡Note: The thrust bearing on the 3.8L and 5.0L engines is the number three main bearing cap location. It has an upper and lower thrust bearing shell.

5   Loosen the main bearing cap bolts 1/4-turn at a time each, until they can be removed by hand. Note if any stud bolts are used and make sure they're returned to their original locations when the crankshaft is reinstalled.

4.6L ENGINES

▶ Refer to illustrations 14.6a, 14.6b, 14.7 and 14.8

6   The 4.6L engines have a more complex crankshaft removal and assembly procedure than 5.0L engines because of the number of bolts used to fasten the main cap to the cylinder block (see illustrations). On 4.6L SOHC models, there are two main cap bolts, two jack screws and two side bolts on each of the number one through number four main

14.4 The main bearing caps are usually marked to indicate their locations (arrows). They should be numbered consecutively from the front of the engine to the rear

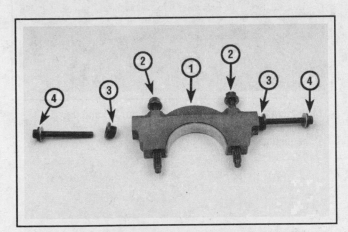

14.6a 4.6 SOHC engines use main bearing caps that are fastened to the block through the use of a set of bolts and specific adjustment procedures

1 Main bearing cap
2 Main bearing bolts
3 Jack screws (left handed thread)
4 Side bolts

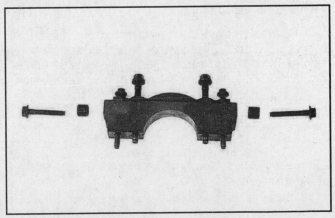

14.6b Main cap bolt arrangement, 4.6L DOHC - there are four vertical bolts

14.7 Remove the side bolts - 4.6L

14.8 Following the reverse order of the tightening sequence (see Section 23), remove the main bearing cap bolts, loosening them 1/4 turn at a time until they can be removed by hand

caps. The 4.6L DOHC engine has four vertical fasteners, (including studs used on four of the caps), along with the same side bolts and adjusting screws as the SOHC engine.

➡ **Note: The number five main bearing cap is the thrust bearing location and has upper and lower thrust bearing halves. It is bolted to the block with two main cap bolts; no jack screws or side bolts are used, although it is drilled for jack screws. It is extremely important to follow the removal and the installation procedure to ensure correct assembly and operation.**

7   Remove all side bolts (see illustration), and back off the adjusting screws on the sides. Follow the reverse of the tightening sequences (see Section 23).

8   Remove the main bearing cap bolts (see illustration).

❋❋ **CAUTION:**

The main bearing cap bolts are "torque-to-yield" bolts and are NOT reusable. A pre-determined stretch of the bolt, calculated by the manufacturer, gives the added rigidity required with this cylinder block. Once removed they must be replaced. The side bolts and jack screws are reusable.

ALL ENGINES

▶ **Refer to illustration 14.9**

9   Gently tap the caps with a soft-face hammer, then separate them from the engine block. If necessary, use the bolts as levers to remove the caps. Try not to drop the bearing inserts if they come out with the caps. All main caps should have an arrow cast in to indicate the front

of the engine, and a number to indicate which position they have on the block. On 4.6L engines, the number is stamped in on the left side of the cap (see illustration).

10   Carefully lift the crankshaft out of the engine. It may be a good idea to have an assistant available, since the crankshaft is quite heavy. With the bearing inserts in place in the engine block and main bearing caps, return the caps to their respective locations on the engine block and tighten the bolts finger tight.

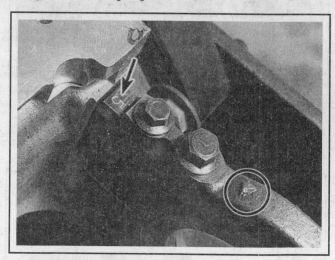

14.9 Main caps should be numbered (arrow) and have an indicator (circle) of the direction facing the front of the engine

15 Engine block - cleaning

▶ Refer to illustrations 15.1a, 15.1b, 15.8 and 15.10

❋❋ CAUTION:

The core plugs (also known as freeze plugs or soft plugs) may be difficult or impossible to retrieve if they're driven into the block coolant passages.

1   Using the wide end of a punch (see illustration) tap in on the outer edge of the core plug to turn the plug sideways in the bore. Then, using a pair of pliers, pull the core plug from the engine block (see illustration). Don't worry about the condition of the old core plugs as they are being removed because they will be replaced on reassembly with new plugs.

2   Using a gasket scraper, remove all traces of gasket material from the engine block. Be very careful not to nick or gouge the gasket sealing surfaces.

3   Remove the main bearing caps and separate the bearing inserts from the caps and the engine block (see Section 14). Tag the bearings, indicating which cylinder they were removed from and whether they were in the cap or the block, then set them aside.

4   Remove all of the threaded oil gallery plugs from the block. The plugs are usually very tight - they may have to be drilled out and the holes re-tapped. Use new plugs when the engine is reassembled.

5   If the engine is extremely dirty it should be taken to an automotive machine shop to be steam cleaned or hot tanked.

6   After the block is returned, clean all oil holes and oil galleries one more time. Brushes specifically designed for this purpose are available at most auto parts stores. Flush the passages with warm water until the water runs clear, dry the block thoroughly and wipe all machined surfaces with a light, rust preventive oil. If you have access to compressed air, use it to speed the drying process and to blow out all the oil holes and galleries.

❋❋ WARNING:

Wear eye protection when using compressed air!

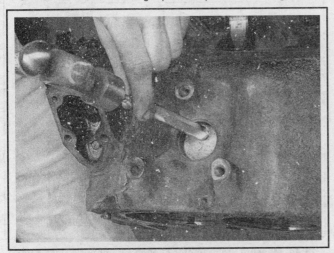

15.1a A hammer and a large punch can be used to knock the core plugs sideways in their bores

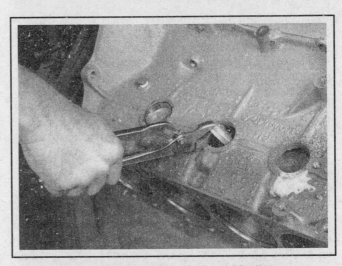

15.1b Pull the core plugs from the block with pliers

15.8 All bolt holes in the block - particularly the main bearing cap and head bolt holes - should be cleaned and restored with a tap (be sure to remove debris from the holes after this is done)

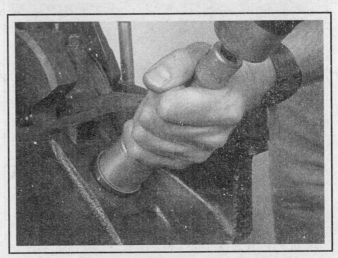

15.10 A large socket on an extension can be used to drive the new core plugs into the bores

7   If the block isn't extremely dirty or sludged up, you can do an adequate cleaning job with hot soapy water and a stiff brush. Take plenty of time and do a thorough job. Regardless of the cleaning method used, be sure to clean all oil holes and galleries very thoroughly, dry the block completely and coat all machined surfaces with light oil.

8   The threaded holes in the block must be clean to ensure accurate torque readings during reassembly. Run the proper size tap into each of the holes to remove rust, corrosion, thread sealant or sludge and restore damaged threads (see illustration). If possible, use compressed air to clear the holes of debris produced by this operation. Now is a good time to clean the threads on the head bolts and the main bearing cap bolts as well.

9   Reinstall the main bearing caps and tighten all bolts finger tight.

10 After coating the sealing surfaces of the new core plugs with Permatex no. 2 sealant, install them in the engine block (see illustration). Make sure they're driven in straight and seated properly or leakage could result. Special tools are available for this purpose, but a large socket, with an outside diameter that will just slip into the core plug, a 1/2-inch drive extension and a hammer will work just as well.

11 Apply non-hardening sealant (such as Permatex no. 2 or Teflon pipe sealant) to the new oil gallery plugs and thread them into the holes in the block. Make sure they're tightened securely.

12 If the engine isn't going to be reassembled right away, cover it with a large plastic trash bag to keep it clean.

16 Engine block - inspection

▶ **Refer to illustrations 16.4a, 16.4b and 16.4c**

1   Before the block is inspected, it should be cleaned as described in Section 15.

2   Visually check the block for cracks, rust and corrosion. Look for stripped threads in the threaded holes. It's also a good idea to have the block checked for hidden cracks by an automotive machine shop that has the special equipment to do this type of work. If defects are found, have the block repaired, if possible, or replaced.

3   Check the cylinder bores for scuffing and scoring.

4   Check the cylinders for taper and out-of-round conditions as follows (see illustrations).

5   Measure the diameter of each cylinder at the top (just under the ridge area), center and bottom of the cylinder bore, parallel to the crankshaft axis.

6   Next measure each cylinder's diameter at the same three locations perpendicular to the crankshaft axis.

7   The taper of the cylinder is the difference between the bore diameter at the top of the cylinder and the diameter at the bottom. The out-of-round specification of the cylinder bore is the difference between the parallel and perpendicular readings. Compare your results to those listed in this Chapter's Specifications.

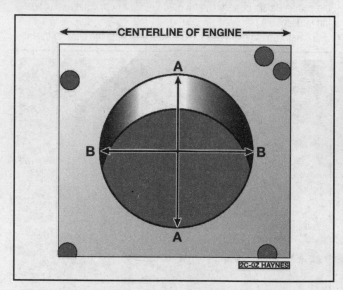

16.4a Measure the diameter of each cylinder at a right angle to the engine centerline (A), and parallel to engine centerline (B) - out-of-round is the difference between A and B; taper is the difference between A and B at the top of the cylinder and A and B at the bottom of the cylinder

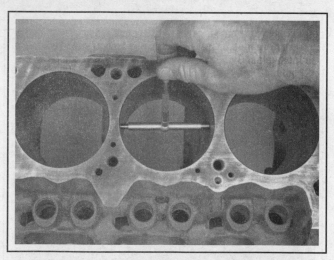

16.4b The ability to "feel" when the telescoping gauge is at the correct point will be developed over time, so work slowly and repeat the check until you're satisfied the bore measurement is accurate

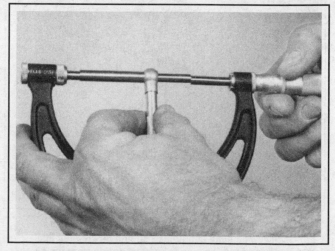

16.4c The gauge is then measured with a micrometer to determine the bore size

8   Repeat the procedure for the remaining pistons and cylinders.

9   If the cylinder walls are badly scuffed or scored, or if they're out-of-round or tapered beyond the limits given in this Chapter's Specifications, have the engine block rebored and honed at an automotive machine shop. If a rebore is done, oversize pistons and rings will be required.

10 If the cylinders are in reasonably good condition and not worn to the outside of the limits, and if the piston-to-cylinder clearances can be maintained properly, then they don't have to be rebored. Honing is all that's necessary (see Section 17).

17 Cylinder honing

▶ **Refer to illustrations 17.3a and 17.3b**

1   Prior to engine reassembly, the cylinder bores must be honed so the new piston rings will seat correctly and provide the best possible combustion chamber seal.

➡**Note: If you don't have the tools or don't want to tackle the honing operation, most automotive machine shops will do it for a reasonable fee.**

2   Before honing the cylinders, install the main bearing caps and tighten the bolts to the torque listed in this Chapter's Specifications. Make sure you use only the original main cap bolts, not the new ones for final assembly.

3   Two types of cylinder hones are commonly available - the flex hone or "bottle brush" type and the more traditional surfacing hone with spring-loaded stones. Both will do the job, but for the less experienced mechanic the "bottle brush" hone will probably be easier to use. You'll also need some kerosene or honing oil, rags and an electric drill motor. Proceed as follows:

a) *Mount the hone in the drill motor, compress the stones and slip it into the first cylinder (see illustration). Be sure to wear safety goggles or a face shield!*

b) *Lubricate the cylinder with plenty of honing oil, turn on the drill and move the hone up-and-down in the cylinder at a pace that will produce a fine crosshatch pattern on the cylinder walls. Ideally, the crosshatch lines should intersect at approximately a 60-degree angle (see illustration). Be sure to use plenty of lubricant and don't take off any more material than is absolutely necessary to produce the desired finish.*

➡**Note: Piston ring manufacturers may specify a smaller cross-hatch angle than the traditional 60-degrees - read and follow any instructions included with the new rings.**

c) *Don't withdraw the hone from the cylinder while it's running. Instead, shut off the drill and continue moving the hone up-and-down in the cylinder until it comes to a complete stop, then compress the stones and withdraw the hone. If you're using a "bottle brush" type hone, stop the drill motor, then turn the chuck in the normal direction of rotation while withdrawing the hone from the cylinder.*

d) *Wipe the oil out of the cylinder and repeat the procedure for the remaining cylinders.*

4   After the honing job is complete, chamfer the top edges of the cylinder bores with a small file so the rings won't catch when the pistons are installed. Be very careful not to nick the cylinder walls with the end of the file.

5   The entire engine block must be washed again very thoroughly with warm, soapy water to remove all traces of the abrasive grit produced during the honing operation.

➡**Note: The bores can be considered clean when a lint-free white cloth - dampened with clean engine oil - used to wipe them out doesn't pick-up any more honing residue, which will show up as gray areas on the cloth. Be sure to run a brush through all oil holes and galleries and flush them with running water.**

6   After rinsing, dry the block and apply a coat of light rust preventive oil to all machined surfaces. Wrap the block in a plastic trash bag to keep it clean and set it aside until reassembly.

17.3a A "bottle brush" hone will produce better results if you've never honed cylinders before

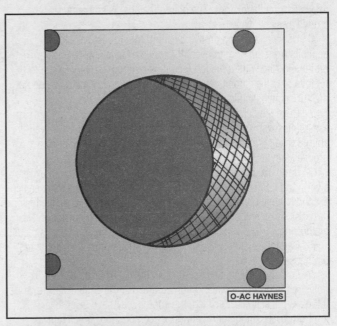

17.3b The cylinder hone should leave a smooth, crosshatch pattern with the lines intersecting at approximately a 60- degree angle

18 Pistons/connecting rods - inspection

18.4a The piston ring grooves can be cleaned with a special tool, as shown here . . .

18.4b . . . or a section of a broken ring

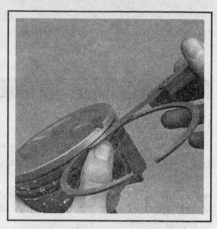

18.10 Check the ring side clearance with a feeler gauge at several points around the groove

▶ Refer to illustrations 18.4a, 18.4b, 18.10 and 18.11

1 Before the inspection process can be carried out, the piston/connecting rod assemblies must be cleaned and the original piston rings removed from the pistons.

➡ Note: Always use new piston rings when the engine is reassembled.

2 Using a piston ring installation tool, carefully remove the rings from the pistons (see illustration 22.11). Be careful not to nick or gouge the pistons in the process.

3 Scrape all traces of carbon from the top of the piston. A hand-held wire brush or a piece of fine emery cloth can be used once the majority of the deposits have been scraped away. Do not, under any circumstances, use a wire brush mounted in a drill motor to remove deposits from the pistons. The piston material is soft and may be eroded away by the wire brush.

4 Use a piston ring groove cleaning tool to remove carbon deposits from the ring grooves. If a tool isn't available, a piece broken off the old ring will do the job (see illustrations). Be very careful to remove only the carbon deposits - don't remove any metal and do not nick or scratch the sides of the ring grooves.

5 Once the deposits have been removed, clean the piston/rod assemblies with solvent and dry them with compressed air (if available). Make sure the oil return holes in the back sides of the ring grooves are clear.

6 If the pistons and cylinder walls aren't damaged or worn excessively, and if the engine block is not rebored, new pistons won't be necessary. Normal piston wear appears as even vertical wear on the piston thrust surfaces and slight looseness of the top ring in its groove. New piston rings, however, should always be used when an engine is rebuilt.

7 Carefully inspect each piston for cracks around the skirt, at the pin bosses and at the ring lands.

8 Look for scoring and scuffing on the thrust faces of the skirt, holes in the piston crown and burned areas at the edge of the crown. If the skirt is scored or scuffed, the engine may have been suffering from overheating and/or abnormal combustion, which caused excessively high operating temperatures. The cooling and lubrication systems should be checked thoroughly. A hole in the piston crown is an indication that abnormal combustion (pre-ignition) was occurring.

Burned areas at the edge of the piston crown are usually evidence of spark knock (detonation). If any of the above problems exist, the causes must be corrected or the damage will occur again. The causes may include intake air leaks, incorrect fuel/air mixture, incorrect ignition timing and EGR system malfunctions.

9 Corrosion of the piston, in the form of small pits, indicates that coolant is leaking into the combustion chamber and/or the crankcase. Again, the cause must be corrected or the problem may persist in the rebuilt engine.

10 Measure the piston ring side clearance by laying a new piston ring in each ring groove and slipping a feeler gauge in beside it (see illustration). Check the clearance at three or four locations around each groove. Be sure to use the correct ring for each groove - they are different. If the side clearance is greater than the figure listed in this Chapter's Specifications, new pistons will have to be used.

11 Check the piston-to-bore clearance by measuring the bore (see Section 16) and the piston diameter. Make sure the pistons and bores are correctly matched. Measure the piston across the skirt, at a 90-degree angle to, and in line with, the piston pin (see illustration). Sub-

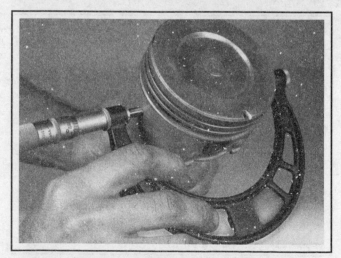

18.11 Measure the piston diameter at a 90-degree angle to the piston pin and in line with it

tract the piston diameter from the bore diameter to obtain the clearance. If it's greater than specified, the block will have to be rebored and new pistons and rings installed.

12 Check the piston-to-rod clearance by twisting the piston and rod in opposite directions. Any noticeable play indicates excessive wear, which must be corrected. The piston/connecting rod assemblies should be taken to an automotive machine shop to have the pistons and rods resized and new pins installed.

13 If the pistons must be removed from the connecting rods for any reason, they should be taken to an automotive machine shop. While they are there have the connecting rods checked for bend and twist,

since automotive machine shops have special equipment for this purpose.

➡ **Note: Unless new pistons and/or connecting rods must be installed, do not disassemble the pistons and connecting rods.**

14 Check the connecting rods for cracks and other damage. Temporarily remove the rod caps, lift out the old bearing inserts, wipe the rod and cap bearing surfaces clean and inspect them for nicks, gouges and scratches. After checking the rods, replace the old bearings, slip the caps into place and tighten the nuts finger tight.

➡ **Note: If the engine is being rebuilt because of a connecting rod knock, be sure to install new rods.**

19 Crankshaft - inspection

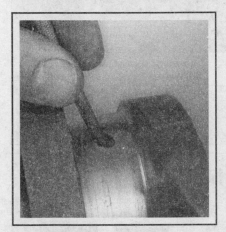

19.1 The oil holes should be chamfered so sharp edges don't gouge or scratch the new bearings

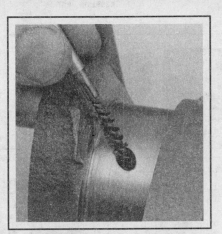

19.2 Use a wire or stiff plastic bristle brush to clean the oil passages in the crankshaft

19.5 Measure the diameter of each crankshaft journal at several points to detect taper and out-of-round conditions

▶ **Refer to illustrations 19.1, 19.2, 19.5 and 19.7**

1   Remove all burrs from the crankshaft oil holes with a stone, file or scraper (see illustration).

2   Clean the crankshaft with solvent and dry it with compressed air (if available). Be sure to clean the oil holes with a stiff brush (see illustration) and flush them with solvent.

3   Check the main and connecting rod bearing journals for uneven wear, scoring, pits and cracks.

4   Check the rest of the crankshaft for cracks and other damage. It should be magnafluxed to reveal hidden cracks - an automotive machine shop will handle the procedure.

5   Using a micrometer, measure the diameter of the main and connecting rod journals and compare the results to this Chapter's Specifications (see illustration). By measuring the diameter at a number of points around each journal's circumference, you'll be able to determine whether or not the journal is out-of-round. Take the measurement at each end of the journal, near the crank throws, to determine if the journal is tapered.

6   If the crankshaft journals are damaged, tapered, out-of-round or worn beyond the limits given in the Specifications, have the crankshaft reground by an automotive machine shop. Be sure to use the correct size bearing inserts if the crankshaft is reconditioned.

7   Check the oil seal journals at each end of the crankshaft for wear and damage. If the seal has worn a groove in the journal, or if it's nicked or scratched (see illustration), the new seal may leak when the

engine is reassembled. In some cases, an automotive machine shop may be able to repair the journal by pressing on a thin sleeve. If repair isn't feasible, a new or different crankshaft should be installed.

8   Refer to Section 20 and examine the main and rod bearing inserts.

19.7 If the seals have worn grooves in the crankshaft journals, or if the seal contact surfaces are nicked or scratched, the new seals will leak

ENGINE BEARING ANALYSIS

Debris

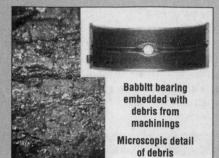

Babbitt bearing embedded with debris from machinings

Microscopic detail of debris

Microscopic detail of gouges

Overplated copper alloy bearing gouged by cast iron debris

Aluminum bearing embedded with glass beads

Microscopic detail of glass beads

Damaged lining caused by dirt left on the bearing back

Misassembly

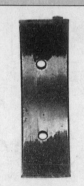

Result of a lower half assembled as an upper - blocking the oil flow

Excessive oil clearance is indicated by a short contact arc

Polished and oil-stained backs are a result of a poor fit in the housing bore

Result of a wrong, reversed, or shifted cap

Overloading

Damage from excessive idling which resulted in an oil film unable to support the load imposed

Damaged upper connecting rod bearings caused by engine lugging; the lower main bearings (not shown) were similarly affected

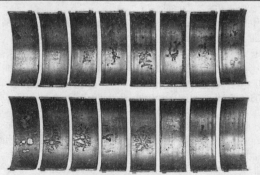

The damage shown in these upper and lower connecting rod bearings was caused by engine operation at a higher-than-rated speed under load

Misalignment

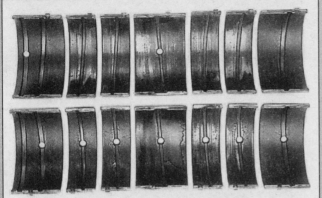

A poorly finished crankshaft caused the equally spaced scoring shown

A tapered housing bore caused the damage along one edge of this pair

A bent connecting rod led to the damage in the "V" pattern

A warped crankshaft caused this pattern of severe wear in the center, diminishing toward the ends

Corrosion

Microscopic detail of corrosion

Corrosion is an acid attack on the bearing lining generally caused by inadequate maintenance, extremely hot or cold operation, or interior oils or fuels

Lubrication

Result of dry start: The bearings on the left, farthest from the oil pump, show more damage

Microscopic detail of cavitation

Example of cavitation - a surface erosion caused by pressure changes in the oil film

Result of a low oil supply or oil starvation

Severe wear as a result of inadequate oil clearance

Damage from excessive thrust or insufficient axial clearance

Bearing affected by oil dilution caused by excessive blow-by or a rich mixture

20 Main and connecting rod bearings - inspection

♦ **Refer to illustration 20.1**

1 Even though the main and connecting rod bearings should be replaced with new ones during the engine overhaul, the old bearings should be retained for close examination, as they may reveal valuable information about the condition of the engine (see illustration).

2 Bearing failure occurs because of lack of lubrication, the presence of dirt or other foreign particles, overloading the engine and corrosion. Regardless of the cause of bearing failure, it must be corrected before the engine is reassembled to prevent it from happening again.

3 When examining the bearings, remove them from the engine block, the main bearing caps, the connecting rods and the rod caps and lay them out on a clean surface in the same general position as their location in the engine. This will enable you to match any bearing problems with the corresponding crankshaft journal.

4 Dirt and other foreign particles get into the engine in a variety of ways. It may be left in the engine during assembly, or it may pass through filters or the PCV system. It may get into the oil, and from there into the bearings. Metal chips from machining operations and normal engine wear are often present. Abrasives are sometimes left in engine components after reconditioning, especially when parts are not thoroughly cleaned using the proper cleaning methods. Whatever the source, these foreign objects often end up embedded in the soft bearing material and are easily recognized. Large particles will not embed in the bearing and will score or gouge the bearing and journal. The best prevention for this cause of bearing failure is to clean all parts thoroughly and keep everything spotlessly clean during engine assembly. Frequent and regular engine oil and filter changes are also recommended.

5 Lack of lubrication (or lubrication breakdown) has a number of interrelated causes. Excessive heat (which thins the oil), overloading (which squeezes the oil from the bearing face) and oil leakage or throw off (from excessive bearing clearances, worn oil pump or high engine speeds) all contribute to lubrication breakdown. Blocked oil passages, which usually are the result of misaligned oil holes in a bearing shell, will also oil starve a bearing and destroy it. When lack of lubrication is the cause of bearing failure, the bearing material is wiped or extruded from the steel backing of the bearing. Temperatures may increase to the point where the steel backing turns blue from overheating.

6 Driving habits can have a definite effect on bearing life. Low

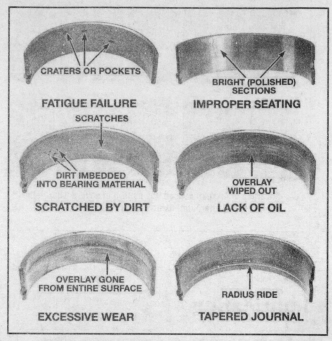

20.1 Typical bearing failures

speed operation in too high a gear (lugging the engine) puts very high loads on bearings, which tends to squeeze out the oil film. These loads cause the bearings to flex, which produces fine cracks in the bearing face (fatigue failure). Eventually the bearing material will loosen in pieces and tear away from the steel backing. Short trip driving leads to corrosion of bearings because insufficient engine heat is produced to drive off the condensed water and corrosive gases. These products collect in the engine oil, forming acid and sludge. As the oil is carried to the engine bearings, the acid attacks and corrodes the bearing material.

7 Incorrect bearing installation during engine assembly will lead to bearing failure as well. Tight fitting bearings leave insufficient bearing oil clearance and will result in oil starvation. Dirt or foreign particles trapped behind a bearing insert result in high spots on the bearing which lead to failure.

21 Engine overhaul - reassembly sequence

1 Before beginning engine reassembly, make sure you have all the necessary new parts (including new head bolts, rod bolts and main cap bolts on 4.6L engines), gaskets and seals as well as the following items on hand:

Common hand tools
A 1/2-inch drive torque wrench
A 3/8-inch drive torque wrench (inch-lb. measurement)
Piston ring installation tool
Piston ring compressor
Vibration damper installation tool
Short lengths of rubber or plastic hose to fit over connecting rod bolts (pushrod engines)
Connecting rod guide bolts (4.6L engines)
Plastigage
Feeler gauges
A fine-tooth file
New engine oil
Engine assembly lube or moly-base grease
Gasket sealant
Thread locking compound

2 In order to save time and avoid problems, engine reassembly must be done in the following general order:

3.8L and 5.0L engines

New camshaft bearings (recommended to be done by an automotive machine shop)

Piston rings
Crankshaft and main bearings

Piston/connecting rod assemblies
Oil pump
Oil pan
Camshaft
Valve lifters
Timing chain and sprockets
Timing chain cover
Cylinder heads
Rocker arms and pushrods
Intake and exhaust manifolds
Valve covers
Driveplate

4.6L engines

Piston rings

Crankshaft and main bearings
Piston/connecting rod assemblies
Oil pump
Oil pan
Cylinder heads
Valve lifters
Rocker arms
Camshaft(s)
Camshaft cap cluster assemblies
Timing chains and sprockets
Timing chain guides and tensioners
Timing chain cover
Intake and exhaust manifolds
Valve covers
Driveplate

22 Piston rings - installation

▶ **Refer to illustrations 22.3, 22.4, 22.8a, 22.8b and 22.11**

1   Before installing the new piston rings, the ring end gaps must be checked. It's assumed that the piston ring side clearance has been checked and verified correct (see Section 18).

2   Lay out the piston/connecting rod assemblies and the new ring sets so the ring sets will be matched with the same piston and cylinder during the end gap measurement and engine assembly.

3   Insert the top (number one) ring into the first cylinder and square it up with the cylinder walls by pushing it in with the top of the piston (see illustration). The ring should be near the bottom of the cylinder, at the lower limit of ring travel.

4   To measure the end gap, slip feeler gauges between the ends of the ring until a gauge equal to the gap width is found (see illustra-tion). The feeler gauge should slide between the ring ends with a slight amount of drag. Compare the measurement to this Chapter's Specifications. If the gap is larger or smaller than specified, double-check to make sure you have the correct rings before proceeding. If there is any doubt contact the parts store where the rings were purchased, to verify that the correct ring set is being used.

5   Excess end gap isn't critical unless it's greater than 0.040-inch. Again, double-check to make sure you have the correct rings for your engine.

6   Repeat the procedure for each ring that will be installed in the first cylinder and for each ring in the remaining cylinders. Remember to keep rings, pistons and cylinders matched up.

7   Once the ring end gaps have been checked/corrected, the rings can be installed on the pistons.

22.3 When checking piston ring end gap, the ring must be square in the cylinder bore (this is done by pushing the ring down with the top of a piston as shown)

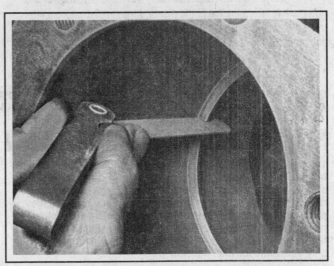

22.4 With the ring square in the cylinder, measure the end gap with a feeler gauge

22.8a Installing the spacer/expander in the oil control ring groove . . .

22.8b . . . followed by the side rails - DO NOT use a piston ring installation tool when installing the oil ring side rails

8   The oil control ring (lowest one on the piston) is usually installed first. It's composed of three separate components. Slip the spacer/expander into the groove (see illustration). Next, install the lower side rail. Don't use a piston ring installation tool on the oil ring side rails, as they may be damaged. Instead, place one end of the side rail into the groove between the spacer/expander and the ring land, hold it firmly in place and slide a finger around the piston while pushing the rail into the groove (see illustration). Next, install the upper side rail in the same manner.

9   After the three oil ring components have been installed, check to make sure that both the upper and lower side rails can be turned smoothly in the ring groove.

10   The number two (middle) ring is installed next. It's usually stamped with a mark which must face up, toward the top of the piston.

➠**Note: Always follow the instructions printed on the ring package or box - different manufacturers may require different approaches. Do not mix up the top and middle rings, as they have different cross sections.**

11   Use a piston ring installation tool and make sure the identification mark is facing the top of the piston, then slip the ring into the middle groove on the piston (see illustration). Don't expand the ring any more than necessary to slide it over the piston.

12   Install the number one (top) ring in the same manner. Make sure

22.11 Installing the compressor rings with a ring expander - the mark (arrow) must face up

the mark is facing up. Be careful not to confuse the number one and number two rings.

13   Repeat the procedure for the remaining pistons and rings.

23   Crankshaft - installation and main bearing oil clearance check

✳✳ CAUTION:

The main bearing cap bolts on the 4.6L engine are all "torque-to-yield" bolts and are NOT reusable. A pre-determined stretch of the bolt, calculated by the manufacturer, gives the added rigidity required with this cylinder block. Once removed they must be replaced with new bolts. The main cap side bolts and jack screws are reusable. During clearance checks using Plastigage, use the old bolts and torque to Specifications, but use only new bolts for final assembly.

1   Crankshaft installation is the first step in engine reassembly. It's assumed at this point that the engine block and crankshaft have been cleaned, inspected and repaired or reconditioned.

2   Position the engine with the bottom facing up.

3   Remove the main bearing cap bolts and lift out the caps. Lay

them out in the proper order to ensure correct installation.

4   If they're still in place, remove the original bearing inserts from the block and the main bearing caps. Wipe the bearing surfaces of the block and caps with a clean, lint-free cloth. They must be kept spotlessly clean.

MAIN BEARING OIL CLEARANCE CHECK

▶ **Refer to illustrations 23.11, 23.12 and 23.15**

5   Clean the back sides of the new main bearing inserts and lay one in each main bearing saddle in the block. If one of the bearing inserts from each set has a large groove in it, make sure the grooved insert is installed in the block. Lay the other bearing from each set in the corresponding main bearing cap. Make sure the tab on the bearing insert fits into the recess in the block or cap.

23.11 Lay the Plastigage strips (arrow) on the main bearing journals, parallel to the crankshaft centerline

23.12 On 4.6L engines tap the main caps down with a brass hammer before installing any top or side bolts - the cap must be square to the block before tapping it down

❋❋ CAUTION:

The oil holes in the block must line up with the oil holes in the bearing insert. Do not hammer the bearing into place and don't nick or gouge the bearing faces. No lubrication should be used at this time.

6   The flanged thrust bearing must be installed in the third cap and saddle on 3.8L or 5.0L engines, or the fifth cap and saddle on 4.6L engines.

7   Clean the faces of the bearings in the block and the crankshaft main bearing journals with a clean, lint-free cloth.

8   Check or clean the oil holes in the crankshaft, as any dirt here can go only one way - straight through the new bearings.

9   Once you're certain the crankshaft is clean, carefully lay it in position in the main bearings.

10   Before the crankshaft can be permanently installed, the main bearing oil clearance must be checked.

11   Cut several pieces of the appropriate-size Plastigage (they must be slightly shorter than the width of the main bearings) and place one piece on each crankshaft main bearing journal, parallel with the journal axis (see illustration).

12   Clean the faces of the bearings in the caps and install the caps in their respective positions (don't mix them up) with the arrows pointing toward the front of the engine (see Section 14). Don't disturb the Plastigage.

➡Note: On all 4.6L engines, the caps should be seated with a brass hammer or a dead-blow plastic mallet before installing any main cap bolts (see illustration).

13   Starting with the center main and working out toward the ends, tighten the main bearing cap bolts, in three steps, to the torque listed in this Chapter's Specifications.

➡Note: On the 4.6L engine it is not necessary to install the jack screws or the side bolts for Plastigage measurement purposes. Don't rotate the crankshaft at any time during this operation.

14   Remove the bolts and carefully lift off the main bearing caps. Keep them in order. Don't disturb the Plastigage or rotate the crankshaft. If any of the main bearing caps are difficult to remove, tap them gently from side-to-side with a soft-face hammer to loosen them.

15   Compare the width of the crushed Plastigage on each journal to

23.15 Compare the width of the crushed Plastigage to the scale on the envelope to determine the main bearing oil clearance (always take the measurement at the widest point of the Plastigage); be sure to use the correct scale - standard and metric ones are included

the scale printed on the Plastigage envelope to obtain the main bearing oil clearance (see illustration). Check the Specifications to make sure it's correct.

16   If the clearance is not as specified, the bearing inserts may be the wrong size (which means different ones will be required). Before deciding that different inserts are needed, make sure that no dirt or oil was between the bearing inserts and the caps or block when the clearance was measured. If the Plastigage was wider at one end than the other, the journal may be tapered (refer to Section 19).

17   Carefully scrape all traces of the Plastigage material off the main bearing journals and/or the bearing faces. Use your fingernail or the edge of a credit card - don't nick or scratch the bearing faces.

FINAL CRANKSHAFT INSTALLATION

18   Carefully lift the crankshaft out of the engine.

19   Clean the bearing faces in the block, then apply a thin, uniform layer of moly-base grease or engine assembly lube to each of the bearing surfaces. Be sure to coat the thrust faces as well as the journal face

of the thrust bearing.

20 Make sure the crankshaft journals are clean, then lay the crankshaft back in place in the block.

21 Clean the faces of the bearings in the caps, then apply lubricant to them.

22 Install the caps in their respective positions with the arrows pointing toward the front of the engine.

3.8L and 5.0L engines

23 Install the main cap bolts.

24 Tighten all, except the thrust bearing cap bolts (number 3) to the torque listed in this Chapter's Specifications (work from the center out and approach the final torque in three steps).

25 Tighten the thrust bearing cap bolts finger tight.

26 Pry the crankshaft forward and while holding pressure on the crankshaft, pry the thrust bearing cap backward. Forcing these two in opposite directions, against each other, will align the thrust bearing surfaces.

27 While keeping forward pressure on the crankshaft, re-tighten ALL main bearing cap bolts to the torque listed in this Chapter's Specifications, starting with cap #3, then #2, #4, #5 and #1.

28 Rotate the crankshaft a number of times by hand to check for any obvious binding.

29 The final step is to check the crankshaft endplay with a feeler gauge or a dial indicator (see Section 13) The endplay should be correct if the crankshaft thrust faces aren't worn or damaged and new bearings have been installed.

30 Install the rear main oil seal (see Chapter 2, Part A).

4.6L engines

♦ **Refer to illustrations 23.32, 23.34a and 23.34b**

31 Install the jack screws into the main caps and bottom them lightly against the caps, this must be done before the caps are placed into the block.

32 Lubricate the upper thrust washer with moly-base grease and install it in the block (see illustration). The side of the washer with the oil grooves must face the crankshaft.

33 Place the main caps on their correct journals and tap the caps into place with a brass or soft-face hammer.

23.32 "Roll" the lubricated crankshaft thrust washer (arrow) into place in front of the last crankshaft journal on 4.6L engines - the grooved side of the thrust washer must face the crankshaft (away from the main bearing saddle)

> ✳✳ **CAUTION:**
>
> **All main bearing caps MUST be tapped into position prior to tightening. Failure to do so may result in improper torque.**

34 Install the NEW main cap bolts and tighten them to 10-to-12 ft-lbs in the recommended sequence (see illustrations).

35 Push the crankshaft forward using a screwdriver or prybar to seat the thrust bearing.

> ✳✳ **CAUTION:**
>
> **Once the crankshaft is pushed fully forward, to seat the thrust bearing, leave the screwdriver in position so that pressure stays placed on the crankshaft until after all main bearing cap bolts have been tightened.**

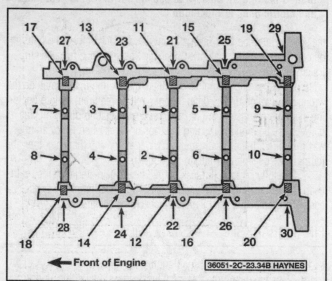

23.34a Main cap bolt/screw tightening sequence - 4.6L SOHC engines

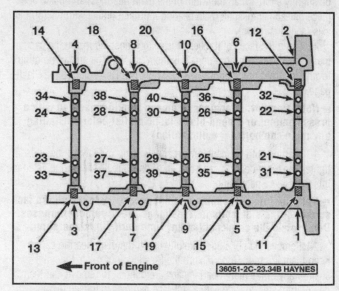

23.34b Main cap bolt/screw tightening sequence - 4.6L DOHC engines

36 Tighten the main bearing cap bolts in two steps in the sequence shown and to the torque and angle indicated in the Specifications listed at the end of this Chapter.

37 Tighten all jack screws in two steps and in the sequence shown to the Specifications listed at the end of this Chapter.

38 Tighten all side bolts in two steps and in the sequence shown to the Specifications listed at the end of this Chapter.

39 Check crankshaft endplay again and verify that it is correct (see Section 14).

40 Rotate the crankshaft a number of times by hand to check for any obvious binding.

41 Install the rear main oil seal (see Chapter 2, Part B).

24 Pistons/connecting rods - installation and rod bearing oil clearance check

✳✳ CAUTION:

The connecting rod bolts on the 4.6L engine are all "torque-to-yield" bolts and are NOT reusable. A pre-determined stretch of the bolt, calculated by the manufacturer, gives the added rigidity required with this cylinder block. Once removed they must be replaced with new bolts. During clearance checks using Plastigage, use the old bolts and torque to Specifications, but use only new bolts for final assembly.

1 Before installing the piston/connecting rod assemblies, the cylinder walls must be perfectly clean, the top edge of each cylinder must be chamfered, and the crankshaft must be in place.

2 Remove the cap from the end of the number one connecting rod (refer to the marks made during removal). Remove the original bearing inserts and wipe the bearing surfaces of the connecting rod and cap with a clean, lint-free cloth. They must be kept spotlessly clean.

CONNECTING ROD BEARING OIL CLEARANCE CHECK

▶ **Refer to illustrations 24.3, 24.5, 24.9, 24.10a, 23.10b, 23.12, 24.14 and 24.18**

3 Clean the back side of the new upper bearing insert, then lay it in place in the connecting rod (see illustration). Make sure the tab on the bearing fits into the recess in the rod. Don't hammer the bearing insert into place and be very careful not to nick or gouge the bearing face.

Don't lubricate the bearing at this time.

4 Clean the back side of the other bearing insert and install it in the rod cap. Again, make sure the tab on the bearing fits into the recess in the cap, and don't apply any lubricant. It's critically important that the mating surfaces of the bearing and connecting rod are perfectly clean and oil free when they're assembled.

5 Position the piston ring gaps at intervals around the piston (see illustration).

6 On 5.0L engines, slip a section of plastic or rubber hose over each connecting rod bolt (see illustration 13.7).

➡**Note: 4.6L engines use cap bolts that are screwed into the rod after the rod and cap are assembled on the crankshaft.**

7 Lubricate the piston and rings with clean engine oil and attach a piston ring compressor to the piston. Leave the skirt protruding about 1/4-inch to guide the piston into the cylinder. The rings must be compressed until they're flush with the piston.

8 Rotate the crankshaft until the number one connecting rod journal is at BDC (bottom dead center) and apply a coat of engine oil to the cylinder walls.

9 With the arrow or notches on top of the piston (see illustration) facing the front of the engine, gently insert the piston/connecting rod

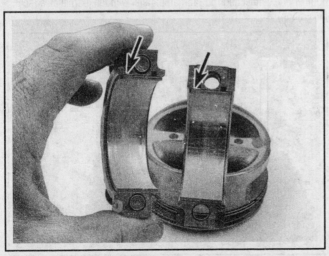

24.3 Insert the connecting rod bearing halves, making sure the bearing tab (arrows) are in the notches in the rod and cap

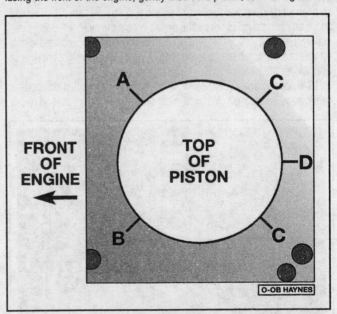

24.5 Ring end gap positions - Align the oil ring spacer gap at D, the oil ring side rails at C (one inch either side of the pin centerline), and the compression rings at A and B, one inch either side of the pin centerline

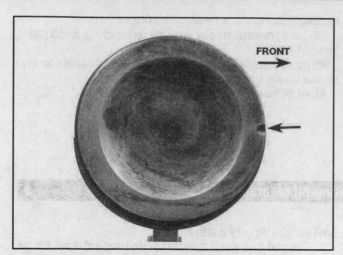

24.9 Turn the piston when installing it to make sure the mark/notch in the piston faces the front of the engine as they are installed

assembly into the number one cylinder bore and rest the bottom edge of the ring compressor on the engine block.

➡**Note: Use short lengths of rubber hose over the rod bolts on 3.8L and 5.0L engines to protect the crank journals.**

10 On 4.6L engines, the rod bolts are pressed lightly into the rod caps. They must be replaced with new bolts, so tap out two of the old ones (see illustration). Take these and cut the heads off, slip rubber hose over them, and screw them into the connecting rod to use as alignment devices during piston/rod installation (see illustration).

11 Tap the top edge of the ring compressor to make sure it's contacting the block around its entire circumference.

12 Gently tap on the top of the piston with the end of a wooden hammer handle (see illustration) while guiding the end of the connecting rod into place on the crankshaft journal. The piston rings may try to pop out of the ring compressor just before entering the cylinder bore, so keep some downward pressure on the ring compressor. Work slowly, and if any resistance is felt as the piston enters the cylinder, stop immediately. Find out what's hanging up and fix it before proceeding. Do not, for any reason, force the piston into the cylinder - you might break a ring and/or the piston.

13 Once the piston/connecting rod assembly is installed, the connecting rod bearing oil clearance must be checked before the rod cap is

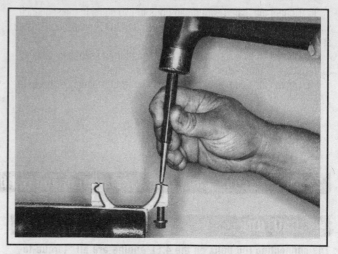

24.10a Hold the 4.6L rod cap lightly in a vise while driving out the old rod bolts - it takes only a little tap to drive them out; then drive new bolts in

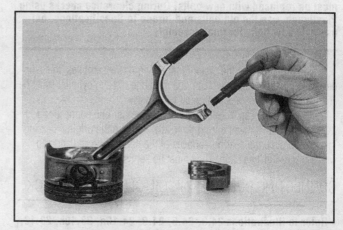

24.10b Two old rod bolts can be used (with the heads cut off) as rod installation guides with rubber hose over them

permanently bolted in place.

14 Cut a piece of the appropriate-size Plastigage slightly shorter than the width of the connecting rod bearing and lay it in place on the number one connecting rod journal, parallel with the journal axis (see illustration).

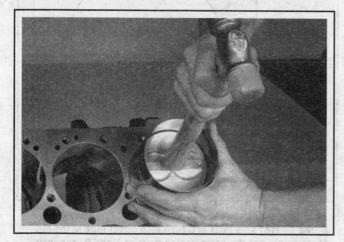

24.12 The piston can be driven gently into the cylinder bore with the end of a wooden or plastic hammer handle

24.14 Lay the Plastigage strips on each rod bearing journal, parallel to the crankshaft centerline

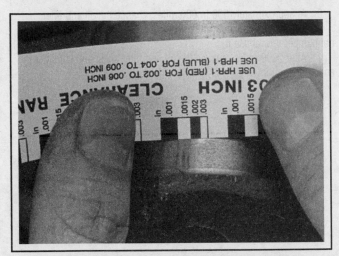

24.18 Measuring the width of the crushed Plastigage to determine the rod bearing oil clearance (be sure to use the correct scale - standard and metric ones are included)

15 Clean the connecting rod cap bearing face, remove the protective hoses from the connecting rod bolts and install the rod cap. Make sure the mating mark on the cap is on the same side as the mark on the connecting rod.

16 Install the nuts or bolts and tighten them to the torque listed in this Chapter's Specifications, working up to it in three steps.

→Note: Use a thin-wall socket to avoid erroneous torque readings that can result if the socket is wedged between the rod cap and nut/bolt. If the socket tends to wedge itself between the nut and the cap, lift up on it slightly until it no longer contacts the cap. Do not rotate the crankshaft at any time during this operation.

17 Remove the nuts/bolts and detach the rod cap, being very careful not to disturb the Plastigage.

18 Compare the width of the crushed Plastigage to the scale printed on the Plastigage envelope to obtain the oil clearance (see illustration). Compare it to the Specifications to make sure the clearance is correct.

19 If the clearance is not as specified, the bearing inserts may be the wrong size (which means different ones will be required). Before deciding that different inserts are needed, make sure that no dirt or oil was between the bearing inserts and the connecting rod or cap when the clearance was measured. Also, recheck the journal diameter. If the Plas-

tigage was wider at one end than the other, the journal may be tapered (refer to Section 19).

FINAL CONNECTING ROD INSTALLATION

20 Carefully scrape all traces of the Plastigage material off the rod journal and/or bearing face. Be very careful not to scratch the bearing - use your fingernail or the edge of a credit card.

21 Make sure the bearing faces are perfectly clean, then apply a uniform layer of clean moly-base grease or engine assembly lube to both of them. You'll have to push the piston into the cylinder to expose the face of the bearing insert in the connecting rod - be sure to slip the protective hoses over the rod bolts first.

22 Slide the connecting rod back into place on the journal, remove the protective hoses from the rod cap bolts, install the rod cap and tighten the nuts to the torque listed in this Chapter's Specifications. Again, work up to the torque in three steps.

→Note: On 4.6L engines, install new rod bolts into the rod caps (see Step 10).

23 Repeat the entire procedure for the remaining pistons/connecting rods.

24 The important points to remember are:

a) *Keep the back sides of the bearing inserts and the insides of the connecting rods and caps perfectly clean when assembling them.*

b) *Make sure you have the correct piston/rod assembly for each cylinder.*

c) *The notches or mark on the piston must face the FRONT of the engine.*

d) *Lubricate the cylinder walls with clean oil.*

e) *Lubricate the bearing faces when installing the rod caps after the oil clearance has been checked.*

25 After all the piston/connecting rod assemblies have been properly installed, rotate the crankshaft a number of times by hand to check for any obvious binding.

26 As a final step, the connecting rod endplay must be checked. Refer to Section 13 for this procedure.

27 Compare the measured endplay to the Specifications to make sure it's correct. If it was correct before disassembly and the original crankshaft and rods were reinstalled, it should still be right. If new rods or a new crankshaft were installed, the endplay may be inadequate. If so, the rods will have to be removed and taken to an automotive machine shop for resizing.

25 Initial start-up and break-in after overhaul

☼ WARNING:

Have a fire extinguisher handy when starting the engine for the first time.

1 Once the engine has been installed in the vehicle, double-check the engine oil and coolant levels.

2 With the spark plugs out of the engine and the ignition system disabled (see Chapter 1), crank the engine until oil pressure registers on the gauge or the light goes out.

3 Install the spark plugs, hook up the plug wires and restore the ignition system functions.

4 Start the engine. It may take a few moments for the fuel system to build up pressure, but the engine should start without a great deal of effort.

→Note: If backfiring occurs through the throttle body, recheck the valve timing and ignition timing.

5 After the engine starts, it should be allowed to warm up to normal operating temperature. While the engine is warming up, make a thorough check for fuel, oil and coolant leaks.

6 Shut the engine off and recheck the engine oil and coolant levels.

7 Drive the vehicle to an area with no traffic, accelerate from 30 to 50 mph, then allow the vehicle to slow to 30 mph with the throttle closed. Repeat the procedure 10 or 12 times. This will load the piston

rings and cause them to seat properly against the cylinder walls. Check again for oil and coolant leaks.

8   Drive the vehicle gently for the first 500 miles (no sustained high speeds) and keep a constant check on the oil level. It is not unusual for an engine to use oil during the break-in period.

9   At approximately 500 to 600 miles, change the oil and filter.

10 For the next few hundred miles, drive the vehicle normally. Do not pamper it or abuse it.

11 After 2000 miles, change the oil and filter again and consider the engine broken in.

Specifications

General

Oil pressure	
3.8L V6 (engine hot at 2500 rpm)	40 to 60 psi
4.6L V8 (engine hot at 1500 rpm)	20 to 45 psi
5.0L V8 (engine hot at 2000 rpm)	40 to 60 psi
Cylinder head warpage limit	0.003 (in any 6 inches)/0.006 inch overall
Compression pressure	Lowest reading cylinder must be within 15 psi of highest reading cylinder (100 psi minimum)

3.8L V6 engines

Valves and related components

Valve face angle	45.8-degrees
Seat angle	44.5-degrees
Seat width	0.060 to 0.080 inch
Minimum valve margin width	1/32 inch

Valves and related components

Stem diameter	
Intake	0.3423 to 0.3415 inch
Exhaust	0.3418 to 0.3410 inch
Stem-to-guide clearance	
Intake	0.001 to 0.0028 inch
Exhaust	0.0015 to 0.0033 inch
Valve spring	
Free length	Not available
Installed height	1.65 inches
Valve lifter	
Diameter	0.8740 to 0.8745 inch
Lifter-to-bore clearance	
Standard	0.0007 to 0.0027 inch
Service limit	0.005 inch

Crankshaft and connecting rods

Connecting rod journal	
Diameter	2.3103 to 2.3111 inches
Out-of-round limit	0.0003 inch
Taper limit	0.0003 inch per inch
Bearing oil clearance	
Desired	0.001 to 0.0014 inch
Allowable	0.00086 to 0.0027 inch
Connecting rod side clearance (endplay)	
Standard	0.0047 to 0.0114 inch
Service limit	0.014 inch
Main journal	
Diameter*	2.5190 to 2.5198 inches
Out of round limit	0.0003 inch
Taper limit	0.0003 inch per inch
Main bearing oil clearance	
Desired	0.001 to 0.0014 inch
Allowable	0.0005 to 0.0023 inch
Crankshaft endplay	0.004 to 0.008 inch

* Note: The crankshaft journals can't be machined more than 0.010 inch under the standard dimension.

Cylinder bore

Diameter	3.810 inches
Out-of-round limit	0.002 inch
Taper limit	0.002 inch

Pistons and rings

Piston diameter	
1994 and 1995	
Coded red	3.8095 to 3.8101 inches
Coded blue	3.8107 to 3.8113 inches
Coded yellow	3.8119 to 3.8125 inches
1996 and later	
Coded red	3.8103 to 3.8108 inches
Coded blue	3.8108 to 3.8113 inches
Coded yellow	3.8113 to 3.8118 inches
Piston-to-bore clearance limit	
1994 and 1995	0.0014 to 0.0032 inch
1996 and later	0.0007 to 0.0017 inch
Piston ring end gap	
1994 and 1995	
Top compression ring	0.011 to 0.012 inch
Bottom compression ring	0.009 to 0.020 inch
Oil ring	0.015 to 0.0583 inch
1996 and later	
Top compression ring	0.009 to 0.016 inch
Bottom compression ring	0.015 to 0.025 inch
Oil ring	0.006 to 0.026 inch
Piston ring side clearance	
1994 and 1995	0.0016 to 0.0034 inch
1996 and later	0.0012 to 0.0032 inch

3.8L V6 engines (continued)

Torque specifications*	Ft-lbs
Main bearing cap bolts	
Step 1	37
Step 2	Rotate an additional 115 to 125 degrees
Connecting rod cap	
1994 and 1995 (nuts)	
Step 1	31 to 36
Step 2	Loosen two turns
Step 3	31 to 36
1996 (nuts)	
Step 1	29
Step 2	Rotate an additional 90 degrees
1997 and later (bolts)	
Step 1	15 to 18
Step 2	30 to 33
Step 3	Rotate an additional 90 degrees

* Note: Refer to Chapter 2, Part A for additional torque specifications.

4.6L V8 engines

Cylinder bore

Diameter	
Coded red 1	3.5539 to 3.5544 inches
Coded blue 2	3.5544 to 3.5549 inches
Coded yellow 3	3.5549 to 3.5554 inches
Out-of-round	
Standard	0.0006 inch
Service limit	0.0008 inch
Taper	0.0002 inch maximum

Valves and related components

Valve arrangement (front-to-rear)	
Left cylinder head	E-I-E-I-E-I-E-I
Right cylinder head	I-E-I-E-I-E-I-E
Intake valve	
Seat angle	45 degrees
Seat width	0.0749 to 0.0827 inch
Seat runout limit	0.0010 inch maximum (total indicator reading)
Stem diameter	
Standard	0.2756 to 0.2748 inch
0.015 oversize	0.2906 to 0.2898 inch
0.030 oversize	0.2985 to 0.3048 inch
Valve stem-to-guide clearance	0.00749 to 0.0027 inch
Valve face angle	45.5 degrees
Valve face runout limit	0.0020 inch maximum
Exhaust valve	
Seat angle	45 degrees
Seat width	0.0749 to 0.0827 inch
Seat runout limit	0.0010 inch maximum (total indicator reading)

Stem diameter
    Standard   0.02746 to 0.2738 inch
    0.015 oversize   0.2896 to 0.2898 inch
    0.030 oversize   0.3046 to 0.3038 inch
    Valve stem-to-guide clearance   0.0018 to 0.0037 inch
    Valve face angle   45.5 degrees
    Valve face runout limit   0.0020 inch maximum
Valve spring
    Free length
        Intake   1.9523 inches
        Exhaust   1.9523 inches
    Out-of-square limit   2 degrees maximum
    Installed height
        Intake   1.1576 inches
        Exhaust   1.1576 inches
Valve spring
    Pressure
        Intake
            Valve open   433.31 lbs at 1.104 inches
            Valve closed   180.54 lbs at 1.576 inches
        Exhaust
            Valve open   433.31 lbs at 1.104 inches
            Valve closed   180.54 lbs at 1.576 inches
    Valve spring pressure service limit   10 percent pressure loss at 1.104 inches
Hydraulic lash adjuster (lifter)
    Diameter (standard)   0.6304 to 0.6299 inch
    Lifter-to-bore clearance
        Standard   0.0007 to 0.0027 inch
        Service limit   0.0006 inch maximum
    Collapsed tappet gap - desired   0.0335 to 0.0177 inch
    Rocker arm ratio (roller cam followers)   1.75:1

Crankshaft and connecting rods

Crankshaft
    Endplay   0.0051 to 0.0099 inch
    Runout to rear face of block
        Standard   0.002 inch
        Service limit   0.005 inch maximum
Connecting rods
    Connecting rod journal
        Diameter   2.0874 to 2.0891 inches
        Bearing oil clearance
            Desired   0.0011 to 0.0027 inch
            Allowable   0.0011 to 0.0027 inch
    Connecting rod side clearance (endplay)
        Standard   0.0006 to 0.0177 inch
        Service limit   0.0197 inch
    Main bearing journal
        Diameter   2.6578 to 2.6598 inches
        Bearing oil clearance
            Desired   0.0011 to 0.0027 inch
            Allowable   0.0011 to 0.0027 inch

4.6L V8 engines (continued)

Pistons and rings

Piston diameter	
Coded red 1	3.5526 to 3.5531 inches
Coded blue 2	3.5531 to 3.5536 inches
Coded yellow 3	3.5536 to 3.5541 inches
Piston-to-bore clearance limit	0.0008 to 0.0018 inch
Piston ring end·gap	
Compression rings	0.0394 inch
Oil ring	0.0493 inch
Piston ring side clearance	
Compression ring (top)	0.0016 to 0.0035 inch
Compression ring (bottom)	0.0012 to 0.0032 inch
Service limit	0.0006 inch maximum
Oil ring	Snug fit

Torque specifications*   Ft-lbs (unless otherwise indicated)

Main bearing cap bolts (tighten first)	
First step	22 to 25
Second step	Rotate and additional 85 to 95-degrees
Main bearing cap - jack screws (tighten second)	
First step	44 in-lbs
Second step	80 to 97 inch lbs
Main bearing cap - side bolts (tighten third)	
First step	84 in-lbs
Second step	14 to 17
Connecting rod cap nuts	
First step	18 to 25
Second step	Rotate an additional 85 to 95-degrees

* Note: Refer to Chapter 2, Part B for additional torque specifications.

5.0L V8 engine

Cylinder bore

Diameter	4.000 to 4.0048 inches
Out-of-round	
Standard	0.0015 inch
Service limit	0.005 inch
Taper	0.010 inch maximum

Valves and related components

Valve arrangement (front-to-rear)	
Left cylinder head	E-I-E-I-E-I-E-I
Right cylinder head	I-E-I-E-I-E-I-E
Intake valve	
Seat angle	45-degrees
Seat width	0.060 to 0.080 inch
Seat runout limit	0.002 inch maximum (total indicator reading)

Stem diameter
    Standard   0.3416 to 0.3423 inch
    0.015 oversize   0.3566 to 0.3573 inch
    0.030 oversize   0.3716 to 0.3723 inch

Valve stem-to-guide clearance
    Standard   0.0010 to 0.0027 inch
    Service limit   0.0055 inch maximum

Valve face angle   44-degrees
Valve face runout limit   0.002 inch maximum

Exhaust valve
    Seat angle   45-degrees
    Seat width   0.060 to 0.080 inch
    Seat runout limit   0.002 inch maximum (total indicator reading)

    Stem diameter
        Standard   0.3411 to 0.3418 inch
        0.015 oversize   0.3561 to 0.3568 inch
        0.030 oversize   0.3711 to 0.3718 inch

    Valve stem-to-guide clearance
        Standard   0.0015 to 0.0032 inch
        Service limit   0.0055 inch maximum

    Valve face angle   44-degrees
    Valve face runout limit   0.002 inch maximum

Valve spring
    Free length
        Intake   2.02 inches
        Exhaust   1.79 inch
    Installed height
        Intake   1-3/4 to 1-13/16 inches
        Exhaust   1-37/64 to 1-41/64 inches
    Out-of-square limit   5/64 inch
    Pressure
        Intake
            Valve open   211 to 230 lbs at 1.36 inches
           Valve closed   74 to 82 lbs at 1.78 inches
        Exhaust
            Valve open   200 to 226 lbs at 1.15 inches
           Valve closed   77 to 85 lbs at 1.60 inches
    Valve spring pressure service limit   10-percent pressure loss at specified length

Hydraulic lash adjuster (lifter)
    Diameter (standard)   0.8740 to 0.8745
    Lifter-to-bore clearance
        Standard   0.0007 to 0.0027 inch
        Service limit   0.005 inch maximum
    Collapsed tappet gap
        Desired   0.096 to 0.146 inch
        Allowable   0.071 to 0.0171 inch
    Rocker arm ratio   1.59:1

5.0L V8 engine (continued)

Crankshaft and connecting rods

Crankshaft	
Endplay	
Standard	0.004 to 0.008 inch
Service limit	0.012 inch maximum
Runout to rear face of block	0.005 inch maximum (total indicator reading)
Connecting rods	
Connecting rod journal	
Diameter	2.1228 to 2.1236 inches
Out-of-round/taper limit	0.0006 inch per inch maximum
Bearing oil clearance	
Desired	0.0008 to 0.0015 inch
Allowable	0.0008 to 0.0024 inch
Connecting rod side clearance (endplay)	
Standard	0.010 to 0.020 inch
Service limit	0.023 inch maximum
Main bearing journal	
Diameter	2.2490 to 2.2482 inches
Out-of-round limit	0.0006 inch
Taper limit	0.0004 inch per inch
Bearing oil clearance	0.0008 to 0.0015 inch

Pistons and rings

Piston diameter	
Coded red	3.9972 to 3.9980 inch
Coded blue	3.9984 to 3.9992 inch
Coded yellow	3.9996 to 4.0004 inch
Piston-to-bore clearance limit	0.0030 to 0.0038 inch
Piston ring end gap	
Compression rings	0.010 to 0.020 inch
Oil ring	0.015 to 0.055 inch
Piston ring side clearance	
Compression rings	0.002 to 0.004 inch
Service limit	0.006 inch
Oil ring	Snug fit

Torque specifications*

	Ft-lbs
Main bearing cap bolts	60 to 70
Connecting rod cap nuts	19 to 24

* Note: Refer to Chapter 2, Part A for additional torque specifications.

GLOSSARY

B

Backlash - The amount of play between two parts. Usually refers to how much one gear can be moved back and forth without moving gear with which it's meshed.

Bearing Caps - The caps held in place by nuts or bolts which, in turn, hold the bearing surface. This space is for lubricating oil to enter.

Bearing clearance - The amount of space left between shaft and bearing surface. This space is for lubricating oil to enter.

Bearing crush - The additional height which is purposely manufactured into each bearing half to ensure complete contact of the bearing back with the housing bore when the engine is assembled.

Bearing knock - The noise created by movement of a part in a loose or worn bearing.

Blueprinting - Dismantling an engine and reassembling it to EXACT specifications.

Bore - An engine cylinder, or any cylindrical hole; also used to describe the process of enlarging or accurately refinishing a hole with a cutting tool, as to bore an engine cylinder. The bore size is the diameter of the hole.

Boring - Renewing the cylinders by cutting them out to a specified size. A boring bar is used to make the cut.

Bottom end - A term which refers collectively to the engine block, crankshaft, main bearings and the big ends of the connecting rods.

Break-in - The period of operation between installation of new or rebuilt parts and time in which parts are worn to the correct fit. Driving at reduced and varying speed for a specified mileage to permit parts to wear to the correct fit.

Bushing - A one-piece sleeve placed in a bore to serve as a bearing surface for shaft, piston pin, etc. Usually replaceable.

C

Camshaft - The shaft in the engine, on which a series of lobes are located for operating the valve mechanisms. The camshaft is driven by gears or sprockets and a timing chain. Usually referred to simply as the cam.

Carbon - Hard, or soft, black deposits found in combustion chamber, on plugs, under rings, on and under valve heads.

Cast iron - An alloy of iron and more than two percent carbon, used for engine blocks and heads because it's relatively inexpensive and easy to mold into complex shapes.

Chamfer - To bevel across (or a bevel on) the sharp edge of an object.

Chase - To repair damaged threads with a tap or die.

Combustion chamber - The space between the piston and the cylinder head, with the piston at top dead center, in which air-fuel mixture is burned.

Compression ratio - The relationship between cylinder volume (clearance volume) when the piston is at top dead center and cylinder volume when the piston is at bottom dead center.

Connecting rod - The rod that connects the crank on the crankshaft with the piston. Sometimes called a con rod.

Connecting rod cap - The part of the connecting rod assembly that attaches the rod to the crankpin.

Core plug - Soft metal plug used to plug the casting holes for the coolant passages in the block.

Crankcase - The lower part of the engine in which the crankshaft rotates; includes the lower section of the cylinder block and the oil pan.

Crank kit - A reground or reconditioned crankshaft and new main and connecting rod bearings.

Crankpin - The part of a crankshaft to which a connecting rod is attached.

Crankshaft - The main rotating member, or shaft, running the length of the crankcase, with offset throws to which the connecting rods are attached; changes the reciprocating motion of the pistons into rotating motion.

Cylinder sleeve - A replaceable sleeve, or liner, pressed into the cylinder block to form the cylinder bore.

D

Deburring - Removing the burrs (rough edges or areas) from a bearing.

Deglazer - A tool, rotated by an electric motor, used to remove glaze from cylinder walls so a new set of rings will seat.

E

Endplay - The amount of lengthwise movement between two parts. As applied to a crankshaft, the distance that the crankshaft can move forward and back in the cylinder block.

F

Face - A machinist's term that refers to removing metal from the end of a shaft or the face of a larger part, such as a flywheel.

Fatigue - A breakdown of material through a large number of loading and unloading cycles. The first signs are cracks followed shortly by breaks.

Feeler gauge - A thin strip of hardened steel, ground to an exact thickness, used to check clearances between parts.

Free height - The unloaded length or height of a spring.

Freeplay - The looseness in a linkage, or an assembly of parts, between the initial application of force and actual movement. Usually perceived as slop or slight delay.

Freeze plug - See Core plug.

G

Gallery - A large passage in the block that forms a reservoir for engine oil pressure.

Glaze - The very smooth, glassy finish that develops on cylinder walls while an engine is in service.

H

Heli-Coil - A rethreading device used when threads are worn or damaged. The device is installed in a retapped hole to reduce the thread size to the original size.

I

Installed height - The spring's measured length or height, as installed on the cylinder head. Installed height is measured from the spring seat to the underside of the spring retainer.

J

Journal - The surface of a rotating shaft which turns in a bearing.

K

Keeper - The split lock that holds the valve spring retainer in position on the valve stem.

Key - A small piece of metal inserted into matching grooves machined into two parts fitted together - such as a gear pressed onto a shaft - which prevents slippage between the two parts.

Knock - The heavy metallic engine sound, produced in the combustion chamber as a result of abnormal combustion - usually detonation. Knock is usually caused by a loose or worn bearing. Also referred to as detonation, pinging and spark knock. Connecting rod or main bearing knocks are created by too much oil clearance or insufficient lubrication.

L

Lands - The portions of metal between the piston ring grooves.

Lapping the valves - Grinding a valve face and its seat together with lapping compound.

Lash - The amount of free motion in a gear train, between gears, or in a mechanical assembly, that occurs before movement can begin. Usually refers to the lash in a valve train.

Lifter - The part that rides against the cam to transfer motion to the rest of the valve train.

M

Machining - The process of using a machine to remove metal from a metal part.

Main bearings - The plain, or babbitt, bearings that support the crankshaft.

Main bearing caps - The cast iron caps, bolted to the bottom of the block, that support the main bearings.

O

O.D. - Outside diameter.

Oil gallery - A pipe or drilled passageway in the engine used to carry engine oil from one area to another.

Oil ring - The lower ring, or rings, of a piston; designed to prevent excessive amounts of oil from working up the cylinder walls and into the combustion chamber. Also called an oil-control ring.

Oil seal - A seal which keeps oil from leaking out of a compartment. Usually refers to a dynamic seal around a rotating shaft or other moving part.

O-ring - A type of sealing ring made of a special rubberlike material; in use, the O-ring is compressed into a groove to provide the sealing action.

Overhaul - To completely disassemble a unit, clean and inspect all parts, reassemble it with the original or new parts and make all adjustments necessary for proper operation.

P

Pilot bearing - A small bearing installed in the center of the flywheel (or the rear end of the crankshaft) to support the front end of the input shaft of the transmission.

Pip mark - A little dot or indentation which indicates the top side of a compression ring.

Piston - The cylindrical part, attached to the connecting rod, that moves up and down in the cylinder as the crankshaft rotates. When the fuel charge is fired, the piston transfers the force of the explosion to the connecting rod, then to the crankshaft.

Piston pin (or wrist pin) - The cylindrical and usually hollow steel pin that passes through the piston. The piston pin fastens the piston to the upper end of the connecting rod.

Piston ring - The split ring fitted to the groove in a piston. The ring contacts the sides of the ring groove and also rubs against the cylinder wall, thus sealing space between piston and wall. There are two types of rings: Compression rings seal the compression pressure in the combustion chamber; oil rings scrape excessive oil off the cylinder wall.

Piston ring groove - The slots or grooves cut in piston heads to hold piston rings in position.

Piston skirt - The portion of the piston below the rings and the piston pin hole.

Plastigage - A thin strip of plastic thread, available in different sizes, used for measuring clearances. For example, a strip of plastigage is laid across a bearing journal and mashed as parts are assembled. Then parts are disassembled and the width of the strip is measured to determine clearance between journal and bearing. Commonly used to measure crankshaft main-bearing and connecting rod bearing clearances.

Press-fit - A tight fit between two parts that requires pressure to force the parts together. Also referred to as drive, or force, fit.

Prussian blue - A blue pigment; in solution, useful in determining the area of contact between two surfaces. Prussian blue is commonly used to determine the width and location of the contact area between the valve face and the valve seat.

R

Race (bearing) - The inner or outer ring that provides a contact surface for balls or rollers in bearing.

Ream - To size, enlarge or smooth a hole by using a round cutting tool with fluted edges.

Ring job - The process of reconditioning the cylinders and installing new rings.

Runout - Wobble. The amount a shaft rotates out-of-true.

S

Saddle - The upper main bearing seat.

Scored - Scratched or grooved, as a cylinder wall may be scored by abrasive particles moved up and down by the piston rings.

Scuffing - A type of wear in which there's a transfer of material between parts moving against each other; shows up as pits or grooves in the mating surfaces.

Seat - The surface upon which another part rests or seats. For example, the valve seat is the matched surface upon which the valve face rests. Also used to refer to wearing into a good fit; for example, piston rings seat after a few miles of driving.

Short block - An engine block complete with crankshaft and piston and, usually, camshaft assemblies.

Static balance - The balance of an object while it's stationary.

Step - The wear on the lower portion of a ring land caused by excessive side and back-clearance. The height of the step indicates the ring's extra side clearance and the length of the step projecting from the back wall of the groove represents the ring's back clearance.

Stroke - The distance the piston moves when traveling from top dead center to bottom dead center, or from bottom dead center to top dead center.

Stud - A metal rod with threads on both ends.

T

Tang - A lip on the end of a plain bearing used to align the bearing during assembly.

Tap - To cut threads in a hole. Also refers to the fluted tool used to cut threads.

Taper - A gradual reduction in the width of a shaft or hole; in an engine cylinder, taper usually takes the form of uneven wear, more pronounced at the top than at the bottom.

Throws - The offset portions of the crankshaft to which the connecting rods are affixed.

Thrust bearing - The main bearing that has thrust faces to prevent excessive end-play, or forward and backward movement of the crankshaft.

Thrust washer - A bronze or hardened steel washer placed between two moving parts. The washer prevents longitudinal movement and provides a bearing surface for thrust surfaces of parts.

Tolerance - The amount of variation permitted from an exact size of measurement. Actual amount from smallest acceptable dimension to largest acceptable dimension.

U

Umbrella - An oil deflector placed near the valve tip to throw oil from the valve stem area.

Undercut - A machined groove below the normal surface.

Undersize bearings - Smaller diameter bearings used with re-ground crankshaft journals.

V

Valve grinding - Refacing a valve in a valve-refacing machine.

Valve train - The valve-operating mechanism of an engine; includes all components from the camshaft to the valve.

Vibration damper - A cylindrical weight attached to the front of the crankshaft to minimize torsional vibration (the twist-untwist actions of the crankshaft caused by the cylinder firing impulses). Also called a harmonic balancer.

W

Water jacket - The spaces around the cylinders, between the inner and outer shells of the cylinder block or head, through which coolant circulates.

Web - A supporting structure across a cavity.

Woodruff key - A key with a radiused backside (viewed from the side).

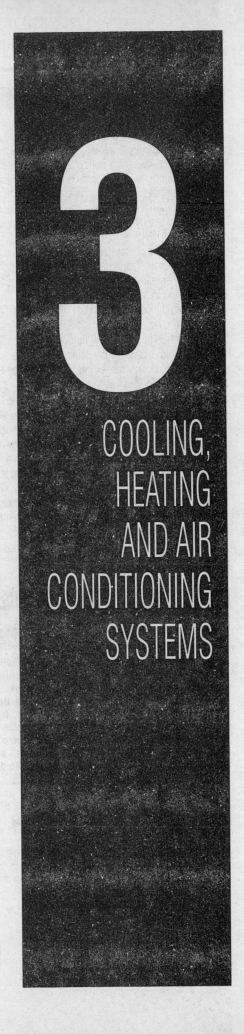

3

COOLING, HEATING AND AIR CONDITIONING SYSTEMS

1 General information

The cooling system consists of a radiator and coolant reserve system, a radiator pressure cap, a thermostat, a temperature-controlled electric cooling fan, and a pulley/belt-driven water pump.

The radiator cooling fan is mounted in a housing/shroud at the engine side of the radiator. It is designed to come on when the engine reaches a certain temperature, and shut off again when the engine cools down some, thereby keeping the engine in the desired operating-temperature range.

The system is pressurized by a spring-loaded radiator cap, which, by maintaining pressure, increases the boiling point of the coolant. If the coolant temperature goes above this increased boiling point, the extra pressure in the system forces the radiator cap valve off its seat and exposes the overflow pipe or hose. The overflow pipe/hose leads to a coolant recovery system. This consists of a plastic reservoir, mounted to the right side of the radiator, into which the coolant that normally escapes due to expansion is retained. When the engine cools, the excess coolant is drawn back into the radiator by the vacuum created as the system cools, maintaining the system at full capacity. This is a continuous process and provided the level in the reservoir is correctly maintained, it is not necessary to add coolant to the radiator.

On 1996 and later models with 4.6L V8 engines, the recovery tank is called a "degas" bottle, and it functions somewhat differently than traditional recovery tanks. Designed to separate any trapped air in the coolant, it is pressurized by the radiator and has a pressure cap on top (the radiator on these models has no cap at all). When the engine's thermostat is closed, no coolant flows in the degas bottle, but when the engine is fully warmed up, coolant flows from the top of the radiator through a small hose that enters the top of the degas bottle. There,

air separates and coolant falls to the approximately one quart coolant reserve in the bottle, which is fed to the cooling system through a larger hose connected to the lower radiator hose. Unlike traditional coolant recovery tanks, the cap on the degas bottle should never be opened when the engine is running, since there is a danger of injury from steam or scalding water (see the **Warning** in Section 5).

Coolant circulates through the radiator, down to the lower radiator hose and into the water pump, where it is forced through the water passages in the cylinder block. The coolant then travels up into the cylinder head, circulates around the combustion chambers and valve seats, travels out of the cylinder head past the open thermostat into the upper radiator hose and back into the radiator.

When the engine is cold, the thermostat restricts the circulation of coolant to the engine. When the minimum operating temperature is reached, the thermostat begins to open, allowing coolant to return to the radiator.

Automatic transmission-equipped models have a cooler element incorporated into the radiator to cool the transmission fluid.

The heating system works by directing air through the heater core, which is like a small radiator mounted behind the dash. Hot engine coolant heats the core, over which air passes to the interior of the vehicle by a system of ducts. Temperature is controlled by mixing heated air with fresh air, using a system of flapper doors in the ducts, and a heater motor.

Air conditioning is an optional accessory, consisting of an evaporator core located under the dash, a condenser in front of the radiator, a accumulator/drier in the engine compartment and a belt-driven compressor mounted at the front of the engine.

2 Antifreeze - general information

✳✳ WARNING:

Do not allow antifreeze to come in contact with your skin or painted surfaces of the vehicle. Rinse off spills immediately with plenty of water. Antifreeze is highly toxic if ingested. Never leave antifreeze lying around in an open container or in puddles on the floor; children and pets are attracted by it's sweet smell and may drink it. Check with local authorities about disposing of used antifreeze. Many communities have collection centers which will see that antifreeze is disposed of safely. Never dump used antifreeze on the ground or pour it into drains.

➡Note: Non-toxic antifreeze is now manufactured and available at local auto parts stores, but even this type should be disposed of properly.

The cooling system should be filled with a water/ethylene glycol based antifreeze solution which will prevent freezing down to at least

-20-degrees F (even lower in cold climates). It also provides protection against corrosion and increases the coolant boiling point. The engines in the covered vehicles have either aluminum heads (V6 and 4.6L SOHC engines) or an aluminum block and heads (4.6L DOHC [Cobra] engine). The manufacturer recommends that only coolant designated as safe for aluminum engine components be used.

The cooling system should be drained, flushed and refilled at least every other year (see Chapter 1). The use of antifreeze solutions for periods of longer than two years is likely to cause damage and encourage the formation of rust and scale in the system.

Before adding antifreeze to the system, check all hose connections. Antifreeze can leak through very minute openings.

The exact mixture of antifreeze to water which you should use depends on the relative weather conditions. The mixture should contain at least 50-percent antifreeze, but should never contain more than 70-percent antifreeze.

3 Thermostat - check and replacement

✳✳ WARNING:

The engine must be completely cool when this procedure is performed.

➡Note: Don't drive the vehicle without a thermostat! The computer may stay in open loop and emissions and fuel economy will suffer.

CHECK

1 Before condemning the thermostat, check the coolant level, drivebelt tension and temperature gauge (or light) operation.

2 If the engine takes a long time to warm up, the thermostat is probably stuck open. Replace the thermostat.

3 If the engine runs hot, check the temperature of the upper radiator hose. If the hose isn't hot, the thermostat is probably stuck shut. Replace the thermostat.

4 If the upper radiator hose is hot, it means the coolant is circulating and the thermostat is open. Refer to the *Troubleshooting* section at the front of this manual for the cause of overheating.

3.8 Thermostat location for the 5.0L engine - arrow indicates the bypass hose

5 If an engine has been overheated, you may find damage such as leaking head gaskets, scuffed pistons and warped or cracked cylinder heads.

REPLACEMENT

▶ Refer to illustrations 3.8, 3.9a, 3.9b, 3.9c and 3.12

6 Drain coolant from the radiator, until the coolant level is below the thermostat housing (See Chapter 1).

7 On some models of the 5.0L engines, it may be necessary to remove the distributor cap in order to remove the thermostat housing (see Chapter 5).

8 Disconnect the upper radiator hose from the thermostat housing. Disconnect the by-pass hose from the thermostat housing on 5.0L engines (see illustration).

9 Remove the bolts and lift the cover off (see illustrations). It may be necessary to tap the cover with a soft-face hammer to break the gasket seal on a 5.0L or 1994 and 1995 3.8L V6 engine. Remove the

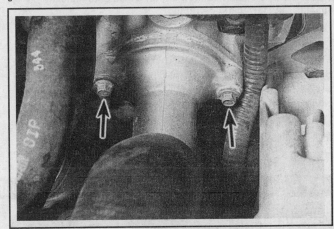

3.9a Thermostat housing bolts - 3.8L V6 models

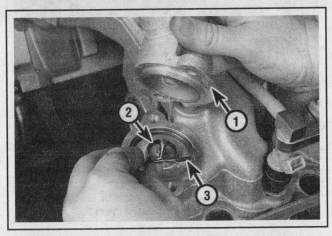

3.9b Once the bolts are removed, separate the housing from the intake manifold in order to remove the gasket and thermostat - 4.6L SOHC

1 Thermostat housing cover	*3 O-ring seal*
2 Thermostat	

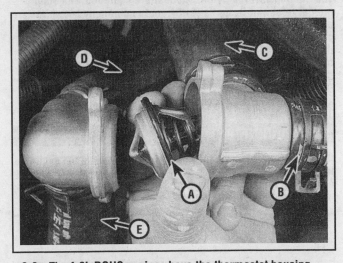

3.9c The 4.6L DOHC engines have the thermostat housing mounted low at the left front of the engine (arrow A indicates the thermostat's O-ring) - supported only by hoses: the water bypass hose B, the hose to the oil cooler C, the hose to the degas bottle D, and the lower radiator hose E (this shot is from below, with the front of the car to the left)

O-ring seal on 1996 and later models.

10 Note how it's installed, then remove the thermostat. Be sure to use a replacement thermostat with the correct opening temperature (see this Chapter's Specifications).

11 On 5.0L and early 3.8L V6 engines, use a scraper or putty knife to remove all traces of old gasket material and sealant from the mating surfaces. On later V6 and all 4.6L engines, the thermostat is sealed with an O-ring, using no gasket or sealer. Make sure no gasket material falls into the coolant passages; it is a good idea to stuff a rag in the passage. Wipe the mating surfaces with a rag saturated with lacquer thinner or acetone.

12 Install the thermostat and make sure the correct end faces out (see illustration) - the spring is directed toward the engine (3.8L, 4.6L SOHC and 5.0L engines). On 4.6L DOHC engines the spring end of the thermostat is directed into the larger portion of the thermostat housing (see illustration 3.9c).

➡**Note 1: On 1998 3.8L engines, the thermostat must be rotated within the thermostat housing so the vent will be positioned at either the 11 o'clock or 1 o'clock position.**

➡**Note 2: On some models, the thermostat housing has a notch that a tab on the thermostat fits into, which automatically locates the thermostat correctly.**

13 On models that use a conventional paper gasket, apply a thin coat of RTV sealant to both sides of the new gasket and position it on the engine side, over the thermostat, and make sure the gasket holes line up with the bolt holes in the housing.

➡**Note: No RTV sealant should be used on the later model O-ring seal.**

14 On models that use an O-ring seal, install the new O-ring into the intake manifold (later 3.8L V6 engines) or onto thermostat housing.

3.12 When installing the thermostat pay special attention to the direction in which it's placed in the engine; the spring will go into the intake manifold

15 Carefully position the cover and install the bolts. Tighten them to the torque listed in this Chapter's Specifications - do not overtighten them or the cover may be cracked or distorted.

16 Reattach the radiator hose to the cover and tighten the clamp - now may be a good time to check and replace the hoses and clamps (see Chapter 1).

17 Refer to Chapter 1 and refill the system, then run the engine and check carefully for leaks.

18 Repeat steps 1 through 5 to be sure the repairs corrected the previous problem(s).

4 Engine cooling fan and circuit - check, removal and installation

✳✳ WARNING 1:

The models covered by this manual are equipped with Supplemental Restraint Systems (SRS), more commonly known as airbags. Always disconnect the negative battery cable, then the positive battery cable and wait two minutes before working in the vicinity of the impact sensors, steering column or instrument panel to avoid the possibility of accidental deployment of the airbag, which could cause personal injury (see Chapter 12). Do not use any electrical test equipment on any of the airbag system wires or tamper with them in any way.

✳✳ WARNING 2:

Do not work with your hands near the fan any time the engine is running or the key is ON. With the key ON, (even with the engine not running) the fan can start at any time, since it is controlled by coolant temperature.

CHECK

▸ **Refer to illustrations 4.1, 4.6, 4.8a and 4.8b**

1 All models have a two-speed electric fan mounted in a plastic shroud attached to the back of the radiator (see illustration).

2 Fan operation is controlled both by the PCM and the Constant

4.1 The electric cooling fan (arrow indicates fan motor) is mounted in a plastic shroud attached to the radiator

Control Relay Module (CCRM), which incorporates the high and low-speed fan relays and the air conditioning relay. The coolant temperature sensor signals the PCM of engine temperature, and the CCRM turns the fan on at LOW speed when coolant temperature reaches 221-degrees F, then turns the fan off when temperature lowers to 200-degrees F. The HIGH speed portion of the fan only operates when the

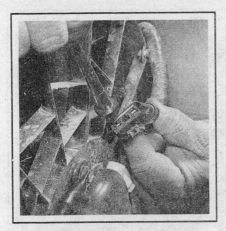

4.6 Pull the connector (arrow) from the fan and check for power under HOT conditions with a voltmeter - 3.8L model shown, test is on red wire

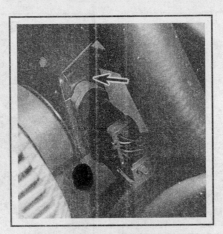

4.8a Location of the CCRM (arrow) on 1994 and 1995 models (to the right of the fan shroud)

4.8b On 1996 and later models, the CCRM (arrow) is located in the right fenderwell - the plastic inner fender shield must be removed for access

engines is hot and the air conditioning is on.

3   If the fan operates continuously, the fault could be the CCRM or the coolant temperature sensor. Refer to Chapter 6 for diagnosis of the sensor.

4   Warm the engine up until the gauge on the instrument panel indicates the high side of NORMAL. The fan should come on. If not, check the cooling fan fuse in the fuse junction panel (see Chapter 12 for fuse locations).

5   If the fuse checked OK, disconnect the electrical connector from the electric fan motor. On 3.8L and 5.0L models, there is only a black ground wire and red power wire. On 4.6L models, there are three wires: a black ground wire, a red/orange (low speed fan operation), and an orange/light blue wire (high speed fan operation).

6   Connect a voltmeter to a chassis ground and probe the connector at the red/orange wire (see illustration). If the engine is hot and the temperature gauge shows above NORMAL, there should be battery voltage at this wire. With the engine still hot, push the air conditioning control on the dash to MAX/AC and probe the terminal on the connector for the orange/light blue wire. There should be battery voltage.

7   Check the ground of the circuit by switching your meter to the ohms scale. Ground one side of the meter and probe the other side at the black wire terminal of the fan connector. Resistance should be no more than 5 ohms. If resistance is high, trace the ground wire (black/white) from the CCRM to the chassis.

8   If there had been no power at the terminals in Step 6, check that power is being supplied to the CCRM. In 1994 and 1995 models the CCRM is mounted to the right of the fan shroud (see illustrations). On later models it is located in the right fenderwell. Refer to Chapter 11 for removing the right inner splash shield for access to the CCRM, and to Chapter 4 for location and pin designations for the CCRM.

9   Two power feed wires (see Chapter 4 for tests) should have battery voltage at all times. Further diagnosis of the sealed CCRM should be performed at your Ford dealer using a factory tool.

REMOVAL AND INSTALLATION

▶ Refer to illustrations 4.10, 4.11, 4.12 and 4.13

10   Leave the electrical connector disconnected from the fan motor as in the above testing. At the right side of the fan shroud, disconnect the plastic clips holding the two wiring harnesses to the fan shroud (see illustration).

11   Remove the two fan shroud bolts and lift out the fan/shroud as an assembly (see illustration).

4.10 Unclip the two wiring harnesses (arrows) attached to the right side of the fan shroud

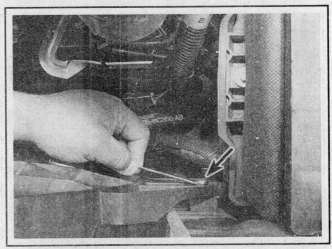

4.11 Remove the two bolts (arrow indicates bolt on left side) and lift out the fan/shroud as an assembly

4.12 Remove the metal clip (arrow) and deburr the motor's shaft to pull the fan from the motor

12 To remove the fan blade from the motor, take off the metal clip and slide the fan off the motor shaft (see illustration).

➡**Note: After removing the clip, file off any slight burrs on the shaft to ease removal of the fan.**

4.13 Remove these bolts (arrows) to separate the fan motor from the shroud

13 To replace the motor, remove the bolts holding it to the fan shroud (see illustration).
14 Installation is the reverse of removal.

5 Radiator, coolant reservoir and degas bottle - removal and installation

❄❄ WARNING 1:

The engine must be completely cool when this procedure is performed.

❄❄ WARNING 2:

The models covered by this manual are equipped with Supplemental Restraint Systems (SRS), more commonly known as airbags. Always disconnect the negative battery cable, then the positive battery cable and wait two minutes before working in the vicinity of the impact sensors, steering column or instrument panel to avoid the possibility of accidental deployment of the airbag, which could cause personal injury (see Chapter 12). Do not use any electrical test equipment on any of the airbag system wires or tamper with them in any way.

COOLANT RESERVOIR OR DEGAS BOTTLE

▶ **Refer to illustrations 5.2a, 5.2b and 5.3**

1 Disconnect the cable from the negative battery terminal.
2 Drain the cooling system as described in Chapter 1, then disconnect the hoses from the coolant reservoir (V6 and 5.0L V8 models) or the pressurized degas bottle (4.6L V8 models) (see illustrations).
3 Remove the bolts and detach the reservoir (see illustration).
4 Prior to installation make sure the reservoir is clean and free of debris which could be drawn into the radiator (wash inside it with soapy water and a long brush if necessary).
5 Installation is the reverse of removal.

5.2a Location of the coolant reservoir on V6 and 5.0L models - arrow indicates upper mounting bolt (the bottom of the reservoir is secured by a tab that fits into a lower bracket)

5.2b Location of the pressurized degas bottle on 4.6L models - disconnect the overflow hose (top arrow) and remove the two mounting bolts (lower arrows)

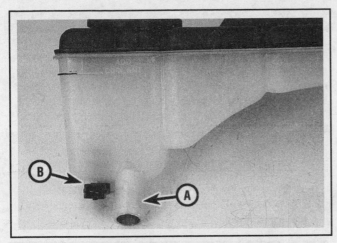

5.3 Degas bottle shown removed for clarity - A is the connection for the hose connecting to the lower radiator hose, B is the connector for the low-coolant sensor

RADIATOR

▶ **Refer to illustrations 5.7, 5.9a, 5.9b and 5.11**

6   Refer to Section 4 and remove the cooling fan and shroud assembly. Refer to above Steps for removal of the coolant reservoir or degas bottle.

7   If equipped with an automatic transmission, detach the cooler lines from the radiator (see illustration) - be careful not to damage the lines or fittings. Plug the ends of the disconnected lines to prevent leakage and stop dirt from entering the system. Have a drip pan ready to catch any spills.

8   Disconnect the upper and lower radiator hoses.

9   Remove the screws (or clips) on some models and remove the plastic shield over the radiator core support (see illustration). Remove the mounting bolts and take off the two upper radiator mounts (see illustration). Carefully lift the radiator out of the vehicle.

10   Prior to installation of the radiator, replace any damaged hose clamps and radiator hoses.

11   Radiator installation is the reverse of removal. When installing the radiator, make sure it seats properly in the lower saddles and that the rubber mounts are intact (see illustration).

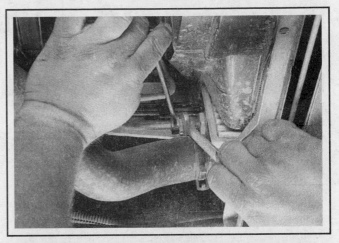

5.7 Use a flare-nut wrench on the line and a back-up wrench at the radiator fitting to prevent damage to the transmission cooler lines when disconnecting them from the radiator

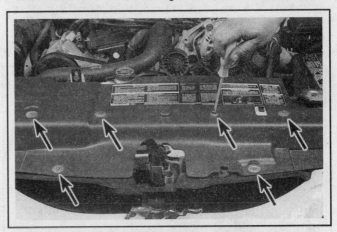

5.9a Remove the screws (arrows) and take off the plastic shield

12   After installation, fill the system with the proper mixture of anti-freeze, and also check the automatic transmission fluid level.

5.9b Remove the two bolts (arrows) and mounts holding the top of the radiator

5.11 Make sure the radiator lower mounts (arrow indicates left mount) are in place before installing the radiator - if they're beginning to deteriorate, now is the time to replace them

6   Coolant temperature sending unit - check and replacement

◆ Refer to illustrations 6.1a, 6.1b, 6.1c and 6.1d

❋ WARNING:

Wait until the engine is completely cool before beginning this procedure.

CHECK

1   The coolant temperature indicator system is composed of a temperature gauge mounted in the dash and a coolant temperature sending unit mounted on the engine (see illustrations). Some vehicles have more than one sending unit, but only one is used for the indicator system and the other is used to send engine temperature information to the computer.

2   If an overheating indication occurs, check the coolant level in the system. Make sure the wiring between the gauge and the sending unit is secure and all fuses are intact.

3   To test the temperature sender, disconnect the electrical connector at the sender and connect an ohmmeter between the sender's terminal and an engine ground. When the engine is cold, resistance should be close to 74 ohms. As the engine warms up, the sender's resistance should drop, and at full operating temperature should read around 9.7 ohms.

REPLACEMENT

4   If the sending unit must be replaced, disconnect the electrical connector and simply unscrew the sensor from the engine and install the replacement.

❋ CAUTION:

The sending unit is made up of metal and plastic and is fragile. Use care not to crack the unit when removing it. Use sealant on the threads. Make sure the engine is cool before removing the defective sending unit. There will be some coolant loss as the unit is removed, so be prepared to catch it. Check the coolant level after the replacement unit has been installed (see Chapter 1).

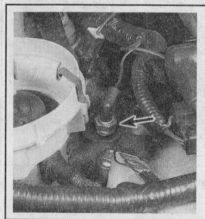

6.1a The coolant temperature sending unit on 5.0L engines is located at the front of the intake manifold near the distributor

6.1b Coolant temperature sending unit (arrow) location - V6 models

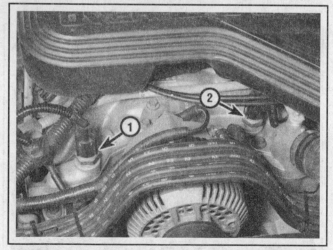

6.1c On the 4.6L SOHC engine, the coolant temperature sending unit is one of two at the front of the intake manifold; be sure to select the correct one for the repair procedure

1   Coolant temperature sending unit (gauge)
2   Coolant temperature sensor (computer)

6.1d The temperature sending unit (A) on 4.6L DOHC engines is in the left pipe of the metal coolant bypass tube; the coolant temperature sensor (B) is for the engine management system

7 Engine oil cooler - replacement

REMOVAL

▶ **Refer to illustrations 7.1, 7.5 and 7.7**

❊ WARNING:

The engine should be completely cool for this procedure.

1 All Cobra models have an engine oil cooler, which is sandwiched between the oil filter and the engine block (see illustration). Coolant flows through the cooler from the block to the lower radiator hose.

2 To replace the oil cooler, refer to Chapter 1 for removal of the oil filter and draining of the cooling system.

3 Disconnect the lower radiator hose from the oil cooler (see illustration 7.1).

4 Disconnect the electrical connector from the oil pressure sending unit on the oil filter adapter.

5 Use a 1/2-inch Allen wrench inside the threaded adapter holding the oil cooler housing to the oil filter adapter housing (see illustration).

6 Pull the oil cooler from the adapter on the block.

7 If only the oil cooler is to be replaced, this is as far as you need to disassemble components. If the oil cooler adapter is to be removed, remove the four bolts holding it to the block and remove it (see illustration).

INSTALLATION

▶ **Refer to illustration 7.9**

8 Clean the block and back of the oil cooler adapter of any old gasket material. Install the adapter to the block with a new gasket and

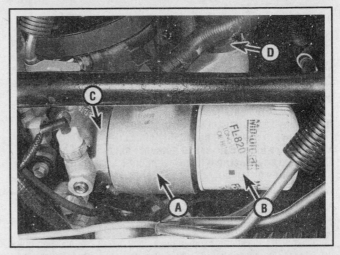

7.1 On Cobra models, the oil cooler (A) is between the oil filter (B) and the oil cooler adapter housing (C) at the lower left side of the engine block - (D) is the lower radiator hose

tighten the bolts to the torque listed in this Chapter's Specifications.

9 Clean the coolant sealing surfaces of the adapter and oil cooler, and install new O-rings (see illustration). Clean the threads of the threaded tube and apply non-hardening thread-locking compound to the end that goes into the oil cooler adapter. Insert it through the oil cooler and tighten it to this Chapter's Specifications.

10 The remainder of installation is the reverse of removal. Install a new oil filter, refill and bleed the cooling system (see Chapter 1), and run the engine to check for oil or coolant leaks.

7.5 Use a 1/2-inch Allen wrench inside the large threaded tube (arrow) in the center of the oil cooler

7.7 Remove the four bolts (arrows) holding the oil cooler adapter to the block

7.9 Install a new O-ring (arrow) on the oil cooler - also replace the O-ring on the adapter housing before installing the oil cooler

8 Water pump - check

▶ **Refer to illustration 8.2**

❈❈ **WARNING:**

The models covered by this manual are equipped with Supplemental Restraint Systems (SRS), more commonly known as airbags. Always disconnect the negative battery cable, then the positive battery cable and wait two minutes before working in the vicinity of the impact sensors, steering column or instrument panel to avoid the possibility of accidental deployment of the airbag, which could cause personal injury (see Chapter 12). Do not use any electrical test equipment on any of the airbag system wires or tamper with them in any way.

1 Water pump failure can cause overheating and serious damage to the engine. There are three ways to check the operation of the water pump while it's installed on the engine. If any one of the following quick checks indicates water pump problems, it should be replaced immediately.

2 A seal protects the water pump impeller shaft bearing from contamination by engine coolant. If this seal fails, a weep hole in the water pump snout will leak coolant (see illustration) (an inspection mirror can be used to look at the underside of the pump if the hole isn't on top). If the weep hole is leaking, shaft bearing failure will follow. Replace the water pump immediately.

➡ **Note: A small amount of gray discoloration is normal. A wet area or heavy brown deposits indicate the pump seal has failed.**

3 Besides contamination by coolant after a seal failure, the water pump impeller shaft bearing can also prematurely wear out. If a noise is coming from the water pump during engine operation, the shaft bearing

8.2 If there's coolant leaking from the weep hole (arrow) the water pump must be replaced

has failed - replace the water pump immediately.

➡ **Note: Do not confuse drivebelt noise with bearing noise. Loose or glazed drivebelts may emit a high-pitched squealing noise.**

4 To identify excessive bearing wear before the bearing actually fails, grasp the water pump pulley (with drivebelt removed) and try to force it up-and-down or from side-to-side. If the pulley can be moved either horizontally or vertically, the bearing is nearing the end of its service life. Replace the water pump.

9 Water pump - removal and installation

❈❈ **WARNING:**

The models covered by this manual are equipped with Supplemental Restraint Systems (SRS), more commonly known as airbags. Always disconnect the negative battery cable, then the positive battery cable and wait two minutes before working in the vicinity of the impact sensors, steering column or instrument panel to avoid the possibility of accidental deployment of the airbag, which could cause personal injury (see Chapter 12). Do not use any electrical test equipment on any of the airbag system wires or tamper with them in any way.

REMOVAL

▶ **Refer to illustrations 9.5, 9.8, 9.9a, 9.9b and 9.9c**

❈❈ **WARNING:**

Wait until the engine is completely cool before starting this procedure.

1 Disconnect the cable from the negative battery terminal.
2 With the engine cold, drain the cooling system (see Chapter 1).
3 Remove the fan shroud and the fan assembly (see Section 4).

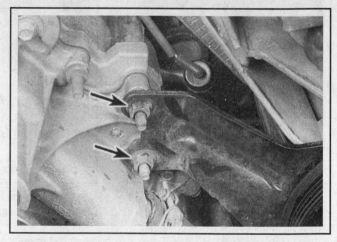

9.5 On V6 engines, the power steering pump bracket fits over the water pump mounting studs (arrows)

4 Remove the drivebelt(s) (see Chapter 1) and remove the water pump pulley.

➡ **Note: It's helpful to loosen the pulley bolts/nuts while the belt is still in place. It helps hold the pulley from turning.**

5 On 5.0L engines, if the power steering pump bracket is retained

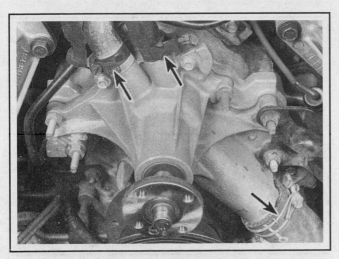

9.8 On 5.0L and V6 engines, detach the radiator hose, heater hose and bypass hose (arrows)

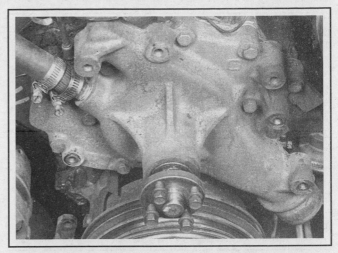

9.9a On 5.0L engines, after the belt-driven accessory brackets have been removed, remove the hoses and the water pump retaining bolts

at the water pump, the power steering pump should be completely removed and laid to one side to facilitate removal of the bracket. On 3.8L V6 engines, remove the power steering pump pulley (see Chapter 10) and remove the brace from the water pump to the power steering pump (see illustration).

9.9b On 4.6L engines, remove the four bolts (arrows) . . .

6   On 5.0L engines equipped with air conditioning, remove the idler pulley and bracket assembly.

7   Remove any accessory brackets that attach to the water pump.

8   On 5.0L and 3.8L V6 engines, remove the lower radiator hose, the heater hose and the by-pass hose from the water pump (see illustration).

9   Remove the water pump retaining bolts and remove the water pump (see illustrations). On 5.0L and V6 engines, take note of the installed positions of the various length bolts and studs (see illustration 9.8 for V6 mounting bolts). On 4.6L V8 engines, the water pump is retained by only four bolts.

INSTALLATION

▶ **Refer to illustrations 9.11, 9.12a and 9.12b**

10   Before installation, remove and clean all gasket or sealant material from the water pump, cylinder front cover, or cylinder block.

11   On 4.6L engines, inspect the O-ring and sealing surface of water pump housing in the block for dirt and/or debris (see illustration). Clean them thoroughly before reassembly.

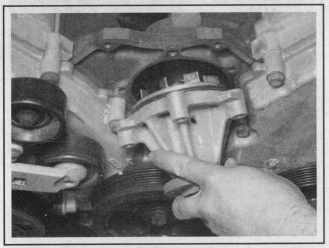

9.9c . . . and remove the water pump from out of the engine block - if it sticks, knock it loose with a soft-face hammer (or a hammer and a block of wood)

9.11 On 4.6L engines, inspect the sealing surface (arrow) in the pump cavity for dirt or signs of pitting

9.12a On 4.6L engines, install a new O-ring seal on the water pump

9.12b On V6 engines, apply sealant to the threads of the bolt for this location (arrow)

12 On 5.0L engines, position new gaskets on the water pump and coat them on both sides with RTV sealant. On 4.6L engines, lubricate a new O-ring seal with clean antifreeze and install it to the water pump (see illustration). On 3.8L V6 engines, coat the threads of the lower right bolt of the right water passage with sealant before installation (see illustration).

13 Install the water pump and tighten the bolts to the torque listed in this Chapter's Specifications.

14 On 5.0L engines, it may be necessary to transfer some hose ports and/or fittings from the old pump if you are replacing it with a new one.

15 On 5.0L and V6 engines, install the lower radiator hose, heater hose and by-pass hose to the water pump. Replace the hose clamps with new ones, if necessary.

16 Install the remaining components to the water pump and engine in the reverse order of removal.

17 Fill the cooling system with the proper coolant mixture.

18 Start the engine and make sure there are no leaks. Check the level frequently during the first few weeks of operation to ensure there are no leaks and that the level in the system is stable.

10 Heater and air conditioning blower motor circuit -check

▶ Refer to illustrations 10.5a, 10.5b, 10.6, 10.7 and 10.9

❊❊ WARNING:

The models covered by this manual are equipped with Supplemental Restraint Systems (SRS), more commonly known as airbags. Always disconnect the negative battery cable, then the positive battery cable and wait two minutes before working in the vicinity of the impact sensors, steering column or instrument panel to avoid the possibility of accidental deployment of the airbag, which could cause personal injury (see Chapter 12). Do not use any electrical test equipment on any of the airbag system wires or tamper with them in any way.

➡Note: The blower motor is switched on the ground-side of the circuit.

1 Check the fuse and all connections in the circuit for looseness and corrosion.

2 Make sure the battery is fully charged.

3 With the transmission in Park, the parking brake securely set, turn the ignition switch to the On position. It isn't necessary to start the vehicle.

4 Switch the heater controls to FLOOR and the blower speed to HI. Listen at the ducts to hear if the blower is operating. If it is, then switch the blower speed to LO and listen again. Try all the speeds.

5 The blower motor resistor assembly is located on the evapora-

10.5a Blower motor resistor location on the duct above the blower motor - disconnect the wiring connector and remove the two screws (arrows)

tor case under the dash (see illustrations). Refer to Chapter 11 for the procedure to remove the glove box for access to the blower and blower motor resistor. There are three resistor elements mounted on the resistor board to provide low and medium blower speeds (HI

10.5b The thermal limiter (arrow) protects the components from excessive heat - check the thermal limiter for damage

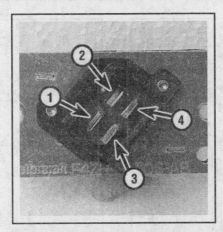

10.6 Test the terminals of the blower resistor with an ohmmeter for continuity

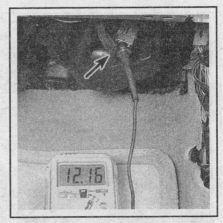

10.7 Backprobe the battery feed wire at the blower motor connector (arrow) - there should be voltage with the mode switch in any position other than Off and the ignition key On

bypasses the resistor). The blower operates continuously, anytime the ignition switch is On and the mode switch is in any position other than Off. A thermal limiter resistor is integrated into the circuits to prevent heat damage to the components. If the thermal limiter circuit has been opened as a result of excessive heat, it should be replaced only with the identical replacement part.

➡Note: Do not replace your blower resistor with a resistor that does not incorporate the thermal limiter.

6   With the resistor removed from the vehicle, visually check the limiter for damage, indicated by the material melting out between the contacts of the limiter. Check the resistor block for continuity between all terminals (see illustration). There should be continuity between terminals 3 and 4 with a resistance of approximately 1.3 to 1.5 ohms; continuity between terminals 2 and 4 with a resistance of 1.8 to 2.0 ohms, and continuity between terminals 1 and 4 with total resistance of 2.3 to 2.5 ohms. If any of the resistor elements do not pass the tests, replace the blower resistor.

7   Locate the electrical connector at the blower motor. Backprobe the dark blue/light green wire terminal; there should be battery voltage with the mode switch in any position other than Off and the ignition switch On (see illustration). If not, there is a problem in the circuit from the fuse panel to the heater/air conditioning control panel, or from the control panel to the blower.

8   If there is voltage at the feed wire, but the blower does not operate, backprobe the black wire and connect it to a known good chassis ground with a jumper wire. If the blower now operates there is a problem in the ground circuit. If it still doesn't operate, replace the blower motor.

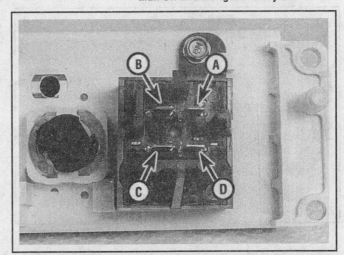

10.9 Check the blower speed switch for continuity (see text)

9   If the blower operates, but not at all speeds and you have already checked the blower resistor, refer to Section 12 and remove the heater/air conditioning control panel. Disconnect the electrical connector from the back of the blower speed switch and test the terminals for continuity (see illustration). In the Medium 1 position, there should be continuity between terminals B and D; in Medium 2 position, there should be continuity between terminals B and C; and in HI position, there should be continuity between terminals B and A. If the continuity is not as described, replace the blower speed switch.

11 Heater and air conditioning blower motor - removal and installation

▸ Refer to illustrations 11.2a, 11.2b and 11.3

❉❉ WARNING:

The models covered by this manual are equipped with Supplemental Restraint Systems (SRS), more commonly known as airbags. Always disconnect the negative battery cable, then the positive battery cable and wait two minutes before working in the vicinity of the impact sensors, steering column or instru-

ment panel to avoid the possibility of accidental deployment of the airbag, which could cause personal injury (see Chapter 12). Do not use any electrical test equipment on any of the airbag system wires or tamper with them in any way.

1   Disconnect the blower motor electrical connector from the motor (see illustration 10.5a).
2   Remove the three blower motor retaining screws. Separate the

11.2a Remove the three blower motor mounting screws (arrows)

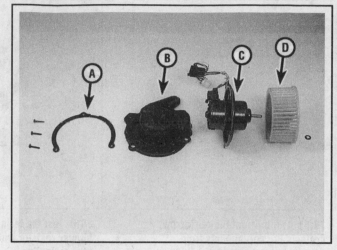

11.2b Blower motor components

A	Stiffener plate	C	Blower motor
B	Blower motor cover	D	Fan

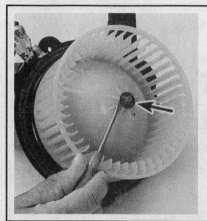

11.3 Pry off the retaining clip (arrow) retaining the blower fan to the blower motor shaft

blower motor from the blower motor cover and stiffener plate (see illustrations).

3   If the blower motor is being replaced, the fan wheel should be transferred to the new motor at this time. It is attached to the blower motor shaft with a push nut. Grasp the nut with a pliers and pull it off or pry it off with a small screwdriver, being careful not to crack the push nut (see illustration). To reinstall the nut, simply push it on to the shaft.

4   The remainder of the installation is the reverse of removal.

12 Heater and air conditioning control assembly - removal and installation

✳✳ WARNING:

The models covered by this manual are equipped with Supplemental Restraint Systems (SRS), more commonly known as airbags. Always disconnect the negative battery cable, then the positive battery cable and wait two minutes before working in the vicinity of the impact sensors, steering column or instrument panel to avoid the possibility of accidental deployment of the airbag, which could cause personal injury (see Chapter 12). Do not use any electrical test equipment on any of the airbag system wires or tamper with them in any way.

REMOVAL

▶ **Refer to illustrations 12.2, 12.3a, 12.3b and 12.3c**

1   Refer to Chapter 11 for removal of the center dash bezel, around the control assembly and radio.

2   Remove the four screws retaining the control assembly to the instrument panel (see illustration).

12.2 After the trim is removed, remove the four screws (arrows) and pull the control assembly out of the dash

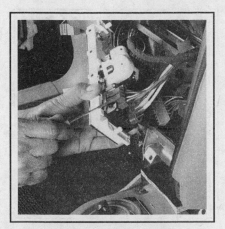

12.3a Disconnect the electrical connectors by gently prying up the clips and pulling the connectors off

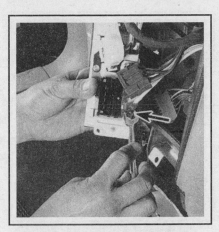

12.3b The vacuum connector can be disconnected by removing this nut (arrow)

12.3c Remove the two screws to disconnect the temperature control cable

3   Pull the control assembly out of the instrument panel and disconnect the electrical connectors, vacuum harness and temperature control cable (see illustrations).

➡**Note: When disconnecting the vacuum lines, be careful to avoid cracking the plastic connectors and causing a vacuum** leak (possibly internal within the control head).

4   Refer to Section 10 for electrical checks of the blower motor speed switch.

5   Installation is the reverse of the removal procedure.

13   Heater core - removal and installation

❋❋ WARNING 1:

The models covered by this manual are equipped with Supplemental Restraint Systems (SRS), more commonly known as airbags. Always disconnect the negative battery cable, then the positive battery cable and wait two minutes before working in the vicinity of the impact sensors, steering column or instrument panel to avoid the possibility of accidental deployment of the airbag, which could cause personal injury (see Chapter 12). Do not use any electrical test equipment on any of the airbag system wires or tamper with them in any way.

❋❋ WARNING 2:

The air conditioning system is under high pressure. DO NOT loosen any fittings or remove any components until after the system has been discharged. Air conditioning refrigerant should be properly discharged into an EPA-approved container at a dealer service department or an automotive air conditioning repair facility. Always wear eye protection when disconnecting air conditioning system fittings.

➡**Note: On 2001 and later models, refer to Section 19 for disconnecting and connecting of the heater hose couplings.**

REMOVAL

▸ **Refer to illustrations 13.3, 13.5, 13.6a, 13.6b, 13.6c, 13.7, 13.8a and 13.8b**

1   Take the vehicle to a dealer service department or automotive air conditioning shop and have the air conditioning system discharged.

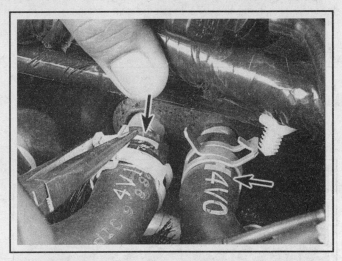

13.3 Slide the clamps back and disconnect the heater hoses from the heater core inlet and outlet pipes (arrows) at the right side of the firewall

2   Disconnect the cable from the negative battery terminal. Drain the cooling system (see Chapter 1).

3   On 1994 through 2000 models, disconnect the heater hoses from the heater core inlet and outlet tubes at the firewall (see illustration). Disconnect and plug the evaporator lines at the firewall (see Section 18). Plug the heater core tubes to avoid spilling any coolant during removal. Cap the evaporator lines to prevent the entry of dirt and moisture.

4   Remove the instrument panel (see Chapter 11).

13.5 Disconnect the main vacuum connector (arrow) from the engine to the heater/evaporator housing, and pull the hose through the firewall into the interior

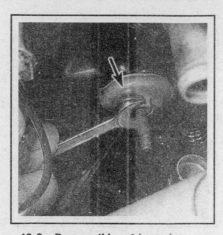

13.6a Remove this nut (arrow), located on the firewall just below the heater hose connections

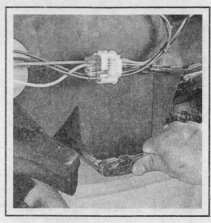

13.6b Working inside the vehicle, use an extension and socket to reach the center bolt at the bottom of the heater/evaporator housing

5   Disconnect the main vacuum line from the heater/evaporator housing to the engine (see illustration). It is located above the rear of the right valve cover. Pull the hose through the firewall into the interior.

6   Remove the heater/evaporator housing fasteners, which include a bolt near the top center of the unit, a nut at the top right, a bolt near the bottom, and a nut on the engine side of the firewall (see illustrations).

7   Making sure no other wires or hoses are connected to the housing, pull the heater/evaporator housing out from under the cowl and remove it from the vehicle (see illustration).

8   Remove the four screws and the heater core cover, then pull out the heater core, being careful not to tear the foam sealing material (see illustrations).

INSTALLATION

▶ **Refer to illustration 13.9**

9   When reinstalling the heater core in the housing, make sure the original foam sealing material is intact and in place (see illustration).

13.6c Remove the bolt and nut (arrows) retaining the heat/AC unit to the cowl

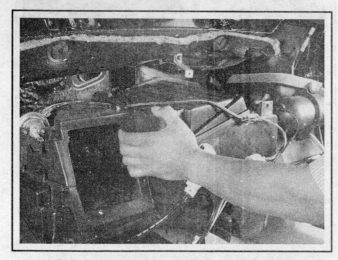

13.7 Carefully pull the housing out from under the cowl - remove it from the vehicle without tilting it, so coolant isn't spilled on the carpeting

13.8a Remove the four screws (arrows) and retaining cover . . .

13.8b . . . then lift the heater core from the assembly

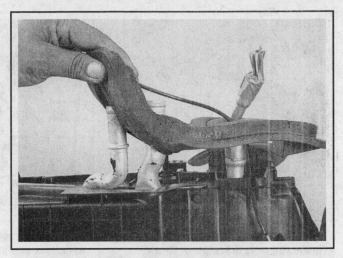

13.9 When reinstalling the heater/evaporator housing, make sure the foam sealing is in place and not torn

10 Route the vacuum supply hose through the dash panel and seat the grommet in the opening.

11 Position the assembled heater/evaporator unit under the cowl. Insert the heater core tubes, evaporator lines and mounting studs through their respective holes in the firewall.

12 The remainder of the installation is the reverse of removal.

13 Fill the cooling system (see Chapter 1). Run the engine and check for coolant leaks. Have the air conditioning system charged and check for proper operation of the system.

14 Air conditioning and heating system - check and maintenance

❄❄ WARNING:

The air conditioning system is under high pressure. DO NOT loosen any fittings or remove any components until after the system has been discharged. Air conditioning refrigerant should be properly discharged into an EPA-approved container at a dealer service department or an automotive air conditioning repair facility. Always wear eye protection when disconnecting air conditioning system fittings.

1 The following maintenance steps should be performed on a regular basis to ensure that the air conditioner continues to operate at peak efficiency.

  a) *Check the tension of the drivebelt and adjust if necessary (see Chapter 1).*
  b) *Check the condition of the hoses. Look for cracks, hardening and deterioration.*

❄❄ WARNING:

Do not replace air conditioning hoses until the system has been discharged by a dealer or air conditioning shop.

  c) *Check the fins of the condenser for leaves, bugs and other foreign material. A soft brush and compressed air can be used to remove them.*
  d) *Check the wire harness for correct routing, broken wires, damaged insulation, etc. Make sure the harness connections are clean and tight.*
  e) *Maintain the correct refrigerant charge.*

2 The system should be run for about 10 minutes at least once a month. This is particularly important during the winter months because long-term non-use can cause hardening of the internal seals.

3 Because of the complexity of the air conditioning system and the special equipment required to effectively work on it, accurate troubleshooting of the system should be left to a professional technician. One probable cause for poor cooling that can be determined by the home mechanic is low refrigerant charge. Should the system lose its cooling ability, the following procedure will help you pinpoint the cause.

CHECK

▶ **Refer to illustration 14.7**

4 Warm the engine up to normal operating temperature.

5 Place the air conditioning temperature selector at the coldest setting and put the blower at the highest setting. Open the doors (to make sure the air conditioning system doesn't cycle off as soon as it cools the passenger compartment).

6 After the system reaches operating temperature, feel the two pipes connected to the evaporator at the firewall.

7 The pipe (thinner tubing) leading from the condenser outlet to the evaporator should be cold, and the evaporator outlet line (the thicker tubing that leads back to the compressor) should be slightly colder (3 to 10 degrees F). If the evaporator outlet is considerably warmer than the inlet, the system needs a charge. Insert a thermometer in the center air distribution duct (see illustration) while operating the air conditioning system - the temperature of the output air should be 35 to 40 degrees F below the ambient air temperature (down to approximately 40 degrees F). If the ambient (outside) air temperature is very high, say

14.7 Place an accurate thermometer in the center dash vent, turn the air conditioning on and check the output temperature

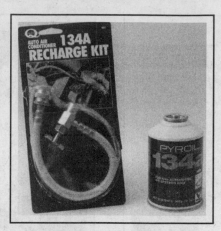

14.9 A basic charging kit for R-134a systems is available at most auto parts stores - it must say R-134a (not R-12) and so must the can of refrigerant

14.12 Add R-134a only to the low-side port (arrow) - the procedure is easier if you wrap the can with a warm, wet towel to prevent icing

110 degrees F, the duct air temperature may be as high as 60 degrees F, but generally the air conditioning is 35 to 40 degrees F cooler than the ambient air. If the air isn't as cold as it used to be, the system probably needs a charge. Further inspection or testing of the system is beyond the scope of the home mechanic and should be left to a professional.

ADDING REFRIGERANT

▶ **Refer to illustrations 14.9, 14.12**

➡**Note: All models covered by this manual use refrigerant R-134a.**

8   When recharging or replacing air conditioning components, use only refrigerant, refrigerant oil and seals compatible with this system. The seals and compressor oil used with older, conventional R-12 refrigerant are not compatible with the components in this system.

9   Buy an automotive charging kit at an auto parts store. A charging kit includes a 14-ounce can of R-134a refrigerant, a tap valve and a short section of hose that can be attached between the tap valve and the system low side service valve (see illustration). Because one can of refrigerant may not be sufficient to bring the system charge up to the proper level, it's a good idea to buy a couple of additional cans. Try to find at least one can that contains red refrigerant dye. If the system is leaking, the red dye will leak out with the refrigerant and help you pinpoint the location of the leak.

10   Connect the charging kit by following the manufacturer's instructions.

11   Back off the valve handle on the charging kit and screw the kit onto the refrigerant can, making sure first that the O-ring or rubber seal inside the threaded portion of the kit is in place.

❋❋ **WARNING:**

Wear protective eye wear when dealing with pressurized refrigerant cans.

12   Remove the dust cap from the low-side charging port and attach the quick-connect fitting on the kit hose (see illustration).

❋❋ **WARNING:**

DO NOT hook the charging kit hose to the system high side! The fittings on the charging kit are designed to fit only on the low side of the system.

13   Warm the engine to normal operating temperature and turn on the air conditioning. Keep the charging kit hose away from the fan and other moving parts.

14   Turn the valve handle on the kit until the stem pierces the can, then back the handle out to release the refrigerant. You should be able to hear the rush of gas. Add refrigerant to the low side of the system until both the outlet and the evaporator inlet pipe feel about the same temperature. Allow stabilization time between each addition.

❋❋ **WARNING:**

Never add more than two cans of refrigerant to the system. The can may tend to frost up, slowing the procedure. Wrap a shop towel wet with hot water around the bottom of the can to keep it from frosting.

15   Put your thermometer back in the center register and check that the output air is getting colder.

16   When the can is empty, turn the valve handle to the closed position and release the connection from the low-side port. Replace the dust cap.

17   Remove the charging kit from the can and store the kit for future use with the piercing valve in the UP position, to prevent inadvertently piercing the can on the next use.

HEATING SYSTEMS

▶ **Refer to illustration 14.22**

18   If the air coming out of the heater vents isn't hot, the problem could stem from any of the following causes:

a)   *The thermostat is stuck open, preventing the engine coolant from warming up enough to carry heat to the heater core. Replace the thermostat (see Section 3).*

14.22 Check the evaporator drain tube (arrow) for blockage that could lead to mildew on the core - this view is from below on the right side, near the exhaust manifold-to-pipe connection (pipe removed for clarity)

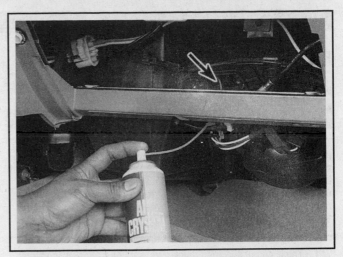

14.26 Remove the blower resistor and spray disinfectant through the hole (arrow) onto the core to destroy mildew that causes air conditioning odors

ELIMINATING AIR-CONDITIONING ODORS

b) *A heater hose is blocked, preventing the flow of coolant through the heater core. Feel both heater hoses at the firewall. They should be hot. If one of them is cold, there is an obstruction in one of the hoses or in the heater core, or the heater control valve is shut. Detach the hoses and back flush the heater core with a water hose. If the heater core is clear but circulation is impeded, remove the two hoses and flush them out with a water hose.*

c) *If flushing fails to remove the blockage from the heater core, the core must be replaced. (see Section 13).*

19 If the blower motor speed does not correspond to the setting selected on the blower switch, the problem could be a bad fuse, circuit, control panel or blower resistor (see Section 10).

20 If there isn't any air coming out of the vents:

a) *Turn the ignition ON and activate the fan control. Place your ear at the heating/air conditioning register (vent) and listen. Most motors are audible. Can you hear the motor running?*

b) *If you can't (and have already verified that the blower switch and the blower motor resistor are good), the blower motor itself is probably bad (see Section 11).*

21 If the carpet under the heater core is damp, or if antifreeze vapor or steam is coming through the vents, the heater core is leaking. Remove it (see Section 13) and install a new unit (most radiator shops will not repair a leaking heater core).

22 Inspect the drain hose from the heater/evaporator assembly at the right side of the firewall, make sure it is not clogged (see illustration). If there is a humid mist coming from the system ducts, this hose may be plugged with leaves or road debris.

▶ **Refer to illustration 14.26**

23 Unpleasant odors that often develop in air-conditioning systems are caused by the growth of a fungus, usually on the surface of the evaporator core. The warm, humid environment there is a perfect breeding ground for mildew to develop.

24 The evaporator core on most vehicles is difficult to access, and factory dealerships have a lengthy, expensive process for eliminating the fungus by opening up the evaporator case and using a powerful disinfectant and rinse on the core until the fungus is gone. You can service your own system at home, but it takes something much stronger than basic household germ-killers or deodorizers.

25 Aerosol disinfectants for automotive air-conditioning systems are available in most auto parts stores, but remember when shopping for them that the most effective treatments are also the most expensive. The basic procedure for using these sprays is to start by running the system in the RECIRC mode for ten minutes with the blower on its highest speed. Use the highest heat mode to dry out the system and keep the compressor from engaging by disconnecting the wiring connector at the compressor (see Section 16).

26 The disinfectant can usually comes with a long spray hose. Remove the blower motor resistor (see Section 10), point the nozzle inside the hole and spray, according to the manufacturer's recommendations (see illustration). Try to cover the whole surface of the evaporator core, by aiming the spray up, down and sideways. Follow the manufacturer's recommendations for the length of spray and waiting time between applications.

27 Once the evaporator has been cleaned, the best way to prevent the mildew from coming back again is to make sure your evaporator housing drain tube is clear (see illustration 14.22).

15 Air conditioning accumulator/ drier - removal and installation

REMOVAL

♦ **Refer to illustrations 15.3, 15.4a, 15.4b and 15.5**

⁂ WARNING:

The air conditioning system is under high pressure. DO NOT loosen any fittings or remove any components until after the system has been discharged. Air conditioning refrigerant should be properly discharged into an EPA-approved container at a dealer service department or an automotive air conditioning repair facility. Always wear eye protection when disconnecting air conditioning system fittings.

1   The accumulator/drier stores refrigerant and removes moisture from the system. When any major air conditioning component (compressor, condenser, evaporator) is replaced, or the system has been apart and exposed to air for any length of time, the accumulator/drier must be replaced.

2   Take the vehicle to a dealer service department or automotive air conditioning shop and have the air conditioning system discharged. Disconnect the cable at the negative battery terminal.

3   Disconnect the electrical connector at the compressor clutch cycling switch on top of the accumulator/drier (see illustration).

4   Disconnect the refrigerant inlet and outlet lines (see illustrations). Remove the metal clips first, then use spring-lock coupling tools to disconnect the two lines from accumulator/drier. To disconnect a fitting, close the two halves of the tool over the connection and push the tool towards the garter spring. This expands the spring to release its hold. While the spring is expanded and tool is still in place, pull in opposite directions on the two lines to separate the connection. Cap or plug the open lines immediately.

➡**Note: Special spring lock coupling tools are required to release the connectors used on the refrigerant lines throughout the air conditioning system, and are available at most auto parts stores in a set.**

5   Remove the nut from the mounting bracket and slide the accumulator/drier assembly up and out of the mounting bracket (see illustration).

15.3 Disconnect the electrical connector (arrow) at the compressor clutch cycling switch

15.4a Pull off the metal clip at each connection . . .

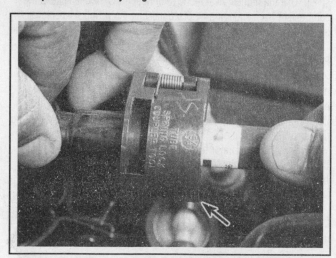

15.4b . . . and use the spring-lock coupling tool according to the tool manufacturer's recommendations to separate the line connections

15.5 Remove the mounting nut in the clamp (arrow), spread the clamp slightly and pull the accumulator/drier up and out

INSTALLATION

6   If you are replacing the accumulator/drier, drain the refrigerant oil from the old accumulator/drier. Add the same amount plus two ounces of clean refrigerant oil to the new accumulator. This will maintain the correct oil level in the system after the repairs are completed.

➡**Note: The manufacturer recommends that to properly drain all of the oil from the accumulator/drier for an accurate measurement, you should drill two half-inch holes in the bottom of the accumulator/drier.**

7   Place the new accumulator/drier into position, tighten the mounting bracket screw lightly, still allowing the accumulator drier to be turned to align the line connections.

8   Install the inlet and outlet lines. Lubricate the O-rings using clean refrigerant oil and reconnect the lines. Now tighten the clamp bolt securely and reconnect the electrical connector.

9   Connect the cable to the negative terminal of the battery.

10 Have the system evacuated, recharged and leak tested by a dealer service department or an air conditioning repair facility.

---

16 Air conditioning compressor - removal and installation

✳ WARNING:

The air conditioning system is under high pressure. DO NOT loosen any fittings or remove any components until after the system has been discharged. Air conditioning refrigerant should be properly discharged into an EPA-approved container at a dealer service department or an automotive air conditioning repair facility. Always wear eye protection when disconnecting air conditioning system fittings.

➡**Note: Special spring-lock coupling tools are required to release the connectors used on the refrigerant lines throughout the air conditioning system. There are different special tools for each line size; these tools can usually be found at local auto parts stores, often in a set. See Section 15 for tool description and use.**

REMOVAL

▸ **Refer to illustrations 16.3a, 16.3b, 16.4 and 16.5**

✳ CAUTION:

Whenever a compressor is replaced, it will be necessary to replace the accumulator/drier.

16.3a Unbolt the refrigerant line block from the back of the compressor (shown removed from vehicle)

1   Take the vehicle to a dealer service department or automotive air conditioning shop and have the air conditioning system discharged. Disconnect the cable from the negative battery terminal.

2   Remove the accessory drivebelt(s) (see Chapter 1). On V6 models, remove the air filter assembly. On 5.0L V8 models, remove the battery and the battery tray.

3   Disconnect the refrigerant lines from the compressor (see illustration).

4   Disconnect the electrical connection at the compressor clutch (see illustration).

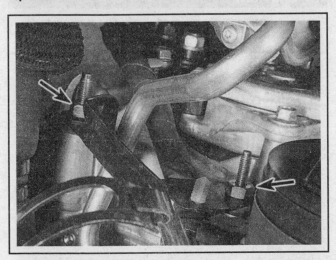

16.3b At the front of the compressor, remove these two nuts (arrows) to release the support bracket on the line carrying the inline filter - this view is looking up from below

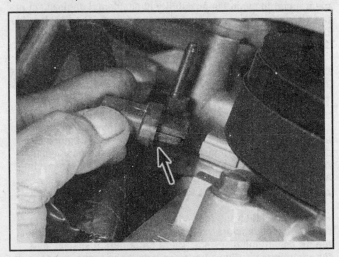

16.4 Disconnect the electrical connector (arrow) at the bottom front of the compressor

16.5 Remove the mounting bolts (arrows) and remove the air conditioning compressor from the engine compartment

5   Remove the compressor mounting bolts (see illustration).

6   Remove the compressor from the mounting location. Drain and measure the refrigerant oil from the compressor.

INSTALLATION

▶ **Refer to illustration 16.9**

7   If the compressor is being replaced, drain any shipping oil that may be in the new compressor.

8   If the amount of refrigerant oil drained from the old compressor

16.9 Use new O-rings (arrows), lubricated with refrigerant oil, when reattaching the line block to the compressor

was 3 ounces or less, add a total of 6 ounces of new oil to the new compressor. If the amount drained was more than 5 ounces, add that amount of new oil, and if the drained amount was between 3 and 5 ounces, add that amount plus an extra ounce to the new compressor.

9   Installation procedures are the reverse of those for removal. When installing the fitting block, use new O-rings and lubricate them with clean refrigerant oil (see illustration).

10   After the compressor is installed, have the system evacuated, recharged and leak tested by a dealer service department or an air conditioning repair facility.

---

17   Air conditioning condenser - removal and installation

✳✳ WARNING 1:

The models covered by this manual are equipped with Supplemental Restraint Systems (SRS), more commonly known as airbags. Always disconnect the negative battery cable, then the positive battery cable and wait two minutes before working in the vicinity of the impact sensors, steering column or instrument panel to avoid the possibility of accidental deployment of the airbag, which could cause personal injury (see Chapter 12). Do not use any electrical test equipment on any of the airbag system wires or tamper with them in any way.

✳✳ WARNING 2:

The air conditioning system is under high pressure. DO NOT loosen any fittings or remove any components until after the system has been discharged. Air conditioning refrigerant should be properly discharged into an EPA-approved container at a dealer service department or an automotive air conditioning repair facility. Always wear eye protection when disconnecting air conditioning system fittings.

➡Note: Special spring-lock coupling tools are required to release the connectors used on the refrigerant lines throughout the air conditioning system. There are different special tools for each line size; these tools can usually be found at local auto parts stores, often in a set. See Section 15 for tool description and use.

REMOVAL

▶ **Refer to illustrations 17.6 and 17.7**

✳✳ CAUTION:

Whenever a condenser is replaced, it will be necessary to replace the accumulator/drier (see Section 15).

1   Take the vehicle to a dealer service department or automotive air conditioning shop and have the air conditioning system discharged.

2   Disconnect the battery cables and remove the battery and battery tray (refer to Chapter 5).

3   Refer to Section 4 and remove the cooling fan and shroud assembly.

4   On 4.6L models, refer to Chapter 6 and remove the air cleaner assembly.

5   Refer to Section 5 and remove the coolant reservoir, upper radiator hose and radiator top mounting brackets.

6   Use spring-lock coupling tools to disconnect the two lines at the right side of the condenser (see illustration). See Section 15 for tool use procedure.

7   Remove the two condenser mounting brackets bolted to the radiator support (see illustration). Carefully tilt the radiator to the rear and lift the condenser out of the bottom cradle supports.

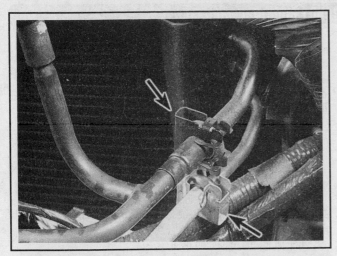

17.6 Using the special spring-lock coupling tool, disconnect the spring lock couplers (arrows) on the right side of the condenser

17.7 The condenser is mounted to the radiator support in rubber blocks (A), remove the bolt (B) on each side and pull the condenser back (toward the engine) from under the radiator support, then up and out

INSTALLATION

8 If the condenser is being replaced with a new one, transfer the brackets and mounts from the old unit to the new one.

9 When replacing the condenser add one ounce of refrigerant oil to the condenser before reassembly. This will maintain the correct oil level in the system after the repairs are completed.

10 Before installation, check the bracket assemblies and mounts for excessive wear or damage. Replace them if necessary.

11 The installation procedures are the reverse of those for removal. When installing the hose and fittings, use new O-rings and lubricate them with clean refrigerant oil.

12 After the condenser is installed have the system evacuated, recharged and leak tested by a dealer service department or an air conditioning repair facility.

18 Air conditioning evaporator - removal and installation

✷✷ WARNING 1:

The models covered by this manual are equipped with Supplemental Restraint Systems (SRS), more commonly known as airbags. Always disconnect the negative battery cable, then the positive battery cable and wait two minutes before working in the vicinity of the impact sensors, steering column or instrument panel to avoid the possibility of accidental deployment of the airbag, which could cause personal injury (see Chapter 12). Do not use any electrical test equipment on any of the airbag system wires or tamper with them in any way.

✷✷ WARNING 2:

The air conditioning system is under high pressure. DO NOT loosen any fittings or remove any components until after the system has been discharged. Air conditioning refrigerant should be properly discharged into an EPA-approved container at a dealer service department or an automotive air conditioning repair facility. Always eye wear protection when disconnecting air conditioning system fittings.

1 The removal of the evaporator core is a difficult job, and a replacement evaporator core is only available with an entirely-new heater/evaporator housing assembly. If the core is to be replaced, all of the ducting, vacuum motors, vacuum tank, heater core, blower motor and other components will have to be removed from the old assembly and mounted on the replacement housing.

➡Note: **Before replacing an evaporator core, determine for certain that the core is leaking by having a leak test performed with special equipment at dealer service department or automotive air conditioning repair facility.**

2 Refer to Section 13 for removal of the heater/evaporator housing. This procedure requires the removal of the instrument panel (see Chapter 11).

➡Note: **Whenever the evaporator core is replaced with a new one, the accumulator/drier will also have to be replaced (see Section 15). Also remove the accumulator/drier mounting bracket from the firewall.**

3 Obtain the new replacement evaporator core/housing assembly and transfer all of the components from the old unit to the new one.

4 Installation is the reverse of the removal process.

5 Have the system evacuated, recharged and leak tested by the dealer service department or an air conditioning repair facility.

19 Heater hose couplings – disconnect and connect (2001 and later models)

1   On 2001 and later models, Ford uses a coupling on the heater/evaporator housing hoses. This type of coupling must be disconnected and connected as described in this procedure to ensure correct installation of the hoses. Whenever the coupling is disconnected, the retainer portion within the coupling must be replaced. To disconnect this coupling, you will need to obtain the disconnect tool, available at most auto supply stores.

2   Push the hose toward the heater/evaporator housing tube projecting from the firewall to fully expose the locking tabs on the coupling retainer.

3   Using the special disconnect tool, hold it perpendicular to and on the highest point of the coupling. Push the special tool over the coupling retainer windows and compress the retainer's locking tabs. While pushing down on the retainer locking tabs, slightly twist the coupling

and hose and disconnect it from the housing tube. Remove the special tool.

➡ **Note: If the heater/evaporator hose is easily accessible, the retainer locking tabs may be compressed by hand using a small flat blade screwdriver.**

4   Spread the retainer tabs apart and slide the retainer off the housing tube. Discard the retainer since it cannot be reused.

5   Clean the housing tube and lubricate with coolant or clean water.

6   Install a new retainer into the coupling housing until it bottoms out.

7   Push the hose and coupling onto heater/evaporator hose until it is locked into place. Pull on the hose to ensure it is securely locked in place.

8   Repeat for the remaining hose.

Specifications

Cooling system capacity
    V6 engine   11.8 quarts
    V8 engines
        1998 and earlier   14.1 quarts
        1999 and later   17.9 quarts
Coolant type   50/50 mixture of non-phosphate ethylene glycol antifreeze
Thermostat
    V6 engine
        Opening temperature   193 to 200 degrees
        Fully open temperature   221 degrees
    V8 engines
        Opening temperature   188 to 195 degrees
        Fully open temperature   212 degrees
Radiator pressure cap
    Specified cap pressure   16 psi
    Test pressure   18 to 19 psi
Refrigerant type   R-134a
Refrigerant capacity   34.0 ounces

Torque specifications   Ft-lbs (unless otherwise indicated)

Thermostat housing bolts	
V6 engine	
1994 and 1995	15 to 22
1996 and later	71 to 97 In-lbs
5.0L V8 engine	12 to 18
4.6L V8 engine	15 to 22
Water pump-to-engine bolts	
V6 engine	
Nuts	53 to 71 in-lbs
Bolts	15 to 22
5.0L V8 engine	15 to 21
4.6L V8 engine	
1998 and earlier	15 to 22
1999 and later	18
Water pump pulley to hub	15 to 21
Transmission oil line fitting-to-radiator	12 to 18
Engine oil cooler insert fastener	
1998 and earlier	41 to 53
1999 and later	43
Oil cooler adapter to block bolts	15 to 22
Fan shroud-to-radiator	24 to 48 in-lbs

Notes

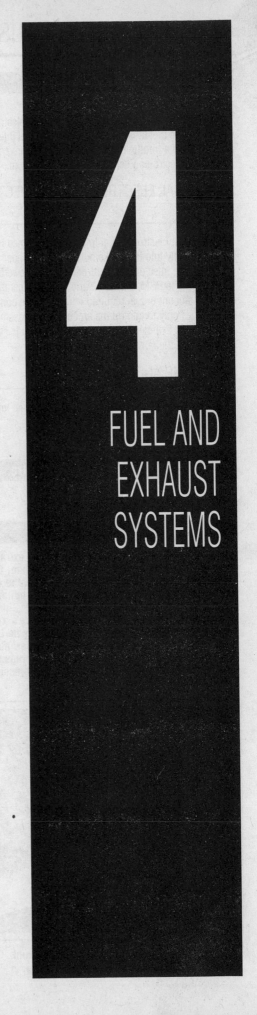

4

FUEL AND EXHAUST SYSTEMS

Section

Reference to other Chapters

1 General information

The fuel system consists of a fuel tank, an electric fuel pump (located in the fuel tank), a fuel pump relay, fuel injectors, an air cleaner assembly and a throttle body unit. All models are equipped with a Sequential Electronic Fuel Injection (SEFI) system.

SEQUENTIAL ELECTRONIC FUEL INJECTION (SEFI) SYSTEM

Sequential Electronic Fuel Injection uses timed impulses to inject the fuel directly into the intake port of each cylinder according to its firing order. The injectors are controlled by the Powertrain Control Module (PCM). The PCM monitors various engine parameters and delivers the exact amount of fuel required into the intake ports. The throttle body serves only to control the amount of air passing into the system. Because each cylinder is equipped with its own injector, much better control of the fuel/air mixture ratio is possible.

FUEL PUMP AND LINES

Fuel is circulated from the fuel tank to the fuel injection system, and back to the fuel tank, through a pair of metal lines running along the underside of the vehicle. An electric fuel pump is located inside the fuel tank. A vapor return system routes all vapors back to the fuel tank through a separate return line.

The fuel pump will operate as long as the engine is cranking or running and the PCM is receiving ignition reference pulses from the electronic ignition system. If there are no reference pulses, the fuel pump will shut off after two or three seconds.

EXHAUST SYSTEM

The exhaust system includes an exhaust manifold fitted with an exhaust oxygen sensor, a catalytic converter, an exhaust pipe, and a muffler.

The catalytic converter is an emission control device added to the exhaust system to reduce pollutants. A single-bed converter is used in combination with a three-way (reduction) catalyst. Refer to Chapter 6 for more information regarding the catalytic converter.

2 Fuel pressure relief procedure

◗ Refer to illustrations 2.1 and 2.4

✳✳ WARNING:

Gasoline is extremely flammable, so take extra precautions when you work on any part of the fuel system. Don't smoke or allow open flames or bare light bulbs near the work area, and don't work in a garage where a gas-type appliance (such as a water heater or a clothes dryer) is present. Since gasoline is carcinogenic, wear latex gloves when there's a possibility of being exposed to fuel, and, if you spill any fuel on your skin, rinse it off immediately with soap and water. Mop up any spills immediately and do not store fuel-soaked rags where they could ignite. The fuel system is under constant pressure, so, if any fuel lines are to be disconnected, the fuel pressure in the system must be relieved first. When you perform any kind of work on the fuel system, wear safety glasses and have a Class B type fire extinguisher on hand.

➡Note: After the fuel pressure has been relieved. it's a good idea to lay a shop towel over any fuel connection to be disassembled, to absorb the residual fuel that may leak out when servicing the fuel system.

1 The fuel pump switch - sometimes called the "inertia switch" - which shuts off fuel to the engine in the event of a collision, affords a simple and convenient means by which fuel pressure can be relieved

2.1 The inertia switch is located in the trunk. Disconnect the electrical connector to disable the fuel pump

2.4 If necessary, push the reset button after connecting the inertia switch to energize the fuel pump

before servicing fuel injection components. The switch is located in the luggage compartment (see illustration) and is usually covered by the carpet which comes up the sides of the trunk.

2   Unplug the inertia switch electrical connector.

3   Start the engine and allow it to run until it stops. This should take only a few seconds, but it may take up to 10 minutes.

4   The fuel system pressure is now relieved. When you're finished working on the fuel system, simply plug the electrical connector back into the switch. If the inertia switch was "popped" (activated) during this procedure, push the reset button on the top of the switch (see illustration).

3   Fuel pump/fuel pressure - check

✳✳ WARNING:

Gasoline is extremely flammable, so take extra precautions when you work on any part of the fuel system. See the Warning in Section 2.

➥**Note 1: To perform the fuel pressure test, you will need to obtain a fuel pressure gauge and adapter set (fuel line fittings).**

➥**Note 2: The fuel pump will operate as long as the engine is cranking or running and the PCM is receiving ignition reference pulses from the electronic ignition system. If there are no reference pulses, the fuel pump will shut off after two or three seconds.**

➥**Note 3: After the fuel pressure has been relieved, it's a good idea to lay a shop towel over any fuel connection to be disassembled, to absorb the residual fuel that may leak out when servicing the fuel system.**

PRELIMINARY INSPECTION

♦ **Refer to illustrations 3.3a and 3.3b**

1   Should the fuel system fail to deliver the proper amount of fuel, or any fuel at all, inspect it as follows. Remove the fuel filler cap. Have an assistant turn the ignition key to the On position (engine not running) while you listen at the fuel filler opening. You should hear a whirring sound that lasts for a couple of seconds.

2   If you don't hear anything, check the fuel pump fuse (see Chap-

ter 12). If the fuse is blown, replace it and see if it blows again. If it does, trace the fuel pump circuit for a short.

3   Check for battery voltage to the fuel pump relay connector and the power relay connector (see illustrations). If there is battery voltage present, have the CCRM tested at a dealer service department or other qualified automotive repair shop.

➥**Note 1: The fuel pump relay, the PCM power relay, the EDF relay and the EDF relay control are all located in the Constant Control Relay Module (CCRM) which is located on the right side fenderwell on OBD II models and up front near the radiator on OBD I models.**

➥**Note 2: 1998 and earlier 4.6L DOHC engines are equipped with another fuel pump relay that is located in the passenger's side kick panel near the PCM. Be sure to check for battery voltage to the relay.**

➥**Note 3: The inertia switch is an electrical device wired into the fuel pump circuit that will shut down power to the fuel pump in an accident. Be sure to check that the inertia switch is activated and in working order if the fuel pump is not receiving the proper voltage (see Section 2).**

4   If there is no voltage present, check the fuse(s) and the wiring circuit for the fuel pump relay and/or power relay (see Chapter 12). If voltage is present, check for battery voltage at the fuel pump connector.

OPERATING PRESSURE CHECK

♦ **Refer to illustrations 3.7 and 3.15**

5   Relieve the fuel system pressure (see Section 2).

6   Detach the cable from the negative battery terminal.

3.3a Remove the center bolt, disconnect the CCRM harness connector and check for battery voltage on terminal number 11 with the ignition key ON (engine not running). This checks power from the 20 amp fuel pump fuse

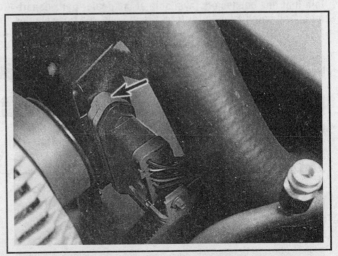

3.3b The CCRM is located up front near the radiator on 5.0L engines (arrow)

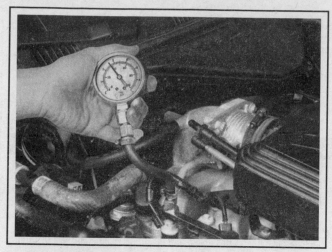

3.7 If you don't have the correct adapter, it is possible to remove the Schrader valve from the fitting and install a standard fuel pressure gauge, using a hose clamp (4.6L SOHC engine shown)

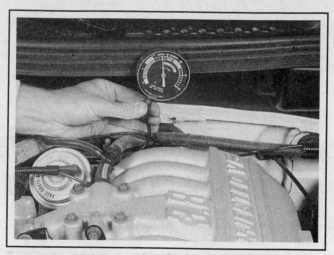

3.15 Detach the vacuum line from the fuel pressure regulator and see if vacuum is present when the engine is running (3.8L engine shown)

7   Remove the cap from the fuel pressure test port and attach a fuel pressure gauge (see illustration). If you don't have the correct adapter for the test port, remove the Schrader valve and connect the gauge hose to the fitting, using a hose clamp.

8   Attach the cable to the negative battery terminal.

9   Start the engine.

10 Check the fuel pressure at idle. Compare your readings with the values listed in this Chapter's Specifications. Disconnect the vacuum hose from the fuel pressure regulator and watch the fuel pressure gauge - the fuel pressure should jump up considerably as soon as the hose is disconnected. If it doesn't, check for a vacuum signal to the fuel pressure regulator (see Step 15).

11 If the fuel pressure is low, pinch the fuel return line shut and watch the gauge. If the pressure doesn't rise, the fuel pump is defective or there is a restriction in the fuel feed line. If the pressure rises sharply, replace the pressure regulator.

➡**Note: If the vehicle is equipped with a nylon fuel return line (or fuel lines made up of steel or other rigid material), it will be necessary to install a special fuel testing harness between the fuel rail and the return line. This can be made up from compatible fuel line connectors (available at the dealer parts department and some auto parts stores), fuel hose and hose clamps.**

12 If the fuel pressure is too high, turn the engine off. Disconnect the fuel return line and blow through it to check for a blockage. If there is no blockage, replace the fuel pressure regulator.

13 Hook up a hand-held vacuum pump to the port on the fuel pressure regulator.

14 Read the fuel pressure gauge with vacuum applied to the fuel pressure regulator and also with no vacuum applied. The fuel pressure should decrease as vacuum increases (and increase as vacuum decreases).

15 Connect a vacuum gauge to the pressure regulator vacuum hose. Start the engine and check for vacuum (see illustration). If there isn't vacuum present, check for a clogged hose or vacuum port. If the amount of vacuum is adequate, replace the fuel pressure regulator.

16 Turn the ignition switch to OFF, wait five minutes and recheck the pressure on the gauge. Compare the reading with the hold pressure listed in this Chapter's Specifications. If the hold pressure is less than specified:

a) *The fuel lines may be leaking.*

b) *The fuel pressure regulator may be allowing the fuel pressure to bleed through to the return line.*

c) *A fuel injector (or injectors) may be leaking.*

d) *The fuel pump may be defective.*

4   Fuel lines and fittings - replacement

✳✳ WARNING:

Gasoline is extremely flammable, so take extra precautions when you work on any part of the fuel system. See the Warning in Section 2.

PUSH-CONNECT FITTINGS - DISASSEMBLY AND REASSEMBLY

1   Ford uses two different push-connect fitting designs. Fittings used with 3/8 and 5/16-inch diameter lines have a "hairpin" type clip; fittings used with 1/4-inch diameter lines have a "duck bill" type clip. The procedure used for releasing each type of fitting is different. The clips should be replaced whenever a connector is disassembled.

2   Disconnect all push-connect fittings from fuel system components such as the fuel filter, the fuel charging assembly, the fuel tank, etc. before removing the assembly.

3/8 and 5/16-inch fittings (hairpin clip)

◆ **Refer to illustration 4.5**

3   Inspect the internal portion of the fitting for accumulations of dirt. If more than a light coating of dust is present, clean the fitting before disassembly.

4.5 A hairpin clip type pushconnect fitting

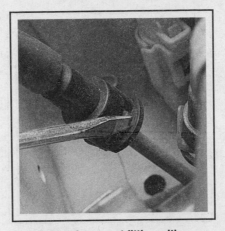

4.10 A push-connect fitting with a duck bill clip

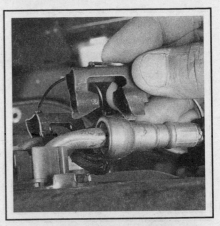

4.13 Remove the safety clamp

4 Some adhesion between the seals in the fitting and the line will occur over a period of time. Twist the fitting on the line, then push and pull the fitting until it moves freely.

5 Remove the hairpin clip from the fitting by bending the shipping tab down until it clears the body. Then, using nothing but your hands, spread each leg about 1/8-inch to disengage the body and push the legs through the fitting. Remember, don't use any tools to perform this part of the procedure. Finally, pull lightly on the triangular end of the clip and work it clear of the line and fitting (see illustration).

6 Grasp the fitting and hose and pull it straight off the line.

7 Do not reuse the original clip in the fitting. A new clip must be used.

8 Before reinstalling the fitting on the line, wipe the line end with a clean cloth. Inspect the inside of the fitting to ensure that it's free of dirt and/or obstructions.

9 To reinstall the fitting on the line, align them and push the fitting into place. When the fitting is engaged, a definite click will be heard. Pull on the fitting to ensure that it's completely engaged. To install the new clip, insert it into any two adjacent openings in the fitting with the triangular portion of the clip pointing away from the fitting opening. Using your index finger, push the clip in until the legs are locked on the outside of the fitting.

1/4-inch fittings (duck bill clip)

▶ **Refer to illustrations 4.10, 4.13 and 4.14**

10 The duck bill clip type fitting consists of a body, spacers, O-rings and the retaining clip (see illustration). The clip holds the fitting securely in place on the line. One of the two following methods must be used to disconnect this type of fitting.

11 Before attempting to disconnect the fitting, check the visible internal portion of the fitting for accumulations of dirt. If more than a light coating of dust is evident, clean the fitting before disassembly.

12 Some adhesion between the seals in the fitting and line will occur over a period of time. Twist the fitting on the line, then push and pull the fitting until it moves freely.

13 Remove the safety clamp from the fuel line (see illustration).

14 The preferred method used to disconnect the fitting requires a special tool, available at most auto parts stores. To disengage the line from the fitting, align the slot in the push-connect disassembly tool with either tab on the clip (90-degrees from the slots on the side of the fitting) and insert the tool (see illustration). This disengages the duck bill from the line.

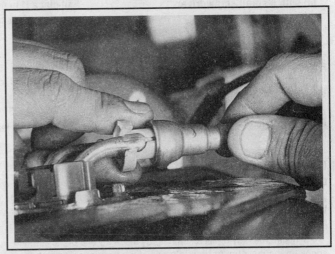

4.14 Duck bill clip fitting disassembly using the special tool

➡**Note: Some fuel lines have a secondary bead which aligns with the outer surface of the clip. The bead can make tool insertion difficult. If necessary, use the alternative disassembly method described in Step 16.**

Holding the tool and the line with one hand, pull the fitting off.

➡**Note: Only moderate effort is necessary if the clip is properly disengaged. The use of anything other than your hands should not be required.**

15 After disassembly, inspect and clean the line sealing surface. Also inspect the inside of the fitting and the line for any internal parts that may have been dislodged from the fitting. Any loose internal parts should be immediately reinstalled (use the line to insert the parts).

16 The alternative disassembly procedure requires a pair of small adjustable pliers. The pliers must have a jaw width of 3/16-inch or less.

17 Align the jaws of the pliers with the openings in the side of the fitting and compress the portion of the retaining clip that engages the body. This disengages the retaining clip from the body (often one side of the clip will disengage before the other - both sides must be disengaged).

18 Pull the fitting off the line.

➡**Note: Only moderate effort is required if the retaining clip has been properly disengaged. Do not use any tools for this procedure.**

19 Once the fitting is removed from the line end, check the fitting

4.26a If the spring lock couplings are equipped with safety clips, pry them off with a small screwdriver

4.26b Open the spring-loaded halves of the spring lock coupling tool and place it in position around the coupling, then close it

4.26c To disconnect the coupling, push the tool into the cage opening to expand the garter spring and release the female fitting, then pull the male and female fittings apart

and line for any internal parts that may have been dislodged from the fitting. Any loose internal parts should be immediately reinstalled (use the line to insert the parts).

20 The retaining clip will remain on the line. Disengage the clip from the line bead to remove it. Do not reuse the retaining clip - install a new one!

21 Before reinstalling the fitting, wipe the line end with a clean cloth. Check the inside of the fitting to make sure that it's free of dirt and/or obstructions.

22 To reinstall the fitting, align it with the line and push it into place. When the fitting is engaged, a definite click will be heard. Pull on the fitting to ensure that it's fully engaged.

23 Install the new replacement clip by inserting one of the serrated edges on the duck bill portion into one of the openings. Push on the other side until the clip snaps into place.

SPRING LOCK COUPLINGS - DISASSEMBLY AND REASSEMBLY

▶ **Refer to illustrations 4.26a, 4.26b and 4.26c**

24 The fuel supply and return lines used on SEFI engines utilize spring lock couplings at the engine fuel rail end instead of plastic push-connect fittings. The male end of the spring lock coupling, which is girded by two O-rings, is inserted into a female flared end engine fitting. The coupling is secured by a garter spring which prevents disengagement by gripping the flared end of the female fitting. On later models, a cup-tether assembly provides additional security.

25 To disconnect the 1/2-inch (12.7 mm) spring lock coupling supply fitting, you will need to obtain a spring lock coupling tool, available at most auto parts stores.

26 Study the accompanying illustrations carefully before detaching either spring lock coupling fitting (see illustrations).

5   Fuel tank - removal and installation

▶ **Refer to illustrations 5.5, 5.6, 5.8, 5.9 and 5.10**

❈❈ WARNING:

Gasoline is extremely flammable, so take extra precautions when you work on any part of the fuel system. See the Warning in Section 2.

➡ **Note: Don't begin this procedure until the gauge indicates that the tank is empty or nearly empty. If the tank must be removed when it's full (for example, if the fuel pump malfunctions), siphon any remaining fuel from the tank prior to removal.**

1   Unless the vehicle has been driven far enough to completely empty the tank, it's a good idea to siphon the residual fuel out before removing the tank from the vehicle.

❈❈ WARNING:

DO NOT start the siphoning action by mouth! Use a siphoning kit (available at most auto parts stores).

2   Relieve the fuel pressure (refer to Section 2).
3   Detach the cable from the negative terminal of the battery.
4   Raise the vehicle and support it securely on jackstands.
5   Remove the fuel tank filler pipe lower bracket bolt (see illustration).

5.5 Remove the lower bracket bolt from the filler pipe

5.6 Remove the bolts (arrows) from the fuel filler neck on the inside of the fenderwell

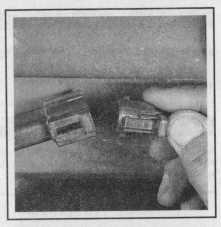

5.8 Disconnect the electrical connector from the fuel pump harness

6 Remove the fuel tank filler neck bracket bolts securing the fuel filler neck and the fuel tank filler pipe retainer (see illustration) and slide the assembly from the vehicle.

➡**Note: On 1999 and later models it may be necessary to cut out the fuel tank filler pipe grommet from the fuel tank to allow removal of the filler pipe and to avoid damage to the filler pipe check valve. Always replace the grommet with a new one.**

7 Disconnect the fuel lines (see Section 4) and vapor lines.

8 Disconnect the electric fuel pump and sending unit electrical connector with a screwdriver (see illustration).

9 Place a floor jack under the tank and position a block of wood between the jack pad and the tank. Raise the jack until it's supporting the tank.

10 Remove the bolts or nuts from the front ends of the fuel tank straps (see illustration). The straps are hinged at the other end so you can swing them out of the way.

11 Lower the tank far enough to unplug any vapor lines or wire harness brackets that may be difficult to reach when the fuel tank is in the vehicle.

12 Slowly lower the jack while steadying the tank. Remove the tank from the vehicle.

13 If you're replacing the tank, or having it cleaned or repaired, refer to Section 6.

14 Refer to Section 7 to remove and install the fuel pump or sending unit.

15 Installation is the reverse of removal with the following excep-

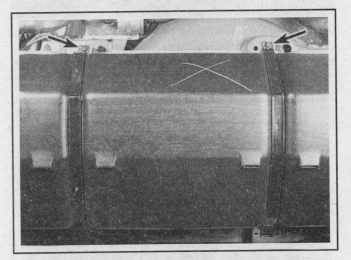

5.10 Remove the bolts (arrows) from the fuel tank straps

tions: Always install a new fuel tank filler neck grommet (if removed or damaged) onto the fuel tank. Clean engine oil can be used as an assembly aid when pushing the fuel filler neck back into the tank.

16 Make sure the fuel tank heat shields are assembled correctly onto the fuel tank before reinstalling the tank in the vehicle.

17 Carefully angle the fuel tank filler neck into the filler pipe assembly and lift the tank into place.

6 Fuel tank - cleaning and repair

1 The fuel tanks installed in the vehicles covered by this manual are made of plastic and are not repairable.

2 If the fuel tank is removed from the vehicle, it should not be placed in an area where sparks or open flames could

ignite the fumes coming out of the tank. Be especially careful inside a garage where a natural gas-type appliance is located, because the pilot light could cause an explosion.

7 Fuel pump - removal and installation

♦ Refer to illustrations 7.6, 7.7, 7.9a, 7.9b, 7.10 and 7.11

1994 THROUGH 1997 MODELS

✳✳ WARNING:

Gasoline is extremely flammable, so take extra precautions when you work on any part of the fuel system. See the Warning in Section 2.

1 Unless the vehicle has been driven far enough to completely empty the tank, it's a good idea to siphon the residual fuel out before removing the fuel pump from the vehicle.

✳✳ WARNING:

DO NOT start the siphoning action by mouth! Use a siphoning kit (available at most auto parts stores).

2 Relieve the fuel pressure (refer to Section 2).

3 Detach the cable from the negative terminal of the battery.
4 Raise the vehicle and support it securely on jackstands.
5 Remove the fuel tank from the vehicle (see Section 5).
6 Using a brass punch or wood dowel only, tap the lock ring counterclockwise until it's loose (see illustration).
7 Carefully pull the fuel pump assembly from the tank (see illustration).
8 Remove the old lock ring gasket and discard it.
9 If you're planning to reinstall the original fuel pump unit, remove the strainer (see illustrations) by prying it off with a screwdriver, wash it in clean solvent, then push it back into place on the pump. If you're

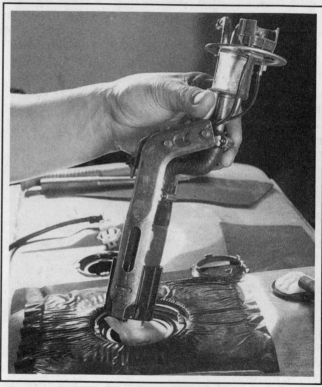

7.7 Carefully angle the fuel pump out of the fuel tank without damaging the fuel strainer

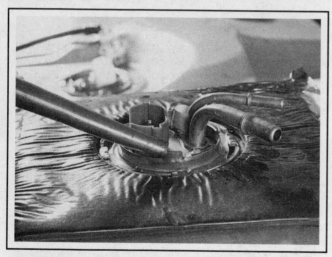

7.6 Use a brass punch to turn the locking ring

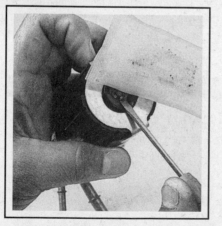

7.9a Remove the C-clip from the base of the fuel pump . . .

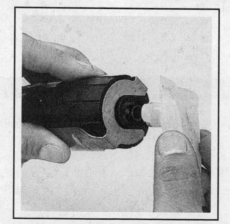

7.9b . . . then separate the strainer from the fuel pump

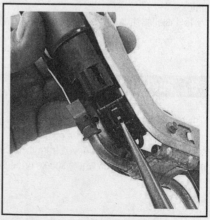

7.10 Disconnect the fuel pump electrical connector from the fuel pump

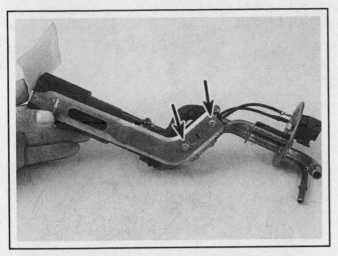

7.11 Disconnect the fuel pump mounting bolts (arrows)

installing a new pump/sending unit, the assembly will include a new strainer.

10 To separate the fuel pump from the assembly, remove the clamp and disconnect the electrical connector from the fuel pump (see illustration).

11 Remove the fuel pump mounting bolts (see illustration).

12 Clean the fuel pump mounting flange and the tank mounting surface and seal ring groove.

13 Installation is the reverse of removal. Apply a thin coat of heavy grease to the new seal ring to hold it in place during assembly.

1998 AND LATER MODELS

➡**Note: The fuel pump module can't be disassembled as on previous models.**

14 Perform Steps 1 through 5 of this procedure.

15 Remove any dirt surrounding the mounting flange.

16 Remove the fuel pump module sender plate mounting bolts.

17 Carefully pull the fuel pump module partially up out of the fuel tank.

18 Reach through the fuel pump module openings, squeeze both locking tabs to release them from the fuel tank opening, then carefully withdraw the fuel pump module from the tank.

19 Remove the large O-ring gasket and discard it.

20 Installation is the reverse of removal. Apply a thin coat of heavy grease to the new O-ring gasket to hold it in place during installation. Make sure both locking tabs are properly engaged with the fuel tank retainer and have snapped into place. Tighten the bolts to the torque listed in this Chapter's Specifications.

8   Fuel level sending unit - check and replacement

CHECK

▶ **Refer to illustrations 8.3 and 8.5**

1   Raise the vehicle and support it securely on jackstands.

2   Disconnect the electrical connector for the fuel level sending unit.

3   Position the ohmmeter probes into the electrical connector and check the resistance (see illustration). Use the 200-ohm scale on the ohmmeter.

4   On 1994 through 1997 models, the resistance should be about

160 ohms with the tank completely full. With the fuel tank nearly empty, the resistance should be 15.0 ohms. On 1998 and later models, with the tank completely full, the resistance should be about 145 ohms and with the fuel tank nearly empty, the resistance should be about 22 ohms.

5   If the readings are incorrect, replace the sending unit.

➡**Note: A more accurate check of the sending unit can be made by removing it from the fuel tank and checking its resistance while manually operating the float arm (see illustration).**

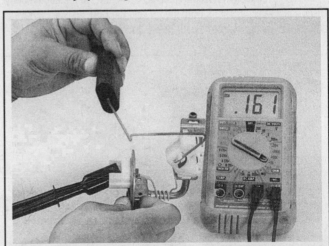

8.5 A more accurate check of the fuel level sending unit can be performed with the assembly on the bench, the ohmmeter probes on the connector and the float positioned on "empty" and "full". Check for a smooth change in resistance between these positions

8.3 Using an ohmmeter, probe the terminals of the fuel sending unit assembly to check the resistance (1997 and earlier shown)

8.7 Use a brass punch or wood dowel to turn the locking ring on the fuel level sending assembly counterclockwise

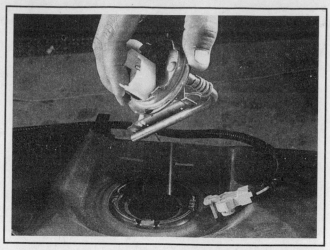

8.8 Lift the sending unit from the fuel tank without damaging the float unit

REPLACEMENT (1994 THROUGH 1997 MODELS)

▶ Refer to illustrations 8.7 and 8.8

➡Note: On 1998 and later models, the fuel level sending unit is an integral part of the fuel pump module and cannot be replaced separately.

6 Remove the fuel tank (see Section 5).
7 To prevent possible sparks, use a brass punch or wood dowel only, tapping the lock ring counterclockwise until it's loose (see illustration).

8 Carefully angle the sending unit out of the opening without damaging the fuel level float located at the bottom of the assembly (see illustration).

9 Installation is the reverse of removal.

10 If the float arm and float wire loop were damaged or bent during removal and installation, adjust the angle and travel distance.

11 Be sure to install a new rubber gasket.

9 Air cleaner housing - removal and installation

▶ Refer to illustrations 9.2 and 9.5

1 Detach the cable from the negative terminal of the battery.
2 Loosen the clamp securing the air intake duct to the throttle body. Disconnect the connectors from the IAT and the MAF sensor. Remove any remaining hoses from the air intake duct (see illustration).

3 Unclip the upper half of the air cleaner housing assembly and remove it (see Chapter 1).
4 Remove the air filter element.
5 Remove the air cleaner housing mounting bolt and detach the assembly (see illustration).
6 Installation is the reverse of removal.

9.2 Remove the air intake duct mounting clamp and pull the assembly off the throttle body

9.5 Remove the mounting bolt from the air cleaner housing assembly

10 Accelerator cable - removal, installation and adjustment

REMOVAL

▶ **Refer to illustrations 10.2a, 10.2b, 10.3, 10.5 and 10.6**

1   Remove the air intake duct from the throttle body and intake manifold area (see Section 9).

2   On all models except 2001 and later 3.8L models, detach the accelerator cable from the throttle lever (see illustration). On 2001 and later 3.8L models, detach the accelerator cable from the throttle wheel.

3   Remove the cruise control cable from the cable bracket (see illustration).

4   Separate the accelerator cable from the cable bracket.

5   Push the accelerator cable nylon bushing out of the accelerator pedal and shaft arm, pull the cable end out from the accelerator pedal recess in the driver's compartment (see illustration).

6   Disconnect any cable clips or brackets securing the accelerator cable (see illustration). On 2001 and later models, remove the bolts securing the cable bracket to the firewall.

7   Remove the throttle cable through the firewall from the engine compartment.

INSTALLATION

8   Installation is the reverse of removal. Be sure the cable is routed correctly and the grommet seats completely in the firewall.

9   If necessary, at the engine compartment side of the firewall, apply sealant around the accelerator cable to prevent water from entering the passenger compartment.

ADJUSTMENT

10 Measure the freeplay by firmly gripping the cable and push it down from the cable housing. There should be a slight amount of slack that will allow cable freeplay.

11 If there is no movement on the cable and the cable is binding not allowing the throttle lever to completely close, replace the cable.

10.2a Remove the accelerator cable end from the throttle lever by twisting until the flattened edge aligns with the keyed slot (3.8L engine shown)

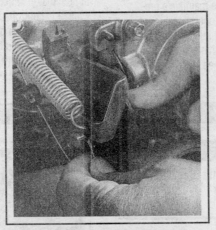

10.2b On 4.6L DOHC engines, rotate the cable until the slot in the throttle lever aligns with the cable and slide it out of the bracket

10.3 Remove the cruise control cable from the throttle lever

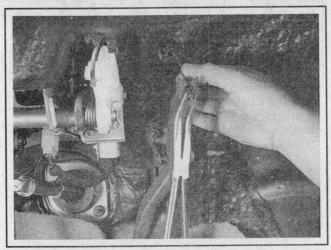

10.5 Working under the dash in the driver's side compartment, pull the cable end from the accelerator pedal recess (4.6L DOHC shown)

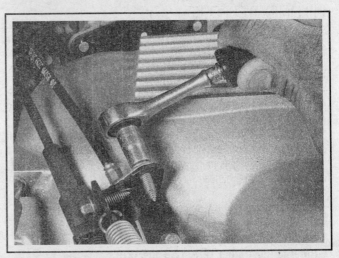

10.6 Unbolt the cable from the bracket on the air intake plenum (typical)

11 Fuel injection system - general information

SEQUENTIAL ELECTRONIC FUEL INJECTION (SEFI)

The Sequential Electronic Fuel Injection (SEFI) system is a multi-point fuel injection system. On the SEFI system, fuel is metered into each intake port in sequence with the engine firing order in accordance with engine demand through one injector per cylinder mounted on a tuned intake manifold. The intake manifold incorporates an air intake plenum to aid in air flow and distribution. Each engine uses a slightly different plenum design and fuel rail arrangement. The 3.8L and 5.0L engines use a one-piece plenum mounted with six long bolts. The air intake plenum bolts to the intake manifold which sits directly in the middle of the engine block. The 4.6L SOHC engine does not incorporate an air intake plenum but instead the throttle body is mounted near the center of the large intake manifold assembly. The 4.6L DOHC engine uses a large air intake plenum mounted onto two intake manifold plates.

This system incorporates an on-board Electronic Engine Control (EEC-IV) computer that accepts inputs from various engine sensors to compute the required fuel flow rate necessary to maintain a prescribed air/fuel ratio throughout the entire engine operational range. The computer then outputs a command to the fuel injectors to meter the approximate quantity of fuel. The system automatically senses and compensates for changes in altitude, load and speed.

➡Note: The computer terminology has changed from Electronic Control Module (ECM) to the Powertrain Control Module (PCM) due to standardization of the Self Diagnosis system within the automotive industry.

The fuel delivery systems include an electric in-tank fuel pump which forces pressurized fuel through a series of metal and plastic lines and an inline fuel filter/reservoir to the fuel charging manifold assembly. The SEFI system uses a single high-pressure pump mounted inside the tank.

The fuel rail assembly incorporates an electrically actuated fuel injector directly above each intake port. When energized, the injectors spray a metered quantity of fuel into the intake air stream.

A constant fuel pressure drop is maintained across the injector nozzles by a pressure regulator. The regulator is positioned downstream from the fuel injectors. Excess fuel passes through the regulator and returns to the fuel tank through a fuel return line.

On the SEFI system, each injector is energized once every other crankshaft revolution in sequence with engine firing order. The period of time that the injectors are energized (known as "on time" or "pulse width") is controlled by the PCM. Air entering the engine is sensed by speed, pressure and temperature sensors. The outputs of these sensors are processed by the PCM. The computer determines the needed injector pulse width and outputs a command to the injector to meter the exact quantity of fuel.

12 Fuel injection system - check

⁕⁕ WARNING:

Gasoline is extremely flammable, so take extra precautions when you work on any part of the fuel system. See the Warning in Section 2.

➡Note: The following procedure is based on the assumption that the fuel pump is working and the fuel pressure is adequate (see Section 3).

PRELIMINARY CHECKS

1   Check all electrical connectors that are related to the system. Loose electrical connectors and poor grounds can cause many problems that resemble more serious malfunctions.

2   Check to see that the battery is fully charged, as the control unit and sensors depend on an accurate supply voltage in order to properly meter the fuel.

3   Check the air filter element - a dirty or partially blocked filter will severely impede performance and economy (see Chapter 1).

4   If a blown fuse is found, replace it and see if it blows again. If it does, search for a grounded wire in the harness to the fuel pump (see Chapter 12).

SYSTEM CHECKS

♦ Refer to illustration 12.7, 12.8 and 12.9

5   Check the condition of the vacuum hoses connected to the intake manifold.

12.7 Use a stethoscope or screwdriver to determine if the injectors are working properly - they should make a steady clicking sound that rises and falls with engine speed changes

6   Remove the air intake duct from the throttle body and check for dirt, carbon or other residue build-up in the throttle body, particularly around the throttle plate. If it's dirty, clean it with carburetor cleaner and a toothbrush (this is permissible on 5.0L V8 engines only - see the **Caution** preceding Step 24).

7   With the engine running, place an automotive stethoscope against each injector, one at a time, and listen for a clicking sound, indicating operation (see illustration). If you don't have a stethoscope, you can place the tip of a long screwdriver against the injector and lis-

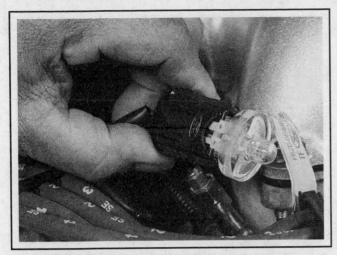

12.8 Install the fuel injector test light or "noid light" into the fuel injector electrical connector and confirm that it blinks when the engine is running

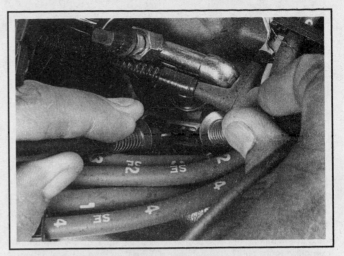

12.9 Measure the resistance of each injector. It should be within Specifications

ten through the handle.

8   If an injector isn't functioning (not clicking), purchase a special injector test light (sometimes called a "noid" light) and install it into the injector electrical connector (see illustration). Start the engine and check to see if the noid light flashes. If it does, the injector is receiving proper voltage. If it doesn't flash, further diagnosis should be performed

by a dealer service department or other repair shop.

9   With the engine OFF and the fuel injector electrical connectors disconnected, measure the resistance of each injector (see illustration). Check the Specifications listed in this Chapter for the correct injector resistance.

10   The remainder of the system checks can be found in Section 13 and Chapter 6.

13   Sequential Electronic Fuel Injection (SEFI) system - component check and replacement

AIR INTAKE PLENUM (UPPER INTAKE MANIFOLD) WITH THROTTLE BODY

➡Note: Refer to Chapter 2 for the complete removal and installation procedure for the upper intake manifold and lower intake manifold (plates) on the 4.6L DOHC engine.

3.8L and 5.0L engines

Removal

▶ Refer to illustrations 13.7 and 13.9

1   Detach the cable from the negative terminal of the battery.

2   If equipped, remove the engine compartment brace (see Chapter 2B).

3   Unplug the electrical connectors at the IAC valve, throttle position sensor (TPS) and EGR position sensor (see Chapter 6).

4   Detach the accelerator cable (see Section 10) and cruise control cable (if equipped) from the throttle body assembly.

5   Remove the accelerator cable/throttle valve (TV) cable bracket from the intake manifold (see Section 10) and position the bracket and cables out of the way.

6   Clearly label, then detach, the vacuum lines from the upper intake manifold, the EGR valve and the fuel pressure regulator. On 1999 and

13.7 Remove the air intake plenum mounting bracket bolt (3.8L engine shown)

later models remove the EGR solenoid bracket and the ignition coil.

7   Remove the bracket that retains the air intake manifold to the engine (see illustration).

8   Remove the PCV tube from the air intake plenum and the PCV valve on the valve cover. Remove the EGR valve (see Chapter 6) from

the air intake plenum.

9 Remove the air intake plenum mounting bolts (see illustration).

10 Remove the upper intake manifold and throttle body as an assembly from the lower intake manifold.

Installation

11 Be sure to clean and inspect the mounting faces of the lower intake manifold (see Chapter 2A) and the air intake plenum before positioning the new gasket(s) onto the lower intake mounting face. The use of alignment studs may be helpful. Install the air intake plenum and throttle body assembly onto the lower intake manifold. Ensure the gasket remains in place (if alignment studs are not used). Install the air intake plenum retaining bolts and tighten them in three stages to the specified torque. Always tighten the bolts in a criss cross pattern starting at the center of the manifold and working outward towards the ends of the manifold. Ford recommends treating the air intake plenum mounting bolts with Teflon before installing them into the intake manifold.

4.6L DOHC engines

Removal

▶ **Refer to illustrations 13.16, 13.17 and 13.23**

12 Detach the cable from the negative terminal of the battery.

13 If equipped, remove the engine compartment brace (see Chapter 2B).

14 Remove the air cleaner intake duct (see Section 9).

15 Unplug the electrical connectors at the IAC valve, throttle position sensor (TPS) and EGR valve (see Chapter 6).

16 Detach the accelerator cable (see Section 10) and cruise control cable (if equipped) from the throttle body assembly. Remove the accelerator cable bracket from the air intake plenum and position the bracket and cables out of the way (see illustration).

17 Disconnect the fuel feed and return lines from the fuel rail (see illustration). Refer to Section 4 for additional information concerning fuel line disconnections.

18 Clearly label, then detach, the vacuum lines from the upper intake manifold vacuum tree, the EGR valve and the fuel pressure regulator.

13.9 Location of the air intake plenum mounting bolts on the 3.8L engine (1998 and earlier shown)

19 Detach the PCV system by disconnecting the hose from the left hand valve cover.

20 If equipped, detach the canister purge line or lines from the throttle body and detach the EGR valve.

21 Remove the air intake plenum mounting bolts (see illustration 13.23).

22 Remove the upper intake manifold and throttle body as an assembly from the lower intake manifold.

Installation

23 Be sure to clean and inspect the mounting faces of the lower intake manifold (see Chapter 2A) and the air intake plenum before positioning the new gasket(s) onto the lower intake mounting face. The use of alignment studs may be helpful. Install the air intake plenum and throttle body assembly onto the upper intake manifold. Ensure the gasket remains in place (if alignment studs are not used). Install the seven air intake plenum retaining bolts and tighten them to the torque listed in this Chapter's Specifications (see illustration). Installation is otherwise the reverse of removal.

13.16 Remove the accelerator cable and cruise control cable mounting bolts (arrows) from the air intake plenum

13.17 Use a special spring lock tool to uncouple the fuel line connector from the fuel rail

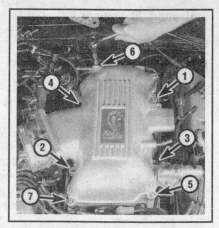

13.23 Air intake plenum tightening sequence on the 4.6L DOHC engine (1997 model shown)

13.28 Throttle body mounting bolts (arrows) on the 3.8L engine

THROTTLE BODY

> ### ✲✲ CAUTION:
>
> **The throttle body on 3.8L and 4.6L models is coated with a sludge-resistant material designed to protect the bore and throttle plate. Do not attempt to clean the interior of the throttle body with carburetor or other spray cleaners. This throttle body is designed to resist sludge accumulation and cleaning will impair the performance of the engine.**

Removal

▸ **Refer to illustrations 13.28**

24 Detach the cable from the negative terminal of the battery.

25 Detach the throttle position sensor (TPS) and Idle Air Control (IAC) valve electrical connectors.

26 Disconnect the accelerator cable (see Section 10) and the Throttle Valve (TV) cable (if equipped) from the throttle body.

27 If equipped, remove the PCV vent closure hose at the throttle body (see Chapter 6).

28 Remove the four throttle body mounting nuts (see illustration).

29 Remove and discard the throttle body gasket.

Installation

30 Clean the gasket mating surfaces. If scraping is necessary, be careful not to damage the gasket surfaces or allow material to drop into the manifold. Installation is the reverse of removal. Be sure to tighten the throttle body mounting nuts to the torque listed in this Chapter's Specifications.

THROTTLE POSITION (TP) SENSOR

31 Refer to Chapter 6, Section 4 for the check and replacement procedures for the TP sensor.

IDLE AIR CONTROL (IAC) VALVE

32 Refer to Section 14 for the check, adjustment and replacement procedures for the IAC valve.

FUEL RAIL ASSEMBLY

▸ **Refer to illustration 13.36a, 13.36b, 13.36c, 13.37 and 13.38**

Removal

33 Relieve the fuel pressure (see Section 2).

34 Detach the cable from the negative terminal of the battery.

35 Remove the air intake plenum assembly (see Steps 1 through 23). On 1999 and later 4.6L SOHC engines, remove the throttle body and any vacuum hoses or electrical connections interfering with the removal of the fuel rail assembly.

36 Using a special spring lock coupler tool (available at most auto parts stores), disconnect the fuel feed and return lines from the fuel rail assembly (see illustrations).

➡**Note: Refer to Section 4 for additional information on disconnecting fuel lines.**

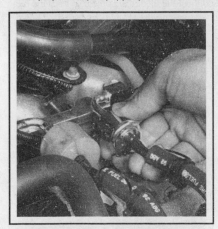

13.36a Press down to release the safety clamp from the fuel line connectors

13.36b Install the correct diameter spring lock coupling tool and push away from the fuel rail to release the internal locking mechanism

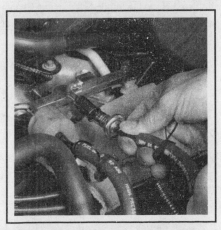

13.36c Detach the fuel line from the fuel rail

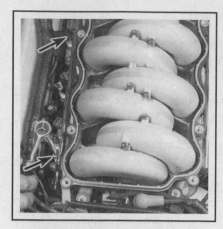

13.37 Fuel rail mounting bolt locations (arrows) on the 4.6L DOHC engine

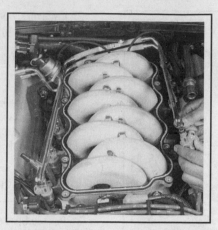

13.38 Lift the fuel rail and separate the fuel injectors from the fuel rail assembly

13.48 Use an Allen wrench to remove the fuel pressure regulator bolts (4.6L DOHC engine shown)

37 Detach the electrical connectors from the fuel injectors. Remove the four fuel rail retaining bolts (two on each side) (see illustration).

38 Carefully disengage the fuel rail from the fuel injectors and remove the fuel rail (see illustration).

➡Note: It may be easier to remove the injectors with the fuel rail as an assembly.

39 Use a rocking, side-to-side motion while lifting to remove the injectors from the fuel rail.

Installation

➡Note: It's a good idea to replace the injector O-rings whenever the fuel rail is removed.

40 Ensure that the injector caps are clean and free of contamination.

41 Place the fuel rail over each of the injectors and seat the injectors into the fuel rail. Ensure that the injectors are well seated in the fuel rail assembly.

➡Note: It may be easier to seat the injectors in the fuel rail and then seat the entire assembly in the lower intake manifold.

42 Secure the fuel rail assembly with the four retaining bolts and tighten them to the torque listed in this Chapter's Specifications.

43 The remainder of installation is the reverse of removal.

FUEL PRESSURE REGULATOR

Check

➡Note: This procedure assumes the fuel filter is in good condition.

44 Refer to the fuel system pressure checks in Section 3.

Replacement

▶ Refer to illustration 13.48

➡Note: Removal and installation of the fuel pressure regulator on models since 1996 is the same as on previous years. The illustrations shown in this procedure are shown on a pre-1996 4.6L engine which is equipped with a different type of intake manifold.

45 Relieve the fuel pressure from the system (see Section 2). Disconnect the cable from the negative terminal of the battery.

46 Clean any dirt from around the fuel pressure regulator.

47 Detach the vacuum hose from the fuel pressure regulator. On 1999 and later models disconnect the electrical connector from the fuel pressure regulator.

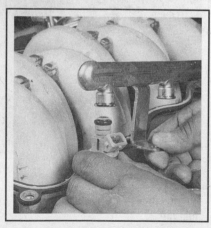

13.54 Remove the fuel injector from the fuel rail

13.57a Remove the O-ring from the top of the fuel injector . . .

13.57b . . . then remove the lower O-ring from the injector

48 Remove the two Allen head bolts that retain the fuel pressure regulator (see illustration) and detach the regulator from the fuel rail.

49 Install new O-rings on the pressure regulator and lubricate them with a light coat of oil.

50 Installation is the reverse of removal. Tighten the pressure regulator mounting bolts securely.

FUEL INJECTOR

▶ **Refer to illustrations 13.54, 13.57a and 13.57b**

Removal

51 Relieve the system fuel pressure (see Section 2).

52 Remove the air intake plenum assembly (see Steps 1 through 23).

53 Remove the fuel rail assembly (see above).

54 Carefully lift the assembly to gain access to the injectors (see illustration).

➡**Note: If all of the injectors are going to be replaced, remove the entire fuel rail.**

55 Carefully detach the electrical connectors from the individual injectors as required.

56 Grasping the injector body, pull up while gently rocking the injector from side-to-side.

57 Inspect the injector O-rings (two per injector) for signs of deterioration (see illustrations). Replace as required.

➡**Note: As long as you have the fuel rail off, it's a good idea to replace all of the the O-rings.**

58 Inspect the injector plastic "hat" (covering the injector pintle) and washer for signs of deterioration. Replace as required. If the hat is missing, look for it in the intake manifold.

Installation

59 Lubricate the new O-rings with light grade oil and install two on each injector.

⁂ **CAUTION:**

Do not use silicone grease. It will clog the injectors.

60 Using a light twisting motion, install the injector(s).

61 The remainder of installation is the reverse of removal.

14 Idle Air Control (IAC) valve - check, removal and adjustment

⁂ **CAUTION:**

The throttle body on 3.8L and 4.6L OBD II models is coated with a sludge resistant material designed to protect the bore and throttle plate. Do not attempt to clean the interior of the throttle body with carburetor or other spray cleaners. This throttle body is designed to resist sludge accumulation and subsequent cleaning will impair the performance of the engine.

➡**Note: The minimum idle speed is pre-set at the factory and should not require adjustment under normal circumstances; however, if the throttle body has been replaced or you suspect the minimum idle speed has been tampered with (for example, if the idle stop screw was removed), follow this procedure.**

CHECK

▶ **Refer to illustration 14.2**

1 The Idle Air Control (IAC) valve controls the amount of air that bypasses the throttle body assembly throttle valve and consequently controls the engine idle speed. This output actuator is mounted on the throttle body and is controlled by voltage pulses sent from the PCM (computer). The IAC valve within the body moves in or out allowing more or less intake air into the system according to the engine conditions. To increase idle speed, the PCM extends the IAC valve from the seat and allows more air to bypass the throttle bore. To decrease idle speed, the PCM retracts the IAC valve towards the seat, reducing the air flow.

2 To check the system, first check for the voltage signal from the PCM. Turn the ignition key On (engine not running) and with a voltmeter, probe the wires of the terminals of the IAC valve electrical connector. It should be approximately 10.5 to 12.5 volts (see illustration).

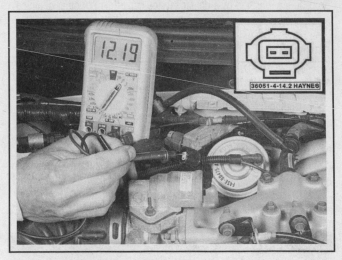

14.2 Disconnect the electrical connector from the IAC valve and check for voltage with the ignition key ON (engine not running)

This indicates that the IAC valve is receiving the proper signal from the PCM.

3 Next, remove the valve (proceed to Step 10) and check the pintle for excessive carbon deposits. If necessary, clean it with carburetor cleaner spray. Also clean the valve housing to remove any deposits.

ADJUSTMENT (5.0L ENGINE)

▶ **Refer to illustrations 14.6a and 14.6b**

4 Place the transmission in Park (automatic transmission models) and set the emergency brake for safety. Start the engine and allow it to

run until it reaches normal operating temperatures.

5   Check the OBD I self diagnosis system for any stored trouble codes (see Chapter 6). If trouble codes exist, be sure to follow through with the diagnosis and repair any problem that might exist in the engine management system before attempting to adjust the idle speed.

6   Remove the service plug from the throttle orifice and turn the throttle screw clockwise to increase idle speed. Watch carefully for any idle fluctuations caused by an air intake leak. Install a tachometer according to the manufacturers specifications and set the idle speed between 550 and 600 rpm by turning the throttle plate adjusting screw (see illustration).

➡ **Note: The throttle lever pad must be in contact with the screw after the adjustment.**

7   Verify that the throttle plate is not stuck in the throttle bore at idle position and the linkage is not preventing the throttle from closing. Depress the accelerator quickly and allow the engine rpm to settle back down to idle. The PCM and IAC valve should adjust the idle from this point. If idle quality suffers (high or low) run a complete diagnosis of the fuel injection and emission control system (see Chapter 6). Also, check the throttle valve (TV) cable adjustment (see Chapter 7).

ADJUSTMENT (3.8L/4.6L ENGINES)

8   The idle speed on the 3.8L and 4.6L is not adjustable. This procedure requires a special SCAN tool to extract working parameters (voltage signals) from the EEC-V system while it is running. Have the procedure performed by a dealer service department or other qualified repair shop.

REMOVAL

▶ **Refer to illustration 14.10**

9   Unplug the electrical connector and the hose (on 4.6L SOHC engines) from the IAC valve.

10 Remove the two valve attaching screws and withdraw the assembly (see illustration).

11 Check the condition of the O-ring. If it's hardened or deteriorated, replace it.

12 Clean the sealing surface and the bore of the throttle body assembly to ensure a good seal.

※※ CAUTION:

The IAC valve itself is an electrical component and must not be soaked in any liquid cleaner, as damage may result.

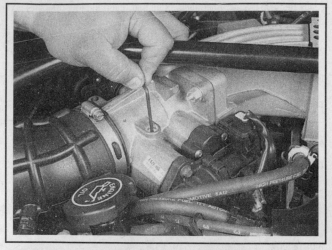

14.6 First, remove the rubber plug, then adjust the idle speed using an Allen wrench

14.10 Removing the IAC mounting bolts on a 3.8L engine

INSTALLATION

13 Position the new O-ring on the IAC valve. Lubricate the O-ring with a light film of engine oil.

14 Install the IAC valve and tighten the screws securely.

15 Plug in the electrical connector at the IAC valve assembly.

---

15   Intake Manifold Runner Control (IMRC) system (2001 and later 3.8L and all 4.6L DOHC engines)

GENERAL INFORMATION

1   The IMRC system controls the air intake charge by opening or closing the butterfly valve on the secondary intake valve directly at the intake manifold. By closing the butterfly to the secondary intake valves under 3,000 rpm, low end driveability is improved. Above 3,000 rpm the butterfly valves open to increase high-end performance. The butterfly valves are controlled by the IMRC actuator and cable assembly.

2   The IMRC system is difficult to check and requires a special SCAN tool to access the PCM for information and operating conditions. Have the system diagnosed by a dealer service department or other qualified repair shop.

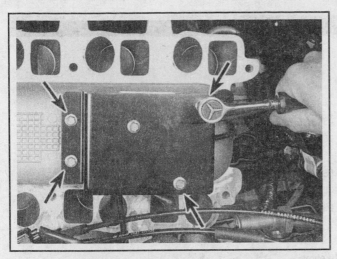

15.4 Remove the IMRC mounting bolts (arrows)

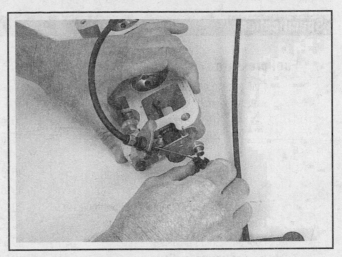

15.5 Remove the actuator cable end from the lever on the lower intake manifold runner (plate)

REPLACEMENT

▶ **Refer to illustrations 15.4 and 15.5**

3   Remove the upper intake manifold from the engine (see Chapter 2).

4   Remove the bolts that retain the IMRC actuator assembly to the bottom of the upper intake manifold (see illustration).
5   Disconnect the actuator cable from the lever on the intake manifold runner (see illustration).
6   Installation is the reverse of removal.

16 Exhaust system servicing - general information

✳✳ WARNING:

Inspection and repair of exhaust system components should be done only after enough time has elapsed after driving the vehicle to allow the system components to cool completely. Also, when working under the vehicle, make sure it is securely supported on jackstands.

1   The exhaust system consists of the exhaust manifold(s), the catalytic converter, the muffler, the tailpipe and all connecting pipes, brackets, hangers and clamps. The exhaust system is attached to the body with mounting brackets and rubber hangers. If any of the parts are improperly installed, excessive noise and vibration will be transmitted to the body.
2   Conduct regular inspections of the exhaust system to keep it safe and quiet. Look for any damaged or bent parts, open seams, holes, loose connections, excessive corrosion or other defects which could allow exhaust fumes to enter the vehicle. Deteriorated exhaust system components should not be repaired; they should be replaced with new parts.
3   If the exhaust system components are extremely corroded or rusted together, welding equipment will probably be required to remove them. The convenient way to accomplish this is to have a muffler repair shop remove the corroded sections with a cutting torch. If, however, you want to save money by doing it yourself (and you don't have a welding outfit with a cutting torch), simply cut off the old components with a hacksaw. If you have compressed air, special pneumatic cutting chisels can also be used. If you do decide to tackle the job at home, be sure to wear safety goggles to protect your eyes from metal chips and work gloves to protect your hands.
4   Here are some simple guidelines to follow when repairing the exhaust system:

a) Work from the back to the front when removing exhaust system components.
b) Apply penetrating oil to the exhaust system component fasteners to make them easier to remove.
c) Use new gaskets, hangers and clamps when installing exhaust systems components.
d) Apply anti-seize compound to the threads of all exhaust system fasteners during reassembly.
e) Be sure to allow sufficient clearance between newly installed parts and all points on the underbody to avoid overheating the floor pan and possibly damaging the interior carpet and insulation. Pay particularly close attention to the catalytic converter and heat shield.

Specifications

Fuel pressure

Fuel system pressure (at idle)	
Vacuum hose attached	
1998 and earlier	30 to 45 psi
1999 and later	35 to 50 psi
Vacuum hose detached	
1998 and earlier	40 to 50 psi
1999 and later	45 to 55 psi
Fuel system hold pressure (after 5 minutes)	30 to 40 psi
Fuel pump pressure (maximum)	65 psi
Fuel pump hold pressure	50 psi
Injector resistance	13.5 to 19 ohms

Torque specifications   Ft-lbs (unless otherwise indicated)

Air intake plenum mounting bolts	
3.8L and 5.0L engines	
1998 and earlier	
First stage	96 in-lbs
Second stage	15
Third stage	24
1999 and later	
First stage	53 in-lbs
Second stage	71 in-lbs
Third stage	Turn an additional 90-degrees
4.6L DOHC engines (follow sequence in illustration 13.23)	71 to 106 in-lbs
Throttle body mounting nuts	12 to 18
EGR valve-to-throttle body	12 to 18
Fuel rail mounting bolts	70 to 105 in-lbs
Exhaust pipe-to-exhaust manifold bolts	25 to 35
Fuel pump module mounting bolts (1998)	80 to 106 in-lbs

Section

Reference to other Chapters

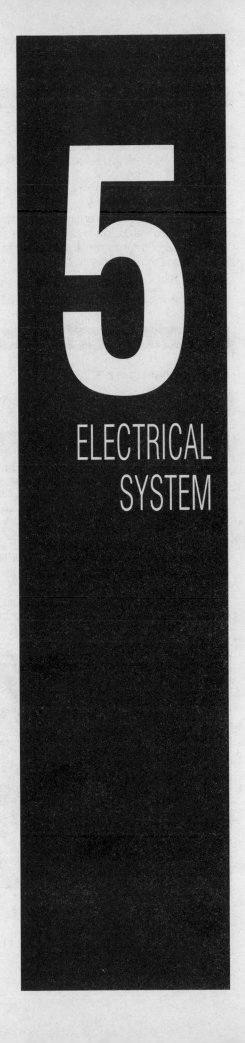

5

ELECTRICAL SYSTEM

1 General information

The engine electrical systems include all ignition, charging and starting components. Because of their engine-related functions, these components are considered separately from chassis electrical devices like the lights, instruments, etc.

Be very careful when working on the engine electrical components. They are easily damaged if checked, connected or handled improperly. The alternator is driven by an engine drivebelt which could cause serious injury if your hands, hair or clothes become entangled in it with the engine running. Both the starter and alternator are connected directly to the battery and could arc or even cause a fire if mishandled, overloaded or shorted out.

Never leave the ignition switch on for long periods of time with the engine off. Don't disconnect the battery cables while the engine is running. Correct polarity must be maintained when connecting battery cables from another source, such as another vehicle, during jump starting. Always disconnect the negative cable first and hook it up last or the battery may be shorted by the tool being used to loosen the cable clamps.

Additional safety related information on the engine electrical systems can be found in *Safety first* near the front of this manual. It should be referred to before beginning any operation included in this Chapter.

2 Battery - removal and installation

▶ **Refer to illustrations 2.1, 2.2 and 2.4**

1   Disconnect both cables from the battery terminals (see illustration).

✳ CAUTION:

Always disconnect the negative cable first and hook it up last or the battery may be shorted by the tool being used to loosen the cable clamps.

2   Remove the bolt and wedge from the battery tray (see illustration).

3   Lift out the battery. Use the special straps that attach to the battery posts - lifting and moving the battery is much easier if you use one.

4   If necessary for access to other components, remove the bolts that secure the battery tray to the engine compartment (see illustration).

5   Installation is the reverse of removal.

2.1 Detach the battery cables - negative first, then positive

2.2 Remove the bolt and the wedge that holds the base of the battery to the battery tray

2.4 Remove the mounting bolts for the battery tray (arrows)

3 Battery - emergency jump starting

Refer to the *Booster battery (jump) starting procedure* at the front of this manual.

4 Battery cables - check and replacement

1 Periodically inspect the entire length of each battery cable for damage, cracked or burned insulation and corrosion. Poor battery cable connections can cause starting problems and decreased engine performance.

2 Check the cable-to-terminal connections at the ends of the cables for cracks, loose wire strands and corrosion. The presence of white, fluffy deposits under the insulation at the cable terminal connection is a sign that the cable is corroded and should be replaced. Check the terminals for distortion, missing mounting bolts and corrosion.

3 When replacing the cables, always disconnect the negative cable first and hook it up last or the battery may be shorted by the tool used to loosen the cable clamps. Even if only the positive cable is being replaced, be sure to disconnect the negative cable from the battery first.

4 Disconnect and remove the cable. Make sure the replacement cable is the same length and diameter.

5 Clean the threads of the relay or ground connection with a wire brush to remove rust and corrosion. Apply a light coat of petroleum jelly to the threads to prevent future corrosion.

6 Attach the cable to the relay or ground connection and tighten the mounting nut/bolt securely.

7 Before connecting the new cable to the battery, make sure that it reaches the battery post without having to be stretched. Clean the battery posts thoroughly and apply a light coat of petroleum jelly to prevent corrosion.

8 Connect the positive cable first, followed by the negative cable.

5 Ignition system - general information

DISTRIBUTOR IGNITION (DI) SYSTEM

1 1994 and 1995 5.0L engines are equipped with the Distributor Ignition (DI) system. These ignition systems are a solid state electronic design consisting of an ignition module (externally mounted on the firewall), coil, distributor, stator (Hall Effect switching device), the spark plug wires and the spark plugs. Mechanically, the system is similar to a breaker point system, except that the distributor cam and ignition points are replaced by a Hall Effect switching device and a rotary vane cup. The coil primary circuit is controlled by an amplifier module. Refer to the wiring schematics at the end of Chapter 12 for additional information.

2 When the ignition is switched on, the ignition primary circuit is energized. When the distributor rotary vane passes through the Hall Effect switching device (stator), voltage is induced which signals the amplifier to turn off the coil primary current. A timing circuit in the amplifier module turns the coil current back on after the coil field has collapsed.

➡Note: The DI systems are equipped with either the Push Start ignition module control or the Computer Control Dwell (CCD) system. The more simple push start systems control the ON-TIME of the coil according to the revolutions of the engine. Push Start inferring that the vehicle could be push started in gear (manual transmission), crankshaft revolutions detected and spark applied to the spark plugs. CCD ignition control systems use the SPOUT signal to control the coil ON TIME. The ignition control module does not determine when to turn the coil ON as it does on the push start system but instead responds directly to the SPOUT signal it receives.

3 When it's on, current flows from the battery through the ignition switch, the coil primary winding, the amplifier module and then to ground. When the current is interrupted, the magnetic field in the ignition coil collapses, inducing a high voltage in the coil secondary windings. The voltage is conducted to the distributor where the rotor directs it to the appropriate spark plug. This process is repeated continuously.

4 Distributor Ignition (DI) systems control the ignition module with the Electronic Engine Control IV (EEC-IV) computer. Ignition timing is handled by the computer. The computer uses information from the Profile Ignition Pick-up (PIP) and Cylinder Identification (CID) to determine the proper point to fire the coil. The ignition control module sends the Spark Output (SPOUT) signal to the Ignition Control Module to turn the coil ON and OFF. The Ignition Control Module also generates an Ignition Diagnostic Monitor (IDM) signal so that the EEC module can check the ignition system operation. These signals are important in diagnosing problems with the ignition system.

➡Note: 1994 and 1995 5.0L engines are equipped with EEC-IV and OBD I engine management and self-diagnosis system. The diagnostic codes are accessible and the procedure is detailed in Chapter 6. 3.8L V6 and 4.6L SOHC and DOHC engines are equipped with the EEC-V and OBD II systems. This system requires a special SCAN tool to access self diagnosis codes and data stream information.

ELECTRONIC DISTRIBUTORLESS IGNITION (EDIS) TYPE

5 The Electronic Distributorless Ignition System (EDIS) is a complete electronically controlled ignition system that does not incorporate a distributor or rotor and cap. The EDIS system consists of a crankshaft timing sensor (variable reluctance sensor) camshaft sensor (1996 and later), EDIS module, ignition coil packs, an EEC V module (PCM), the spark plug wires and the spark plugs. This engine is equipped with an

ignition coil for each pair of spark plugs. The EDIS system features a waste-spark method of spark distribution. Each cylinder is paired with its companion cylinder in the firing order (1-5, 2-6, 3-4 [V6 engine]) or (1-6, 5-3, 4-7, 2-8 [V8 engine]) so one cylinder under compression fires simultaneously with its opposing cylinder, where the piston is on the exhaust stroke. Since the cylinder on the exhaust stroke requires very little of the available voltage to fire its plug, most of the voltage is used to fire the plug under compression.

→Note: The EDIS system on 1994 and 1995 3.8L V6 engines differs from the EDIS systems on 1996 and later 3.8L V6 and 4.6L SOHC and DOHC engines. 1994 and 1995 EDIS systems are equipped with a crankshaft sensor, an ignition module and a PCM. 1996 and later models are equipped with a crankshaft sensor, camshaft sensor and PCM (no ignition module). Here the PCM functions as the overall controller of the ignition system by receiving engine speed and crankshaft position signals and determining the correct ignition timing and injector ON-TIME (rich/lean) but also functions as the controller of the ignition coil(s) primary circuit which was basically the job of the ignition module.

6   This ignition system does not have any moving parts (no distributor) and all engine timing and spark distribution is handled electronically. This system has fewer parts that require replacement and provides more accurate spark timing. During engine operation, the DIS ignition module calculates spark angle and determines the turn-on and firing time of the ignition coil.

7   The crankshaft timing sensor is a variable reluctance sensor mounted above the front pulley timing gear. This passive electromagnetic device senses movement of the teeth on the pulley timing gear and generates an A/C voltage signal which increases with engine rpm. This sensor provides engine speed and crankshaft position signals to the PCM. The main function of the EDIS module is to synchronize the ignition coils so they are turned ON an OFF in the proper sequence for accurate spark control.

6   Ignition system - check

❊❊ WARNING:

Because of the very high secondary (spark plug) voltage generated by the ignition system, extreme care should be taken when this check is done.

CALIBRATED IGNITION TESTER METHOD

▶ **Refer to illustration 6.2**

1   If the engine turns over but won't start, disconnect the spark plug lead from any spark plug and attach it to a calibrated ignition tester (available at most auto parts stores). Make sure the tester is designed for Ford ignition systems if a universal tester isn't available.

2   Connect the clip on the tester to a bolt or metal bracket on the engine (see illustration), crank the engine and watch the end of the tester to see if bright blue, well-defined sparks occur.

3   If sparks occur, sufficient voltage is reaching the plug to fire it (repeat the check at the remaining plug wires to verify that the distributor cap and rotor are OK). However, the plugs themselves may be fouled, so remove and check them as described in Chapter 1 or install new ones.

Distributor Ignition (DI) systems

▶ **Refer to illustration 6.6**

4   If no sparks or intermittent sparks occur, remove the distributor cap and check the cap and rotor as described in Chapter 1. If moisture is present, dry out the cap and rotor, then reinstall the cap and repeat the spark test.

5   If there's still no spark, detach the coil secondary wire from the distributor cap and hook it up to the tester (reattach the plug wire to the spark plug), then repeat the spark check.

6   If no sparks occur, check the primary (small) wire connections at the coil to make sure they're clean and tight. Check the ignition coil

6.2 To use a calibrated ignition tester, simply disconnect a spark plug wire, clip the tester to a convenient ground (like a valve cover bolt) and operate the starter - if there is enough power to fire the plug, sparks will be visible between the electrode tip and the tester body (4.6L DOHC engine shown)

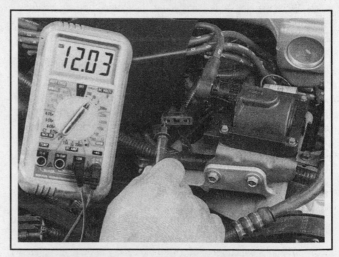

6.6 Check for battery voltage to the ignition coil (DI system shown)

supply voltage circuit (see illustration). Make any necessary repairs, then repeat the check again.

7   If sparks now occur, the distributor cap, rotor, plug wire(s) or spark plug(s) (or all of them) may be defective.

8   If there's still no spark, the coil-to-cap wire may be bad (check the resistance with an ohmmeter and compare it to the Specifications). If a known good wire doesn't make any difference in the test results, the ignition coil, module or other internal components may be defective (see Sections 7 and 10).

Electronic Distributorless Ignition (EDIS) system

♦ **Refer to illustration 6.9**

9   If no sparks or intermittent sparks occur, check for battery voltage to the ignition coil (see illustration). Check for a bad spark plug wire by swapping wires. Check the coils and DIS ignition module (see Sections 7 and 10).

ALTERNATIVE METHOD (DISTRIBUTOR IGNITION SYSTEM)

➡**Note: If you're unable to obtain a calibrated ignition tester, the following method will allow you to determine if the ignition system has spark, but it won't tell you if there's enough voltage produced to actually initiate combustion in the cylinders.**

10   Remove the wire from one of the spark plugs. Using an insulated tool, hold the wire about 1/4-inch from a good ground and have an assistant crank the engine.

11   If bright blue, well-defined sparks occur, sufficient voltage is reaching the plug to fire it. However, the plug(s) may be fouled, so remove and check them as described in Chapter 1 or install new ones.

12   If there's no spark, check the remaining wires in the same manner. A few sparks followed by no spark is the same condition as no spark at all.

13   If no sparks occur, remove the distributor cap and check the cap and rotor as described in Chapter 1. If moisture is present, dry out the cap and rotor, then reinstall the cap and repeat the spark test.

14   If there's still no spark, disconnect the secondary coil wire from the distributor cap, hold it about 1/4-inch from a good engine ground and crank the engine again.

15   If no sparks occur, check the primary (small) wire connections at the coil to make sure they're clean and tight.

16   If sparks do occur, the distributor cap and rotor, plug wire(s) or spark plug(s) may be defective.

17   If there's still no spark, the coil-to-cap wire may be bad (check

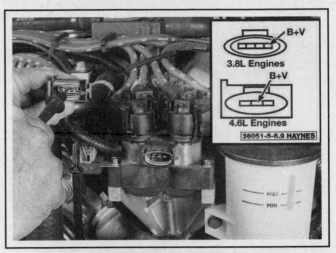

6.9 Disconnect the electrical connector from the ignition coil and check for battery voltage to the coil with the ignition key on (4.6L DOHC engine shown)

the resistance with an ohmmeter and compare it to the Specifications). If a known good wire doesn't make any difference in the test results, the ignition coil, module or other internal components may be defective. Refer further testing to a Ford dealer or qualified electrical specialist.

ALL SYSTEMS

18   Check for battery voltage to the ignition module. 1994 and 1995 5.0L engines are equipped with the DI system. The ignition module is under the air cleaner assembly. 1994 and 1995 3.8L engines are equipped with the EDIS system and the ignition module is also located under the air cleaner assembly. 1996 and later 3.8L, 4.6L SOHC and DOHC engines are not equipped with an ignition module but instead the PCM houses the complete components for the fuel injection, emission and ignition system. Refer to Section 10 for the checks and replacement procedures.

19   On 1994 and 1995 5.0L engines, check for battery voltage to the stator. Also, check the condition of the distributor and the stator (see Section 10).

20   Check the operation of the crankshaft sensors and the camshaft sensors (see Chapter 6).

21   If all the components and the ignition system checks are correct, have the system diagnosed by a dealer service department.

---

7   Ignition coil - check and replacement

DISTRIBUTOR IGNITION (DI) SYSTEM

Check

Primary and secondary coil resistance

♦ **Refer to illustrations 7.1 and 7.2**

1   With the ignition off, disconnect the wires from the coil. Connect an ohmmeter across the coil primary (low voltage) terminals (see illus-

tration). The resistance should be as listed in this Chapter's Specifications. If not, replace the coil.

2   Connect an ohmmeter between the negative primary terminal and the secondary terminal (see illustration) (the one that the distributor cap wire connects to). The resistance should be as listed in this Chapter's Specifications. If not, replace the coil.

Ignition coil primary winding-to-case resistance

3   Measure the resistance from the positive primary terminal to the case of the ignition coil.

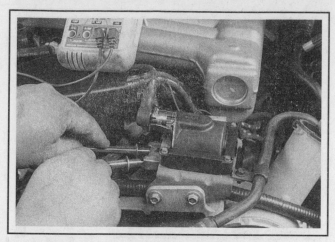

7.1 Checking the coil primary resistance on a Distributor Ignition system

4   If the indicated resistance is less than the resistance listed in this Chapter's Specifications, replace the ignition coil.

5   Reconnect the ignition coil wires.

Replacement

▶ **Refer to illustration 7.9**

6   Detach the cable from the negative terminal of the battery.

7   Detach the wires from the primary terminals on the coil.

8   Unplug the coil secondary lead.

9   Remove both bracket bolts and detach the coil (see illustration).

10   Installation is the reverse of removal.

ELECTRONIC DISTRIBUTORLESS IGNITION (EDIS) SYSTEM

1996 and later models without Coil Over Plug (COP)

Check

▶ **Refer to illustrations 7.11 and 7.12**

11   With the ignition off, disconnect the electrical connector(s) from the coil. Connect an ohmmeter across the coil primary terminal (+) and

7.9 To replace the ignition coil, detach the cable from the negative terminal of the battery, unplug the coil primary connection, detach the coil secondary lead and remove both coil bracket bolts (arrows)

7.2 Checking the coil secondary resistance on a Distributor Ignition system

the outer terminal(s) (-) (see illustration). The resistance should be as listed in this Chapter's Specifications. If not, replace the coil.

12   Connect an ohmmeter between the secondary terminals (see illustration) (the one that the spark plug wires connect to) of each coil pack. The resistance should be as listed in this Chapter's Specifications.

➥**Note: Each coil pack is paired according to the companion cylinders.**

3.8L V6 engines	1/5, 2/6, 3/4
4.6L SOHC and DOHC engines	7/4, 8/2, 1/6 and 3/5

Be sure to check resistance with these designated terminals only. If not, replace the coil.

Replacement

▶ **Refer to illustration 7.16**

13   Disconnect the negative cable from the battery.

14   Disconnect the ignition coil electrical connector(s) from each individual coil pack.

15   Disconnect the ignition wires by squeezing the locking tabs and

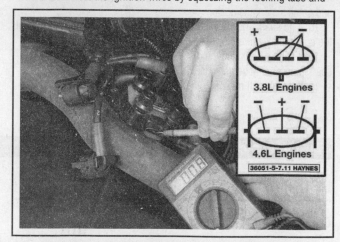

7.11 To check the primary resistance of the EDIS coil, connect the probes to the positive (+) terminal and negative (-) terminal of the coil. Be sure to check the other coil pack (opposite terminal) and then the other coil pack assembly mounted on the right engine bank. The resistance should be the same for all four tests

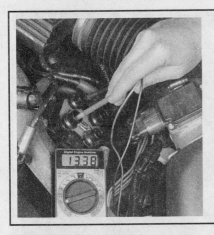

7.12 Check the coil secondary resistance by probing the paired companion cylinders (7/4, 8/2, 1/6 and 3/5) (4.6L SOHC coil shown)

7.16 Remove the coil pack mounting screws (arrows) and lift it from the engine

twisting while pulling. DO NOT just pull on the wires to disconnect them. Disconnect all spark plug leads.

16 Remove the bolts securing the ignition coil to the mounting bracket on the engine (see illustration).

17 Installation is the reverse of the removal procedure with the following additions:

    a) *Prior to installing the spark plug lead into the ignition coil, coat the entire interior of the rubber boot with silicone dielectric compound, available at most auto parts stores.*

    b) *Insert each spark plug wire into the proper terminal of the ignition coil. Push the wire into the terminal and make sure the boots are fully seated and both locking tabs are engaged properly.*

➡**Note: Refer to the EDIS firing order schematic in Chapter 2 Specifications to correctly identify each cylinder and its corresponding coil pack terminal.**

1999 and later models with Coil Over Plug (COP) system

Check

▶ **Refer to illustrations 7.18 and 7.19**

18 With the ignition off, disconnect the electrical connector(s) from each coil assembly. Connect an ohmmeter across the coil primary terminal (+) and the negative terminal (-) (see illustration). The resistance should be as listed in this Chapter's Specifications. If not, replace the coil.

19 Remove the COP assembly from the cylinder head (see Step 20). Connect an ohmmeter between the secondary terminals (see illustration) (the one that fits over the spark plug). The resistance should be as listed in this Chapter's Specifications.

Replacement

▶ **Refer to illustration 7.23**

20 Disconnect the negative cable from the battery.

21 On 4.6L DOHC engines, remove the ignition coil access cover from the top of the valve cover.

22 Disconnect the ignition coil electrical connector(s) from each individual coil. Mark each electrical connector with tape to prevent mix-ups during reassembly.

23 On 4.6L SOHC engines, remove the bolt securing the ignition coil (see illustration).

24 Pull the coil from the cylinder head.

25 Installation is the reverse of the removal procedure with the following additions:

    a) *Prior to installing the coil over plug (COP) assembly into the cylinder head, coat the entire interior of the assembly with Silicone Dielectric Compound or equivalent.*

    b) *Connect each COP electrical connector to its correct coil and make sure they are tight and secure.*

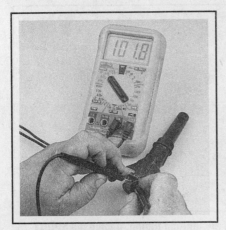

7.18 Check to COP assembly primary resistance

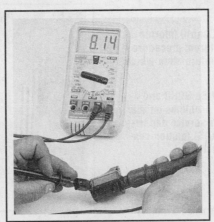

7.19 Check the COP assembly secondary resistance

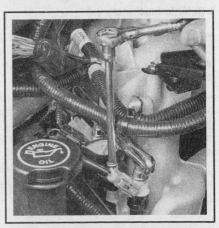

7.23 Remove the COP mounting bolt and lift the assembly from the cylinder head

8 Distributor (5.0L engines) - removal and installation

REMOVAL

▶ **Refer to illustration 8.3**

1 Unplug the primary lead from the coil.

2 Unplug the electrical connector for the module. Follow the wires as they exit the distributor to find the connector.

3 Note the raised "1" on the distributor cap (see illustration). This marks the location for the number one cylinder spark plug wire terminal.

4 Remove the distributor cap (see Chapter 1) and turn the engine over until the rotor is pointing toward the number one spark plug terminal (see the TDC locating procedure in Chapter 2).

5 Make a mark on the edge of the distributor base directly below the rotor tip and in line with it. Also, mark the distributor base and the engine block to ensure that the distributor is installed correctly.

6 Remove the distributor hold-down bolt and clamp, then pull the distributor straight up to remove it. Be careful not to disturb the intermediate driveshaft.

> **⁂ CAUTION:**
>
> **DO NOT turn the engine while the distributor is removed, or the alignment marks will be useless.**

INSTALLATION

7 Insert the distributor into the engine in exactly the same relationship to the block that it was in when removed.

8 To mesh the helical gears on the camshaft and the distributor, it may be necessary to turn the rotor slightly. If the distributor doesn't seat completely, the hex shaped recess in the lower end of the distributor shaft is not mating properly with the oil pump shaft. Recheck the alignment marks between the distributor base and the block to verify that the

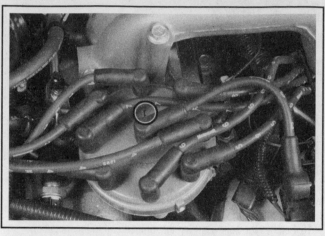

8.3 The number "1" on the distributor cap marks the location of the spark plug wire terminal for the number 1 cylinder spark plug

distributor is in the same position it was in before removal. Also check the rotor to see if it's aligned with the mark you made on the edge of the distributor base.

➡**Note: If the crankshaft has been moved while the distributor is out, locate Top Dead Center (TDC) for the number one piston (see Chapter 2) and position the distributor and rotor accordingly.**

9 Place the hold-down clamp in position and loosely install the bolt.

10 Install the distributor cap and tighten the cap screws securely.

11 Plug in the module electrical connector.

12 Reattach the spark plug wires to the plugs (if removed).

13 Connect the cable to the negative terminal of the battery.

14 Check and, if necessary, adjust the ignition timing (refer to Section 9) and tighten the distributor hold-down bolt securely.

9 Ignition timing (5.0L engine) - check and adjustment

▶ **Refer to illustration 9.3**

➡**Note 1: Always check the Vehicle Emission Control Information (VECI) label on your vehicle to see if a different procedure is specified. The VECI label contains detailed information which is specific to your vehicle.**

➡**Note 2: Ignition timing on the 3.8L and the 4.6L SOHC and DOHC engines cannot be adjusted. Any timing problems on the these engines will have to repaired by a dealer service department. Ignition timing on the Distributorless (EDIS) Ignition system is computer controlled and cannot be adjusted.**

1 Apply the parking brake and block the wheels. Place the transmission in DRIVE (parking brake applied). Turn off all accessories (heater, air conditioner, etc.).

2 Start the engine and warm it up. Once it has reached operating temperature, turn it off.

3 Unplug the single wire connector or SPOUT (Spark Output) located immediately above the electrical connector for the module (see illustration).

9.3 Before adjusting the ignition timing, unplug the SPOUT (arrow) (single wire connector) attached to the ignition module wire harness (if you do not, the EEC-IV system will still be controlling the base ignition timing)

➡ **Note: The SPOUT controls the ignition signal from the computer. Disconnecting the SPOUT will display only the base timing settings without any changes from the computer.**

4   Connect an inductive timing light and a tachometer in accordance with the manufacturer's instructions.

> ✪ **CAUTION:**
>
> **Make sure that the timing light and tachometer wires don't hang anywhere near the cooling fan or they may become entangled in the fan blades when the fan begins to rotate.**

5   Locate the timing marks on the crankshaft pulley (see Chapter 2).
6   Start the engine again.
7   Point the timing light at the pulley timing marks and note whether the specified timing mark (see the VECI label) is aligned with the timing pointer on the front of the timing chain cover.

8   If the proper mark isn't aligned with the stationary pointer, loosen the distributor hold-down bolt. Turn the distributor clockwise (to advance timing) or counterclockwise (to retard timing) until the correct timing mark on the crankshaft pulley is aligned with the stationary pointer. Tighten the distributor hold-down bolt securely when the timing is correct and recheck it to make sure it didn't change when the bolt was tightened.

9   Turn off the engine.
10 Plug in the SPOUT connector located in the harness near the air cleaner assembly.
11 Restart the engine and check the idle speed. The specified rpm for each vehicle is different (see your VECI Label). On vehicles with an adjustable idle speed, see Chapter 4 for adjustment procedure.
12 Turn off the engine.
13 Remove the timing light and tachometer.

10 Ignition module and stator - check and replacement

> ✪ **CAUTION:**
>
> **The ignition module is a delicate and relatively expensive electronic component. Failure to follow the step-by-step procedures could result in damage to the module and/or other electronic devices, including the EEC-IV or V microprocessor itself. Additionally, all devices under computer control are protected by a Federally mandated extended warranty. Check with your dealer concerning this warranty before attempting to diagnose and replace the module yourself.**

DISTRIBUTOR IGNITION (DI) MODULE (1994 AND 1995 5.0L ENGINES)

Check

▶ Refer to illustrations 10.1, 10.2, 10.3, 10.4 and 10.5

➡ **Note: Refer to the ignition checking procedure in Section 6 and the wiring schematics at the end of Chapter 12 for additional information.**

1   Distributor Ignition (DI) systems are equipped with an external ignition module located under the air cleaner assembly (see illustration).
2   Check for power to the ignition module. Using a voltmeter, probe the red/light green wire (terminal 4) to the module (see illustration). With the ignition ON (engine not running), there should be battery voltage.
3   Check the PIP signal from the stator (Hall Effect switching device) in the distributor to the ignition module. Backprobe the dark green wire (terminal 1) on the ignition control module (see illustration) with an LED test light, crank the engine over and confirm that the test light flashes. If there are no flashes, check the distributor.
4   Check for power to the stator. Probe the red/light green wire (terminal 4) to the module (see illustration). With the ignition ON (engine not running), there should be battery voltage. If battery voltage exists and there is still no response (LED flashes) from the distributor (see Step 3), replace the stator.

10.1 The ignition module is located under the air cleaner housing on the fenderwell on 5.0L engines

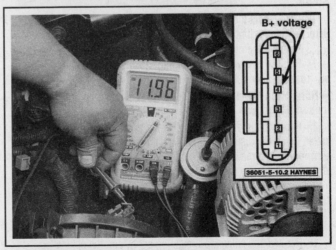

10.2 Check battery voltage to the ignition module on terminal number 4

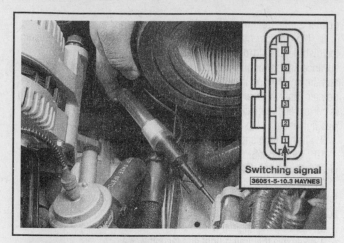

10.3 Have an assistant crank the engine while backprobing terminal number 1 on the ignition control module. The test light should flash as the ignition module switches primary voltage

5   Check the SPOUT signal from the ignition module. Backprobe the pink wire (terminal 2) with an LED test light, have an assistant crank the engine over and observe flashes (see illustration) on the test light.

6   Check for the GROUND for the ignition module. Disconnect the ignition module harness connector, install one probe of the ohmmeter onto the negative battery terminal and probe the black/light blue wire (terminal 6) (see illustration 10.2). There should be less than 5.0 ohms resistance. If the resistance is excessive, repair the ground or the Hall Effect switching device in the distributor.

7   If battery voltage is not reaching the ignition module or distributor, trace the circuit to the ignition switch and battery (see Chapter 12) and check for open circuits or a damaged wire harness. If any of the other test results are incorrect, replace the ignition module with a new part.

Replacement

Ignition module

8   Detach the cable from the negative terminal of the battery.
9   Unplug the electrical connectors.
10 Remove the mounting screws and detach the module.
11 Installation is the reverse of removal.

Stator

12 Disconnect the cable from the negative terminal of the battery. Remove the distributor cap and rotor (see Chapter 1).
13 Remove the distributor (see Section 8).
14 Remove the two screws holding the armature and lift the assembly from the distributor.

➡**Note: Hold the distributor drive gear not the armature to loosen the screws.**

15 Remove and discard the pin in the distributor drive gear and collar. Invert the distributor and place the assembly in a vice. Using an appropriate size pin punch, drive the roll pin from the distributor gear and shaft. Press the gear off the shaft and remove the shaft assembly from the distributor base. If necessary, deburr and clean the distributor shaft so it slides out of the base easily.
16 Press off the drive gear.
17 Remove the shaft from the distributor.
18 Remove the octane rod retaining screw and the octane rod.
19 Remove the distributor stator mounting screws and remove the stator from the distributor.

10.4 Test for battery voltage to the Hall Effect switching device at the harness connector on terminal number 4

10.5 Backprobe the SPOUT connector with a LED test light and check for a flashing signal

20 Inspect the distributor base bushing. If the bushing is damaged, replace the entire distributor.
21 Inspect the distributor base O-ring and replace it if necessary.
22 Installation is the reverse of removal with the following additions:

a) *Apply a light coat of clean engine oil to the distributor shaft before installation.*

b) *Align the hole in the gear and shaft exactly, before pressing the gear on. DO NOT use a drift punch to align the holes.*

c) *Drive a NEW roll pin through the gear and shaft until it's flush with the gear.*

d) *Replace the distributor base O-ring.*

ELECTRONIC DISTRIBUTORLESS IGNITION SYSTEM (EDIS) MODULE

Ignition coil primary circuit (all EDIS systems)

▶ **Refer to illustration 10.25**

23 Unplug the ignition coil wiring harness connectors and inspect them for dirt, corrosion and damage.
24 Check for battery voltage to the ignition coil(s) (see illustration 6.9). Attach a 12 volt test light to the battery negative (-) terminal. Disconnect the coil harness connector and check for power to the positive

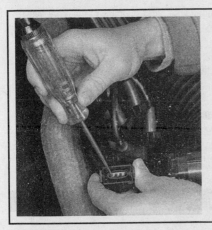

10.25 Connect a LED test light on the coil negative (-) terminals on the ignition coil connectors and watch for a blinking light when the engine is cranked (4.6L SOHC shown) (1997 4.6L SOHC shown)

(+) terminal. Battery voltage should be available with the ignition key ON (engine not running). If there is no battery voltage, check the 20 amp fuse that governs the ignition circuit (see Chapter 12 for additional information on the fuses and the wiring schematics).

25 If battery voltage is available, attach a 12 volt test light to the battery positive (+) terminal and the coil harness connector negative terminal (-) (see illustration) and crank the engine.

➡️Note: Make sure the primary (low voltage) electrical connectors are disconnected from both coils to prevent the engine from starting.

Confirm that the test light flashes.

✳️ CAUTION:

Do not probe the positive (+) wire. This is battery voltage source. Refer to illustration 7.11 for the correct terminals. This test checks for the trigger signal (ground) from the computer. Check the other wires to the ignition coil(s) using only an LED test light to avoid damaging the circuits. This will indicate that the coil(s) are receiving the proper signal.

➡️Note: On 1999 and later models with the Coil Over Plug (COP) system, check for battery voltage at the coil connector first, then use an LED test light to check the trigger signal on the other wire. These systems only have two wires running to each ignition coil: a positive and a negative. It will be necessary to perform this test on all eight coils.

26 The test light should flash with each output signal from the EDIS ignition module through the coil primary circuit as the engine fires.

➡️Note: It will be necessary to check each circuit that governs each coil pack. Install the test light into the appropriate terminals on the harness connector and repeat the test. Follow the wiring schematics at the end of Chapter 12 for the correct color wires to the coil drivers in the PCM.

Sensor checks (all EDIS systems)

➡️Note: 1994 and 1995 EDIS systems on the 3.8L engines are equipped with a variable reluctance type crankshaft sensor. This type of crankshaft sensor can be checked on the bench using an A/C voltmeter. 1996 and later 3.8L and 4.6L SOHC and DOHC engines are equipped with a camshaft sensor as well as a crankshaft sensor. The camshaft sensor on the 3.8L 1996 and later signals the PCM to begin sequential pulsation of the fuel injectors. This camshaft sensor is a Hall Effect switching device activated by a single vane. This type of sensor must be checked on the vehicle with voltage applied to the sensor by the PCM. The 3.8L 1996 and later camshaft sensor is mounted on the

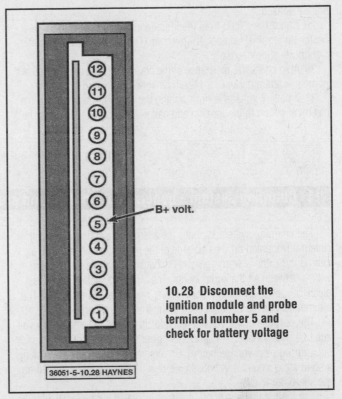

10.28 Disconnect the ignition module and probe terminal number 5 and check for battery voltage

B+ volt.

36051-5-10.28 HAYNES

top of the engine where the distributor used to be installed in the older 3.8L engines. The camshaft sensor in the 4.6L SOHC and DOHC engines is a variable reluctance device which is triggered by the high point mark on the camshaft. These sensors are mounted on the front of the cylinder head near the camshaft sprocket. These camshaft sensors signal the PCM to start up fuel injector pulsation as well as misfire detection.

27 The crankshaft sensor and camshaft sensor are an integral component of the ignition systems on 3.8L and 4.6L SOHC and DOHC engines. These sensors are difficult to reach for testing purposes but it is of major importance that they be checked when dealing with ignition system diagnostics. In the event the crankshaft sensor or camshaft sensor is defective (or both), replace them with new parts and continue checking the ignition system to verify the working condition of all ignition system components. Refer to Chapter 6 for all the locations, checking and replacement procedures on the crankshaft sensor and camshafts sensors.

Ignition module checks (1994 and 1995 3.8L engines)

◆ Refer to illustration 10.28

➡️Note: The EDIS system on the 1994 and 1995 3.8L engines differ from the EDIS systems on the 1996 and later 3.8L and 4.6L SOHC and DOHC engines. 1994 and 1995 EDIS systems are equipped with a crankshaft sensor, an ignition module and a PCM. 1996 and later models are equipped with a crankshaft sensor, camshaft sensor and PCM (no ignition module). Here the PCM functions as the overall controller of the ignition system by receiving engine speed and crankshaft position signals and determining the correct ignition timing and injector ON-TIME (rich/lean) but also functions as the controller of the ignition coil(s) primary circuit which was basically the job of the ignition module.

28 Check for power to the ignition module. Using a voltmeter, probe terminal number 5 (red wire [+]) and check for battery voltage (see illustration). With the ignition ON (engine not running), there should be

battery voltage.

29 Check the circuit from the ignition module to the SPOUT connector on terminal number 10 (pink wire [+]) for a complete circuit. Continuity should exist.

30 Also check the resistance of the crankshaft sensor on terminals number 7 and number 8. It should be between 1.0 and 1.5 ohms.

31 If battery voltage is not reaching the ignition module, trace the electrical circuit to the ignition and battery (see Chapter 12) and check

for open circuits or a damaged wire harness. If any of the other test results are incorrect, replace the ignition module with a new one.

Replacement

32 Disconnect the negative cable from the battery.

33 Disconnect the electrical connector from the EDIS ignition module.

34 Remove the screws securing the EDIS module to the fenderwell.

35 Installation is the reverse of the removal procedure.

11 Charging system - general information and precautions

The charging system includes the alternator, a voltage regulator (integral [mounted on the backside of the alternator] or internal), a charge indicator or warning light, the battery, a fusible link and the wiring between all the components. The charging system supplies electrical power for the ignition system, the lights, the radio, etc. The alternator is driven by a drivebelt at the front of the engine.

The purpose of the voltage regulator is to limit the alternator's voltage to a preset value. This prevents power surges, circuit overloads, etc., during peak voltage output. On integral voltage regulator systems, a solid state regulator is housed inside a plastic module mounted on the alternator itself.

The fusible link is a short length of insulated wire integral with the engine compartment wiring harness. The link is several wire gauges smaller in diameter than the circuit it protects. Production fusible links and their identification flags are identified by the flag color. Refer to

Chapter 12 for additional information on fusible links.

The charging system doesn't ordinarily require periodic maintenance. However, the drivebelt, battery and wires and connections should be inspected at the intervals outlined in Chapter 1.

Be very careful when making electrical circuit connections to a vehicle equipped with an alternator and note the following:

a) *When reconnecting wires to the alternator from the battery, be sure to note the polarity.*

b) *Before using arc welding equipment to repair any part of the vehicle, disconnect the wires from the alternator and the battery terminals.*

c) *Never start the engine with a battery charger connected.*

d) *Always disconnect both battery cables before using a battery charger (negative cable first, positive cable last).*

12 Charging system - check

▶ **Refer to illustration 12.2**

1 If a malfunction occurs in the charging circuit, do not immediately assume that the alternator is causing the problem. First check the following items:

a) *The battery cables where they connect to the battery. Make sure the connections are clean and tight.*

b) *The battery electrolyte specific gravity. If it is low, charge the battery.*

c) *Check the external alternator wiring and connections.*

d) *Check the drivebelt condition and tension (see Chapter 1).*

e) *Check the alternator mounting bolts for tightness.*

f) *Run the engine and check the alternator for abnormal noise.*

2 Using a voltmeter, check the battery voltage with the engine off. It should be approximately 12-volts (see illustration).

3 Start the engine and check the battery voltage again. It should now be approximately 14 to 15-volts.

4 If the indicated voltage reading is less or more than the specified charging voltage, replace the voltage regulator. If replacing the regulator fails to restore the voltage to the specified range, the problem may be within the alternator.

➡**Note: Due to the special equipment necessary to test or service the alternator, it is recommended that if a fault is suspected the vehicle be taken to a dealer or a shop with the proper equipment. Because of this, the home mechanic should limit**

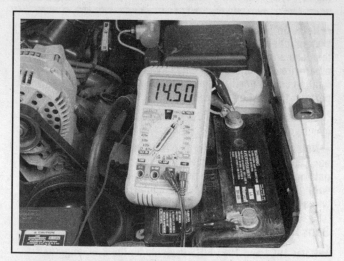

12.2 To measure charging voltage, attach the voltmeter leads to the battery terminals, start the engine and record the voltage reading

maintenance to checking connections, fuses and fusible links that govern the charging system.

5 Check the ALT fuse in the engine compartment fuse box (see Chapter 12). Also, check the fusible links A and B.

6   Some models are equipped with an ammeter on the instrument panel that indicates charge or discharge - current passing in or out of the battery. With all electrical equipment switched ON, and the engine idling, the gauge needle may show a discharge condition. At fast idle or normal driving speeds the needle should stay on the charge side of the gauge, with the charged state of the battery determining just how far over (the lower the battery state of charge, the farther the needle should swing toward the charge side).

7   Some models are equipped with a voltmeter on the instrument panel that indicates battery voltage with the key on and engine off, and alternator output when the engine is running.

8   The charge light on the instrument panel illuminates with the key on and engine not running, and should go out when the engine runs.

9   If the gauge does not show a charge when it should or the alternator light (if equipped) remains on, there is a fault in the system. Before inspecting the brushes or replacing the alternator, the battery condition, alternator belt tension and electrical cable connections should be checked.

13 Alternator - removal and installation

▶ **Refer to illustrations 13.5a, 13.5b and 13.5c**

1   Detach the cable from the negative terminal of the battery.
2   Unplug the electrical connectors from the alternator.
3   Remove the drivebelt (see Chapter 1).
4   On 4.6L engines, remove the ignition wire assembly from the intake manifold area.

5   Remove the bolts and separate the alternator from the engine (see illustrations).
6   Installation is the reverse of removal.
7   After the alternator is installed, install the drivebelt and reconnect the cable to the negative terminal of the battery.

13.5a On 4.6L engines, remove the lower mounting bolts (arrows) . . .

13.5b . . . then remove the four mounting bolts (arrows) and separate the alternator bracket from the air intake plenum (4.6L DOHC engine shown)

13.5c Alternator mounting bolts - 3.8L V6 engine

14 Voltage regulator/alternator brushes (integral regulator) - replacement

▶ **Refer to illustrations 14.3, 14.4, 14.5 and 14.9**

➡**Note: On some later models, the voltage regulator and brush holder are not replaceable. If they are replaceable, you will be able to see the plastic regulator assembly and attaching screws on the back of the alternator.**

1   Remove the alternator (see Section 13).
2   Set the alternator on a clean workbench.
3   Remove the four voltage regulator mounting screws (see illustration).
4   Detach the voltage regulator (see illustration).
5   Detach the rubber plugs and remove the brush lead retaining screws and nuts to separate the brush leads from the holder (see illustration). Note that the screws have Torx heads and require a special screwdriver.
6   After noting the relationship of the brushes to the brush holder assembly, remove both brushes. Don't lose the springs.

14.3 To detach the voltage regulator/brush holder assembly, remove the four screws

14.4 Lift the assembly from the alternator

14.5 To remove the brushes from the voltage regulator/brush holder assembly, detach the rubber plugs from the two brush lead screws and remove both screws (arrows)

14.9 Before installing the voltage regulator/brush holder assembly, insert a paper clip as shown to hold the brushes in place during installation - after installation, simply pull the paper clip out

7   If you're installing a new voltage regulator, insert the old brushes into the brush holder of the new regulator. If you're installing new brushes, insert them into the brush holder of the old regulator. Make sure the springs are properly compressed and the brushes are properly inserted into the recesses in the brush holder.

8   Install the brush lead retaining screws and nuts.

9   Insert a short section of wire, like a paper clip, through the hole in the voltage regulator (see illustration) to hold the brushes in the retracted position during regulator installation.

10   Carefully install the regulator. Make sure the brushes don't hang up on the rotor.

11   Install the voltage regulator screws and tighten them securely.

12   Remove the wire or paper clip.

13   Install the alternator (see Section 13).

15   Starting system - general information and precautions

1   The function of the starting system is to crank the engine to start it. The system is composed of the starter motor, starter relay, battery, switch and connecting wires.

2   Turning the ignition key to the Start position actuates the starter relay through the starter control circuit. The starter relay then connects the battery to the starter. The battery supplies the electrical energy to the starter motor, which does the actual work of cranking the engine.

3   These models are equipped with a starter/solenoid assembly that is mounted to the transmission bellhousing.

4   Vehicles equipped with an automatic transmission are equipped with a Transmission Range sensor in the starter control circuit, which

prevents operation of the starter unless the shift lever is in Neutral or Park. Manual transmission vehicles are equipped with a starter clutch pedal position switch. The starter will not crank with the foot off the clutch pedal.

5   The starter circuit is equipped with a starter relay. This relay is located in the engine compartment fuse panel.

6   Never operate the starter motor for more than 15 seconds at a time without pausing to allow it to cool for at least two minutes. Excessive cranking can cause overheating, which can seriously damage the starter.

16 Starter motor and circuit - in-vehicle check

➡️**Note: Before diagnosing starter problems, make sure the battery is fully charged.**

GENERAL CHECK

1   If the starter motor doesn't turn at all when the switch Is operated, make sure the shift lever is in Neutral or Park.

2   Make sure the battery is charged and that all cables at the battery and starter solenoid terminals are secure.

3   If the starter motor spins but the engine doesn't turn over, then the drive assembly in the starter motor is slipping and the starter motor must be replaced (see Section 17).

4   If, when the switch is actuated, the starter motor doesn't operate at all but the starter solenoid operates (clicks), then the problem lies with either the battery, the starter solenoid contacts or the starter motor connections.

5   If the starter solenoid doesn't click when the ignition switch is actuated, either the starter solenoid circuit is open or the solenoid itself is defective. Check the starter solenoid circuit (see the wiring diagrams at the end of this book) or replace the solenoid (see Section 18).

6   To check the starter solenoid circuit, remove the push-on connector from the solenoid wire. Make sure that the connection is clean and secure. If the connections are good, check the operation of the solenoid with a jumper wire. To do this, place the transmission in Park.

Remove the push-on connector from the solenoid. Connect a jumper wire between the battery positive terminal and the exposed terminal on the solenoid. If the starter motor now operates, the starter solenoid is okay. The problem is in the ignition switch, Transmission Range sensor Clutch Pedal Position switch or in the starting circuit wiring (look for open or loose connections).

7   If the starter motor still doesn't operate, replace the starter solenoid (see Section 18).

8   If the starter motor cranks the engine at an abnormally slow speed, first make sure the battery is fully charged and all terminal connections are clean and tight. Also check the connections at the starter solenoid and battery ground. Eyelet terminals should not be easily rotated by hand. Also check for a short to ground. If the engine is partially seized, or has the wrong viscosity oil in it, it will crank slowly.

9   Check the starter circuit. Consult the wiring diagrams at the end of Chapter 12. On automatics, it will be necessary to check the condition of the Transmission Range sensor (see Chapter 6) or the Clutch Pedal Position switch (see Chapter 7) on manual transmission vehicles.

10 Check the operation of the starter relay. Check for battery voltage to the relay and correct operation of the relay. Refer to Chapter 12 for additional information on the locations of relays and how to test them.

11 If he vehicle is equipped with the a anti-theft alarm, check the circuit and the control module for shorts or damaged components (see Chapter 12).

17 Starter motor - removal and installation

♦ **Refer to illustration 17.4**

1   Detach the cable from the negative terminal of the battery.

2   Raise the vehicle and support it securely on jackstands.

3   Disconnect the large cable from the terminal on the starter motor and the solenoid terminal connections.

4   Remove the starter motor mounting bolts (see illustration) and detach the starter from the engine.

5   If necessary, turn the wheels to one side to provide removal access.

6   Installation is the reverse of removal.

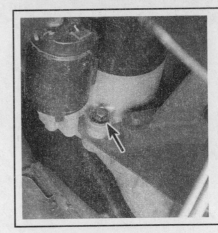

17.4 Remove the starter/solenoid assembly bolts (arrow) and separate the assembly from the transmission bellhousing. The top bolt is hidden from view

18 Starter solenoid - replacement

1   Remove the starter assembly from the engine compartment (see Section 17).

2   Remove the positive brush connector from the solenoid M terminal.

3   Remove the solenoid mounting bolts and separate the solenoid from the starter body.

4   Installation is the reverse of removal.

Specifications

Battery voltage

Engine off	12-volts
Engine running	14-to-15 volts
Firing order	See Chapter 2
Ignition coil-to-distributor cap wire resistance	5,000 ohms per foot

Ignition coil resistance

Distributor Ignition (DI) systems

Primary resistance	0.8 to 1.6 ohms
Secondary resistance	7.7 to 10.5 K-ohms
Primary winding-to-case resistance	10 M-ohms

Distributorless Ignition Systems (DIS) systems
1996 and later without Coil Over Plug (COP)

Primary resistance	0.3 to 1.0 ohms
Secondary resistance	6.5 to 11.5 K-ohms

1999 and later with Coil Over Plug (COP)

Primary resistance	0.55 ohms
Secondary resistance	5.5 K-ohms

Ignition timing

5.0L engines	10-degrees BTDC with SPOUT disconnected
3.8L and 4.6L engines	Timing not adjustable

Alternator brush length

New	1/2 inch
Minimum	1/4 inch

Section

Reference to other Chapters

6

EMISSIONS AND ENGINE CONTROL

1 General information

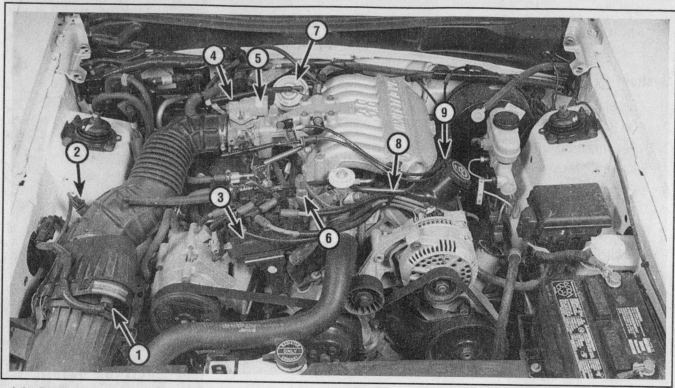

1.1a Emission and engine control system component locations - 1998 and earlier 3.8L V6 engine

1	MAF sensor	4	TPS	6	ECT	8	PCV tube
2	IAT sensor	5	IAC valve	7	EGR valve	9	PCV valve
3	EDIS coil pack						

1.1b Emission and engine control system component locations - 5.0L V8 engine

1	MAF sensor	3	Breather hose	5	IAC valve	7	Ignition coil
2	IAT sensor	4	Diagnostic connector	6	TPS	8	ECT

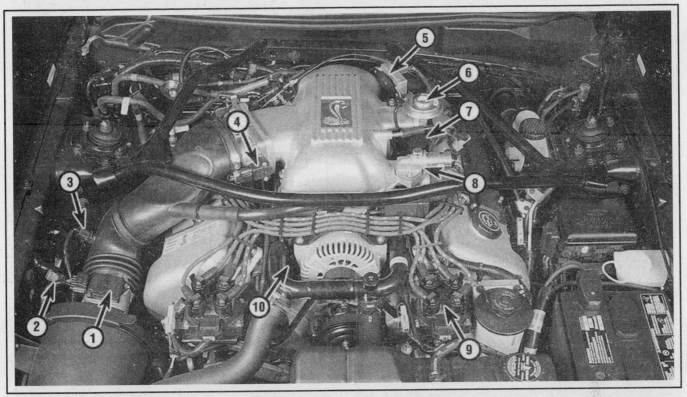

1.1c Emission and engine control system component locations - 4.6L DOHC V8 engine

1	MAF sensor	5	Differential Pressure Regulator	8	IAC valve
2	SPOUT		(DPFE)	9	Ignition coil pack (left side)
3	IAT sensor	6	EGR valve	10	ECT
4	TPS	7	EGR vacuum regulator valve		

▶ **Refer to illustrations 1.1a, 1.1b, 1.1c, 1.7a and 1.7b**

To prevent pollution of the atmosphere from incompletely burned and evaporating gases, and to maintain good driveability and fuel economy, a number of emission control systems are incorporated (see illustrations). They include the:

Electronic Engine Control system (EEC-IV) OBD I
Electronic Engine Control system (EEC-V) OBD II
Evaporative Emission Control System (EECS)
Positive Crankcase Ventilation (PCV) system
Exhaust Gas Recirculation (EGR) system
Air Injection (AIR) system
Catalytic converter

All of these systems are linked, directly or indirectly, to the emission control system.

The Sections in this Chapter include general descriptions, checking procedures within the scope of the home mechanic and component replacement procedures (when possible) for each of the systems listed above.

Before assuming that an emissions control system is malfunctioning, check the fuel and ignition systems carefully. The diagnosis of some emission control devices requires specialized tools, equipment and training. If checking and servicing become too difficult or if a procedure is beyond your ability, consult a dealer service department. Remember, the most frequent cause of emissions problems is simply a loose or broken vacuum hose or wire, so always check the hose and wiring connections first.

This doesn't mean, however, that emission control systems are

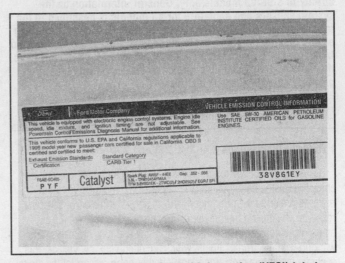

1.7a The Vehicle Emission Control Information (VECI) label is located in the engine compartment on the radiator support and contains information on the emission devices on your vehicle, vacuum line routing, etc. (3.8L V6 engine shown)

particularly difficult to maintain and repair. You can quickly and easily perform many checks and do most of the regular maintenance at home with common tune-up and hand tools.

➡**Note: Because of a Federally mandated extended warranty which covers the emission control system components, check with your dealer about warranty coverage before working on** any emissions-related systems. Once the warranty has expired, you may wish to perform some of the component checks and/or replacement procedures in this Chapter to save money.

Pay close attention to any special precautions outlined in this Chapter. It should be noted that the illustrations of the various systems may not exactly match the system installed on the vehicle you're working on because of changes made by the manufacturer during production or from year-to-year.

A Vehicle Emissions Control Information (VECI) label is located in the engine compartment (see illustrations). This label contains important emissions specifications and adjustment information, as well as a vacuum hose schematic with emissions components identified. When servicing the engine or emissions systems, the VECI label in your particular vehicle should always be checked for up-to-date information.

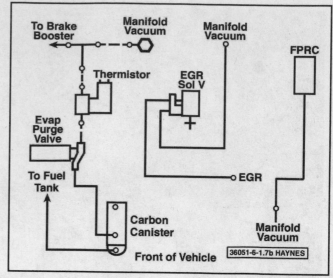

1.7b Vacuum hose routing - 3.8L V6 engine

2 On Board Diagnosis (OBD) system and trouble codes

➡ **Note: The diagnostic system and trouble codes for 3.8L V6 and all 4.6L V8 engines are only accessible using expensive specialized equipment. The codes indicated in the text apply strictly to 5.0L V8 models only. General information on the system sensors and actuators for all models is described in the following text. See the Troubleshooting section at the beginning of this manual for some basic diagnostic aids. If the Malfunction Indicator Light illuminates on a 3.8L V6 or 4.6L V8 model, have the vehicle diagnosed by a dealer service department or other properly equipped repair facility.**

DIAGNOSTIC TOOL INFORMATION

◆ **Refer to illustrations 2.1, 2.2, 2.3 and 2.4**

1   A digital multimeter is necessary for checking fuel injection and emission related components (see illustration). A digital volt-ohm-meter is preferred over the older style analog multimeter for several reasons. The analog multimeter cannot display the volts-ohms or amps measurement in hundredths and thousandths increments. When working with electronic circuits which are often very low voltage, this accurate reading is most important. Another good reason for the digital multimeter is the high impedance circuit. The digital multimeter is equipped with a high resistance internal circuitry (10 million ohms). Because a voltmeter is hooked up in parallel with the circuit when testing, it is vital that none of the voltage being measured should be allowed to travel the parallel path set up by the meter itself. This dilemma does not show itself when measuring larger amounts of voltage (9 to 12 volt circuits) but if you are measuring a low voltage circuit such as the oxygen sensor signal voltage, a fraction of a volt may be a significant amount when diagnosing a problem. Obtaining the diagnostic trouble codes is one exception where using an analog voltmeter

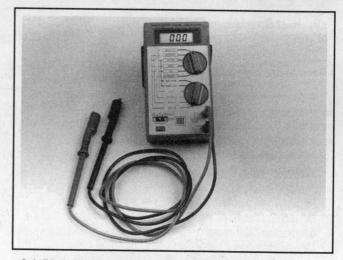

2.1 Digital multimeters can be used for testing all types of circuits; because of their high impedance, they are much more accurate than analog meters for measuring millivoltage-voltage in low-voltage computer circuits

is necessary.

2   Hand-held scanners are the most powerful and versatile tools for analyzing engine management systems used on later model vehicles (see illustration). Early model scanners handle codes and some diagnostics for many OBD I systems. Each brand scan tool must be examined carefully to match the year, make and model of the vehicle you are working on. Often interchangeable cartridges are available to access the particular manufacturer (Ford, GM, Chrysler, etc.). Some manufacturers will specify by continent (Asia, Europe, USA, etc.) With the arrival of the Federally mandated emission control system (OBD II), a specially

2.2 Scanners like the Actron Scantool and the AutoXray XP240 are powerful diagnostic aids - programmed with comprehensive diagnostic information, they can tell you just about anything you want to know about your engine management system

designed scanner must be used. At this time, several manufacturers plan to release OBD II scan tools for the home mechanic. Ask the parts salesman at a local auto parts store for additional information concerning dates and costs.

➡ Note: Although OBD II codes cannot be accessed on 1994 and 1995 3.8L V6 models and all 1996 and later models (at this time), follow the simple component checks in Section 4.

3   Software is available for a desktop computer or laptop computer that allows the desktop computer to interface with the engine management computer (see illustration). This software can output trouble codes, identify problems without even lifting the hood.

4   Another type of code reader and less expensive is available at parts stores (see illustration). These tools simplify the procedure for extracting codes from the engine management computer by simply "plugging in" to the diagnostic connector on the vehicle wiring harness.

➡ Note: Some diagnostic connectors are located under the dash, kick panel or glovebox while others are located in the engine compartment.

OBD SYSTEM GENERAL DESCRIPTION

5   Vehicles equipped with the 5.0L V8 engine use the Electronic Engine Control (EEC) IV system. Vehicles equipped with the 3.8L V6 or 4.6L V8 engines use the EEC-V system. Both systems consist of an onboard computer, known as the Powertrain Control Module (PCM), and information sensors, which monitor various functions of the engine and send data to the PCM. Based on the data and the information programmed Into the computer's memory, the PCM generates output signals to control various engine functions via control relays, solenoids and other output actuators.

6   The PCM, located under the instrument panel, is the "brain" of the EEC-IV system. It receives data from a number of sensors and other electronic components (switches, relays, etc.). Based on the information it receives, the PCM generates output signals to control various relays, solenoids and other actuators. The PCM is specifically calibrated to optimize the emissions, fuel economy and driveability of the vehicle.

7   Because of a Federally-mandated extended warranty which covers the EEC-IV system components and because any owner-induced dam-

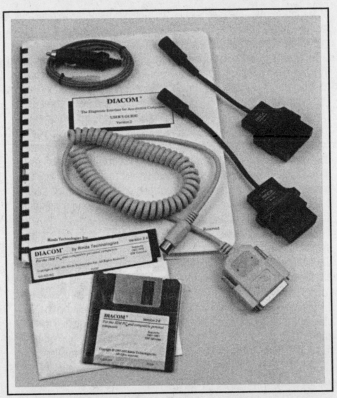

2.3 Diagnostic software, such as this kit from Diacom, turns your IBM compatible computer into the scan tool, saving the extra cost of buying a scanner but providing you with all the same information

age to the PCM, the sensors and/or the control devices may void the warranty, it isn't a good idea to attempt diagnosis or replacement of the PCM at home while the vehicle is under warranty. Take the vehicle to a dealer service department if the PCM or a system component malfunctions.

INFORMATION SENSORS

8   When battery voltage is applied to the air conditioning compressor clutch, a signal is sent to the PCM, which interprets the signal as an added load created by the compressor and increases engine idle speed accordingly to compensate.

9   The Intake Air Temperature sensor (IAT), threaded into a runner

2.4 Trouble code tools simplify the task of extracting the trouble codes

of the intake manifold (see Section 4), provides the PCM with fuel/air mixture temperature information. The PCM uses this information to control fuel flow, ignition timing and EGR system operation.

10 The Engine Coolant Temperature (ECT) sensor, which is threaded into a coolant passage in the intake manifold, monitors engine coolant temperature. The ECT sends the PCM a voltage signal which influences PCM control of the fuel mixture, ignition timing and EGR operation.

11 The Heated Exhaust Gas Oxygen (HEGO) sensors, which are threaded into the exhaust manifolds, constantly monitor the oxygen content of the exhaust gases. A voltage signal which varies in accordance with the difference between the oxygen content of the exhaust gases and the surrounding atmosphere is sent to the PCM. The PCM converts this exhaust gas oxygen content signal to the fuel/air ratio, compares it to the ideal ratio for current engine operating conditions and alters the signal to the injectors accordingly.

12 The Throttle Position Sensor (TPS), which is mounted on the side of the throttle body (see Section 4) and connected directly to the throttle shaft, senses throttle movement and position, then transmits an electrical signal to the PCM. This signal enables the PCM to determine when the throttle is closed, in its normal cruise condition or wide open.

13 The Mass Air Flow (MAF) sensor, which is mounted in the air cleaner intake passage, measures the mass of the air entering the engine (see Section 4). Because air mass varies with air temperature (cold air is denser than warm air), measuring air mass provides the PCM with a very accurate way of determining the correct amount of fuel to obtain the ideal fuel/air mixture.

OUTPUT ACTUATORS

14 The EEC power relay, which is activated by the ignition switch, supplies battery voltage to the EEC-IV or V system components when the switch is in the Start or Run position.

➡Note: The fuel pump relay, the PCM power relay, the EDF relay and the EDF relay control are all located in the Constant Control Relay Module (CCRM) which is located on the right side fenderwell on 3.8L V6 and 4.6L V8 models and up front near the radiator on 5.0L V8 models.

15 The canister purge solenoid (CANP) switches manifold vacuum to operate the canister purge valve when a signal is received from the PCM. Vacuum opens the purge valve when the solenoid is energized, allowing fuel vapor to flow from the canister to the intake manifold.

16 The solenoid-operated fuel injectors are located above the intake ports (see Chapter 4). The PCM controls the length of time the injector is open. The "open" time of the injector determines the amount of fuel delivered. For information regarding injector replacement, refer to Chapter 4.

17 The fuel pump relay is activated by the PCM with the ignition switch in the On position. When the ignition switch is turned to the On position, the relay is activated to supply initial line pressure to the system. For information regarding fuel pump check and replacement, refer to Chapter 4.

18 The EDIS ignition module (see Chapter 5) installed on all 3.8L and 4.6L engines, triggers the ignition coils and determines dwell. The PCM uses a signal from the Profile Ignition Pick-Up (PIP) to determine crankshaft position. Ignition timing is determined by the PCM, which then signals the module to fire the coil. For further information regarding the ignition module, refer to the appropriate Section in Chapter 5.

➡Note: This module is an integral part of the PCM on 1996 and later models.

OBTAINING OBD-I SYSTEM CODES ON THE 5.0L V8 ENGINE

19 The diagnostic codes for the EEC-IV systems are arranged in such a way that a series of tests must be completed in order to extract ALL the codes from the system. If one portion of the test is performed without the others, there may be a chance the trouble code that will pinpoint a problem in your particular vehicle will remain stored in the PCM without detection. The tests start first with a Key On, Engine Off (KOEO) test followed by a computed timing test then finally a Engine Running (ER) test. Here is a brief overview of the code extracting procedures of the EEC-IV system followed by the actual test:

Quick Test - Key On Engine Off (KOEO)

20 The following tests are all included with the key on, engine off:

Self test codes - These codes are accessed on the test connector by using a jumper wire and an analog voltmeter or the factory diagnostic tool called the Star tester. These codes are also called Hard Codes.

Separator pulse codes - After the initial Hard Codes, the system will flash a code 111 and then will flash a series of Soft (or Continuous Memory) Codes.

Continuous Memory Codes - These codes indicate a fault that may or may not be present at the time of testing. These codes usually indicate an intermittent failure. Continuous Memory codes are stored in the system and they will flash after the normal Hard Codes. These codes are three digit codes. These codes can indicate chronic or intermittent problems. Also called Soft Codes.

Fast codes - These codes are transmitted 100 times faster than normal codes and can only be read by a Ford Star Tester or an equivalent SCAN tool.

Engine running codes (KOER) or (ER)

21 **Running tests** - These tests make it possible for the PCM to pick-up a diagnostic trouble code that cannot be set while the engine is in KOEO. These problems usually occur during driving conditions. Some codes are detected by cold or warm running conditions, some are detected at low rpm or high rpm and some are detected at closed throttle or WOT.

ID Pulse codes - These codes indicate the type of engine (6 or 8 cylinder) or the correct module and Self Test mode access.

Computed engine timing test - This engine running test determines base timing for the engine and starts the process of allowing the engine to store running codes.

Wiggle test - This engine running test checks the wiring system to the sensors and output actuators as the engine performs.

Cylinder balance test - This engine running test determines injector balance as well as cylinder compression balance.

➡Note: This test should be performed by a dealer service department.

BEGINNING THE TEST

◗ **Refer to illustration 2.23**

22 Position the parking brake ON, Shift lever in PARK, block the drive wheels and turn off all electrical loads (air conditioning, radio, heater fan blower etc.). Make sure the engine is warmed to normal operating temperature (if possible).

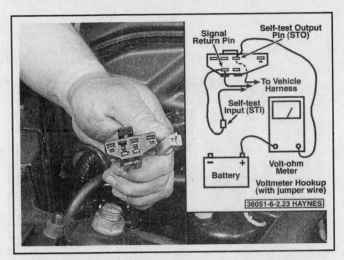

2.23 To read any stored trouble codes, connect a voltmeter to the Diagnostic Test connector as shown, then connect a jumper wire between the self test input and pin number 2 on the larger connector - turn the ignition key ON and watch the voltmeter needle or CHECK ENGINE light (5.0L engine shown)

23 Perform the KOEO tests:

a) *Turn the ignition key off for at least 10 seconds*

b) *Locate the Diagnostic Test connector inside the engine compartment. Install the analog voltmeter leads onto the battery and pin number 4 (STO) of the test connector (see illustration). Install a jumper wire from the test terminal to pin number 2 of the Diagnostic Test terminal (STI).*

c) *Turn the ignition key ON (engine not running) and observe the needle sweeps on the analog voltmeter. For example on code 123, the voltmeter will sweep once and then pause. There will be a two second pause between digits and then there will be two distinct sweeps of the needle to indicate the second digit of the code number. There will be another pause and then three distinct sweeps of the meter. It is possible to also observe the CHECK ENGINE light flash the codes. Additional codes will be separated by a four second pause and then the indicated sweeps on the voltmeter. Be aware that the code sequence may continue into the continuous memory codes (read further).*

➡**Note: These models will flash the CHECK ENGINE light on the dash in place of the voltmeter.**

24 Interpreting the continuous memory codes:

a) *After the KOEO codes are reported, there will be a short pause and any stored Continuous Memory codes will appear in order. Remember that the "Separator" code is 111. The computer will not enter the Continuous Memory mode without flashing the separator pulse code.*

b) *The Continuous Memory codes are read the same as the initial codes or "Hard Codes". Record these codes onto a piece of paper and continue the test.*

25 Perform the Engine Running (ER) tests.

a) *Remove the jumper wires from the Diagnostic Test connector to start the test.*

b) *Run engine until it reaches normal operating temperature.*

c) *Turn the engine OFF for at least 10 seconds.*

d) *Install the jumper wire onto Diagnostic Test connector (see illustration 2.23) and start the engine.*

e) *Observe that the voltmeter or CHECK ENGINE light will flash the engine identification code. This code indicates 1/2 the number of cylinders of the engine. For example, 4 flashes represent an 8 cylinder engine, or 3 flashes represent a six cylinder engine.*

f) *Within 1 to 2 seconds of the ID code, turn the steering wheel at least 1/2 turn and release. This will store any power steering pressure switch trouble codes.*

g) *Depress the brake pedal and release.*

➡**Note: Perform the steering wheel and brake pedal procedure in succession immediately (1 to 2 seconds) after the ID codes are flashed.**

h) *Observe all the codes and record them on a piece of paper. Be sure to count the sweeps or flashes very carefully as you jot them down.*

26 On some models the PCM will request a Dynamic Response check. This test quickly checks the operation of the TPS, MAF or MAP sensors in action. This will be indicated by a code 1 or a single sweep of the voltmeter needle (one flash on CHECK ENGINE light). This test will require the operator to simply full throttle ("goose") the accelerator pedal for one second. DO NOT throttle the accelerator pedal unless it is requested.

27 The next part of this test makes sure the system can advance the timing. This is called the Computed Timing test. After the last ER code has been displayed, the PCM will advance the ignition timing a fixed amount and hold it there for approximately 2 minutes. Use a timing light to check the amount of advance. The computed timing should equal the base timing plus 20 BTDC. The total advance should equal 27 to 33 degrees advance. If the timing is out of specification, have the system checked at a dealer service department.

➡**Note: Remember to remove the SPOUT from the connector as described in the ignition timing procedure in Chapter 5. This will remove the computer from the loop and give base timing.**

28 Finally perform the Wiggle Test. This test can be used to recreate a possible intermittent fault in the harness wiring system.

a) *Use a jumper wire to ground the STI lead on the Diagnostic Test connector (see illustration 2.23).*

b) *Turn the ignition key ON (engine not running).*

c) *Now deactivate the self test mode (remove the jumper wire) and then immediately reactivate the self-test mode. Now the system has entered Continuous Monitor Test Mode.*

d) *Carefully wiggle, tap or remove any suspect wiring to a sensor or output actuator. If a problem exists, a trouble code will be stored that indicates a problem with the circuit that governs the particular component. Record the codes that are indicated.*

e) *Next, enter Engine Running Continuous Monitor Test Mode to check for wiring problems only when the engine is running. Start first by deactivating the Diagnostic Test connector and turning the ignition key OFF. Now start the engine and allow it to idle.*

f) *Use a jumper wire to ground the STI lead on the Diagnostic Test connector (see illustration 2.23). Wait ten seconds and then deactivate the test mode and reactivate it again (install jumper wire). This will enter Engine Running Continuous Monitor Test Mode.*

g) *Carefully wiggle, tap or remove any suspect wiring to a sensor or output actuator. If a problem exists, a trouble code will be stored that indicates a problem with the circuit that governs the particular component. Record the codes that are indicated.*

29 If necessary, perform the Cylinder Balance Test. This test must be performed by a dealer service department.

CLEARING CODES

30 To clear the codes from the PCM memory, start the KOEO self test diagnostic procedure (see illustration 2.23) and install the jumper wire into the Diagnostic Test connector. When the codes start to display themselves on the voltmeter or CHECK ENGINE light, remove the jumper wire from the Diagnostic Test connector. This will erase any stored codes within the system.

✳✳ CAUTION:

Do not disconnect the battery from the vehicle to clear the codes. This will erase stored operating parameters from the KAM (Keep Alive Memory) and cause the engine to run rough for a period of time while the computer relearns the information.

OBTAINING OBD II SYSTEM CODES (3.8L AND 4.6L V8 MODELS)

▶ **Refer to illustration 2.32**

31 On OBD-II systems, the PCM will illuminate the Malfunction Indicator Light on the dash if it recognizes a component fault for two consecutive drive cycles. It will continue to set the light until the PCM does not detect any malfunction for three or more consecutive drive cycles. Because the OBD-II system requires a SCAN tool to reset the light, if the tool is not available for diagnostics, have the system checked by a dealer service department or other qualified repair facility.

32 The diagnostic codes for the EEC-V (OBD-II) systems can be extracted from the PCM using a special SCAN tool that is programmed to interface with this new system by plugging into the DLC (see illustration). If the tool is not available, have the vehicle checked at a dealer service department.

2.32 Typical Data Link Connector (DLC) on an OBD-II vehicle

CLEARING CODES

33 To clear the codes from the PCM memory, install the OBD-II SCAN tool, scroll the menu for the function that describes "CLEARING CODES' and follow the prescribed method for that particular SCAN tool. If necessary, have the codes cleared by a dealer service department or other qualified repair facility.

✳✳ CAUTION:

Do not disconnect the battery from the vehicle to clear the codes. This will erase stored operating parameters from the memory and cause the engine to run rough for a period of time while the computer relearns the information.

OBD-I Trouble Codes

➡**Note: Not all codes apply to all models.**

Code	Test Condition*	Probable Cause
111	O, C, R	Pass
112	O, R	Intake Air Temperature sensor circuit indicates circuit grounded/above 245 degrees F
113	O, R	Intake Air Temperature sensor circuit indicates open circuit/below –40 degrees F
114	O, R	Intake Air Temperature sensor out of self-test range
116	O, R	Coolant Temperature sensor out of self-test range
117	O, C	Coolant Temperature circuit below minimum voltage/indicates above 245 degrees F
118	O, C	Coolant Temperature sensor circuit above maximum voltage/ indicates below –40 degrees F
121	O, C, R	Throttle Position sensor out of self-test range
122	O, C	Throttle Position sensor below minimum voltage
123	O, C	Throttle Position sensor above maximum voltage
124	C	Throttle Position Sensor voltage higher than expected
125	C	Throttle Position Sensor voltage lower than expected
136	R	Heated oxygen sensor indicates lean condition, left side

O = Key On, Engine Off; C = Continuous Memory; R = Engine Running

Code	Test Condition*	Probable Cause
137	R	Heated oxygen sensor indicates rich condition, left side
139	C	No heated oxygen sensor switching detected, left side
141	C	Fuel system indicates lean
144	C	No heated oxygen sensor switching detected, right side
157	R,C	Mass Air Flow Sensor below minimum voltage
158	O, R,C	Mass Air Flow Sensor above maximum voltage
159	O, R	Mass Air Flow Sensor out of self-test range
167	R	Insufficient Throttle Position Sensor change during Dynamic Response Check
171	C	Heated oxygen sensor unable to switch, right side
172	R,C	Heated oxygen sensor indicates lean condition, right side
173	R,C	Heated oxygen sensor indicates rich condition, right side
174	C	Heated oxygen sensor switching slow, right side
175	C	Heated oxygen sensor unable to switch, left side
176	C	Heated oxygen sensor indicates lean condition, left side
177	C	Heated oxygen sensor indicates rich condition, left side
178	C	Heated oxygen sensor switching slow, left side
179	C	Adaptive Fuel lean limit reached at part throttle, system rich, right side
181	C	Adaptive Fuel rich limit reached at part throttle, right side
184	C	Mass Air Flow higher than expected
185	C	Mass Air Flow lower than expected
186	C	Injector Pulse-width higher than expected
187	C	Injector Pulse-width lower than expected
188	C	Adaptive Fuel lean limit reached, left side
189	C	Adaptive Fuel rich limit reached, left side
191	C	Adaptive Fuel lean limit reached at idle, left side
192	C	Adaptive Fuel rich limit reached at idle, left side
193	O	Flexible Fuel (FF) sensor circuit failure
211	C	Profile Ignition Pick-up circuit fault
212	C	Ignition module circuit failure/SPOUT circuit grounded
213	R	SPOUT circuit open
214	C	Cylinder identification (CID) circuit failure
215	C	PCM detected coil 1 primary circuit failure
216	C	PCM detected coil 2 primary circuit failure
217	C	PCM detected coil 3 primary circuit failure
218	C	Loss of ignition diagnostic monitor (IDM) signal - left side
219	C	Spark timing defaulted to 10 degrees SPOUT circuit open
221	C	Spark timing error
222	C	Loss of ignition diagnostic monitor (IDM) signal - right side
223	C	Loss of dual plug Inhibit (DPI) control
224	C	PCM detected coil 1,2,3 or 4 primary circuit failure
225	C	Knock sensor not detected during dynamic response test KOER
226	O	Ignition Diagnostic Module (IDM) signal not received
232	C	PCM detected coil 1,2,3 or 4 primary circuit failure

*O = Key On, Engine Off; C = Continuous Memory; R = Engine Running

OBD-I Trouble Codes (continued)

➡ Note: Not all codes apply to all models.

Code	Test Condition*	Probable Cause
238	C	PCM detected coil 4 primary circuit failure
241	C	ICM to PCM - IDM pulse width transmission error
244	R	CID circuit fault present when cylinder balance test requested
311	R	AIR system inoperative during KOER (Bank number 1 with dual heated oxygen sensors)
312	R	AIR misdirected during KOER
313	R	AIR not bypassed during KOER
314	R	AIR system inoperative during KOER (Bank number 2 with dual heated oxygen sensors)
326	C,R	EGR (PFE/DPFE) circuit voltage lower than expected
327	O, C, R	EGR (EGRP/EVP/PFE/DPFE) circuit below minimum voltage
328	O, C, R	EGR valve position sensor voltage below closed limit
332	C,R	Insufficient EGR valve opening detected
334	O, C, R	EGR valve position sensor voltage above closed limit
335	O	EGR Sensor voltage out-of-range
336	R	EGR (PFE/DPFE) circuit higher than expected
337	O, C, R	EGR (EGRP/EVP/PFE/DPFE) circuit above maximum voltage
338	R	ECT lower than expected
339	R	ECT higher than expected
341	O	Octane adjust service pin open
381	C	Frequent air conditioning clutch cycling
411	R	Unable to control RPM during Low RPM Self-test
412	R	Unable to control RPM during High PRM Self-test
415	R	Idle Air Control (IAC) system at maximum adaptive lower limit
416	C	Idle Air Control (IAC) system at upper adaptive learning limit
452	C	No input from Vehicle Speed Sensor
453	R	Servo leaking down (KOER IVSC test)
454	R	Servo leaking up (KOER IVSC test)
455	R	Insufficient rpm increase (KOER IVSC test)
456	R	Insufficient rpm decrease (KOER IVSC test)
457	O	Speed control command switch(s) circuit not functioning (KOEO IVSC test)
458	O	Speed control command switch(s) stuck/circuit grounded (KOEO IVSC test)
459	O	Speed control ground circuit open (KOEO IVSC test)
511	O	Read Only Memory test failed - replace PCM
512	C	Keep Alive Memory test failed
513	O	Internal voltage failure in PCM
519	O	Power steering pressure switch (PSP) circuit open
521	R	Power steering pressure switch (PSP) circuit did not change states
522	O	Transmission Range (TR) sensor circuit open/vehicle in gear
525	O	Indicates vehicle in gear, air conditioning on
527	O	Transmission Range (TR) sensor circuit open, air conditioning on during KOEO
528	O	Clutch pedal position (CPP) switch failure

*O = Key On, Engine Off; C = Continuous Memory; R = Engine Running

Code	Test Condition*	Probable Cause
529	C	Data Communication Link (DCL) or PCM circuit failure
532	C	Cluster Control Assembly (CCA) circuit failure
533	C	Data Communications Link (DCL) or Electronic Instrument Cluster (EIC) circuit failure
536	C,R	Brake ON/Off (BOO) circuit failure/not activated during the KOER
538	R	Insufficient change in RPM/operator error in Dynamic Response Check
539	O	Air conditioning on during Self-test
542	O, C	Fuel Pump circuit open; PCM to motor
543	O, C	Fuel Pump circuit open; Battery to PCM
551	O	Idle Air Control (IAC) circuit failure KOEO
552	O	Secondary Air Injection Bypass (AIRB) circuit failure (KOEO)
553	O	Secondary Air Injection Diverter (AIRB) circuit failure (KOEO)
554	O	Fuel Pressure Regulator Control (FPRC) circuit failure
556	O, C	Primary Fuel Pump circuit failure
557	O, C	Low speed fuel pump primary circuit failure
558	O	EGR Vacuum Regulator circuit failure
559	O	Air Conditioning On (ACON) relay circuit failure
563	O	High fan control (HFC) circuit failure
564	O	Fan control (FC) circuit failure
565	O	Canister Purge circuit failure
567	O	Speed Control Vent (SCVNT) circuit failure (KOEO IVSC test)
568	O	Speed Control Vacuum (SCVAC) circuit failure (KOEO IVSC test)
569	O	Auxiliary Canister Purge (CANP2) circuit failure KOEO
571	O	EGRA solenoid circuit failure KOEO
572	O	EGRV solenoid circuit failure KOEO
578	C	Air conditioning pressure sensor circuit shorted
579	C	Insufficient air conditioning pressure change
581	C	Power to Fan circuit over current
582	O	Fan circuit open
583	C	Power to Fuel pump over current
584	C	VCRM Power ground circuit open (VCRM Pin 1)
585	C	Power to air conditioning clutch over current
586	C	Air conditioning clutch circuit open
587	O, C	Variable Control Relay Module (VCRM) communication failure
617	C	1-2 shift error
618	C	2-3 shift error
619	C	3-4 shift error
621	O, C	Shift Solenoid 1 (SS 1) circuit failure KOEO
622	O	Shift Solenoid 2 (SS2) circuit failure KOEO
623	O	Transmission Control Indicator Light (TCIL) circuit failure
624	O, C	Electronic Pressure Control (EPC) circuit failure
625	O, C	Electronic Pressure Control (EPC) driver open in PCM
626	O	Coast Clutch Solenoid (CCS) circuit failure KOEO
627	O	Torque Converter Clutch (TCC) solenoid circuit failure

*O = Key On, Engine Off; C = Continuous Memory; R = Engine Running

OBD-I Trouble Codes (continued)

➡Note: Not all codes apply to all models.

Code	Test Condition*	Probable Cause
628	C	Excessive converter clutch slippage
629	O, C	Torque Converter Clutch (TCC) solenoid circuit failure
631	O	Transmission Control Indicator Lamp (TCIL) circuit failure KOEO
632	R	Transmission Control Switch (TCS) circuit did not change states during KOER
634	O, C, R	Transmission Range (TR) sensor voltage higher or lower than expected
636	O, R	Transmission Fluid Temp (TFT) higher or lower than expected
637	O, C	Transmission Fluid Temp (TFT) sensor circuit above maximum voltage/ -40 degrees F indicated / circuit open
638	O, C	Transmission Fluid Temp (TFT) sensor circuit below minimum voltage/ 290 degrees F indicated / circuit shorted
639	R,C	Insufficient input from Transmission Speed Sensor (TSS)
641	O, C	Shift Solenoid 3 (SS3) circuit failure
643	O, C	Torque Converter Clutch (TCC) circuit failure
645	C	Incorrect gear ratio obtained for first gear
646	C	Incorrect gear ratio obtained for second gear
647	C	Incorrect gear ratio obtained for third gear
648	C	Incorrect gear ratio obtained for fourth gear
649	C	Electronic Pressure Control (EPC) higher or lower than expected
651	C	Electronic Pressure Control (EPC)circuit failure
652	O	Torque Converter Clutch (TCC) solenoid circuit failure
653	R	Transmission Control Switch (TCS) did not change states during KOER
654	O	Transmission Range (TR) sensor not indicating PARK during KOEO
656	C	Torque Converter Clutch continuous slip error
657	C	Transmission over temperature condition occurred
659	C	High vehicle speed in park indicated
667	C	Transmission Range sensor circuit voltage below minimum voltage
668	C	Transmission Range circuit voltage above maximum voltage
675	C	Transmission Range sensor circuit voltage out of range
998	O	Hard fault present

OBD-II Trouble Codes

Code	Probable cause
P0102	Mass Airflow (MAF) sensor circuit low input
P0103	Mass Airflow (MAF) sensor circuit high input
P0112	Intake Air Temperature (IAT) sensor circuit low input
P0113	Intake Air Temperature (IAT) sensor circuit high input
P0117	Electronic Coolant Temperature (ECT) sensor circuit low input
P0118	Electronic Coolant Temperature (ECT) sensor circuit high input
P0121	In range Throttle Position Sensor (TPS) fault

*O = Key On, Engine Off; C = Continuous Memory; R = Engine Running

Code	Probable cause
P0122	Throttle Position Sensor (TPS) circuit low input
P0123	Throttle Position Sensor (TPS) circuit high input
P0131	Upstream heated O2 sensor circuit low voltage (Bank 1)
P0133	Upstream heated O2 sensor circuit slow response (Bank 1)
P0135	Upstream heated O2 sensor heater circuit fault (Bank 1)
P0136	Downstream heated O2 sensor fault (Bank 1)
P0141	Downstream heated O2 sensor heater circuit fault (Bank 1)
P0151	Upstream heated O2 sensor circuit low voltage (Bank 2)
P0153	Upstream heated O2 sensor circuit slow response (Bank 2)
P0155	Upstream heated O2 sensor heater circuit fault (Bank 2)
P0156	Downstream heated O2 sensor fault (Bank 2)
P0161	Downstream heated O2 sensor heater circuit fault (Bank 2)
P0171	System Adaptive fuel too lean (Bank 1)
P0172	System Adaptive fuel too rich (Bank 1)
P0174	System Adaptive fuel too lean (Bank 2)
P0172	System Adaptive fuel too rich (Bank 2)
P0191	Injector Pressure sensor system performance
P0192	Injector Pressure sensor circuit low input
P0193	Injector Pressure sensor circuit high input
P0301	Cylinder no. 1 misfire detected
P0302	Cylinder no. 2 misfire detected
P0303	Cylinder no. 3 misfire detected
P0304	Cylinder no. 4 misfire detected
P0305	Cylinder no. 5 misfire detected
P0306	Cylinder no. 6 misfire detected
P0307	Cylinder no. 7 misfire detected
P0308	Cylinder no. 8 misfire detected
P0325	Knock sensor circuit fault
P0326	Knock sensor circuit performance
P0351	Ignition coil no. 1 primary circuit fault
P0352	Ignition coil no. 2 primary circuit fault
P0353	Ignition coil no. 3 primary circuit fault
P0354	Ignition coil no. 4 primary circuit fault
P0355	Ignition coil no. 5 primary circuit fault
P0356	Ignition coil no. 6 primary circuit fault
P0357	Ignition coil no. 7 primary circuit fault
P0358	Ignition coil no. 8 primary circuit fault
P0400	EGR flow fault
P0401	EGR insufficient flow detected
P0402	EGR excessive flow detected
P0420	Catalyst system efficiency below threshold (Bank 1)
P0421	Catalyst system efficiency below threshold (Bank 1)

*O = Key On, Engine Off; C = Continuous Memory; R = Engine Running

OBD-II Trouble Codes (continued)

Code	Probable cause
P0430	Catalyst system efficiency below threshold (Bank 2)
P0431	Catalyst system efficiency below threshold (Bank 2)
P0442	EVAP small leak detected
P0443	EVAP VMV circuit fault
P0452	EVAP fuel tank pressure sensor low input
P0453	EVAP fuel tank pressure sensor high input
P0500	VSS fault
P0505	IAC valve system fault
P0603	PCM Keep Alive Memory test error
P0605	PCM Read Only Memory test error

O = Key On, Engine Off; C = Continuous Memory; R = Engine Running

---

3   Powertrain Control Module (PCM) - replacement

1   The Powertrain Control Module (PCM) is located in the passenger compartment behind the passenger's side kick panel. The PCM is easily distinguished by the aluminum casing surrounding the module.

2   Disconnect the negative battery cable from the battery.

✷✷ WARNING:

Some models have airbags. Always disconnect the negative battery cable, then the positive battery cable and wait 2 minutes before working in the vicinity of the impact sensors, steering column or instrument panel to avoid the possibility of accidental deployment of the airbag, which could cause personal injury (see Chapter 12).

3   Remove the passenger side kick panel (see Chapter 11 if necessary). Remove the bolt that retains the electrical connector to the PCM.

✷✷ CAUTION:

The ignition switch must be turned OFF when pulling out or plugging in the electrical connectors to prevent damage to the PCM.

4   Remove the retaining nuts from the PCM studs.

5   Carefully slide the PCM out far enough to clear the kick panel.

➡Note: Avoid any static electricity damage to the computer by using gloves and a special anti-static pad to store the PCM on once it is removed.

6   Installation is the reverse of removal.

---

4   Information sensors

➡Note: If any of the following checks indicate that a sensor is good (and not the cause of the driveability problem or trouble code), check the wiring harness and electrical connectors between the sensor and the PCM for an open or short-circuit condition. If no problems are found, have the vehicle checked by a dealer service department or other qualified repair shop.

ENGINE COOLANT TEMPERATURE (ECT) SENSOR

▶ Refer to illustrations 4.1, 4.2, 4.3 and 4.4

General description

1   The coolant sensor is a thermistor (a resistor which varies the value of its voltage output in accordance with temperature changes) (see illustration). The change in the resistance values will directly affect the voltage signal from the coolant sensor. As the sensor temperature DECREASES, the resistance values will INCREASE. As the sensor temperature INCREASES, the resistance values will DECREASE. On 5.0L V8 models, a failure in the coolant sensor circuit should set a Code 116, 117 or 118. These codes indicate a failure in the coolant temperature circuit, so in most cases the appropriate solution to the problem will be either repair of a wire or replacement of the sensor.

Check

2   Check the resistance value of the coolant temperature sensor while it is completely cold (50 to 65-degrees F = 58,750 to 40,500 ohms). Next, start the engine and warm it up until it reaches operating temperature (see illustration). The resistance should be lower (180 to 220-degrees F = 3,600 to 1,840 ohms).

➡Note: Access to the coolant temperature sensor makes it difficult to position electrical probes on the terminals. If necessary, remove the sensor and perform the tests in a pan of heated water to simulate the conditions.

3   If the resistance values on the sensor are correct, check the refer-

4.1 Location of the coolant temperature sensor (ECT) on the 4.6L-DOHC engine (typical)

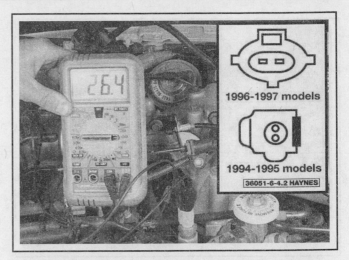

4.2 Check the resistance of the coolant temperature sensor with the engine completely cold and then with the engine at operating temperature. Resistance should decrease as temperature increases (3.8L engine shown)

ence voltage from the PCM to the sensor (see illustration). The reference voltage should be approximately 5.0 volts.

Replacement

4   Before installing the new sensor, wrap the threads with Teflon sealing tape to prevent leakage and thread corrosion (see illustration).

5   To remove the sensor, unplug the electrical connector, then carefully unscrew it.

> ❄ **CAUTION:**

Handle the coolant sensor with care. Damage to this sensor will affect the operation of the entire fuel injection system. Install the sensor and tighten it securely.

OXYGEN SENSOR

▶ **Refer to illustrations 4.6, 4.8 and 4.17**

General description and check

6   The heated oxygen sensors (HEGO), which are located in the exhaust manifolds, monitor the oxygen content of the exhaust gas stream (see illustration). The oxygen content in the exhaust reacts with the oxygen sensor to produce a voltage output which varies from 0.1-volt (high oxygen, lean mixture) to 0.9-volts (low oxygen, rich mixture).

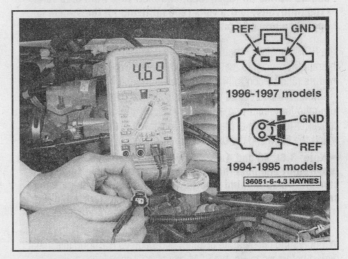

4.3 Working on the harness side, check the reference voltage from the PCM to the coolant temperature sensor with the ignition key ON and the engine not running. It should be approximately 5.0 volts

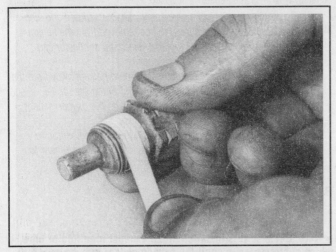

4.4 To prevent leakage, wrap the threads of the coolant temperature sensor with Teflon tape before installing it

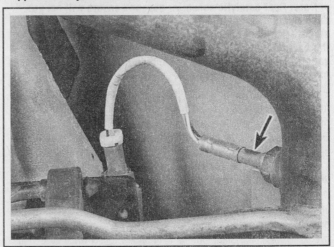

4.6 The oxygen sensor (arrow) is located in the exhaust pipe (3.8L V6 shown)

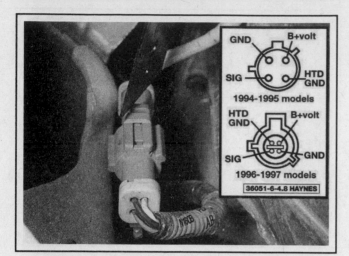

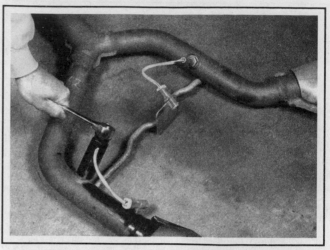

4.8 Using pins or paper clips, backprobe SIG (+) and GND (-) and check for a varying millivolt signal as the system adjusts the air/fuel ratio. Voltage should remain steady as the engine warms-up (open loop) and then vary from 0.10 volts (100 millivolts) to 0.9 volts (900 millivolts) if the system is operating properly (closed loop)

The PCM constantly monitors this variable voltage output to determine the ratio of oxygen to fuel in the mixture. The PCM alters the air/fuel mixture ratio by controlling the pulse width (open time) of the fuel injectors. A mixture ratio of 14.7 parts air to 1 part fuel is the ideal mixture ratio for minimizing exhaust emissions, thus allowing the catalytic converter to operate at maximum efficiency. It is this ratio of 14.7 to 1 which the PCM and the oxygen sensor attempt to maintain at all times.

➡**Note: 3.8L V6 and 4.6L V8 models are equipped with dual pre (upstream) and post (downstream) catalytic converter oxygen sensors. Keep in mind that the voltage values for the oxygen sensors mounted ahead of the catalytic converters will differ from the oxygen sensors mounted after the catalytic converters.**

7   The oxygen sensor produces no voltage when it is below its normal operating temperature of about 600-degrees F. During this initial period before warm-up, the PCM operates in open loop mode.

8   Allow the engine to reach normal operating temperature and check that the oxygen sensor is producing a varying signal voltage between 0.1 and 0.9-volts (see illustration).

➡**Note: Post-catalytic converter oxygen sensors will not produce fluctuating voltage but instead a steady high voltage signal (rich) will indicate few oxygen molecules available after the oxygen molecules catalyzed with hydrogen to form water vapors. Low voltage values will indicate the presence of excess oxygen but not a lean mixture.**

9   A delay of two minutes or more between engine start-up and normal operation of the sensor, followed by a low or a high voltage signal or a short in the sensor circuit, will cause the PCM to also set a code. On 5.0L V8 models, the codes that indicate problems in the oxygen sensor system are 136, 137, 139, 144 and 171 through 178.

10 Also check to make sure the oxygen sensor heater(s) is supplied with battery voltage (see illustration 4.8). Backprobe the HTR GND and the B+ Volt. terminals with the ignition key ON. Because battery voltage is supplied to the oxygen sensors through a relay, voltage will only be delivered for a very short time (3 seconds) when the ignition key is cycled. Have an assistant turn the ignition key to ON while observing the voltmeter. Refer to Chapter 12 for additional information on the wiring schematics and relays.

11 When any of the above codes occur, the PCM operates in the

4.17 Use the slotted portion of the oxygen socket to slide over the harness connector then remove the oxygen sensor (exhaust system removed for clarity)

open loop mode - that is, it controls fuel delivery in accordance with a programmed default value instead of feedback information from the oxygen sensor.

12 The proper operation of the oxygen sensor depends on four conditions:

a) *Electrical - The low voltages generated by the sensor depend upon good, clean connections which should be checked whenever a malfunction of the sensor is suspected or indicated.*

b) *Outside air supply - The sensor is designed to allow air circulation to the internal portion of the sensor. Whenever the sensor is removed and installed or replaced, make sure the air passages are not restricted.*

c) *Proper operating temperature - The PCM will not react to the sensor signal until the sensor reaches approximately 600-degrees F. This factor must be taken into consideration when evaluating the performance of the sensor.*

d) *Unleaded fuel - The use of unleaded fuel is essential for proper operation of the sensor. Make sure the fuel you are using is of this type.*

13 In addition to observing the above conditions, special care must be taken whenever the sensor is serviced.

a) *The oxygen sensor has a permanently attached pigtail and electrical connector which should not be removed from the sensor. Damage or removal of the pigtail or electrical connector can adversely affect operation of the sensor.*

b) *Grease, dirt and other contaminants should be kept away from the electrical connector and the louvered end of the sensor.*

c) *Do not use cleaning solvents of any kind on the oxygen sensor.*

d) *Do not drop or roughly handle the sensor.*

e) *The silicone boot must be installed in the correct position to prevent the boot from being melted and to allow the sensor to operate properly.*

Replacement

▸ **Refer to illustration 4.17**

➡**Note: Because it is installed in the exhaust manifold or pipe, which contracts when cool, the oxygen sensor may be very difficult to loosen when the engine is cold. Rather than risk damage to the sensor (assuming you are planning to reuse it in another**

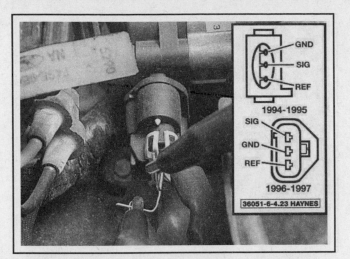

4.23 Backprobe the TPS using pins or paper clips on SIG (+) and GND (-) and with the throttle completely closed, check the signal voltage. It should be 0.5 to 1.0 volts at closed throttle

manifold or pipe), start and run the engine for a minute or two, then shut it off. Be careful not to burn yourself during the following procedure.

14 Disconnect the cable from the negative terminal of the battery.
15 Raise the vehicle and place it securely on jackstands.
16 Carefully disconnect the electrical connector from the sensor.
17 Carefully unscrew the sensor from the exhaust manifold (see illustration).

❋❋ CAUTION:

Excessive force may damage the threads.

18 Anti-seize compound must be used on the threads of the sensor to facilitate future removal. The threads of new sensors will already be coated with this compound, but if an old sensor is removed and reinstalled, recoat the threads.

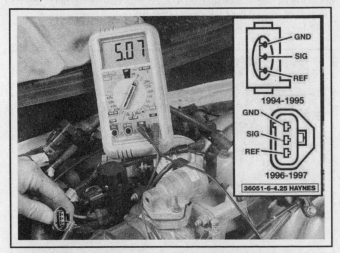

4.25 Check the reference voltage to the TPS with a voltmeter. Backprobe terminal REF with the positive (+) probe and GND (-) with the negative probe of the voltmeter and make sure the reference voltage is approximately 5.0 volts

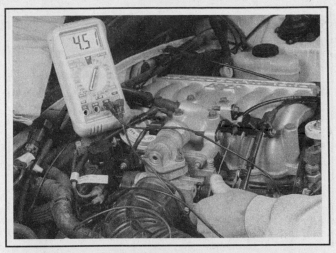

4.24 Rotate the accelerator completely to wide open throttle and observe the voltage increase steadily to 4.5 to 5.0 volts

19 Install the sensor and tighten it securely.
20 Reconnect the electrical connector of the pigtail lead to the main engine wiring harness.
21 Lower the vehicle and reconnect the cable to the negative terminal of the battery.

THROTTLE POSITION SENSOR (TPS)

General description

22 The Throttle Position Sensor (TPS) is located on the end of the throttle shaft on the throttle body. By monitoring the output voltage from the TPS, the PCM can determine fuel delivery based on throttle valve angle (driver demand). A broken or loose TPS can cause intermittent bursts of fuel from the injector and an unstable idle because the PCM thinks the throttle is moving. Any problems in the TPS or circuit on 5.0L V8 models, will set a code 122 through 125.

Check

▶ Refer to illustrations 4.23, 4.24 and 4.25

23 To check the TPS, turn the ignition switch to ON (engine not running) and install the probes of the voltmeter into the ground wire and signal wire on the backside of the electrical connector (see illustration). This test checks for the proper signal voltage from the TPS.

➡Note: Be careful when backprobing the electrical connector. Do not damage the wiring harness or pull on any connectors to make clean contact.

24 The sensor should read 0.50 to 1.0-volt at idle. Have an assistant depress the accelerator pedal to simulate full throttle and the sensor should increase voltage to 4.0 to 5.0-volts (see illustration). If the TPS voltage readings are incorrect, replace it with a new unit.

25 Also, check the TPS reference voltage. With the ignition key ON (engine not running), install the positive (+) probe of the voltmeter (see illustration) onto the voltage reference wire. There should be approximately 5.0 volts sent from the PCM to the TPS.

Replacement

26 The TPS is a non-adjustable unit. Remove the two retaining screws and separate the TPS from the throttle body.
27 Installation is the reverse of removal.

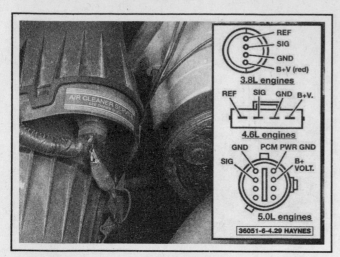

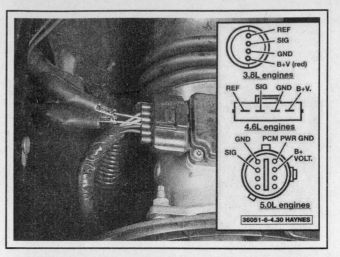

4.29 Check for battery voltage to the B+V terminal on the MAF sensor (key ON engine not running)

4.30 Use pins and backprobe the SIG (+) terminal and the GND (−) terminal of the MAF sensor and check signal voltage (0.2 to 1.5 volts at idle)

MASS AIRFLOW SENSOR (MAF)

General Information

▶ **Refer to illustrations 4.29, 4.30 and 4.36**

28 The Mass Airflow Sensor (MAF) is located on the air intake duct. This sensor uses a hot wire sensing element to measure the amount of air entering the engine. The air passing over the hot wire causes it to cool. Consequently, this change in temperature can be converted into an analog voltage signal to the PCM which in turn calculates the required fuel injector pulse width.

Check

29 Check for power to the MAF sensor. Disconnect the MAF sensor electrical connector, work on the harness side and probe the connector to check for battery voltage (see illustration). Use the B+ Voltage terminal (+) and the GND (−) for the voltmeter probes.

30 Reconnect the electrical connector and backprobe the MAF SIG and GND (see illustration) with the voltmeter and check for the voltage. The voltage should be 0.2 to 1.5 volts at idle.

31 Raise the engine rpm. The signal voltage from the MAF sen-

sor should increase to about 2.0 volts at 60 mph. It is impossible to simulate these conditions in the driveway at home but it is necessary to observe the voltmeter for a fluctuation in voltage as the engine speed is raised. The vehicle will not be under load conditions but it should manage to vary slightly. This parameter is easily monitored on a SCAN tool. Look for a steady increase in the voltage signal.

32 Disconnect the MAF harness connector and use an ohmmeter and probe the terminals MAF SIG and GND. If the hot wire element inside the sensor has been damaged it will be indicated by an open circuit (infinite resistance).

33 If the voltage readings are correct, check the wiring harness for open circuits or a damaged harness (see Chapter 12).

Replacement

34 Disconnect the electrical connector from the MAF sensor.

35 Remove the upper section of the air cleaner assembly (see Chapter 4).

36 On 3.8L and 5.0L engines detach the tabs securing the MAF sensor to the air cleaner housing; on 4.6L engines remove the nuts (see illustration) and lift the MAF sensor from the engine compartment.

37 Installation is the reverse of removal.

4.36 Disconnect the air inlet duct, remove the nuts (arrows) and separate the MAF sensor from the air cleaner housing

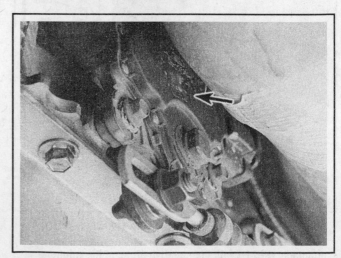

4.38 Location of the Transmission Range sensor (TR)

TRANSMISSION RANGE (TR) SENSOR

General description

▶ Refer to illustration 4.38

38 The Transmission Range (TR) sensor, located on the transmission (see illustration) indicates to the PCM when the transmission is in Park, Neutral, Drive or Reverse. This information is used for starting, Transmission Converter Clutch (TCC), Exhaust Gas Recirculation (EGR) and Idle Air Control (IAC) valve operation. For example, if the signal wire(s) become grounded, it may be difficult to start the engine in Park or Neutral. On 5.0L V8 models, a problem with the Transmission Range (TR) sensor will flash a code 522.

Check

▶ Refer to illustration 4.40

39 In the event there is a problem with the Transmission Range (TR) sensor, first check the terminal connectors for proper attachment.

40 Working on the TR sensor harness on the computer side, use a voltmeter and with the ignition key ON (engine not running), check for power (see illustration) to the switch on terminal number 2. There should be voltage present.

41 Disable the ignition system (see Chapter 5) and have an assistant

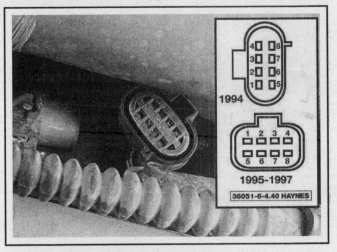

4.40 Check for battery voltage to the TR sensor on terminal number 2

turn the ignition key to Start and check for cranking voltage to the TR sensor on terminal number 1. Cranking voltage should be more than 9 volts but less than battery voltage.

42 Check the resistance between the indicated TR sensor terminals following the different gear selections. Refer to the test chart.

Circuits	Terminals for ohmmeter probes	Gear selection positions	Known good values
Transmission Circuits	Terminal 7 and Terminal 6.	Park.	3,770 to 4,607 ohms
		Reverse	1,304 to 1,593 ohms
		Neutral	660 to 807 ohms
		Overdrive	361 to 442 ohms
		Drive	190 to 232 ohms
		First gear	78 to 95 ohms
Back-up lamp circuit	Terminal 2 and Terminal 3	Park.	Greater than 100 K-ohms
		Reverse	Less than 5.0 ohms
		Neutral	Greater than 100 K-ohms
		Overdrive	Greater than 100 K-ohms
		Drive	Greater than 100 K-ohms
		First gear	Greater than 100 K-ohms
Starter Relay Circuit	Terminal 4 and Terminal 1.	Park.	Greater than 100 K-ohms
		Reverse	Less than 5.0 ohms
		Neutral	Greater than 100 K-ohms
		Overdrive	Greater than 100 K-ohms
		Drive	Greater than 100 K-ohms
		First gear	Less than 5.0 ohms

43 Check the adjustment of the switch. If the switch is out of adjustment, perform the procedure and clear the codes. Recheck the system for any other problems.

Adjustment

44 Follow the transmission shift control cable adjustment in Chapter 7 and check for a distinct "click" when the shift lever selects each gear (Park, Reverse, Neutral, Drive etc.).

45 The shift button should release smoothly and there should not be any cable binding preventing smooth transition between gears.

AIR CONDITIONING CLUTCH CONTROL

▶ Refer to illustration 4.47

46 During air conditioning operation, the PCM controls the application of the air conditioning compressor clutch. The PCM controls the air conditioning clutch control relay to delay clutch engagement after the air conditioning is turned ON to allow the ISC valve to adjust the idle speed of the engine to compensate for the additional load. The PCM also controls the relay to disengage the clutch in the event of an

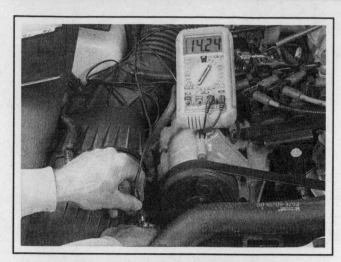

4.47 Disconnect the air conditioning clutch harness connector and check for battery voltage with the system activated (ignition key ON - engine not running)

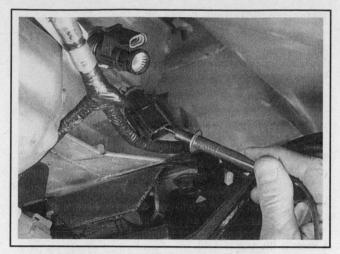

4.52 Disconnect the VSS harness connector and check for battery voltage

excessively high or low pressure within the system or an overheating problem.

47 First, check for battery voltage to the air conditioning clutch with the engine running, the air conditioning system activated and the air conditioning clutch harness connector disconnected (see illustration). Battery voltage should be available. If not, check the air conditioning clutch relay.

➡Note: The air conditioning clutch relay is housed in the Computer Controlled Relay Module (CCRM). Refer to Chapter 4 for detailed information concerning the location of the CCRM module.

48 Use a jumper wire from the battery positive terminal (+) and apply voltage to the air conditioning clutch. There should be a definite "click" when the clutch is activated.

49 Check for battery voltage to the air conditioning clutch relay on terminal 21.

➡Note: The air conditioning clutch relay is housed in the Computer Controlled Relay Module (CCRM). Refer to Chapter 4 for detailed information concerning the location of the CCRM

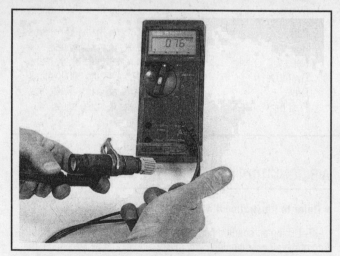

4.53 Remove the VSS and check for a pulsing AC voltage signal as the VSS gear is slowly turned

module. If no power exists, then check the air conditioning high pressure cut-out fan switch, the air conditioning clutch cycling pressure switch, the air conditioning/heater control assembly (see Chapter 3) and the 15 amp fuse that protects the circuit (see Chapter 12).

50 In most cases, if the air conditioning does not function, the problem is probably related to the air conditioning system relays and switches and not the PCM. Refer to Chapter 3 for additional information on the air conditioning system and diagnostics.

VEHICLE SPEED SENSOR (VSS)

General description

51 The Vehicle Speed Sensor (VSS) is located near the rear section of the transmission. This sensor is a variable reluctance sensor that produces a pulsing voltage proportional to the speed of the vehicle. These pulses are translated by the PCM and provided for other systems for fuel and transmission shift control. The VSS is part of the Transmission Converter Clutch (TCC) system.

Check

▶ **Refer to illustrations 4.52 and 4.53**

52 To check the vehicle speed sensor, remove the electrical connector in the wiring harness near the sensor. Using a voltmeter, check for reference voltage to the sensor (see illustration). With the ignition key ON (engine not running), the reference wire should have 5 volts available. If there is no voltage available, have the PCM diagnosed by a dealer service department or other qualified repair shop.

53 Place the VSS on a bench and check for a pulsing voltage. Backprobe the harness connector using two pins and while slowly spinning the VSS gear, observe that the voltage signal pulses from 0 to 0.5 volts. Use the AC scale on the voltmeter (see illustration).

Replacement

54 To replace the VSS, disconnect the electrical connector from the VSS.

55 Remove the retaining bolt and withdraw the VSS from the transmission.

56 Installation is the reverse of removal.

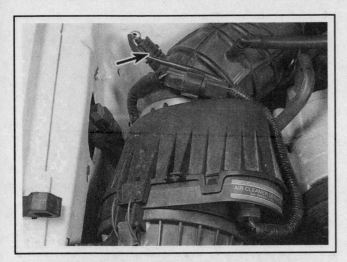

4.57 Location of the IAT sensor on the 3.8L engine

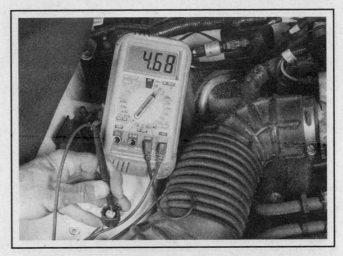

4.59 Check for reference voltage to the IAT sensor with the ignition key ON (engine not running). It should be approximately 5.0 volts

INTAKE AIR TEMPERATURE (IAT) SENSOR

General description

▶ Refer to illustration 4.57

57 The Intake Air Temperature (IAT) sensor is located inside the air intake duct (see illustration). This sensor acts as a resistor which changes value according to the temperature of the air entering the engine. Low temperatures produce a high resistance value (for example, at 68 degrees F the resistance is 27.3 K-ohms) while high temperatures produce low resistance values (at 212-degrees F the resistance is 2.0 K-ohms. The PCM supplies approximately 5-volts (reference voltage) to the IAT sensor. The voltage will change according to the temperature of the incoming air. The voltage will be high when the air temperature is cold and low when the air temperature is warm. Any problems with the IAT sensor will usually set a code 112, 113 or 114 on 5.0L V8 models.

Check

▶ Refer to illustrations 4.59 and 4.61

58 To check the IAT sensor, disconnect the two prong electrical connector and turn the ignition key ON but do not start the engine.

59 Measure the reference voltage. Reference voltage should be approximately 5-volts (see illustration).

60 If the voltage signal is not correct, have the PCM diagnosed by a dealer service department or other repair shop.

61 Measure the resistance across the sensor terminals (see illustration). The resistance should be HIGH when the air temperature is LOW. Next, start the engine and let it idle (cold). Wait until engine reaches operating temperature. Turn the ignition OFF, disconnect the IAT sensor and measure the resistance across the terminals. The resistance should be LOW when the air temperature is HIGH. If the sensor does not exhibit this change in resistance, replace it with a new part.

POWER STEERING PRESSURE SWITCH

62 Turning the steering wheel increases power steering fluid pressure and engine load. The pressure switch will close before the load can cause an idle problem.

63 A pressure switch that will not open or an open circuit from the

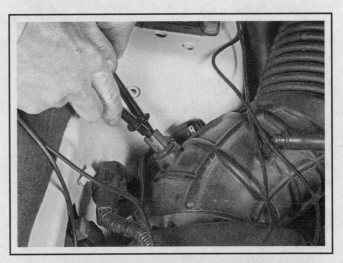

4.61 Remove the electrical connector from the IAT sensor (located in air cleaner housing), then check the resistance of the IAT sensor cold and warm. It may be necessary to use simulated conditions to obtain accurate results

PCM will cause timing to retard at idle and this will affect idle quality.

64 A pressure switch that will not close or an open circuit may cause the engine to die when the power steering system is used heavily.

65 Any problems with the power steering pressure switch or circuit should be repaired by a dealer service department or other qualified repair shop.

CRANKSHAFT POSITION SENSOR (CKP)

General information

▶ Refer to illustrations 4.66a and 4.66b

66 3.8L V6 and 4.6L V8 models are equipped with a crankshaft position sensor. The crankshaft position sensor (see illustrations) is mounted adjacent to a pulse wheel located on the crankshaft. The crankshaft sensor monitors the pulse wheel as the teeth pass under the magnetic field created by the sensor. The pulse wheel has 35 teeth and

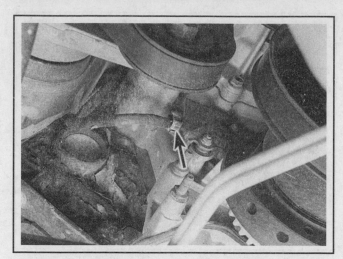

4.66a Location of the crankshaft sensor (arrow) on the 3.8L V6 engine

4.66b Location of the crankshaft sensor (arrow) on the 4.6L V8 engine

a spot where one tooth is missing. By monitoring the lost tooth, the crankshaft sensor determines the piston travel, crankshaft position and speed information and sends the information to the PCM.

Check

▶ **Refer to illustration 4.68**

67 Disconnect the CKP sensor electrical connector and with the ignition key ON (engine not running), check for battery voltage to the CKP sensor.

68 Install a voltmeter onto the crankshaft sensor and using the AC scale, check the voltage pulses as the gear is slowly rotated (see illustration). Use a large socket and breaker bar to rotate the crankshaft pulley.

69 If no pulsing voltage signal is produced, replace the crankshaft sensor.

Replacement

70 Remove the electrical connector and the retaining bolt and lift the assembly from the engine block.

71 Installation is the reverse of removal.

CAMSHAFT POSITION SENSOR

General information

72 3.8L V6 and 4.6L V8 models are equipped with a camshaft sensor as well as a crankshaft sensor. The camshaft sensor signals the PCM to begin sequential pulsation of the fuel injectors. This camshaft sensor on the 3.8L is a Hall Effect switching device activated by a single vane. This camshaft sensor is mounted on the top of the engine in the normal location of the distributor on an older 3.8L V6 engine. The camshaft sensor in the 4.6L is a variable reluctance device which is triggered by the high point mark on the camshaft. The sensor is mounted on the front of the cylinder head near the camshaft sprocket.

Check

3.8L V6 models

73 Check the signal voltage. Backprobe the signal wire (dark blue/ orange) from the computer and the ground wire (black/white) and while slowly rotating the engine, observe that the voltage pulses from 0 to 5.0 volts.

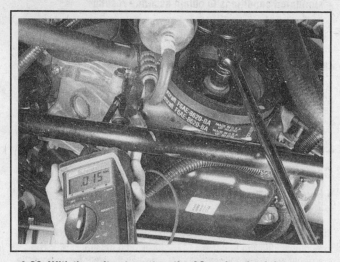

4.68 With the voltmeter set on the AC scale, check for a pulsing voltage signal between 0 and 0.05 volts as the engine is slowly rotated

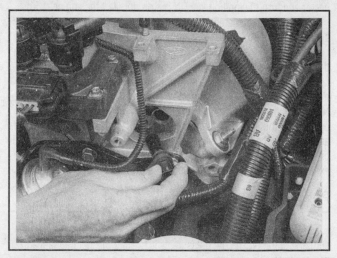

4.76 First remove the power steering fluid reservoir from the cylinder head to gain access to the camshaft position sensor

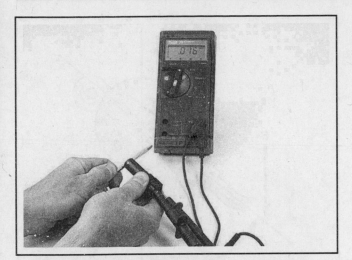

4.77 Working on the bench, carefully pass a metal object close to the tip of the camshaft sensor and observe the AC voltage fluctuate. If the camshaft sensor does not exhibit any reaction as the magnetic field is broken, the sensor must be replaced

➡️**Note: Do not crank the engine over using the starter but instead install a breaker bar and socket onto the front crankshaft pulley bolt and rotate the engine slowly by hand.**

74 If there is no pulsing signal voltage, have the PCM diagnosed by a dealer service department.

4.6L V8 models

▶ **Refer to illustrations 4.76 and 4.77**

75 Check for battery voltage to the camshaft position sensor with the ignition key ON (engine not running).

76 Remove the camshaft sensor from the engine and place it on a clean workbench (see illustration).

77 Check the AC voltage output. Install the probes of a voltmeter set on the AC scale onto the camshaft sensor and observe that it produces a voltage pulse as a metal object is passed over the tip of the sensor (see illustration).

78 If no pulsing voltage signal is produced, replace the camshaft sensor.

Replacement

3.8L V6 models

▶ **Refer to illustrations 4.82 and 4.86**

➡️**Note: 3.8L models equipped with a camshaft position sensor are mounted on a synchronizer assembly, which is essentially a drive unit for the sensor. If you are simply replacing the cam position sensor it is not necessary to remove the synchronizer assembly from the engine - just remove the screws from the sensor, detach it from the synchronizer and install the new sensor. However, many engine repair procedures require removal of the synchronizer assembly, in which case it will be necessary to perform the following procedure to time the synchronizer. This procedure requires the use of a Ford special tool to properly align the sensor, read through the entire procedure and obtain the necessary tool before beginning.**

79 On a 1994 and 1995 model, position the number 1 cylinder at 26-degrees ATDC. On a 1996 model, position the number 1 cylinder at 10-degrees ATDC. On a 1997 and later model, position the number 1 piston at TDC. Refer to Chapter 2B for the procedure.

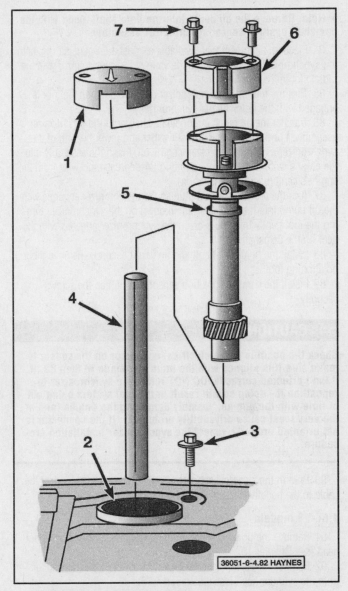

36051-6-4.82 HAYNES

4.82 Exploded view of the camshaft position sensor and synchronizer assembly - 3.8L V6

1   Syncro positioning tool
2   Timing chain cover
3   Clamp
4   Oil pump intermediate shaft
5   Camshaft Position sensor housing
6   Camshaft Position sensor
7   Bolt

4.86 With the housing seated against the engine block, the

80 Disconnect the battery negative cable.

81 Mark the relative position of the camshaft position sensor electrical connector so the assembly can be oriented properly upon installation (this is only necessary if the synchronizer assembly will be removed). Disconnect the electrical connector from the camshaft position sensor. Remove the screws and detach the sensor from the synchronizer assembly.

82 Remove the sensor mounting screws (see illustration) and lift the sensor from the housing.

83 If you will be removing the synchronizer assembly, remove the bolt and withdraw the synchronizer from the engine.

➡️**Note: Remove the oil pump intermediate shaft along with the camshaft position sensor synchronizer assembly.**

84 Place an alignment tool, available at most auto parts stores, onto the synchronizer assembly. Align the vane of the synchronizer with the radial slot in the special tool.

85 Turn the tool on the synchronizer until the boss on the tool is engaged with the notch on the synchronizer.

86 Transfer the oil pump intermediate shaft onto the synchronizer assembly. Lubricate the gear, thrust washer and lower bearing of the synchronizer assembly with clean engine oil. Insert the assembly into the engine, with the arrow tool pointing 54-degrees clockwise from the engine's centerline (see illustration).

87 Turn the tool clockwise a little so the synchronizer engages with the oil pump intermediate shaft. Push down on the synchronizer, turning the tool gently until the gear on the synchronizer engages with the gear on the camshaft.

88 Install the hold-down bolt and tighten it securely. Remove the positioning tool.

89 Install the camshaft position sensor and tighten the screws securely.

❊❊ **CAUTION:**

Check the position of the electrical connector on the sensor to make sure it is aligned with the mark you made in Step 82. If it isn't oriented correctly, DO NOT rotate the synchronizer to reposition it - doing so will result in the fuel system being out of time with the engine, possibly damaging the engine (and at the very least cause driveability problems). If the connector is not oriented properly, repeat the synchronizer installation procedure.

90 Plug in the electrical connector to the sensor and reconnect the cable to the negative terminal of the battery.

4.6L V8 models

91 Remove the power steering fluid reservoir from the left cylinder head (see Chapter 10).

92 Remove the retaining screw and separate the camshaft sensor from the cylinder head (see illustration 4.76).

93 Installation is the reverse of removal.

BRAKE ON/OFF (BOO) SWITCH

General Information

94 The brake On/Off switch informs the PCM when the brakes are being applied. The switch closes when brakes are applied and opens when the brakes are released. The switch is located on the brake pedal assembly.

95 The brake light circuit and bulbs are wired into the switch circuit so it is important in diagnosing any driveability problems to make sure all the brake light bulbs are working properly (not burned out) or the driver may feel poor idle quality (see Chapter 7).

Check

96 Disconnect the electrical connector from the Brake On/Off switch and using a 12 volt test light, check for battery voltage to the switch.

97 Also, check continuity from the switch to the brake light bulbs. Change any burned out bulbs or damaged wire looms.

Replacement

98 Refer to Chapter 9 for the replacement procedure.

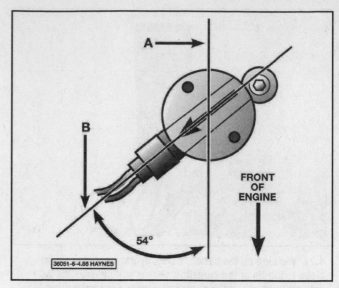

arrow on the tool (B) should point 54-degrees from the left of centerline (A) on 1998 and earlier models - On 1999 and later models the arrow on the tool (B) should point 54- degrees to the right of centerline (A)

KNOCK SENSOR (4.6L DOHC MODELS ONLY)

General description

▸ **Refer to illustration 4.99**

99 The knock sensor is located in the engine block under the intake manifold (see illustration). The knock sensor detects abnormal vibration in the engine. The sensor produces an AC output voltage which increases with the severity of the knock. The signal is fed into the PCM and the timing is retarded up to 10 degrees to compensate for severe detonation. Any problems with the knock sensor can only be monitored using a special OBD II SCAN tool.

Check

100 Because the knock sensors are difficult to access, have a dealer service department check the system for correct operation.

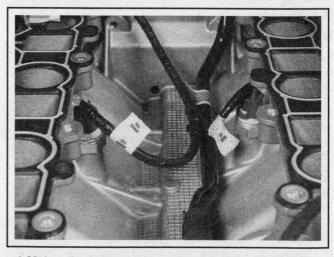

4.99 Location of the knock sensors on the 4.6L-DOHC engine

5 Exhaust Gas Recirculation (EGR) system

GENERAL DESCRIPTION

▶ **Refer to illustrations 5.2a and 5.2b**

1   The EGR system is used to lower oxides of nitrogen (NOx) emission levels caused by high combustion temperatures. The EGR recirculates a small amount of exhaust gases into the intake manifold. The additional mixture lowers the temperature of combustion thereby reducing the formation of NOx compounds.

2   The EGR flow rate is determined by monitoring the pressure across a fixed metering orifice as exhaust gasses pass through it. The more simplified system called the Pressure Feedback (PFE) system (see illustration), monitors only the downstream (after) pressure after the exhaust gasses have passed through the metering orifice. This backpressure coefficient is relayed to the PCM and the correct amount of EGR (duty cycle) is applied to the EGR vacuum regulator control (EVR). The more complex system called the Differential Pressure Feedback (DPFE) system (see illustration) monitors upstream (before) and downstream (after) exhaust backpressure. By calculating the difference between the two pressures, the PCM determines exactly the EGR flow rate at all driving conditions. The DPFE is more accurate in that the computer does not have to guess at the upstream pressure coefficient to determine EGR flow rate as the engine drives through various road conditions such as hard acceleration, downshifting, engine misfire, poor fuel combustion, etc. All these conditions will cause the exhaust backpressure to vary and requires more strict and responsive EGR control to limit NOx emission levels.

3   Different engine options are equipped with different EGR systems:

   a) *5.0L V8 models are equipped with the Pressure Feedback Exhaust Gas Recirculation (PFE) system. This system relies upon the PCM for EGR control. The control module (PCM) calculates the desired flow of exhaust gases into the combustion chamber and subsequently controls the EGR valve position with the EGR vacuum regulator (EVR) using an analog voltage signal or duty cycle (On/Off time). A duty cycle of 50-percent would hold the EGR valve half way open.*

   b) *3.8L V6 and 4.6L V8 models are equipped with the Differential Pressure Feedback EGR (DPFE) system. This operates in the same way as the PFE except it monitors the pressure drop across the orifice allowing for a more precise measurement of the exhaust gas pressures.*

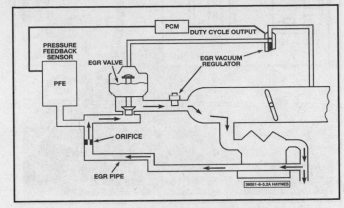

5.2a Typical Pressure Feedback EGR (PFE) system

CHECK

4   Too much EGR flow tends to weaken combustion, causing the engine to run rough or stop. When EGR flow is excessive, the engine can stop after a cold start or at idle after deceleration, the vehicle can surge at cruising speeds or the idle may be rough. If the EGR valve remains constantly open, the engine may not idle at all.

5   Too little or no EGR flow allows combustion temperatures to get too high during acceleration and load conditions. This can cause spark knock (detonation), engine overheating or emission test failure.

6   The following checks will help you pinpoint problems in the EGR system. Where the procedure says to lift up on the EGR valve diaphragm, it's a good idea to wear a heat-resistant glove to prevent burns.

EGR valve

▶ **Refer to illustration 5.9**

7   The EGR valve is controlled by a normally open EGR vacuum regulator (EVR) which allows vacuum to pass when energized. The PCM energizes the EVR to turn on the EGR. The PCM controls the EGR when three conditions are present: engine coolant is above 113-degrees F, the TPS is at part throttle and the MAF sensor is in its mid-range.

8   Make sure the vacuum hoses are in good condition and hooked up correctly.

9   To perform a leakage test, hook up a vacuum pump to the EGR

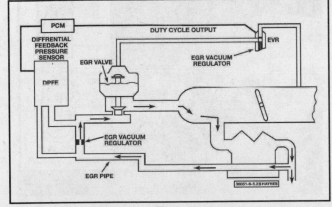

5.2b Typical Differential Pressure Feedback EGR (DPFE) system

5.9 Apply vacuum to the EGR valve and check with the tip of your finger for movement of the diaphragm. It should move smoothly without any binding when vacuum is applied

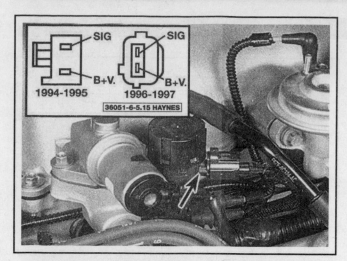

5.15 Working on the harness side of the Electronic Vacuum Regulator (arrow) electrical connector, check for battery voltage

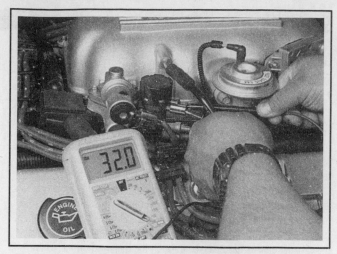

5.16 Check the resistance of the EGR vacuum regulator. It should be 30 to 70 ohms

valve (see illustration). Apply a vacuum of 5 to 6 in-Hg to the valve. The vacuum pump should hold vacuum.

10 If access is possible, position your finger tip under the vacuum diaphragm and apply vacuum to the EGR valve. You should feel movement of the EGR diaphragm.

⁜ WARNING:

The EGR valve becomes very hot during engine operation - it's a good idea to wear a glove when performing this check.

11 Remove the EGR valve (see Step 20) and clean the inlet and outlet ports with a wire brush or scraper. Do not sandblast the valve or clean it with gasoline or solvents. These liquids will destroy the EGR valve diaphragm.

12 If the specified conditions are not met, replace the EGR valve.

EGR control system

▸ **Refer to illustrations 5.15, 5.16 and 5.17**

13 If a code is displayed there are several possibilities for EGR failure. Engine coolant temperature sensor, TPS, MAF sensor, TCC system and the engine rpm govern the parameters the EGR system use for distinguishing the correct ON time.

14 All systems use an Electronic Vacuum Regulator (EVR) to control the amount of exhaust gas through the EGR valve. The valve is normally open (engine at operating temperature) and the vacuum source is a ported signal. The PCM uses a controlled "pulse width" or electronic signal to turn the EGR ON and OFF (the "duty cycle"). The duty cycle should be zero percent (no EGR) when in Park or Neutral, when the TPS input is below the specified value or when Wide Open Throttle (WOT) is indicated.

15 To check the EGR vacuum regulator, disconnect the electrical connector to the EGR vacuum regulator, turn the ignition key ON (engine not running) and check for battery voltage to the solenoid (see illustration). Battery voltage should be present.

16 Next, use an ohmmeter and check the resistance of the EGR vacuum regulator. It should be between 30 and 70 ohms (see illustration).

17 Check for reference voltage to the DPFE sensor. With the ignition key on (engine not running), check for voltage on the harness side of

the electrical connector (see illustration) on terminal VREF. It should be between 4.0 and 6.0 volts. If the test results are incorrect, replace the DPFE sensor.

18 Check the operation of the Pressure Feedback EGR (PFE) or Differential Pressure Feedback (DPFE) sensor.

➡**Note: The DPFE sensor on the Differential Pressure Feedback EGR systems have two exhaust lines hooked into the EGR tube.**

Check for signal voltage to the sensor. Backprobe the correct terminals and check for a voltage signal while the engine is running first at cold temperatures and then at warm operating temperatures. With the engine cold there should be NO EGR therefore the voltage should be approximately 0.20 to 0.70 volts. As the engine starts to warm and EGR is signaled by the computer, voltage values should increase to approximately 4.0 to 6.0 volts.

COMPONENT REPLACEMENT

EGR valve

▸ **Refer to illustration 5.23**

19 When buying a new EGR valve, make sure that you have the right EGR valve. Use the stamped code located on the top of the EGR valve.

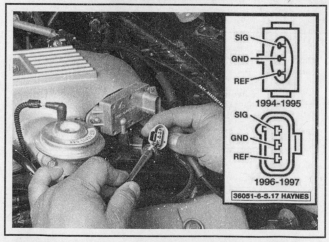

5.17 Check for the correct reference voltage to the DPFE sensor with the ignition key ON (engine not running)

5.23 Remove the EGR pipe from the EGR valve

5.37 Remove the DPFE sensor mounting bolts

20 Detach the cable from the negative terminal of the battery.
21 Remove the air cleaner housing assembly (see Chapter 4).
22 Detach the vacuum line from the EGR valve.
23 Raise the vehicle and support it securely on jackstands. Remove the EGR pipe from the exhaust manifold (see illustration). Lower the vehicle.
24 Remove the bolts securing the EGR valve to the intake manifold/air intake plenum.
25 Remove the EGR valve and gasket from the manifold. Discard the gasket.
26 With a wire wheel, buff the exhaust deposits from the EGR valve mounting surface on the manifold and, if you plan to use the same valve, the mounting surface of the valve itself. Look for exhaust deposits in the valve outlet. Remove deposit build-up with a screwdriver.

❊ CAUTION:

Never wash the valve in solvents or degreaser - both agents will permanently damage the diaphragm. Sand blasting is also not recommended because it will affect the operation of the valve.

27 If the EGR passage contains an excessive build-up of deposits, clean it out with a wire wheel. Make sure that all loose particles are completely removed to prevent them from clogging the EGR valve or from being ingested into the engine.
28 Installation is the reverse of removal.

EGR vacuum regulator

29 Detach the cable from the negative terminal of the battery.
30 Unplug the electrical connector from the solenoid.
31 Clearly label and detach both vacuum hoses.
32 Remove the solenoid mounting screw and remove the solenoid.
33 Installation is the reverse of removal.

DPFE sensor

▶ **Refer to illustration 5.37**

34 Detach the cable from the negative terminal of the battery.
35 Unplug the electrical connector from the sensor.
36 Clearly label and detach both vacuum hoses.
37 Remove the sensor mounting screws (see illustration) and remove the assembly.
38 Installation is the reverse of removal.

6 Air Injection (AIR) system

GENERAL INFORMATION

1 The Air Injection system (AIR) controls emissions during the first 20 to 120 seconds of the engine operation through its warm-up cycle. 1994 and 1995 models are equipped with a mechanical air pump while later models are equipped with a electronically controlled air pump. Both pumps force air down into the exhaust manifolds to oxidize the hydrocarbons (HC) and carbon monoxide (CO) created by the rich running conditions.
2 Early systems consist of an air pump, bypass valve, diverter valve, injection manifolds and hose routing, upstream and downstream check valves and three-way catalytic converters. Later systems are equipped with an electric air pump, dual combination AIR bypass valves, an AIR diverter valve, a solid state relay, PCM and connecting harness and vacuum lines.

3 Later systems operate electronically. The PCM receives ECT, IAT and engine rpm information from the information sensors to initiate Secondary AIR activation. The solid state relay provides the start-up signal to the air pump. The electric pump provides the necessary air to oxidize the emission gasses created by the rich running start-up condition.

CHECK

Air pump

Mechanical air pump

4 Check and adjust the drivebelt tension (see Chapter 1).
5 Disconnect the air supply hose at the air bypass valve inlet.
6 The pump is operating satisfactorily if airflow is felt at the pump

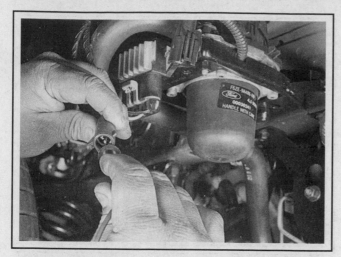

6.9 With the ignition key ON (engine not running), check for battery voltage to the air pump

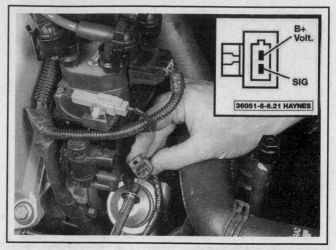

6.21 Check for battery voltage to the air diverter valve

6.33 Air pump mounting bolts (arrows) (4.6L V8 engine shown)

outlet with the engine running at idle, increasing as the engine speed is increased.

7 If the air pump doesn't pass the above tests, replace it with a new or rebuilt unit.

Electric air pump

▶ **Refer to illustration 6.9**

8 With the engine cold, disconnect the AIR line at the check valve, start the engine and observe that fresh air is being pumped to the exhaust system. If no air is felt, continue checking the system.

9 Check for battery voltage to the air pump. With the engine completely cooled down, turn the ignition key ON (engine not running) and check for battery voltage to the air pump (see illustration). Check for battery voltage to the CCRM. Power to the AIR system components is supplied by the CCRM (see Chapter 4). If no battery voltage is present, have the PCM and the AIR circuit diagnosed by a dealer service department.

10 Check the operation of the electric air pump. Disconnect the air pump electrical connector and using jumper wires, apply battery voltage. The pump should activate and there should be a noticeable sound as the pump produces air volume. If there is no sound, replace the air pump.

11 Physically inspect the air pump and lines for damage, broken connectors or water that might have been ingested into the impeller housing from the motor cup (bowl) attached to the body.

Bypass valve

12 With the engine running at idle, disconnect the hose from the valve outlet.

13 Remove the vacuum hose from the port and remove or bypass any restrictors or delay valves in the vacuum hose.

14 Verify that vacuum is present in the vacuum hose by putting your finger over the end.

15 Reconnect the vacuum hose to the port.

16 With the engine running at 1500 rpm, the air pump supply air should be felt or heard at the air bypass valve outlet.

17 With the engine running at 1500 rpm, disconnect the vacuum hose. Air at the valve outlet should be decreased or shut off and air pump supply air should be felt or heard at the silencer ports.

18 Reconnect all hoses.

19 If the normally closed air bypass valve doesn't successfully pass

the above tests, check the air pump (refer to Steps 4 through 7).

20 If the air pump is operating satisfactorily, replace the air bypass valve with a new one.

Air diverter valve

▶ **Refer to illustration 6.21**

21 On computer controlled diverter valves, check for battery voltage to the diverter valve (see illustration) with the ignition key ON (engine not running).

22 If no battery voltage is present, have the PCM and circuit checked by a dealer service department.

Check valve

23 Disconnect the hoses from both ends of the check valve, carefully noting the installed position of the valve and the hoses.

24 Blow through both ends of the check valve, verifying that air flows in one direction only.

25 If air flows in both directions or not at all, replace the check valve with a new one.

26 When reconnecting the valve, make sure it is installed in the proper direction.

Mechanical air pump noise test

27 Check for unusual noises from the air pump. Under normal conditions, noise rises in pitch as the engine speed increases. To determine if noise is the fault of the air injection system, detach the drivebelt (after verifying that the belt tension is correct) and operate the engine. If the noise disappears, proceed with the following diagnosis.

✳✳ CAUTION:

The pump must accumulate 500 miles (vehicle miles) before the following check is valid.

28 If the belt noise is excessive:

a) *Check for a loose belt and tighten as necessary (refer to Chapter 1).*
b) *Check for a seized pump and replace it if necessary.*
c) *Check for a loose pulley. Tighten the mounting bolts as required.*
d) *Check for loose, broken or missing mounting brackets or bolts. Tighten or replace as necessary.*

29 If there is excessive mechanical noise:

a) *Check for an overtightened mounting bolt.*
b) *Check for an overtightened drivebelt (see Chapter 1).*
c) *Check for excessive flash on the air pump adjusting arm boss and remove as necessary.*
d) *Check for a distorted adjusting arm and, if necessary, replace the arm.*

30 If there is excessive thermactor system noise (whirring or hissing sounds):

a) *Check for a leak in the hoses (use a soap and water solution to find the leaks) and replace the hose(s) as necessary.*
b) *Check for a loose, pinched or kinked hose and reassemble, straighten or replace the hose and/or clamps as required.*
c) *Check for a hose touching other engine parts and adjust or reroute the hose to prevent further contact.*

d) *Check for an inoperative bypass valve (refer to Step 12 through 19) and replace if necessary.*
e) *Check for an inoperative check valve (refer to Step 22 through 25) and replace if necessary.*
f) *Check for loose pump or pulley mounting fasteners and tighten as necessary.*
g) *Check for a restricted or bent pump outlet fitting. Inspect the fitting and remove any casting flash blocking the air passageway. Replace bent fittings.*
h) *Check for air dumping through the bypass valve (only at idle). On many vehicles, the thermactor system has been designed to dump air at idle to prevent overheating the catalytic converter. This condition is normal. Determine that the noise persists at higher speeds before proceeding.*
i) *Check for air dumping through the bypass valve (the decel and idle dump). On many vehicles, the thermactor air is dumped into the air cleaner or the remote silencer. Make sure that the hoses are connected properly and not cracked.*

31 If there is excessive pump noise, make sure the pump has had sufficient break-in time (at least 500 miles). Check for a worn or damaged pump and replace as necessary.

COMPONENT REPLACEMENT

▶ **Refer to illustration 6.33**

32 To replace the air bypass valve, air supply control valve, check valve, combination air bypass/air control valve or the silencer, clearly label, then disconnect, the hoses leading to them, replace the faulty component and reattach the hoses to the proper ports. Make sure the hoses are in good condition. If not, replace them with new ones.

33 To replace the air supply pump, first loosen the engine drivebelt (see Chapter 1), then remove the pump mounting bolts (see illustration) from the mounting bracket.

34 On mechanical air pumps, after the new pump is installed, adjust the drivebelts (see Chapter 1).

7 Evaporative Emissions Control System (EECS)

GENERAL DESCRIPTION

▶ **Refer to illustrations 7.2a and 7.2b**

1 This system is designed to trap and store fuel vapors that evaporate from the fuel tank, throttle body and intake manifold during non-operation or idling, store them in the charcoal canister and then route into the combustion chamber to be burned during engine operation.

2 The Evaporative Emission Control System (EECS) consists of a charcoal-filled canister (see illustration) and the lines connecting the canister to the fuel tank, canister purge regulator valve (see illustration), ported vacuum and intake manifold vacuum.

3 Fuel vapors are transferred from the fuel tank, throttle body and intake manifold to a canister where they are stored when the engine is not operating. When the engine is running, the fuel vapors are purged from the canister by a purge control solenoid which is PCM controlled and consumed in the normal combustion process.

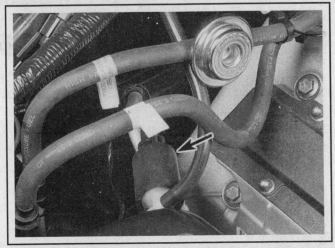

7.2a Location of the canister purge regulator valve (arrow) (4.6L V8 engine shown)

CHECK

4   Poor idle, stalling and poor driveability can be caused by an inoperative canister purge regulator valve, a damaged canister, split or cracked hoses or hoses connected to the wrong tubes.

5   Evidence of fuel loss or fuel odor can be caused by fuel leaking from fuel lines or the throttle body, a cracked or damaged canister, an inoperative bowl vent valve, an inoperative purge valve, disconnected, misrouted, kinked, deteriorated or damaged vapor or control hoses or an improperly seated air cleaner or air cleaner gasket.

6   Inspect each hose attached to the canister for kinks, leaks and breaks along its entire length. Repair or replace as necessary.

7   Inspect the canister. If it is cracked or damaged, replace it.

8   Look for fuel leaking from the bottom of the canister. If fuel is leaking, replace the canister and check the hoses and hose routing.

9   Apply a short length of hose to the lower tube of the purge valve assembly and attempt to blow through it. Little or no air should pass into the canister (a small amount of air will pass because the canister has a constant purge hole).

10   With a hand-held vacuum pump, apply vacuum through the control vacuum signal tube near the throttle body to the purge control solenoid diaphragm.

11   If the purge control solenoid does not hold vacuum for at least 20 seconds, the purge control solenoid is leaking and must be replaced.

12   If the diaphragm holds vacuum, apply battery voltage to the purge control solenoid and observe that vacuum (vapors) are allowed to pass through to the intake system.

7.2b   Location of the charcoal canister (4.6L V8 engine shown)

COMPONENT REPLACEMENT

13   Clearly label, then detach, all vacuum lines from the canister.

14   Loosen the canister mounting clamp bolt and pull the canister out.

15   Installation is the reverse of removal.

---

8   Positive Crankcase Ventilation (PCV) system

1   The Positive Crankcase Ventilation (PCV) system reduces hydrocarbon emissions by scavenging crankcase vapors. It does this by circulating fresh air from the air cleaner through the crankcase, where it mixes with blow-by gases and is then rerouted through a PCV valve to the intake manifold.

2   The main components of the PCV system are the PCV valve, a fresh air filtered inlet and the vacuum hoses connecting these two components with the engine and the EECS system.

3   To maintain idle quality, the PCV valve restricts the flow when the intake manifold vacuum is high. If abnormal operating conditions arise, the system is designed to allow excessive amounts of blow-by gases to flow back through the crankcase vent tube into the air cleaner to be consumed by normal combustion.

4   Checking and replacement of the PCV valve and filter is covered in Chapter 1.

---

9   Catalytic converter

GENERAL DESCRIPTION

1   The catalytic converter is an emission control device added to the exhaust system to reduce pollutants from the exhaust gas stream. A single-bed converter design is used in combination with a three-way (reduction) catalyst. The catalytic coating on the three-way catalyst contains platinum and rhodium, which lowers the levels of oxides of nitrogen (NOx) as well as hydrocarbons (HC) and carbon monoxide (CO).

CHECK

2   The test equipment for a catalytic converter is expensive and highly sophisticated. If you suspect that the converter on your vehicle is malfunctioning, take it to a dealer or authorized emissions inspection facility for diagnosis and repair.

3   Whenever the vehicle is raised for servicing of underbody components, check the converter for leaks, corrosion and other damage. If damage is discovered, the converter should be replaced.

REPLACEMENT

4   Because the converter is part of the exhaust system, converter replacement requires removal of the exhaust pipe assembly (see Chapter 4). Take the vehicle, or the exhaust system, to a dealer or a muffler shop.

Section

Reference to other Chapters

7A

MANUAL TRANSMISSION

1   General information

All vehicles covered in this manual come equipped with either a 5-speed manual transmission or a four-speed automatic transmission. All information on the manual transmission, is included in this Part of Chapter 7. Information for the automatic transmission can be found in Part B of this Chapter.

The manual transmission used in most models is a 5-speed unit known as the T5. 1996 and later models with the 4.6L engine use a heavier-duty unit known as the T45.

Due to the complexity, unavailability of replacement parts and the special tools necessary, internal repair procedures for these two units are not recommended for the home mechanic. The information contained within this manual will be limited to general information and removal and installation of the transmission assembly.

Depending on the expense involved in having a faulty transmission overhauled, it may be an advantage to consider replacing the unit with either a new or rebuilt one. Your local dealer or transmission shop should be able to supply you with information concerning cost, availability and exchange policy. Regardless of how you decide to remedy a transmission problem, you can still save considerable expense by removing and installing the unit yourself.

2   Shift lever - removal and installation

▶ Refer to illustrations 2.1 and 2.3

1   Remove the shift lever knob (see illustration).
2   Remove the shift lever trim bezel and boot (see Chapter 11).
3   Remove the two shift lever retaining bolts (see illustration).

4   To install, place the shift lever in position and install the retaining bolts. Tighten the bolts to the torque listed in this Chapter's Specifications.
5   Install the shift lever trim bezel and boot (see Chapter 11).
6   Install the shift lever knob and tighten it securely.

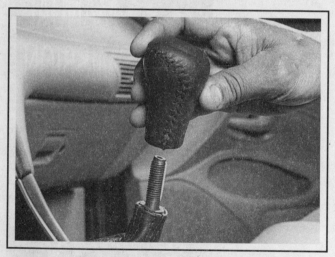

2.1 To remove the shift lever knob from the shift lever, simply unscrew it

2.3 To detach the shift lever, remove these two bolts (arrows)

3   Oil seal replacement

EXTENSION HOUSING SEAL

▶ Refer to illustrations 3.3 and 3.5

1   Oil leaks frequently occur due to wear of the extension housing oil seal and bushing (if equipped), and/or the speedometer drive gear oil seal and O-ring. Replacement of these seals is relatively easy, since the repairs can usually be performed without removing the transmission from the vehicle. The extension housing oil seal is located at the extreme rear of the transmission, where the driveshaft is attached. If leakage at the seal is suspected, raise the vehicle and support it securely on jackstands. If the seal is leaking, transmission lubricant will be built up on the front of the driveshaft and may be dripping from the rear of the transmission.

2   Disconnect the driveshaft from the transmission (see Chapter 8).

3   Using a seal removal tool or screwdriver (see illustrations), carefully pry the oil seal out of the rear of the transmission. Do not damage the splines on the transmission output shaft.

4   If the oil seal cannot be removed with a screwdriver or prybar, a special oil seal puller (available at auto parts stores) will be required.

5   Using a large section of pipe or a very large deep socket as a drift, install the new oil seal. Drive it into the bore squarely and make sure it's completely seated (see illustration).

6   Lubricate the splines of the transmission output shaft and the

3.3 Use a seal removal tool or screwdriver to pry the seal out of the transmission extension housing; make sure you don't gouge the seal bore

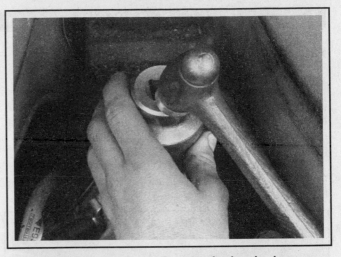

3.5 Place the seal square to the extension housing bore, then use a large socket to drive it into the bore; the outside diameter of the socket should be slightly smaller than the outside diameter of the seal

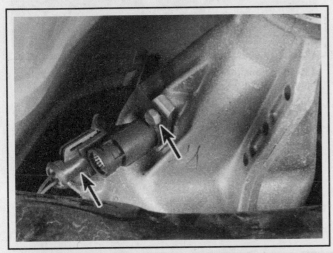

3.7 The vehicle speed sensor is located on the left side of the extension housing. To remove the sensor, unplug the electrical connector, then remove the hold-down bolt (arrows)

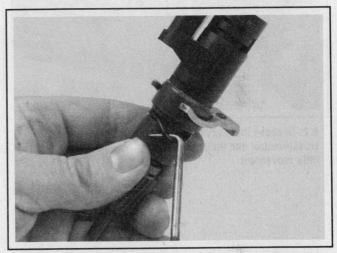

3.9 To replace the O-ring on the speed sensor, simply pull it off with a hooked tool, but be careful not to scratch the seal groove; be sure to lubricate the new O-ring with clean oil so it doesn't become twisted when the sensor is installed

outside of the driveshaft sleeve yoke with lightweight grease, then install the driveshaft. Be careful not to damage the lip of the new seal.

VEHICLE SPEED SENSOR O-RING

▶ **Refer to illustrations 3.7 and 3.9**

7   The vehicle speed sensor (see illustration) is located on the side of the extension housing. Look for transmission oil around the cable housing to determine if the seal and O-ring are leaking.

8   Unplug the electrical connector, remove the hold-down bolt (see illustration 3.7) and remove the sensor.

9   Remove the O-ring and install a new one (see illustration).

10 Installation is the reverse of removal. Be sure to lubricate the new seal with clean oil or multi-purpose grease before inserting the sensor into the transmission. Tighten the sensor hold-down bolt securely.

4   Transmission mount - check and replacement

▶ **Refer to illustrations 4.2 and 4.3**

1   Raise the vehicle and place it securely on jackstands.

2   Insert a large screwdriver or prybar into the space between the transmission extension housing and the crossmember and try to pry the transmission up slightly (see illustration). The transmission should not move away from the mount much at all. If it does, replace the mount.

3   To replace the mount, remove the bolts attaching the mount to the crossmember and to the transmission extension housing (see illustration).

4   Raise the transmission slightly with a jack and remove the mount.

5   Installation is the reverse of the removal procedure. Be sure to tighten the bolts securely.

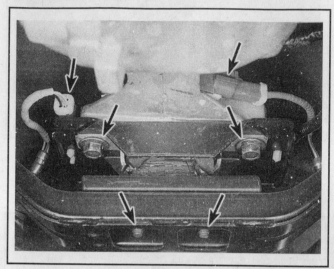

4.3 To replace the transmission mount, remove the bolts (middle arrows) that attach the mount to the transmission extension housing and the nuts (lower arrows) that attach the mount to the crossmember; it's not necessary to unplug the two electrical connectors (upper arrows) for the oxygen sensors, or detach the connectors from the extension housing, unless you're planning to remove the transmission

4.2 To check the transmission mount, pry between the crossmember and the mount - there should be very little movement

5   Manual transmission - removal and installation

▶ **Refer to illustrations 5.2, 5.4, 5.10, 5.11a and 5.11b**

REMOVAL

1   Disconnect the negative cable at the battery.

2   From inside the vehicle, remove the shift lever trim bezel (see Chapter 11) and the shift lever (see Section 2). Remove the lower shift lever dust boot (see illustration).

3   Raise the vehicle and support it securely on jackstands.

4   Unplug the electrical connectors for the vehicle speed sensor (see illustration 3.7), the back-up light switch (see illustration) and the oxygen sensors (see illustration 4.3). Unclip the left oxygen sensor connector from the transmission extension housing and the right connector from the rear crossmember, then tuck the electrical leads out of the way. Trace the other leads and make sure that any clips or brackets attaching them to the rear crossmember or transmission case are removed.

5   Disengage the clutch cable from the release lever (see Chapter 8).

6   Disconnect the driveshaft from the transmission (see Chapter 8).

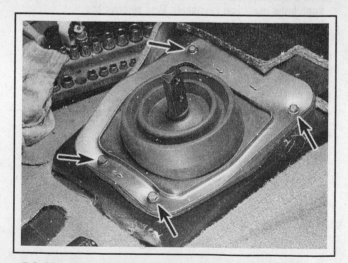

5.2 After removing the shift lever trim bezel and the shift lever, remove these four bolts (arrows) and remove the lower shift lever dust boot

5.4 Unplug the electrical connector from the back-up light switch

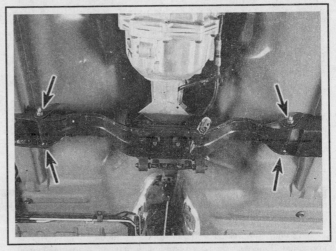

5.10 After you've unbolted the transmission mount from the transmission, raise the transmission slightly and remove the crossmember bolts and nuts (arrows)

Use a plastic bag to cover the end of the transmission to prevent fluid loss and contamination.

7   Remove the exhaust system components as necessary for clearance (see Chapter 4).

8   Support the engine. This can be done from above by using an engine hoist, or by placing a jack (with a block of wood as an insulator) under the engine oil pan. The engine should remain supported at all times while the transmission is out of the vehicle.

9   Support the transmission with a jack - preferably a special jack made for this purpose. Safety chains will help steady the transmission on the jack.

10   Unbolt the transmission mount from the transmission extension housing (see Section 4), raise the transmission slightly and remove the rear crossmember (see illustration).

11   Remove the bolts securing the transmission to the bellhousing (all models except 1996 and later models with a 4.6L engine). On 1996 and later models with a 4.6L engine, remove the bolts securing the transmission to the engine (see illustrations).

12   Make a final check that all wires and hoses have been disconnected from the transmission and then move the transmission and jack toward the rear of the vehicle until the transmission input shaft is clear of the bellhousing (3.8L and 5.0L models) or the clutch hub (4.6L models). Keep the transmission level as this is done.

13   Once the input shaft is clear, lower the transmission and remove it from under the vehicle.

14   Inspect the clutch components while the transmission is removed (see Chapter 8). (On 3.8L and 5.0L models, you'll have to remove the bellhousing.) In general, it's always a good idea to install new clutch components anytime the transmission is removed.

INSTALLATION

15   If removed, install the clutch components (see Chapter 8) and, on 3.8L and 5.0L models, the bellhousing.

16   With the transmission secured to the jack as on removal, raise the transmission into position, then carefully slide it forward, engaging the input shaft with the splines in the clutch hub. Do not use excessive force to install the transmission - if the input shaft does not slide into place, readjust the angle of the transmission so it is level and/or turn the input shaft so the splines engage properly with the clutch hub.

17   Install the transmission-to-bellhousing bolts (3.8L and 5.0L models) or the transmission bellhousing-to-engine bolts (4.6L models). Tighten the bolts to the torque listed in this Chapter's Specifications.

18   Install the rear crossmember and transmission mount (see Sec-

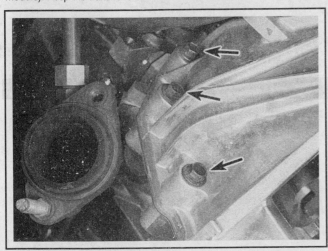

5.11a Left side transmission-to-engine bolts (arrows)

5.11b Right side transmission-to-engine bolts (arrows)

tion 4). Tighten all nuts and bolts securely.

19 Remove the jacks supporting the transmission and the engine.

20 Install the various items removed previously, referring to Chapter 8 for the installation of the driveshaft and Chapter 4 for information regarding the exhaust system components.

21 Reattach the clutch cable and install the release lever housing.

22 Reroute the electrical harnesses for the back-up light switch, the vehicle speed sensor and the oxygen sensors. Plug in all electrical con-nectors. Make sure the oxygen sensor connectors are clipped into the crossmember and transmission.

23 Fill the transmission with the recommended lubricant (see Chapter 1).

24 Remove all jackstands and lower the vehicle.

25 From inside the vehicle connect the shift lever (see Section 2).

26 Connect the negative battery cable. Road test the vehicle for proper operation and check for leakage.

6 Manual transmission overhaul - general information

Overhauling a manual transmission is a difficult job for the do-it-yourselfer. It involves the disassembly and reassembly of many small parts. Numerous clearances must be precisely measured and, if necessary, changed with select fit spacers and snap-rings. If transmission problems arise, you can remove and install the transmission yourself, but overhaul should be left to a transmission repair shop. Rebuilt trans-missions may be available - check with your dealer parts department and auto parts stores. At any rate, the time and money involved in an overhaul is almost sure to exceed the cost of a rebuilt unit.

Nevertheless, it's not impossible for an inexperienced mechanic to rebuild a transmission if the special tools are available and the job is done in a deliberate step-by-step manner so nothing is overlooked.

The tools necessary for an overhaul include internal and external snap-ring pliers, a bearing puller, a slide hammer, a set of pin punches, a dial indicator and possibly a hydraulic press. In addition, a large, sturdy workbench and a vise or transmission stand will be required.

During disassembly of the transmission, make careful notes of how each piece comes off, where it fits in relation to other pieces and what holds it in place. Be sure to note how the parts are installed as you remove them; this will make it much easier to get the transmission back together.

Before taking the transmission apart for repair, it will help if you have some idea what area of the transmission is malfunctioning. Certain problems can be closely tied to specific areas in the transmission, which can make component examination and replacement easier. Refer to the *Troubleshooting* section at the front of this manual for informa-tion regarding possible sources of trouble.

Specifications

General

Transmission type	
1996 and 1997 4.6L V8 models	T45
1998 and later V8 models	T50 D
2001 and later GT models	TR3650
All other models	T5
Lubricant type	See Chapter 1

Torque specifications

	Ft-lbs
Shift lever retaining bolts	23 to 31
Transmission-to-bellhousing bolts (T5)	45 to 64
Transmission bellhousing-to-engine bolts	
1998 4.6L engine	39 to 54
All other engines and years	28 to 38

Section

1　General information
2　Diagnosis - general
3　Shift cable - check, adjustment and replacement
4　Neutral start switch - general information
5　Shift interlock system - description and check
6　Automatic transmission - removal and installation

Reference to other Chapters

7B

AUTOMATIC TRANSMISSION

1 General information

The vehicles covered in this manual are equipped with either a five-speed manual or a four-speed automatic transmission. Information on manual transmissions can be found in Chapter 7 Part A. This part of Chapter 7 covers the automatic transmission. 1994 and 1995 models use an AODE (overdrive electronic four-speed); 1996 and later models use a 4R70W (overdrive electronic four-speed) automatic transmission.

Due to the complexity of the automatic transmissions covered in this manual and the need for specialized equipment to perform most service operations, this Chapter contains only general diagnosis, rou-tine maintenance, adjustment and removal and installation procedures. For information regarding the diagnostic trouble codes for AODE transmissions, refer to Chapter 6.

If the transmission requires major repair work, it should be left to a dealer service department or an automotive transmission repair shop. You can, however, remove and install the transmission yourself and save the expense, even if the repair work is done by a transmission shop.

2 Diagnosis - general

➡Note: Automatic transmission malfunctions may be caused by five general conditions: poor engine performance, improper adjustments, hydraulic malfunctions, mechanical malfunctions or malfunctions in the computer or its signal network. Diagnosis of these problems should always begin with a check of the easily repaired items: fluid level and condition (see Chapter 1), shift linkage adjustment and throttle linkage adjustment. Next, perform a road test to determine if the problem has been corrected or if more diagnosis is necessary. If the problem persists after the preliminary tests and corrections are completed, additional diagnosis should be done by a dealer service department or transmission repair shop. Refer to the troubleshooting Section at the front of this manual for information on symptoms of transmission problems.

PRELIMINARY CHECKS

1   Drive the vehicle to warm the transmission to normal operating temperature.

2   Check the fluid level as described in Chapter 1:

a) If the fluid level is unusually low, add enough fluid to bring the level within the designated area of the dipstick, then check for external leaks (see below).

b) If the fluid level is abnormally high, drain off the excess, then check the drained fluid for contamination by coolant. The presence of engine coolant in the automatic transmission fluid indicates that a failure has occurred in the internal radiator walls that separate the coolant from the transmission fluid (see Chapter 3).

c) If the fluid is foaming, drain it and refill the transmission, then check for coolant in the fluid or a high fluid level.

3   Check the engine idle speed.

➡Note: If the engine is malfunctioning, do not proceed with the preliminary checks until it has been repaired and runs normally.

4   Inspect the shift control linkage (see Section 3). Make sure that it's properly adjusted and that the linkage operates smoothly.

FLUID LEAK DIAGNOSIS

5   Most fluid leaks are easy to locate visually. Repair usually consists of replacing a seal or gasket. If a leak is difficult to find, the following procedure may help.

6   Identify the fluid. Make sure it's transmission fluid and not engine oil or brake fluid (automatic transmission fluid is a deep red color).

7   Try to pinpoint the source of the leak. Drive the vehicle several miles, then park it over a large sheet of cardboard. After a minute or two, you should be able to locate the leak by determining the source of the fluid dripping onto the cardboard.

8   Make a careful visual inspection of the suspected component and the area immediately around it. Pay particular attention to gasket mating surfaces. A mirror is often helpful for finding leaks in areas that are hard to see.

9   If the leak still cannot be found, clean the suspected area thoroughly with a degreaser or solvent, then dry it.

10   Drive the vehicle for several miles at normal operating temperature and varying speeds. After driving the vehicle, visually inspect the suspected component again.

11   Once the leak has been located, the cause must be determined before it can be properly repaired. If a gasket is replaced but the sealing flange is bent, the new gasket will not stop the leak. The bent flange must be straightened.

12   Before attempting to repair a leak, check to make sure that the following conditions are corrected or they may cause another leak.

➡Note: Some of the following conditions cannot be fixed without highly specialized tools and expertise. Such problems must be referred to a transmission repair shop or a dealer service department.

GASKET LEAKS

13   Check the pan periodically. Make sure the bolts are tight, no bolts are missing, the gasket is in good condition and the pan is flat (dents in the pan may indicate damage to the valve body inside).

14   If the pan gasket is leaking, the fluid level or the fluid pressure may be too high, the vent may be plugged, the pan bolts may be too tight, the pan sealing flange may be warped, the sealing surface of the transmission housing may be damaged, the gasket may be damaged or the transmission casting may be cracked or porous. If sealant instead of gasket material has been used to form a seal between the pan and the transmission housing, it may be the wrong sealant.

SEAL LEAKS

15   If a transmission seal is leaking, the fluid level or pressure may be too high, the vent may be plugged, the seal bore may be damaged, the seal itself may be damaged or improperly installed, the surface of the shaft protruding through the seal may be damaged or a loose bear-

ing may be causing excessive shaft movement.

16 Make sure the dipstick tube seal is in good condition and the tube is properly seated. Periodically check the area around the speedometer gear or sensor for leakage. If transmission fluid is evident, check the O-ring for damage.

CASE LEAKS

1/ If the case itself appears to be leaking, the casting is porous and will have to be repaired or replaced.

18 Make sure the oil cooler hose fittings are tight and in good condition.

FLUID COMES OUT VENT PIPE OR FILL TUBE

19 If this condition occurs, the transmission is overfilled, there is coolant in the fluid, the case is porous, the dipstick is incorrect, the vent is plugged or the drain-back holes are plugged.

ELECTRONIC CONTROL SYSTEM

20 The Powertrain Control Module has special diagnostic trouble codes for the transmission. For information on these codes, refer to Chapter 6.

---

3 Shift cable - check, adjustment and replacement

CHECK

1 Try to start the engine in each shift lever position; the starter should operate in Park and Neutral only. If the starter does not operate in Park or Neutral or operates in any position other than Park and Neutral, the shift linkage is in need of adjustment or the Transmission Range sensor is defective (see Chapter 6).

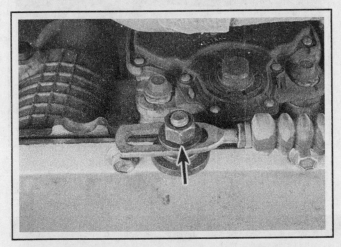

3.4 Loosen this nut to adjust the shift cable (remove it to replace the cable)

ADJUSTMENT

▶ **Refer to illustrations 3.4, 3.5a and 3.5b**

2 Put the shift lever in the Drive position; make sure the shift lever is positioned against the rear Drive stop.

3 Raise the vehicle and support it securely on jackstands.

4 Loosen the shift cable-to-manual lever retaining nut (see illustration).

5 Move the manual lever to the Drive position by moving the lever all the way forward, until it stops, then pulling it back three detent positions (see illustrations).

6 With both the shift lever and manual lever now in the Drive positions, tighten the shift cable-to-manual lever adjusting nut securely.

7 After adjustment, check the operation of the transmission in each shift lever position.

REPLACEMENT

▶ **Refer to illustrations 3.10, 3.11, 3.13 and 3.14**

8 Put the shift lever in the Drive position.

9 Raise the vehicle, if you haven't already done so.

10 Locate the shift cable bracket (see illustration) on the left side of the driveshaft tunnel, just behind the shift lever, and remove the bracket retaining bolts.

3.5a To adjust the shift cable, move the manual lever all the way forward . . .

3.5b . . . then pull it back three clicks; it's now in the Drive position

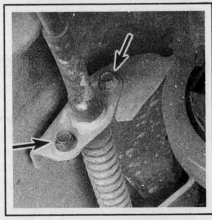

3.10 To detach this shift cable bracket from the left side of the driveshaft tunnel, remove these bolts (arrows)

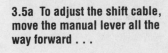

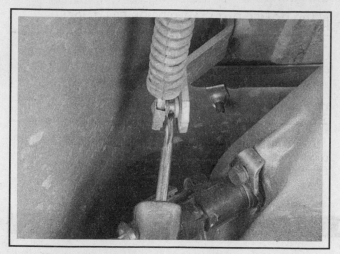

3.11 To detach the shift cable from the shift lever ball stud, pry it off with a screwdriver

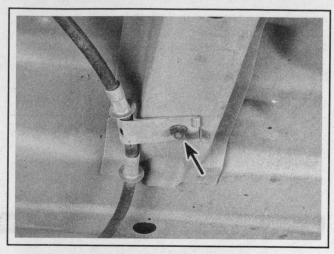

3.13 To detach the shift cable from the floorpan, remove this bolt (arrow)

11 Detach the shift cable from the shift lever ball stud (see illustration).

12 Raise the vehicle and place it securely on jackstands.

13 Remove the shift cable clip retaining bolt from the floorpan (see illustration).

14 Remove the shift cable bracket retaining bolts (see illustration) from the transmission.

15 Remove the shift cable-to-manual lever retaining nut (see illustration 3.4) and detach the shift cable from the manual lever.

16 Installation is the reverse of removal. Make sure the cable is adjusted properly (see Steps 2 through 7).

17 Check the operation of the transmission in each shift lever position. Verify that the Transmission Range sensor is functioning properly (see Chapter 6).

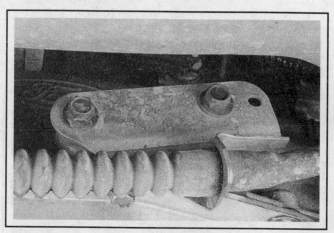

3.14 To detach this shift cable bracket from the transmission, remove these two bolts

4   Neutral start switch - general information

The AODE and 4R70W transmissions used on the vehicles covered in this manual do not have a neutral start switch. That function had been incorporated into an information sensor known as the Transmission Range (TR) sensor. For information on checking and replacing the TR sensor, refer to Chapter 6.

5   Shift interlock system - description and check

DESCRIPTION

1   The shift interlock system prevents the shift lever from being moved out of the Park position unless the brake pedal is depressed. The system consists of a shift lock actuator assembly at the key interlock assembly. When the ignition key is turned to the On position, the solenoid is energized, locking the shift lever in the Park position. When the brake pedal is depressed, the brake light switch is activated, which deactivates the shift solenoid, allowing the shift lever to be moved out of Park.

CHECK

♦ **Refer to illustration 5.7**

2   Make sure the shift lever is in the Park position, then start the engine.

3   With the ignition switch in the Run position, and with your foot off the brake, verify that the shift lever can't be moved out of the Park position.

4   Apply the brake pedal, then verify that the shift lever can be

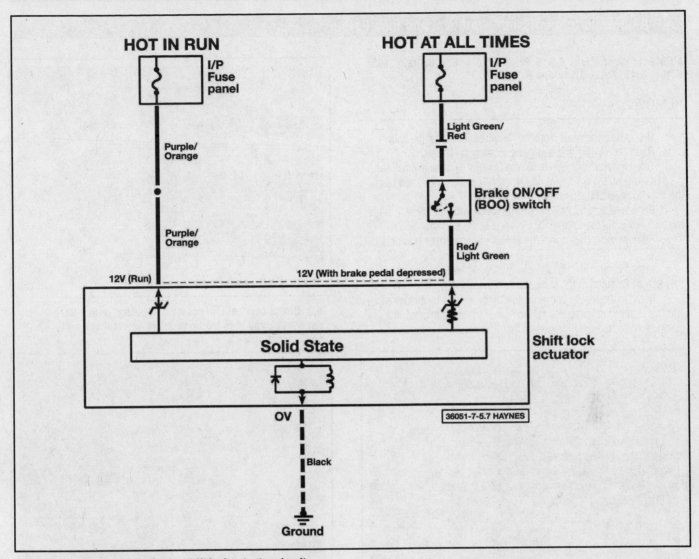

5.7 Electrical schematic for the shift lock actuator circuit

shifted out of Park.

5   Shift into the Reverse position, then verify that the ignition key can't be turned to the Lock position.

6   Shift into the Park position, then verify that the ignition key can be turned to the Lock position.

7   If the transmission can be shifted out of Park when the ignition switch is in the Run position and the brake pedal is not depressed, either:

a) *There's no power to the shift lock actuator: Check Fuse 1 (see Chapter 12).*

b) *There's an open ground circuit: check continuity of the black wire between the shift lock actuator and ground (see illustration).*

c) *The shift lock actuator or the cable is defective: with the shift lock actuator energized, there should be no cable freeplay at the shift lever; with the actuator de-energized, the there should be cable freeplay at the shift lever.*

8   If the transmission can't be shifted out of Park when the ignition switch in the Run position and the brake pedal is depressed, either:

a) *The brake on/off switch is inoperative: connect a jumper wire across the brake on/off switch with the ignition switch in the Run position. If the actuator unlocks, check the brake on/off switch. If the actuator remains locked, check the continuity of the red and light green wire between the brake on/off switch and the shift lock actuator (see illustration 5.7).*

b) *The shift lock actuator or the cable is defective: with the shift lock actuator energized, there should be no cable freeplay at the shift lever; with the actuator de-energized, the there should be cable freeplay at the shift lever.*

6 Automatic transmission - removal and installation

♦ Refer to illustrations 6.3, 6.5a, 6.5b, 6.6, 6.7, 6.10a, 6.10b, 6.10c, 6.16, 6.17, 6.18a and 6.18b

REMOVAL

1 Disconnect the cable from the negative terminal of the battery.

2 Raise the vehicle and support it securely on jackstands.

3 Drain the transmission fluid (see Chapter 1), then reinstall the pan. Disconnect the oil cooler line fittings (see illustration) and plug the lines to prevent contamination.

4 Remove any exhaust components which will interfere with transmission removal (see Chapter 4).

5 Remove the torque converter access plug and plate (see illustrations).

6 Mark the relationship of the torque converter to the driveplate so they can be installed in the same position (see illustration).

7 Remove the torque converter-to-driveplate nuts (see illustration). Turn the crankshaft for access to each nut. Turn the crankshaft in a clockwise direction only (as viewed from the front).

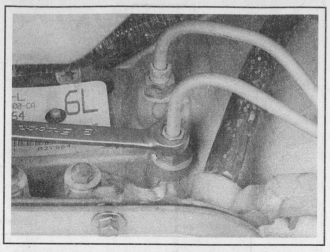

6.3 Disconnect both oil cooler line fittings with a flare-nut wrench and plug the lines to prevent leakage and contamination

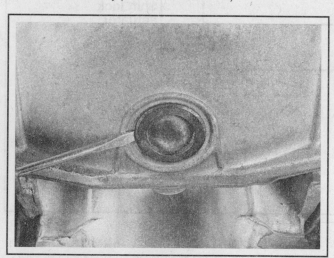

6.5a Pry off the torque converter access plug . . .

6.5b . . . and the torque converter access plate

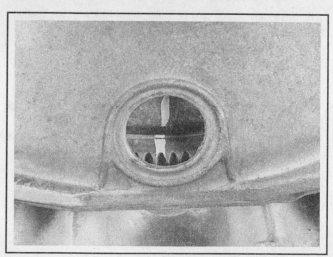

6.6 Mark the relationship of the torque converter to the driveplate to preserve the converter's balance when it's installed again

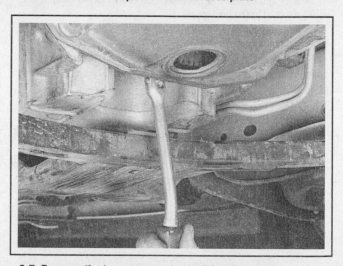

6.7 Remove the torque converter-to-driveplate nuts

6.10a Unplug the electrical connectors from the speed sensor . . .

6.10b . . . the Transmission Range sensor . . .

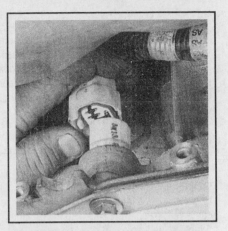

6.10c . . . and the torque converter clutch solenoid

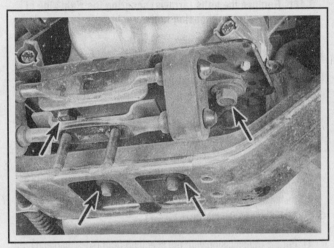

6.16 Remove the transmission mount-to-crossmember nuts and bolts (arrows)

8   Rotate the torque converter until the drain plug is at its lowest point. Place the pan under the torque converter, remove the drain plug and allow the fluid to drain. Install the drain plug and tighten it securely.

9   Remove the driveshaft (see Chapter 8).

10 Unplug the electrical connectors from the speed sensor, the Transmission Range sensor, the torque converter clutch solenoid (see illustrations) and any other electrical devices located on the transmission.

11 Detach all wiring harnesses from the transmission and secure them out of the way so they won't be damaged during transmission removal and installation.

12 Disconnect the shift cable from the manual lever and from the transmission cable bracket (see Section 3).

13 Remove the starter motor (see Chapter 5).

14 Support the engine with a hoist from above or with a jack from below. If a jack is used, place a block of wood under the oil pan to spread the load.

15 Support the transmission with a jack - preferably a jack made for this purpose. Safety chains will help secure the transmission to the jack.

16 Remove the transmission mount-to-crossmember nuts and bolts (see illustration).

17 Raise the transmission slightly, remove the crossmember-to-frame nuts and bolts (see illustration), then remove the crossmember and lower the jack a few inches (as this is done, the engine will have to be lowered, too.

18 Remove the bolts securing the lower part of the transmission bellhousing to the engine (see illustrations).

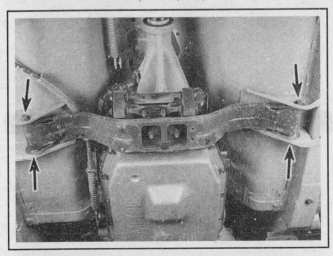

6.17 Remove the crossmember-to-frame nuts and bolts (arrows), then remove the crossmember

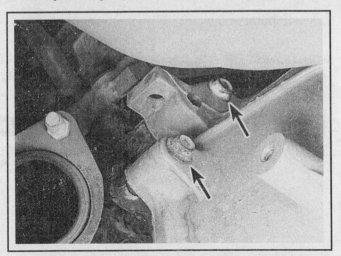

6.18a Remove the bolts (arrows) securing the left side of the transmission bellhousing to the engine

19 Lower the transmission slightly.

20 Remove the upper transmission bellhousing-to-engine bolts.

21 Remove the transmission dipstick tube.

22 Move the transmission to the rear to disengage it from the engine block dowel pins and make sure the torque converter is detached from the driveplate. Secure the torque converter to the transmission so it won't fall out during removal.

INSTALLATION

23 Prior to installation, make sure the torque converter hub is securely engaged in the pump. This can be done by turning the torque converter while pushing it in toward the transmission. If the converter was not fully engaged, it will "clunk" into place (it may even "clunk" more than once).

24 With the transmission secured to the jack, raise it into position. Be sure to keep it level so the torque converter does not slide forward.

25 Turn the torque converter to line up the studs with the holes in the driveplate. The marks on the torque converter and driveplate made in Step 5 must line up.

26 Move the transmission forward carefully until the dowel pins and the torque converter are engaged.

27 Install the transmission-to-engine bolts. Tighten them to the torque listed in this Chapter's Specifications.

✳✳ CAUTION:

Do not force the engine and transmission together by tightening the bolts.

28 Install the torque converter-to-driveplate nuts. Tighten the nuts to the torque listed in this Chapter's Specifications.

29 Connect the transmission fluid cooler lines.

30 Install the transmission mount and crossmember through-bolts.

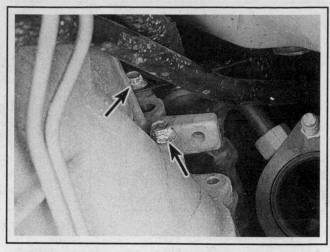

6.18b Remove the bolts (arrows) securing the right side of the transmission bellhousing to the engine

Tighten the bolts and nuts securely.

31 Remove the jacks supporting the transmission and the engine.

32 Install the dipstick tube. Install the oil cooler line fittings and tighten them securely.

33 Install the starter motor (see Chapter 5).

34 Connect the shift cable (see Section 3).

35 Plug in all transmission electrical connectors.

36 Install the torque converter cover plate and plug.

37 Install the driveshaft (see Chapter 8).

38 Adjust the shift cable (see Section 3).

39 Install any exhaust system components that were removed or disconnected (see Chapter 4).

40 Lower the vehicle.

41 Fill the transmission with the specified fluid (see Chapter 1), run the engine and check for fluid leaks.

Specifications

General

Transmission type	
1994 and 1995	AODE
1996 and later	4R70W

Torque specifications

	Ft-lbs
Transmission-to-engine bolts	40 to 50
Torque converter-to-driveplate nuts	20 to 33

Section

Reference to other Chapters

8

CLUTCH AND DRIVETRAIN

1 General information

The information in this Chapter deals with the components from the rear of the engine to the rear wheels, except for the transmission, which is dealt with in the previous Chapter. For the purposes of this Chapter, these components are grouped into three categories; clutch, driveshaft and rear axle. Separate Sections within this Chapter offer general descriptions and checking procedures for each of these three groups.

Since nearly all the procedures covered in this Chapter involve working under the vehicle, make sure it's securely supported on sturdy jackstands or on a hoist where the vehicle can be easily raised and lowered.

2 Clutch - description and check

1   All vehicles with a manual transmission use a single dry plate, diaphragm spring type clutch. The clutch disc has a splined hub which allows it to slide along the splines of the transmission input shaft. The clutch and pressure plate are held in contact by spring pressure exerted by the diaphragm in the pressure plate.

2   The clutch release system is cable operated. The release system includes the clutch pedal, the clutch cable, the release lever and the release bearing.

3   When the clutch pedal is depressed, it pulls the clutch cable, which pulls the release lever forward. As the lever is pulled forward, it slides the release bearing forward along the input shaft, and the release bearing pushes against the fingers of the diaphragm spring in the pressure plate assembly, which releases the clutch plate.

4   Terminology can be a problem regarding the clutch components because common names have in some cases changed from that used by the manufacturer. For example, the driven plate is also called the clutch plate or disc and the clutch release bearing is sometimes called a throwout bearing.

5   Unless you're replacing components with obvious damage, perform some preliminary checks to diagnose a clutch system malfunction.

a) To check "clutch spin down time," run the engine at normal idle speed with the transmission in Neutral (clutch pedal up - engaged). Disengage the clutch (pedal down), wait nine seconds and shift the transmission into Reverse. No grinding noise should be heard. A grinding noise would most likely indicate a problem in the pressure plate or the clutch disc.

b) To check for complete clutch release, run the engine (with the parking brake applied to prevent movement) and hold the clutch pedal approximately 1/4-inch from the floor. Shift the transmission between 1st gear and Reverse several times. If the shift is not smooth, component failure is indicated.

c) Visually inspect the clutch pedal bushing at the top of the clutch pedal to make sure there is no sticking or excessive wear.

d) A clutch pedal that is difficult to operate is most likely caused by a faulty clutch cable. Check the cable where it enters the casing for fraying, rust or other signs of corrosion. If it looks good, lubricate the cable with penetrating oil. If pedal operation improves, the cable is worn out and should be replaced.

3 Clutch cable and adjuster mechanism - replacement

CLUTCH CABLE

▶ **Refer to illustrations 3.2, 3.4, 3.5, 3.6a and 3.6b**

1   Remove the lower steering column trim panel (see Chapter 11).

2   Using a flashlight, locate the clutch pedal adjuster quadrant, which is located on the end of a shaft above the accelerator pedal. Pull the clutch pedal to the rear as far as it will go to disengage the adjuster pawl from the quadrant. Push the quadrant forward, unhook the cable (see illustration) and let the quadrant return slowly to its normal position.

✳ WARNING:

Allowing the quadrant - which is under spring tension - to snap back into position could cause possible injury. While the cable is removed, inspect the adjuster mechanism. If the teeth on the quadrant and/or the pawl are worn, the adjuster mechanism will slip instead of tensioning the cable. If the cable adjuster mechanism is faulty, replace it (refer to the following procedure).

3   Raise the vehicle and place it securely on jackstands.

4   Remove the clutch dust cover bolt (see illustration) and remove the cover.

5   Disengage the clutch cable from the clutch release lever (see illustration).

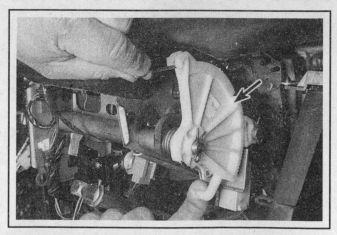

3.2 Using a flashlight, locate the clutch pedal adjuster quadrant (arrow), which is located above the accelerator pedal, pull the clutch pedal to the rear as far as it will go to disengage the adjuster pawl from the quadrant, push the quadrant forward, unhook the cable and let the quadrant return slowly to its normal position

✳ WARNING:

The quadrant is spring-loaded! Don't let it snap back into position or you could be injured

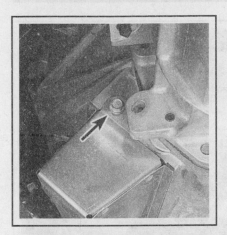

3.4 Remove the clutch dust cover bolt (arrow) and remove the cover

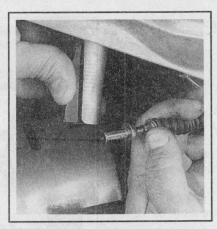

3.5 Push the release lever forward and disengage the clutch cable from the clutch release lever

3.6a Remove the C-clip . . .

6 Remove the C-clip and pull the cable through the cable guide boss on the transmission (see illustrations).

7 Unbolt the cable clamps from the left inner fender housing and the master cylinder.

8 Remove the screws that retain the cable housing to the firewall.

9 Pull the cable out of the firewall from the engine compartment side.

10 Insert the cable through the firewall from the engine compartment side, attach the cable housing to the firewall and tighten the screws securely.

11 Working under the dash, lift up on the clutch pedal, rotate the quadrant forward and hook the cable end into the quadrant. Slowly release the quadrant.

12 Install the clutch cable clamps on the master cylinder and left inner fender housing.

13 Route the cable through the cable guide boss on the transmission and install the C-clip.

14 Have an assistant pull back on the clutch pedal, rotate the quadrant forward and hold it there while you connect the cable to the clutch release lever. Depress the clutch pedal a few times to adjust the cable.

15 Install the lower steering column trim panel.

16 Check for proper operation of the clutch components before placing the vehicle in normal service.

ADJUSTER MECHANISM

▶ **Refer to illustrations 3.18, 3.19, 3.22, 3.23, 3.24, 3.25a, 3.25b, 3.26, 3.27, 3.29, 3.30a and 3.30b**

17 Disconnect the clutch cable (see clutch cable replacement above).

18 Remove the retainer from the quadrant pin (see illustration), disengage the quadrant spring from the clutch pedal shaft lever and remove the quadrant from the pin.

19 Remove the retainer from the pawl pin (see illustration), disengage the pawl spring from the clutch pedal shaft lever and remove the pawl from the pin.

20 Unplug the electrical connectors from the clutch pedal position switch (see Section 7), the brake light switch (see Chapter 9) and the cruise control switch (the switch located just below the pawl).

21 Disconnect the power brake pushrod and the brake light switch from the brake pedal (see Chapter 9).

22 Remove the pedal bracket assembly (see illustration). Besides the upper bracket retaining bolt, you will have to remove the four bracket-to-firewall nuts (see Chapter 9, "Power brake booster - check, removal, installation and adjustment").

23 Remove the clutch pedal shaft retaining nut (see illustration).

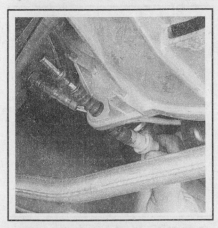

3.6b . . . and pull the cable forward, through the cable guide boss on the transmission

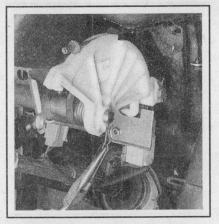

3.18 Remove the quadrant retainer from the quadrant pivot pin

3.19 Remove the pawl retainer from the pawl pivot pin

24 Pull the clutch pedal shaft out of the pedal bracket assembly (see illustration).

25 Remove the shaft bushings (see illustrations) and inspect them for wear; if they're worn, replace them.

26 Pry the pawl return spring off the pedal shaft lever (see illustration) and remove the pawl.

27 Install a new pawl on the lever. Make sure the pawl return spring is installed properly (see illustration). Install the retainer; use a new retainer if the old one is loose or weak.

28 Lubricate the clutch pedal shaft bushings with a little multi-purpose grease, install the bushings and install the clutch pedal shaft. Tighten the shaft retaining nut securely.

29 Install the return spring on the quadrant (see illustration). The straight end of the spring should be seated against the stop on the quadrant as shown.

30 Install the quadrant on the clutch pedal shaft lever, engage the hooked end of the quadrant return spring around the lower edge of the lever (see illustration), push the quadrant onto the lever pin and install the retainer (see illustration); use a new retainer if the old one is loose or weak.

31 Install the pedal bracket assembly. Tighten the bolts securely.

32 Reattach the power brake pushrod and the brake light switch to the brake pedal (see Chapter 9).

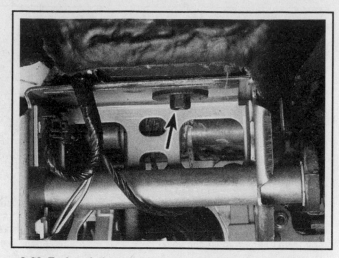

3.22 To detach the pedal bracket assembly from the vehicle, remove the upper bracket retaining bolt (arrow); you'll also have to remove the three bracket-to-firewall nuts and a fourth nut which can be accessed from the engine compartment side of the firewall (there are photos showing the location of these four nuts in Chapter 9)

3.23 Remove the clutch pedal shaft retaining nut

3.24 Pull the clutch pedal shaft out of the pedal bracket assembly

3.25a Remove the left clutch pedal shaft bushing . . .

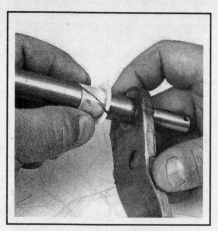

3.25b . . . and the right shaft bushing; inspect both bushings for cracks and wear, and replace them if necessary

3.26 To disengage the pawl from the clutch pedal shaft lever, pry off the return spring

3.27 Make sure the pawl return spring is properly installed as shown

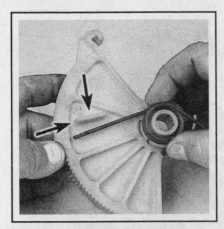

3.29 Install the quadrant return spring with the straight end of the spring seated against this stop on the quadrant

3.30a Make sure the hooked end of the quadrant return spring wraps around the lower edge of the clutch pedal shaft lever

3.30b Install the retainers in the pivot pins for the quadrant (shown) and the pawl

33 Plug in the electrical connectors for the clutch pedal position switch (see Section 7), the brake light switch (see Chapter 9) and the cruise control switch (the switch below the pawl).

34 Connect the clutch cable to the quadrant (see above).

35 Install the lower steering column trim panel (see Chapter 11).

4 Clutch components - removal, inspection and installation

✳✳ WARNING:

Dust produced by clutch wear and deposited on clutch components is hazardous to your health. DO NOT blow it out with compressed air and DO NOT inhale it. DO NOT use gasoline or petroleum-based solvents to remove the dust. Brake system cleaner should be used to flush the dust into a drain pan. After the clutch components are wiped clean with a rag, dispose of the contaminated rags and cleaner in a covered container.

REMOVAL

▶ **Refer to illustration 4.6**

1 Access to the clutch components is normally accomplished by removing the transmission, leaving the engine in the vehicle. If, of course, the engine is being removed for major overhaul, then the opportunity should always be taken to check the clutch for wear and replace worn components as necessary. The following procedures assume that the engine will stay in place.

2 Remove the transmission (see Chapter 7A). Support the engine while the transmission is out. An engine hoist is preferable. If a jack is used underneath the engine, make sure a piece of wood is used between the jack and oil pan to spread the load.

✳✳ CAUTION:

The pickup for the oil pump is very close to the bottom of the oil pan. If the pan is bent or distorted in any way, engine oil starvation could occur.

3 On 3.8L and 5.0L models, remove the bellhousing-to-engine

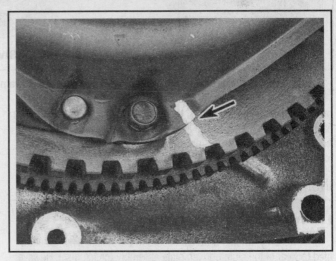

4.6 If you're going to re-use the same clutch pressure plate, but there are no existing marks, mark the relationship of the pressure plate to the flywheel

bolts and remove the bellhousing. If it's stuck, pry it off the alignment dowels with a screwdriver or prybar. On 2003 4.6L models, remove the starter motor (see Chapter 5).

4 The clutch fork and release bearing can remain attached to the housing for the time being.

5 To support the clutch disc during removal, install a clutch alignment tool through the clutch disc hub.

6 Carefully inspect the flywheel and pressure plate for indexing marks. The marks are usually an X, an O or a white letter. If they cannot be found, scribe marks yourself so the pressure plate and the flywheel will be in the same alignment during installation (see illustration).

7 Turning each bolt only 1/4-turn at a time, slowly loosen the

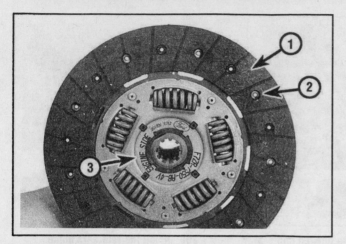

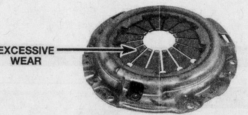

4.11 The clutch disc

1 *Lining* - this will wear down in use
2 *Rivets* - these secure the lining and will damage the flywheel or pressure plate if allowed to contact the surfaces
3 *Marks* - "flywheel side" or something similar

4.14a Examine the pressure plate friction surface for score marks, cracks and evidence of overheating (blue spots)

NORMAL FINGER WEAR **EXCESSIVE FINGER WEAR** **BROKEN OR BENT FINGERS**

EXCESSIVE WEAR

4.14b Replace the pressure plate if any of these conditions are noted

pressure plate-to-flywheel bolts. Work in a diagonal pattern and loosen each bolt a little at a time until all spring pressure is relieved. Then hold the pressure plate securely and completely remove the bolts, followed by the pressure plate and clutch disc.

INSPECTION

▶ **Refer to illustrations 4.11, 4.14a and 4.14b**

8 Ordinarily, when a problem occurs in the clutch, it can be attributed to wear of the clutch driven plate assembly (clutch disc). However, all components should be inspected at this time.

9 Inspect the flywheel for cracks, heat checking, grooves or other signs of obvious defects. If the imperfections are slight, a machine shop can machine the surface flat and smooth, which is highly recommended regardless of the surface appearance. Refer to Chapter 2 for the flywheel removal and installation procedure.

10 Inspect the pilot bearing (see Section 5).

11 Inspect the lining on the clutch disc. There should be at least 1/16-inch of lining above the rivet heads. Check for loose rivets, distortion, cracks, broken springs and other obvious damage (see illustration).

12 As mentioned above, ordinarily the clutch disc is replaced as a matter of course, so if in doubt about the condition, replace it with a new one.

13 Ordinarily, the release bearing is also replaced along with the clutch disc (see Section 5).

4.16 Center the clutch with an alignment tool, then tighten the bolts in a criss-cross fashion to the torque listed in this Chapter's Specifications

14 Check the machined surfaces and the diaphragm spring fingers of the pressure plate (see illustrations). If the surface is grooved or otherwise damaged, take it to a machine shop for possible machining or replacement. Also check for obvious damage, distortion, cracking, etc. Light glazing can be removed with medium grit emery cloth. If a new pressure plate is indicated, new or factory-rebuilt units are available.

INSTALLATION

▶ **Refer to illustration 4.16**

15 Before installation, carefully wipe the flywheel and pressure plate machined surfaces clean. It's important that no oil or grease is on these surfaces or the lining of the clutch disc. Handle these parts only with clean hands.

16 Position the clutch disc and pressure plate with the clutch held in place with an alignment tool (see illustration). Make sure it's Installed properly (most replacement clutch plates will be marked "flywheel side" or something similar - if not marked, install the clutch disc with the damper springs toward the transmission).

17 Tighten the pressure plate-to-flywheel bolts only finger tight, working around the pressure plate.

18 Center the clutch disc by inserting the alignment tool through the splined hub and into the pilot bearing in the crankshaft. Tighten the pressure plate-to-flywheel bolts a little at a time, working in a criss-cross pattern to prevent distorting the cover. After all of the bolts are snug, tighten them to the specified torque. Remove the alignment tool.

19 Using high temperature grease, lubricate the inner groove of the release bearing (see Section 5). Also place grease on the release lever contact areas.

20 Install the clutch release bearing (see Section 4).

21 On 3.8L and 5.0L models, install the bellhousing and tighten the bolts to the torque listed in this Chapter's Specifications. On 2003 4.6L models, install the starter motor (see Chapter 5).

22 Install the transmission (see Chapter 7A).

5 Clutch release bearing - removal, inspection and installation

REMOVAL

▶ **Refer to illustration 5.4**

1 Raise the vehicle and place it securely on jackstands.

2 Remove the transmission (see Chapter 7A).

3 Remove the bellhousing (see Section 4).

4 Remove the clutch release lever from the ball stud, then remove the bearing from the lever (see illustration).

INSPECTION

▶ **Refer to illustrations 5.5a, 5.5b and 5.5c**

5 Hold the center of the bearing and rotate the outer portion while applying pressure (see illustration). If the bearing doesn't turn smoothly or if it's noisy, replace it with a new one. Wipe the bearing with a clean rag and inspect it for damage, wear and cracks. The bearing is sealed for life, so don't immerse it in solvent or you'll ruin it. Inspect the friction surfaces and the bearing retainer on the release lever (see illustrations). If the friction surfaces are worn excessively, or the retainer fingers are weak, bent or broken, replace the release lever.

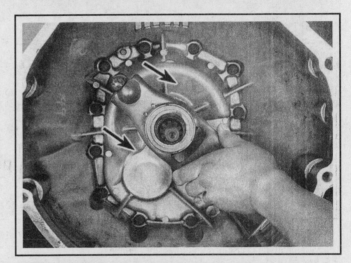

5.4 To disengage the clutch release lever from the fulcrum ball stud, pull the release lever in the direction of the arrows until it pops loose

5.5a To check the release bearing, hold it by the outer cage and rotate the inner race while applying a side load to it - the bearing should turn smoothly and easily; if it doesn't, replace it

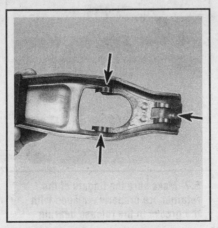

5.5b Inspect the fulcrum ball stud socket (right arrow) for wear and make sure the retainer fingers (arrows) are still strong; if the socket is worn, or the fingers are weak, bent or broken, replace the release lever

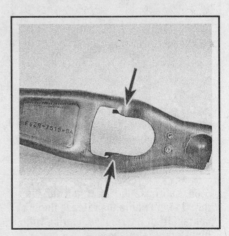

5.5c Flip the release lever over and inspect the friction surfaces (arrows) that push the release bearing; if they're excessively worn, replace the release lever

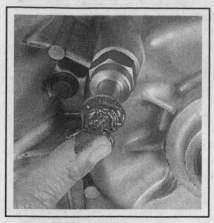

5.6a Lubricate the release lever fulcrum stud . . .

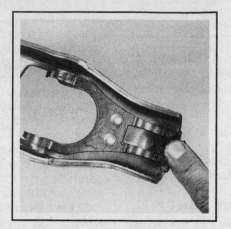

5.6b . . . the fulcrum ball stud socket . . .

5.6c . . . the retainer fingers . . .

INSTALLATION

▶ Refer to illustrations 5.6a, 5.6b, 5.6c, 5.6d, 5.6e, 5.7 and 5.8

6   Lightly lubricate the release lever fulcrum ball stud, the release lever and the release bearing with high temperature grease (see illustrations).

7   Attach the release bearing to the clutch lever (see illustration).

8   Push the release lever onto the ball stud until it's firmly seated (see illustration).

9   Apply a light coat of high temperature grease to the face of the release bearing, where it contacts the pressure plate diaphragm fingers.

10 On 3.8L and 5.0L models, install the bellhousing and tighten the bolts to the torque listed in this Chapter's Specifications.

11 Install the transmission (see Chapter 7A).

12 Remove the jackstands and lower the vehicle.

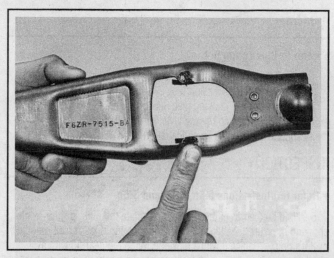

5.6d . . . and the friction surfaces of the release lever

5.6e Lubricate the inner hub and the thrust side (where the release fingers contact it) of the release bearing with high-temperature grease

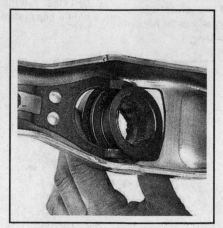

5.7 Make sure the fingers of the retainer are properly engaged with the groove in the release bearing

5.8 This is how the release bearing and release lever should look when properly installed; don't forget to lubricate the front bearing surface (arrows) of the release bearing

6   Pilot bearing - inspection and replacement

▶ **Refer to illustrations 6.1, 6.5, 6.8, 6.9 and 6.10**

1   The clutch pilot bearing (see illustration) is a needle roller type bearing which is pressed into the rear of the crankshaft. It is greased at the factory and does not require additional lubrication. Its primary purpose is to support the front of the transmission input shaft. The pilot bearing should be inspected whenever the clutch components are removed from the engine. Due to its inaccessibility, if you are in doubt as to its condition, replace it with a new one.

➡ **Note: If the engine has been removed from the vehicle, disregard the following steps which do not apply.**

2   Remove the transmission (see Chapter 7A)
3   Remove the clutch components (see Section 4).
4   Inspect for any excessive wear, scoring, lack of grease, dryness or obvious damage. If any of these conditions are noted, the bearing should be replaced. A flashlight will be helpful to direct light into the recess.

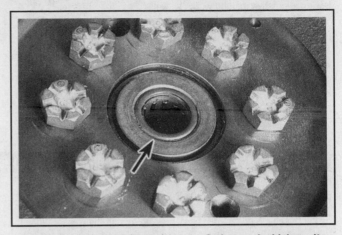

6.1 The pilot bearing (arrow) has an O-ring seal which can't be replaced separately; if there's any sign of leakage, or if the bearing is dry, replace the bearing and seal - neither can be replaced separately; make sure the seal faces out (toward the transmission)

6.5 Remove the old pilot bearing with a small slide-hammer, as shown, if you've got one

6.8 If you don't have a small slide-hammer, pack the cavity behind the pilot bearing with grease . . .

6.9 . . . then force out the bearing hydraulically with a steel rod or wood dowel slightly smaller in diameter than the bearing bore - when the hammer strikes the rod or dowel, the grease will transmit this force to the backside of the bearing and push it out

6.10 Use a large socket and hammer, or a soft-faced hammer, to install the new pilot bearing; make sure the O-ring seal faces out (toward the transmission) and make sure the bearing is fully seated

5 The pilot bearing can be removed with a special puller and slide hammer (see illustration), but if you don't have a suitable tool, the following alternative method works as well.

6 Obtain a solid steel bar or wood dowel which is slightly smaller in diameter than the bearing.

7 Check the bar or dowel for fit - it should just slip into the bearing with very little clearance.

8 Pack the bearing and the area behind it (in the crankshaft recess) with heavy grease (see illustration). Pack it tightly to eliminate as much air as possible.

9 Insert the bar or dowel into the bearing bore and strike it sharply with a hammer (see illustration); this will force the grease to the back-side of the bearing and push it out. Remove the bearing and clean all grease from the crankshaft recess.

10 To install the new bearing, lightly lubricate the outside surface with lithium-based grease, then drive it into the recess with a large socket (see illustration). Make sure that the seal faces out, toward the transmission.

11 Install the clutch components, transmission and all other components removed previously, tightening all fasteners properly.

7 Clutch pedal position switch - check and replacement

♦ **Refer to illustrations 7.1, 7.4, 7.6a and 7.6b**

1 The clutch pedal must be depressed to start the engine. When the pedal is depressed, the clutch pedal position switch closes the circuit between the ignition switch and the rest of the starting circuit (which includes the battery, starter relay and starter motor and, on some models, an anti-theft system). The switch (see illustration) is located at the top of the clutch pedal. To access the switch, remove the lower steering column trim panel (see Chapter 11).

2 The switch plunger contacts the clutch pedal when the pedal is in its normal position; the plunger is depressed and the circuit is open. When the clutch pedal is depressed, the spring-loaded plunger protrudes from the switch, closing the starter relay circuit, which in turn allows full battery voltage to the starter motor.

3 To check the switch, verify that the engine can be started only when the clutch pedal is depressed.

4 If the engine can be started without depressing the clutch pedal, the switch may be shorted. Unplug the switch connector and hook up an ohmmeter to the connector terminals for the red and blue wire and the white and pink wire (see illustration). There should be no continuity when the clutch pedal is released (switch plunger depressed), and continuity when the pedal is depressed (plunger released). If the switch doesn't operate as described, replace it.

5 If the engine can't be started even when the clutch pedal is depressed, either the switch is bad, the electrical connector is unplugged, or there's a ground, open or short in the circuit between the ignition switch and the clutch pedal position switch, or between the pedal position switch and the rest of the starter circuit. Check the

7.1 The clutch pedal position switch (arrow) is located at the top of the clutch pedal

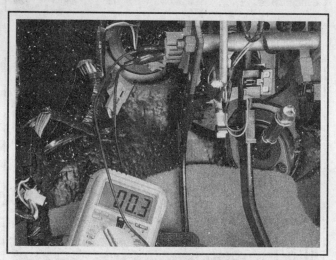

7.4 To check the operation of the switch, unplug the switch electrical connector and hook up an ohmmeter to the terminals for the red and light blue and the pink and white wires; with the clutch pedal released, there should be no continuity, but when the pedal is depressed, there should be continuity (shown)

7.6a To remove the clutch pedal position switch, unplug the switch electrical connector, remove the cotter pin that secures the switch pushrod to the pin at the top of the clutch pedal . . .

7.6b . . . remove the switch retaining bolt (arrow) and slide the pushrod to the right to disengage it from the clutch pedal pin

switch as described in the previous step. If the switch is okay, refer to the *Wiring Diagrams* at the end of Chapter 12 and troubleshoot the circuit.

6   To remove the clutch pedal position switch, disconnect the negative battery cable, unplug the switch electrical connector, remove the cotter pin (see illustration) that secures the switch pushrod to the pin at the top of the clutch pedal, remove the switch mounting bolt (see illustrations). and push the pushrod off the clutch pedal pin at the top of the clutch pedal.

7   Installation is the reverse of removal.

8   Driveshaft - inspection

1   Raise the rear of the vehicle and support it securely on jackstands.

2   Crawl under the vehicle and visually inspect the driveshaft. Look for any dents or cracks in the tubing. If any are found, the driveshaft must be replaced.

3   Check for any oil leakage at the front and rear of the driveshaft. Leakage where the driveshaft enters the transmission indicates a defective transmission rear seal. Leakage where the driveshaft enters the differential indicates a defective pinion seal.

4   While under the vehicle, have an assistant turn the rear wheel so

the driveshaft will rotate. As it does, make sure the universal joints are operating properly without binding, noise or looseness.

5   The universal joints can also be checked with the driveshaft motionless, by gripping your hands on either side of the joint and attempting to twist the joint. Any movement at all in the joint is a sign of considerable wear. Lifting up on the shaft will also indicate movement in the universal joints.

6   Finally, check the driveshaft mounting bolts at the ends to make sure they are tight.

9   Driveshaft - removal and installation

▶ **Refer to illustrations 9.2 and 9.3**

1   Raise the rear of the vehicle an support it securely on jackstands.

2   Mark the relationship of the driveshaft to the differential companion flange (see illustration).

3   Remove the bolts and separate the driveshaft from the differential companion flange with a 12-point socket or box end wrench (see illus-

tration). Pull the driveshaft toward the rear to remove it.

4   Wrap a plastic bag tightly around the extension housing of the transmission to prevent fluid loss.

5   Installation is the reverse of removal. Be sure to align the reference marks made during removal.

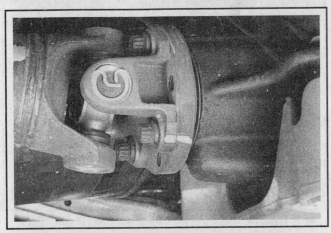

9.2 Mark the relationship of the driveshaft to the differential companion flange to ensure that the driveshaft retains its dynamic balance after reinstalling it

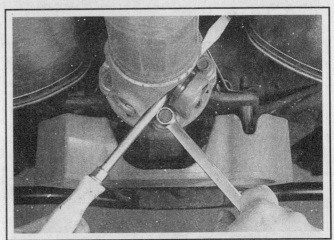

9.3 To remove the bolts that attach the driveshaft to the differential companion flange, insert a small prybar or large screwdriver through the rear U-joint and hold the driveshaft while you break loose the four flange bolts

10 Universal joints - replacement

▶ Refer to illustrations 10.2a, 10.2b, 10.4 and 10.9

➡**Note: A press or large vise will be required for this procedure. It may be advisable to take the driveshaft to a local dealer service department, service station or machine shop where the universal joints can be replaced for you, normally at a reasonable charge.**

1 Remove the driveshaft as outlined in the previous Section.

2 Using a small pair of pliers, remove the snap-rings from the spider (see illustrations).

3 Supporting the driveshaft, place it in position on a workbench equipped with a vise.

4 Place a piece of pipe or a large socket with the same inside diameter over one of the bearing caps. Position a socket which is of slightly smaller diameter than the cap on the opposite bearing cap (see illustration) and use the vise or press to force the cap out (inside the pipe or large socket), stopping just before it comes completely out of the yoke. Use the vise or large pliers to work the cap the rest of the way out.

5 Transfer the sockets to the other side and press the opposite bearing cap out in the same manner.

6 Pack the new universal joint bearings with grease. Ordinarily, specific instructions for lubrication will be included with the universal joint servicing kit and should be followed carefully.

7 Position the spider in the yoke and partially install one bearing cap in the yoke.

8 Start the spider into the bearing cap and then partially install the other cap. Align the spider and press the bearing caps into position, being careful not to damage the dust seals.

9 Install the snap-rings. If difficulty is encountered in seating the snap-rings, strike the driveshaft yoke sharply with a hammer (see illustration). This will spring the yoke ears slightly and allow the snap-rings to seat in the groove.

10 Install the grease fitting and fill the joint with grease. Be careful not to overfill the joint, as this could blow out the grease seals.

11 Install the driveshaft, tightening the companion flange bolts to the torque listed in this Chapter's Specifications.

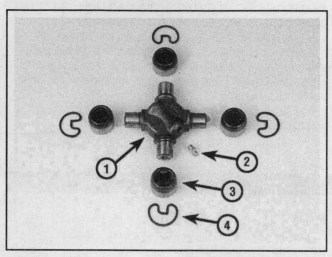

10.2a Exploded view of the universal joint components

1	Spider	3	Seal, bearings and cap
2	Grease fitting	4	Snap ring

10.2b A pair of needle-nose pliers can be used to remove the universal joint snap-rings

10.4 To press the universal joint out of the driveshaft yoke, set it up in a vise with the small socket pushing the joint and bearing cap into the large socket

10.9 If the snap-ring will not seat in the groove, strike the yoke with a brass hammer - this will relieve the tension that has set up in the yoke, and slightly spring the yoke ears (this should also be done if the joint feels tight when assembled)

11 Differential pinion oil seal - replacement

▶ **Refer to illustrations 11.4, 11.5, 11.6a, 11.6b, 11.7 and 11.8**

1   Raise the rear of the vehicle and place it securely on jackstands.

2   Remove the rear wheels and brake drums (see Chapter 9).

3   Mark the driveshaft and companion flange for ease of realignment during reassembly, then remove the driveshaft (see Section 9).

4   Mark the relationship between the pinion and companion flange (see illustration).

5   Using an inch-pound torque wrench, measure and record the torque required to turn the pinion nut through several revolutions (see illustration). This value, known as pinion bearing preload, will be used when the pinion flange is reinstalled.

6   Using a suitable tool, hold the companion flange and remove the pinion nut (see illustration). Using a suitable puller (see illustration), remove the companion flange.

7   Pry out the old seal with a seal removal tool (see illustration).

8   Clean the oil seal mounting surface, then tap the new seal into place, taking care to insert it squarely as shown (see illustration).

9   Inspect the splines on the pinion shaft for burrs and nicks. Remove any rough areas with a crocus cloth. Wipe the splines clean.

11.4 Mark the relationship between the pinion and flange as shown

10 Install the companion flange, aligning it with the marks made during removal. Gently tap the flange on with a soft-faced hammer until you can start the pinion nut on the pinion shaft.

11 Using a suitable tool, hold the companion flange while tightening the pinion nut to the minimum torque listed in this Chapter's Specifica-

11.5 Using an inch-pound torque wrench, measure the pinion bearing preload (turning torque) and jot down this measurement

11.6a To keep the flange from turning while you're loosening and removing the pinion nut, hold the flange with a punch jammed through a hole in the flange and wedged under the reinforcing rib on the side of the differential housing

11.6b If necessary, use a small puller to separate the pinion flange from the pinion shaft

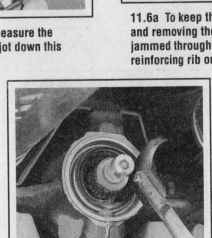

11.7 Pry out the old seal with a seal removal tool

11.8 Using a seal driver or a large socket, tap the new pinion seal into place with the seal square to the bore

tions. Continue tightening, take frequent rotational torque measurements, using the inch-pound torque wrench, until the measurement recorded in Step five is reached.

> **CAUTION:**
>
> If the measurement recorded in Step five was less than the pinion bearing preload torque listed in this Chapter's Specifications, continue tightening until the specified torque is reached. If it was more than specified, continue tightening until the

recorded measurement is reached. Under no circumstances should the pinion nut be backed off to reduce pinion bearing preload. Increase the nut torque in small increments and check the preload after each increase.

12 Reinstall the driveshaft, brake drums and wheels.
13 Check the differential oil level and fill as necessary.
14 Lower the vehicle and take a test drive to check for leaks.

12 Axleshaft - removal and installation

▶ **Refer to illustrations 12.4a, 12.4b, 12.4c, 12.5 and 12.6**

1 Loosen the wheel lug nuts, raise the rear of the vehicle, support it securely on jackstands and remove the wheel.
2 Remove the brake caliper and disc (see Chapter 9).
3 Remove the cover from the differential carrier and allow the lubricant to drain into a container (see Chapter 1).
4 Remove the lock bolt from the differential pinion shaft. Slide the notched end of the pinion shaft out of the differential case as far as it

will go (see illustrations).
5 Push in the outer (flanged) end of the axleshaft and remove the C-lock from the inner end of the shaft (see illustration).
6 Withdraw the axleshaft, taking care not to damage the oil seal in the end of the axle housing as the splined end of the axleshaft passes through it (see illustration).
7 Installation is the reverse of removal. Tighten the differential pinion shaft lock bolt to the torque listed in this Chapter's Specifications.
8 Install the differential cover (see Chapter 1).
9 Refill the axle with the correct quantity and grade of lubricant (see Chapter 1).

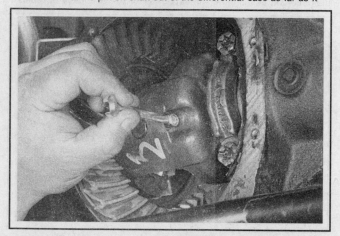

12.4a Position a large screwdriver between the rear axle case and a ring gear bolt to keep the differential case from turning, then loosen the pinion shaft lock bolt . . .

12.4b . . . remove the lock bolt . . .

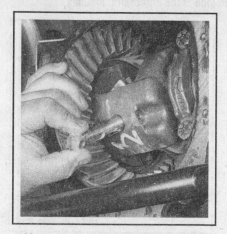

12.4c . . . and slide out the pinion shaft

12.5 Push in on the axle flange and remove the C-lock from the inner end of the axleshaft (a magnet is handy for this job)

12.6 Pull the axle out of the housing, supporting it with one hand to prevent damage to the seal

13 Axleshaft oil seal - replacement

▶ **Refer to illustrations 13.2a, 13.2b and 13.3**

1   Remove the axleshaft (see Section 12).

2   Pry the old oil seal out of the end of the axle housing, using a seal removal tool or the inner end of the axleshaft itself as a lever (see illustrations).

3   Using a seal driver or a large socket, tap the seal into position so that the lips are facing in and the metal face is visible from the end of the axle housing (see illustration). When correctly installed, the face of the oil seal should be flush with the end of the axle housing. Lubricate the lips of the seal with gear oil.

4   Install the axleshaft (see Section 12).

13.2a Use a seal removal tool to remove the old seal from the axle housing

13.2b If a seal removal tool isn't available, a prybar or even the end of the axle can be used to pry the seal out of the housing

13.3 Use a seal driver or a large socket to tap the new axleshaft oil seal into place

14 Axleshaft bearing - replacement

▶ **Refer to illustrations 14.2a, 14.2b and 14.4**

1   Remove the axleshaft (see Section 12) and the oil seal (see Section 13).

2   You'll need a bearing puller (see illustrations), or you'll need to fabricate a similar tool.

3   Attach a slide hammer and pull the bearing out of the axle housing.

4   Clean out the bearing recess and drive in the new bearing with a bearing driver or a large socket (see illustration). Lubricate the new bearing with gear lubricant. Make sure that the bearing is seated into the full depth of its recess.

5   Discard the old oil seal and install a new one (see Section 13), then install the axleshaft (see Section 12).

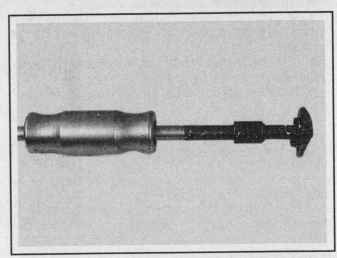

14.2a A typical axleshaft bearing removal tool (available at stores which carry automotive tools)

14.2b To remove the axle bearing, insert a bearing removal tool attached to a slide hammer through the center, pull the tool up against the back side and use the slide hammer to drive the bearing from the axle housing

14.4 A correctly-sized bearing driver must be used to drive the bearing into the housing

15 Rear axle assembly - removal and installation

REMOVAL

♦ **Refer to illustration 15.8**

1   Disconnect the cable from the negative battery terminal.

2   Loosen, but do not remove the rear wheel lug nuts. Block the front wheels and raise the rear of the vehicle. Support it securely on jackstands placed under the frame. Remove the rear wheels.

3   Remove the brake calipers and discs (see Chapter 9).

4   Remove the differential cover and allow the lubricant to drain (see Chapter 1).

5   If the vehicle is equipped with ABS, remove the sensors (see Chapter 9).

6   Remove both rear axleshafts (see Section 12).

7   Disconnect all clips for the ABS sensor wires, hydraulic brake lines and parking brake cables from the axle housing.

8   Remove the four bolts that attach the torque plates to the axle housing (see illustration). Detach the torque plate assemblies from the axle housing.

9   Unbolt the driveshaft from the differential companion flange (see Section 9) and secure it out of the way.

10 Place a floor jack under the differential and raise the rear axle slightly.

11 Place a safety chain through the coil springs.

12 Disconnect the rear axle dampers (see Chapter 10).

13 Remove the shock absorber lower mounting bolts (see Chapter 10).

14 Remove the upper suspension arm-to-rear axle housing nuts and bolts (see Chapter 10).

15 Lower the axle housing until the coil springs are fully extended, then remove them.

16 Remove the lower suspension arm-to-axle housing nuts and bolts (see Chapter 10).

17 Lower the axle housing and guide it out from underneath the vehicle.

15.8 To remove the brake backing plate (the aluminum shield), remove these three bolts (arrows); to remove the rear brake caliper anchor plate from the axle assembly, remove these four bolts (arrows)

INSTALLATION

18 Raise the rear axle assembly into place and install the upper suspension arm-to-axle housing bolts and nuts. Don't completely tighten the nuts at this time.

19 Install the coil springs (see Chapter 10) and connect the lower suspension arms to the rear axle assembly.

20 Raise the axle housing to simulate normal ride height and tighten the upper and lower suspension arm-to-axle housing nuts to the torque listed in the Chapter 10 Specifications.

21 Connect the lower ends of the shock absorbers to the rear axle housing and tighten the bolts/nuts to the torque listed in the Chapter 10 Specifications.

22 Connect the rear axle dampers to the rear axle housing and tighten the bolts/nuts to the torque listed in the Chapter 10 Specifications.

23 Connect the driveshaft to the differential companion flange, align the matchmarks and tighten the companion flange bolts to the torque listed in this Chapter's Specifications.

24 Attach the brake torque plates to the axle housing and tighten the bolts securely.

25 Connect the brake sensor wires, the brake lines and the parking brake cables to their clips on the axle housing.

26 Install the axleshafts (see Section 12).

27 Install the brake discs and calipers (see Chapter 9).

28 Install the differential cover and fill the differential with the recommended oil (see Chapter 1).

29 Install the wheels and lug nuts. Lower the vehicle and tighten the lug nuts to the torque listed in the Chapter 1 Specifications.

Specifications

Torque specifications   Ft-lbs (unless otherwise indicated)

Bellhousing-to-engine bolts (3.8L and 5.0L models)	28 to 38
Driveshaft U-joint-to-pinion flange bolts	70 to 95
Pressure plate-to-flywheel bolts	12 to 24
Companion flange/pinion nut (minimum)	140
Pinion bearing preload (minimum, original bearings)	8 to 14 in-lbs
Differential pinion shaft lock bolt	15 to 30

Notes

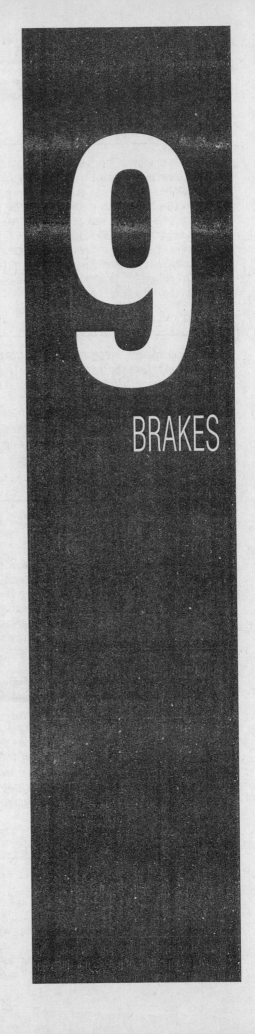

9

BRAKES

Section

Reference to other Chapters

1 General information

GENERAL DESCRIPTION

All models covered in this manual are equipped with hydraulically-operated, power assisted brake systems. All front and rear brakes are disc type: all later models and Cobra models are equipped with dual-piston front calipers; all other models use a single-piston front caliper. Some models are equipped with an Anti-lock Brake System (ABS) (see Section 2). All brakes are self-adjusting.

The hydraulic system is a "split" design, meaning there are separate circuits for the front and rear brakes. If one circuit fails, the other circuit will remain functional and a warning indicator will light up on the dashboard, showing that a failure has occurred.

MASTER CYLINDER

The master cylinder - recognizable by the large plastic fluid reservoir on top - is mounted on the front of the power brake booster. The reservoir is partitioned to prevent total fluid loss in the event of a front or rear brake hydraulic system failure.

The master cylinder, which is designed for the split system, has separate primary and secondary piston assemblies: the piston nearest the firewall, which applies hydraulic pressure to the front brakes, is the primary piston.

BRAKE PRESSURE CONTROL VALVE

The brake pressure control valve is located below the master cylinder, against the left inner fender panel. The control valve contains a proportioning valve and a shuttle valve.

The proportioning valve regulates the hydraulic pressure in the rear brake system. When the brake pedal is applied, the rear brake fluid pressure passes through the proportioning valve to the rear brake system until the valve's split point is reached. Above its split point, the proportioning valve begins to reduce the hydraulic pressure to the rear brakes thereby balancing the braking condition between the front and rear brakes. This condition will prevent the rear wheel from locking up and the vehicle from skidding out of control.

If the brake hydraulic system loses pressure, the shuttle valve closes the circuit for the low brake fluid pressure warning system, turning on a warning light on the instrument cluster.

The brake pressure control valve is not serviceable - if a problem develops with the valve, it must be replaced as an assembly.

PARKING BRAKE

The parking brake system is cable-operated and self-adjusting. When the parking brake lever is applied, it pulls a front cable, which pulls on two rear cables, which in turn move levers on the rear calipers, applying the rear pistons via screw mechanisms. A spring-loaded ratcheting mechanism on the parking brake lever automatically takes up the slack as the cables stretch, so the cable never has to be adjusted.

PRECAUTIONS

There are some general cautions and warnings involving the brake system on this vehicle:

a) *Use only brake fluid conforming to DOT 3 specifications.*

b) *The brake pads contain fibers which are hazardous to your health if inhaled. Whenever you work on brake system components, clean all parts with brake system cleaner or denatured alcohol. Do not allow the fine dust to become airborne.*

c) *Safety should be paramount whenever any servicing of the brake components is performed. Do not use parts or fasteners which are not in perfect condition, and be sure that all clearances and torque specifications are adhered to. If you are at all unsure about a certain procedure, seek professional advice. Upon completion of any brake system work, test the brakes carefully in a controlled area before putting the vehicle into normal service.*

If a problem is suspected in the brake system, don't drive the vehicle until it's fixed.

2 Anti-lock Brake System (ABS) - general information

Some models are equipped with an Anti-lock Brake System (ABS). The ABS system is designed to maintain vehicle steerability, directional stability and optimum deceleration under severe braking conditions and on most road surfaces. It does so by monitoring the rotational speed of each wheel and controlling the brake line pressure to each wheel during braking. This prevents the wheel from locking-up and provides maximum vehicle controllability.

HYDRAULIC CONTROL UNIT (HCU)

♦ **Refer to illustration 2.2**

The hydraulic control unit (see illustration) is located in the lower right front corner of the engine compartment. It consists of a brake pressure control valve block, a pump motor and a hydraulic control unit reservoir with a fluid level indicator assembly.

During normal braking conditions, brake hydraulic fluid from the master cylinder enters the hydraulic control unit through two inlet ports and passes through four normally open inlet valves, one to each wheel.

When the anti-lock brake control module senses that a wheel is about to lock up, the anti-lock brake control module closes the appropriate inlet. This prevents any more fluid from entering the affected brake. If the module determines that the wheel is still decelerating, the module opens the outlet valve, which bleeds off pressure in the affected brake.

WHEEL SENSORS

♦ **Refer to illustrations 2.6a and 2.6b**

The ABS system uses four "variable-reluctance" sensors to monitor wheel speed ("reluctance" is a term used to indicate the amount of resistance to the passage of flux lines - lines of force in a magnetic field - through a given material). Each sensor contains a small inductive coil that generates an electromagnetic field. When paired with a toothed sensor ring which interrupts this field as the wheels turn, each

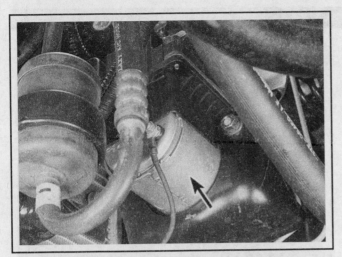

2.2 The ABS hydraulic control unit (arrow) is located in the lower right front corner of the engine compartment

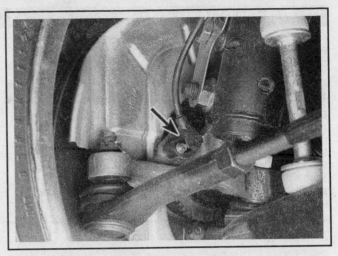

2.6a ABS front wheel sensor (arrow)

sensor generates a low-voltage analog (continuous) signal. This voltage signal, which rises and falls in proportion to wheel rotation speed, is continuously sampled (monitored) by the control module, converted into digital data inside the module and processed (interpreted).

The front wheel sensors (see illustration) are mounted in the steering knuckle in close proximity to the toothed sensor rings, which are pressed onto the wheel hubs. The rear wheel sensors (see illustration) are mounted in the caliper torque plate and the sensor rings are pressed onto the axleshafts.

BRAKE CONTROL MODULE

The brake control module is also mounted in the right front corner of the engine compartment (it's an integral part of the HCU). The control module is the "brain" of the ABS system. The module constantly monitors the incoming analog voltage signals from the four ABS wheel sensors, converts these signals to digital form, processes this digital data by comparing it to the map (program), makes decisions, converts these (digital) decisions to analog form and sends them to the hydraulic control unit, which opens and closes the front and/or rear circuits as necessary.

The module also has a self-diagnostic capability which operates during both normal driving as well as ABS system operation. If a mal-

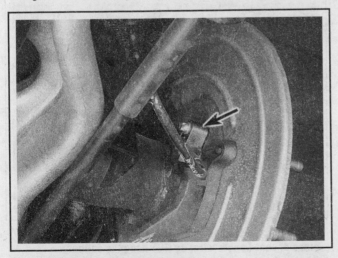

2.6b ABS rear wheel sensor (arrow)

function occurs, a red "BRAKE" warning indicator or an amber "CHECK ANTI-LOCK BRAKES" warning indicator will light up on the dash.

 a) *If the red BRAKE light glows, the brake fluid level in the master cylinder reservoir has fallen below the level established by the fluid level switch. Top up the reservoir and verify that the light goes out.*
 b) *If the amber CHECK ANTI-LOCK BRAKES light glows, the ABS and, if equipped, Traction Assist, have been turned off because of a symptom detected by the module. Normal power-assisted braking is still operational, but the wheels can now lock up if you're involved in a panic-stop situation. A diagnostic code is also stored in the module when a warning indicator light comes on; when retrieved by a service technician, the code indicates the area or component where the problem is located. Once the problem is fixed, the code is cleared. These procedures, however, are beyond the scope of the home mechanic.*

DIAGNOSIS AND REPAIR

❈❈ **WARNING:**

If a dashboard warning light comes on and stays on while the vehicle is in operation, the ABS system requires immediate attention!

Although a special electronic ABS diagnostic tester is necessary to properly diagnose the system, the home mechanic can perform a few preliminary checks before taking the vehicle to a dealer who is equipped with this tester.

 a) *Check the brake fluid level in the reservoir.*
 b) *Verify that the control module electrical connector is securely connected.*
 c) *Check the electrical connectors at the hydraulic control unit.*
 d) *Check the fuses.*
 e) *Follow the wiring harness to each wheel and check that all connections are secure and that the wiring is not damaged.*

If the above preliminary checks do not rectify the problem, the vehicle should be diagnosed by a dealer service department or other qualified repair shop. Due to the rather complex nature of this system, all actual repair work must be done by the dealer service department or repair shop.

3 Brake pads - replacement

◆ Refer to illustrations 3.6a through 3.6m, 3.7a through 3.7q and 3.8a through 3.8m

❋❋ WARNING:

Disc brake pads must be replaced on both front wheels or both rear wheels at the same time - never replace the pads on only one wheel. Also, the dust created by the brake system is harmful to your health. Never blow it out with compressed air and don't inhale any of it. An approved filtering mask should be worn when working on the brakes. Do not, under any circumstances, use petroleum-based solvents to clean brake parts. Use brake system cleaner only!

1 Remove the cover from the brake fluid reservoir and siphon out about 1/2 of the brake fluid.

2 Loosen the wheel lug nuts, raise the vehicle and support it securely on jackstands.

3 Remove the wheels. Work on one brake assembly at a time, using the assembled brake for reference if necessary.

3.6a Wash down the brake caliper assembly and the disc with brake cleaner to remove brake dust; do NOT blow off brake dust with compressed air

3.6b To make room for the new brake pads, compress the piston into the caliper with a large C-clamp

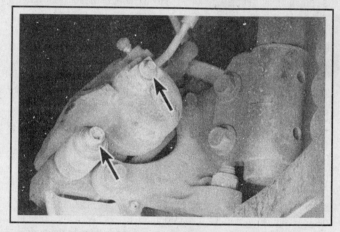

3.6c Remove the caliper mounting bolt (lower arrow); upper arrow points at brake hose-to-caliper banjo bolt - it's not necessary to remove this bolt unless you're removing the caliper for overhaul

3.6d Pivot the caliper up, off the brake pads, and slide it off the pin at the top

3.6e Hang the caliper from the coil spring with a piece of coat-hanger wire; do NOT hang the caliper from its brake hose!

3.6f Remove the outer brake pad

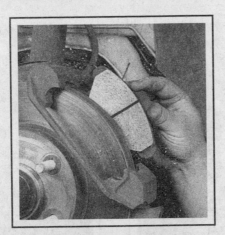

3.6g Remove the inner brake pad

3.6h Apply some anti-squeal compound to the backing plates of the new pads

3.6i Install the inner brake pad

3.6j Install the outer brake pad

3.6k Apply high temperature grease to the caliper mounting pin

4   Inspect the brake disc carefully as outlined in Section 5.

5   If machining is necessary, follow the information in that Section to remove the disc, at which time the pads can be removed from the caliper as well.

6   If you're replacing the front brake pads on a single-piston caliper,

follow the accompanying photos, beginning with illustration 3.6a, for the front brake pad replacement procedure. Be sure to stay in order and read the caption under each illustration.

7   If you're replacing the front brake pads on a dual-piston caliper,

3.6l Make sure the anti-rattle spring is seated firmly in the caliper

3.6m Slide the caliper onto the upper mounting pin, pull it down over the new pads, install the caliper bolt and tighten it to the torque listed in this Chapter's Specifications

3.7a Wash down the caliper and brake disc with brake cleaner to remove brake dust; do NOT blow off brake dust with compressed air

3.7b Insert a socket in one of the holes in the caliper and install a C-clamp, as shown, with one clamping pad on the caliper body and one on the socket, then compress the pistons until they bottom out

follow the photos beginning with illustration 3.7a. Be sure to stay in order and read the caption under each illustration.

8 If you're replacing the rear brake pads, follow the photos

beginning with illustration 3.8a. Be sure to stay in order and read the caption under each illustration.

9 When reinstalling calipers (except for Cobra front calipers), be

3.7c Pry off the old C-clip with a small screwdriver and discard the clip; remove the washer

3.7d Pull out the brake pad retainer pin

3.7e Lift off the caliper

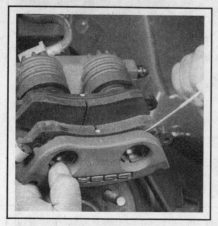

3.7f Pry off the old outer brake pad . . .

3.7g . . . and remove it from the caliper

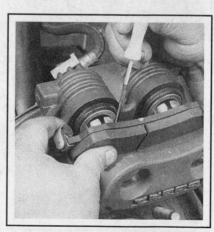

3.7h Pry off the old inner pad and remove it from the caliper

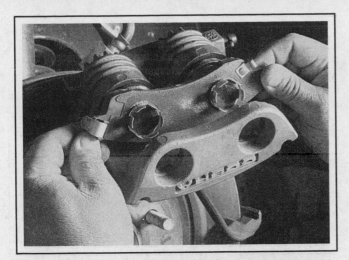

3.7i Install the new outer pad; make sure that the retainers are fully seated in their respective holes in the caliper body

3.7j Pop the new inner brake pad into place; again, make sure the retainers are seated all the way into the recesses in the pistons

sure to tighten the caliper bolt(s) to the torque listed in this Chapter's Specifications. After the job has been completed, firmly depress the brake pedal a few times to bring the pads into contact with the disc.

10 Check the brake fluid level and add some, if necessary, to bring it to the appropriate level (see Chapter 1).

3.7k Remove the dust boot and sliding pin from the anchor bracket . . .

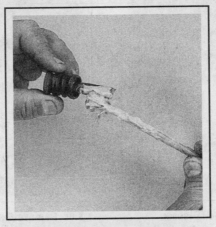

3.7l . . . and lubricate the sliding pin with high-temperature grease (anchor bracket removed for clarity)

3.7m Install the caliper over the pads

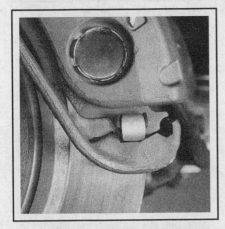

3.7n Make sure the clips on the pads are properly seated, as shown, in the recesses in the anchor bracket . . .

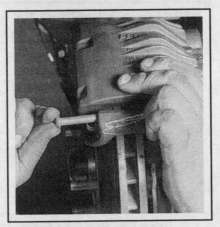

3.7o . . . then insert the caliper pin . . .

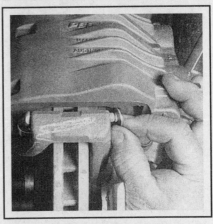

3.7p . . . and install the washer . . .

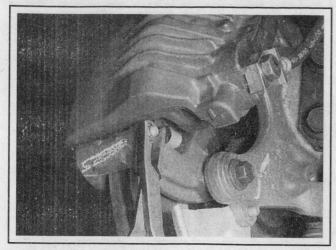

3.7q ... and a new C-clip

3.8a Wash down the caliper and brake disc with brake cleaner to remove brake dust; do NOT blow off brake dust with compressed air

3.8b Remove the caliper bolts (arrows); do NOT loosen the banjo bolt for the brake hose unless you're planning to overhaul the caliper or replace the brake hose

3.8c Remove the brake caliper

3.8d Hang the caliper from the axle damper with a piece of coat-hanger wire

3.8e Remove the outer brake pad

3.8f Remove the inner brake pad

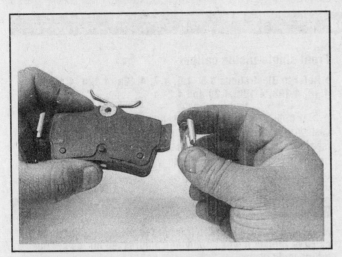

3.8g Remove these clips from each brake pad . . .

3.8h . . . and swap them over to the new pads; make sure they're installed exactly as shown

3.8i Pull out the two caliper pins (arrows), remove the dust boots, inspect for excessive wear and damage and replace if necessary. Be sure to wipe off the pins and lubricate with high-temperature grease before installation

3.8j Install the new inner brake pad

3.8k Install the new outer brake pad

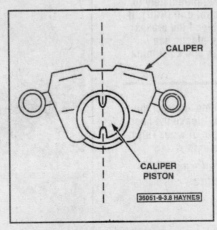

3.8l Rotate the **piston** clockwise with a brake **piston tool** or needle-nose pliers - **screw** the piston in all the way and **align the** notches in the piston with **the openings in the** caliper, as **shown**

3.8m Install the brake caliper, install the caliper bolts and tighten them to the torque listed in this Chapter's Specifications

4 Brake caliper - removal, overhaul and installation

❊❊ WARNING 1:

Dust created by the brake system is harmful to your health. Never blow it out with compressed air and don't inhale any of it. An approved filtering mask should be worn when working on the brakes. Do not, under any circumstances, use petroleum-based solvents to clean brake parts. Use brake system cleaner only!

❊❊ WARNING 2:

If the vehicle is equipped with ABS, make sure you plug the brake hose immediately after disconnecting it from the brake caliper, to prevent the fluid from draining out of the line and air entering the HCU. The HCU on an ABS system cannot be bled without a very expensive tool.

➡ **Note:** If an overhaul is indicated (usually because of fluid leakage) explore all options before beginning the job. New and factory-rebuilt calipers are available on an exchange basis, which makes this job quite easy. If it is decided to rebuild the calipers, make sure that a rebuild kit is available before proceeding. Always rebuild the calipers in pairs- never rebuild just one of them.

REMOVAL

▶ **Refer to illustration 4.2**

1   Apply the parking brake and block the wheels opposite the end being worked on. Loosen the wheel lug nuts, raise the vehicle and support it securely on jackstands. Remove the wheel.

2   Unscrew the brake hose banjo bolt (see illustration) and detach the hose from the caliper - remove the sealing washers from each side of the hose fitting and discard them. New sealing washers must be installed.

❊❊ CAUTION:

On ABS-equipped models, plug the brake hose immediately to prevent air from getting into the hydraulic control unit (HCU). If air gets into the HCU, you will not be able to bleed the brakes properly at home. On non-ABS models, wrap a plastic bag around the end of the hose to prevent fluid loss and contamination.

➡ **Note:** If the caliper will not be completely removed from the vehicle - as for pad inspection or disc removal - leave the hose connected and suspend the caliper with a length of wire. This will save the trouble of bleeding the brake system.

3   Refer to the first six steps in Section 3 to separate the caliper from the steering knuckle (front) or the torque plate (rear) - it's part of the brake pad replacement procedure.

OVERHAUL

4   Clean the exterior of the caliper with brake system cleaner. Never use gasoline, kerosene or other petroleum-based cleaning solvents. Place the caliper on a clean workbench.

Front single-piston caliper

▶ Refer to illustrations 4.5, 4.6, 4.7, 4.12a, 4.12b, 4.14, 4.17, 4.18, 4.19a, 4.19b, 4.20 and 4.21

5   Position a wood block or rags in the center of the caliper as a cushion, then use compressed air to remove the piston from the caliper (see illustration). Use only enough air to ease the piston out of the bore. If the piston is blown out, even with the cushion in place, it may be damaged.

❊❊ WARNING:

Never place your fingers in front of the piston in an attempt to catch or protect it when applying compressed air, as serious injury could occur.

4.2 If you're removing the caliper for overhaul, remove this banjo bolt and detach the banjo fitting - shove a piece of rubber hose through the banjo fitting to plug the hose (rear caliper shown; front caliper banjo bolts similar)

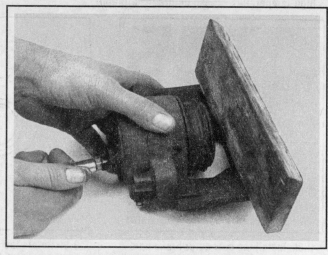

4.5 With the caliper padded to catch the piston, use compressed air to force the piston out of its bore - make sure your hands and fingers are not between the piston and the caliper!

4.6 Remove the dust boot from the caliper bore groove by carefully tapping it out with a hammer and punch; make sure you don't scratch or gouge the piston

6   Pry the dust boot out of the caliper bore (see illustration).

7   Using a wood or plastic tool, remove the piston seal from the caliper bore (see illustration). Metal tools may cause bore damage.

8   Carefully examine the piston for nicks, burrs, cracks, loss of plating, corrosion or any signs of damage. If surface defects are present, the parts must be replaced.

9   Check the caliper bore in a similar way. Light polishing with crocus cloth is permissible to remove light corrosion and stains.

10   Remove the bleeder valve and rubber cap.

11   Inspect the caliper bolts for corrosion and damage. Replace them with new ones if necessary.

12   Remove the dust boots and the caliper bolt bushing from the caliper ears (see illustrations).

13   Use brake system cleaner to clean all the parts.

✳✳ WARNING:

Do not, under any circumstances, use petroleum-based solvents to clean brake parts. Allow all parts to dry, preferably using compressed air to blow out all passages. Make sure the compressed air is filtered, as a harmful lubricant residue or moisture may be present in unfiltered systems.

14   Push the new caliper dust boots into place (see illustration).

15   Check the fit of the piston in the bore by sliding it into the caliper. The piston should move smoothly but firmly. Don't install it yet.

16   Thread the bleeder valve into the caliper and tighten it securely. Install the rubber cap.

17   Lubricate the new piston seal and caliper bore with clean brake fluid. Position the seal in the caliper bore groove, making sure it doesn't twist (see illustration).

4.7 To remove the seal from the caliper bore, use a plastic or wooden tool, such as a pencil

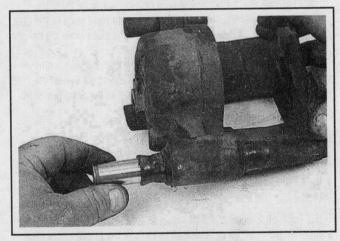

4.12a Remove the caliper bolt bushing . . .

4.12b . . . grab the ends of the caliper bolt dust boots and, using a twisting motion, push them through the caliper ears

4.14 Push the new dust boots through the holes in the caliper ears, making sure they're installed all the way

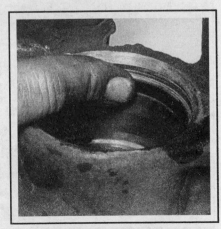

4.17 Push the new seal into the groove with your fingers, then check to see that it isn't twisted or kinked

4.18 Install the dust boot in the upper groove in the caliper bore, making sure it's completely seated, then gently tap it into place

18 Fit the new dust boot in the caliper bore upper groove; make sure it's properly seated (see illustration).

19 Lubricate the caliper piston with clean brake fluid. Push the piston into the caliper, using a turning motion to roll the lip of the dust boot over the piston (see illustrations). Push the piston into the caliper by hand as far as possible.

20 Using a C-clamp and a block of wood, push the piston all the way to the bottom of the bore. Work slowly, keeping an eye on the side of the piston, making sure it enters the bore perfectly straight with no resistance (see illustration).

21 Seat the lip of the dust boot in the groove on the piston (see illustration).

Front dual-piston caliper

▶ Refer to illustrations 4.22a, 4.22b, 4.22c, 4.23, 4.30, 4.31 and 4.32

22 Position a wood block or rags in the center of the caliper as a cushion, then use compressed air to remove the pistons from the

4.20 Use a C-clamp and a block of wood to bottom the piston in the caliper bore - make sure it goes in perfectly straight, or the sides of the piston may be damaged, rendering it useless

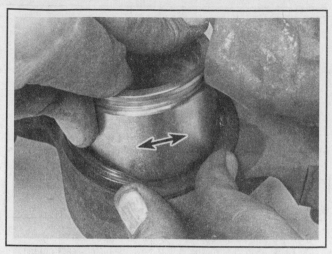

4.19a Lubricate the piston and bore with clean brake fluid, insert the piston into the dust boot (NOT the bore) at an angle, then, using a rotating motion, work the piston completely into the dust boot . . .

caliper (see illustrations). Use only enough air to ease the pistons out of the bore. If the piston is blown out, even with the cushion in place, it may be damaged.

4.19b . . . and push it straight into the caliper as far as possible by hand

4.21 Install the lip of the dust boot in the groove on the caliper piston

4.22a Using a block of wood as shown, or a shop rag, to cushion the blow, pop out the pistons with a squirt of compressed air . . .

Never place your fingers in front of the piston in an attempt to catch or protect it when applying compressed air, as serious injury could occur. If you're unable to extract the pistons using the above method, try the following variation: Clamp one piston with a small block of wood and pop the other piston out first (see illustration), then clamp the bore without a piston, and pop the other piston out.

23 Pry the dust boots out of the caliper bore (see illustration).

24 Using a wood or plastic tool, remove the piston seal from the caliper bore (see illustration 4.7). Metal tools may cause bore damage.

25 Carefully examine the piston for nicks, burrs, cracks, loss of plating, corrosion or any signs of damage. If surface defects are present, the parts must be replaced.

26 Check the caliper bore in a similar way. Light polishing with crocus cloth is permissible to remove light corrosion and stains.

27 Remove the bleeder valve and rubber cap.

28 Use brake system cleaner to clean all the parts.

Do not, under any circumstances, use petroleum-based solvents to clean brake parts. Allow all parts to dry, preferably using compressed air to blow out all passages. Make sure the compressed air is filtered, as a harmful lubricant residue or moisture may be present in unfiltered systems.

4.23 Remove the old dust boots

4.22b . . . then pull out the pistons

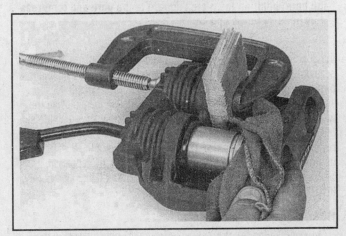

4.22c If the pistons are cocked or stuck, compress one all the way into the caliper, clamp it in place with a small block of wood and a C-clamp and remove the other piston; then move the block of wood and C-clamp to the bore of the piston you just removed and remove the other piston

29 Lubricate the new piston seal and caliper bore with clean brake fluid. Position the seal in the lower groove in the caliper bore, making sure it doesn't twist.

30 Lubricate the pistons with clean brake fluid, then slide the new dust boots onto the pistons (see illustration).

31 Position each piston square to the bore, seat the outer edge of

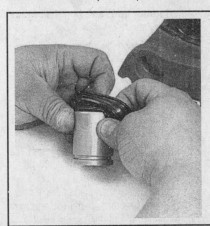

4.30 Lubricate the pistons with clean brake fluid and install the new dust boots onto the bottom of each piston

4.31 Seat the outer edge of the dust boot into its groove in the bore, position the piston square to the bore and compress it by hand as far as you can

4.32 Use a C-clamp to finish the job; be sure to seat the lip of the seal into its groove in the piston just before the piston is fully compressed

the dust boot into its groove in the caliper bore, make sure it's properly seated, lubricate the piston with a little more clean brake fluid, then push it into the caliper by hand (see illustration).

32 Using a C-clamp and a block of wood, push the piston all the way to the bottom of the bore. Work slowly, keeping an eye on the side of the piston, making sure it enters the bore perfectly straight with no resistance (see illustration). Be sure to seat the lip of the dust boot in its groove on the piston just before the piston is fully depressed.

33 Thread the bleeder valve into the caliper and tighten it securely. Install the rubber cap.

Rear caliper

34 Overhauling the rear caliper is extremely difficult without the right tools. If it's leaking or malfunctioning, we recommend that you replace it with a new or rebuilt unit.

INSTALLATION

35 Refer to Section 3 for the caliper installation procedure - it's part of the brake pad replacement procedure.

36 Connect the brake hose to the caliper, using new sealing washers. Tighten the banjo bolt to the torque listed in this Chapter's Specifications.

37 Bleed the brakes as outlined in Section 8. This is not necessary if the banjo bolt was not loosened or removed (if the caliper was removed for access to other components, for example).

38 Install the wheel and lower the vehicle. Tighten the lug nuts to the torque listed in the Chapter 1 Specifications. Pump the brake pedal several times to bring the pads into contact with the disc.

39 Test the operation of the brakes before placing the vehicle into normal service.

---

5   Brake disc - inspection, removal and installation

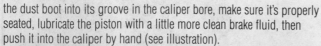

INSPECTION

♦ **Refer to illustrations 5.5a, 5.5b, 5.6a and 5.6b**

➡ **Note: This procedure applies to both front and rear disc brake assemblies.**

1   Loosen the wheel lug nuts, raise the vehicle and support it securely on jackstands. Remove the wheel.

2   Remove the brake caliper as outlined in Section 4. It's not necessary to disconnect the brake hose for this procedure. After removing the caliper bolts, suspend the caliper out of the way with a piece of wire. Don't let the caliper hang by the hose and don't stretch or twist the hose.

3   Reinstall three lug nuts (inverted) to hold the disc against the hub. It may be necessary to install washers between the disc and the lug nuts to take up space.

4   Visually check the disc surface for score marks and other damage. Light scratches and shallow grooves are normal after use and may not always be detrimental to brake operation, but deep score marks

5.5a To check disc runout, mount a dial indicator as shown and rotate the disc

5.5b Using a swirling motion, remove the glaze from the disc with sandpaper or emery cloth

5.6a The minimum thickness limit is cast into the inside of the disc

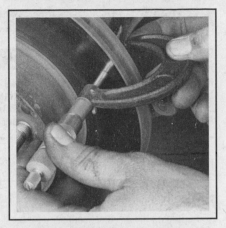

5.6b Use a micrometer to measure disc thickness at several points, about 1/2-inch from the edge

- over 0.015-inch - require disc removal and refinishing by an automotive machine shop. Be sure to check both sides of the disc. If pulsating has been noticed during application of the brakes, suspect disc runout.

5 To check disc runout, place a dial indicator at a point about 1/2-inch from the outer edge of the disc (see illustration). Set the indicator to zero and turn the disc. The indicator reading should not exceed the specified allowable runout limit. If it does, the disc should be refinished by an automotive machine shop.

➡Note: **Professionals recommend resurfacing of brake discs regardless of the dial indicator reading (to produce a smooth, flat surface that will eliminate brake pedal pulsations and other undesirable symptoms related to questionable discs). At the very least, if you elect not to have the discs resurfaced, deglaze the brake pad surface with emery cloth or sandpaper (use a swirling motion to ensure a non-directional finish) (see illustration).**

6 The disc must not be machined to a thickness less than the specified minimum refinish thickness. The minimum wear (or discard) thickness is cast into the inside of the disc (see illustration). The disc thickness can be checked with a micrometer (see illustration).

REMOVAL AND INSTALLATION

▶ **Refer to illustrations 5.7a, 5.7b and 5.8**

7 Remove the caliper anchor plate (see illustrations).

8 Remove the disc. If it's stuck, make sure you have removed any lug nuts installed during inspection. If the disc has never been removed, it may have some wave washers securing it to the lug nut studs; cut them off (see illustration) and discard them.

9 Install the disc onto the hub assembly.

10 Install the caliper and brake pad assembly over the disc and position it on the steering knuckle (front), or on the torque plate (rear) (see Section 4). Install the caliper bolts and tighten them to the torque listed in this Chapter's Specifications.

11 Install the wheel, then lower the vehicle to the ground. Depress the brake pedal a few times to bring the brake pads into contact with the rotor. Bleeding of the system will not be necessary unless the brake hose was disconnected from the caliper. Check the operation of the brakes carefully before placing the vehicle into normal service.

5.7a Front caliper anchor plate bolts (arrows) (anchor plate for dual-piston caliper shown; single-piston anchor plate similar)

5.7b Rear caliper anchor plate bolts (arrows)

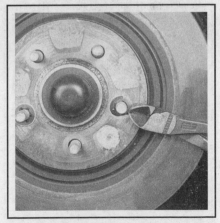

5.8 If the disc has wave-type retainer washers like these, simply cut them off and discard them

6 Master cylinder - removal, overhaul and installation

❊❊ WARNING:

If the vehicle is equipped with ABS, make sure you plug the brake line immediately after disconnecting it from the master cylinder, to prevent air from entering the HCU. The HCU on this ABS system cannot be bled without a very expensive tool.

❊❊ CAUTION:

Brake fluid will damage paint. Cover all body parts and be careful not to spill fluid during this procedure. Unscrew the tube nuts at the master cylinder (see illustration). On models with a 4.6L engine, unscrew the tube nuts at the lower ends of the master cylinder brake lines, where they're connected to the brake control valve (see illustration) (the brake lines can be unscrewed from the underside of the master cylinder on these models, but they're very difficult to reach). To prevent rounding off the flats on these nuts, a flare-nut wrench, which wraps around the fitting, should be used. Pull the brake lines away from the master cylinder slightly and plug the ends to prevent contamination.

REMOVAL

◆ **Refer to illustrations 6.1a, 6.1b, 6.2, 6.3a, 6.3b and 6.4**

1   Unplug the electrical connector for the fluid level sensor (see illustrations).

2   Detach the bracket for the shift interlock cable (automatic transmission) or the clutch cable (manual transmission) (see illustration).

3   Place rags under the brake line fittings and prepare caps or plastic bags to cover the ends of the lines once they are disconnected.

4   Remove the two master cylinder mounting nuts (see illustration) and detach the master cylinder from the power brake booster.

5   Remove the reservoir cap, then discard any fluid remaining in the reservoir.

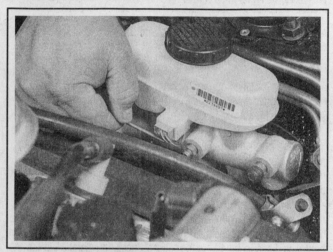

6.1a Release the locking tab on the bottom of the electrical connector for the fluid level sensor . . .

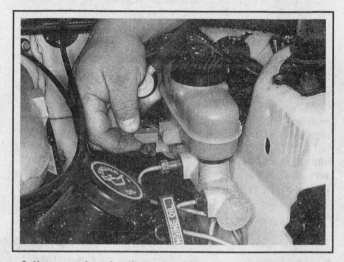

6.1b . . . and unplug the connector

6.2 To detach the clutch cable bracket from the master cylinder, remove this bolt (arrow) (a similar setup is used for the shift interlock cable on models with an automatic transmission)

6.3a On non-4.6L models, use a flare-nut wrench to unscrew the brake line tube nuts at the master cylinder; plug the ends of both lines immediately to prevent contamination

6.3b On 4.6L models, unscrew the tube nuts from the rear of the brake control valve instead (the valve is located directly below the master cylinder); plug the ends of both lines immediately to prevent contamination

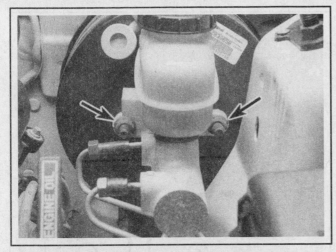

6.4 To detach the master cylinder from the power brake booster, remove these two mounting nuts (arrows)

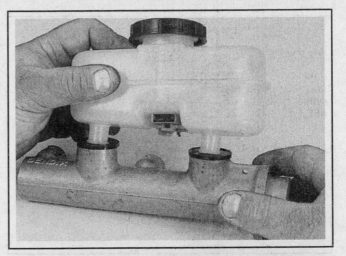

6.7a Remove the fluid reservoir if the grommets are leaking or if the reservoir is broken; if the reservoir is difficult to remove, gently pry it off with a screwdriver or small prybar

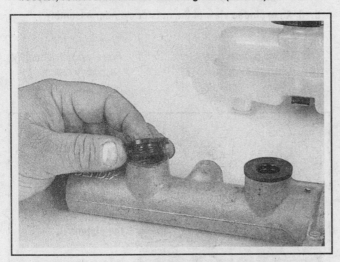

6.7b Remove the old reservoir grommets and discard them

OVERHAUL

▶ Refer to illustrations 6.7a, 6.7b, 6.8a, 6.8b, 6.9, 6.10, 6.12a, 6.12b, 6.12c, 6.13 and 6.17

➡Note: Before deciding to overhaul the master cylinder, check on the availability and cost of a new or factory rebuilt unit and also the availability of a rebuild kit.

6   Mount the master cylinder in a bench vise with the vise jaws clamping on the mounting flange.

7   If fluid has been leaking past the reservoir grommets, pry the reservoir from the cylinder body with a screwdriver and remove it, then remove the grommets (see illustrations). Clean the master cylinder body and components with brake system cleaner.

❊❊ WARNING:

DO NOT use petroleum-based solvents to clean brake parts - use brake system cleaner only.

8   Remove the primary piston assembly from the cylinder bore (see illustrations).

6.8a Put the master cylinder in a bench vise, then use a Phillips head screwdriver to push the primary piston into the cylinder just far enough to remove the snap ring with a pair of suitable snap-ring pliers

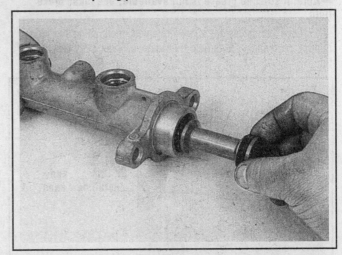

6.8b Remove the primary piston assembly from the cylinder

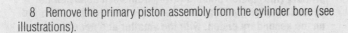

6.9 Tap the master cylinder against a block of wood to eject the secondary piston assembly

9   Remove the secondary piston assembly from the cylinder bore. It may be necessary to remove the master cylinder from the vise and invert it, carefully tapping it against a block of wood to expel the piston (see illustration).

10 Wash all the parts thoroughly with clean brake fluid and lay them out for inspection (see illustration).

11 Inspect the cylinder bore for corrosion and damage. If any corrosion or excessive wear is found, replace the master cylinder assembly - abrasives cannot be used on the bore. Usually, if the bore of the master cylinder is corroded or worn, the primary and secondary pistons and springs are damaged as well.

12 Remove the old seals from the pistons and install the new seals (see illustrations).

13 Lubricate the cylinder bore and primary and secondary piston assemblies with clean brake fluid (see illustration).

14 Insert the secondary piston assembly into the cylinder.

15 Install the primary piston assembly in the cylinder bore, depress it and install the snap-ring.

16 Lubricate the new reservoir grommets with silicone grease and press them into the master cylinder body. Make sure they're properly seated.

➡**Note: If silicone grease is not available, use clean brake fluid.**

17 Lube the insides of the new grommets, then, using a rocking motion, press the reservoir into the master cylinder body (see illustration).

6.12b . . . and install new ones

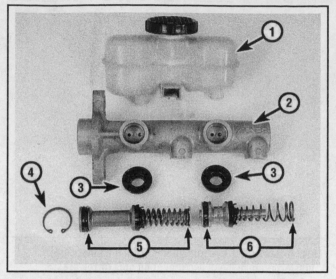

6.10 An exploded view of the master cylinder assembly

1 Reservoir	4 Snap ring
2 Master cylinder body	5 Primary piston assembly
3 Reservoir-to-master cylinder grommets	6 Secondary piston assembly

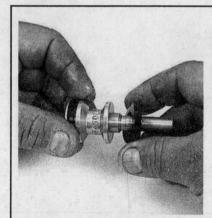

6.12a Remove the old seals from the pistons . . .

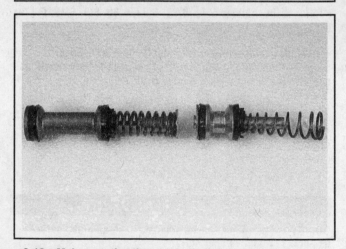

6.12c Make sure that the new seals face forward on the primary (left) piston and out (away from each other) on the secondary (right) piston; also note how the spring in installed on the secondary piston, with the smaller end near the piston

6.13 Coat the pistons and new seals with clean brake fluid and install them in the master cylinder, spring end first

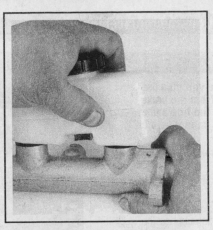

6.17 After the new grommets have been installed and lubricated with clean brake fluid, install the reservoir

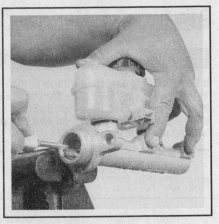

6.22 If you don't have a couple of plugs that will fit the primary and secondary outlet ports, just use your fingers!

18 Inspect the reservoir cap and diaphragm for cracks and deformation. Replace any damaged parts with new ones and attach the diaphragm to the cap.

➡**Note: Whenever the master cylinder is removed, the complete hydraulic system must be bled. The time required to bleed the system can be reduced if the master cylinder is filled with fluid and bench bled (refer to Steps 18 through 22) before the master cylinder is installed on the vehicle.**

19 Insert threaded plugs of the correct size into the cylinder outlet holes and fill the reservoirs with brake fluid. The master cylinder should be supported in such a manner that brake fluid will not spill during the bench bleeding procedure.

20 Loosen one plug at a time, starting with the secondary outlet port first, and push the piston assembly into the bore to force air from the master cylinder. To prevent air from being drawn back into the cylinder, the appropriate plug must be replaced before allowing the piston to return to its original position. Stroke the piston three or four times for each outlet to ensure that all air has been expelled.

21 Since high pressure is not involved in the bench bleeding procedure, you can use your fingers instead of threaded plugs. Before pushing in on the piston assembly, place your fingers over the holes (see illustration). When you release the piston, make sure your fingers are pressed tightly over the holes to keep air from being drawn back into the master cylinder. Wait several seconds for the brake fluid to be drawn from the reservoir to the piston bore, then repeat the procedure. When you push down on the piston it will force your finger off the hole, allowing the air inside to be expelled. When only brake fluid is being ejected from both holes, the master cylinder is ready for installation.

INSTALLATION

▶ **Refer to illustration 6.25**

22 Install the master cylinder over the studs on the power brake booster and tighten the nuts only finger tight at this time.

23 Thread the brake line fittings onto the master cylinder. Since the master cylinder is still a bit loose, you can move it slightly to facilitate threading the hydraulic line tube nuts. Make sure you don't strip the threads as the tube nuts are screwed on.

24 Tighten the master cylinder mounting nuts to the torque listed in this Chapter's Specifications. Tighten the brake line tube nuts securely.

25 Fill the master cylinder reservoir with fluid, then bleed the lines at the master cylinder, followed by bleeding the remainder of the brake system (see Section 8). To bleed the lines at the master cylinder, have an assistant depress the brake pedal and hold it down. Loosen the fitting to allow air and fluid to escape (see illustration). Tighten the fitting, then allow your assistant to return the pedal to its rest position. Repeat this procedure on both fittings until the fluid is free of air bubbles, then bleed the rest of the system. Check the operation of the brake system carefully before driving the vehicle.

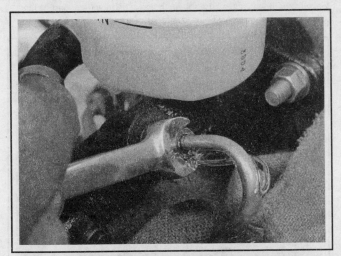

6.25 Have an assistant depress the brake pedal and hold it down, then loosen the fitting nut, allowing the air and fluid to escape; repeat this procedure on both fittings until the fluid is clear of air bubbles

※ **WARNING:**

If you do not have a firm brake pedal upon completion of the brake bleeding procedure, or if you have any doubts regarding the effectiveness of the brake system, DO NOT drive the vehicle. Have it towed to a dealer service department or other qualified repair shop for diagnosis.

7   Brake hoses and lines - inspection and replacement

> **⁘ CAUTION:**
>
> If the vehicle is equipped with ABS, make sure you plug the brake line immediately after disconnecting it from the brake hose, to prevent the fluid from draining out of the line and air entering the HCU. The HCU on an ABS system cannot be bled without a very expensive tool.

INSPECTION

1   About every six months, the rubber hoses which connect the steel brake lines to the front and rear calipers should be inspected. These are critical yet vulnerable parts of the brake system, so your inspection should be thorough. Raise the vehicle and support it securely on jackstands. Look for cracks, chafing of the outer cover, leaks, blisters and any other damage (a light and mirror are helpful). If a hose exhibits any of the above conditions, replace it with a new one.

REPLACEMENT

Flexible hose

▶ Refer to illustrations 7.2, 7.3a and 7.3b

2   To disconnect a front brake hose from a metal brake line, use a flare nut wrench to disconnect the metal brake line from the hose fitting, being careful not to bend the frame bracket or brake line (see illustration), then remove the large retaining clip from the bracket and slip the hose through the bracket.

> **⁘ CAUTION:**
>
> On ABS-equipped models, plug the metal brake line immediately to prevent air from getting into the hydraulic control unit (HCU). If air gets into the HCU, you will not be able to bleed the brakes properly at home.

3   To disconnect a rear brake hose from the metal line(s), unscrew the tube nut(s) from the junction block (see illustrations), then unbolt

7.2 To disconnect the fitting that attaches the flexible brake hose to the metal brake line at the bracket in the wheel well, unscrew the tube nut with a flare nut wrench, then remove the large retainer clip (arrow) and pull the hose through the bracket

the junction block mounting bracket from the frame.

4   Remove the banjo bolt from the caliper (see illustration 4.2) and discard the sealing washers.

5   Connect the hose to the caliper, using new sealing washers. Tighten the banjo bolt to the torque listed in this Chapter's Specifications.

6   Without twisting the hose, connect the other end of the line to the bracket on the chassis (front hose) or bolt the junction block to the frame (rear hose).

7   Connect the metal brake line tube nut(s) to the hose fitting or junction block by hand, then, using a flare nut wrench, tighten the fitting(s) securely.

8   When the brake hose installation is complete, there should be no kinks in the hose. Make sure the hose doesn't contact any part of the suspension. Check this by turning the wheels to the extreme left and

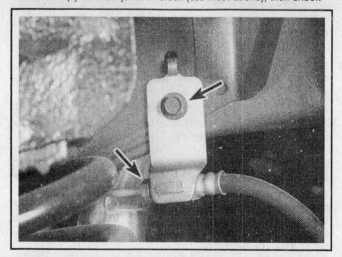

7.3a To detach the left rear junction block, unscrew the tube nut, then remove the bracket bolt (arrow)

7.3b To detach the right rear junction block, unscrew the tube nuts (one line is from the proportioning valve, the other goes to the left junction block), then unscrew the bracket bolt (arrow)

right positions. If the hose makes contact, remove it and correct the installation as necessary.

Metal brake line

9   When replacing brake lines be sure to use the correct parts. Don't use copper tubing for any brake system components. Purchase steel brake lines from a dealer or auto parts store.

10   Prefabricated brake line, with the tube ends already flared and fit-

tings installed, is available at auto parts stores and dealers. These lines are also sometimes bent to the proper shapes.

11   When installing the new line make sure it's securely supported in the brackets and has plenty of clearance between moving or hot components.

12   After installation, check the master cylinder fluid level and add fluid as necessary. Bleed the brake system as outlined in the next Section and test the brakes carefully before driving the vehicle in traffic.

---

8   Brake hydraulic system - bleeding

▶ **Refer to illustration 8.8**

➡Note: Bleeding the hydraulic system is necessary to remove any air that manages to find its way into the system when it's been opened during removal and installation of a hose, line, caliper or master cylinder.

1   It will probably be necessary to bleed the system at all four brakes if air has entered the system due to low fluid level, or if the brake lines have been disconnected at the master cylinder.

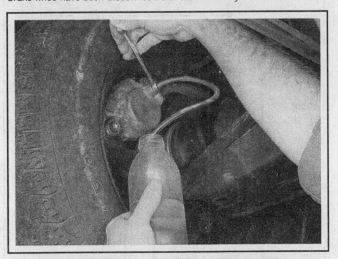

8.8   When bleeding the brakes, a hose is connected to the bleed screw at the caliper or wheel cylinder and then submerged in brake fluid - air will be seen as bubbles in the tube and container (all air must be expelled before moving to the next wheel)

2   If a brake line was disconnected only at a wheel, then only that caliper or wheel cylinder must be bled.

3   If a brake line is disconnected at a fitting located between the master cylinder and any of the brakes, that part of the system served by the disconnected line must be bled.

4   Remove any residual vacuum from the brake power booster by applying the brake several times with the engine off.

5   Remove the master cylinder reservoir cover and fill the reservoir with brake fluid. Reinstall the cover.

➡Note: Check the fluid level often during the bleeding operation and add fluid as necessary to prevent the fluid level from falling low enough to allow air bubbles into the master cylinder.

6   Have an assistant on hand, as well as a supply of new brake fluid, an empty clear plastic container, a length of 3/16-inch plastic, rubber or vinyl tubing to fit over the bleeder valve and a wrench to open and close the bleeder valve.

7   Beginning at the right rear wheel, loosen the bleeder valve slightly, then tighten it to a point where it is snug but can still be loosened quickly and easily.

8   Place one end of the tubing over the bleeder valve and submerge the other end in brake fluid in the container (see illustration).

9   Have the assistant pump the brakes slowly a few times to get pressure in the system, then hold the pedal firmly depressed.

10   While the pedal is held depressed, open the bleeder valve just enough to allow a flow of fluid to leave the valve. Watch for air bubbles to exit the submerged end of the tube. When the fluid flow slows after a couple of seconds, close the valve and have your assistant release the pedal.

11   Repeat Steps 9 and 10 until no more air is seen leaving the tube, then tighten the bleeder valve and proceed to the left rear wheel, the right front wheel and the left front wheel, in that order, and perform the same procedure. Be sure to check the fluid in the master cylinder reservoir frequently.

12   Never use old brake fluid. It contains moisture which will deteriorate the brake system components.

13   Refill the master cylinder with fluid at the end of the operation.

14   Check the operation of the brakes. The pedal should feel solid when depressed, with no sponginess. If necessary, repeat the entire process.

9   Power brake booster - check, removal, installation and adjustment

VACUUM BOOSTER

1   The power brake booster unit requires no special maintenance apart from periodic inspection of the vacuum hose and the case.

2   Dismantling of the brake booster requires special tools and is not ordinarily done by the home mechanic. If a problem develops, install a new or factory rebuilt unit.

Check

3   Begin the power booster check by depressing the brake pedal several times with the engine off and make sure that there is no change in the pedal reserve distance. The reserve distance is the distance between the pedal and the floor when the pedal is fully depressed.

4   Now, depress the pedal and start the engine. If the pedal goes down slightly, operation is normal. Release the brake pedal and let the engine run for a couple of minutes.

5   Turn off the engine and depress the brake pedal several times slowly. If the pedal goes down farther the first time but gradually rises after the second or third depression, the booster is airtight.

6   Start the engine and depress the brake pedal, then stop the engine with the pedal still depressed. If there is no change in the reserve distance after holding the pedal for about 30-seconds, the booster is airtight.

7   If the pedal feels "hard" when the engine is running, the booster isn't operating properly or there is a vacuum leak in the hose to the booster.

Removal

▶ **Refer to illustration 9.9**

8   Remove the nuts attaching the master cylinder to the booster (see Section 8) and carefully pull the master cylinder forward until it clears the mounting studs. Use caution so as not to bend or kink the brake lines.

9   Detach the manifold vacuum hose from the booster check valve (see illustration).

10 Working in the passenger compartment under the steering column, unplug the electrical connector from the brake light switch (see Section 11), then remove the pushrod retaining clip and nylon washer from the brake pedal pin and slide the pushrod off the pin (see Section 11).

11 Remove the nuts attaching the brake booster to the firewall.

12 Carefully detach the booster from the firewall and lift it out of the engine compartment.

Installation

13 Place the booster into position on the firewall and tighten the mounting nuts to the torque listed in this Chapter's Specifications. Connect the pushrod and brake light switch to the brake pedal. Install the retaining clip in the brake pedal pin.

14 Install the master cylinder to the booster, tightening the nuts to the torque listed in this Chapter's Specifications.

15 Carefully check the operation of the brakes before driving the vehicle in traffic.

Adjustment

▶ **Refer to illustrations 9.16 and 9.20**

16 The booster has an adjustable pushrod. It's matched to the

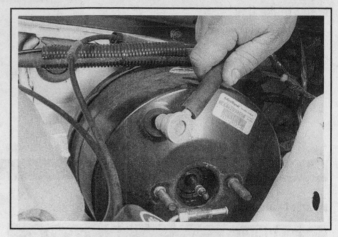

9.9 Detach the intake manifold vacuum hose from the power brake booster (vacuum type booster)

booster at the factory and most likely will not require adjustment, but if a misadjusted pushrod is suspected, a gauge can be fabricated out of heavy gauge sheet metal using the accompanying template (see illustration).

17 Some common symptoms caused by a misadjusted pushrod include dragging brakes (if the pushrod is too long) or excessive brake pedal travel accompanied by a groaning sound from the brake booster (if the pushrod is too short).

18 To check the pushrod length, unbolt the master cylinder from the booster and position it to one side. It isn't necessary to disconnect the hydraulic lines, but be careful not to bend them.

19 Block the front wheels, apply the parking brake and place the transmission in Park.

20 Start the engine and place the pushrod gauge against the end of

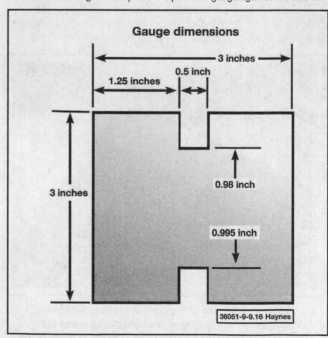

Gauge dimensions

3 inches

1.25 inches   0.5 inch

3 inches

0.98 inch

0.995 inch

36051-9-9.16 Haynes

9.16 If you want to measure the power brake booster pushrod exactly, fabricate a pushrod gauge template to these dimensions

9.20 You can also measure the pushrod with a ruler, but this method is a little more difficult and potentially less accurate

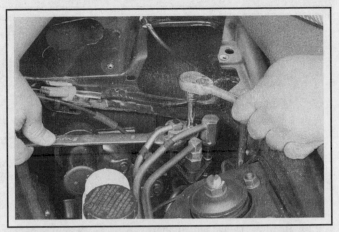

9.32 Disconnect the three hydraulic lines from the Hydro-Boost unit or, as shown here, from the remote junction bracket located next to the booster (the short lines from the junction to the booster can be more easily removed after the booster is out of the car)

the pushrod, exerting a force of approximately five pounds to seat the pushrod in the power unit.

➡ **Note: If you have a vacuum pump, you can simply apply vacuum to the booster instead of starting the engine.**

The rod measurement should fall somewhere between the minimum and maximum cutouts on the gauge. If it doesn't, adjust it by holding the knurled portion of the pushrod with a pair of pliers and turning the end with a wrench. If you don't have a template, use a steel pocket ruler to measure how far the pushrod protrudes from the booster (see illustration).

21 When the adjustment is complete, reinstall the master cylinder and check for proper brake operation before driving the vehicle in traffic.

HYDRAULIC BOOSTER

Check

22 Check the fluid in the master cylinder. If the fluid level isn't within 1/4-inch of the top of the master cylinder reservoirs, top it off with brake fluid (see Chapter 1).

23 Check the power steering pump fluid level with the engine off and the fluid at operating temperature (see Chapter 1).

24 Check the power steering pump belt tension and adjust it if necessary (see Chapter 1).

25 Inspect all power steering system hoses for leaks and kinks. If the fluid smells burned, check the hoses and cooler for restrictions.

26 Check the engine idle speed and adjust it to specifications (see Chapter 1).

27 Check the power steering hydraulic fluid for aeration (indicated by bubbles in the fluid). If there is any air in the system, bleed the power steering system (see Chapter 10).

28 If, after completing the above preliminary checks, you still can't find the cause of the condition, perform the following functional test of the system:

    a) *Check the brake system for leaks or insufficient fluid in the master cylinder reservoir.*

    b) *With the transmission in Neutral, stop the engine and apply the brake pedal several times to deplete all accumulator reserve.*

    c) *Hold the pedal depressed and start the engine. If the Hydro-Boost unit is operating correctly, the brake pedal will fall slightly, then it will push back against your foot. If you don't feel this "push-back" right after starting the engine, the Hydro-Boost unit is not working correctly.*

    d) *Start the engine and operate it at idle speed. Turn the steering wheel to the stop. Hold for a maximum of five seconds. Return*

the steering wheel to center and turn off the engine.

    e) *Depress and release the brake pedal. Repeat this procedure until a "hard pedal" is obtained. There should be at least two power-assisted brake applications with pressure applied to the pedal.*

    f) *Restart the engine and let it idle. Turn the steering wheel to the stop. There should be a light hissing sound as the accumulator is charged. Hold lightly against the stop for a maximum of five seconds. Return the steering wheel to center and turn off the engine.*

    g) *Wait one hour and apply the brake pedal (do not restart the engine). There should still be at least two power-assisted brake applications when the pedal is depressed before you feel a "hard pedal."*

29 If the Hydro-Boost unit is working correctly, the problem lies somewhere in the brake system; if the Hydro-Boost unit is not working properly, verify that the power steering is operating normally. You'll have to take the vehicle to a dealer service department to have the power steering pump tested for flow and pressure.

30 If power steering operation is normal, and the Hydro-Boost unit is suspect, refer to the *Troubleshooting* Section at the front of this manual and check those items related to the Hydro-Boost system. If the Hydro-Boost unit itself is the problem, do not attempt to overhaul it; replace it with a new or rebuilt unit.

Removal

▶ **Refer to illustrations 9.32, 9.33, 9.34a and 9.34b**

31 Discharge the accumulator by repeatedly depressing the brake pedal until a "hard pedal" is obtained.

32 Remove the two nuts attaching the master cylinder to the Hydro-Boost unit (see illustration), pull it off and secure it to one side, with the metal hydraulic lines still attached (make sure you don't kink or bend these lines, or they will have to be replaced).

33 Disconnect the pressure, steering gear and return lines from the booster (see illustration). Plug the lines and the ports in the Hydro-Boost unit to prevent dirt from contaminating the system.

34 From under the dashboard, disconnect the Hydro-Boost pushrod from the brake pedal assembly as follows (refer to Section 11 for help in disconnecting the brake light switch):

    a) *Unplug the brake light switch electrical connector.*

    b) *Remove the retainer from the clevis pin.*

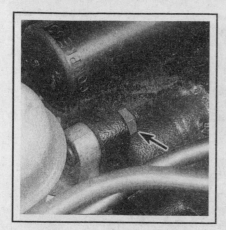

9.33 Remove the two nuts (upper nut shown) that attach the master cylinder to the Hydro-Boost unit

9.34a To detach the Hydro-Boost unit from the firewall, remove these retaining nuts (arrows) from inside the vehicle . . .

9.34b . . . and this nut (arrow) from the engine compartment side of the firewall

c) Slide the brake light switch off the brake pedal pin just far enough for the switch outer hole to clear the pin, then remove the switch from the pin.
d) Loosen the Hydro-Boost-to-firewall locknuts (see illustrations). There are three nuts on the inside of the vehicle and one in the engine compartment.
e) Slide the Hydro-Boost pushrod and the nylon washers and bushing off the brake pedal pin.

35 Remove the Hydro-Boost-to-firewall locknuts and remove the Hydro-Boost unit, sliding the pushrod link out from the engine side of the hole in the firewall. Don't lose the rubber dust boot.

Installation

36 Place the Hydro-Boost assembly in position on the firewall and insert the pushrod and boot through the hole in the firewall. Loosely install the Hydro-Boost-to-firewall locknuts.

37 Working under the dash, connect the Hydro-Boost pushrod to the brake pedal assembly as follows (refer to Section 11 if necessary):

a) Install the inner nylon washer, the Hydro-Boost pushrod and the bushing on the brake pedal pin.
b) Position the switch so that it straddles the pushrod with the switch slot on the pedal pin and the switch outer hole just clear-

ing the pin. Slide the switch completely onto the pin and install the nylon washer. Be careful not to deform the switch.
c) Secure these parts to the pin with the hairpin retainer.
d) Plug in the brake light switch connector and install the wires in the retaining clip.
e) Tighten the Hydro-Boost-to-firewall locknuts securely.

38 Install the master cylinder on the Hydro-Boost unit and tighten the master cylinder mounting nuts to the torque listed in this Chapter's Specifications.

39 Remove the plugs and connect the fluid pressure, steering gear and return hoses to the Hydro-Boost unit. Tighten the fittings securely.

40 Remove the coil wire to disable the engine. Fill the power steering pump reservoir and, while engaging the starter, apply the brakes with a pumping action. Do NOT turn the steering wheel lock-to-lock until all residual air has been purged from the Hydro-Boost.

41 Check the fluid level and add fluid as necessary.

42 Install the coil wire, start the engine and apply the brakes with a pumping action. Turn the steering wheel lock-to-lock several times. Check for leaks.

43 If you hear a whining noise after installing a Hydro-Boost unit, fluid aeration may be the problem. Bleed the power steering system (see Chapter 10).

10 Parking brake cables - replacement

FRONT CABLE

◆ **Refer to illustration 10.5, 10.6 and 10.7**

1 Remove the center console (see Chapter 11).
2 Release the parking brake lever completely.
3 Raise the vehicle and support it securely on jackstands.
4 Get inside the vehicle. Have an assistant under the vehicle pull the parking brake equalizer to the rear about 2-1/2 inches to rotate the self-adjusting reel counterclockwise.
5 Insert a steel gage pin or drill bit through the holes in the parking brake lever, the lever base assembly and the adjuster reel (see illustration).

✳✳ CAUTION:

Do NOT remove the gage pin or drill bit until the parking brake cable has been reinstalled. If you do so, the spring-loaded adjuster reel will unwind and the entire parking brake lever assembly will have to be removed in order to rewind the adjuster mechanism.

6 Disengage the cable from the adjuster reel (see illustration).
7 Underneath the vehicle, disengage the cable equalizer from the two rear cables (see illustration).
8 Pull the cable down through the grommet in the floorpan and remove it.

10.5 Insert a steel gage pin, drill bit or punch through the hole in the parking brake lever and through the adjuster reel; do NOT remove the gage pin, drill bit or punch until the front parking brake cable has been reinstalled. If you do, the spring-loaded adjuster reel will unwind and the entire parking brake lever assembly will have to be removed in order to rewind the adjuster mechanism

10.6 Disengage the front parking brake cable from the adjuster reel

9   Installation is the reverse of removal. Don't remove the gage pin or drill bit from the adjuster reel until you have connected the cable to the reel and the equalizer to the rear cables.

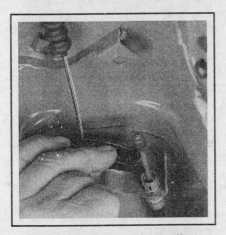

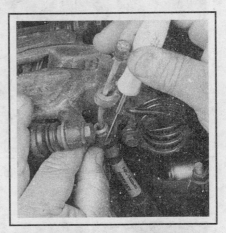

10.7 Disengage the cable equalizer from the two rear cables

10.12a To remove a rear parking brake cable, disengage the cable from the caliper lever . . .

10.12b . . . remove this C-clip from the cable boss on the rear caliper . . .

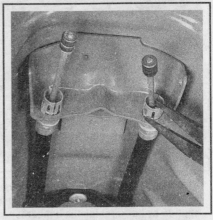

10.12c . . . remove this cable bracket bolt (arrow) from the lower suspension arm . . .

10.12d . . . remove this cable bracket bolt (arrow) from the underside of the pan . . .

10.12e . . . then squeeze the tangs of the cable housing together and disengage the cable from this bracket

REAR CABLES

▶ **Refer to illustrations 10.12a through 10.12e**

10 Make sure the parking brake is released. Release cable tension as described in Steps 4 and 5.

11 Raise the rear of the vehicle and place it securely on jackstands.

12 To disconnect the rear cable, follow the accompanying procedure (see illustrations).

13 Installation is the reverse of removal.

11 Brake light switch - check and replacement

CHECK

▶ **Refer to illustrations 11.1 and 11.4**

1   The brake light switch (see illustration), which is located near the top of the brake pedal, closes the circuit for the brake lights when the brake pedal is applied. If the switch doesn't operate as described, either it's not getting voltage, or there's a problem in the circuit between the switch and the brake lights, or the switch is bad.

2   Check the brake light circuit fuse (see Chapter 12).

3   If the fuse is okay, remove the lower steering column trim panel (see Chapter 11), then backprobe the switch electrical connector (light green wire with a red stripe and ground) to verify that the switch is getting voltage.

4   If the switch is getting voltage, verify that there's continuity on the brake light side of the switch when the brake pedal is applied by backprobing the light green wire with a red stripe (power to the switch) and the red wire with a light green stripe (brake light circuit) (see illustration) and that there's no continuity when the pedal is released.

5   If the switch is operating correctly, troubleshoot the circuit between the switch and the brake lights (see the Wiring Diagrams at the end of Chapter 12).

REPLACEMENT

▶ **Refer to illustrations 11.7a, 11.7b, 11.7c, 11.7d, 11.8 and 11.10**

6   Remove the lower steering column trim panel (see Chapter 11).

7   Remove the retainer, remove the white nylon washer, remove the switch and remove the nylon bushing (see illustrations).

8   Use a small screwdriver to unlock the electrical connector (see illustration), then unplug the connector from the brake light switch.

9   Plug the new switch into the electrical connector; make sure it snaps into place.

10 To reconnect the switch assembly to the brake pedal, position

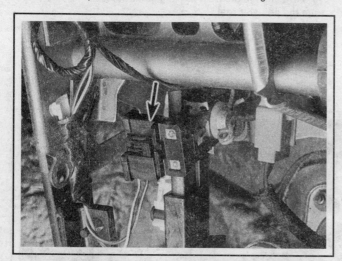

11.1 The brake light switch (arrow) is located near the top of the brake pedal

11.4 Hook up an ohmmeter to verify that there's continuity on the brake light side of the switch when the brake pedal is applied by backprobing the light green wire with a red stripe (power to the switch) and the red wire with a light green stripe (brake light circuit) and that there's no continuity when the pedal is released

11.7a To detach the brake light switch from the power brake pushrod, remove the switch retainer . . .

11.7b . . . remove the white nylon washer . . .

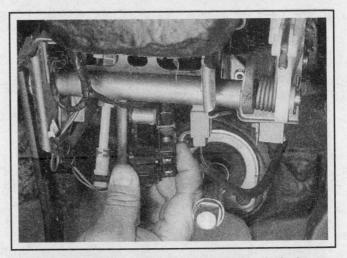

11.7c . . . disengage the switch from the pin on the brake pedal and remove the switch

11.7d Don't lose this nylon bushing; when you install the switch, the bushing goes between the pushrod and the pin at the top of the pedal, between the two sideplates of the switch

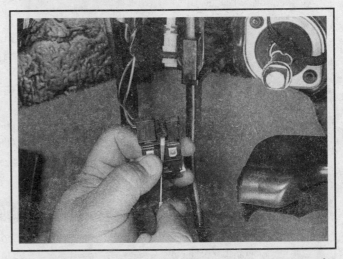

11.8 Pry open the locking tab on the electrical connector and unplug the connector from the switch

the switch so that the U-shaped side faces the brake pedal, position the master cylinder pushrod and nylon bushing between the switch sideplates (see illustration), then push the switch forward, install the white plastic washer on the pin and install the hairpin retainer clip.

11 Install the lower steering column trim panel (see Chapter 11).

12 Check the brake lights for proper operation.

11.10 When installing the brake light switch, make sure the U-shaped side faces the brake pedal and make sure the master cylinder pushrod and nylon bushing are positioned correctly, between the switch sideplates

Specifications

Brake fluid type	See Chapter 1

Disc brakes

Minimum brake pad thickness	See Chapter 1
Front brake disc	
Standard thickness	
Cobra	1.10 inches
All other models	1.03 inches
Minimum thickness*	
Cobra	1.04 inches
All other models	0.97 inch
Runout limit	0.001 inch
Thickness variation (parallelism)	0.0004 inch
Rear brake disc	
Standard thickness	
Cobra	0.71 inch
All other models	0.55 inch
Minimum thickness*	
Cobra	0.66 inch
All other models	0.50 inch
Runout limit	0.002 inch
Thickness variation (parallelism)	0.0003 inch

Refer to marks stamped on the disc (they supersede information printed here)

Torque specifications

	Ft-lbs
Front anchor plate bolts	85 to 95
Rear anchor plate bolts	65 to 87
Brake caliper (front) bolt (except Cobra)	
1997 and earlier	65
1998 and later	23
Brake caliper (rear) bolts	23 to 26
Brake hose-to-front caliper banjo bolts	29
Brake hose-to-rear caliper banjo bolts	30 to 44
Master cylinder to-power brake booster	
mounting nuts	16 to 22
Power brake booster-to-firewall mounting nuts	16 to 21

Section

Reference to other Chapters

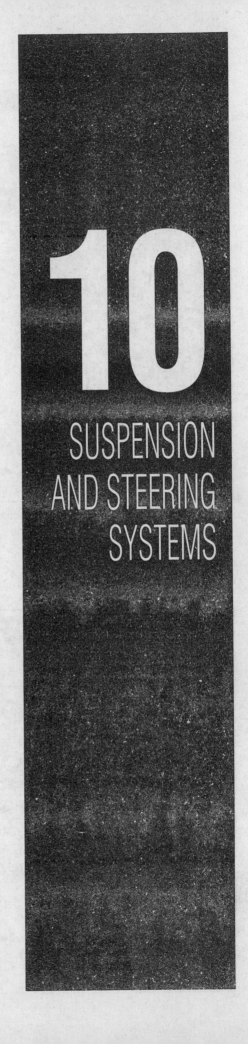

10

SUSPENSION AND STEERING SYSTEMS

1 General information

1.1a Front suspension and steering components

1	Front stabilizer bar
2	Stabilizer bar clamp
3	Stabilizer bar-to-lower control arm link
4	Lower control arm
5	Lower control arm rear pivot bolt/nut
6	Lower control arm front pivot bolt/nut
7	Tie-rod end
8	Tie-rod end jam nut
9	Steering gear/tie-rod dust boot
10	Steering gear assembly
11	Coil spring
12	Strut assembly

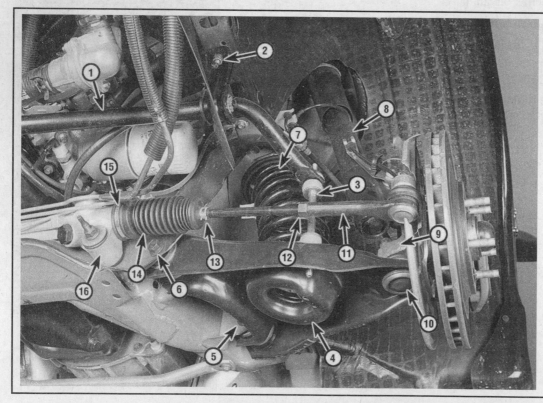

1.1b A close-up view of the front suspension

1   Stabilizer bar
2   Stabilizer bar clamp
3   Stabilizer bar-to-lower control arm link
4   Lower control arm
5   Control arm pivot bolt/ nut
6   Control arm pivot bolt/ nut
7   Coil spring
8   Strut assembly
9   Steering knuckle
10   Balljoint
11   Tie-rod end
12   Tie-rod end jam nut
13   Steering gear dust boot outer clamp
14   Steering gear dust boot
15   Steering gear dust boot inner clamp
16   Steering gear

1.2a Rear suspension components

1   Stabilizer bar
2   Lower suspension arm pivot bolt/nut

3   Lower suspension arm-to-rear axle bolt/
nut
4   Upper suspension arm pivot bolt/nut

5   Shock absorber
6   Shock absorber-to-rear axle bolt/nut
7   Coil spring

▶ **Refer to illustrations 1.1a, 1.1b, 1.2a and 1.2b**

✳✳ WARNING:

Whenever any of the suspension or steering fasteners are loosened or removed they must be inspected and if necessary, replaced with new ones of the same part number or of original equipment quality and design. Torque specifications must be followed for proper reassembly and component retention. Never attempt to heat, straighten or weld any suspension or steering component. Instead, replace any bent or damaged part with a new one.

➡Note: These vehicles use a combination of standard and metric fasteners on the various suspension and steering components, so it would be a good idea to have both types of tools available when beginning work.

The front suspension (see illustrations) is fully independent, allowing each wheel to compensate for road surface irregularities without appreciably affecting the other. Each wheel is connected to the frame by a steering knuckle, a balljoint, a lower control arm and a strut assembly positioned vertically between the steering knuckle and the vehicle body. A coil spring is mounted between the lower control arm and the front suspension crossmember. Body side roll is controlled by a stabilizer

1.2b A close-up view of the upper suspension arms

1   Upper suspension arm pivot bolt/nut
2   Upper suspension arm-to-rear axle bolt/nut

bar attached to the frame and to the lower control arms.

The rear suspension (see illustrations) consists of the axle, two coil springs, a pair of shock absorbers, and four - two lower and two upper - suspension arms. Body roll is controlled by a stabilizer bar attached to the two lower suspension arms.

The steering system consists of the steering wheel, steering column, intermediate shaft, rack-and-pinion steering gear, power steering pump and a pair of tie-rods, which connect the steering gear to the steering knuckles.

2 -Strut (front) - removal and installation

REMOVAL

▶ **Refer to illustrations 2.3, 2.4 and 2.5**

1   Loosen the front wheel lug nuts, raise the vehicle and support it securely on jackstands. Remove the wheels.

2   Place a floor jack under the lower control arm and raise it slightly. The lower control arm must be supported throughout the entire procedure.

3   If the vehicle is equipped with ABS, remove the nut (see illustration) which attaches the bracket for the ABS lead to the strut.

4   Remove the strut-to-steering knuckle nuts and bolts (see illustration).

5   Unscrew the three upper mount-to-body retaining bolt and nuts (see illustration).

6   Separate the strut assembly from the steering knuckle and remove it from the vehicle. Don't allow the steering knuckle to fall outward, as the brake hose could be damaged.

7   Installation is the reverse of removal. Be sure to tighten all fasteners to the torque listed in this Chapter's Specifications.

8   Remove the jack from under the lower control arm, install the

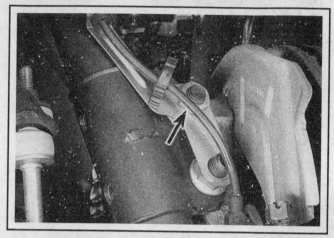

2.3 If the vehicle is equipped with ABS, remove this nut (arrow) and detach the bracket for the ABS lead

wheels, lower the vehicle and tighten the lug nuts to the torque listed in the Chapter 1 Specifications.

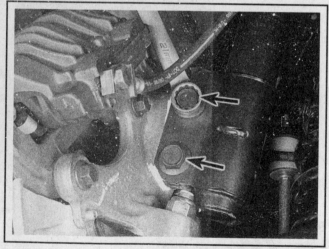

2.4 To detach the lower end of the strut from the steering knuckle, remove these two bolts (arrows); note the alignment marks painted on the strut, along the edge of the strut bracket, to ensure that correct camber is restored when the new strut is installed

2.5 To detach the upper end of the strut from the vehicle, remove this bolt and these nuts (arrows)

3   Stabilizer bar (front) - removal and installation

REMOVAL

▶ **Refer to illustrations 3.2a, 3.2b and 3.3**

1   Raise the vehicle and support it securely on jackstands. Apply the parking brake.

2   Remove the stabilizer bar-to-link nuts (see illustration), noting how the washers and bushings are positioned. Clamp a pair of locking pliers to the stabilizer bar link to prevent it from turning. Inspect the bushings for wear. If they're cracked or torn, replace them. To detach the lower end of either link from the lower control arm, remove the lower nut (see illustration) located underneath the control arm.

3   Remove the stabilizer bar bracket nuts (see illustration) and detach the bar from the vehicle.

4   Pull the brackets off the stabilizer bar and inspect the bushings for cracks, hardening and other signs of deterioration. If the bushings are damaged, cut them off the bar and discard them.

INSTALLATION

5   Lubricate the new stabilizer bar bushings with a rubber lubricant (such as a silicone spray) and slide the bushings onto the bar. The bushings should be installed with the seam facing forward.

6   Push the brackets over the bushings and raise the bar up to the frame. Install the bracket nuts but don't tighten them completely at this time.

3.2a To disconnect the stabilizer bar from the links, remove the nut (arrow) from each stabilizer bar link; make sure to note the order in which the bushings and washers are installed - they must be installed in the same sequence when the stabilizer is installed

7   Install the stabilizer bar link washers and rubber bushings and tighten the nuts.

8   Tighten the bracket nuts and the stabilizer link nuts to the torque listed in this Chapter's Specifications.

3.2b To disconnect either link from a lower control arm, remove this nut; be sure to note the order in which the washers and bushings are installed

3.3 To detach the stabilizer bar from the frame, remove these nuts (arrows) that attach the bushing clamps to the frame (left bushing clamp shown)

4 Coil spring (front) - removal and installation

REMOVAL

♦ **Refer to illustrations 4.5, 4.8a, 4.8b, 4.8c and 4.8d**

✳✳ WARNING:

The following procedure is potentially dangerous if the proper safety precautions are not taken. You should use a coil spring compressor designated for this purpose to safely perform this procedure.

1 Loosen the wheel lug nuts on the side to be disassembled. Raise the vehicle, support it securely on jackstands and remove the wheel.
2 Disconnect the tie-rod end from the steering knuckle (see Section 15).
3 Disconnect the stabilizer bar link from the lower control arm (see Section 3).
4 Remove the steering gear bolts (see Section 17). (The steering gear must be raised slightly in order to remove the front pivot bolt from either lower control arm.)
5 On 3.8L models, install a suitable spring compressor tool, available at most auto parts stores, (see illustration); insert the upper plate of the tool through the spring upper pocket in the crossmember with the hooks on the plate pointing towards the center of the spring.
6 On 5.0L and 4.6L models, install a spring compressor tool with a plate between the coils near the top of the spring.
7 Guide the compression rod up through the hole in the lower control arm and the coil spring, then insert the end of the compression rod into the upper plate. Install the lower plate, ball nut, thrust washer and bearing and the forcing nut on the compression rod. Tighten the forcing nut until the coil spring can be wiggled, indicating that all spring pressure has been taken up.
8 Remove the lower control arm-to-crossmember nuts and pivot bolts (see illustrations).
9 Remove the spring compressor compression rod then maneuver the coil spring out from between the lower control arm and crossmember.

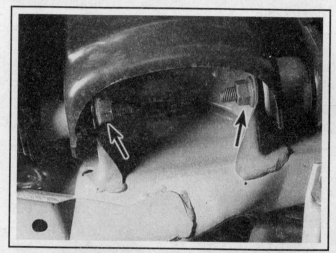

4.8a To detach the lower control arm from the front suspension crossmember, remove these nuts (arrows) and bolts . . .

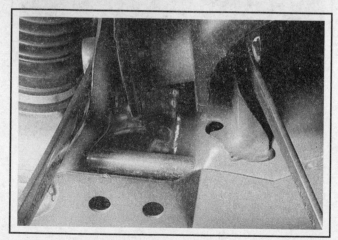

4.5 A typical aftermarket internal spring compressor tool - the hooked arms grip the upper coils of the spring, the plate is inserted below the lower coils, and when the nut on the threaded rod is turned, the spring is compressed

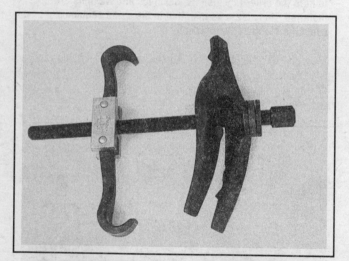

4.8b . . . using two wrenches

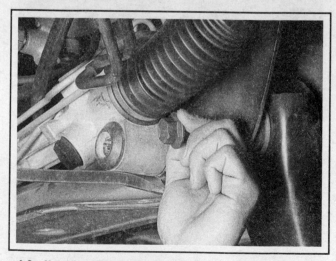

4.8c Note that the steering gear has been unbolted and raised up to provide sufficient clearance to remove the front pivot bolt for the lower control arm

INSTALLATION

10 Install the coil spring insulator on the top of the spring.

11 Install the spring in between the lower control arm and the spring upper pocket in the suspension crossmember.

12 Position the bottom of the spring so that the pigtail covers only one of the drain holes, but leaves the other one open.

13 Locate the spring in the upper seat in the crossmember. Install the spring compressor tool as described in Steps 3 and 4, then tighten the forcing nut until the lower control arm bushing holes align with the pivot bolt holes in the crossmember.

14 Install the lower control arm pivot bolts and nuts with the bolt heads facing out (away from each other). Don't tighten them completely at this time.

15 Remove the spring compressor tool. Position a floor jack under the outer end of the lower control arm and raise it to simulate a normal ride position. Now tighten the pivot bolt nuts to the torque listed in this Chapter's Specifications.

16 Reattach the steering gear (see Section 17) and tighten the steering gear bolts to the torque listed in this Chapter's Specifications.

17 Reconnect the stabilizer bar link to the lower control arm (see Section 3).

18 Reattach the tie-rod end to the steering knuckle (see Section 15).

19 Install the front wheel, remove the jackstands and lower the

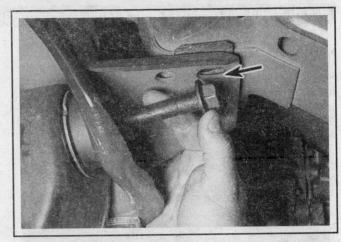

4.8d The suspension crossmember bolt (arrow) must be removed before the rear pivot bolt for the lower control arm can be removed

vehicle. Tighten the wheel lug nuts to the torque listed in the Chapter 1 Specifications.

20 Have the alignment checked by a dealer service department or an alignment shop.

5   Lower control arm (front) - removal and installation

1 Loosen the wheel lug nuts, raise the vehicle and support it securely on jackstands. Remove the wheel.

2 Remove the coil spring (see Section 4).

3 Unscrew the balljoint nut, strike the steering knuckle sharply with a hammer to break the ballstud loose and remove the control arm from the vehicle. A "pickle fork" type balljoint separator can be used, but it will damage the balljoint seal, so avoid a pickle fork unless you're planning to replace the balljoint.

4 Installation is the reverse of the removal procedure. Be sure to tighten all of the fasteners to the torque listed in this Chapter's Specifications. Tighten the lug nuts to the torque listed in the Chapter 1 Specifications.

5 Have the alignment checked by a dealer service department or an alignment shop.

6   Balljoint - check and replacement

CHECK

▶ **Refer to illustration 6.3**

1 Raise the front end of the vehicle and place it securely on jackstands.

2 Place a floor jack under the lower control arm and raise the jack just enough to support the arm.

3 Grasp the top and bottom of the tire, then try to simultaneously push in at the top and pull out at the bottom of the tire (see illustration), then the opposite (push in on the bottom while pulling out on the top). Replace the balljoint if there is any movement in the balljoint area.

REPLACEMENT

4 Remove the lower control arm (see Section 5).

5 Have the old balljoint pressed out of the arm and a new balljoint pressed in by an automotive machine shop.

6 Install the lower control arm (see Section 5).

7 Have the alignment checked by a dealer service department or an alignment shop.

6.3 To check a balljoint, raise the front of the vehicle and place it securely on jackstands, support the lower control arm with a floor jack, then try to rock the wheel in and out; if there's any play in the balljoint, replace it

7 Hub and bearing assembly - removal and installation

♦ **Refer to illustrations 7.3 and 7.4**

→**Note: The front wheel bearings are part of the hub and bearing assembly and are not serviced separately.**

1 Loosen the wheel lug nuts, apply the parking brake and raise the vehicle. Support it securely on jackstands placed under the frame. Remove the wheel.

2 Remove the brake caliper and hang it out of the way with a section of wire, then remove the caliper anchor and the brake disc (see Chapter 9).

3 Remove the grease cap from the hub and bearing assembly (see illustration).

4 Remove the hub and bearing retaining nut and washer (see illustration overleaf).

5 Remove the hub and bearing assembly. If the hub does not come off easily use an appropriate puller.

6 Installation is the reverse of removal. Be sure to clean off the spindle and lubricate it with wheel bearing grease, install the washer, then tighten the hub and bearing nut to the torque listed in this Chapter's Specifications. Tighten the lug nuts to the torque listed in the Chapter 1 Specifications.

7.3 To remove the hub and bearing retaining nut, first remove the grease cap with a hammer and chisel

7.4 To detach the hub and bearing assembly from the steering knuckle, remove the retaining nut and pull the hub from the spindle (this nut is very tight, so make sure the vehicle is supported securely)

8 Steering knuckle - removal and installation

1 Loosen the wheel lug nuts, apply the parking brake and raise the vehicle. Support it securely on jackstands placed under the frame. Remove the wheel.

2 Remove the brake caliper and hang it out of the way with a section of wire, then remove the caliper anchor and the brake disc (see Chapter 9).

3 Remove the hub and bearing assembly (see Section 7).

4 Loosen the strut-to-steering knuckle nuts (see Section 2), but don't remove the bolts yet.

5 Separate the tie-rod end from the steering knuckle (see Section 15).

6 Remove the lower control arm (see Section 5).

7 Remove the strut-to-steering knuckle nuts and bolts and remove the steering knuckle.

8 Remove the splash shield from the steering knuckle. The splash shield is riveted onto the steering knuckle with three rivets. Cut the backs off the rivets and drive out the rivets with a punch.

9 Install the splash shield. You can use appropriately sized bolts and self-locking nuts instead of rivets.

10 Installation is otherwise the reverse of removal. Be sure to tighten all fasteners to the torque listed in this Chapter's Specifications.

11 Install the wheel and lug nuts. Lower the vehicle to the ground and tighten the nuts to the torque listed in the Chapter 1 Specifications.

12 Have the alignment checked by a dealer service department or an alignment shop.

9 Stabilizer bar (rear) - removal and installation

▶ **Refer to illustrations 9.2 and 9.3**

1   Raise the rear of the vehicle and support it securely on jackstands. Place the jackstands under the frame, not under the axle housing. The axle housing must be free to hang down so that the shock absorbers are fully extended.

2   Detach the ABS lead, if equipped (see illustration), from the lower suspension arm.

3   Remove the four bolts (two on each arm) that attach the stabilizer

bar to the lower suspension arms (see illustration) and remove the bar.

4   Installation is the reverse of the removal procedure. Be sure to tighten all fasteners to the torque values listed in this Chapter's Specifications.

5   Remove the jackstands and lower the vehicle.

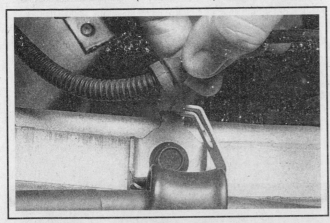

9.2. If the vehicle is equipped with ABS, disengage the ABS lead from its bracket on the lower suspension arm

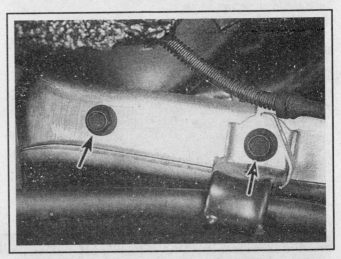

9.3 To detach the rear stabilizer bar from the lower suspension arms, remove these two bolts (arrows) from each arm (left lower suspension arm shown)

10 Shock absorber (rear) - removal and installation

▶ **Refer to illustrations 10.3 and 10.4**

1   Raise the rear of the vehicle and support it securely on jackstands placed under the frame, not under the axle housing.

2   Support the rear axle with a floor jack to prevent it from dropping when the shock absorber is disconnected.

3   Locate the upper retaining nut for the shock absorber inside the trunk (see illustration). To prevent the piston rod from turning, hold it

with a wrench or locking pliers while you break loose the nut. Remove the nut, washer and upper insulator. Discard the nut.

4   Remove the lower retaining nut and bolt (see illustration) and remove the shock absorber from the vehicle.

5   Installation is the reverse of removal. Be sure to tighten the upper and lower shock absorber fasteners to the torque listed in this Chapter's Specifications.

6   Remove the jackstands and lower the vehicle.

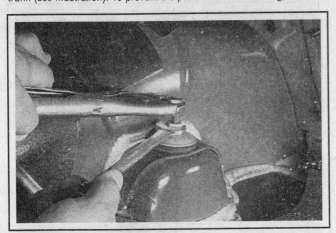

10.3 Locate the upper retaining nut for the shock absorber inside the trunk; to prevent the piston rod from turning, hold it with a wrench or locking pliers while you break loose the nut

10.4 Remove the lower retaining nut and bolt (arrows) and disengage the shock absorber from the axle bracket

11 Coil spring (rear) - removal and installation

REMOVAL

➡Note: Rear coil springs should always be replaced in pairs.

1 Loosen the wheel lug nuts, raise the rear of the vehicle and support it securely on jackstands placed under the frame. Remove the wheel and block the front wheels.

2 Remove the rear stabilizer bar (see Section 9).

3 Support the rear axle assembly with a floor jack placed under the axle housing.

4 Pass a length of chain up through the suspension arm and coil spring, then bolt the chain together. This will prevent the spring from flying out before it's fully extended. Be sure to leave enough slack in the chain to allow the coil spring to extend fully.

5 Detach the parking brake cable clips from the lower suspension arm (see Chapter 9).

6 Place a floor jack under the lower suspension arm pivot bolt and remove the pivot bolt and nut (see illustration 12.12).

7 Slowly lower the jack under the suspension arm until all tension is removed from the coil spring. Remove the chain, coil spring and insulators from between the suspension arm and the spring upper seat.

INSTALLATION

8 Set the upper insulator on top of the spring, using tape to hold it in place, if necessary.

9 Place the spring between its seat on the axle tube and the frame seat, so that the pigtail (the lower end of the spring) is at the rear and pointing toward the left side of the vehicle. Install the safety chain.

10 Raise the lower suspension arm with the floor jack and install the arm pivot bolt and nut (see Section 12).

11 Repeat Steps 4 through 7 for the other spring.

12 Reattach the parking brake cables to the lower suspension arms (see Chapter 10).

13 Install the rear stabilizer bar (see Section 9).

14 Install the wheel and lug nuts. Lower the vehicle and tighten the lug nuts to the torque listed in the Chapter 1 Specifications.

12 Suspension arms (rear) - removal and installation

❉❉ WARNING:

If you're going to remove both the upper and the lower arms at the same time, then remove the coil springs first (see Section 11).

➡Note: If one upper arm requires replacement, replace the other upper arm as well. The manufacturer recommends installing new fasteners when reassembling the rear suspension components.

1 Loosen the rear wheel lug nuts. Raise the rear of the vehicle and support it securely on jackstands placed beneath the frame rails. Block the front wheels. Remove the rear wheels.

2 Position a jack under the differential housing to support the axle.

UPPER ARM

▶ **Refer to illustrations 12.3 and 12.4**

3 Remove the upper arm-to-rear axle pivot bolt and nut (see illustration).

4 Remove the upper arm-to-frame pivot bolt and nut (see illustration) and remove the arm from the vehicle.

5 Inspect the bushings at both ends of the arm. If either bushing is damaged or worn, have it replaced by an automotive machine shop.

6 Position the leading end of the new suspension arm in the frame bracket. Install a new pivot bolt and nut with the bolt head facing forward. Don't fully tighten the nut at this time.

7 Attach the other end of the arm to the axle housing with a new

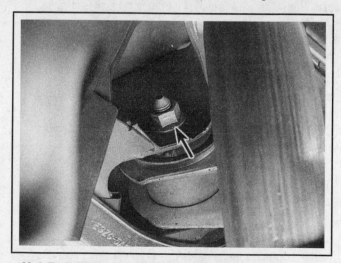

12.3 To disconnect an upper rear suspension arm from the axle, remove this bolt (arrow) and nut; note that the bolt head faces out

12.4 To disconnect an upper rear suspension arm from the vehicle, remove this nut (arrow) and bolt; note that the nut faces out

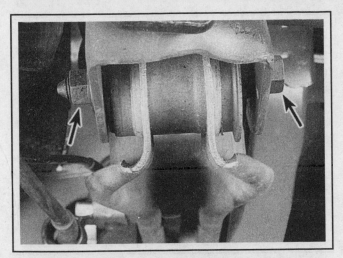

12.12 To disconnect a lower rear suspension arm from the axle bracket, remove this nut and bolt (arrows)

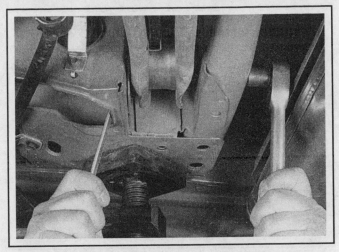

12.14 To disconnect a lower rear suspension arm from the vehicle, remove the nut and pivot bolt

pivot bolt and nut. The bolt head should be facing to the rear. It may be necessary to jack up the rear axle to align the holes. Don't fully tighten the nut yet.

8   Repeat Steps 3 through 6 and replace the other upper suspension arm, then proceed to Step 21.

LOWER ARM

▶ **Refer to illustrations 12.12 and 12.14**

➡**Note: If one lower arm requires replacement, replace the other lower arm as well. Also, the manufacturer recommends installing new fasteners when reassembling the rear suspension components.**

9   Detach the ABS lead (see illustration 9.2), if equipped, from the lower suspension arm.

10 Remove the stabilizer bar (see Section 9).

11 Chain the coil spring to the lower suspension arm (see Section 11).

12 Place a jack under the lower suspension arm-to-axle pivot bolt and remove the pivot bolt and nut (see illustration).

13 Carefully lower the jack until all tension is removed from the spring.

14 Remove the lower arm-to-frame pivot bolt and nut (see illustra-

tion), then remove the arm from the vehicle.

15 Inspect the bushings at both ends of the arm. If either bushing is damaged or worn, have it replaced by an automotive machine shop.

16 Position the new lower arm in the frame mounting bracket and install a new pivot bolt and nut, with the nut facing out. Do not tighten the nut completely at this time.

17 Position the other end of the lower arm in the axle bracket and install a new bolt and nut (again, nut facing out). Do not fully tighten the nut at this time.

18 Repeat Steps 11 through 17 and replace the other lower suspension arm.

19 Remove both jacks (from underneath the differential and whichever lower suspension arm you just replaced) and place the two jacks underneath either end of the axle tube, then raise the axle until the rear of the vehicle is supported by the axle (this is the normal ride height). Tighten all pivot bolt nuts to the torque listed in this Chapter's Specifications.

20 Install the stabilizer bar (see Section 9).

UPPER OR LOWER ARM

21 Install the wheel and lug nuts. Remove the jackstands and floor jack, lower the vehicle and tighten the lug nuts to the torque listed in the Chapter 1 Specifications.

13 Axle damper - removal and installation

REMOVAL

▶ **Refer to illustrations 13.2 and 13.3**

1   Loosen the wheel lug nuts, raise the vehicle and support it on jackstands. Remove the wheel and place a floor jack under the rear axle

to support it, just in case it shifts when the axle damper is removed.

2   Remove the axle damper front attaching nut and bolt from the axle bracket (see illustration).

3   Remove the rear attaching nut (see illustration). Remove the bolts that hold the rear mounting bracket to the frame sidemember and remove the damper from the vehicle.

13.2 To disconnect the axle damper from the axle bracket, remove this nut (arrow)

13.3 To disconnect the axle damper from the vehicle bracket, remove this nut (arrow)

INSTALLATION

4   Place the rear bracket onto the axle damper and install the nut (don't tighten it yet).

5   Position the rear bracket on the frame sidemember and install the bolts, tightening them securely.

6   Swing the axle damper into the mount on the rear axle and install the pivot bolt and attaching nut, tightening them securely.

7   Tighten the rear retaining nut securely.

8   Install the wheel and lug nuts and lower the vehicle. Tighten the lug nuts to the torque listed in the Chapter 1 Specifications.

14   Steering wheel - removal and installation

▶ Refer to illustrations 14.3a, 14.3b, 14.4a, 14.4b, 14.5, 14.6, 14.7, 14.8 and 14.9

❊❊ WARNING:

The models covered by this manual are equipped with Supplemental Restraint Systems (SRS), more commonly known as airbags. Always disconnect the negative battery cable, then the positive battery cable and wait two minutes before working in the vicinity of the impact sensors, steering column or instrument panel to avoid the possibility of accidental deployment of the airbag, which could cause personal injury (see Chapter 12).

Do not use electrical test equipment on any of the airbag system wiring or tamper with them in any way. The steering column must not be rotated while the steering wheel is removed; to do so could damage the airbag contact assembly.

1   Position the front wheels in the straight-ahead position and lock the steering column.

2   To disable the airbag system, disconnect the cable from the negative terminal of the battery, disconnect the positive terminal of the battery, then wait two minutes before beginning work.

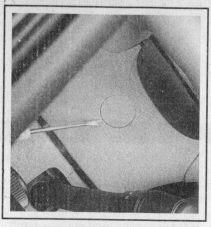

14.3a To remove the airbag module, pry off the small covers on either side of the steering wheel . . .

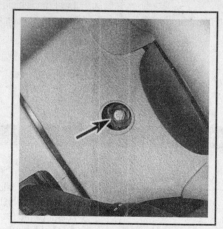

14.3b . . . then remove the airbag module retaining bolts (left side shown)

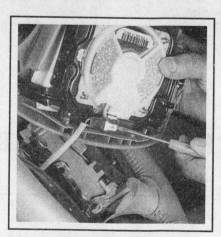

14.4a Lift the airbag module off the steering wheel, release the locking tab for the module electrical connector . . .

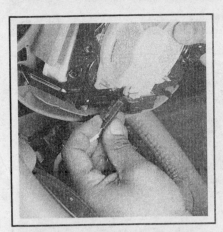

14.4b . . . and unplug the connector

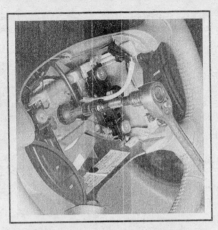

14.5 Remove and discard the steering wheel retaining bolt (Torx T50)

14.6 Unplug the electrical connector for cruise control, if equipped

3   Remove the two steering wheel covers for the airbag module retaining bolts, then remove the airbag module retaining bolts (see illustrations).

4   Lift the module off the steering wheel and unplug the module electrical connector (see illustrations).

> **WARNING:**
>
> **When handling an airbag module, always carry the module with the airbag side facing away from your body. Place the airbag in a safe location with the airbag side pointing up.**

5   Remove the steering wheel retaining bolt (see illustration).

> **WARNING:**
>
> **Discard the hub bolt. Use a new one during installation.**

6   Unplug the electrical connector for the cruise control, if equipped (see illustration).

7   There should already be an alignment mark on the upper edge of the steering shaft and another mark on the steering wheel hub. If not, then mark the relationship of the steering shaft to the hub (if marks don't already exist or don't line up) to simplify installation and ensure correct steering wheel alignment (see illustration).

8   Use a steering wheel puller to detach the steering wheel from the shaft (see illustration). Don't use an impact puller and don't pound on the steering wheel or shaft. Route the contact assembly wire harness through the steering wheel as the wheel is lifted off the shaft.

9   Before installing the steering wheel, make sure that the steering column shaft alignment mark is at the 12 o'clock position (see illustration).

10 To install the wheel, align the mark on the steering wheel hub with the mark on the shaft and slip the wheel onto the shaft. Install a new bolt and tighten it to the torque listed in this Chapter's Specifications.

11 Plug in the cruise control connector, if equipped.

12 Connect the airbag electrical connector and install the airbag module.

13 Install the airbag module retaining bolts and tighten them to the torque listed in this Chapter's Specifications.

14 Connect the positive, then the negative, battery cables.

14.7 Make sure there are alignment marks on the upper edge of the steering shaft and on the steering wheel hub - if there aren't, make marks

14.8 Install a steering wheel puller as shown to remove the steering wheel from the steering shaft

14.9 Before installing the steering wheel, make sure the steering shaft alignment mark is at the 12 o'clock position

15 Tie-rod ends - removal and installation

REMOVAL

▶ **Refer to illustrations 15.2a, 15.2b and 15.4**

1 Loosen the wheel lug nuts. Block the rear wheels and set the parking brake. Raise the front of the vehicle and support it securely. Remove the front wheel.

2 Loosen the jam nut enough to mark the position of the tie-rod end in relation to the threads (see illustrations).

3 Remove the cotter pin and loosen the nut on the tie-rod end stud.

4 Disconnect the tie-rod from the spindle arm with a puller (see illustration). Remove the nut and separate the tie-rod.

5 Unscrew the tie-rod end from the tie-rod.

INSTALLATION

6 Thread the tie-rod end on to the marked position and insert the tie-rod stud into the spindle arm. Tighten the jam nut securely.

7 Install a new nut on the stud and tighten it to the torque listed in this Chapter's Specifications. Install a new cotter pin.

8 Install the wheel and lug nuts. Lower the vehicle and tighten the

15.2a Before separating a tie-rod end from the steering knuckle, back off the jam nut . . .

lug nuts to the torque listed in the Chapter 1 Specifications.

9 Have the alignment checked by a dealer service department or an alignment shop.

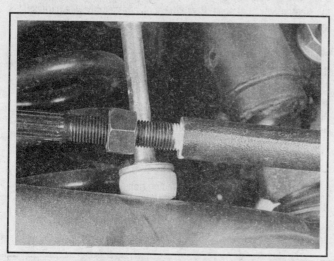

15.2b . . . and mark the relationship of the tie-rod end to the inner tie rod by marking the threads with paint; when you install the new tie-rod end, simply screw it back on up to this mark

15.4 Use a suitable small puller to separate the tie-rod end from the steering knuckle. Note that - as a safety measure - the castellated nut has been loosened, but NOT removed; that way, if the ballstud pops out of the knuckle with a lot of force, there's no danger of the tie-rod end flying out violently enough to cause injury

16 Steering gear boots - replacement

▶ **Refer to illustrations 16.3a and 16.3b**

1 Loosen the lug nuts, raise the vehicle and support it securely on jackstands. Remove the wheel.

2 Remove the tie-rod end (see Section 15).

3 Remove the steering gear boot clamps (see illustrations) and slide off the boot.

4 Before installing the new boot, wrap the threads and serrations on the end of the inner tie rod with a layer of tape so the small end of

the new boot isn't damaged.

5 Slide the new boot into position on the steering gear until it seats in the groove in the steering gear and install new clamps.

6 Remove the tape from the inner tie rod and install the tie-rod end (see Section 15).

7 Install the wheel and lug nuts. Lower the vehicle and tighten the lug nuts to the torque listed in this Chapter's Specifications.

8 Have the alignment checked by a dealer service department or an alignment shop.

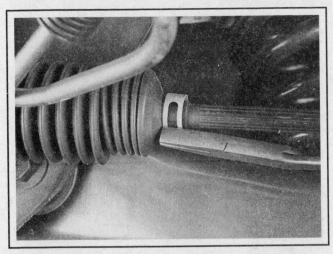

16.3a Before removing a steering gear dust boot, remove the outer boot clamp . . .

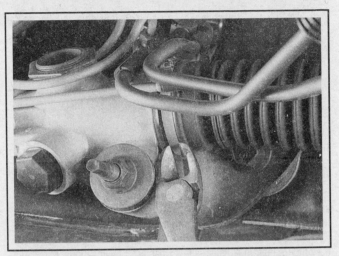

16.3b . . . and cut off the inner clamp; discard both clamps and use new ones with the new boot

17 Steering gear - removal and installation

✳✳ WARNING 1:

The models covered by this manual are equipped with Supplemental Restraint Systems (SRS), more commonly known as airbags. Always disconnect the negative battery cable, then the positive battery cable and wait two minutes before working in the vicinity of the impact sensors, steering column or instrument panel to avoid the possibility of accidental deployment of the airbag, which could cause personal injury (see Chapter 12).

✳✳ WARNING 2:

Do not allow the steering column to rotate while the steering gear is removed; damage to the airbag contact assembly could occur.

REMOVAL

◗ Refer to illustrations 17.4, 17.5 and 17.7

1   Position the front wheels in the straight-ahead position and lock the steering column.

2   To disable the airbag system, disconnect the cable from the negative terminal of the battery, disconnect the positive terminal of the battery, then wait two minutes before beginning work.

3   Raise the front of the vehicle and support it securely on jackstands. Apply the parking brake.

4   Place a drain pan under the steering gear. Disconnect the power steering pressure and return lines (see illustration) and cap the ends to prevent excessive fluid loss and contamination.

17.4 Disconnect the power steering pressure and return line fittings (arrows) and plug the lines to prevent contamination

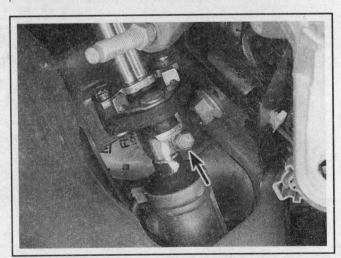

17.5 Mark the relationship of the steering shaft flexible coupling to the steering gear input shaft, then loosen and remove this pinch bolt (arrow)

5   Mark the relationship of the steering shaft flexible coupling to the steering gear input shaft, then remove the pinch bolt (see illustration).

6   Separate the tie-rod ends from the steering knuckles (see Section 15).

7   Support the steering gear and remove the steering gear-to-crossmember mounting nuts and bolts (see illustration). Lower the unit, separate the steering shaft from the steering gear input shaft and remove the steering gear from the vehicle.

INSTALLATION

8   Raise the steering gear into position, align the marks you made on the steering column shaft flexible coupling and steering gear input shaft, connect the steering gear input shaft to the flexible coupling. Install the pinch bolt but don't tighten it yet.

9   Install the steering gear mounting bolts and washers and tighten the nuts to the torque listed in this Chapter's Specifications. Make sure the bolt heads face to the rear and the nuts face forward.

10 Tighten the steering shaft flexible coupling pinch bolt to the torque listed in this Chapter's Specifications.

11 Connect the tie-rod ends to the steering knuckles (see Section 15).

12 Connect the power steering pressure and return hoses to the steering gear and fill the power steering pump reservoir with the recom-

17.7 To detach the steering gear from the front suspension crossmember, remove these nuts (arrows) and bolts; be sure to save all washers and install them exactly as removed

mended fluid (see Chapter 1).

13 Remove the jackstands and lower the vehicle.

14 Bleed the steering system (see Section 19).

18 Power steering pump - removal and installation

REMOVAL

♦ **Refer to illustrations 18.3a, 18.3b, 18.4 and 18.5**

1   Relieve tension on the serpentine belt (see Chapter 1).

2   On 3.8L and 5.0L engines, the pump can be accessed from above. On 4.6L engines, raise the front of the vehicle and place it securely on jackstands (the pump is more easily accessed from underneath the vehicle on these models).

3   Locate the pump on the left (driver's) side of the engine block. Disconnect the fluid return hose, drain the fluid from the pump reservoir, and disconnect the pressure hose (see illustrations). Plug the lines

to prevent contamination.

4   On 3.8L and 5.0L engines, the pump is mounted on a bracket bolted to the engine. You'll have to remove the pulley before you can remove the pump-to-bracket mounting bolts. A special puller for this purpose (see illustration) is available at most auto parts stores. On 4.6L engines, the pump is mounted directly on the block, so the pulley doesn't cover up the mounting bolts. On these models, it's easier to remove the pulley on the bench after you've removed the pump assembly.

5   Remove the pump mounting bolts (see illustration) and remove the pump.

18.3a To disconnect the power steering lines from the pump on a 4.6L model, remove this small bolt and remove the high pressure line bracket . . .

18.3b . . . then unscrew the high pressure fitting (arrow), squeeze the big hose clamp (arrow) and detach the return hose; to unbolt the pump from the block, remove all four mounting bolts (arrows)

18.4 You'll need a special puller to remove the power steering pump pulley on 3.8L and 5.0L models (on 4.6L models, this can be done off the vehicle)

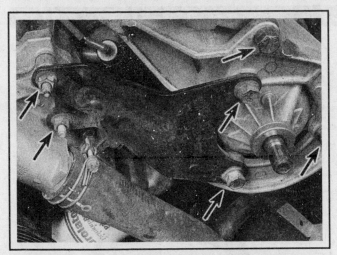

18.5 On 3.8L and 5.0L models, remove the pump bracket bolts (arrows) and the bracket, then remove the power steering pump bolts (arrows); on 4.6L models, the pump is bolted directly to the block (see illustration 18.3b)

INSTALLATION

◆ **Refer to illustration 18.6**

6   Installation is the reverse of the above procedure. On 3.8L and 5.0L engines, you'll need a special pulley installer tool (see illustration), available at most auto parts stores, to install the pulley once the

18.6 You'll also need a special pulley installer tool to press the pulley onto the pump shaft; NEVER hammer a pulley onto the shaft - you could damage the pump

pump is bolted to its mounting bracket.

7   Install the serpentine belt (see Chapter 1).

8   Install the pressure and return lines and fill the reservoir with an approved fluid. Start the engine and turn the steering wheel from lock to lock several times to distribute the fluid, then recheck the fluid level and top-off if necessary.

9   Bleed the power steering system (see Section 19).

19 Power steering system - bleeding

1   Following any operation in which the power steering fluid lines have been disconnected, the power steering system must be bled to remove all air and obtain proper steering performance.

2   With the front wheels in the straight ahead position, check the power steering fluid level and, if low, add fluid until it reaches the Cold mark on the dipstick.

3   Start the engine and allow it to run at fast idle. Recheck the fluid level and add more if necessary to reach the Cold mark on the dipstick.

4   Bleed the system by turning the wheels from side-to-side, without hitting the stops. This will work the air out of the system. Keep the reservoir full of fluid as this is done.

5   When the air is worked out of the system, return the wheels to the straight ahead position and leave the vehicle running for several more minutes before shutting it off.

6   Road test the vehicle to be sure the steering system is functioning normally and noise free.

7   Recheck the fluid level to be sure it is up to the Hot mark on the dipstick while the engine is at normal operating temperature. Add fluid if necessary (see Chapter 1).

20 Wheels and tires - general information

♦ **Refer to illustration 20.1**

All models covered by this manual are equipped with metric-sized radial tires (see illustration overleaf). Use of other size or type of tires may affect the ride and handling of the vehicle. Don't mix different types of tires, such as radials and bias belted, on the same vehicle as handling may be seriously affected. It's recommended that tires be replaced in pairs on the same axle, but if only one tire is being replaced, be sure it's the same size, structure and tread design as the other.

Because tire pressure has a substantial effect on handling and wear, the pressure on all tires should be checked at least once a month or before any extended trips (see Chapter 1).

Wheels must be replaced if they are bent, dented, leak air, have elongated bolt holes, are heavily rusted, out of vertical symmetry or if the lug nuts won't stay tight. Wheel repairs that use welding or peening are not recommended.

Tire and wheel balance is important to the overall handling, braking and performance of the vehicle. Unbalanced wheels can adversely affect handling and ride characteristics as well as tire life. Whenever a tire is installed on a wheel, the tire and wheel should be balanced by a shop with the proper equipment.

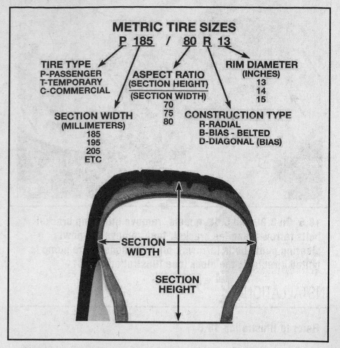

20.1 Metric tire size code

21 Front end alignment - general information

♦ **Refer to illustration 21.1**

A front end alignment refers to the adjustments made to the front wheels so they are in proper angular relationship to the suspension and the ground. Front wheels that are out of proper alignment not only affect steering control, but also increase tire wear (see illustration).

Getting the proper front wheel alignment is a very exacting process,

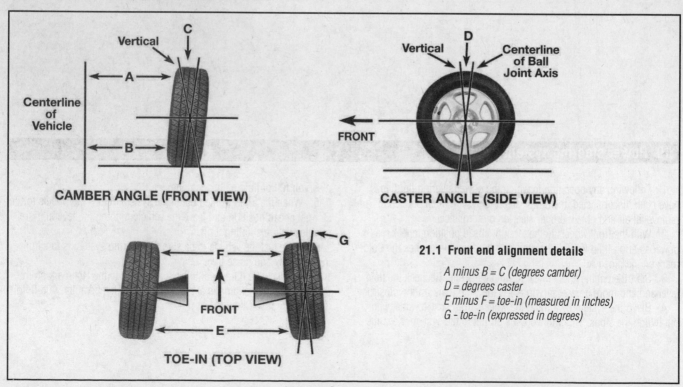

21.1 Front end alignment details

A minus B = C (degrees camber)
D = degrees caster
E minus F = toe-in (measured in inches)
G - toe-in (expressed in degrees)

one in which complicated and expensive machines are necessary to perform the job properly. Because of this, you should have a technician with the proper equipment perform these tasks. We will, however, use this space to give you a basic idea of what is involved with front end alignment so you can better understand the process and deal intelligently with the shop that does the work.

Toe-in is the turning in of the front wheels. The purpose of a toe specification is to ensure parallel rolling of the front wheels. In a vehicle with zero toe-in, the distance between the front edges of the wheels will be the same as the distance between the rear edges of the wheels. The actual amount of toe-in is normally only a fraction of an inch. Toe-in adjustment is controlled by the tie-rod end position on the tie-rod. Incorrect toe-in will cause the tires to wear improperly by making them scrub against the road surface.

Camber is the tilting of the front wheels from the vertical when viewed from the front of the vehicle. When the wheels tilt out at the top, the camber is said to be positive (+). When the wheels tilt in at the top the camber is negative (-). The amount of tilt is measured in degrees from the vertical and this measurement is called the camber angle. This angle affects the amount of tire tread which contacts the road and compensates for changes in the suspension geometry when the vehicle is cornering or traveling over an undulating surface.

Caster is the tilting of the top of the front steering axis from the vertical. A tilt toward the rear is positive caster and a tilt toward the front is negative caster. Specifications

Torque specifications	Ft-lbs (unless otherwise indicated)

Front suspension

Balljoint-to-steering knuckle nut	109 to 149
Hub and bearing retaining nut	221 to 295
Lower control arm pivot bolts/nuts	141 to 191
Stabilizer bar	
Stabilizer bar bracket nuts	44 to 59
Stabilizer bar link nuts	132 to 192 in-lbs
Strut	
Strut-to-steering knuckle bolts/nuts	141 to 191
Strut-to-vehicle bolt and nuts	25 to 34

Rear suspension

Axle damper	
Axle damper-to-axle bolt/nut	57 to 75
Axle damper-to-vehicle nut	57 to 75
Lower arm	
Lower arm-to-axle bolt/nut	71 to 97
Lower arm-to-frame bolt/nut	71 to 97
Shock absorber	
Shock absorber-to-axle bolt/nut	57 to 75
Shock absorber-to-vehicle nut	25 to 34
Stabilizer bar-to-lower arm bolts	29 to 37
Upper arm	
Upper arm-to-frame bolt/nut	71 to 97
Upper arm-to-axle bolt/nut	71 to 97

Steering

Airbag module retaining bolts	35 to 53 in-lbs
Tie-rod end-to-steering knuckle nut	35 to 47
Steering gear to-crossmember bolts	30 to 40
Steering shaft-to-steering gear U-joint pinch bolt	30 to 40
Steering wheel retaining bolt	22 to 33

Notes

Section

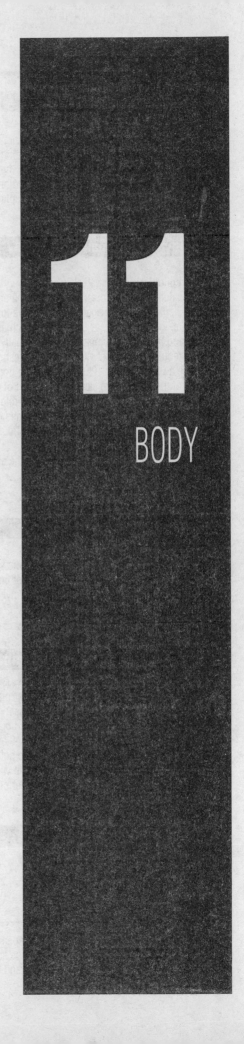

11

BODY

1 General information

These models feature a "unibody" construction, using a floor pan with front and rear frame side rails which support the body components, front and rear suspension systems and other mechanical components. Certain components are particularly vulnerable to accident damage and can be unbolted and repaired or replaced. Among these parts are the body moldings, bumpers, hood and trunk lids and all glass.

Only general body maintenance practices and body panel repair procedures within the scope of the do-it-yourselfer are included in this Chapter.

2 Body - maintenance

1   The condition of your vehicle's body is very important, because the resale value depends a great deal on it. It's much more difficult to repair a neglected or damaged body than it is to repair mechanical components. The hidden areas of the body, such as the wheel wells, the frame and the engine compartment, are equally important, although they don't require as frequent attention as the rest of the body.

2   Once a year, or every 12,000 miles, it's a good idea to have the underside of the body steam cleaned. All traces of dirt and oil will be removed and the area can then be inspected carefully for rust, damaged brake lines, frayed electrical wires, damaged cables and other problems. The front suspension components should be greased after completion of this job.

3   At the same time, clean the engine and the engine compartment with a steam cleaner or water soluble degreaser.

4   The wheel wells should be given close attention, since undercoating can peel away and stones and dirt thrown up by the tires can cause the paint to chip and flake, allowing rust to set in. If rust is found, clean down to the bare metal and apply an anti-rust paint.

5   The body should be washed about once a week. Wet the vehicle thoroughly to soften the dirt, then wash it down with a soft sponge and plenty of clean soapy water. If the surplus dirt is not washed off very carefully, it can wear down the paint.

6   Spots of tar or asphalt thrown up from the road should be removed with a cloth soaked in solvent.

7   Once every six months, wax the body and chrome trim. If a chrome cleaner is used to remove rust from any of the vehicle's plated parts, remember that the cleaner also removes part of the chrome, so use it sparingly.

3 Vinyl trim - maintenance

Don't clean vinyl trim with detergents, caustic soap or petroleum-based cleaners. Plain soap and water works just fine, with a soft brush to clean dirt that may be ingrained. Wash the vinyl as frequently as the rest of the vehicle.

After cleaning, application of a high quality rubber and vinyl protectant will help prevent oxidation and cracks. The protectant can also be applied to weatherstripping, vacuum lines and rubber hoses (which often fail as a result of chemical degradation) and to the tires.

4 Upholstery and carpets - maintenance

1   Every three months remove the carpets or mats and clean the interior of the vehicle (more frequently if necessary). Vacuum the upholstery and carpets to remove loose dirt and dust.

2   Leather upholstery requires special care. Stains should be removed with warm water and a very mild soap solution. Use a clean, damp cloth to remove the soap, then wipe again with a dry cloth. Never use alcohol, gasoline, nail polish remover or thinner to clean leather upholstery.

3   After cleaning, regularly treat leather upholstery with a leather wax. Never use car wax on leather upholstery.

4   In areas where the interior of the vehicle is subject to bright sunlight, cover leather seats with a sheet if the vehicle is to be left out for any length of time.

5 Body repair - minor damage

See photo sequence

REPAIR OF MINOR SCRATCHES

1   If the scratch is superficial and does not penetrate to the metal of the body, repair is very simple. Lightly rub the scratched area with a fine rubbing compound to remove loose paint and built-up wax. Rinse the area with clean water.

2   Apply touch-up paint to the scratch, using a small brush. Continue to apply thin layers of paint until the surface of the paint in the scratch is level with the surrounding paint. Allow the new paint at least two weeks to harden, then blend it into the surrounding paint by rubbing with a very fine rubbing compound. Finally, apply a coat of wax to the scratch area.

3   If the scratch has penetrated the paint and exposed the metal of the body, causing the metal to rust, a different repair technique is required. Remove all loose rust from the bottom of the scratch with a

pocket knife, then apply rust inhibiting paint to prevent the formation of rust in the future. Using a rubber or nylon applicator, coat the scratched area with glaze-type filler. If required, the filler can be mixed with thinner to provide a very thin paste, which is ideal for filling narrow scratches. Before the glaze filler in the scratch hardens, wrap a piece of smooth cotton cloth around the tip of a finger. Dip the cloth in thinner and then quickly wipe it along the surface of the scratch. This will ensure that the surface of the filler is slightly hollow. The scratch can now be painted over as described earlier in this Section.

REPAIR OF DENTS

4   When repairing dents, the first job is to pull the dent out until the affected area is as close as possible to its original shape. There is no point in trying to restore the original shape completely as the metal in the damaged area will have stretched on impact and cannot be restored to its original contours. It is better to bring the level of the dent up to a point which is about 1/8-inch below the level of the surrounding metal. In cases where the dent is very shallow, it is not worth trying to pull it out at all.

5   If the back side of the dent is accessible, it can be hammered out gently from behind using a soft-face hammer. While doing this, hold a block of wood firmly against the opposite side of the metal to absorb the hammer blows and prevent the metal from being stretched.

6   If the dent is in a section of the body which has double layers, or some other factor makes it inaccessible from behind, a different technique is required. Drill several small holes through the metal inside the damaged area, particularly in the deeper sections. Screw long, self-tapping screws into the holes just enough for them to get a good grip in the metal. Now the dent can be pulled out by pulling on the protruding heads of the screws with locking pliers.

7   The next stage of repair is the removal of paint from the damaged area and from an inch or so of the surrounding metal. This is done with a wire brush or sanding disk in a drill motor, although it can be done just as effectively by hand with sandpaper. To complete the preparation for filling, score the surface of the bare metal with a screwdriver or the tang of a file, or drill small holes in the affected area. This will provide a good grip for the filler material. To complete the repair, see the subsection on filling and painting later in this Section.

REPAIR OF RUST HOLES OR GASHES

8   Remove all paint from the affected area and from an inch or so of the surrounding metal using a sanding disk or wire brush mounted in a drill motor. If these are not available, a few sheets of sandpaper will do the job just as effectively.

9   With the paint removed, you will be able to determine the severity of the corrosion and decide whether to replace the whole panel, if possible, or repair the affected area. New body panels are not as expensive as most people think and it is often quicker to install a new panel than to repair large areas of rust.

10 Remove all trim pieces from the affected area except those which will act as a guide to the original shape of the damaged body, such as headlight shells, etc. Using metal snips or a hacksaw blade, remove all loose metal and any other metal that is badly affected by rust. Hammer the edges of the hole in to create a slight depression for the filler material.

11 Wire brush the affected area to remove the powdery rust from the surface of the metal. If the back of the rusted area is accessible, treat it with rust inhibiting paint.

12 Before filling is done, block the hole in some way. This can be done with sheet metal riveted or screwed into place, or by stuffing the hole with wire mesh.

13 Once the hole is blocked off, the affected area can be filled and painted. See the following subsection on filling and painting.

FILLING AND PAINTING

14 Many types of body fillers are available, but generally speaking, body repair kits which contain filler paste and a tube of resin hardener are best for this type of repair work. A wide, flexible plastic or nylon applicator will be necessary for imparting a smooth and contoured finish to the surface of the filler material. Mix up a small amount of filler on a clean piece of wood or cardboard (use the hardener sparingly). Follow the manufacturer's instructions on the package, otherwise the filler will set incorrectly.

15 Using the applicator, apply the filler paste to the prepared area. Draw the applicator across the surface of the filler to achieve the desired contour and to level the filler surface. As soon as a contour that approximates the original one is achieved, stop working the paste. If you continue, the paste will begin to stick to the applicator. Continue to add thin layers of paste at 20-minute intervals until the level of the filler is just above the surrounding metal.

16 Once the filler has hardened, the excess can be removed with a body file. From then on, progressively finer grades of sandpaper should be used, starting with a 180-grit paper and finishing with 600-grit wet-or-dry paper. Always wrap the sandpaper around a flat rubber or wooden block, otherwise the surface of the filler will not be completely flat. During the sanding of the filler surface, the wet-or-dry paper should be periodically rinsed in water. This will ensure that a very smooth finish is produced in the final stage.

17 At this point, the repair area should be surrounded by a ring of bare metal, which in turn should be encircled by the finely feathered edge of good paint. Rinse the repair area with clean water until all of the dust produced by the sanding operation is gone.

18 Spray the entire area with a light coat of primer. This will reveal any imperfections in the surface of the filler. Repair the imperfections with fresh filler paste or glaze filler and once more smooth the surface with sandpaper. Repeat this spray-and-repair procedure until you are satisfied that the surface of the filler and the feathered edge of the paint are perfect. Rinse the area with clean water and allow it to dry completely.

19 The repair area is now ready for painting. Spray painting must be carried out in a warm, dry, windless and dust free atmosphere. These conditions can be created if you have access to a large indoor work area, but if you are forced to work in the open, you will have to pick the day very carefully. If you are working indoors, dousing the floor in the work area with water will help settle the dust which would otherwise be in the air. If the repair area is confined to one body panel, mask off the surrounding panels. This will help minimize the effects of a slight mismatch in paint color. Trim pieces such as chrome strips, door handles, etc., will also need to be masked off or removed. Use masking tape and several thickness of newspaper for the masking operations.

20 Before spraying, shake the paint can thoroughly, then spray a test area until the spray painting technique is mastered. Cover the repair area with a thick coat of primer. The thickness should be built up using several thin layers of primer rather than one thick one. Using 600-grit wet-or-dry sandpaper, rub down the surface of the primer until it is very smooth. While doing this, the work area should be thoroughly rinsed with water and the wet-or-dry sandpaper periodically rinsed as well. Allow the primer to dry before spraying additional coats.

21 Spray on the top coat, again building up the thickness by using

These photos illustrate a method of repairing simple dents. They are intended to supplement Body repair - minor damage in this Chapter and should not be used as the sole instructions for body repair on these vehicles.

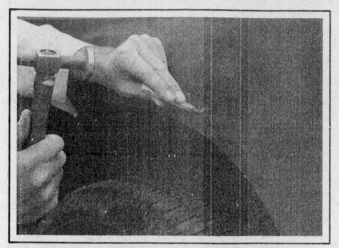

1   If you can't access the backside of the body panel to hammer out the dent, pull it out with a slide-hammer-type dent puller. In the deepest portion of the dent or along the crease line, drill or punch hole(s) at least one inch apart . . .

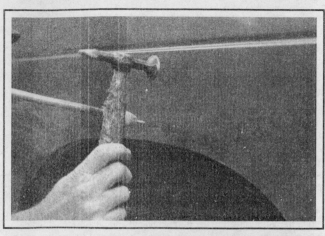

2   . . . then screw the slide-hammer into the hole and operate it. Tap with a hammer near the edge of the dent to help 'pop' the metal back to its original shape. When you're finished, the dent area should be close to its original contour and about 1/8-inch below the surface of the surrounding metal

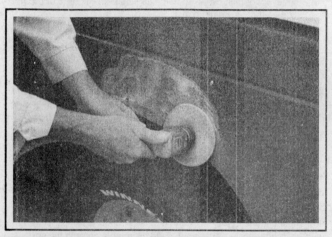

3   Using coarse-grit sandpaper, remove the paint down to the bare metal. Hand sanding works fine, but the disc sander shown here makes the job faster. Use finer (about 320-grit) sandpaper to feather-edge the paint at least one inch around the dent area

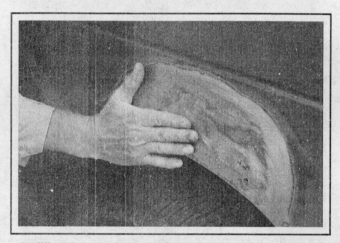

4   When the paint is removed, touch will probably be more helpful than sight for telling if the metal is straight. Hammer down the high spots or raise the low spots as necessary. Clean the repair area with wax/silicone remover

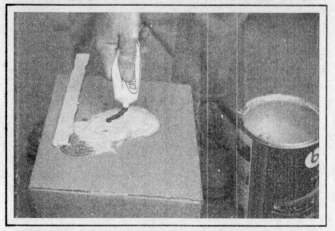

5   Following label instructions, mix up a batch of plastic filler and hardener. The ratio of filler to hardener is critical, and, if you mix it incorrectly, it will either not cure properly or cure too quickly (you won't have time to file and sand it into shape)

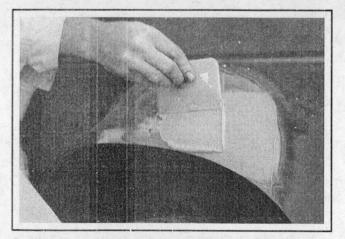

6   Working quickly so the filler doesn't harden, use a plastic applicator to press the body filler firmly into the metal, assuring it bonds completely. Work the filler until it matches the original contour and is slightly above the surrounding metal

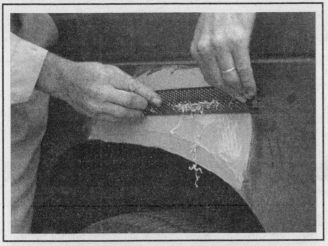

7 Let the filler harden until you can just dent it with your fingernail. Use a body file or Surform tool (shown here) to rough-shape the filler

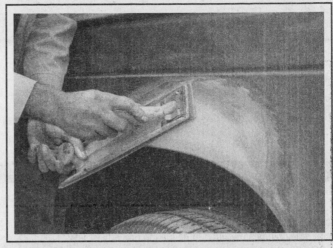

8 Use coarse-grit sandpaper and a sanding board or block to work the filler down until it's smooth and even. Work down to finer grits of sandpaper - always using a board or block - ending up with 360 or 400 grit

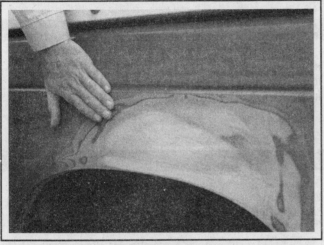

9 You shouldn't be able to feel any ridge at the transition from the filler to the bare metal or from the bare metal to the old paint. As soon as the repair is flat and uniform, remove the dust and mask off the adjacent panels or trim pieces

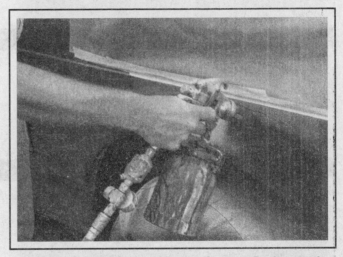

10 Apply several layers of primer to the area. Don't spray the primer on too heavy, so it sags or runs, and make sure each coat is dry before you spray on the next one. A professional-type spray gun is being used here, but aerosol spray primer is available inexpensively from auto parts stores

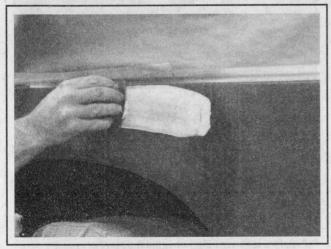

11 The primer will help reveal imperfections or scratches. Fill these with glazing compound. Follow the label instructions and sand it with 360 or 400-grit sandpaper until it's smooth. Repeat the glazing, sanding and respraying until the primer reveals a perfectly smooth surface

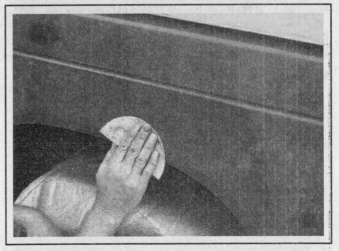

12 Finish sand the primer with very fine sandpaper (400 or 600-grit) to remove the primer overspray. Clean the area with water and allow it to dry. Use a tack rag to remove any dust, then apply the finish coat. Don't attempt to rub out or wax the repair area until the paint has dried completely (at least two weeks)

several thin layers of paint. Begin spraying in the center of the repair area and then, using a circular motion, work out until the whole repair area and about two inches of the surrounding original paint is covered. Remove all masking material 10 to 15 minutes after spraying on the final coat of paint. Allow the new paint at least two weeks to harden, then use a very fine rubbing compound to blend the edges of the new paint into the existing paint. Finally, apply a coat of wax.

6   Body repair - major damage

1   Major damage must be repaired by an auto body shop specifically equipped to perform unibody repairs. These shops have the specialized equipment required to do the job properly.
2   If the damage is extensive, the body must be checked for proper alignment or the vehicle's handling characteristics may be adversely affected and other components may wear at an accelerated rate.

3   Due to the fact that all of the major body components (hood, fenders, etc.) are separate and replaceable units, any seriously damaged components should be replaced rather than repaired. Sometimes the components can be found in a wrecking yard that specializes in used vehicle components, often at considerable savings over the cost of new parts.

7   Hinges and locks - maintenance

Once every 3000 miles, or every three months, the hinges and latch assemblies on the doors, hood and trunk should be given a few drops of light oil or lock lubricant. The door latch strikers should also be lubricated with a thin coat of grease to reduce wear and ensure free movement. Lubricate the door and trunk locks with spray-on graphite lubricant.

8   Windshield and fixed glass - replacement

Replacement of the windshield and fixed glass requires the use of special fast-setting adhesive/caulk materials and some specialized tools. It is recommended that these operations be left to a dealer or a shop specializing in glass work.

9   Hood - removal, installation and adjustment

➡Note: The hood is heavy and somewhat awkward to remove and install - at least two people should perform this procedure.

REMOVAL AND INSTALLATION

◆ Refer to illustrations 9.2 and 9.4

1   Use blankets or pads to cover the cowl area of the body and fenders. This will protect the body and paint as the hood is lifted off.
2   Make marks or scribe a line around the hood hinge to ensure proper alignment during installation (see illustration).
3   Disconnect any cables or wires that will interfere with removal.
4   Have an assistant support the hood. Remove the hinge-to-hood nuts or bolts (see illustration).
5   Lift off the hood.
6   Installation is the reverse of removal.

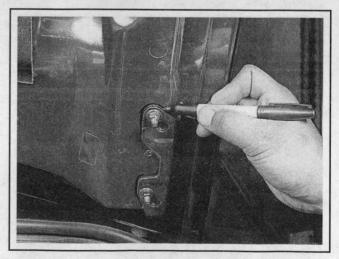

9.2 Before removing the hood, draw a mark around the hinge plate

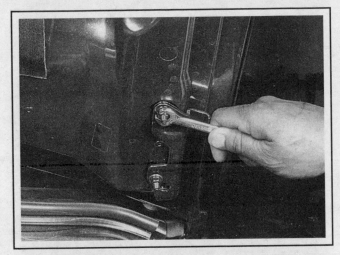

9.4 Remove the hinge to hood retaining bolts and lift off the hood with the help of an assistant

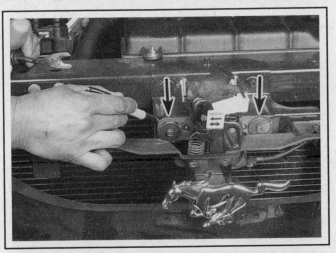

9.10 Scribe a line around the hinge to use as a reference point - To adjust the hood latch, loosen the retaining bolts (arrows), move the latch and retighten bolts, then close the hood to check the fit

ADJUSTMENT

▶ **Refer to illustrations 9.10 and 9.11**

7 Fore-and-aft and side-to-side adjustment of the hood is done by moving the hinge plate slot after loosening the bolts or nuts.

8 Scribe a line around the entire hinge plate so you can determine the amount of movement (see illustration 9.2).

9 Loosen the bolts or nuts and move the hood into correct alignment. Move it only a little at a time. Tighten the hinge bolts and carefully lower the hood to check the position.

10 If necessary after installation, the entire hood latch assembly can be adjusted up-and-down as well as from side-to-side on the radiator support so the hood closes securely and flush with the fenders. To make the adjustment, scribe a line or mark around the hood latch mounting bolts to provide a reference point, then loosen them and reposition the latch assembly, as necessary (see illustration). Following adjustment, retighten the mounting bolts.

11 Finally, adjust the hood bumpers on the radiator support so the hood, when closed, is flush with the fenders (see illustration).

12 The hood latch assembly, as well as the hinges, should be periodically lubricated with white, lithium-base grease to prevent binding and wear.

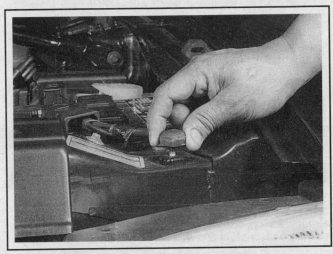

9.11 Adjust the hood closing height by turning the hood bumpers in or out

10 Hood release latch and cable - removal and installation

LATCH

▶ **Refer to illustration 10.2**

1 Scribe a line around the latch to aid alignment when installing, then detach the latch retaining bolts to the radiator support (see illustration 9.10) and remove the latch.

2 Disconnect the hood release cable by disengaging the cable from the latch assembly (see illustration).

3 Installation is the reverse of the removal procedure.

➡ **Note: Adjust the latch so the hood engages securely when closed and the hood bumpers are slightly compressed.**

CABLE

▶ **Refer to illustration 10.6**

4 Disconnect the hood release cable from the latch assembly as described above.

5 Attach a piece of stiff wire to the end of the cable, then follow the cable back to the firewall and detach all the cable retaining clips.

6 Working in the passenger compartment, remove the driver side kick panel. Then remove the two release lever mounting bolts and detach the hood release lever (see illustration).

7 Pull the cable and grommet rearward into the passenger com-

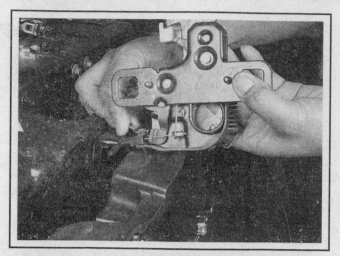

10.2 Unscrew the cable retaining bolt from the backside of the hood latch assembly, then disengage the cable

10.6 Remove the hood release lever retaining screws (arrow) and pull the cable rearward into the passenger compartment

partment until you can see the wire. Ensure that the new cable has a grommet attached, then remove the old cable from the wire and replace it with the new cable.

8   Working from engine compartment pull the wire back through the firewall.

9   Installation is the reverse of the removal

➡**Note: Push on the grommet with your fingers from the passenger compartment to seat the grommet in the firewall correctly.**

11 Bumpers - removal and installation

✻ WARNING:

The models covered by this manual are equipped with Supplemental Restraint systems (SRS), more commonly known as airbags. Always disconnect the negative battery cable, then the positive battery cable and wait two minutes before working in the vicinity of the impact sensors, steering column or instrument panel to avoid the possibility of accidental deployment of the airbag, which could cause personal injury (see Chapter 12). Do not use electrical test equipment on any of the airbag system wiring or tamper with them in any way.

FRONT BUMPER

◗ Refer to illustrations 11.3, 11.4, 11.5, 11.6 and 11.8

1   Apply the parking brake, raise the vehicle and support it securely on jackstands.

2   Disconnect the negative battery cable. then the positive battery cable and wait two minutes before proceeding any further.

3   Working under the vehicle, detach the plastic clips securing the lower edges of the bumper cover (see illustration).

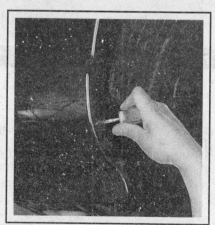

11.3 Pull downward on the center pin to release the clips from the lower edge of the bumper cover

11.4 Detach the retaining screws securing the bumper cover to the inner fenderwell splash shield

11.5 Peel back the splash shield and remove the bumper cover to fender retaining bolts (arrows)

11.6 Drill out two rivets securing the upper half of the bumper cover

11.8 Use a long extension and socket to remove the bumper retaining bolts (arrows)

11.11a Use a trim removal tool or a small screwdriver to pry out the plastic clips securing the lower edge of the bumper cover

4   Working in the front wheel opening, detach the retaining screws securing the bumper cover to inner fenderwell splash shield (see illustration).

5   Pry out the lower edge of the splash shield, then reach up behind the bumper cover and remove the bumper cover to fender retaining nuts (see illustration).

6   Remove the two retaining rivets securing the upper portion of the bumper cover and pull the bumper cover assembly out and away from the vehicle (see illustration).

7   Disconnect any electrical connections which would interfere with removal.

8   Remove the bumper retaining bolts and pull the bumper assembly out and away from the vehicle (see illustration).

9   Installation is the reverse of removal.

REAR BUMPER

▶ **Refer to illustrations 11.11a, 11.11b, 11.12a, 11.12b, 11.13a and 11.13b**

10   Apply the parking brake, raise the vehicle and support it securely on jackstands.

11   Working under the vehicle, detach the plastic clips and screws

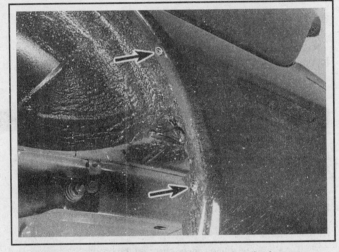

11.11b Remove the screws (arrows) securing the bumper cover to the wheel opening

securing the lower edges of the bumper cover (see illustrations).

12   Working in the trunk, pry out the plastic clips securing the drivers side, passenger side, and rear inside trunk finishing panels to allow

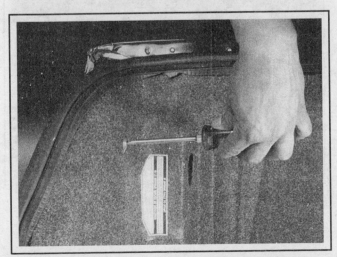

11.12a Remove the clips and screws securing the trunk compartment rear finishing panel

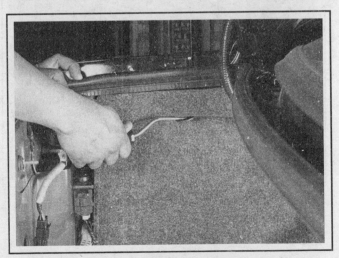

11.12b Pry out the clips securing the trunk compartment driver and passenger side finishing panels

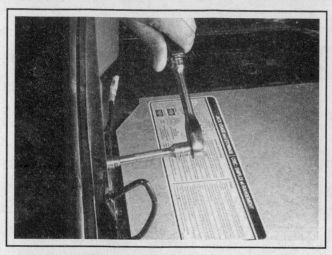

11.13a Detach five retaining nuts securing the bumper cover to the taillight panel

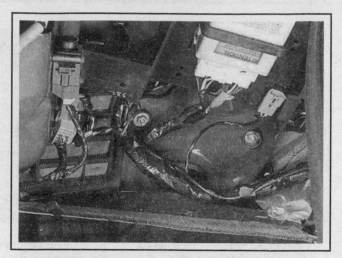

11.13b Detach the retaining nuts on each side of the trunk securing the bumper cover to rear quarter panels

access to the bumper cover retaining bolts (see illustrations).

13 Detach the retaining nuts securing the bumper cover to the tail light panel and right and left quarter panels (see illustrations), Pull the bumper cover assembly out and away from the vehicle.

14 Remove the bumper retaining bolts and pull the bumper assembly out and away from the vehicle (see illustration 11.8).

15 Installation is the reverse of removal.

12 Front fender - removal and installation

▶ Refer to illustrations 12.3, 12.4a, 12.4b, 12.6a, 12.6b, 12.6c and 12.6d

1 Raise the vehicle, support it securely on jackstands and remove the front wheel.

2 Remove the headlight and parking light assemblies (see Chapter 12).

3 Detach the retaining screws securing the headlight housing panel (see illustration).

4 Detach the inner fenderwell splash shield and the front flair molding from the fender (see illustrations).

5 Remove the front bumper cover assembly (see Section 11).

6 Remove the remaining fender mounting bolts (see illustrations).

7 Detach the fender. It's a good idea to have an assistant support the fender while it's being moved away from the vehicle to prevent damage to the surrounding body panels.

8 Installation is the reverse of removal.

12.3 Detach the retaining bolts (arrows) located behind the headlight assemblies

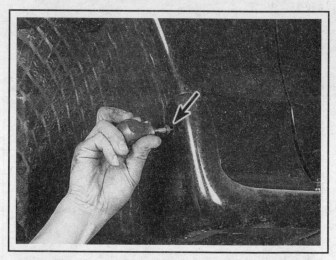

12.4a Working in the wheel opening remove the screws and clips securing the front flair molding to the fender (arrows)

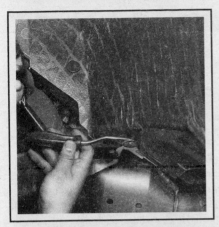

12.4b Remove the clips securing the inner fenderwell splash shield

12.6a Remove the fender to radiator support bolts (arrows)

12.6b Remove the fender to rocker panel bolts (arrows)

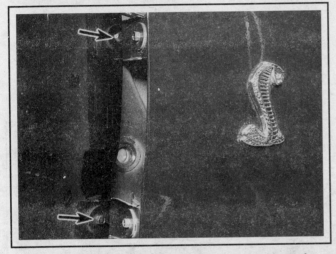

12.6c Open the door to access and remove the fender to door pillar bolts (arrows)

12.6d Detach the remaining bolts located in the hood opening

13 Trunk lid support struts - removal and installation

Refer to illustration 13.2

➡Note: The rear trunk lid is heavy and somewhat awkward to hold - at least two people should perform this procedure.

1 Open the hood or rear trunk lid and support it securely.

2 Using a small screwdriver, detach the retaining clips at both ends of the support strut. Then pry or pull sharply to detach it from the vehicle (see illustration).

3 Installation is the reverse of removal.

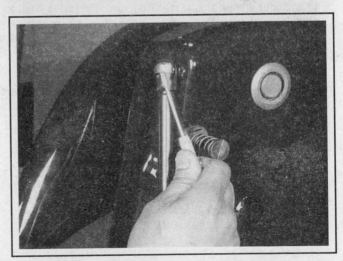

13.2 Use a small screwdriver to pry the clip out of its locking groove, then detach the end of the strut from the locating stud

14 Trunk lid - removal, installation and adjustment

➡Note: The trunk lid is heavy and somewhat awkward to remove and install - at least two people should perform this procedure.

REMOVAL AND INSTALLATION

◆ Refer to illustration 14.5

1   Open the trunk lid and cover the edges of the trunk compartment with pads or cloths to protect the painted surfaces when the lid is removed.

2   Disconnect any cables or wire harness connectors attached to the trunk lid that would interfere with removal.

3   Remove the trunk lid support struts (see Section 13).

4   Make alignment marks around the hinge mounting bolts with a marking pen.

5   While an assistant supports the trunk lid, remove the lid-to-hinge bolts (see illustration) on both sides of the trunk and lift it off.

6   Installation is the reverse of removal.

➡Note: When reinstalling the trunk lid, align the lid-to-hinge bolts with the marks made during removal.

ADJUSTMENT

◆ Refer to illustrations 14.10a and 14.10b

7   Fore-and-aft and side-to-side adjustment of the trunk lid is accomplished by moving the lid in relation to the hinge after loosening the bolts or nuts.

8   Scribe a line around the entire hinge plate as described earlier in this Section so you can determine the amount of movement.

9   Loosen the bolts or nuts and move the trunk lid into correct alignment. Move it only a little at a time. Tighten the hinge bolts or nuts and carefully lower the trunk lid to check the alignment.

10 If necessary after installation, the entire trunk lid striker assembly can be adjusted up and down as well as from side to side on the trunk lid so the lid closes securely and is flush with the rear quarter panels. To do this, scribe a line around the trunk lid striker assembly to provide a reference point. Then loosen the bolts and reposition the striker as necessary (see illustrations). Following adjustment, retighten the mounting bolts.

11 The trunk lid latch assembly, as well as the hinges, should be periodically lubricated with white lithium-base grease to prevent sticking and wear.

14.5 Scribe a mark around the hinge plate for realignment purposes - then remove the retaining bolts (arrows) on each side of the trunk lid

14.10a Scribe a mark around the striker assembly as a reference point to aid in the adjustment procedure

14.10b Loosen the bolts and move the striker assembly as necessary (arrows) to adjust the trunk lid flush with the quarter panels in the closed position

15 Trunk lid latch and lock cylinder - removal and installation

TRUNK LID LATCH

◆ Refer to illustration 15.3

1   Open the trunk and scribe a line around the trunk lid latch assembly for a reference point to aid the installation procedure.

2   Disconnect the electrical connectors and the door lock actuator from the door lock cylinder.

3   Detach the retaining bolts and remove the latch (see illustration).

4   Installation is the reverse of removal. See Section 14 for adjustment procedures.

TRUNK LOCK CYLINDER

◆ Refer to illustrations 15.5 and 15.7

5   Working from the outside of the trunk lid, remove the license plate and the license plate trim panel (see illustration).

6   Disconnect any electrical connectors and the door lock actuator from the door lock cylinder.

7   Drill out the lock cylinder retaining rivet, then remove the lock cylinder from the vehicle (see illustration).

8   Installation is the reverse of removal.

15.3 Disconnect the electrical connectors and the lock actuator from the lock cylinder, then detach the retaining bolts (arrows) to remove the trunk lid latch

15.5 Detach the bolts (arrows) and remove the license plate trim panel

15.7 Drill out the retaining rivet, then rotate the lock cylinder to remove it

16 Rear spoiler - removal and installation

▶ **Refer to illustration 16.3**

1   Open the trunk lid.
2   Working on the inside of the trunk lid, remove the plastic caps covering the rear spoiler mounting bolts.
3   Detach the bolts (see illustration) and remove the spoiler.
4   Installation is the reverse of removal.

16.3 Detach the rear spoiler retaining nuts (arrows) from each side of the trunk lid

17 Door trim panel - removal and installation

▶ **Refer to illustrations 17.2, 17.3a, 17.3b, 17.4, 17.5, 17.6a and 17.6b**

1   Disconnect the negative cable from the battery.
2   On manual window equipped models, remove the window crank, using a hooked tool to remove the retainer clip (see illustration). A special tool is available for this purpose, but it's not essential. With the clip removed, pull off the handle.
3   On power window equipped models, pry out the armrest switch control plate and disconnect the electrical connections (see illustrations).
4   Detach the retaining screws located behind the armrest switch control plate (see illustration).
5   Using a wide putty knife, a thin screwdriver or a special trim panel removal tool, pry out the plastic retaining clip

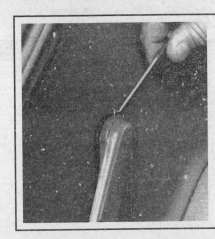

17.2 Use a hooked tool like this to remove the window crank retaining clip

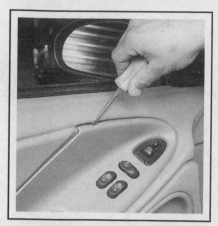

17.3a Using a small screwdriver, pry out the armrest switch control plate

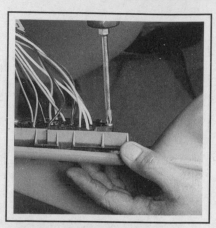

17.3b Detach the electrical connector from the backside of the armrest switch control plate

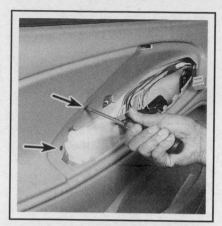

17.4 Remove the retaining screws (arrows) located behind the armrest switch control plate

17.5 Detach the plastic clip (arrow) securing the front edge of the door trim panel

17.6a Pull straight out to remove the side view mirror trim cover or speaker cover (if equipped)

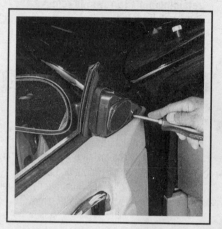

17.6b Detach the screws securing the speaker (if equipped)

securing the front edge of the door trim panel (see illustration).

6   Detach the side view mirror trim cover by pulling straight out. Some models are equipped with an optional door speaker at this location. Pull straight out on the speaker cover then detach the speaker retaining screws and remove the speaker assembly from the vehicle (see illustrations).

7   Once all of the clips and screws are disengaged, detach the trim panel, disconnect any electrical connectors and remove the trim panel from the vehicle by gently pulling it up and out.

8   For access to the inner door, peel back the watershield, taking care not to tear it. To install the trim panel, first press the watershield back into place. If necessary, add more sealant to hold it in place.

9   The remainder of the installation is the reverse of removal.

18 Door - removal, installation and adjustment

➡Note: The door is heavy and somewhat awkward to remove and install - at least two people should perform this procedure.

REMOVAL AND INSTALLATION

▸ **Refer to illustration 18.8**

1   Lower the window completely in the door and then disconnect the negative cable from the battery

2   Open the door all the way and support it on jacks or blocks covered with rags to prevent damaging the paint.

3   Remove the door trim panel and water deflector as described in (see Section 17).

4   Remove the door speaker (see Chapter 12).

5   Unplug all electrical connections, ground wires and harness retaining clips from the door.

➡Note: It is a good idea to label all connections to aid the reassembly process.

6   Working through the door speaker hole and the door opening, detach the rubber conduit between the body and the door. Then pull wiring harness through conduit hole and remove from door.

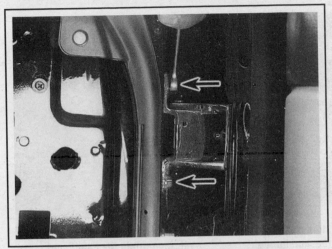

18.8 Before loosening the door retaining bolts (arrows), draw a line around the hinge plate for a reinstallation reference

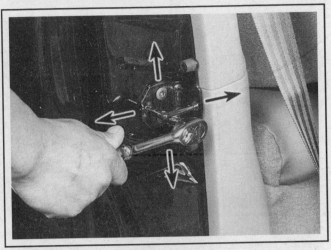

18.13 Adjust the door lock striker by loosening the mounting screws and gently tapping the striker in the desired direction (arrows)

7   Mark around the door hinges with a pen or a scribe to facilitate realignment during reassembly.

8   Have an assistant hold the door, remove the hinge to door bolts (see illustration) and lift the door off.

9   Installation is the reverse of the removal.

ADJUSTMENT

▶ **Refer to illustration 18.13**

10   Having proper door to body alignment is a critical part of a well functioning door assembly. First check the door hinge pins for excessive play. Fully open the door and lift up and down on the door without lifting the body. If a door has 1/16-inch or more excessive play, the hinges should be replaced.

11   Door to body alignment adjustments are made by loosening the hinge-to-body or hinge to door bolts and moving the door. Proper body alignment is achieved when the top of door is aligned with the top of front fender and rear quarter panel and the bottom of the door is aligned with the lower rocker panel. If these goals can't be reached by adjusting the hinge to body or hinge to door bolts, body alignment shims may have to be purchased and inserted behind the hinges to achieve correct alignment.

12   To adjust the door closed position, first check that the door latch is contacting the center of the latch striker. If not remove striker and add or subtract shims to achieve correct alignment.

13   Finally adjust latch striker as necessary (up and down or sideways) to provide positive engagement with the latch mechanism (see illustration) and the door panel is flush with rear quarter panel.

19 Door latch, lock cylinder and handles - removal and installation

DOOR LATCH

▶ **Refer to illustration 19.2**

1   Raise the window then remove the door trim panel and watershield as described in (Section 17).

2   Remove the screws securing the latch to the door (see illustration).

3   Working through the large access hole, position the latch as necessary to disengage the outside door handle and outside lock cylinder to latch rods and the inside handle to latch cable.

4   All door locking rods are attached by plastic clips. The plastic clips can be removed by unsnapping the portion engaging the connecting rod and then by pulling the rod out of its locating hole.

5   Position the latch as necessary to disengage the door lock actuator hook. Then remove the latch assembly from the door.

6   Installation is the reverse of removal.

19.2 Remove the latch retaining screws (arrows) from the end of the door, then detach the locking rods and cable and pull the latch assembly through the access hole

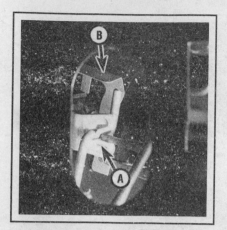

19.9 To remove the lock cylinder, detach the plastic clip securing the lock rod (A) then pry off the lock cylinder retaining clip (B)

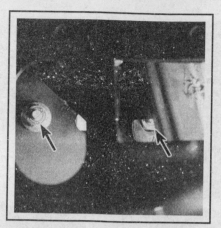

19.11 The outside handle retaining nuts (arrows) can be reached through the access hole in the door frame

19.14 Drill out the handle retaining rivet, then rotate the handle out and detach the latch cable from the backside

DOOR LOCK CYLINDER AND OUTSIDE HANDLE

▶ **Refer to illustrations 19.9 and 19.11**

7   To remove the lock cylinder, raise the window and remove the door trim panel and watershield as described in Section 17.

8   Working through the large access hole, disengage the plastic clip that secures the lock cylinder to latch rod.

9   Using a screwdriver, slide the lock cylinder retaining clip out of engagement and remove the lock cylinder from the door (see illustration).

10   To remove the outside handle, work through the access hole and disengage the plastic clip that secures the outside handle-to-latch rod.

11   Remove the outside handle retaining nuts (see illustration) and

pull the handle from the door.

12   Installation is the reverse of removal.

INSIDE HANDLE AND CABLE

▶ **Refer to illustration 19.14**

13   Remove the door trim panel as described in Section 17 and peel away the watershield.

14   Drill out the rivet securing the inside handle (see illustration). Pull rearward on the handle to disengage it from the inner door panel.

15   Detach the latch cable from the backside of the handle and remove it from the vehicle.

16   Installation is the reverse of removal.

20 Door window glass - removal and installation

▶ **Refer to illustrations 20.4 and 20.5**

1   Remove the door trim panel and the plastic watershield (see Section 17).

2   Lower the window glass all the way down into the door.

3   Carefully pry the inner and outer weatherstripping out of the door window opening.

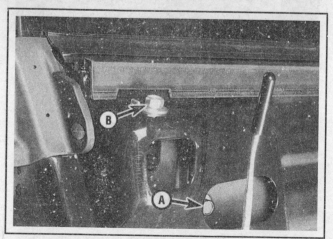

20.4 Detach the window stabilizer brackets (A) and the window up-stop brackets (B) from each end of the door

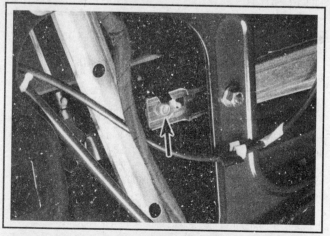

20.5 Raise the window just enough to access the glass retaining rivets (arrow) through the hole in the door frame - drill out the rivets securing the glass to the equalizer arm

4   Remove the window stabilizer and up-stop brackets (see illustration).

5   Raise the window just enough to access the window retaining rivets through the hole in the door frame (see illustration).

6   Place a rag over the glass to help prevent scratching the glass, then drill out the two glass mounting rivets.

7   Remove the glass by pulling it up and out.

8   Installation is the reverse of removal.

21 Door window glass regulator - removal and installation

▶ Refer to illustrations 21.4a and 21.4b

✳✳ WARNING:

The regulator arms are under extreme pressure and can cause serious injury if the motor or counter balance spring is removed without locking the sector gear. This can be done by inserting a bolt and nut through the holes in the backing plate and sector gear to lock them together.

1   Remove the door trim panel and the plastic watershield (see Section 17).

2   Remove the window glass assembly (see Section 20).

3   On power operated windows, disconnect the electrical connector from the window regulator motor.

4   Remove the equalizer arm bracket and the regulator mounting bolts (see illustrations).

5   Pull the equalizer arm and regulator assemblies through the service hole in the door frame to remove it.

6   Installation is the reverse of removal.

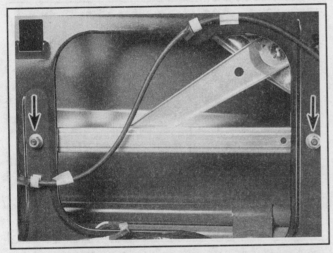

21.4a Detach the window equalizer arm bracket retaining nuts (arrows) . . .

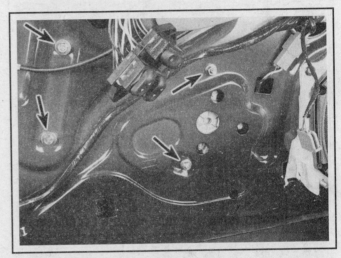

21.4b . . . then remove the window regulator bolts (arrows)

22 Sideview mirrors - removal and installation

▶ Refer to illustration 22.4

1   Remove the door trim panel and the plastic watershield (see Section 17).

2   Pry off the mirror trim cover.

3   Disconnect the electrical connector from the mirror.

4   Remove the three mirror retaining nuts and detach the mirror from the vehicle (see illustration).

5   Installation is the reverse of removal.

22.4 Disconnect the electrical connector, then detach the mirror retaining nuts (arrows) and remove the mirror from the vehicle

23 Center console - removal and installation

▸ Refer to illustrations 23.2, 23.3, 23.4 and 23.5

✳✳ WARNING:

The models covered by this manual are equipped with Supplemental Restraint systems (SRS), more commonly known as airbags. Always disconnect the negative battery cable, then the positive battery cable and wait two minutes before working in the vicinity of the impact sensors, steering column or instrument panel to avoid the possibility of accidental deployment of the airbag, which could cause personal injury (see Chapter 12). Do not use electrical test equipment on any of the airbag system wiring or tamper with them in any way.

1   Disconnect the negative battery cable, then the positive battery cable and wait two minutes before proceeding any further.

2   Pry out the gear selector trim bezel (see illustration). Vehicles equipped with manual transmissions will require unscrewing the shift lever knob to remove the trim bezel.

3   Detach the retaining screws securing the front half of the console (see illustration).

4   Working in the console glove box, pry out the rubber bumpers located along the front edge, then detach the retaining screws and remove the glove box (see illustration).

5   Detach the retaining screws securing the rear half of the console (see illustration).

6   Apply the parking brake, then move the gear selector to the towards the rear of the vehicle.

7   Lift the console up and over the shift lever. Disconnect any electrical connections and remove the console from the vehicle.

8   Installation is the reverse of removal.

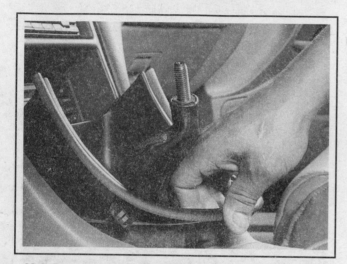

23.2 Pry out the gear selector trim bezel

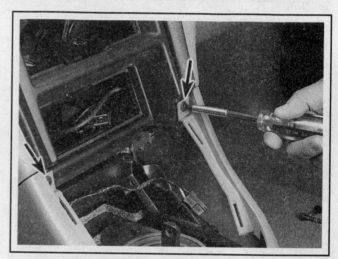

23.3 Remove the screws (arrows) located under the gear selector trim plate

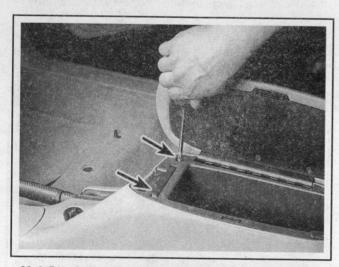

23.4 Detach the rubber bumpers and the retaining screws (arrows), then remove the glove box from the console

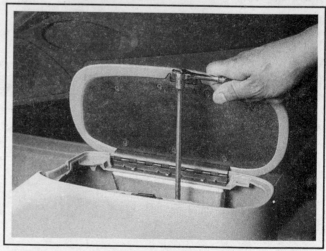

23.5 Remove the screws located under the console glove box

24 Instrument cluster bezel - removal and installation

▶ Refer to illustration 24.3

WARNING:

The models covered by this manual are equipped with Supplemental Restraint systems (SRS), more commonly known as airbags. Always disconnect the negative battery cable, then the positive battery cable and wait two minutes before working in the vicinity of the impact sensors, steering column or instrument panel to avoid the possibility of accidental deployment of the airbag, which could cause personal injury (see Chapter 12). Do not use electrical test equipment on any of the airbag system wiring or tamper with them in any way.

1   Disconnect the negative battery cable, then the positive battery cable and wait two minutes before proceeding any further.

2   Pull the headlight switch outward to the On position. Push the release tab at the bottom of the knob to remove it (see Chapter 12).

3   Remove the bezel retaining screws (see illustration).

4   Tilt the steering wheel down to the lowest position. Pull the top of the instrument cluster bezel outward while disengaging the lower clips

24.3 Detach the bezel retaining screws (arrows) then pull the bezel outward to disengage the lower clips

on the bezel. Remove the bezel from the vehicle.

5   Installation is the reverse of removal.

25 Dashboard trim panels - removal and installation

WARNING:

The models covered by this manual are equipped with Supplemental Restraint systems (SRS), more commonly known as airbags. Always disconnect the negative battery cable, then the positive battery cable and wait two minutes before working in the vicinity of the impact sensors, steering column or instrument panel to avoid the possibility of accidental deployment of the airbag, which could cause personal injury (see Chapter 12). Do not use electrical test equipment on any of the airbag system wiring or tamper with them in any way.

1   Disconnect the negative battery cable, then the positive battery cable and wait two minutes before proceeding any further.

KNEE BOLSTER

▶ Refer to illustration 25.2

2   Working in the drivers side passenger compartment, detach the retaining screws along the lower edge of the knee bolster (see illustration).

3   Pull outward on the lower edge of the knee bolster and detach it from the vehicle.

4   Detach the retaining screws securing the knee bolster reinforcement panel.

5   Installation is the reverse of removal.

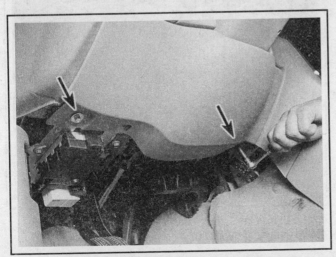

25.2 Detach the screws (arrows) at the lower edge of the knee bolster - pull straight up to remove it

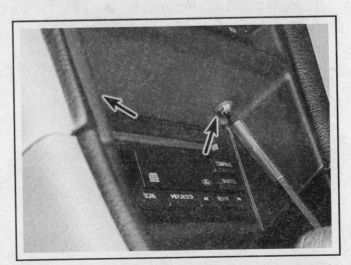

25.7a Remove the screws (arrows) securing the lower half of the center trim panel

25.7b Remove the screw (arrow) located behind the radio

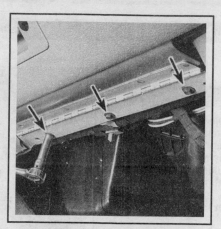

25.10 Detach the glove box door hinge retaining screws (arrows)

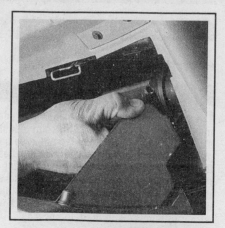

25.11 Push inward to release the glove box door stops - pull straight out to remove it from the vehicle

CENTER TRIM PANEL

♦ **Refer to illustrations 25.7a and 25.7b**

6 Remove the radio and compact disc player, if equipped (see Chapter 12).

7 Detach the retaining screws from the lower half of the trim panel (see illustrations).

8 Using a small screwdriver, pry out the clips securing the top of the bezel then unsnap the clips in the center of the trim panel and remove it from the vehicle.

9 Installation is the reverse of removal.

GLOVE BOX

♦ **Refer to illustrations 25.10 and 25.11**

10 Detach the door hinge retaining screws along the lower edge of the glove box (see illustration).

11 Open the glove box door. Release the door stops by pressing in on the sides, then pull straight out to remove the glove box assembly (see illustration).

12 Installation is the reverse of removal.

26 Steering column cover - removal and installation

♦ **Refer to illustration 26.3**

1 Remove the driver side knee bolster (see Section 25).

2 Remove the key lock cylinder (see Chapter 12).

3 Remove the screws from the lower steering column cover (see illustration).

4 Separate the cover halves and detach them from the steering column.

5 Installation is the reverse of removal.

26.3 Detach the screws - then separate the steering column cover halves to remove them from the steering column

27 Instrument panel - removal and installation

27.6 Remove the bolt (arrow) securing the steering column to the steering shaft

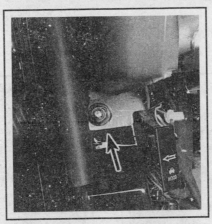

27.7a Remove two bolts (one arrowed) securing the instrument panel to the driver side door pillar

27.7b Peel the carpeting back to access the instrument-panel-to-floor-pan bolts

▶ Refer to illustrations 27.6, 27.7a, 27.7b, 27.7c and 27.8

❈❖ WARNING:

The models covered by this manual are equipped with Supplemental Restraint systems (SRS), more commonly known as airbags. Always disconnect the negative battery cable, then the positive battery cable and wait two minutes before working in the vicinity of the impact sensors, steering column or instrument panel to avoid the possibility of accidental deployment of the airbag, which could cause personal injury (see Chapter 12). Do not use electrical test equipment on any of the airbag system wiring or tamper with them in any way.

➡Note: The instrument panel is heavy and somewhat awkward to remove and install - at least two people should perform this procedure.

1   Disconnect the negative battery cable, then the positive battery cable and wait two minutes before proceeding any further.

❈❖ CAUTION:

Always use extreme care when working around airbag modules.

Never strike, pry or bump airbag modules to avoid the possibility of accidental deployment.

2   Position the steering wheel in the lock position.

➡Note: Make sure the steering wheel remains in the lock position during the entire procedure or damage to the airbag sliding contact will occur.

3   Remove the radio and compact disc player, if equipped (see Chapter 12).

4   Remove the dashboard trim panels (see Section 25) and the center floor console (see Section 23).

5   Remove the air conditioning and heater control panel (see Chapter 3).

6   Detach the bolt securing the steering shaft (see illustration).

7   Remove the nuts and bolts securing the lower half of the instrument panel (see illustrations).

8   Pry out the defroster grilles and remove the screws securing the upper edge of the instrument panel (see illustration).

9   Detach any electrical connectors interfering with removal, then pull the instrument panel towards the rear of the vehicle to remove it.

10   Installation is the reverse of removal.

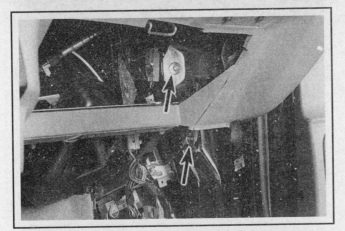

27.7c Remove two bolts (arrows) securing the instrument panel to the passenger side door pillar

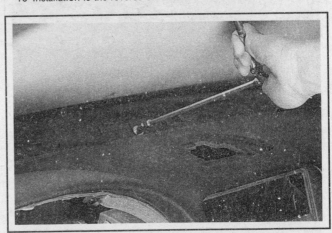

27.8 Pry out the defroster grille and remove the bolts retaining the upper half of the instrument panel

28 Cowl cover - removal and installation

▶ **Refer to illustrations 28.3 and 28.4**

1 Remove the windshield wiper arms (see Chapter 12).
2 Detach the hood seal from the cowl cover.

3 Pry off the cowl top cover (see illustration).
4 Remove the retaining screws securing the lower cowl cover (see illustration).
5 Installation is the reverse of removal.

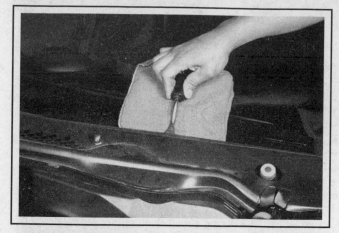

28.3 Detach the retaining clips securing the top cowl cover . . .

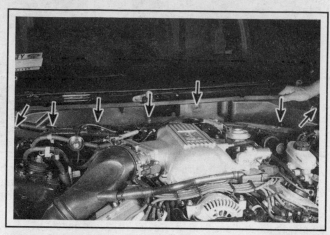

28.4 . . . then remove the screws (arrows) from the lower cowl cover

29 Seats - removal and installation

FRONT SEAT

▶ **Refer to illustration 29.2**

1 Position the seat all the way forward or all the way to the rear to access the front seat retaining bolts.
2 Detach any bolt trim covers and remove the retaining bolts (see illustration).
3 Tilt the seat upward to access the underneath, then disconnect any electrical connectors and lift the seat from the vehicle.
4 Installation is the reverse of removal.

REAR SEAT

▶ **Refer to illustration 29.5**

5 Then lift up on the front edge of the cushion and release the seat cushion retaining tabs (see illustration). Remove the cushion from the vehicle.
6 Detach the retaining bolts at the lower edge of the seat back.
7 Lift up on the lower edge of the seat back and remove it from the vehicle.
8 Installation is the reverse of removal.

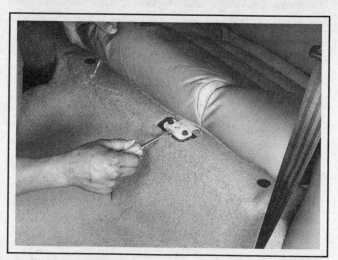

29.2 Detach the trim covers to access the front seat retaining bolts

29.5 Press down on the release button to remove the rear seat cushion

Section

12

CHASSIS ELECTRICAL SYSTEM

1   General information

The electrical system is a 12-volt, negative ground type. Power for the lights and all electrical accessories is supplied by a lead/acid-type battery which is charged by the alternator.

This Chapter covers repair and service procedures for the various electrical components not associated with the engine.

Information on the battery, alternator, distributor and starter motor can be found in Chapter 5.

It should be noted that when portions of the electrical system are serviced, the negative battery cable should be disconnected from the battery to prevent electrical shorts and/or fires.

2   Electrical troubleshooting - general information

A typical electrical circuit consists of an electrical component, any switches, relays, motors, fuses, fusible links or circuit breakers related to that component and the wiring and connectors that link the component to both the battery and the chassis. To help you pinpoint an electrical circuit problem, wiring diagrams are included at the end of this Chapter.

Before tackling any troublesome electrical circuit, first study the appropriate wiring diagrams to get a complete understanding of what makes up that individual circuit. Trouble spots, for instance, can often be narrowed down by noting if other components related to the circuit are operating properly. If several components or circuits fail at one time, chances are the problem is in a fuse or ground connection, because several circuits are often routed through the same fuse and ground connections.

Electrical problems usually stem from simple causes, such as loose or corroded connections, a blown fuse, a melted fusible link or a failed relay. Visually inspect the condition of all fuses, wires and connections in a problem circuit before troubleshooting the circuit.

If test equipment and instruments are going to be utilized, use the diagrams to plan ahead of time where you will make the necessary connections in order to accurately pinpoint the trouble spot.

The basic tools needed for electrical troubleshooting include a circuit tester or voltmeter (a 12-volt bulb with a set of test leads can also be used), a continuity tester, which includes a bulb, battery and set of test leads, and a jumper wire, preferably with a circuit breaker incorporated, which can be used to bypass electrical components. Before attempting to locate a problem with test instruments, use the wiring diagram(s) to decide where to make the connections.

VOLTAGE CHECKS

Voltage checks should be performed if a circuit is not functioning properly. Connect one lead of a circuit tester to either the negative battery terminal or a known good ground. Connect the other lead to a connector in the circuit being tested, preferably nearest to the battery or fuse. If the bulb of the tester lights, voltage is present, which means that the part of the circuit between the connector and the battery is problem free. Continue checking the rest of the circuit in the same fashion. When you reach a point at which no voltage is present, the problem lies between that point and the last test point with voltage. Most of the time the problem can be traced to a loose connection.

➡Note: Keep in mind that some circuits receive voltage only when the ignition key is in the Accessory or Run position.

FINDING A SHORT

One method of finding shorts in a circuit is to remove the fuse and connect a test light or voltmeter in place of the fuse terminals. There should be no voltage present in the circuit. Move the wiring harness from side-to-side while watching the test light. If the bulb goes on, there is a short to ground somewhere in that area, probably where the insulation has rubbed through. The same test can be performed on each component in the circuit, even a switch.

GROUND CHECK

Perform a ground test to check whether a component is properly grounded. Disconnect the battery and connect one lead of a self-powered test light, known as a continuity tester, to a known good ground. Connect the other lead to the wire or ground connection being tested. If the bulb goes on, the ground is good. If the bulb does not go on, the ground is not good.

CONTINUITY CHECK

A continuity check is done to determine if there are any breaks in a circuit - if it is passing electricity properly. With the circuit off (no power in the circuit), a self-powered continuity tester can be used to check the circuit. Connect the test leads to both ends of the circuit (or to the "power" end and a good ground), and if the test light comes on the circuit is passing current properly. If the light doesn't come on, there is a break somewhere in the circuit. The same procedure can be used to test a switch, by connecting the continuity tester to the switch terminals. With the switch turned On, the test light should come on.

FINDING AN OPEN CIRCUIT

When diagnosing for possible open circuits, it is often difficult to locate them by sight because oxidation or terminal misalignment are hidden by the connectors. Merely wiggling a connector on a sensor or in the wiring harness may correct the open circuit condition. Remember this when an open circuit is indicated when troubleshooting a circuit. Intermittent problems may also be caused by oxidized or loose connections.

Electrical troubleshooting is simple if you keep in mind that all electrical circuits are basically electricity running from the battery, through the wires, switches, relays, fuses and fusible links to each electrical component (light bulb, motor, etc.) and to ground, from which it is passed back to the battery. Any electrical problem is an interruption in the flow of electricity to and from the battery.

3 Fuses - general information

◆ **Refer to illustrations 3.1a, 3.1b and 3.2**

The electrical circuits of the vehicle are protected by a combination of fuses, circuit breakers and fusible links. All models covered in this manual have two fuse blocks, one for standard fuses located under the instrument panel on the left side of the dashboard and one for high current fuses in the engine compartment, adjacent to the battery (see illustrations). Disconnect the cable to the negative battery terminal before replacing high current fuses.

Miniaturized fuses are employed in the fuse block in the passenger compartment. These compact fuses, with blade terminal design, allow fingertip removal and replacement. If an electrical component fails, always check the fuse first. The best way to check the fuses is with a test light. Check for power at the exposed terminal tips of each fuse. If power is present at one side of the fuse but not the other, the fuse is blown. A blown fuse can also be identified by visually inspecting it (see illustration).

Be sure to replace blown fuses with the correct type. Fuses of different ratings are physically interchangeable, but only fuses of the proper rating should be used. Replacing a fuse with one of a higher or lower value than specified is not recommended. Each electrical circuit needs a specific amount of protection. The amperage value of each fuse is molded into the fuse body.

If the replacement fuse immediately fails, don't replace it again until

3.1a The passenger compartment fuse block is located under the driver's side of the dash - release the clip by inserting a screwdriver, then pull sharply down to remove the cover

the cause of the problem is isolated and corrected. In most cases, the cause will be a short circuit in the wiring caused by a broken or deteriorated wire.

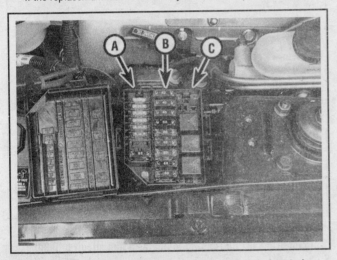

3.1b The fuse block in the engine compartment is located adjacent to the battery - it contains miniaturized fuses (A), cartridge type fusible links (B) and relays (C)

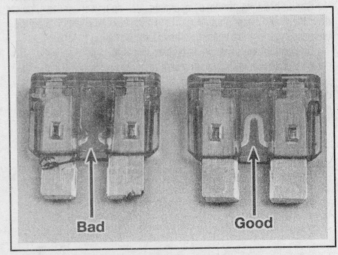

3.2 When a fuse blows, the center element melts - the fuse on the left is blown, the fuse on the right is good

4 Fusible links - general information

◆ **Refer to illustrations 4.2**

Some circuits are protected by fusible links. The links are used in circuits which are not ordinarily fused, such as the ignition circuit.

In addition to the conventional type of fusible link (described below) which is located in the wiring harness (see illustration), there is also cartridge type fusible links located in the engine compartment fuse

block that are similar to a large fuses (see illustration 3.1b), and, after disconnecting the negative battery cable, are simply unplugged and replaced by a unit of the same amperage. Some fusible links are held in place by a screw which must be loosened before removing the link.

Conventional type fusible links cannot be repaired, a new link of the same size wire should be installed in its place. The procedure is as follows:

a) Disconnect the cable from the negative battery terminal.

b) Disconnect the fusible link from the wiring harness.

c) Cut the damaged fusible link out of the wiring just behind the connector.

d) Strip the insulation back approximately 1/2-inch.

e) Position the connector on the new fusible link and crimp it into place.

f) Use rosin core solder at each end of the new link to obtain a good solder joint.

g) Use plenty of electrical tape around the soldered joint. No wires should be exposed.

h) Connect the battery ground cable. Test the circuit for proper operation.

4.2 Conventional type fusible links can be found exiting the engine compartment fuse block (arrow)

5   Circuit breakers - general information

▶ **Refer to illustration 5.2**

Circuit breakers protect components such as power windows, power door locks and headlights. Most of the circuit breakers are located in the passenger compartment fuse box (see illustration 3.1a).

On some models the circuit breaker resets itself automatically, so an electrical overload in a circuit breaker protected system will cause the circuit to fail momentarily, then come back on. If the circuit does not come back on, check it immediately (see illustration). Once the condition is corrected, the circuit breaker will resume its normal function.

5.2 Perform a continuity test with an ohmmeter to check a circuit breaker - no reading indicates a bad circuit breaker

6   Relays - general information and testing

GENERAL INFORMATION

1   Several electrical accessories in the vehicle, such as the fuel injection system, horns, starter, and fog lamps use relays to transmit the electrical signal to the component. Relays use a low-current circuit (the control circuit) to open and close a high-current circuit (the power circuit). If the relay is defective, that component will not operate properly. The various relays are mounted in engine compartment (see illustration 3.1b) and several locations throughout the vehicle (see Chapter 5). If a faulty relay is suspected, it can be removed and tested using the procedure below or by a dealer service department or a repair shop. Defective relays must be replaced as a unit.

TESTING

▶ **Refer to illustration 6.4**

2   It's best to refer to the wiring diagram for the circuit to determine the proper hook-ups for the relay you're testing. However, if you're not able to determine the correct hook-up from the wiring diagrams, you may be able to determine the test hook-ups from the information that follows.

3   On most relays, two of the terminals are the relay's control circuit (they connect to the relay coil which, when energized, closes the large contacts to complete the circuit). The other terminals are the power

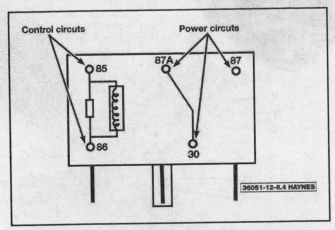

6.4 Most relays are marked on the outside to easily identify the control and power circuits

circuit (they are connected together within the relay when the control-circuit coil is energized).

4   The relays are marked as an aid to help you determine which terminals are the control circuit and which are the power circuit (see illustration).

5   Remove the relay from the vehicle and check for continuity between the relay power circuit terminals. There should be no continuity between terminal 30 and 87.

6   Connect a fused jumper wire between one of the two control circuit terminals and the positive battery terminal. Connect another jumper wire between the other control circuit terminal and ground. When the connections are made, the relay should click. On some relays, polarity may be critical, so, if the relay doesn't click, try swapping the jumper wires on the control circuit terminals.

7   With the jumper wires connected, check for continuity between the power circuit terminals. Now, there should be continuity between terminals 30 and 87.

8   If the relay fails any of the above tests, replace it.

7   Turn signal/hazard flasher - check and replacement

♦ Refer to illustration 7.1

❊❊ WARNING:

The models covered by this manual are equipped with Supplemental Restraint systems (SRS), more commonly known as airbags. Always disconnect the negative battery cable, then the positive battery cable and wait two minutes before working in the vicinity of the impact sensors, steering column or instrument panel to avoid the possibility of accidental deployment of the airbag, which could cause personal injury (see Section 27). Do not use electrical test equipment on any of the airbag system wiring or tamper with them in any way.

1   The turn signal and hazard flashers are controlled from a single electronic flasher unit which is mounted to the side of the interior fuse block (see illustration).

2   When the flasher unit is functioning properly, an audible click can be heard during its operation. If the turn signals fail on one side or the other and the flasher unit does not make its characteristic clicking sound, a faulty turn signal bulb is indicated.

3   If both turn signals fail to blink, the problem may be due to a blown fuse, a faulty flasher unit, a broken switch or a loose or open connection. If a quick check of the fuse box indicates that the turn signal fuse has blown, check the wiring for a short before installing a new fuse.

7.1 The electronic flasher unit (arrow) is mounted to the side of the passenger compartment fuse block

4   To replace the flasher, simply disconnect the electrical connectors, then remove the screw securing the flasher retaining bracket.

5   Make sure that the replacement unit is identical to the original. Compare the old one to the new one before installing it.

6   Installation is the reverse of removal.

8   Steering column switches - check and replacement

❊❊ WARNING:

The models covered by this manual are equipped with Supplemental Restraint systems (SRS), more commonly known as airbags. Always disconnect the negative battery cable, then the positive battery cable and wait two minutes before working in the vicinity of the impact sensors, steering column or instrument panel to avoid the possibility of accidental deployment of the airbag, which could cause personal injury (see Section 27). Do not use electrical test equipment on any of the airbag system wiring or tamper with them in any way.

MULTI-FUNCTION SWITCH

Check

♦ Refer to illustrations 8.3a, 8.3b, 8.3c and 8.3d

1   The multi-function switch is located on the left side of the steering column. It incorporates the turn signal, headlight dimmer and windshield wiper/washer functions into one switch.

2   Remove the multi-function switch (see Step 4).

3   Using an ohmmeter or self-powered test light and the accompanying diagrams, check for continuity between the indicated switch terminals with the switch in each of the indicated positions (see illustrations). If the continuity isn't as specified, replace the switch.

Replacement

▶ **Refer to illustration 8.6**

4   Disconnect the negative battery cable, then the positive battery cable and wait two minutes before proceeding any further.

5   Remove the lower steering column trim cover and the steering column covers (see Chapter 11).

6   Disconnect the electrical connectors, remove the retaining screws then detach the switch from the steering column (see illustration).

7   Installation is the reverse of removal.

CRUISE CONTROL SWITCHES

Check

▶ **Refer to illustrations 8.10a, 8.10b, 8.10c, and 8.10d**

8   Remove the left front fender splash shield (see Chapter 11).

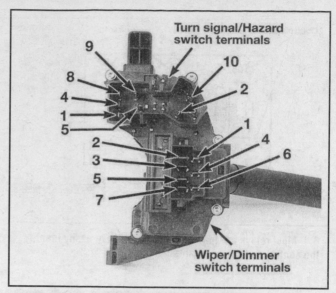

8.3a Multi- function switch terminal identification guide

Switch positions	Hazard warning	Continuity between
Neutral	OFF	9 and 10; 9 and 2
	ON	4 and 10; 4 and 2
		4 and 5; 4 and 8
Left	OFF	1 and 10; 1 and 8
Right	OFF	1 and 2; 1 and 5

36051-12-8.3b HAYNES

8.3b Turn signal and hazard switch continuity chart

Switch positions	Continuity between
Flash to Pass hold lever in this position	5 and 7
	2 and 3
High beam	2 and 5
Low beam	2 and 3

36051-12-8.3c HAYNES

8.3c Headlight dimmer switch continuity chart

Switch positions	Test terminals	Ohmmeter readings (+ or -10%)
Wiper OFF	1 and 4	47.6 K-ohms
Wash OFF	4 and 6	103.3 K-ohms
Intermitent	1 and 4	11.3 K-ohms
Low	1 and 4	4.08 K-ohms
High	1 and 4	0-ohms
Wash ON Wiper OFF	4 and 6	0-ohms
Delay control knob @ maximum position	4 and 6	103.3 K-ohms
Delay control knob @ minimum position	4 and 6	3.3 K-ohms

36051-12-8.3d HAYNES

8.3d Windshield wiper switch continuity chart

8.6 Remove the retaining screws (arrows) and unplug the connectors, then remove the multi-function switch

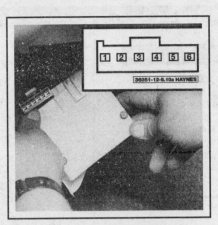

8.10a 1994 and 1995 cruise control amplifier terminal identification guide

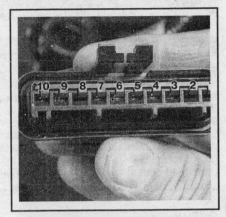

8.10b 1996 and later cruise control amplifier terminal identification guide

Switch positions	Test terminals	Ohmmeter readings (+ or -10%)
OFF	1 and 5	0 and 1 K-ohms
ON with ignition in RUN position	1 and 5	Battery voltage
SET/ACCEL	1 and 5	714 and 646 K-ohms
COAST	1 and 5	126 and 114 K-ohms
RESUME	1 and 5	2310 and 2090 K-ohms

Rotate the steering wheel through its full range of travel while performing each of the above tests.

36051-12-8.10c HAYNES

8.10c 1994 and 1995 cruise control actuator switch continuity chart

Switch positions	Test terminals	Ohmmeter readings (+ or -10%)
OFF	5 and 6	less than 4 K-ohms
ON with ignition in RUN position	5 and 10	Battery voltage
SET/ACCEL	5 and 6	714 and 646 K-ohms
COAST	5 and 6	126 and 114 K-ohms
RESUME	5 and 6	2310 and 2090 K-ohms

Rotate the steering wheel through its full range of travel while performing each of the above tests.

36051-12-8.10d HAYNES

8.10d 1996 and later cruise control actuator switch continuity chart

9   Disconnect the electrical connector from the cruise control amplifier located under the driver's side instrument panel on 1994 and 1995 models or behind the driver's side inner wheel well on 1996 and later models.

10 Using an ohmmeter and the accompanying diagrams, check for continuity between the indicated switch terminals with the switch in each of the indicated positions (see illustrations). If the continuity isn't as specified, replace the switch.

Replacement

♦ Refer to illustration 8.14

11 Disconnect the negative battery cable, then the positive battery cable and wait two minutes before proceeding any further.

12 Remove the drivers side airbag module (see Chapter 10, Section 14).

13 Disconnect the electrical connections from each switch.

14 Detach the switch retaining screws (see illustration). Then pry the steering wheel back cover outward to allow removal of the switch.

15 Installation is the reverse of removal.

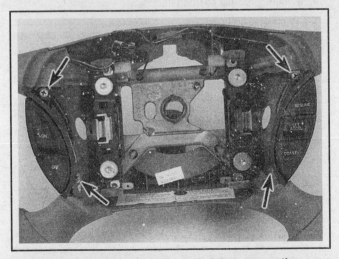

8.14 Detach the driver side airbag module to access the cruise control actuator switch retaining screws (arrows)

9   Ignition switch - check and replacement

✷✷ WARNING:

The models covered by this manual are equipped with Supplemental Restraint systems (SRS), more commonly known as airbags. Always disconnect the negative battery cable, then the positive battery cable and wait two minutes before working in the vicinity of the impact sensors, steering column or instrument panel to avoid the possibility of accidental deployment of the airbag, which could cause personal injury (see Section 27). Do not use electrical test equipment on any of the airbag system wiring or tamper with them in any way.

CHECK

▶ **Refer to illustrations 9.2a, 9.2b and 9.2c**

1   The ignition switch is mounted below the steering column behind the knee bolster. To check the switch it must first be removed (see Step 3).

2   Using an ohmmeter or self-powered test light and the accompanying diagrams, check for continuity between the indicated switch terminals with the switch in each of the indicated positions (see illustrations). If the continuity isn't as specified, replace the switch.

REPLACEMENT

▶ **Refer to illustration 9.6**

3   Disconnect the negative battery cable, then the positive battery cable and wait two minutes before proceeding any further.

4   Turn the ignition key lock cylinder to the Run position.

➡ **Note: On 1999 and later models the ignition switch should be left in the Off position.**

5   Remove the driver side knee bolster and the lower steering column cover (see Chapter 11).

6   Unplug the ignition switch electrical connector and remove the switch retaining screws (see illustration).

7   Disengage the ignition switch from the actuator pin and remove the switch from the vehicle.

8   Make sure the actuator pin slot in the new ignition switch is in the Run position (see illustration 9.2b).

➡ **Note: A new replacement switch assembly will be set in this position.**

Switch positions	Continuity between
ACC	B5 and A1
LOCK	P1 and P2
OFF	P1 and P2
RUN	B1 and A1; B2 and A2 B3 and A3; B4 and A4 B5 and I1
START	B1 and I2; B4 and STA B5 and I1; P1 and GND P2 and GND

36051-12-9.2c HAYNES

9.2c Ignition switch continuity chart

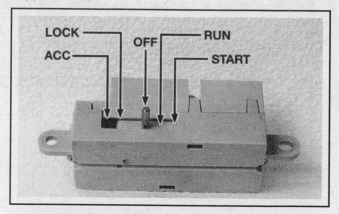

9.2a Check the ignition switch terminals for continuity in each of the indicated positions

9   Place the new switch in position on the actuator pin and install the retaining screws. It may be necessary to move the switch back and forth to line up the screw holes.

10   The remainder of the installation is the reverse of removal. Check for proper operation of the ignition switch in the lock, start and accessory positions.

9.2b Ignition switch position details

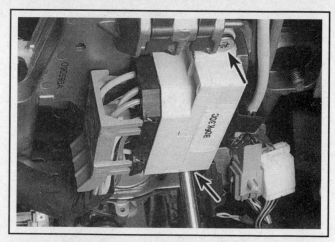

9.6 Unplug the electrical connector and remove the ignition switch retaining screws (arrows)

10 Ignition lock cylinder - removal and installation

♦ Refer to illustration 10.3

REMOVAL

1   Disconnect the negative battery cable, then the positive battery cable and wait two minutes before proceeding any further.
2   Turn the ignition key/lock cylinder to the Run position.
3   Insert an 1/8-inch punch into the hole at the bottom of the steering column cover surrounding the lock cylinder. Depress the punch while pulling out on the lock cylinder to remove it from the column housing (see illustration).

INSTALLATION

4   Depress the retaining pin on the side of the lock cylinder and rotate the ignition key/lock cylinder to the Run position.

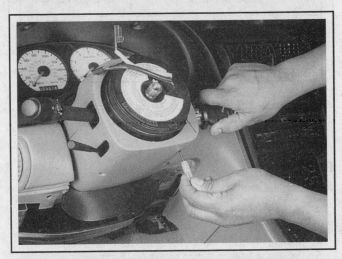

10.3 To remove the ignition lock cylinder, place the key in the "RUN" position, push in on the release tab with a screwdriver and pull the cylinder straight out

5   Install the lock cylinder into the steering column housing, making sure it's fully seated and aligned in the interlocking washer.
6   Rotate the key back to the Off position. This will allow the retaining pin to extend itself back into the locating hole in the steering column housing.
7   Turn the lock to ensure that operation is correct in all positions.
8   The remainder of installation is the reverse of removal.

11 Instrument panel switches - check and replacement

HEADLIGHT SWITCH

Check

♦ Refer to illustrations 11.2a and 11.2b

1   To check the switch it must first be removed (see Step 3).
2   Using an ohmmeter or self-powered test light and the accompanying diagrams, check for continuity between the indicated switch

11.2a Headlight switch terminal identification guide

terminals with the switch in each of the indicated positions (see illustrations). If the continuity isn't as specified, replace the switch.

Switch positions	Continuity between
OFF	B1 and H; B2 and R open circuit
PARK	B2 and R
ON	B1 and H; B2 and R
KNOB rotated to full left position	D1 and D2
KNOB rotating right from the full left position	R and I varied resistance

36051-12-11.2b HAYNES

11.2b Headlight switch continuity chart

Replacement

▸ **Refer to illustrations 11.3 and 11.5**

3   Detach the headlight switch knob by pushing the release tab at the bottom of the knob (see illustration).

4   Remove the instrument cluster bezel (see Chapter 11).

5   Detach the switch retaining screws (see illustration).

6   Unplug the electrical connector and remove the switch from the vehicle.

7   Installation is the reverse of removal.

REAR WINDOW DEFOGGER SWITCH

Check

▸ **Refer to illustration 11.10**

8   To check the switch it must first be removed (see Step 10).

9   Using several conventional type jumper wires, a fused jumper wire and an ohmmeter perform the following tests.

10 Ground terminal 4, then apply battery voltage to terminal 3. With

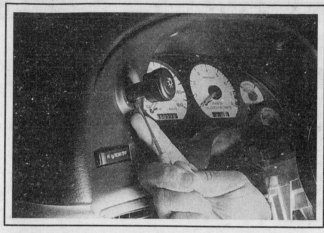

11.3 Using a small screwdriver depress the headlight switch knob retaining clip

the switch in the ON position check for continuity between terminals 1 and 2 (see illustration). If the switch fails the test procedure, replace the switch.

Replacement

▸ **Refer to illustrations 11.13**

11 Detach the headlight switch knob (see Step 3).

12 Remove the instrument cluster bezel (see Chapter 11).

13 Detach the plastic locking tabs on each side of the switch (see illustration).

14 Unplug the electrical connector from the back side of the switch, then remove it from the vehicle.

15 Installation is the reverse of removal.

11.5 Detach the switch retaining screws (arrows) - unplug the electrical connector and withdraw the switch from the instrument panel

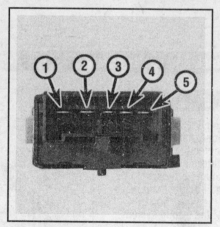

11.10 Rear defogger switch terminal guide

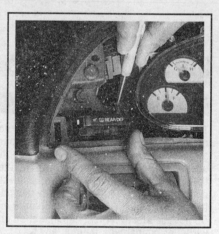

11.13 Detach the retaining clips on each side of the rear defogger switch

12 Radio/CD player and speakers - removal and installation

※ WARNING:

The models covered by this manual are equipped with Supplemental Restraint systems (SRS), more commonly known as airbags. Always disconnect the negative battery cable, then the positive battery cable and wait two minutes before working in the vicinity of the impact sensors, steering column or instrument panel to avoid the possibility of accidental deployment of the airbag, which could cause personal injury (see Section 27). Do not use electrical test equipment on any of the airbag system wiring or tamper with them in any way.

1   Disconnect the negative battery cable, then the positive battery cable and wait two minutes before proceeding any further.

RADIO AND CD PLAYER

♦ **Refer to illustrations 12.3a and 12.3b**

➡**Note: On 2001 and later models, the radio/CD player is secured with 2 bolts and the U-shaped wire is no longer required for removal.**

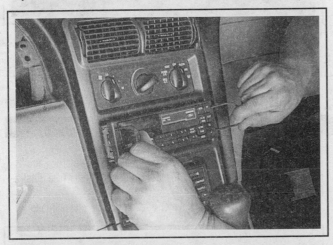

12.3a Insert the tools until they seat, then push outward simultaneously on both tools to release the clips and withdraw the radio from the dash

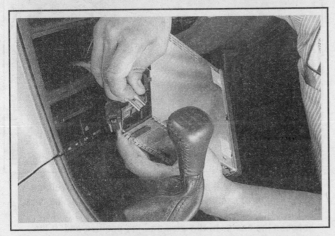

12.3b Detach the electrical connector and the antenna lead from the back side of the radio

2   On 1994 through 2000 models, for theft protection, the radio receiver and CD player assemblies are retained in the instrument panel by special clips. Releasing these clips requires the use of two sets of a special removal tool, available at most auto parts stores, or two short lengths of coat hanger wire bent into U-shapes. Insert the tools into the holes at the corners of the radio and CD player assemblies until you feel the internal clips release.

3   On 1994 through 2000 models, with the clips released, push outward simultaneously on both tools and pull the assembly out of the instrument panel, disconnect the antenna and electrical connectors and remove the unit from the vehicle (see illustrations).

4   Install by plugging in the electrical connectors, then sliding the radio or CD player along the track and into the instrument panel until the clips can be felt snapping in place.

SPEAKERS

♦ **Refer to illustration 12.6**

Door mounted

5   Remove the door trim panel (see Chapter 11).
6   Remove the mounting screws, withdraw the speaker, unplug the electrical connector and remove the speaker from the vehicle (see illustration).
7   Installation is the reverse of removal.

Rear quarter panel mounted

8   Remove the rear seat and the rear quarter trim panels (see Chapter 11).
9   Remove the speaker retaining screws, withdraw the speaker, unplug the electrical connector and remove the speaker from the vehicle.
10 Installation is the reverse of removal

Package shelf mounted

11 Remove the rear seat and package shelf (see Chapter 11).
12 Remove the speaker retaining screws, withdraw the speaker, unplug the electrical connector and remove the speaker from the vehicle.
13 Installation is the reverse of removal

12.6 After removing the door trim panel, the speaker retaining screws (arrows) are easy to reach

13 Antenna - removal and installation

▶ **Refer to illustrations 13.2 and 13.4**

1 Detach the radio and disconnect the antenna lead from the rear side of the radio (see Section 12).

2 Working from the outside of the vehicle, use a small wrench and remove the mast (see illustration).

3 Pry off the antenna trim cap.

4 Remove the screws securing the antenna to the body (see illustration), then pull the antenna up and out to remove it.

5 Installation is the reverse of removal.

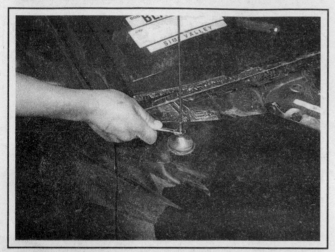

13.2 Use a small wrench to remove the antenna mast

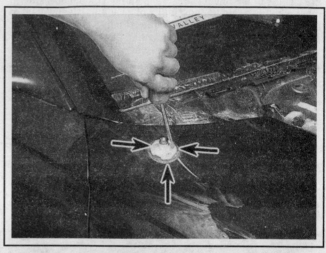

13.4 Remove the retaining screws (arrows) securing the antenna base to the front fender

14 Rear window defogger - check and repair

1 The rear window defogger consists of a number of horizontal elements baked onto the glass surface.

2 Small breaks in the element can be repaired without removing the rear window.

CHECK

▶ **Refer to illustrations 14.4, 14.5 and 14.7**

3 Turn the ignition switch and defogger system switches to the ON position.

4 When measuring voltage during the next two tests, wrap a piece

of aluminum foil around the tip of the voltmeter negative probe and press the foil against the heating element with your finger (see illustration).

5 Check the voltage at the center of each heating element (see

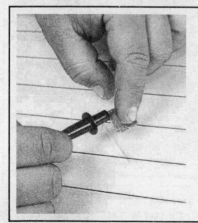

14.4 When measuring the voltage at the rear window defogger grid, wrap a piece of aluminum foil around the negative probe of the voltmeter and press the foil against the wire with your finger

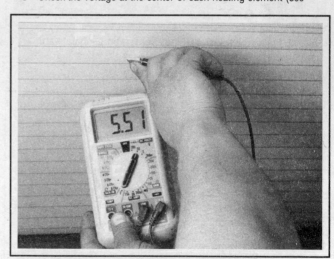

14.5 To determine if a wire has broken, check the voltage at the center of each wire. If the voltage is 6-volts, the wire is unbroken; if the voltage is 12-volts, the wire is broken between the center of the wire and the positive end; if the voltage is 0-volts, the wire is broken between the center of the wire and ground

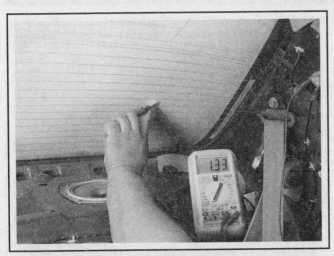

14.7 To find the break, place the voltmeter positive lead against the defogger positive terminal, place the voltmeter negative lead with the foil strip against the heat wire at the positive terminal end and slide it toward the negative terminal end - the point at which the voltmeter deflects from zero to several volts is the point at which the wire is broken

illustration). If the voltage is 6-volts, the element is okay (there is no break). If the voltage is 12-volts, the element is broken between the center of the element and the positive end. If the voltage is 0-volts the element is broken between the center of the element and ground.

6   Connect the negative lead to a good body ground. The reading should stay the same.

7   To find the break, place the voltmeter positive lead against the defogger positive terminal. Place the voltmeter negative lead with the foil strip against the heating element at the positive terminal end and slide it toward the negative terminal end. The point at which the voltmeter deflects from zero to several volts is the point at which the heating element is broken (see illustration).

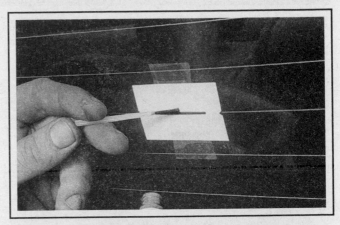

14.13 To use a defogger repair kit, apply masking to the inside of the window at the damaged area, then brush on the special conductive coating

REPAIR

▶ **Refer to illustration 14.13**

8   Repair the break in the element using a repair kit specifically recommended for this purpose, such as Dupont paste No. 4817 (or equivalent). Included in this kit is plastic conductive epoxy.

9   Prior to repairing a break, turn off the system and allow it to cool off for a few minutes.

10 Lightly buff the element area with fine steel wool, then clean it thoroughly with rubbing alcohol.

11 Use masking tape to mask off the area being repaired.

12 Thoroughly mix the epoxy, following the instructions provided with the repair kit.

13 Apply the epoxy material to the slit in the masking tape, overlapping the undamaged area about 3/4-inch on either end (see illustration).

14 Allow the repair to cure for 24 hours before removing the tape and using the system.

15 Headlights - replacement

▶ **Refer to illustrations 15.2 and 15.4**

✳ WARNING:

Halogen gas filled bulbs are under pressure and may shatter if the surface is scratched or the bulb is dropped. Wear eye protection and handle the bulbs carefully, grasping only the base whenever possible. Do not touch the surface of the bulb with your fingers because the oil from your skin could cause it to overheat and fail prematurely. If you do touch the bulb surface, clean it with rubbing alcohol.

1   Open the hood.

2   Detach the plastic clips securing the headlight cover (see illustration). On 1999 and later models, remove the headlight housing (see Section 17).

3   Disconnect the electrical connector from the bulb holder.

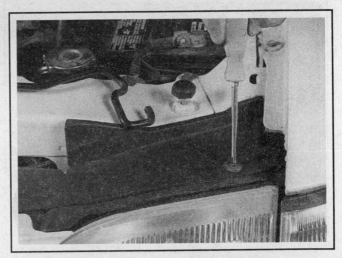

15.2 Detach the headlight cover retaining screws

4   Rotate the headlight bulb retaining ring counterclockwise as viewed from the rear (see illustration).

5   Withdraw the bulb assembly and retaining ring from the headlight housing.

6   Remove the bulb from the socket assembly by pulling it straight out.

7   Without touching the glass with your bare fingers, insert the new bulb into the socket assembly and then into the headlight housing, install and tighten the retaining ring.

8   Plug in the electrical connector. Install the headlight housing on 1999 and later models. Test headlight operation, then close the hood.

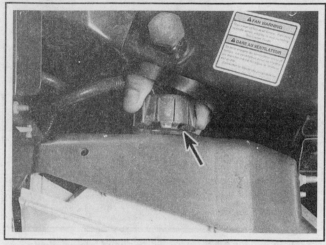

15.4 Rotate the headlight bulb retaining ring counterclockwise and pull the bulb socket assembly out of the housing - when installing the new bulb, don't touch the surface, clean it with rubbing alcohol if you do

16   Headlights - adjustment

♦ Refer to illustrations 16.1a, 16.1b and 16.3

➡**Note: The headlights must be aimed correctly. If adjusted incorrectly they could blind the driver of an oncoming vehicle and cause a serious accident or seriously reduce your ability to see the road. The headlights should be checked for proper aim every 12 months and any time a new headlight is installed or front end body work is performed. It should be emphasized that the following procedure is only an interim step which will provide temporary adjustment until the headlights can be adjusted by a properly equipped shop.**

1   The headlights have three adjusting screws each, one inboard and two outboard. The adjuster located on the outboard lower corner of the headlight housing is accessible from the front of the vehicle. The remaining two adjusters are accessible from the rear of the headlight assembly and are turned using a small wrench or pliers (see illustrations).

2   There are several methods of adjusting the headlights. The simplest method requires masking tape, a blank wall and a level floor.

16.1a The lower outboard headlight adjusting screw can be adjusted from the outside of the vehicle (1998 and earlier shown)

16.1b The remaining headlight adjusting screws must be adjusted from the rear of the headlight housing (1998 and earlier shown)

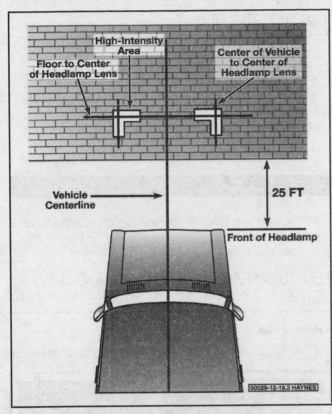

16.3 Headlight adjustment details

3   Position masking tape vertically on the wall in reference to the vehicle centerline and the centerlines of both headlights (see illustration).

4   Position a horizontal tape line in reference to the centerline of all the headlights.

➡Note: It may be easier to position the tape on the wall with the vehicle parked only a few inches away.

5   Adjustment should be made with the vehicle parked 25 feet from the wall, sitting level, the gas tank half-full and no unusually heavy load in the vehicle.

6   Starting with the low beam adjustment, position the high intensity zone so it is two inches below the horizontal line and two inches to the right of the headlight vertical line. Adjustment is made by turning the top adjusting screw clockwise to raise the beam and counterclockwise to lower the beam. The adjusting screw on the side should be used in the same manner to move the beam left or right.

7   With the high beams on, the high intensity zone should be vertically centered with the exact center just below the horizontal line.

➡Note: It may not be possible to position the headlight aim exactly for both high and low beams. If a compromise must be made, keep in mind that the low beams are the most used and have the greatest effect on safety.

8   Have the headlights adjusted by a dealer service department or service station at the earliest opportunity.

17 Headlight housing - removal and installation

✳ WARNING:

The models covered by this manual are equipped with Supplemental Restraint systems (SRS), more commonly known as airbags. Always disconnect the negative battery cable, then the positive battery cable and wait two minutes before working in the vicinity of the impact sensors, steering column or instrument panel to avoid the possibility of accidental deployment of the airbag, which could cause personal injury (see Section 27). Do not use electrical test equipment on any of the airbag system wiring or tamper with them in any way.

1998 AND EARLIER MODELS

▶ **Refer to illustrations 17.3 and 17.4**

1   Disconnect the negative battery cable, then the positive battery cable and wait two minutes before proceeding any further.

2   Remove the headlight bulb(s) (see Section 15).

3   Detach the clip from the upper adjusting screw (see illustration).

4   Squeeze the locking tabs on the lower two adjusting screws while

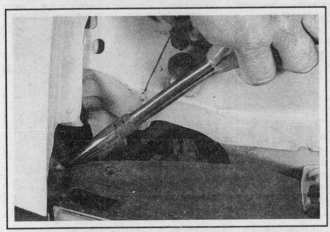

17.3 Detach the metal retaining clip securing the upper adjusting screw

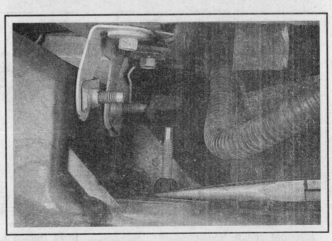

17.4 Using a pair of pliers, squeeze the lower retaining clips while pulling the headlight housing outward

pulling outward on the headlight assembly to detach it from the radiator support (see illustration).

5   When reinstalling the headlight housing, align the adjusting screws with there respective holes, then push straight back until the locking tabs fully engage the radiator support.

6   The remainder of the installation is the reverse of removal.

18 Bulb replacement

FRONT TURN SIGNAL AND SIDE MARKER LIGHTS

▶ **Refer to illustrations 18.2 and 18.3**

1   Detach the headlight trim cover (see Section 15).

2   Detach the side marker light retaining nut(s), then pull the side marker light outward (see illustration). On 1999 and later models remove the headlight housing (see Section 17).

3   Twist the bulb socket a quarter turn counterclockwise, then remove the bulb assembly from the housing (see illustration).

18.2 Detach the side marker light housing retaining nut (arrow)

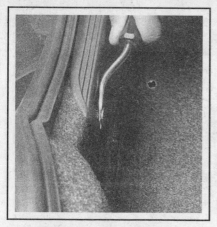

18.6 Detach the clips securing the trunk compartment rear finishing panel

1999 AND LATER MODELS

7   Pull upward on the headlight housing retaining clips located at the top of the housing assembly.

8   Pull the headlight housing outward away from the vehicle.

9   Disconnect the electrical connectors and remove the housing from the vehicle.

10   Installation is the reverse of removal.

4   The defective bulb can then be pulled straight out of the socket and replaced.

5   Installation of the housing is the reverse of removal.

REAR TURN SIGNAL, BRAKE, TAIL AND BACK-UP LIGHTS

▶ **Refer to illustrations 18.6, 18.7a and 18.7b**

6   Working in the trunk compartment, detach the plastic clips secur-

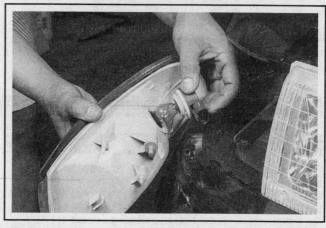

18.3 Rotate the bulb holder counterclockwise and withdraw it from the side marker light housing, then grasp the bulb and pull it straight out

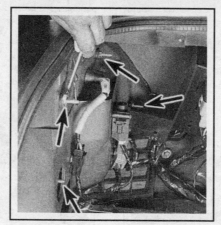

18.7a Detach the tail light housing retaining nuts . . .

18.7b . . . then pull the housing outward to access the tail light bulbs

ing the rear finishing panel, then remove the panel from the vehicle (see illustration).

7 Detach the retaining nuts securing the rear tail light housing, then pull the tail light assembly outward to access the tail light bulbs (see illustrations).

8 Twist the bulb socket a quarter turn counterclockwise, then remove the bulb assembly from the housing.

9 The defective bulb can then be pulled straight out of the socket and replaced.

10 Installation of the tail light housing is the reverse of removal.

LICENSE PLATE LIGHT

▶ **Refer to illustration 18.11**

11 Detach the retaining screws which secure the lens to the trunk lid (see illustration).

12 The defective bulb can then be pulled straight out of the socket and replaced.

13 Installation of the lens is the reverse of removal.

HIGH-MOUNTED BRAKE LIGHT

▶ **Refer to illustration 18.14**

14 The high mounted brake light bulbs can be accessed from the trunk compartment (see illustration).

15 Twist the bulb socket a quarter turn counterclockwise, then remove the bulb assembly from the housing.

16 The defective bulb can then be pulled straight out of the socket and replaced.

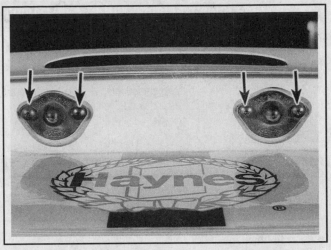

18.11 Detach the screws (arrows) securing the lenses to replace the license plate light bulbs

INTERIOR LIGHTS

▶ **Refer to illustration 18.17**

17 Using a small screwdriver, remove the lens and replace the bulb (see illustration).

INSTRUMENT CLUSTER ILLUMINATION

▶ **Refer to illustration 18.18**

18 To gain access to the instrument cluster illumination lights, the instrument cluster will have to be removed (see Section 21). The bulbs can then be removed and replaced from the rear of the cluster (see illustration).

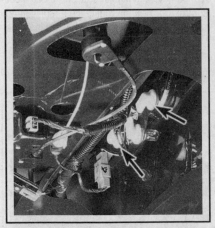

18.14 Twist the bulb holder (arrows) counterclockwise to remove the high mounted brake light bulbs

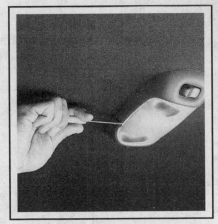

18.17 Use a small screwdriver to pry out the interior light lens

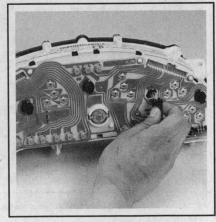

18.18 To remove an instrument cluster bulb, depress the bulb and rotate it counterclockwise

19 Daytime Running Lights (DRL) - general information

The Daytime Running Lights (DRL) system is used on all Canadian models and on all U.S. models since 1998 to illuminate the headlights whenever the engine is running.

The only exception is with the engine running and the parking brake engaged. Once the parking brake is released, the lights will remain on as long as the ignition switch is on, even if the parking brake is later applied.

The DRL system supplies reduced power to the headlights so they won't be too bright for daytime use, while prolonging headlight life.

20 Wiper motor - check and replacement

WIPER MOTOR CIRCUIT CHECK

▶ **Refer to illustration 20.2**

➡**Note: Refer to the wiring diagrams for wire colors and locations in the following checks. Keep in mind that power wires are generally larger in diameter and brighter colors, where ground wires are usually smaller in diameter and darker colors. When checking for voltage, probe a grounded 12-volt test light to each terminal at a connector until it lights; this verifies voltage (power) at the terminal.**

1   If the wipers work slowly, make sure the battery is in good condition and has a strong charge (see Chapter 1). If the battery is in good condition, remove the wiper motor (see below) and operate the wiper arms by hand. Check for binding linkage and pivots. Lubricate or repair the linkage or pivots as necessary. Reinstall the wiper motor. If the wipers still operate slowly, check for loose or corroded connections, especially the ground connection. If all connections look OK, replace the motor.

2   If the wipers fail to operate when activated, check the fuse. If the fuse is OK, connect a jumper wire between the wiper motor and ground, then retest. If the motor works now, repair the ground connection. If the motor still doesn't work, turn the wiper switch to the HI position and check for voltage at the motor (see illustration). If there's voltage at the motor, remove the motor and check it off the vehicle with fused jumper wires from the battery. If the motor now works, check for binding linkage (see Step 1 above). If the motor still doesn't work, replace it. If there's no voltage at the motor, check for voltage at the wiper control module. If there's voltage at the wiper control module and no voltage at the at the wiper motor, check the switch for continuity (see Section 8). If the switch is OK, the wiper control module is probably bad.

3   If the interval (delay) function is inoperative, check the continuity of all the wiring between the switch and wiper control module. If the wiring is OK, check the resistance of the delay control knob of the multi-function switch (see Section 8). If the delay control knob is within the specified resistance, replace the wiper control module.

4   If the wipers stop at the position they're in when the switch is turned off (fail to park), check for voltage at the park feed wire of the wiper motor connector when the wiper switch is OFF but the ignition is ON. If no voltage is present, check for an open circuit between the wiper motor and the fuse panel.

5   If the wipers won't shut off unless the ignition is OFF, disconnect the wiring from the wiper control switch. If the wipers stop, replace the switch. If the wipers keep running, there's a defective limit switch in the motor; replace the motor.

6   If the wipers won't retract below the hood line, check for mechanical obstructions in the wiper linkage or on the vehicle's body which

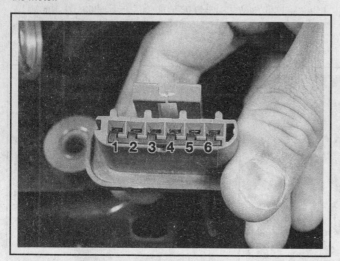

20.2 Windshield wiper motor terminal guide (1998 and earlier).

➡**Note: On later models, the connector is similar, except there is no common terminal. 1 through 5 are the same as 2 through 6 in this photo**

1   *Common terminal*
2   *Park switch terminal*
3   *Park feed power terminal*
4   *Ground terminal*
5   *Low speed terminal*
6   *High speed terminal*

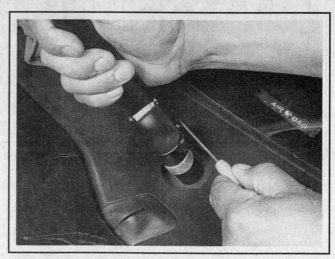

20.7 Pry out the locking tab, then pull straight up to remove the wiper arm assembly

20.10 Detach the wiper motor retaining bolts (arrows)

would prevent the wipers from parking. If there are no obstructions, check the wiring between the switch and motor for continuity. If the wiring is OK, replace the wiper motor.

WIPER MOTOR REPLACEMENT

▶ **Refer to illustrations 20.7 and 20.10**

7   Remove the windshield wiper arms (see illustration).
8   Remove the cowl cover and the cowl vent screen (see Chapter 11).
9   Disconnect the electrical connector from the wiper motor.
10 Remove the wiper motor retaining bolts (see illustration),
11 Pull the wiper motor outward slightly and detach the clip securing the wiper arm linkage to the backside of the motor, then remove the motor from the vehicle.
12 Installation is the reverse of removal.

21   Instrument cluster - removal and installation

▶ **Refer to illustration 21.3**

❋❋ WARNING:

The models covered by this manual are equipped with Supplemental Restraint systems (SRS), more commonly known as airbags. Always disconnect the negative battery cable, then the positive battery cable and wait two minutes before working in the vicinity of the impact sensors, steering column or instrument panel to avoid the possibility of accidental deployment of the airbag, which could cause personal injury (see Section 27). Do not use electrical test equipment on any of the airbag system wiring or tamper with them in any way.

1   Disconnect the negative battery cable, then the positive battery cable and wait two minutes before proceeding any further.
2   Tilt the steering wheel to its lowest position and remove the instrument cluster bezel (see Chapter 11).
3   Remove the instrument cluster retaining screws (see illustration).
4   Pull the instrument cluster out and unplug the electrical connectors from the backside, then remove the cluster from the instru-

21.3 The instrument cluster is held in place by screws (arrows) at both sides of the housing

ment panel.
5   Installation is the reverse of removal.

22   Horn - check and replacement

CHECK

▶ **Refer to illustration 22.3**

➡**Note: Check the fuses before beginning electrical diagnosis.**

1   Disconnect the electrical connector from the horn.
2   To test the horn, connect battery voltage to the two terminals with a pair of jumper wires. If the horn doesn't sound, replace it.
3   If the horn does sound, check for voltage at the terminal when the horn button is depressed (see illustration). If there's voltage at the terminal, check for a bad ground at the horn.
4   If there's no voltage at the horn, check the relay (see Section 6). Note that most horn relays are either the four-terminal or externally grounded three-terminal type.

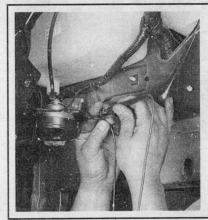

22.3 Connect a voltmeter to the horn wire and ground - test for voltage while the switch is depressed

5   If the relay is OK, check for voltage to the relay power and control circuits. If either of the circuits is not receiving voltage, inspect the wiring between the relay and the fuse panel.

6   If both relay circuits are receiving voltage, depress the horn button and check the circuit from the relay to the horn button for continuity to ground. If there's no continuity, check the circuit for an open. If there's no open circuit, replace the horn button.

7   If there's continuity to ground through the horn button, check for an open or short in the circuit from the relay to the horn.

REPLACEMENT

▶ **Refer to illustration 22.9**

8   To access the horns, the left front fender splash shield must first be removed (see Chapter 11).

9   Disconnect the electrical connectors and remove the bracket bolt (see illustration).

10 Installation is the reverse of removal.

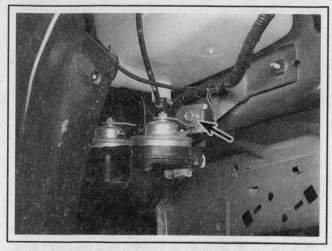

22.9 **Disconnect the electrical connector, remove the bolt (arrow) and detach the horn**

23 Cruise control system - description and check

▶ **Refer to illustrations 23.5a and 23.5b**

1   The cruise control system maintains vehicle speed with a servo motor located in the driver's side wheel well, which is connected to the throttle linkage by a cable. The system consists of the servo motor, brake switch, control switches, a relay and on 1994 and 1995 models, associated vacuum hoses. Some features of the system require special testers and diagnostic procedures which are beyond the scope of this manual. Listed below are some general procedures that may be used to locate common problems.

2   Locate and check the fuse (see Section 3).

3   Have an assistant operate the brake lights while you check their operation (voltage from the brake light switch deactivates the cruise control).

4   If the brake lights don't come on or don't shut off, correct the problem and retest the cruise control.

5   On early models visually inspect the vacuum hose connected to the speed control servo. On all models check the control cable between the cruise control servo/amplifier and the throttle linkage and replace as necessary (see illustrations).

6   The cruise control system uses a speed sensing device. The speed sensor is located in the transmission. To test the speed sensor (see Chapter 6).

7   Test drive the vehicle to determine if the cruise control is now working. If it isn't, take it to a dealer service department or an automotive electrical specialist for further diagnosis.

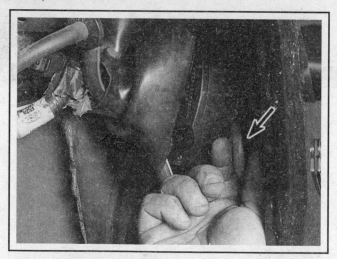

23.5a **The cruise control servo is located in driver side wheel opening - make sure the vacuum hose (arrow) is connected securely**

23.5b **Make sure the cruise control and accelerator linkage mounted on the throttle body are not damaged and that they operate smoothly together when the throttle is opened**

24 Power window system - description and check

♦ **Refer to illustration 24.12**

1   The power window system operates electric motors, mounted in the doors, which lower and raise the windows. The system consists of the control switches, the motors, regulators, glass mechanisms and associated wiring.

2   The power windows can be lowered and raised from the master control switch by the driver or by remote switches located at the individual windows. Each window has a separate motor which is reversible. The position of the control switch determines the polarity and therefore the direction of operation.

3   The circuit is protected by a fuse and a circuit breaker. Each motor is also equipped with an internal circuit breaker, this prevents one stuck window from disabling the whole system.

4   The power window system will only operate when the ignition switch is ON. In addition, many models have a window lockout switch at the master control switch which, when activated, disables the switches at the rear windows and, sometimes, the switch at the passenger's window also. Always check these items before troubleshooting a window problem.

5   These procedures are general in nature, so if you can't find the problem using them, take the vehicle to a dealer service department or other properly equipped repair facility.

6   If the power windows won't operate, always check the fuse and circuit breaker first.

7   If only the rear windows are inoperative, or if the windows only operate from the master control switch, check the rear window lockout switch for continuity in the unlocked position. Replace it if it doesn't have continuity.

8   Check the wiring between the switches and fuse panel for continuity. Repair the wiring, if necessary.

9   If only one window is inoperative from the master control switch, try the other control switch at the window.

➥**Note: This doesn't apply to the drivers door window.**

10 If the same window works from one switch, but not the other, check the switch for continuity.

24.12 If no voltage is found at the motor with the switch depressed - check for voltage at the switch

11 If the switch tests OK, check for a short or open in the circuit between the affected switch and the window motor.

12 If one window is inoperative from both switches, remove the trim panel from the affected door and check for voltage at the switch (see illustration) and at the motor while the switch is operated.

13 If voltage is reaching the motor, disconnect the glass from the regulator (see Chapter 11). Move the window up and down by hand while checking for binding and damage. Also check for binding and damage to the regulator. If the regulator is not damaged and the window moves up and down smoothly, replace the motor. If there's binding or damage, lubricate, repair or replace parts, as necessary.

14 If voltage isn't reaching the motor, check the wiring in the circuit for continuity between the switches and motors. You'll need to consult the wiring diagram for the vehicle. If the circuit is equipped with a relay, check that the relay is grounded properly and receiving voltage.

15 Test the windows after you are done to confirm proper repairs.

25 Power door lock and keyless entry system - description and check

♦ **Refer to illustration 25.9**

1   The power door lock system operates the door lock actuators mounted in each door. The system consists of the switches, actuators, and associated wiring. Diagnosis can usually be limited to simple checks of the wiring connections and actuators for minor faults which can be easily repaired.

2   Power door lock systems are operated by bi-directional solenoids located in the doors. The lock switches have two operating positions: Lock and Unlock. On later models with keyless entry the switches activate a module which in turn connects voltage to the door lock solenoids. Depending on which way the switch is activated, it reverses polarity, allowing the two sides of the circuit to be used alternately as the feed (positive) and ground side. On earlier models with out keyless entry the switches directly activate the door lock motors.

3   If you are unable to locate the trouble using the following general steps, consult your a dealer service department.

4   Always check the circuit protection first. On these models the battery voltage passes through the 20 amp circuit breaker located in the passenger compartment fuse block.

5   Operate the door lock switches in both directions (Lock and Unlock) with the engine off. Listen for the faint click of the door lock solenoid (motor) or relay operating.

6   If there's no click, check for voltage at the switches. If no voltage is present, check the wiring between the fuse block and the switches for shorts and opens.

7   If voltage is present but no click is heard, test the switch for continuity. Replace it if there's no continuity in both switch positions.

8   If the switch has continuity but the solenoid doesn't click, check

25.9 Check for voltage at the lock solenoid while the lock switch is operated

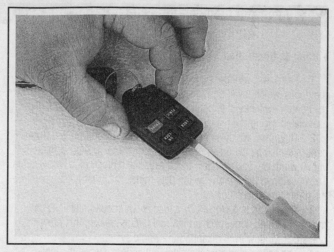

25.13 Use a small screwdriver to separate the transmitter halves

the wiring between the switch and solenoid for continuity. Repair the wiring if there's not continuity.

9   If all but one lock solenoids operate, remove the trim panel from the affected door (see Chapter 11) and check for voltage at the solenoid while the lock switch is operated (see illustration). One of the wires should have voltage in the Lock position; the other should have voltage in the unlock position.

10 If the inoperative solenoid is receiving voltage, replace the solenoid.

➡**Note: It's common for wires to break in the portion of the harness between the body and door (opening and closing the door fatigues and eventually breaks the wires).**

KEYLESS ENTRY SYSTEM

▶ **Refer to illustrations 25.13 and 25.14**

11 The keyless entry system consists of a remote control transmitter that sends a coded infrared signal to a receiver located in the trunk compartment that operates the door lock system.

12 Replace the transmitter batteries when the red LED light on the side of the case doesn't light when the button is pushed.

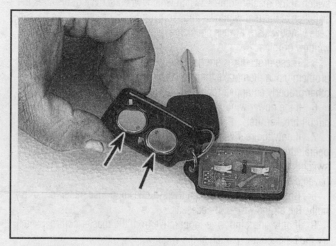

25.14 Replace the lithium batteries (arrows)

13 Use a small screwdriver to carefully separate the case halves (see illustration).

14 Replace the two 3-volt 2016 lithium batteries (see illustration).

15 Snap the case halves together.

26 | Electric side view mirrors - description and check

1   Most electric rear view mirrors use two motors to move the glass; one for up and down adjustments and one for left-right adjustments.

2   The control switch has a selector portion which sends voltage to the left or right side mirror. With the ignition ON but the engine OFF, roll down the windows and operate the mirror control switch through all functions (left-right and up-down) for both the left and right side mirrors.

3   Listen carefully for the sound of the electric motors running in the mirrors.

4   If the motors can be heard but the mirror glass doesn't move, there's probably a problem with the drive mechanism inside the mirror. Remove and disassemble the mirror to locate the problem.

5   If the mirrors don't operate and no sound comes from the mirrors, check the fuse (see Chapter 1).

6   If the fuse is OK, remove the mirror control switch from its mounting without disconnecting the wires attached to it. Turn the ignition ON and check for voltage at the switch. There should be voltage at one terminal. If there's no voltage at the switch, check for an open or short in the wiring between the fuse panel and the switch.

7   If there's voltage at the switch, disconnect it. Check the switch for continuity in all its operating positions. If the switch does not have continuity, replace it.

8   Re-connect the switch. Locate the wire going from the switch to ground. Leaving the switch connected, connect a jumper wire between

this wire and ground. If the mirror works normally with this wire in place, repair the faulty ground connection.

9   If the mirror still doesn't work, remove the mirror and check the wires at the mirror for voltage. Check with ignition ON and the mirror selector switch on the appropriate side. Operate the mirror switch in all its positions. There should be voltage at one of the switch-to-mirror

wires in each switch position (except the neutral "off" position).

10   If there's not voltage in each switch position, check the wiring between the mirror and control switch for opens and shorts.

11   If there's voltage, remove the mirror and test it off the vehicle with jumper wires. Replace the mirror if it fails this test.

27 Airbag - general information

♦ **Refer to illustrations 27.1a and 27.1b**

All models are equipped with a Supplemental Restraint System (SRS), more commonly known as an airbag. This system is designed to protect the driver, and the front seat passenger, from serious injury in the event of a head-on or frontal collision. It consists of an airbag module in the center of the steering wheel and the right side of the instrument panel, two crash sensors mounted at the front of the vehicle and a diagnostic module which also contains a safing sensor is located inside the passenger compartment (see illustrations).

AIRBAG MODULE

Steering wheel-mounted

The airbag inflator module contains a housing incorporating the cushion (airbag) and inflator unit, mounted in the center of the steering wheel The inflator assembly is mounted on the back of the housing over a hole through which gas is expelled, inflating the bag almost instantaneously when an electrical signal is sent from the system. A coil assembly on the steering column under the module carries this signal to the module.

This coil assembly can transmit an electrical signal regardless of steering wheel position. The igniter in the air bag converts the electrical signal to heat and ignites the sodium azide/copper oxide powder, producing nitrogen gas, which inflates the bag.

Instrument panel-mounted

The airbag is mounted above the glove compartment and designated by the letters SRS (Supplemental Restraint System). It consists of an inflator containing an igniter, a bag assembly, a reaction housing and a trim cover.

The air bag is considerably larger that the steering wheel-mounted unit (8 cu ft vs. 2.3 cu ft) and is supported by the steel reaction housing. The trim cover is textured and painted to match the instrument panel and has a molded seam which splits when the bag inflates. As with the steering-wheel-mounted air bag, the igniter electrical signal converts to heat, converting sodium azide/iron oxide powder to nitrogen gas, inflating the bag.

SENSORS

The system has three sensors: two forward crash sensors at the front of the vehicle and a safing sensor mounted inside the airbag diagnostic module which is located in the center console behind the radio.

The forward and passenger compartment sensors are basically pressure sensitive switches that complete an electrical circuit during an impact of sufficient G force. The electrical signal from these sensors is sent to the electronic diagnostic monitor which then completes the circuit and inflates the airbag(s).

ELECTRONIC DIAGNOSTIC MONITOR

The electronic diagnostic monitor supplies the current to the airbag system in the event of the collision, even if battery power is cut off. It checks this system every time the vehicle is started, causing the "AIR BAG" light to go on then off, if the system is operating properly. If there is a fault in the system, the light will go on and stay on, flash, or the dash will make a beeping sound. If this happens, the vehicle should be taken to your dealer immediately for service.

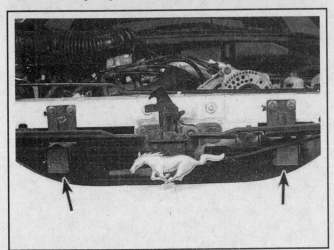

27.1a The front crash sensors are mounted in the front grille opening

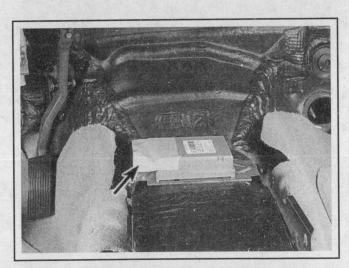

27.1b The airbag diagnostic module is mounted to the transmission tunnel behind the console

DISABLING THE SYSTEM

Whenever working in the vicinity of the steering wheel, steering column or near other components of the airbag system, the system should be disarmed. To do this, perform the following steps:

a) *Turn the ignition switch to Off.*

b) *Detach the cable from the negative battery terminal then detach the positive cable. Wait 2 minutes for the electronic module backup power supply to be depleted.*

ENABLING THE SYSTEM

a) *Turn the ignition switch to the Off position.*

b) *Connect the positive battery cable first, then connect the negative cable.*

28 Wiring diagrams - general information

Since it isn't possible to include all wiring diagrams for every year covered by this manual, the following diagrams are those that are typical and most commonly needed.

Prior to troubleshooting any circuits, check the fuse and circuit breakers (if equipped) to make sure they're in good condition. Make sure the battery is properly charged and check the cable connections (see Chapter 1).

When checking a circuit, make sure that all connectors are clean, with no broken or loose terminals. When unplugging a connector, do not pull on the wires. Pull only on the connector housings themselves.

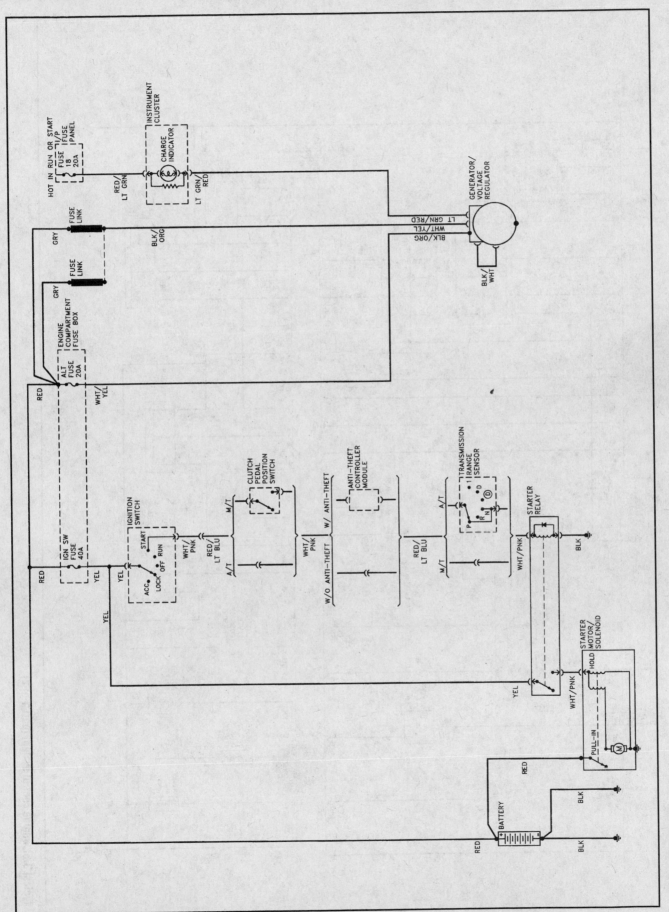

Typical starting and charging system

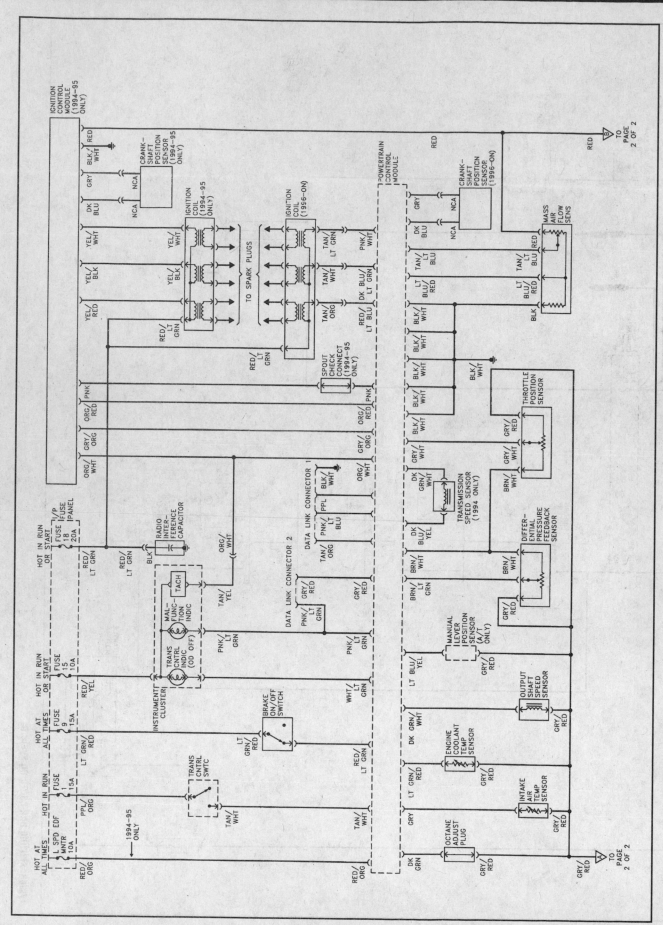

Typical 3.8L engine control system (part 1 of 2)

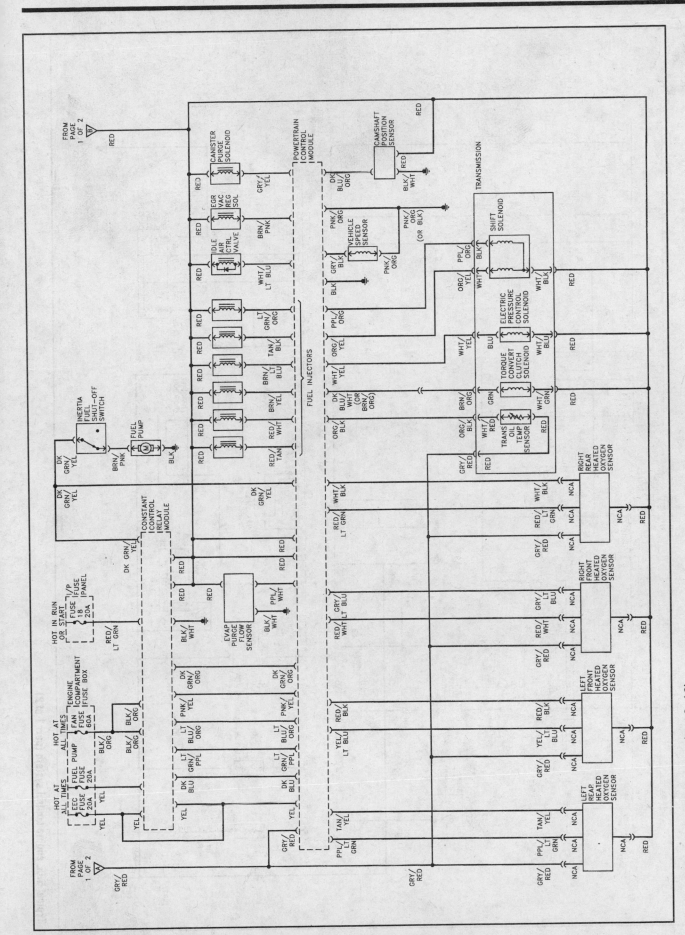

Typical 3.8L engine control system (part 2 of 2)

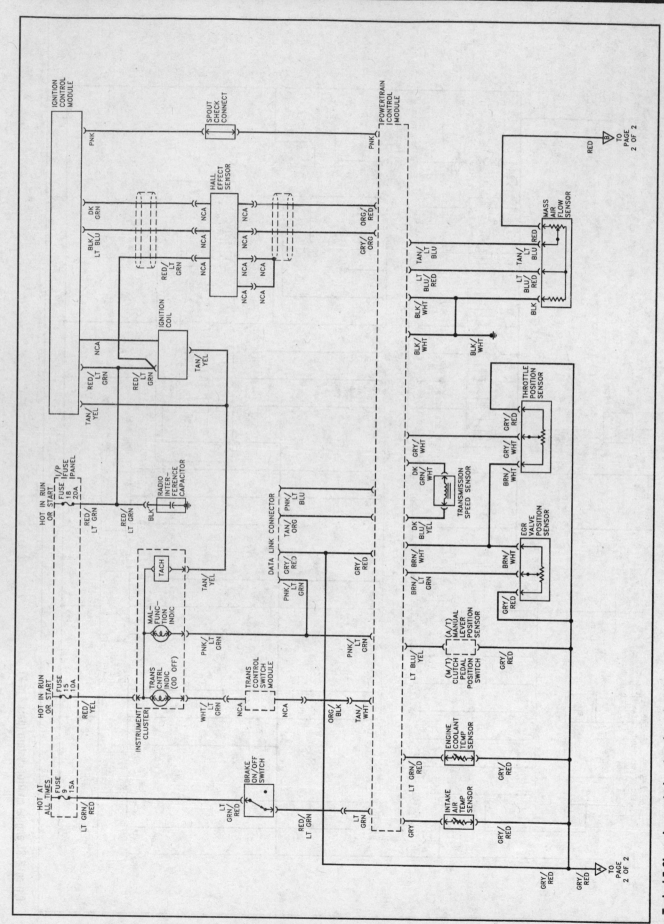

Typical 5.0L engine control system (part 1 of 2)

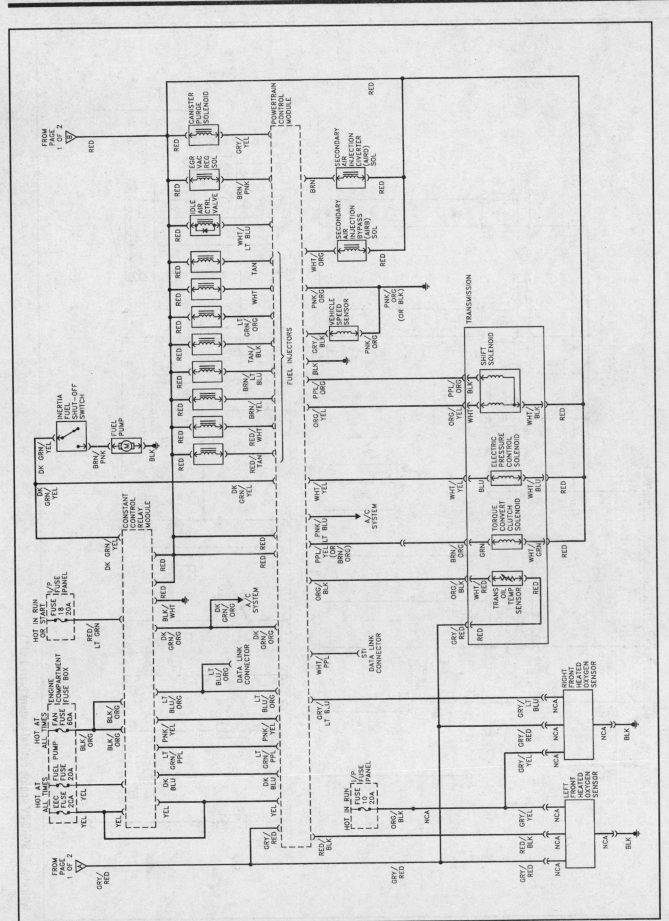

Typical 5.0L engine control system (part 2 of 2)

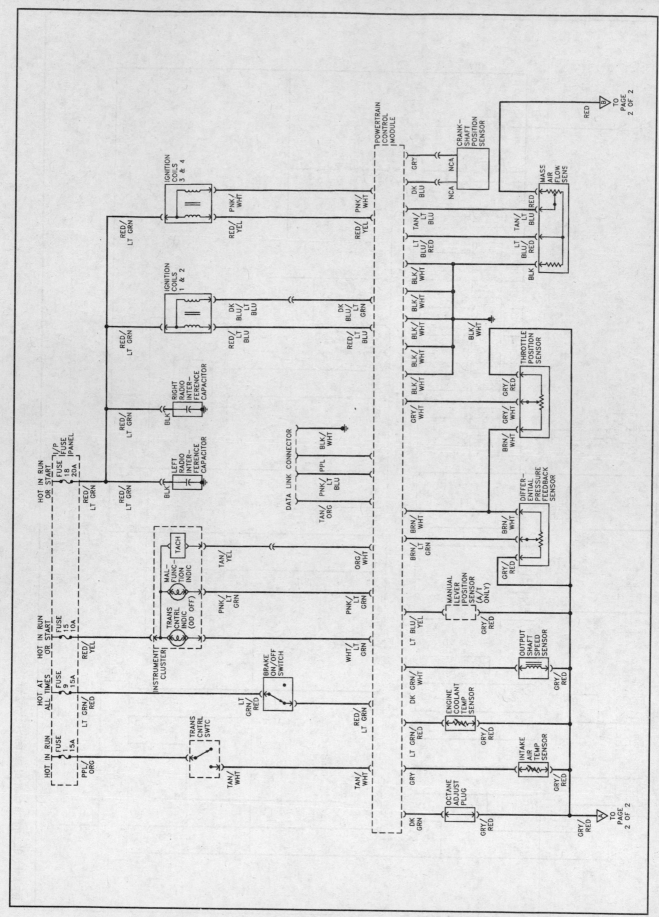

Typical 4.6L SOHC 2V engine control system (part 1 of 2)

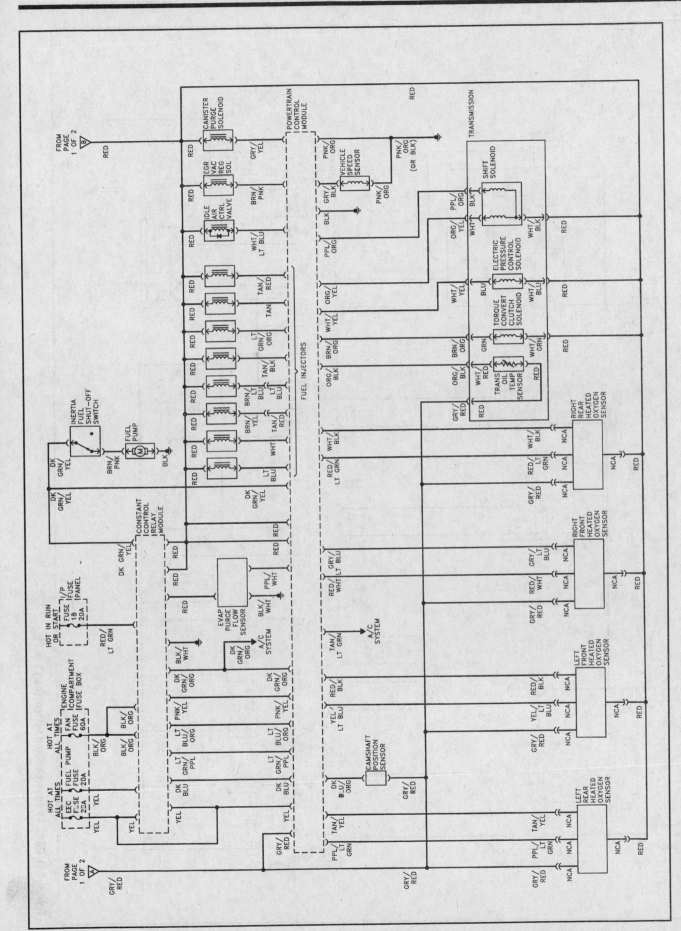

Typical 4.6L SOHC 2V engine control system (part 2 of 2)

Typical 4.6L DOHC 4V engine control system (part 1 of 2)

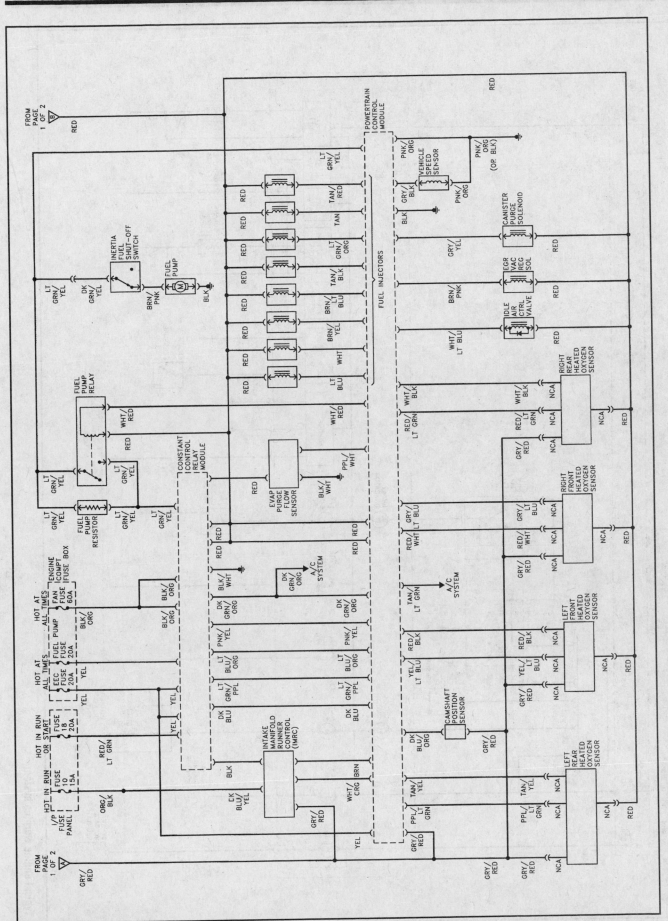

Typical 4.6L DOHC 4V engine control system (part 2 of 2)

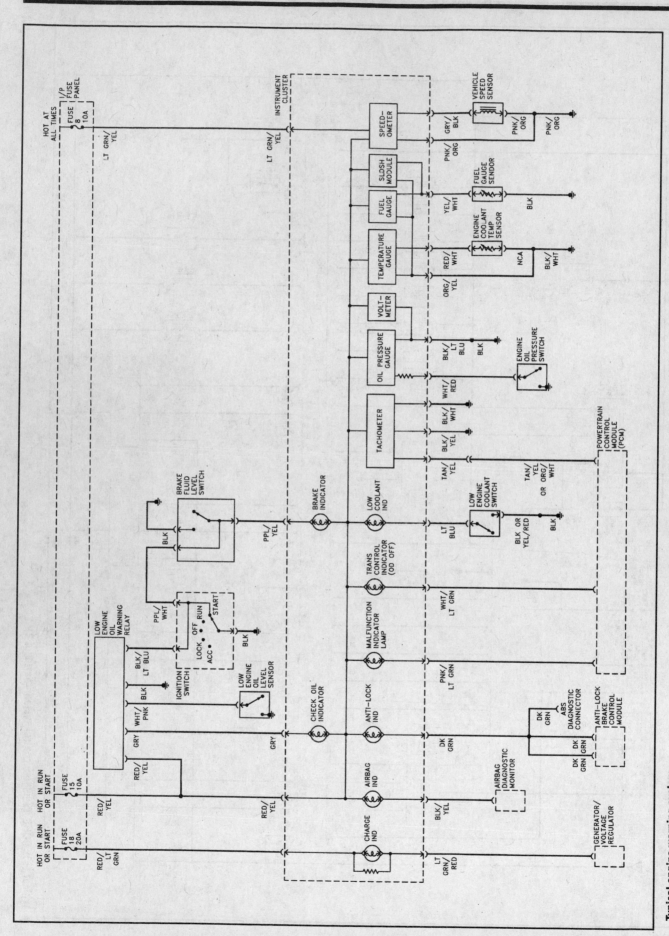

Typical engine warning system

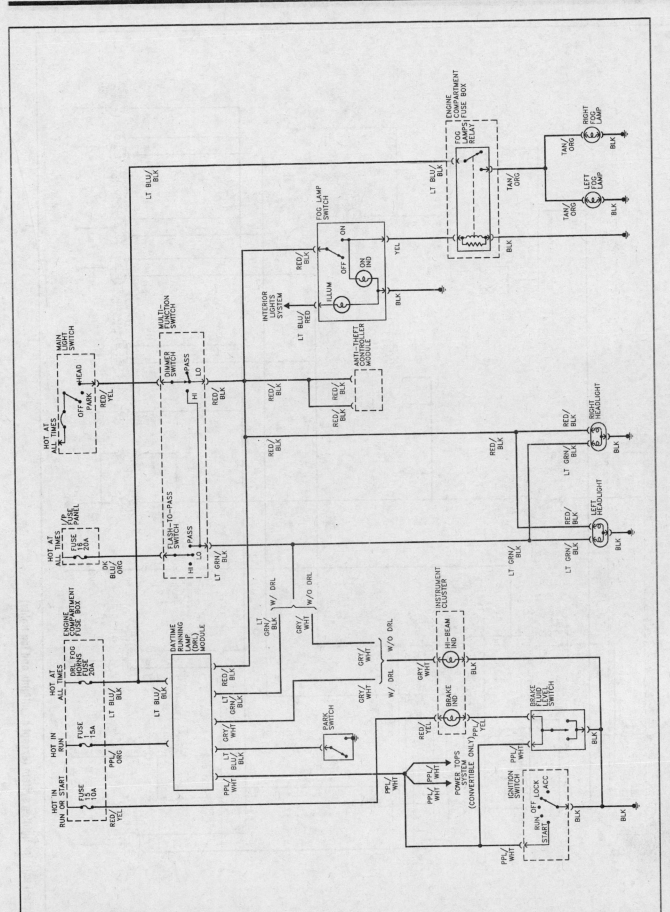

Typical headlight and fog light system

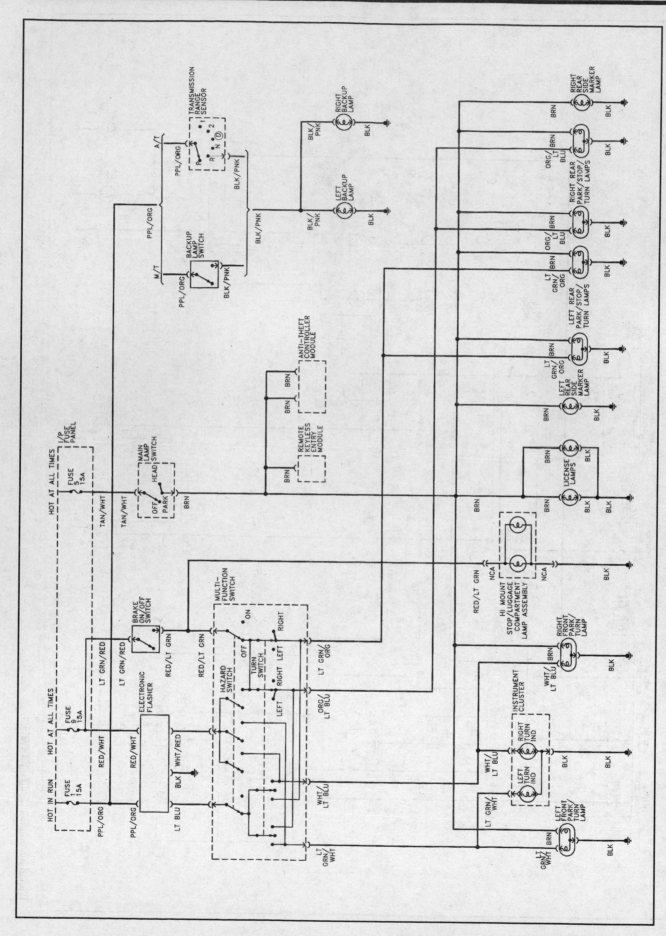

Typical exterior lighting system (except headlights and fog lights)

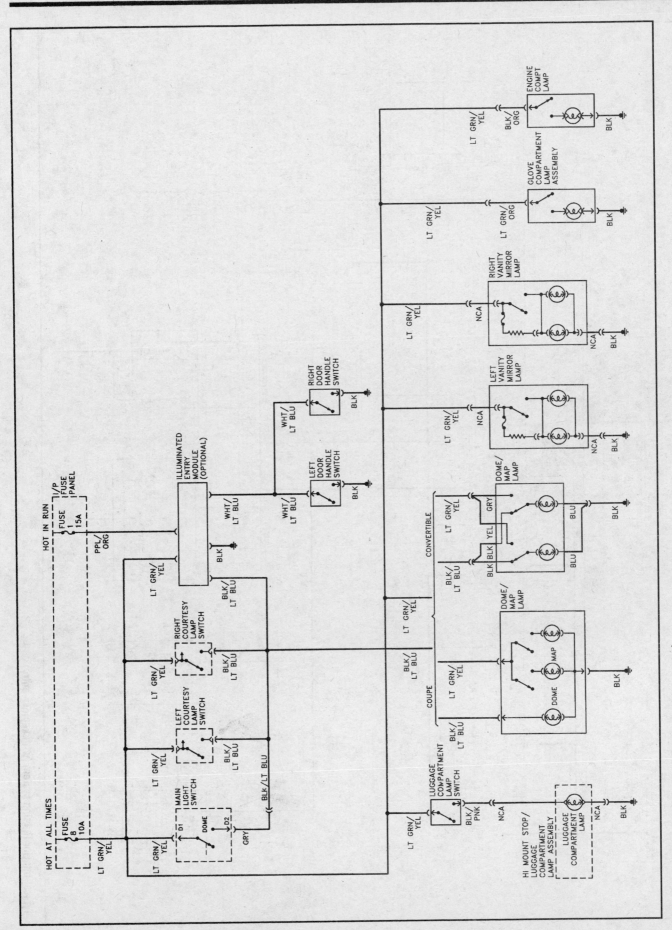

Typical interior lighting system (without keyless entry)

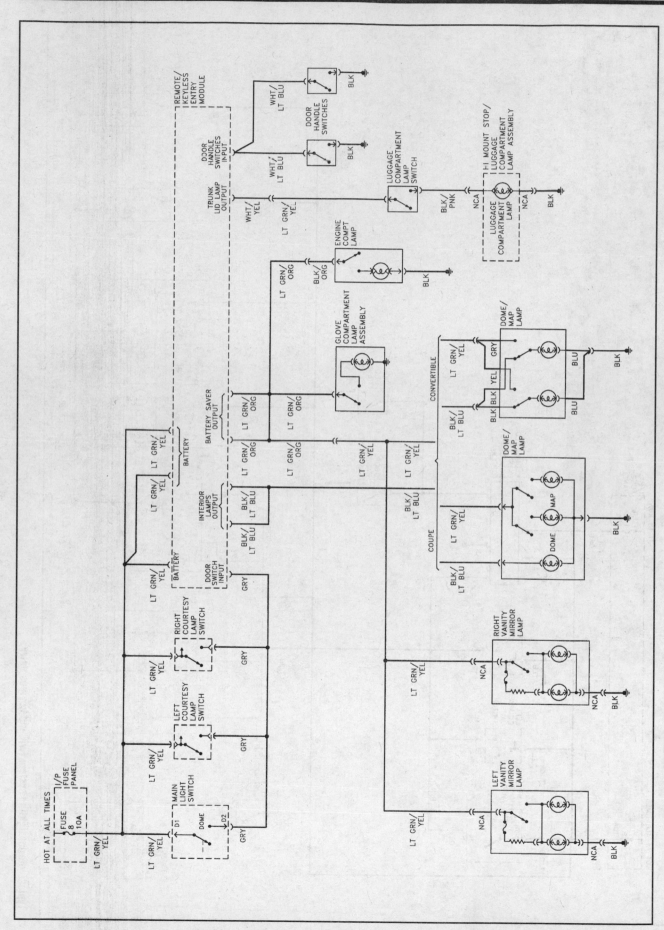

Typical interior lighting system (with keyless entry)

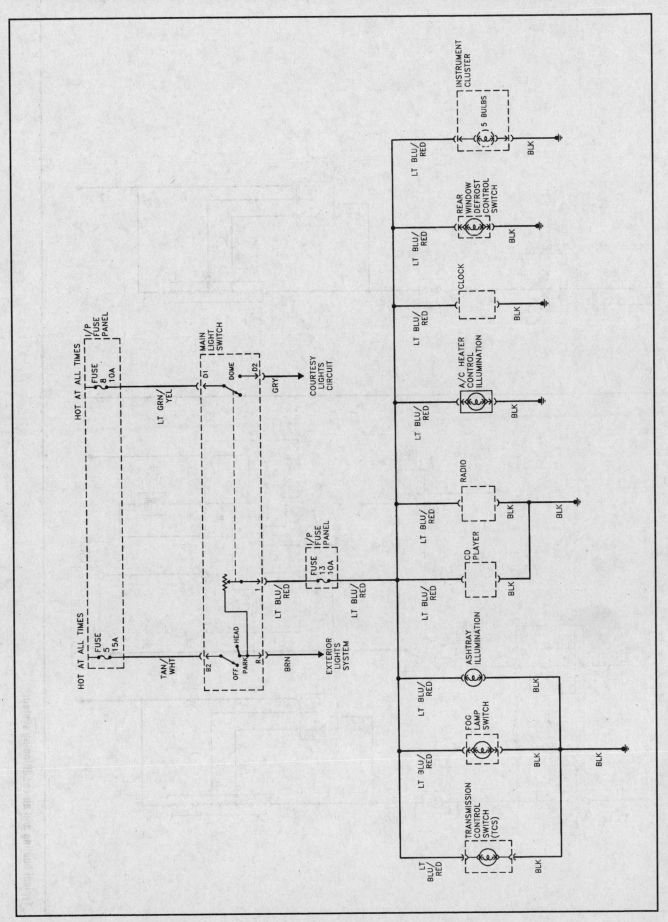

Typical instrument panel illumination system

Typical heating and air conditioning system

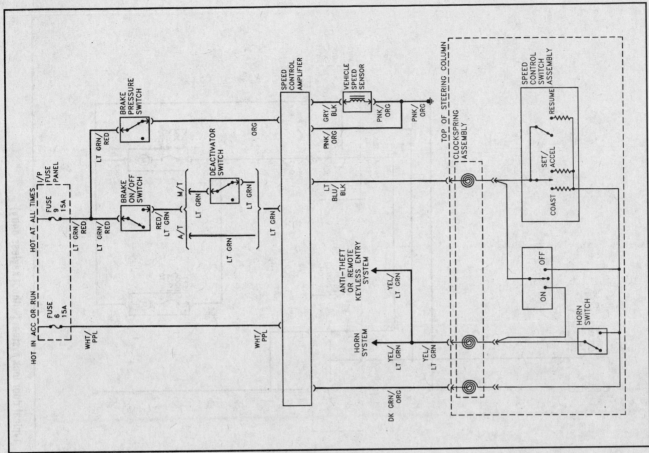

Typical 1996 and later cruise control system

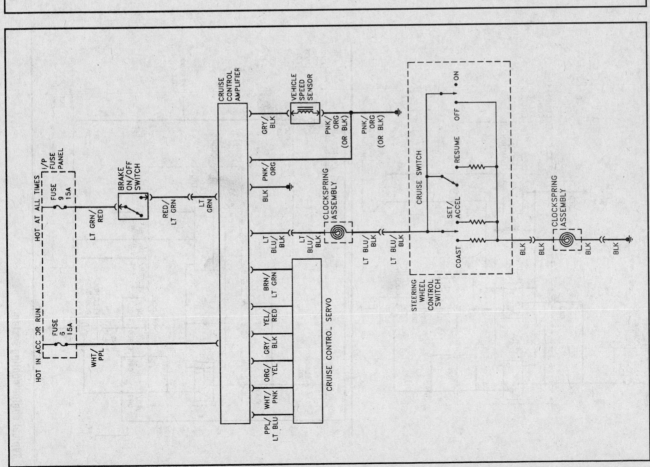

Typical 1995 and earlier cruise control system

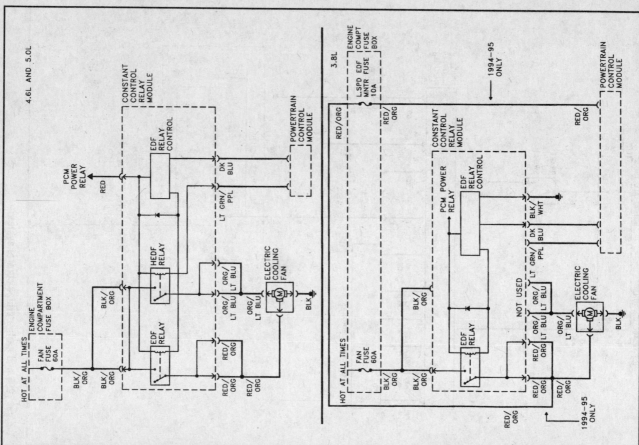

Typical door lock system (without keyless entry)

Typical engine cooling system

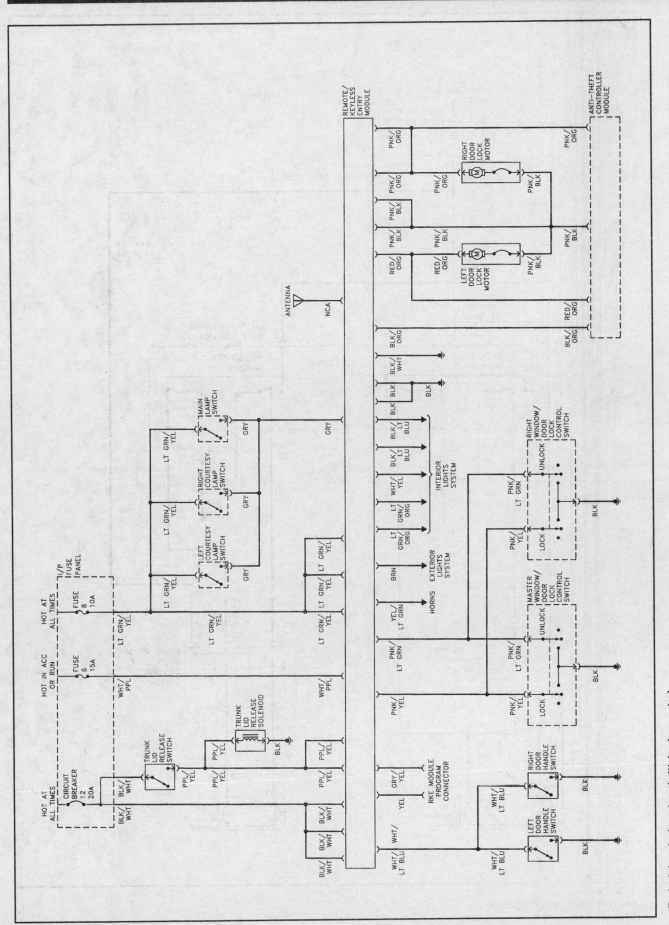

Typical door lock system (with keyless entry)

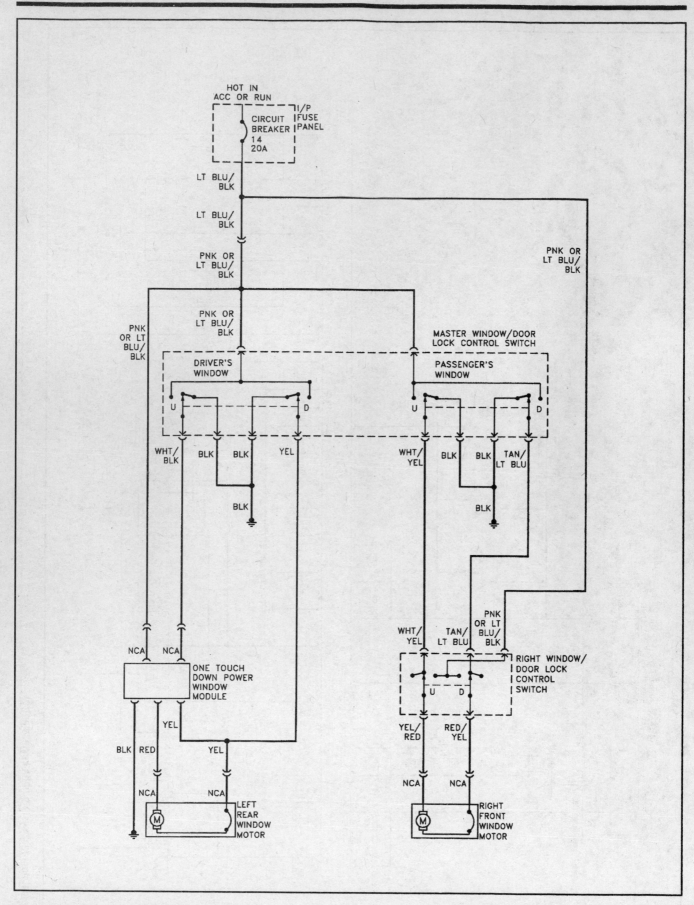

Typical power window system (Coupe)

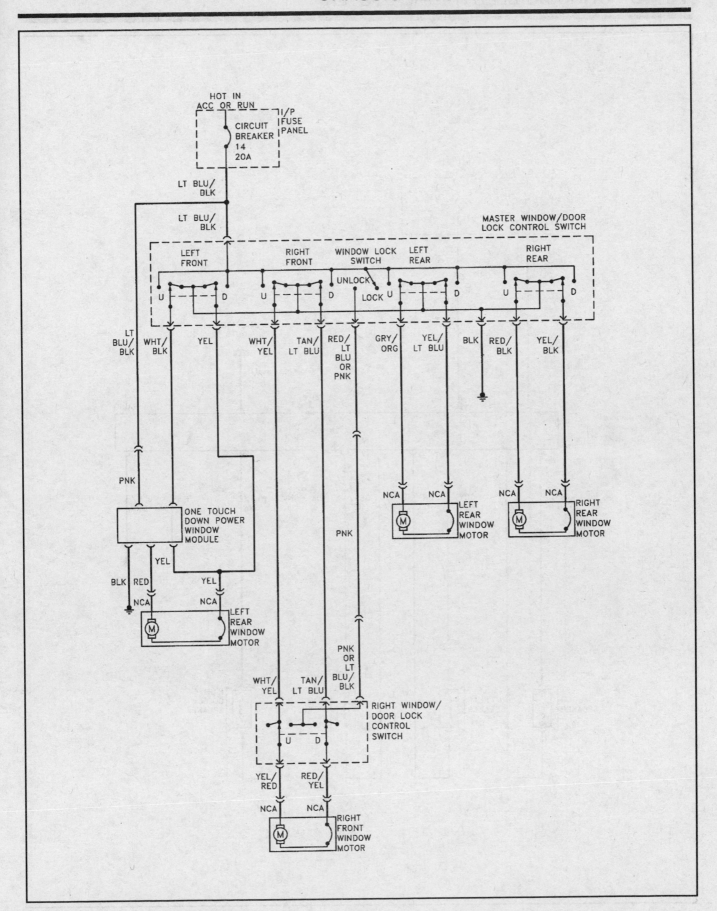

Typical power window system (Convertible)

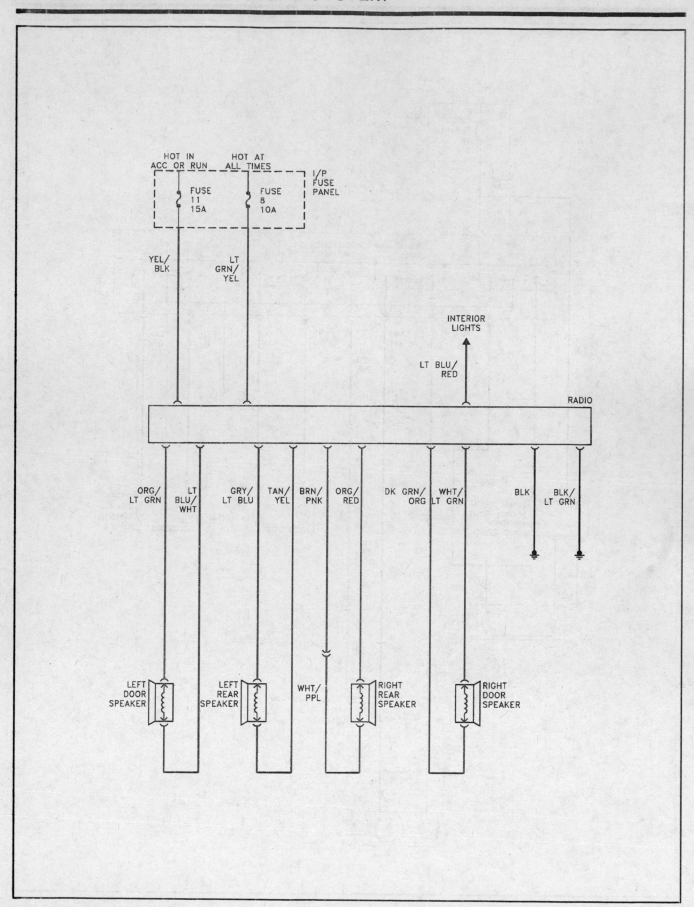

Typical audio system

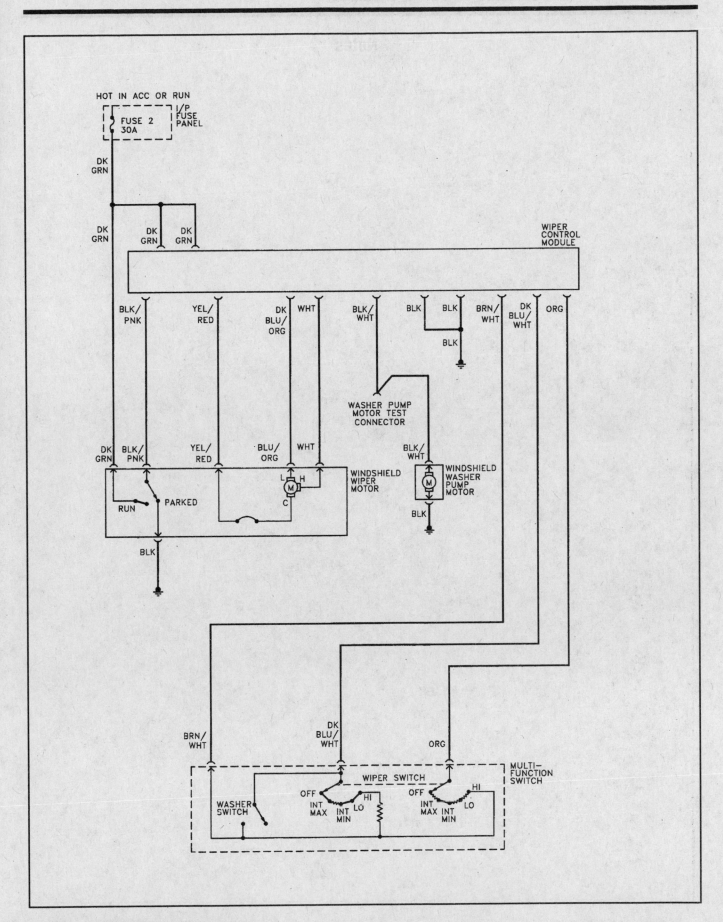

Typical windshield wiper and washer system

Notes

GLOSSARY

AIR/FUEL RATIO: The ratio of air-to-gasoline by weight in the fuel mixture drawn into the engine.

AIR INJECTION: One method of reducing harmful exhaust emissions by injecting air into each of the exhaust ports of an engine. The fresh air entering the hot exhaust manifold causes any remaining fuel to be burned before it can exit the tailpipe.

ALTERNATOR: A device used for converting mechanical energy into electrical energy.

AMMETER: An instrument, calibrated in amperes, used to measure the flow of an electrical current in a circuit. Ammeters are always connected in series with the circuit being tested.

AMPERE: The rate of flow of electrical current present when one volt of electrical pressure is applied against one ohm of electrical resistance.

ANALOG COMPUTER: Any microprocessor that uses similar (analogous) electrical signals to make its calculations.

ARMATURE: A laminated, soft iron core wrapped by a wire that converts electrical energy to mechanical energy as in a motor or relay. When rotated in a magnetic field, it changes mechanical energy into electrical energy as in a generator.

ATMOSPHERIC PRESSURE: The pressure on the Earth's surface caused by the weight of the air in the atmosphere. At sea level, this pressure is 14.7 psi at 32°F (101 kPa at 0°C).

ATOMIZATION: The breaking down of a liquid into a fine mist that can be suspended in air.

AXIAL PLAY: Movement parallel to a shaft or bearing bore.

BACKFIRE: The sudden combustion of gases in the intake or exhaust system that results in a loud explosion.

BACKLASH: The clearance or play between two parts, such as meshed gears.

BACKPRESSURE: Restrictions in the exhaust system that slow the exit of exhaust gases from the combustion chamber.

BAKELITE: A heat resistant, plastic insulator material commonly used in printed circuit boards and transistorized components.

BALL BEARING: A bearing made up of hardened inner and outer races between which hardened steel balls roll.

BALLAST RESISTOR: A resistor in the primary ignition circuit that lowers voltage after the engine is started to reduce wear on ignition components.

BEARING: A friction reducing, supportive device usually located between a stationary part and a moving part.

BIMETAL TEMPERATURE SENSOR: Any sensor or switch made of two dissimilar types of metal that bend when heated or cooled due to the different expansion rates of the alloys. These types of sensors usually function as an on/off switch.

BLOWBY: Combustion gases, composed of water vapor and unburned fuel, that leak past the piston rings into the crankcase during normal engine operation. These gases are removed by the PCV system to prevent the buildup of harmful acids in the crankcase.

BRAKE PAD: A brake shoe and lining assembly used with disc brakes.

BRAKE SHOE: The backing for the brake lining. The term is, however, usually applied to the assembly of the brake backing and lining.

BUSHING: A liner, usually removable, for a bearing; an anti-friction liner used in place of a bearing.

CALIPER: A hydraulically activated device in a disc brake system, which is mounted straddling the brake rotor (disc). The caliper contains at least one piston and two brake pads. Hydraulic pressure on the piston(s) forces the pads against the rotor.

CAMSHAFT: A shaft in the engine on which are the lobes (cams) which operate the valves. The camshaft is driven by the crankshaft, via a belt, chain or gears, at one half the crankshaft speed.

CAPACITOR: A device which stores an electrical charge.

CARBON MONOXIDE (CO): A colorless, odorless gas given off as a normal byproduct of combustion. It is poisonous and extremely dangerous in confined areas, building up slowly to toxic levels without warning if adequate ventilation is not available.

CARBURETOR: A device, usually mounted on the intake manifold of an engine, which mixes the air and fuel in the proper proportion to allow even combustion.

CATALYTIC CONVERTER: A device installed in the exhaust system, like a muffler, that converts harmful byproducts of combustion into carbon dioxide and water vapor by means of a heat-producing chemical reaction.

CENTRIFUGAL ADVANCE: A mechanical method of advancing the spark timing by using flyweights in the distributor that react to centrifugal force generated by the distributor shaft rotation.

CHECK VALVE: Any one-way valve installed to permit the flow of air, fuel or vacuum in one direction only.

CHOKE: A device, usually a moveable valve, placed in the intake path of a carburetor to restrict the flow of air.

CIRCUIT: Any unbroken path through which an electrical current can flow. Also used to describe fuel flow in some instances.

CIRCUIT BREAKER: A switch which protects an electrical circuit from overload by opening the circuit when the current flow exceeds a predetermined level. Some circuit breakers must be reset manually, while most reset automatically.

COIL (IGNITION): A transformer in the ignition circuit which steps up the voltage provided to the spark plugs.

COMBINATION MANIFOLD: An assembly which includes both the intake and exhaust manifolds in one casting.

COMBINATION VALVE: A device used in some fuel systems that routes fuel vapors to a charcoal storage canister instead of venting them into the atmosphere. The valve relieves fuel tank pressure and allows fresh air into the tank as the fuel level drops to prevent a vapor lock situation.

COMPRESSION RATIO: The comparison of the total volume of the cylinder and combustion chamber with the piston at BDC and the piston at TDC.

CONDENSER: 1. An electrical device which acts to store an electrical charge, preventing voltage surges. 2. A radiator-like device in the air conditioning system in which refrigerant gas condenses into a liquid, giving off heat.

CONDUCTOR: Any material through which an electrical current can be transmitted easily.

CONTINUITY: Continuous or complete circuit. Can be checked with an ohmmeter.

COUNTERSHAFT: An intermediate shaft which is rotated by a mainshaft and transmits, in turn, that rotation to a working part.

CRANKCASE: The lower part of an engine in which the crankshaft and related parts operate.

CRANKSHAFT: The main driving shaft of an engine which receives reciprocating motion from the pistons and converts it to rotary motion.

CYLINDER: In an engine, the round hole in the engine block in which the piston(s) ride.

CYLINDER BLOCK: The main structural member of an engine in which is found the cylinders, crankshaft and other principal parts.

CYLINDER HEAD: The detachable portion of the engine, usually fastened to the top of the cylinder block and containing all or most of the combustion chambers. On overhead valve engines, it contains the valves and their operating parts. On overhead cam engines, it contains the camshaft as well.

DEAD CENTER: The extreme top or bottom of the piston stroke.

DETONATION: An unwanted explosion of the air/fuel mixture in the combustion chamber caused by excess heat and compression, advanced timing, or an overly lean mixture. Also referred to as "ping".

DIAPHRAGM: A thin, flexible wall separating two cavities, such as in a vacuum advance unit.

DIESELING: A condition in which hot spots in the combustion chamber cause the engine to run on after the key is turned off.

DIFFERENTIAL: A geared assembly which allows the transmission of motion between drive axles, giving one axle the ability to turn faster than the other.

DIODE: An electrical device that will allow current to flow in one direction only.

DISC BRAKE: A hydraulic braking assembly consisting of a brake disc, or rotor, mounted on an axle, and a caliper assembly containing, usually two brake pads which are activated by hydraulic pressure. The pads are forced against the sides of the disc, creating friction which slows the vehicle.

DISTRIBUTOR: A mechanically driven device on an engine which is responsible for electrically firing the spark plug at a predetermined point of the piston stroke.

DOWEL PIN: A pin, inserted in mating holes in two different parts allowing those parts to maintain a fixed relationship.

DRUM BRAKE: A braking system which consists of two brake shoes and one or two wheel cylinders, mounted on a fixed backing plate, and a brake drum, mounted on an axle, which revolves around the assembly.

DWELL: The rate, measured in degrees of shaft rotation, at which an electrical circuit cycles on and off.

ELECTRONIC CONTROL UNIT (ECU): Ignition module, module, amplifier or igniter. See Module for definition.

ELECTRONIC IGNITION: A system in which the timing and firing of the spark plugs is controlled by an electronic control unit, usually called a module. These systems have no points or condenser.

END-PLAY: The measured amount of axial movement in a shaft.

ENGINE: A device that converts heat into mechanical energy.

EXHAUST MANIFOLD: A set of cast passages or pipes which conduct exhaust gases from the engine.

FEELER GAUGE: A blade, usually metal, or precisely predetermined thickness, used to measure the clearance between two parts.

FIRING ORDER: The order in which combustion occurs in the cylinders of an engine. Also the order in which spark is distributed to the plugs by the distributor.

FLOODING: The presence of too much fuel in the intake manifold and combustion chamber which prevents the air/fuel mixture from firing, thereby causing a no-start situation.

FLYWHEEL: A disc shaped part bolted to the rear end of the crankshaft. Around the outer perimeter is affixed the ring gear. The starter drive engages the ring gear, turning the flywheel, which rotates the crankshaft, imparting the initial starting motion to the engine.

FOOT POUND (ft. lbs. or sometimes, ft.lb.): The amount of energy or work needed to raise an item weighing one pound, a distance of one foot.

FUSE: A protective device in a circuit which prevents circuit overload by breaking the circuit when a specific amperage is present. The device is constructed around a strip or wire of a lower amperage rating than the circuit it is designed to protect. When an amperage higher than that stamped on the fuse is present in the circuit, the strip or wire melts, opening the circuit.

GEAR RATIO: The ratio between the number of teeth on meshing gears.

GENERATOR: A device which converts mechanical energy into electrical energy.

HEAT RANGE: The measure of a spark plug's ability to dissipate heat from its firing end. The higher the heat range, the hotter the plug fires.

HUB: The center part of a wheel or gear.

HYDROCARBON (HC): Any chemical compound made up of hydrogen and carbon. A major pollutant formed by the engine as a byproduct of combustion.

HYDROMETER: An instrument used to measure the specific gravity of a solution.

INCH POUND (inch lbs.; sometimes in.lb. or in. lbs.): One twelfth of a foot pound.

INDUCTION: A means of transferring electrical energy in the form of a magnetic field. Principle used in the ignition coil to increase voltage.

INJECTOR: A device which receives metered fuel under relatively low pressure and is activated to inject the fuel into the engine under relatively high pressure at a predetermined time.

INPUT SHAFT: The shaft to which torque is applied, usually carrying the driving gear or gears.

INTAKE MANIFOLD: A casting of passages or pipes used to conduct air or a fuel/air mixture to the cylinders.

JOURNAL: The bearing surface within which a shaft operates.

KEY: A small block usually fitted in a notch between a shaft and a hub to prevent slippage of the two parts.

MANIFOLD: A casting of passages or set of pipes which connect the cylinders to an inlet or outlet source.

MANIFOLD VACUUM: Low pressure in an engine intake manifold formed just below the throttle plates. Manifold vacuum is highest at idle and drops under acceleration.

MASTER CYLINDER: The primary fluid pressurizing device in a hydraulic system. In automotive use, it is found in brake and hydraulic clutch systems and is pedal activated, either directly or, in a power brake system, through the power booster.

MODULE: Electronic control unit, amplifier or igniter of solid state or integrated design which controls the current flow in the ignition primary circuit based on input from the pick-up coil. When the module opens the primary circuit, high secondary voltage is induced in the coil.

NEEDLE BEARING: A bearing which consists of a number (usually a large number) of long, thin rollers.

OHM: (Ω) The unit used to measure the resistance of conductor-to-electrical flow. One ohm is the amount of resistance that limits current flow to one ampere in a circuit with one volt of pressure.

OHMMETER: An instrument used for measuring the resistance, in ohms, in an electrical circuit.

OUTPUT SHAFT: The shaft which transmits torque from a device, such as a transmission.

OVERDRIVE: A gear assembly which produces more shaft revolutions than that transmitted to it.

OVERHEAD CAMSHAFT (OHC): An engine configuration in which the camshaft is mounted on top of the cylinder head and operates the valve either directly or by means of rocker arms.

OVERHEAD VALVE (OHV): An engine configuration in which all of the valves are located in the cylinder head and the camshaft is located in the cylinder block. The camshaft operates the valves via lifters and pushrods.

OXIDES OF NITROGEN (NOx): Chemical compounds of nitrogen produced as a byproduct of combustion. They combine with hydrocarbons to produce smog.

OXYGEN SENSOR: Use with the feedback system to sense the presence of oxygen in the exhaust gas and signal the computer which can reference the voltage signal to an air/fuel ratio.

PINION: The smaller of two meshing gears.

PISTON RING: An open-ended ring with fits into a groove on the outer diameter of the piston. Its chief function is to form a seal between the piston and cylinder wall. Most automotive pistons have three rings: two for compression sealing; one for oil sealing.

PRELOAD: A predetermined load placed on a bearing during assembly or by adjustment.

PRIMARY CIRCUIT: the low voltage side of the ignition system which consists of the ignition switch, ballast resistor or resistance wire, bypass, coil, electronic control unit and pick-up coil as well as the connecting wires and harnesses.

PRESS FIT: The mating of two parts under pressure, due to the inner diameter of one being smaller than the outer diameter of the other, or vice versa; an interference fit.

RACE: The surface on the inner or outer ring of a bearing on which the balls, needles or rollers move.

REGULATOR: A device which maintains the amperage and/or voltage levels of a circuit at predetermined values.

RELAY: A switch which automatically opens and/or closes a circuit.

RESISTANCE: The opposition to the flow of current through a circuit or electrical device, and is measured in ohms. Resistance is equal to the voltage divided by the amperage.

RESISTOR: A device, usually made of wire, which offers a preset amount of resistance in an electrical circuit.

RING GEAR: The name given to a ring-shaped gear attached to a differential case, or affixed to a flywheel or as part of a planetary gear set.

ROLLER BEARING: A bearing made up of hardened inner and outer races between which hardened steel rollers move.

ROTOR: 1. The disc-shaped part of a disc brake assembly, upon which the brake pads bear; also called, brake disc. 2. The device mounted atop the distributor shaft, which passes current to the distributor cap tower contacts.

SECONDARY CIRCUIT: The high voltage side of the ignition system, usually above 20,000 volts. The secondary includes the ignition coil, coil wire, distributor cap and rotor, spark plug wires and spark plugs.

SENDING UNIT: A mechanical, electrical, hydraulic or electromagnetic device which transmits information to a gauge.

SENSOR: Any device designed to measure engine operating conditions or ambient pressures and temperatures. Usually electronic in nature and designed to send a voltage signal to an on-board computer, some sensors may operate as a simple on/off switch or they may provide a variable voltage signal (like a potentiometer) as conditions or measured parameters change.

SHIM: Spacers of precise, predetermined thickness used between parts to establish a proper working relationship.

SLAVE CYLINDER: In automotive use, a device in the hydraulic clutch system which is activated by hydraulic force, disengaging the clutch.

SOLENOID: A coil used to produce a magnetic field, the effect of which is to produce work.

SPARK PLUG: A device screwed into the combustion chamber of a spark ignition engine. The basic construction is a conductive core inside of a ceramic insulator, mounted in an outer conductive base. An electrical charge from the spark plug wire travels along the conductive core and jumps a preset air gap to a grounding point or points at the end of the conductive base. The resultant spark ignites the fuel/air mixture in the combustion chamber.

SPLINES: Ridges machined or cast onto the outer diameter of a shaft or inner diameter of a bore to enable parts to mate without rotation.

TACHOMETER: A device used to measure the rotary speed of an engine, shaft, gear, etc., usually in rotations per minute.

THERMOSTAT: A valve, located in the cooling system of an engine, which is closed when cold and opens gradually in response to engine heating, controlling the temperature of the coolant and rate of coolant flow.

TOP DEAD CENTER (TDC): The point at which the piston reaches the top of its travel on the compression stroke.

TORQUE: The twisting force applied to an object.

TORQUE CONVERTER: A turbine used to transmit power from a driving member to a driven member via hydraulic action, providing changes in drive ratio and torque. In automotive use, it links the driveplate at the rear of the engine to the automatic transmission.

TRANSDUCER: A device used to change a force into an electrical signal.

TRANSISTOR: A semi-conductor component which can be actuated by a small voltage to perform an electrical switching function.

TUNE-UP: A regular maintenance function, usually associated with the replacement and adjustment of parts and components in the electrical and fuel systems of a vehicle for the purpose of attaining optimum performance.

TURBOCHARGER: An exhaust driven pump which compresses intake air and forces it into the combustion chambers at higher than atmospheric pressures. The increased air pressure allows more fuel to be burned and results in increased horsepower being produced.

VACUUM ADVANCE: A device which advances the ignition timing in response to increased engine vacuum.

VACUUM GAUGE: An instrument used to measure the presence of vacuum in a chamber.

VALVE: A device which control the pressure, direction of flow or rate of flow of a liquid or gas.

VALVE CLEARANCE: The measured gap between the end of the valve stem and the rocker arm, cam lobe or follower that activates the valve.

VISCOSITY: The rating of a liquid's internal resistance to flow.

VOLTMETER: An instrument used for measuring electrical force in units called volts. Voltmeters are always connected parallel with the circuit being tested.

WHEEL CYLINDER: Found in the automotive drum brake assembly, it is a device, actuated by hydraulic pressure, which, through internal pistons, pushes the brake shoes outward against the drums.

NOTES

A

MASTER INDEX

Notes